OREGON
HANDBOOK
SECOND EDITION

OREGON
HANDBOOK
SECOND EDITION

STUART WARREN & TED LONG ISHIKAWA

MOON
PUBLICATIONS INC.

OREGON HANDBOOK
SECOND EDITION

Published by
Moon Publications, Inc.
P.O. Box 3040
Chico, California 95927-3040, USA

Printed by
Colorcraft Ltd.

Library of Congress Cataloging-in-Publication Data

Warren, Stuart, 1958-
  Oregon Handbook / Stuart Warren & Ted Long Ishikawa.
      p.   cm.
  Includes bibliographical references and index.
  ISBN 0-918373-96-4
  1.   Oregon—Guidebooks.   I. Long Ishikawa, Ted, 1958-
II. Title.
F874.3.W37   1993
917.9504'43—dc20   92-21556
                                              CIP

Please send all comments,
corrections, additions,
amendments, and critiques to:

**OREGON HANDBOOK
c/o MOON PUBLICATIONS, INC.
P.O. BOX 3040
CHICO, CA 95927-3040, USA**

Printing History
  1st edition—July 1991
  Reprinted—November 1991
  Reprinted—October 1992
  2nd edition—September 1993

Editors: Taran March, Mark Morris
Copy Editors: Mark Arends, Don Root, Asha Johnson, Nicole Revere
Production and Design: Aaron Yamaguchi, Carey Wilson
Cartographers: Bob Race, Brian Bardwell
Index: Taran March, Julie Mason
Cover photo by Charles Shoffner

To Mr. Ed Hardy, who always said we could.

ACKNOWLEDGEMENTS

Oregon Handbook began in Alaska when Moon's editor-in-chief emeritus and esteemed author Deke Castleman grabbed Stuart and said, "Oregon needs a good book. Just get it down, man." Shortly thereafter "it" got under way and was carried to conclusion largely because of Taran March, the best editor we've run into (and who we hope won't notice that we end with a preposition). Thank you from us and your favorite state, Oregon.

We're also indebted to Rhys Thomas and Theo Trimmell for their wise and witty sidebar about the Oregon Country Fair. However, the biggest contribution to the first edition of *Oregon Handbook* came at the 11th hour when Dave Johnson, the most respected environmental journalist in the state, stepped in to help cover the other side of the mountains.

Special thanks to Anne Long for artistic brilliance, Jennifer and Elliot Gehr for their help on the prehistory section, and also to Bill and Dierdre Dant for their insightful comments about Portland and the north coast, which prevented those sections from reading like a telephone directory. Liam Singer, Phineas Warren, Rhys and Maria Thomas, Bruce Bush, Henning Larson, Marty Immerman, and Brian Litt all played a part in bringing the project to fruition.

In addition to the "Beast of the East," we thank Number 95, "Old Blue," for schoolin'; The Bob, The Big Man, and Larry for being straight shooters; Duke Dunnell for esprit de corps; Bowl-of-Rice for teaching us how to avoid black holes; and The Prez for sage advice. We'd also be remiss if we didn't give a nod to the college boys and overly articulate Bill for "inducing a more sanguine outlook," and to Ralph and April, looking hopefully over our shoulders as we wrote. In this vein, *Oregon Handbook* doles out a special medal of honor to our wives Rebecca Singer and Sawako Ishikawa, who read the text more than anyone should ever have had to, as well as taking photos and riding shotgun on our roadtrips. Last but not least, our gratitude goes out to our parents for their unwavering encouragement, which sustained us through many long months of work.

CONTENTS

MAPS

MAP SYMBOLS

FREEWAY
MAIN HIGHWAY
SECONDARY ROAD
UNPAVED ROAD
FOOT PATH, TRAIL
STATE BORDER
OTHER BORDER
TUNNEL
PASS
RAILROAD
BRIDGE

INTERSTATE HIGHWAY

U.S. HIGHWAY

STATE HIGHWAY

○ LARGE CITY
○ SMALL CITIES & TOWNS
▲ MOUNTAIN

WATERFALL

WATER

SKI AREA

■ POINT OF INTEREST
N.W.R. NATIONAL WILDLIFE REFUGE
N.P. NATIONAL PARK
S.P. STATE PARK

CHARTS

SPECIAL TOPICS

ABBREVIATIONS

AYH—American Youth Hostel

AARP—American Association of
Retired People

B & B—bed and breakfast

BLM—Bureau of Land Management

CCC—Civilian Conservation Corps

NFS—National Forest Service

NRA—National Recreation Area

NWR—National Wildlife Refuge

OMSI—Oregon Museum of Science
and Industry

ORE (plus number)—state highway

pp—per person

RV—recreational vehicle

WISTEC—Willamette Science and
Technology Center

IS THIS BOOK OUT OF DATE?

We strive to keep our books as up to date as possible and would appreciate your help. If you find that a resort is not as we described, or discover a new restaurant or other information that should be included in our book, please let us know. Our mapmakers take extraordinary effort to be accurate, but if you find an error, let us know that as well.

We're especially interested in hearing from female travelers, RVers, outdoor enthusiasts, expatriates, and local residents. We are always interested in hearing from the tourist industry which specializes in accommodating visitors to Oregon. Happy traveling! Please address letters to:

Oregon Handbook
Moon Publications, Inc.
P.O. Box 3040
Chico, CA 95927-3040, USA

INTRODUCTION

Theodore Winthrop, a mid-19th-century adventurer and novelist from New England, made the following observation at the end of his journey to the Oregon Territory:

Our race has never yet come into contact with great mountains as companions of daily life, nor felt that daily development of the finer and more comprehensive senses which these signal facts of nature compel. . . .

These Oregon people, in a climate where being is bliss—where every breath is a draught of vivid life—these Oregon people, carrying to a newer and grander New England of the West a full growth of the American Idea . . . will elaborate new systems of thought and life.

What this boils down to in the language of today is that "these Oregon people" know how to live. Modern travelers to the state will tell you that nowhere else in the country has civilization meshed so peacefully with the environment. Recycling and mass transit maintain a benefi-

cent quality of life in the state's largest cities, and vast tracts of preserved land attest to Oregonians' appreciation of their gemlike coastline and snowcapped mountain ranges.

Most of these trophies of the good life didn't come easily. Just as it took Oregon Trail pioneers many months to cross 2,000 miles of forbidding deserts and treacherous mountain passes to reach the promised land, Oregonians have sacrificed much to blaze trails in the thickets of environmental legislation and jurisprudence. And while the dilemma of one person's conservation being another's unemployment has been a continuous fact of life here, the debate has never raged more fiercely than it does at present. Inevitably, the outcome will bring more change and the regrettable passing of a way of life for many. But as the millennium approaches, one fact becomes clear—if Oregon has erred on the side of conservation, it has at least preserved an increasingly valuable and vanishing commodity: its natural resources. The proof is here for you to see.

THE LAND

GEOGRAPHY

The Overview

If Oregon were part of a jigsaw puzzle of the U.S., it would be a squarish piece with a dip in the center of its top. To the west is the Pacific Ocean; to the east is the Snake River and Idaho. Up top, much of the northern boundary between Oregon and Washington is defined by the Columbia River; the southern border is comprised of the state lines of California and Nevada.

If this puzzle also depicted the vertical relief of topographic features, it would show broad columns of mountains dividing the coast from the inland valleys, as well as peaks cutting off western Oregon from the central and eastern parts of the state. East of the highest central range the Columbia Plateau predominates, broken up in the northeast where mountainous features reassert themselves. In the southeast, many lakes fill the landscape in the least mountainous expanse of the state. The Great Basin desert—characterized by rivers that evaporate, peter out, or disappear into underground aquifers—makes up the bottom third of eastern Oregon. Here, the seven-inch annual rainfall of the Alvord Desert seems more at home in the Great Basin country of Nevada and California than in a state known for blustery rainstorms.

The Peak Experience In Western Oregon

Moving west to east, let's consider the major ranges, beginning with the Coastal and Klamath mountains. The Klamaths comprise the lower quarter of the state's westernmost barrier to the Pacific; the eastern flank of this range is generally referred to as the Siskiyous. As we move north, the Oregon Coast Range, a younger volcanic range, replaces the Klamaths. The highest peaks in each of these cordilleras barely top 4,000 feet and stand in between coastal plateaus on one side and such agricultural centers as the Willamette and the Rogue valleys on the other. East of these valleys are dormant (as of this writing) volcanoes. Known collectively as the Cascades, five of the peaks top 10,000 feet above sea level.

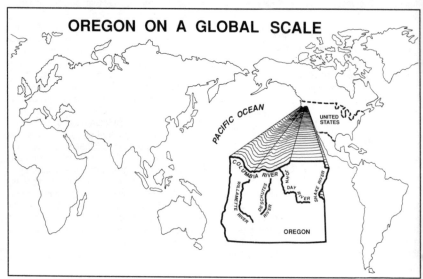

OREGON ON A GLOBAL SCALE

OREGON LANDFORMS

Contrasts In Eastern Oregon

Beyond the Cascades' eastern slope, one finds semiarid high desert conditions contrasting with the Coast Range rainforests and the mild, wet maritime climate which characterizes much of western Oregon. The contrast is repeated in the northeast, where the 10,000-foot elevation of the snowcapped Wallowas lies less than 50 miles from a subtropical enclave—the hot, dry floor of Hell's Canyon, about 1,300 feet above sea level.

In addition to Hell's Canyon, America's biggest hole in the ground (7,900 feet maximum depth), Oregon also boasts the continent's deepest lake: Crater Lake, with a depth of 1,962 feet.

Last Of The Red-hot Lavas

In each part of the state, there are other well-known remnants of Oregon's cataclysmic past. Offshore waters here feature 1,477 volcanic islands. Lava fields dot the approach to the High Cascades. East of the range a volcanic plateau supports cinder cones, lava caves, and lava-cast forests in the most varied array of these phenomena outside of Hawaii.

Seismic events may not be just a thing of the past, according to research which took place on the north Oregon coast in 1990. Scientists unearthed discontinuities in both rock strata and tree rings here, indicating that Tillamook County has experienced major tremors every several hundred years. They estimate that the next one could come within our lifetimes and be of significant magnitude. These coastal quakes are caused by what geologists call *subduction*. This process occurs when one of the giant plates (see "The High Cascades" for more on plate tectonics) that make up the earth's crust slides under another as they collide. In Pacific Northwest coastal regions, this takes place when the Juan de Fuca plate's marine layer is pushed under the continental North American plate. With virtually every part of the state possessing seismic potential that hasn't been released in many years, the pressure along the fault lines is increasing. The fact that Oregon building codes have not yet acknowledged this became evident in March of 1993 when a 5.7 quake centered 30 miles south of Portland accounted for several million dollars worth of damage.

The Great Meltdown

However pervasive the effects of volcanism here, they must still share top billing with the big Ice Age in Oregon's topographic grand epic. When that glacial epoch's final meltdown 12,000 years ago unleashed water dammed up by thousands of feet of ice, great rivers were spawned and existing channels were enlarged. A particularly large inundation was the Missoula Flood, which began with an ice dam breaking up in present-day Montana. Before it subsided, it carved out the contours of what are now the Columbia River Gorge and the Willamette Valley. Other glacial floodwaters found their outlet westward to the sea, digging out silt-ridden estuaries in the process. Pacific wave action washed this debris back up onto the land, helping to create dunes and beaches.

Metes And Bounds

Oregon's 2.9 million people live in the 10th-largest state in the U.S., some 62 million acres. Two counties in eastern Oregon, Harney and Malheur, are bigger than eight other states. Harney County alone could hold Rhode Island eight times.

CLIMATE

The Rain Shadow

Oregon's weather system is best understood as a series of valley microclimates set apart from each other by mountain ranges. Moving west to east, each of these valley zones records progressively lower rainfall levels until one encounters a desert on the eastern side of the state.

It all begins when moisture-laden westerlies off the Pacific slam into the Coast and Klamath ranges. As the clouds climb higher they drop their moisture in the form of rain or snow. That is because rising air cools 3° F every 1,000 feet, and cooler air can't hold as much moisture as warm air. As a consequence, coastal rainfall often exceeds 80 inches a year, while the Willamette and other inland valleys on the other side of the mountains usually record half that total. The rain shadow effect is repeated when the Cascades catch precipitation from eastward-moving cloud masses; consequently, the

PRECIPITATION

ASTORIA
69.60 in.

WASHINGTON
OREGON

PENDLETON
12.20 in.

PORTLAND
37.31 in.

THE DALLES
15.78 in.

LA GRANDE
18.79 in.

BAKER
10.63 in.

PACIFIC OCEAN

NEWPORT
58 in.

EUGENE
46 in.

BEND
11.53 in.

OREGON
IDAHO

BURNS
10.61 in.

ROSEBURG
33.35 in.

CRATER LAKE
66.87 in.

GRANTS PASS
32.31 in.

0   50mi
0   50km

BROOKINGS
86.22 in.

ASHLAND
18.90 in.

KLAMATH FALLS
13.49 in.

OREGON
CALIFORNIA | NEVADA

other side of this range often records annual rainfall totals below 10 inches. This dryness is contrasted by the climate of the western Cascades and Coast Range, where precipitation commonly exceeds 100 inches.

Anyone driving through the Coast Range sees evidence of the "siege mentality" which sets in with each winter monsoon season. Giant TV satellite discs and stacks of covered firewood are common lawn ornaments here in the rainiest part of the state.

Western Oregon
Oregon's location equidistant from the equator and the North Pole subjects her to weather from both tropical and polar air flows. This makes for a pattern of changeability in which calm often alternates with storm, and extreme heat and extreme cold seldom last long. (Coastal conditions will be treated in detail in that region's chapter.)

If there is one constant in western Oregon, it is cloudiness. Portland and the Willamette Valley get only about 45% of maximum potential sunshine; more than 200 days of the year are cloudy and rain falls an average of 150 days. While this might sound bleak, consider that the cloud cover helps moderate the climate by trapping and reflecting the earth's heat. Daily fluctuations in temperature average only 15° F here; the difference between the average temperatures of the warmest month, July, and the coldest one, January, is only about 20°. Best of all, on average, only 44 days of the year record temperatures below freezing. Thus, the region, despite being on a more northerly latitude than parts of Canada, has a milder climate. Except in mountainous areas, snow usually isn't a force to be reckoned with here. Another surprise is that the average annual rainfall of 40 inches is often less than totals recorded in New York, Miami, and Chicago.

While Portland and the rest of the Willamette Valley share mild climates, with wintertime highs of 45° and average summertime mercury readings between 65° and 75°, their weather differ-

The painted hills of
John Day Fossil Beds
National Monument

ences are worth noting. Portland is affected by icy winds coming out of the Columbia River Gorge, originally derived from frigid Rocky Mountain air. At these times, the otherwise mild Portland climate experiences uncharacteristic frosts.

The rest of the Willamette Valley is affected by temperature inversions. In winter, for example, warm air above the valley walls holds in the colder air below, resulting in enduring, but not endearing, fogs. In the southern valleys, fog has a more positive manifestation, as it helps to counterbalance the region's long dry season: Ashland and Medford can sometimes record only half the yearly precipitation of their neighbors to the north, as well as higher wintertime and summertime temperatures. At the same time, these inversions can cause unwelcome pollution to linger.

In much of western Oregon, the day-night differences in temperature are seldom extreme because of cloud cover and vegetation. Both act to keep the air cool and moist during the day and trap heat at night.

Eastern Oregon
By contrast, the scorching deserts of eastern Oregon can give way to cold temperatures at night. This is because clear skies and a dearth of vegetation facilitate the escape of heat. Consider that on May 2, 1968, the difference between the high and low temperatures at Juniper Lake, north of the Alvord Desert in southeastern Oregon, was 81 degrees.

Mountain areas also experience extreme diurnal temperature fluctuations. Thin mountain air does not filter out ultraviolet radiation as effectively as the denser air at lower elevations, so the sun's force is accentuated at higher elevations. At night, chill spreads quickly through this thin air.

The saying, "Only a dude or a fool predicts mountain weather," can apply with equal force to Oregon's high desert, where snow has fallen every month of the year. Sudden storms and cold affect both desert and mountain areas, even in midsummer.

Choose Your Poison
What eastern and western Oregonians have in common is a tendency to poke fun at the others' climate. West of the Cascades, the reigning opinion seems to be that it's so dry in the Oregon desert that the jackrabbits pack canteens. In like measure, the dry-siders will assure you that people in western Oregon don't tan, they rust. A quick look at the extremes of rain, heat, and cold will set the record straight.

As the rainiest places in the state don't have weather stations, we'll have to accord the dubious distinction for precipitous precipitation to a "noncommunity." West of Salem, nestled high in the Coast Range, is Valsetz, a tiny lumber town that once was. Until the town's demise in 1985, its 129.9 inches yearly average (with a record 191.4 inches compiled August 1973 to July 1974) was the highest in the state, although rainfall in the surrounding mountains and over maritime locations commonly exceeds 150 inches. Then, too, the typical winter storm season on the coast usually sees 100-mile-per-hour gales and 12-foot waves near Cape Blanco, Cape Foulweather, and at the mouth of the Columbia River near Astoria. And if that's not enough, the *World Almanac* cites Eugene as having the highest relative humidity on a monthly basis of any place in the U.S. (among the sampling of cities surveyed).

Statistics from the other side of the mountains make it clear that the sectional debate over whose climate is worse can best be summed up by the phrase, "choose your poison." To wit, Pendleton and Prineville have both recorded 119° F days. Two other eastern Oregon communities, Seneca and Ukiah, share the distinction for the lowest temperature, -54° F.

Such statistics should be viewed in their proper context. These climatic aberrations are not the reality that most Oregonians experience. In fact, the extremes of wind, rain, heat, and cold affect less than one percent of the population, leaving the vast majority in mild, temperate conditions.

FLORA AND FAUNA

FLORA

Trees

Oregon is known for its forests. The mixed-conifer ecosystem of western Oregon boasts such record specimens as the 302-foot Finnegan's Fir in the Coast Range outside Coos Bay, once rated the nation's largest Douglas fir by the American Forestry Association based on height, diameter, and crown size. Jumbo-sized western hemlock and Sitka spruce also exist in between Oregon's shoreline and the mid-Cascades. Within this region, the evergreen forest of the wet lowlands is the most productive belt of conifers in the world. This woodland carries up to 1,000 tons of plant matter per hectare and sometimes more.

While the record ponderosa pine outside Bend, the world's tallest Sitka spruce off U.S. 26 near Cannon Beach, the world's largest Monterey cypress in Brookings, and a bevy of similar distinctions might also rate a nod from the *Guinness Book of World Records,* the rainforest-to-desert diversity here is straight out of *Ripley's Believe It or Not!* With only seven percent as much rainfall as the Coast Range forests, 24,000 square miles of eastern Oregon's desert is largely sagebrush and juniper.

Tree lovers will also be taken by such arboreal aberrations as southern Oregon's redwood groves, the huge ponderosa pines in the middle of Christmas Valley desert, and fall color in Portland and Willamette Valley towns from deciduous trees planted by early pioneers. A particularly striking natural display along the McKenzie River mixes red vine maple and sumacs with golden oaks and alders against an evergreen backdrop.

Trees to Know in Oregon, published by the Oregon State University Extension Service in Corvallis, is an excellent aid to tree identification as well as a compendium of useful facts. Oregon schoolchildren first learn to distinguish between fir, spruce, hemlock, and ponderosa pine by a mnemonic device. The needles of a fir are flat, flexible, and friendly. Spruce needles are square, stiff and will stick you. Hemlock needles have a hammocklike configuration, and the crown of the tree is curved like it's tipping its hat. Finally, the ponderosa pine's platelike bark is also distinctive.

Flowers And Fruits

The state of Oregon has forever been associated in the public mind with such sobriquets as the "Emerald Empire" and the "Chlorophyll Commonwealth." While giant conifers and a profuse understory of greenery do in fact surround the state's most populous areas, this ecosystem represents only the most visible part of Oregon's bountiful botany. In between the mist-covered mountains and the deserts exist other worlds.

While not as visually arresting as the evergreens of western Oregon, the several varieties of blackberries in the state are no less pervasive. Found mostly from the coast to the mid-Cascades, blackberries favor clearings, burned-over areas, and people's gardens. Some Oregonians swear that they've seen this hardy vine growing on the fenders of cars! It also takes root in the woods alongside wild strawberries, salmonberries, thimbleberries, currants, and salal. Within this edible realm, wild food connoisseurs especially seek out the thin-leafed huckleberry found in the Wallowa, Blue, Cascade, and Klamath ranges. Prime snacking season for all these berries ranges from midsummer to midfall. During the fall, U-pick orchards are also popular. Apples in the Hood River Valley and on Sauvie Island, pears outside of Medford, and all of the above throughout the Willamette Valley are choice pickin's.

Autumn is also the season for those who covet chanterelle and morel mushrooms, particularly after the first rains. The Coast Range September through November is the prime picking area for chanterelles—a fluted orange or yellow mushroom in the tall second-growth Douglas fir forests. If you plan to sell what you find, you will need to purchase a permit from the National Forest Service for a nominal fee. After picking, don't put them in plastic bags. Use waxed paper or a basket, and leave them uncovered unless it's raining. This mycological harvest, along with the cutting of ferns, helps many residents of forest communities make ends meet. Maidenhair ferns command an especially high price from florists.

Exempt from exploitation but no less prized are the rare plant communities of the Columbia River Gorge and the Klamath/Siskiyou region. A quarter of Oregon's rare and endangered plants are found in the latter area, a portion of which is in the valley of the Illinois River, a Wild and Scenic tributary of the Rogue. One of these anomalies, *Kalmiopsis leachiana,* even has a wilderness named after it. Whole volumes have been dedicated to Oregon's singular ecosystems, such as *Rare Plants Of The Columbia Gorge* by Russ Jolley (Portland: Oregon Historical Society Press, 1990.)

Motorists will treasure such springtime floral fantasias as the dahlias and irises near Canby on I-5; the Easter lilies along U.S. 101 near Brookings; blue lupines alongside ORE 97 in central Oregon; apple blossoms in

the Hood River Valley near the Columbia Gorge; pear blossoms in the Bear Creek Valley near Medford; beargrass, columbines, and Indian paintbrush on Cascade thoroughfares; as well as Scotch broom, rhododendrons, and fireweed along the coast. And on some of the busiest highways in the state, Willamette Valley daffodils chart a springtime yellow brick road through the heart of the Emerald Empire.

Wildflower lovers will notice that in the country east of the Cascades the undergrowth is often more varied than the ground cover in the damp forests on the other side of the mountains. This is because sunny openings in the forest permit room for more species and for plants of different heights. And, in contrast to the white flowers that predominate in the shady forests in western Oregon, "dry-side" wildflowers generally have brighter colors. These blossoms must attract color-sensitive pollinators like bees and butterflies. On the opposite flank of the range, the commonly seen white trillium relies on beetles and ants for propagation, lessening the need for eye-catching pigments.

The hand of man has brought Oregon's horticultural highlights to the notice of flower lovers everywhere. Such world-famous displays as the **Hendricks Park Rhododendron Garden** in Eugene, Brookings's **Azalea State Park,** and the **International Rose Test Garden** in Portland all peak in mid-June. Not surprisingly, nationally known seed companies and nurseries proliferate in the western part of the state.

An especially good book, if you can find it, is *Wild Flowers of the Pacific Coast,* by L.L. Hoskin, published by Binford and Mort, 1934. In any case, there is no shortage of good flower books about each specific section of Oregon. Powell's on Burnside St. in Portland has a good collection. Since the color plates in many of these books make them expensive, you'll appreciate the fact that Powell's sells used editions at a discount.

Pseudotsuga menziessi,
Douglas fir

FAUNA

Wildlife

Oregon's creatures great and small comprise an excitingly diverse group, especially in so developed a country as the United States. Oregon's low population density, abundance of wildlife refuges and nature preserves, as well as biomes running the gamut from rainforest to desert, explain this variety.

Let's begin our overview from the ground up with the venerable Oregon slug. There are few places on earth where these snails-out-of-shells grow as large and in such numbers. The reason is western Oregon's climate: drier than drizzle but moister than mist. This balance and calcium-poor soil enables the native banana slug and the more common European black slug to thrive while being the bane of Oregon gardeners. When these three-to-ten-inch squirts of slime are not eating plants, you'll see them moving along at a snail's pace on some sidewalk or forest trail.

It's altogether fitting that the continent's fastest land mammal, the pronghorn, also walks the earth here . . . when it's not running, that is. Able to log over 60 miles per hour in short bursts, pronghorns prefer open country east of the Cascades. The low brush there suits their excellent vision, which enables them to spot predators. The most dangerous predator of all is kept at a distance by the boundaries of the **Hart Moun-**

Felis concolor, *mountain lion*

tain National Antelope Refuge (see "Lake County").

In like measure, such tracts as the **South Slough Estuary,** the **Malheur Bird/Wildlife Refuge,** the **Jewell Preserve for Roosevelt Elk,** and the **Finley Bird and Wildlife Preserve** provide safe havens for both feathered and furry friends.

While the dominant animals in each of the state's ecosystems are profiled in the relevant chapters, there are certain species whose ubiquitous presence demands an in-depth treatment.

Smaller Scavengers

Many of the most frequently sighted animals in Oregon are smaller scavengers. Even in the most urban parts of the state, it's possible to see raccoons, skunks, chipmunks, squirrels, and opossums. All are frequently encountered in woodsier neighborhoods, often around garbage cans, in parks, and near picnic areas. Urban gardens attract moles and pocket gophers.

West of the Cascades, the dark-colored Townsend's chipmunks are among the most commonly encountered mammals; east of the Cascades, lighter-colored pine chipmunks and golden mantled ground squirrels proliferate in drier interior forests. Expect to see the dark brown, cinnamon-bellied Douglas squirrel on both sides of the Cascades.

Urban jungles, suburbs, and bush communities throughout Oregon have seen an infestation of opossums. These docile nocturnal marsupials are usually sighted during twilight hours and often as road kills. Brought by a contingent of rural folk from Arkansas as a food source back in the '30s and '40s, their numbers have increased exponentially. In fact, people are becoming so used to North America's only marsupial that the opossum is taking on a new life as a domesticated household pet. They can't get rabies or distemper because their body temperatures are too low, and their ability to grasp objects with their tail and the presence of opposable thumbs make opossums fascinating to watch. Just catch them when they're awake. These nearly blind fruit and carrion eaters spend most of their lives asleep.

Raccoons are not so agreeable. These deceptively cute critters are really vicious scavengers who've earned a dubious distinction as

Eutamias townsendi, *chipmunk*

dog-killers. Though no match for many canines on land, they can even the odds by luring a family pet to water to drown. Be especially careful of potentially rabid mothers near cubs.

Eastern Oregon Critters
When talking about this region, it should first be noted that marine fossils dating back 225 million years were found in eastern Oregon creekbeds. These crustaceans were discovered in present-day Lake County, which today is home to such diverse wildlife as pronghorn antelope and wild mustangs. Since 99% of desert animals are nocturnal, it's difficult to see many of them. Nonetheless, their variety and exotic presences should be noted. Horned lizards, the red-and-black ground snake, the kit fox, and a four-inch-long greenish yellow hairy scorpion are some of the more interesting denizens of the desert east of the Cascade mountains. Should you ever have the chance to witness the intelligence of coyotes on the hunt or the nimble-footed bighorn sheep dancing along a precipitous ridge here, you'll never forget it.

Big Game And Fellow Travelers
Sportsmen and wildlife enthusiasts alike appreciate Oregon's big-game herds. Their habitats differ dramatically from one side of the Cascades to the other, with Roosevelt elk and blacktail deer in the west and Rocky Mountain elk and mule deer east of the Cascades. The Columbian whitetail deer is a seldom-seen endangered species that populates western Oregon. Pronghorn reside in the high desert country of southeastern Oregon.

While sightings are rare, the state boasts cougar and wild horse populations. Encounters with these shy creatures will become next to impossible as we approach the millennium, thanks to a state-sanctioned cougar hunt in the Cascades and the slow but sure federal auctioning off of the 60 or so captured wild mustangs which graze in the shadows of the Steens Mountains.

These so-called "Kiger" mustangs are believed to be descendants of horses that the Spanish conquistadores brought to America centuries ago. They are identified by their hooked ears, thin dorsal stripes, two-toned manes, and faint zebra stripes on their legs. Narrow trunks and a short back are other distinguishing physical characteristics. They sometimes can be identified from a distance by the herding instinct bred into them by the Spanish.

Beavers In The Beaver State
Castor canadensis, the Americas largest rodent, has long been the state of Oregon's mascot. For good reason: it was the beaver that inspired the fur brigades and spurred the initial exploration and settlement of the state. Apart from its role in bringing Europeans into the wilderness, the beaver merits a special mention for being perhaps the most important animal in Oregon's forest ecosystem. Contrary to pop-

Servus canadensis, *elk*

Castor canadensis, *beaver*

ular conception, the abilities of Mother Nature's carpenter extend far beyond the mere destruction of trees to dam a waterway. In fact, the activities associated with lodge construction actually serve to maintain the food chain and the health of the forest.

When a mated pair (beavers mate for life) packs sticks and mud to dam a river or stream, the resulting pool of deeper water in which they build their lodge protects these ungainly creatures from predation. The beavers' chances for survival are aided by their ability to enter the lodge underwater and to stay beneath the surface for as long as 20 minutes. Retractable membranes that protect their eyes and ear flaps enable them to dive comfortably, and a flat rudderlike tail helps them to swim. Add a pair of long, sharp middle teeth and beavers are perfectly equipped to cut trees into sticks of exact specifications and float them to the construction site.

The resulting lodge, together with the dammed beaver pond, creates a fertile web of life. Aged trees killed by the intrusion of a pond into a forest become homes for millions of insects, which provide food for woodpeckers and many other birds. Fish, turtles, frogs, and snakes soon inhabit the pond and its surrounding environment, and herons, muskrats, otters, and raccoons arrive later as part of the newly emerging ecosystem. Bears, birds of prey, and deer may come to the shore to drink or feed on smaller animals. Fish may feed on mosquito larvae deposited in the still waters. After the beavers have exhausted the nearby food supply and have moved on, the pond may eventually drain and become a fertile meadow and home to yet other creatures.

The presence of beavers has other positive implications for the nearby human population. In early times, pioneers coveted the fertile soil left from a drained beaver pond. Floods and droughts are tempered in the long run by beaver activities; controlling soil erosion and reducing forest fires are other positive byproducts. All of these benefits result from a beaver complex built of trees that are considered trash species by lumbermen—willow, birch, alder, vine maple, and certain kinds of pine.

The beaver's belated recognition from scientists as Oregon's forest manager comes along with an increased respect for the complexity of its social order. Despite the traditional rodent propensity for violence when living in close quarters, the beaver is distinguished by a peaceable demeanor. Even though the mating pair and their litter (kits) may be crammed into a small lodge, their ability to cooperate is notable. This seems to be due to touching and territoriality. Their instinct to groom one another has a soothing behavioral effect, and information conveyed by imparting their scent to sticks in the pond can serve to ward off other trespassing beavers. Then too, a higher order of rodent is created by the beaver's extra-long lifespan of 25 years. This enables it to socialize its young for several years, thus perfecting an intricate behavioral repertoire.

Beavers are widespread throughout the state, though they're most commonly sighted in second-growth forests after sunset. Oregon's estimated 174,000 of these creatures could be diminished in the future if the state pays heed to complaints from Christmas-tree farmers and orchard owners. To protect their trees, they are requesting that the state mascot become a "marked mammal." Whether or not these concerns are valid, a beaver hunt would be an ironic turn in the Beaver State—a region whose exploration and settlement were dependent on this animal.

Bears

Black bears, *Ursus americanus,* proliferate in remote mountain forests of Oregon. The state's Department of Fish and Wildlife estimates that 14,000 to 19,000 black bears roam the western Cascades and the Coast Range. Adults average between 200 and 500 pounds and have

ANNE LONG

Ursus americanus, *black bear*

dark coats. Despite Washington Cascades sightings of the feared grizzly—a species twice the size of the black bear, with three-inch claws, sharper teeth, and a meaner disposition—no encounters have been reported in the Oregon wilderness since 1931.

Black bears shy away from people except when provoked by the scent of food, when cornered or surprised, or upon human intrusion into territory near their cubs. Female bears tend to have a very strong maternal instinct that may construe any alien presence as an attack upon their young. Authorities often counsel hikers unfortunate or foolish enough to come between mama bear and her cub to lie down and play dead if she charges. Bears can run faster than the fastest human on steroids can sprint, and their retractable claws enable black bears to scramble up trees like squirrels. Furthermore, bears tend to give chase when they see something running.

So if you see a bear at a distance, try to stay upwind and back away slowly. Remember, bears are omnivorous, eating fruits and greens as readily as meat, but it is worth noting that human flesh has no appeal to them. In fact, some studies suggest that our body scent is abhorrent to bears.

Despite their strong sense of smell, bears possess very poor eyesight, which makes an attack by mistake a possibility, particularly when a human on the run evokes the behavior of the bear's prey. Bears can remove a human limb with one swipe of the paw, so an encounter should be avoided at all costs. To this end, campers should place all food in a sack tied to a rope and suspend it 20 feet or more from the ground.

About every third year the female gives birth to cubs. Her one to two young, born blind and helpless, usually in February, stay with her through the first summer and commonly den up with her the following winter. Humans tend to first see the cubs in the spring, when they are five months old, having no idea that at birth they were small enough to fit into a teacup.

Salmon

"To everything there is a season," and spring and fall are prime times to savor the fate as well as the flavor of the Pacific salmon. During these seasons, Oregon's rivers and streams become choked with spawning fish returning to the exact site of their conception, where they mate and die. As with the eruptions of Old Faithful geyser and the return of the swallows to Capistrano, this poignant dance of death affords a look at one of Mother Nature's time clocks.

The salmon's life cycle begins in a freshwater stream when the female deposits her eggs on some coarse sand and papa fertilizes them in vitro. Their bodies then deteriorate to become part of the food chain for young fish. Prior to their death, the adults starve themselves in their journey upriver from the ocean. The resulting weight loss acts as a deterrent to predators along the way. Thus, the optimum time for a fisherman to reel in something fit for dinner is prior to spawning.

Each species varies in the number of years it remains away from its home stream. The largest species, known as king or chinook, can spend as many as seven years away from its nesting (and ultimately its resting) place. For smaller species like chum, it is less than half that. Theories about how the salmon's miraculous homing instinct works range from electromagnetic impulses in the earth to celestial objects in the sky, but one thing has been established with certainty—"the nose knows." When salmon's olfactory orifices were stuffed with cotton and petroleum jelly, they were unable to find their spawning streams. The current belief is that baby salmon imprint the odor of their birth stream, enabling them to find their way home years later.

The salmon's traditional predators like the harbor seal, black bear, and herring gull pale in comparison to the threats posed by modern civilization. Everything from phosphates to nuclear waste have polluted Oregon waters, and until recently hydroelectric turbines threatened to block Oregon's all-important Columbia River spawning route. This was remedied somewhat when the U.S. Army Corps of Engineers built the fish ladders, a series of concrete baffles, at Bonneville Dam to divert the fish from turbine blades that would chop them to bits. These facilities, together with subterranean fish-viewing windows, offer a special perspective on the spawning phenomenon.

While viewing the salmon's life cycle in various rivers and streams in the fall and spring can be inspiring, most people's interests extend beyond food for the soul. Hence, let's briefly survey what's on the menu:

King or **chinook** salmon—the largest, sometimes weighing in at over 60 pounds. Touted as the best-tasting salmon when caught fresh (especially the spring chinook caught off the Rogue River estuary).

Silver or **coho** salmon—coveted by the Europeans for smoked salmon, it is also known as a fighting fish among sportsmen.

Sockeye or **red** salmon—the "money" fish.

Frequently seen in cans, this fish is also smoked and eaten fresh and commands a hefty price.

Chum salmon—known derogatorily as "dog salmon" because Canadian and Alaskan native people thought them only worthy of being fed to their dog teams. (Be aware that Oregon salmon contain a microorganism poisonous to dogs.) Today, this misconception has been replaced by the realization that these fish can be enjoyed canned or smoked.

Another variety, called **pink** salmon, is not caught south of Washington waters, but it is sold in Oregon stores. Among canned varieties, its tastiness rates below sockeye and coho but above chum.

As for fresh fish, you'll notice a variance in price based on how the salmon was caught. Troll salmon (usually chinook and coho in Oregon) are landed in the ocean by hook and line, one at a time. This method permits better handling than the net salmon, which are caught in large groups as they come upriver from the ocean to spawn. Thus, you'll pay more for troll salmon but you can taste the difference.

The results of a study by Swedish scientists completes our gustatory perspective on the Pacific salmon. These researchers found that wild salmon had three times the fat content of hatchery-raised fish. What's significant about this is that fat is what gives this species its flavor and, surprisingly, its healthful properties. The latter owes to the concentration of omega-three fatty acids, a proven inhibitor of heart disease. In addition to food value and flavor, wild salmon possess more vigor to survive the elements than do their hatchery-raised cousins, compelling a

Oncorhynchus tshawytscha, *chinook salmon*

reassessment of aquaculture's domination of the current fish population's gene pool.

Birds

Oregon is rapidly gaining a reputation as one of the best birding states. Seasonal variance in populations is often dramatic. Birdwatchers in the state for a long time, or during the interface of seasons, are best able to appreciate the diversity of the influx. For example, in the winter and summer the outskirts of Klamath Falls become inundated with more bald eagles than anyplace else in the lower 48; other times of year, many of these birds are in Alaska. But southern Oregon hunting season byproducts such as deer carcasses, road kills, and wounded waterfowl provide a ready food source for migrating carnivorous birds.

Birds of prey, or raptors, abound all over the state. Northeast of Enterprise and near Zum-

THE SPOTTED OWL ~ A BIRD IN THE HEADLINES

BOB RACE

The Northwest spotted owl is spoken of so passionately in Oregon that newcomers to the state might have the impression that every other person on the street is an ornithology buff. To the environmentalist, the bird represents the "indicator" species of the old-growth Douglas fir forest, an animal whose health and survival is synonymous with an ecosystem that took centuries to develop. To the loggers, the bird is the scourge of the timber industry, a species whose protection will tie up millions of acres of valuable trees, resulting in the loss of tens of thousands of jobs. To Oregon legislators in Washington, the bird represents a knotty problem, that of balancing the mandates of the 1972 Endangered Species Act and the interests of a public increasingly sensitive to environmental issues with the needs of almost 80,000 people who work in the state's forest-products industries.

The points of contention between the two constituencies are better understood when we examine the spotted owl's habits and habitat. In a 150-year-old Douglas fir forest, hollowed-out trees provide ideal nesting areas for these birds, while voles, snowshoe hares, flying squirrels, and other prey provide an abundant food supply. A mated pair needs 1,000 acres of old-growth forest to feed and reproduce, so the survival of several thousand mated pairs might require that logging of the few remaining ancient stands be stopped. The fact that these forests contain several times more biomass than any other forests in the world makes scientists covet them as a laboratory to study this crucial part of the food chain. They point out that destruction of the old-growth forests is like playing dice with Mother Nature. The counter argument contends that one person's conservation is another person's unemployment.

Old-growth Douglas fir makes straight-grained lumber with no knots. It is prized around the world as a building material par excellence. With lumber prices up worldwide and demand expected to increase 300% by the 21st century, the wood represents an economic bonanza. However dire the consequences to the spotted owl, sustained-yield forestry and the environment must be balanced against the consequences of reduced logging: destruction of families, communities, and the state's economy.

If the tangible concerns seem to cast spotted owl defenders as selfish ideologues, consider that an overall shortage of trees and automation in the mills will phase out logging revenues and employment drastically within the decade anyway. Perhaps extending the life of the spotted owl will extend the life of the logging industry.

ANNE LONG

Branta canadensis,
Canada goose

walt are perhaps the best places to see hawks. Species commonly sighted include the ferruginous, red-tailed, and Swainson's hawks. Along I-5 in the Willamette Valley, look for red-tailed hawks on fenceposts and American kestrels, North America's smallest falcons, sitting on phone wires. Farther south turkey buzzards circle the dry areas during the warmer months. Vultures are commonly sighted above the Rogue River. Along the lower Columbia east of Astoria, over a hundred bald eagles have chosen to winter during the past few years; in 1989 the Twilight Eagle Sanctuary was established in this estuary.

Those motoring on Sauvie Island near Portland will be treated to an amazing variety of birds. The northern third of this island is a protected wildlife refuge. More than 200 bird species come through here on the Pacific Flyway, feeding in grassy clearings.

The best inland locations to take in an array of migratory species are wildlife preserves such as Finley and Malheur. The latter is Oregon's premier bird retreat and stopover point for large groups of Canada and snow geese, whistling swans, and pintail ducks. It's also home to the rare sandhill crane.

Apart from great flocks of geese, gulls, and other shorebirds, the species most travelers notice are Clark's nutcracker and the Steller's jay, whose grating voice and large size (for a jay) often commands the most attention. Mountain hikers are bound to share part of their picnic lunch with these birds. The seven-foot wingspan of the great blue heron is also unforgettable.

Unfortunately, the western meadowlark, the state bird, has nearly vanished from western Oregon due to loss of habitat, but thanks to natural pasture east of the Cascades you can still hear its distinctive song. Just look for this bird's brown plumage with buff and black markings.

The meadowlark also is distinguished by a yellow underside with a black crescent pattern across the breast and white outer tail feathers.

In terms of sheer numbers and variety, the coast's mudflats at low tide and the tidal estuaries are the best birding environments. Rare species like tufted puffins and the snowy plover enjoy special protection here, along with other types of migratory waterfowl. *The Birder's Guide to Oregon,* by Joseph E. Evanich Jr. (Portland: Portland Audubon Society, 1990), will introduce you to the habits and hangouts of Oregon's avian ambassadors and clue you in to where you can break new ground. The author of the book himself candidly admits that much remains to be discovered, especially in the remote northeastern part of the state.

The zeal of **Oregon Birders** (Box 10373, Eugene 97440) is evident from their monthly publication, *Oregon Birds*. In addition to articles on various species and sightings, phone numbers for each part of the state are included for the **Oregon Rare Bird Telephone Network.** Should you see a particular bird of note, you can participate.

The U.S. Fish and Wildlife Service has established viewpoints for wildlife- and birdwatching at 12 Oregon national wildlife refuges. You can obtain specific information from these branches: Hart Mountain, (Room 308, Post Office Bldg., Lakeview 97630; tel. 947-3315), Malheur (Box 245, Princeton 97721; tel. 494-2323 or 494-2364), Umatilla (Box 239, Umatilla 97882; tel. 922-3232), which serves McKay Creek and Cold Springs, and William L. Finley (Route 2, Box 208, Corvallis 97333; tel. 757-7236), which serves Ankeny, Cape Meares, Oregon Islands, Three Arch Rocks, and Bandon Marsh.

Also of interest to serious birders and naturalists is the excellent *Oregon Wildlife Viewing Guide,* put together by Defenders of Wildlife and published by Falcon Press (Box 1718, Helena, MT 59624). Not only does this highly regarded resource list wildlife sites and nearby accommodations, but detailed state and regional maps and several guided nature trails offer independent readers the means to design their own wildlife adventure. Proceeds from the book go toward wildlife site maintenance and publications put out by Defenders of Wildlife.

HISTORY

NATIVE PEOPLES

Early Days

Long before the white man came to this hemisphere, native peoples thrived for thousands of years in the region of present-day Oregon. A popular theory concerning their origins maintains that their ancestors came over from Asia on a land/ice bridge spanning what is now the Bering Strait. Along with archaeological evidence, shipwrecks of Oriental craft on the Pacific coast also support the theory that Native Americans had Asian roots. This contention has been further substantiated by facial features and dental patterns common to both peoples, as well as isolated correspondences in ritual, music, and dialect.

Despite common ancestry, the tribes on the rain-soaked coast and in the Willamette Valley lived quite differently from those on the drier eastern flank of the Cascade Mountains. Tribes west of the Cascades enjoyed abundant salmon, shellfish, berries, and game. Great broad rivers facilitated travel, and rainforests ensured that there was never a dearth of building materials. A mild climate with plentiful food and resources allowed the wet-siders the leisure time to evolve a startlingly complex culture. This was perhaps best evidenced in their artistic endeavors, theatrical pursuits, and in such ceremonial gatherings as the traditional potlatch, where the divesting of one's material wealth was seen as a status symbol. Dentalia and abalone shells, woodpecker feathers, obsidian blades, and hides were especially coveted. Later on, Hud-

an Umpqua Indian

son's Bay blankets were added to this list.

Chinook, an amalgam of Indian tongues with some French and English thrown in, was the common argot among the diverse tribes that gathered in the Columbia Gorge during solstice. It was at these powwows that the coast and valley dwellers would come into contact with their poorer cousins east of the Cascades. These dry-siders led a seminomadic existence in order to follow the game and avoid the climatic extremes of winter and summer in their region. Subsistence needs were thus pushed to the fore in their cultures while recreational endeavors were limited.

The introduction of horses in the mid-1700s made hunting, especially for large bison, much easier. In contrast to the 100- by 40-foot longhouses of their west-of-the-Cascade counterparts, extended families in the eastern tribes inhabited pit houses when not hunting. Hunting necessitated caves or crude rock shelters.

Twelve separate nations populated Oregon. Although these were further divided into 80 tribes, the primary allegiance was to the village. The "nation" status referred to language groupings such as Salish and Athabascan. Tribal names such as Calapooya, Alsea, or Shasta Costa were usually derived from a word in the local argot for "The People," or from what the neighboring tribe called "Them." On occasion, white explorers bestowed a name upon the particular native grouping. An example of this was the "Rogue" Indian appellation. According to one theory, this name came from French fur trappers who referred to the troublesome thieves as "les coquins," which was translated as "the rogues." Another theory was that Rogue was inspired by its ocher riverbed, described as "rouge" by French trappers and subsequently misspelled. Across the region, many Indians were united in their worship of Spilyai, the coyote demigod. Spilyai, as well as many other figures animal and human, formed the subject of a large body of folk tales which explain the origins of the land in ways that are both entertaining and insightful.

The White Man

The coming of the white man meant the usurpation of tribal homelands, exposure to diseases of civilization like smallpox and diphtheria, and the passing of a way of life. Violent conflicts ensued on a large scale with the influx of settlers seeking missionary work and government land giveaways in the 1830s and '40s. In the 1850s, mining activity in southern Oregon and on the coast incited the Rogue River Indian Wars, adding to the strife brought on by annexation to the U.S.

All these events compelled the federal government to send in troops and to eventually set up treaties with Oregon's first inhabitants. The attempts at arbitration in the 1850s added insult to injury. Tribes of different, indeed often incompatible, backgrounds were rounded up and grouped together haphazardly on reservations, often far from their indigenous surroundings. In the century that followed, the evils of modern civilization destroyed much of the ecosystem upon which these cultures were based. An es-

pecially regrettable result of settlement was the decline of the Columbia River salmon runs due to overfishing and loss of habitat through pollution. This not only weakened the food chain but made the spiritual totem of the many tribes along the Columbia an expendable resource.

For a while, there was an attempt to restore the balance. In 1924, the government accorded citizenship to Indians. Ten years later, the Indian Reorganization Act provided for tribal guards and prohibited the sale of land to non-Indians. A decade later a court of treaty claims was established. In the 1960s, however, the government, acting on the premise that the Indians needed to assimilate into white society, terminated several reservations.

Recent government reparations have accorded many native peoples preferential hunting and fishing rights, monetary/land grants, and the restoration of tribal status to certain disenfranchised groups. There are now nine federally recognized tribes and four reservations in Oregon. Nonetheless, most of the 40,000 native people of the region feel they can never regain their birthright.

Archaeological Perspectives

To help measure what we've lost by the passing of the traditional ways, archaeologists have unearthed all manner of native artifacts. One that has evoked considerable controversy is a site found at Fort Rock, east of the Cascades near Bend. Charcoals from a hearth there are thought to be over 13,000 years old, exceeding earlier

The bicentennial wagon train retraced the pioneers' journey along the Oregon Trail.

estimates of the period of human presence in the region by about 4,000 years. A sandal found at the same site dated at 9,500 years old had been the previous standard-bearer. Another significant find is a gallery of 5,000-year-old petroglyphs on the walls of a cave in the foothills just east of the Willamette Valley. The valley itself boasts perhaps the best-known excavation in the state, due to its location on the site of the Oregon Country Fair near Eugene. Relics there have been dated at 8,000 to 10,000 years of age. Other recent finds include coastal and Rogue Valley digs where 9,000-year-old artifacts have been unearthed.

In terms of written history, a manuscript found in a Chinese monastery could have the distinction of being the first written account of a voyage to our continent. A Chinese navigator, Hee-li, was spirited from offshore Cathay waters by a violent storm. Both captain and crew survived the storm but were thrown off course during their return voyage by a cockroach lodged underneath a compass needle. Hee-li persisted in following the cockeyed compass in the direction he thought was west, despite sunsets appearing on the opposite horizon. After miles and miles of open ocean, the ship docked in a country of forests towering around a vast inlet, which the mariners explored. The manuscript, which supposedly dates to 217 B.C., was found 21 centuries later in the archives at Shensi Province by an American missionary to China. In it, a reference to towering trees and redfaced men could well have referred to the Pacific Northwest. In any event, Chinese and Japanese shipwrecks along the Oregon coast have been dated as early as the 5th century A.D. Potsherds and other ceramic artifacts found along the Columbia River also point to early contact with the Orient.

When you look at this evidence, it is clear that while east may be east and west may be west, the two probably *did* meet in the Oregon Country.

The only in-depth overview of Oregon's prehistory currently in print is *Oregon Archaeology*, by Melvin Aikens, obtainable for a nominal fee through the Department of the Interior, BLM, Oregon State Office (Box 2965-825, N.E. Multnomah St., Portland 97208).

EXPLORATION, SETTLEMENT, AND GROWTH

One theory of how Oregon got its name goes back to an encounter between the native peoples and the Spanish mariners who plied West Coast waters in the 17th and 18th centuries. Upon seeing the abalone shell earrings of the coastal Salish Indians, the sailors exclaimed, *"Orejon!"* ("What big ears!"). This was later anglicized to Oregon. Others have pointed out the name's similarity to those of such Spanish locales as Aragon and Obregon (in Mexico). A less fanciful explanation has it that the state's name was inspired by the English word *origin*, conjuring the image of the forest primeval. The French word *ouragan* (hurricane) has also been suggested as the source of the state's name, courtesy of French Canadian fur trappers who became the first permanent white settlers in the region during the early 19th century. In any case, Spanish, English, and Russian vessels came to offshore waters here in search of a sea route connecting the Atlantic with the Pacific. Accounts differ, but the first sightings of the Oregon coast have been credited to either Juan Cabrilho (in 1543) or the English explorer Sir Francis Drake (in 1579). Other voyagers of note included Spain's Vizcaíno and de Alguilar (in 1603) and Heceta (in 1775), and England's Cook and Meares during the late 1770s, as well as Vancouver (in 1792).

Sea otter and beaver pelts added impetus to the search for a trade route connecting the two oceans. While the Northwest Passage turned out to be a myth, the fur trade became a basis of commerce and contention between European, Asian, and eventually American governments. The pattern was repeated inland when the English beaver brigades eventually moved down from Canada to set up headquarters on the Columbia near present-day Portland.

American Expansion In Oregon
The Americans first came into the area when Robert Gray sailed up the Columbia River in 1792. The first American overland excursion into Oregon was made by the Corps of Discovery in 1804-07. Cocaptained by Lewis and Clark,

In 1807, Meriwether Lewis and William Clark arrived in Oregon along with their Corps of Discovery.

the expedition trekked across the continent to the mouth of the Columbia and back to St. Louis. Dispatched by Thomas Jefferson to explore the lands of the Louisiana Purchase and beyond, the expedition threw down the gauntlet for future settlement and eventual annexation of the Oregon Territory by the United States.

Lewis and Clark's exploration and mapping of Oregon wasn't the only impetus to America becoming a two-ocean power. The expedition also initially secured good relations with the Indians, thus establishing the preconditions to trade and the missionary influx. In fact, several decades after the coming of the expedition, the Nez Percé Indians sent a delegation to William Clark in St. Louis to ask for "The Book of Heaven," as well as teachers of the Word.

But before the missionaries came west, there were years of wrangling over America's right to settle in the new territory. John Jacob Astor's Pacific Fur Company was a case in point. The mere threat of British gunboats on the Columbia caused the quick departure of Astor's company during the War of 1812. It wasn't until the Convention of 1818 that the country west of the Rockies, south of Russian America, and north of Spanish America was open for use by American citizens as well as British subjects. The following year, the U.S. and Spain signed a treaty which fixed the present southern border of Oregon.

With the Monroe Doctrine in 1824 opposing European expansion in this hemisphere, another blow was struck toward removing the shackles of British rule in the Northwest.

During the 1820s, the Hudson's Bay Company continued to hold sway over Oregon country by means of Fort Vancouver, on the north shore of the Columbia. Over 500 people settled here under the charismatic leadership of John McLoughlin, who oversaw the planting of crops and the raising of livestock.

Despite the establishment of almost half a dozen Hudson's Bay outposts, several factors harbingered the inevitable demise of British influence in Oregon. Most obvious was the decline of the fur trade as well as England's difficulty in maintaining her far-flung empire. Less apparent but equally influential was the lack of females in a land populated predominantly by white trappers and explorers. If the Americans could attract settlers of both genders, they'd be in a position to create an expanding population base which could dominate the region. The first step in this process was the arrival of the missionaries. In 1834, Methodist soul-seekers led by Jason Lee settled near the Columbia River. Two years later Marcus and Narcissa Whitman's missions started up on the upper Columbia in present-day Washington (until 1853, the Washington area was considered a single entity with Oregon). The missionaries brought alien ways and diseases for which the Indians had no immunity. As if this weren't enough to provoke a violent reaction, the Indians would soon have their homelands inundated by thousands of settlers lured by government land giveaways.

But it wasn't just the Organic Act's 640 free acres that each adult white male could claim in the mid-1840s that fueled the march across the frontier. The westward expansion that Americans regarded as their "manifest destiny" leapt to the fore as a ready solution to the problems of the 1830s. During this decade, the country was in its worst depression yet, with land panics, droughts, and an unstable currency. Despite ignorance of western geography and the hardships it held, the Oregon Trail, a 2,000-mile frontier thoroughfare, was viewed with covetous eyes, especially in Missouri. (By 1840, 400,000 settlers had arrived there, tripling the population in 10 years.) Around Independence, Missouri, the trees thinned, the settlements ended, and the Oregon Trail began.

Over 53,000 people traversed the trail between 1840 and 1850 en route to western Oregon. In 1850, the Land Donation Law cut in half the acreage of the Organic Act, reflecting diminishing availability of real estate. But although a single pioneer man was now entitled to only 320 acres, and single women were totally excluded from land ownership, as part of a couple they could also own an additional 320 free acres. This promoted marriage, and in turn families, and helped to fulfill Secretary of State John C. Calhoun's prediction that American families could outbreed the single HBC trappers, thus winning the battle of the West in the bedroom.

The Land Donation Act also stipulated that non-whites could not own any part of the Oregon Territory, enabling the pioneers to seize native people's lands. The act impeded the growth of towns and industries too, as large parcels of land were given away to relatively small numbers of people, which kept the population geographically distant from one another. This was one reason why urbanization was slow in coming to the Northwest.

Early Government And Statehood
Nevertheless, there was enough unity among American settlers to organize a provisional government in 1843. Then, in 1848, the federal government decided to accord Oregon territorial status. With migration increasing exponentially from 1843 on, there was little doubt in Congress about Oregon's viability. Still, it took frontiersman Joe Meek to coalesce popular opinion. He had first performed this role in Champoeg, at the northern end of the Willamette Valley, in 1843 when he boomed out the rallying cry for regional confederation, "Who's for a divide?" In equally dramatic fashion, he strode into the halls of Congress fresh from the trail in mountain-man regalia to state the case for territoriality.

The Oregon Territory got off to a rousing start thanks to the California gold rush of 1849. The rush occasioned a housing boom in San Francisco and a need for lumber, and the dramatic population influx created instant markets for the agriculture of the Willamette Valley. Portland was located just north of the valley and 110 miles upriver from the Pacific on the Columbia,

near the world's largest supply of accessible softwood timber. The young city was in a perfect position to channel goods from the interior to coastal ports. So great was the need in California for food that wheat from eastern Oregon was declared legal tender. The exchange rate started around one dollar a bushel and went as high as six dollars. The economic benefits from the gold rush notwithstanding, Oregon lost two-thirds of her adult male population to gold fever. Many of the emigrants returned when the news of gold discoveries in southwestern Oregon came out between 1850 and 1860. The resulting influx helped establish the Rogue Valley and coastal population centers.

However, strategic importance and population growth alone do not explain Oregon becoming the 33rd state in the Union. It was no accident that shortly before statehood, the Dred Scott decision had become law in 1857. This had the effect of opening the territory to slavery. While slavery didn't lack for adherents in Oregon, the prevailing sentiment was that this controversial institution was neither necessary nor desirable. Because territorial status would be a potential liability to a Union on the mend, the congressional majority saw an especially compelling reason to open its doors to this new member. When nonslavery status was assured, Oregon entered the Union on Valentine's day, 1859.

Economic Growing Pains
During the years of the Civil War and its aftermath, internal conflicts were the order of the day within the state. By 1861, good Willamette Valley land was becoming scarce, so many farmers moved east of the Cascades to farm wheat, where they ran into violent confrontation with Indians over land. Between 1862 and 1934 the Homestead Act land giveaways helped fuel these fires of resentment. In the 1870s, cattlemen came to eastern Oregon, followed by sheep ranchers, whose presence precipitated range wars with the cattlemen. Just when it appeared that eastern Oregon land was ripe for agricultural promoters and community planners, the bottom fell out. Overproduction of wheat, uncertain markets, and two severe winters were the culprits. In the early 20th century a population influx created further problems by draining the water table. Thus, the glory that was gold,

OREGON ~ HOTBED OF BIOREGIONALISM

Oregonians have a well-deserved reputation for embodying the maverick spirit. Oregon's politicians, for example, don't always vote with a party majority, and even the state's motto, "She flies with her own wings," expresses this outlook. In addition, the state holds unofficial status as a haven to social, religious, and cultural groups who eschew convention. Therefore, it is altogether fitting to find the only serious American secessionist movement outside of the Southern Confederacy here.

At various times since the 1850s, the people of Oregon and northern California have tried to establish a new state. With common interests transcending state boundaries, inhabitants of this region attempted to secede in each of the years 1852-1854, and more recently, in 1941. This last drive, for an independent state of Jefferson (the name of the third president of the United States was chosen because of his vision of America as a self-sufficient agrarian country), was dramatized by a blockade of U.S. 99 at the Oregon-California border. The movement got as far as inaugurating an acting governor, but the U.S. entry into WW II several days later preempted further action.

These days, southern Oregon is once again a hotbed of bioregional revolt. The 1973 book *Eco-topia* by Ernest Callenbach, added fuel to the fire by proposing that northern California break off from the rest of the state to join with Oregon as a single republic based on environmental imperatives. Another bioregional manifesto, *The Nine Nations of North America*, divided the continent into nine bioregions on the basis of their cultural, historical, ethnic, economic, and environmental interests. The region north of San Francisco to Vancouver was identified once again as "Ecotopia."

In recent years the Ashland-Jacksonville area and the surrounding Rogue and Applegate valleys have carried the torch for bioregionalism, often invoking as a rallying cry the name of the late great state-that-never-was, Jefferson. With a constituency ranging from survivalists and radical environmentalists to folks just tired of big government and bureaucracy, this activist region coalesces the spirit of Jefferson throughout the state.

To keep up on the politics and the patrimony of Jefferson, read the excellent publication put out by the Southern Willamette Alliance. It is distributed free in natural-food stores and selected locations throughout the lower Willamette Valley and southern Oregon.

grass, and grain east of the Cascades was short-lived. Many eastern Oregon towns grew up and flourished for a decade, only to fall back into desert, leaving nary a trace of their existence.

Unlike the downturn east of the Cascades, boom times were ahead for the rest of the state as the 20th century approached. In the 1860s and '70s, Jacksonville to the south became the commercial counterpart to Portland, owing to its proximity to the Rogue Valley and south coast goldfields as well as the California border. During this period, transportation links began to consolidate. The first stagecoach, steamship, and rail lines moved south from the Columbia River into the Willamette Valley; by the 1880s, Portland was joined to San Francisco and the east by railroad. Henry Villard was the prime mover in this effort, eventually dominating all commerce in the Northwest by channeling freight and passengers through Portland and along the Columbia. In 1900, Union Pacific mag-nate James J. Hill picked up where Villard left off. By selling 900,000 acres of timberland to lumber baron Frederic Weyerhaeuser at $6 an acre (with the stipulation that Weyerhaeuser build his mills close by Union Pacific tracks), he hitched the destinies of both men and the region to the iron horse.

Progressive Politics

In the modern era, Oregon also blazed trails in the thicket of governmental legislation and reform. The so-called Oregon system of initiative, referendum, and recall was first conceived in the 1890s, coming to fruition in the first decade of this century. The system has since become an integral part of the democratic process.

In like measure, Oregon's extension of suffrage to women in 1912, a 1921 compulsory education law, as well as the first large-scale union activity in the country during the '20s, were red-letter events in American history. This tradition of reform continues to this day with Oregon's bottle bill and progressive land-use statutes. More recently, the Oregon Health Plan will attempt to extend health care coverage to the state's working poor by expanding the procedures covered by Medicaid. The plan's costs will be controlled by prioritizing various services, an idea which could set the precedent for a future federal health insurance plan. But while Oregon's plan has been given the go-ahead by the feds, it still isn't clear if there will be enough funds to pay for it, given huge state budget deficits.

The 1930s were exciting years in the Northwest. Despite widespread poverty, the foundations of future prosperity were laid during this decade. New Deal programs such as the Works Projects Administration and the Civilian Conservation Corps undertook many projects around the state. Building roads and hydroelectric dams created jobs and improved the quality of life in Oregon, in addition to bolstering the country's defense during wartime. Hydroelectric power from the Bonneville Dam, completed in 1938, enabled Portland's shipyards and aluminum plants to thrive. Low utility rates encouraged more employment and settlement, while the Columbia's irrigation water enhanced agriculture.

In addition to laying the foundations for future growth, the war years in Oregon and their immediate aftermath were full of trials for state residents. Vanport, a city of 18,000 (at one time, 45,000) that grew up in the shadow of Kaiser aluminum plants and the shipyards north of Portland, was washed off the map by a Columbia River flood. Tillamook County forests, which supplied Sitka spruce for airplanes, endured several massive fires which destroyed 500 square miles of trees. Along with these natural disasters, Oregon was the only state among the contiguous 48 to have a military installation shelled by a Japanese submarine (see "Astoria"), to endure a Japanese bombing mission on the mainland (see "Brookings and Vicinity"), and to suffer civilian casualties when a balloon bomb exploded (see "Lake County"). While California also sustained an attack when a Japanese surface submarine put a shell into a Southern Pacific Daylight train near Goleta, only Oregon experienced all three wartime mishaps.

With the perfection of the chainsaw in the 1940s, the timber industry could take advantage of the postwar housing boom. Today, Oregon's resource-based economy has followed a boom-bust cycle. The timber and fishing industries have been especially hard hit by the current era of limits. While Oregon's traditionally humanistic outlook and environmental advocacy have been somewhat tempered by these economic tensions of late, the state still enjoys a reputation for being both progressive and pristine.

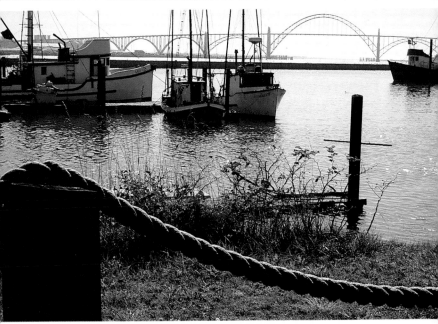

(preceding page) an abandoned boat dock along the Tillamook River (Warren Weber);
(this page, top) surfers at Indian Beach (Mary Orr);
(this page, bottom) Yacquina Bay harbor, Newport (Warren Weber)

ECONOMY AND INDUSTRY

The leading industries within the state are forestry and agriculture, followed by tourism and high-tech enterprises. But these rankings only tell part of the story; the scenario for every sector of Oregon's economy should change dramatically in the coming years.

The ripple effects from the decline in timber will affect many aspects of society in the Northwest. Weyerhaeuser, Georgia Pacific, and other wood-products giants are bracing for a reduction in the allowable cut as well as export restrictions. More timber from private holdings, as opposed to government lands, will be harvested, and jobs will shift to the manufacture of secondary wood products such as doors, window frames, laminated beams, and furniture parts.

In agriculture, specialty products have become the fastest-growing business in Oregon. These products include wine grapes, ginseng, organic produce, chanterelle mushrooms, goat cheese, and other fare prized by "foodies." Larger agribusiness entities that rely on grass seed or bulk produce have had problems due to such environmental safeguards as limitations on field burning and bans on certain pesticides. Restrictions on the use of illegal aliens have also depleted a cheap labor pool. Nonetheless, the booming food-processing and packing industries in Oregon will continue to thrive.

High-tech industries and tourism are often mentioned as the state's future moneymakers. Both owe their rosy reputation to being in the right place at the right time. The region's pure water and low utility rates are ideal for computer chip manufacture; low production costs and a high quality of life have also helped attract the computer industry. Oregon is in a perfect position to be "discovered" as a refuge from California's inflated prices and increasing urbanization. According to Atlas and Allied moving companies, Oregon was the most moved-into state in 1992, and California the most moved-out-of. The Japanese are also expected to come here to take advantage of world-class *kulturfests* and nature on a grand scale.

Cost Of Living/Shopping Opportunities

In 1992, *Money* magazine considered Oregon second only to New York as the state with the heaviest tax burden. This might be true for folks with high incomes such as those in the magazine's survey, but the lack of sales tax here, cheap car-registration fees, and comparatively low real estate prices are boons to the average wage earner. In fact, the U.S. Census Bureau places Oregon in the middle of the pack in its tax burden survey. Those passing through needn't be concerned with the state's income tax. In-

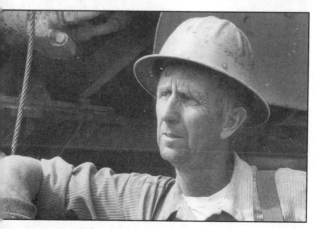

Oregonians depend heavily on a resource-based economy.

stead, they can revel in the shopping opportunities here, which include an abundance of craft fairs, auctions, and garage sales.

The profusion of locally made objets d'art available in **Made in Oregon** shops in the larger cities deserves special mention, as does the potlatch of creations at the Portland and Eugene Saturday markets (for more details, see those cities' chapters). Coastal and mountain resort areas also purvey the work of nationally known potters, woodworkers, painters, jewelers, and glass artisans from Oregon. These homemade items often go for quite a bit less than would be charged in out-of-state markets for work of comparable quality. While these "arts" cottage industries don't have the "bottom line" of timber and agriculture, they are one of the more visible and appreciated forms of economic activity a traveler to this state encounters. The best guide to shopping for indigenous items is *Where to Find Oregon in Oregon,* written and published by Bridget Beattie McCarthy (7277 S.W. Barnes Rd., Portland 97225).

Throughout the Northwest you'll encounter Fred Meyer, the region's leading retailer. In addition to offering good buys on merchandise, this company maintains an orientation in keeping with the state's environmental ethic. Its boycott of drift-net tuna, support of a regional ban on phosphates, and assurance of pesticide-free produce bespeaks this commitment.

LUMBER

Logging and wood products have historically been the most important industries to Oregon in terms of jobs provided and revenue produced. Currently, 79,400 workers are employed in logging, sawmills, and paper production, contributing about 3.1 billion dollars or seven percent of Oregon's gross state product. Timber revenues have also contributed millions to state schools and sociocultural programs. Oregon is the leading supplier of wood products in the nation, providing one-fifth of the country's softwood lumber.

Throughout its history, the Oregon logging industry has been dogged by controversy. In the 1920s, shoddy treatment of workers resulted in the first large-scale unionization in the country and inspired the spadework for the AFL-CIO.

Currently, the forestry and economic practices which are the basis of the industry are being questioned. This could result in the reduction of the allowable cut and devastating losses in employment and revenue. Regardless of the imminent ban on logging in spotted owl habitats and the like, the industry will face a slowdown in the '90s simply because of the lack of trees to cut.

The larger implications of the transition from a timber-based economy hinge on the speed and effectiveness of economic diversification.

a common sight on Oregon highways

But even with Oregon's impressive gains in tourism, high-tech industries, and specialized agriculture, it will be difficult to replace an industry that has permeated every aspect of Oregon life. The new forestry orientation has created job opportunities for tree-planters, since the law mandates that for every one tree cut on federally owned land, at least six must be replanted.

AGRICULTURE

In the 1930s a Woody Guthrie song extolled the "pastures of plenty" in the Northwest. Six decades later, the pastures are still plentiful, only more so. Oregon leads the world in the production of such varied agricultural commodities as filberts, peppermint, blackberries, rhubarb, several kinds of grass seed, and Christmas trees. The Willamette Valley boasts the most diversified farming region on the planet; the Bing and maraschino cherries and elephant garlic were developed here, and the Valley's legendary fertility inspired tens of thousands of Oregon Trail emigrants.

An oft-heard refrain in pioneer days was "Crops never fail west of the Cascades." The Oregon Trail migration and government land giveaways resulted in the settlement of most of the Willamette's good agricultural land by the mid-1850s. In the 1860s, gold-rush activity put a premium on eastern Oregon's wheat. Later on, alfalfa, sheep, and livestock diversified farmers' options on the dry side of the mountains. Today, this region's food-processing plants have enjoyed a boom, particularly with the potato crop; McDonald's gets most of its spuds for french fries from eastern Oregon, as do several of the leading potato-chip and frozen-food manufacturers. Oregonians themselves look to the east side toward Hermiston for the best melons and potatoes in the state.

The golden age of Oregon agriculture began with the tapping of the Columbia River for irrigation water, enabling large-scale farming to get started. At about the same same time, World War II compelled Oregon to develop her own flower-bulb industry, instead of relying upon Japan. Today, Oregon is a leader in nursery crops, ornamental flowers, and flower seed production.

If you're interested in roadside agriculture, certain highways have signs identifying crops and some livestock operations. Look for these signs in Hermiston, Pendleton, The Dalles, Hood River, Madras, Redmond, Medford, Ashland, and Brookings. Agricultural operations are also labeled along I-5 and U.S. 99 in the Willamette Valley, the Sunset Highway between Portland and the coast, ORE 34 from Corvallis to the coast, and ORE 211 out of Molalla.

Oregon grows over 180 different commercial commodities. Only California ranks ahead of Oregon in crop diversity. Agriculture-related employment accounts for 300,000 jobs, with four out of 10 Oregonians involved in getting food from the farm to market.

Perennial leaders among vegetable crops in the state are onions, sweet corn, and snap beans. The top corporate agricultural revenue producers include such giants as Tillamook Cheese and Norpac (the state's largest farmer-owned food processor) While beef, grass seed, dairy products, and wheat have traditionally been the leading economic entities in the state's several-billion-dollar farm economy, specialty crops and processing currently enjoy the fastest rates of growth. In addition, Oregon wineries garner top honors in international competitions, with the bulk of the prizes going to the Pinot Noir and chardonnay varietals from Yamhill County.

GOLD AND MINERALS

While not a major economic force in the modern era, gold mining played a pivotal role in the early growth of towns throughout the state. In the decade following the California gold rush of 1849, thousands of miners came into southern Oregon because of gold finds in the Rogue Valley and on the south coast. The boomtown of Jacksonville was created in 1851 near a gold-bearing creek, and the Applegate Trail became the low-road alternative to the Oregon Trail for cross-country emigrants. Baker, Jacksonville's eastern Oregon counterpart, was located near the main spur of the Oregon Trail. Both places were reputed to be among the wildest towns west of Chicago during the mid-19th century. In any case, Oregon gold production helped the Union win the Civil War. One stretch of Canyon Creek near Canyon City in the John Day area of eastern Oregon yielded $28 million in gold for Union coffers.

BUREAU OF LAND MANAGEMENT

miners at the Greenhorn Mine, circa 1913

In addition to the Canyon City strike, there was other activity that compounded the impression that 1860 was a golden decade. During that era, gold finds launched Jacksonville as a center of commerce. In addition, gold was reported in the foothills surrounding Cottage Grove, near the southern tip of the Willamette Valley. This latter discovery by James "Bohemia" Johnson (so named because of his heritage) in 1863 lay virtually dormant until the early 20th century, due to insufficient technology to mine the million-dollar deposits.

The Bohemia mining country also generated a story, perhaps apocryphal, that part of Cottage Grove was paved with gold-rich gravel from the Row River. So far, no one has been willing to rip up the streets and check. To the south 150 miles, the "streets of gold" story was rehashed with a new twist during the Depression, when residents unearthed tens of thousands of dollars from old claims in their back yards.

In the 1990s, a process that involves the cyanide leaching of gold-laden soils is slated for large-scale implementation in southeastern Oregon, despite the protests of ranchers and environmentalists. Throughout the state, gold is still in "them thar hills," but its price on the world market has to be high enough to make it financially feasible to extract.

Southwestern Oregon is often touted as the part of the state with the most mineral wealth.

The only producing nickel mine and smelter in the U.S. is still operating in Riddle, a small Douglas County town off of I-5. In addition to gold and nickel, deposits of copper, chromium, platinum, manganese, asbestos, mercury, iron, molybdenum, zinc, coal, and limestone have been mined in the region. South coast offshore-oil and mineral-mining leases have been proposed, but environmental restrictions make such operations more likely off the central coast near Newport.

But when all is said and done, the most mundane minerals and aggregates make the most money. Sand, gravel, and limestone for the manufacture of cement account for half of these revenues in the state's 153-million-dollar-a-year mining economy.

FISHING

The exploitation of Oregon's fishing resources has been an enduring aspect of life in the region for thousands of years. Salmon has always been the most valued species. Native Americans on both sides of the Cascades have depended upon it, and commercial fishermen have viewed it as a mainstay for over a century.

The advent of commercial salmon fishing was late in coming due to the pioneer preoccupation with mining, logging, and agriculture. Canning technology and fishing methods first perfected in Alaska made their way down to Oregon in the 1860s in time to meet the demands of emerging domestic and foreign markets. In the modern era, Oregon salmon fisheries have grown into a megabusiness which nets well over a hundred million dollars annually.

Still, the future is troubling to contemplate, given the evolution of the industry. At first, fish wheels (see "Cascade Locks") depleted rivers once so choked with spawning fish that a pioneer pitchfork stuck haphazardly into the water would often yield a salmon. Dam construction and pollution joined overfishing to further reduce the catch. In recent years, Asian drift nets have emerged as the most virulent scourge of all. Northwest fishermen say the 30-mile-long, 50-foot-deep driftnets rake off millions of pounds of baby salmon annually, which would otherwise have returned to waters in the American Northwest.

The salmon shortfall and other outgrowths of the drift-net debacle have motivated increasing diversification. A caviar industry (derived from Columbia River sturgeon) as well as alternative ocean fisheries have developed. Bottom fishing for black ling cod and rockfish, together with the harvest of such long-ignored species as hake, whiting, and pollock have increased in proportion to the decline of salmon, flounder, albacore tuna, smelt, and halibut. Clam, oysters, shrimp, and crab continue to be strong facets of the industry, despite occasional pollution problems. Recently unearthed shellfish middens (mounds) dating back to ancient Indian times indicate that these species were the most enduring part of the Northwest diet.

CAMPING AND OUTDOOR RECREATION

Oregon has more state parks than anyplace else in the country, as well as a natural environment suited to all manner of recreational activities. With a coastline that is largely owned by the public, the nation's first scenic highway in the Columbia Gorge, and the country's fifth national park at Crater Lake, the land ethic was given eloquent voice early here. In order to keep Oregon the way it is, here are some suggestions:

- Stay on the trails so as not to increase the rate of erosion or destroy such fragile vegetation as alpine wildflowers.
- Use established campsites, avoid digging tent trenches or cutting vegetation.
- Camp several hundred feet from water sources.
- Bring a tool to dig a latrine and make it four to six inches deep.
- As for trash, if you pack it in, pack it out. Leave nothing but footprints.
- Avoid feeding wild animals so as not to inhibit their natural instinct to fend for themselves.

TRAILS, EQUIPMENT, AND RESERVATIONS

Trails Information System

The Trails Information System (TRIS) allows the public access, via computer screen, to a data base of trail information from national forests, national parks, and state and local agencies. Boot up your desired info by trail name or number or by a desired experience (e.g., Mt. Hood Lakes). The computer record includes such "specs" as access, length, difficulty, elevation, and management agencies. TRIS screens are available free of charge at such outlets as the Willamette National Forest office and Collin's Cycle Shop in Eugene, the Zig Zag Ranger District on Mt. Hood, and the REI Co-op and the Multnomah County Library in Portland (addresses available in respective chapters). For more information on TRIS and trails in general contact the U.S. Forest Service (319 S.W. Pine St., Portland 97208; tel. 326-2877).

Mountain bikers and hikers on Oregon trails will appreciate the 911 Oregon maps published

With the most state parks in the nation, Oregon offers great odds of finding the perfect campsite.

by the U.S. Geologic Survey. They can be purchased in bookstores and outdoor stores for about $3 each. A few hints might help first-time users. First, the fine squiggly lines covering the map are called "contour lines." When you see them close together, expect steep slopes. Conversely, kinder, gentler terrain is indicated by larger spaces between contour lines.

By molding a pipe cleaner in the pattern of a trail, then straightening it out and superimposing it on the mileage scale at the bottom of the map, you can find out the distance you'll be covering.

User Permits, Equipment

A permit is now a prelude to hiking in three heavily used national forest wilderness areas— Three Sisters, Mt. Jefferson, and Mt. Washington. Between May 23 and October 31, you must pick up these free permits at ranger stations and selected outdoor stores (for overnight camping), or at the trailheads (for day-use). Rangers generally stop short of issuing citations for non-compliance, but there will come a time soon when use restriction in certain areas will mandate punitive enforcement for those who ignore this formality.

As you may know, clothing in layers of polypropylene, wool, and Gore-Tex are the best choices on most Oregon camping trips. Lightweight down vests are always appreciated for their warmth and make great pillows. Those camping in the Columbia Gorge as well as the Coast and Klamath ranges during early spring

might bring along rain pants. Danner boots, made right in Oregon, are tailored specifically to the state's rainforest, alpine, and desert regions. Get discount prices at the factory outlet (12722 N.E. Airport Way, Portland; tel. 251-1111). Whatever brand of boot you buy, it's a safe bet that waterproofing will be useful here.

Lightness, durability, and water-resistance are also the predominant criteria in choosing tents and sleeping bags. Neophyte hikers are reminded that tents and bags should be as compact as possible. These considerations compel the selection of down as the preferable "fill" for sleeping bags, even though these bags can be faulted for becoming useless when wet. Nonetheless, their lightness, warmth, and compressibility supersede the higher resistance to moisture of synthetic fill. To make sure down retains its advantages, bring along a foam mat or Therm-A-Rest inflatable pad in a Gore-Tex stuff bag (or a plastic bag—both waterproof and cheap). The pad provides extra insurance for a comfortable night on the damp, uneven terrain in many locales. The best synthetic fill, according to some, is Quallofil by Du Pont.

While it cools down significantly at night almost everywhere in Oregon during the June to October peak hiking season, the diurnal temperature variations are the most pronounced in the high Cascades and in the Wallowas, necessitating heavier fill in your sleeping bag. Among popular camping areas, coldest of all could well be Steens Mountain in summer, fre-

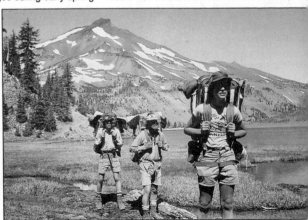

on the trail through the Green Lakes basin

quently recording subfreezing nocturnal temperatures. By contrast, the Willamette and southern Oregon valleys along the I-5 corridor sometimes experience daytime heat continuing into the night; at such times a down bag becomes a sweat lodge. Regardless of the kind of bag you choose, it should have a waterproof cover.

In like measure, tents should have rainflys. Dome tents are the best choice, given their ease of setup and lightweight construction; waterproof ones go for a little over $100. Probably the best selection in the state is available at the **REI Co-op** in Portland's Jantzen Beach Mall (1798 Jantzen Beach Center, Portland 97217; tel. 283-1301), just off I-5 near the Columbia River. There is also an outlet in Tualatin and one in downtown Eugene (306 Lawrence St.). All of these stores have pamphlets on what to look for when buying tents, stoves, packs, etc., as well as helpful staff.

Discount prices are available at **Andy and Bax** (324 S.E. Grand, Portland; tel. 234-7538). Everything from U.S. Army reissue coolers and other G.I. surplus to a wide variety of camping equipment is available here. Specialty items such as Metsker Oregon County maps and whitewater guidebooks will also be appreciated by the outdoorsperson.

As long as we're on the subject of camping-gear outfitters, it should be mentioned that Oregon is one of the best places in the world to purchase equipment. First of all, Portland, Bend, and the two college towns of Eugene and Corvallis boast many stores and equipment manufacturers that cater to the Oregonian love affair with the outdoors. Since these purchases tend to run into higher figures wherever you shop, Oregon's comparatively low overhead and lack of sales tax helps keep costs down. Look for markdowns on items with "blems" or cosmetic defects, as well as "annex" stores selling same or closeout items. If you need a high level of sophistication in your gear, chances are you'll find state-of-the-art hardware within the Beaver State.

One item many travelers might have to purchase on-site will be fuel for cookstoves, since its transport is prohibited on commercial airlines. White gas is the best, but for flexibility, bring a stove that uses a variety of fuels. Propane rates highly with many campers because of its low

cost and compatibility with other camping implements. Nonetheless, its volatility makes it potentially hazardous. Stoves are very important to have on many treks because of the shortage of dry firewood.

Flashlights or lanterns are essential for comfort and safety. Commonsense items like water-purification tablets, sunscreen, a canteen, a Swiss army knife, cooking and eating utensils, freeze-dried food, maps and compasses, plastic bags, and nylon twine will also ensure a bon voyage. Certain trips will also require mosquito repellent and wooden matches dipped in nail polish or wax (for waterproofing). Finally, a safety kit containing iodine, lip balm or Chapstick, diarrhea medication, aloe vera, aspirin, antibiotics, and bandages or Band-Aids is also a good idea; add eye drops, antihistamine and/or allergy medicine if you're camping in or near the Willamette Valley from April till July.

Fire Lookouts

A relatively new and romantic option for campers is the opening-up of fire-lookout stations for overnight stays. We say "campers" because these places all have wood heat, no electricity, and an outhouse. Although there are sometimes furnishings, you have to bring your own bedding, and getting there sometimes can involve an uphill hike of as much as several miles. In some cases, cross-country skis or snowshoes are required to get to your hideaway. To reserve one of these ultimate rooms-with-a-view, contact the Forest Service ranger districts which maintain these facilities, most of which are either out-of-service or out-of-season lookouts. Rent per night is usually in the $20-30 range.

At this writing, several ranger districts with lookouts are available for overnights, but there are many more in the process of restoration. The program has proved so popular that weekends are usually booked up well in advance, but weekdays are frequently open. In addition to the places listed below, you can get updates on new lookouts which are opening up for overnights by writing to the **Oregon Lookout Association** (Box 11501, Eugene 97440).

The existing facilities include Ludlum House, Snow Camp, and Packers Cabin on the south coast (c/o Chetco Ranger Station, 555 Fifth St., Brookings 97415; tel. 469-2196), Acker Rock (c/o Tiller Rock Ranger Station, 27812 Tiller Trail, Tiller 97484; tel. 825-3201) in southwestern Oregon, and Five Mile and Flag Point lookouts in the Cascade foothills (c/o Barlow Ranger District, Box 67, Dufur 97021; tel 462-2291). In contrast to the summertime availability of their counterparts, the Barlow lookouts are available November through May. If the skies are clear here, you can see north to Mt. Adams, Mt. St. Helens, and Mt. Rainier, with Mt. Hood to the west.

Camping Reservations

Reservations are accepted at 13 high-use state park campgrounds in Oregon from Memorial Day through Labor Day. Reservations are not necessarily required, but are advisable, particularly at the coastal sites. Applications can be procured by mail or in person from the State Park Headquarters (525 Trade St., Salem 97310, tel. 378-6305), as well as from Department of Motor Vehicles offices, police stations, chambers of commerce throughout the state, or any one of the 13 campgrounds. The campsite info phone (238-7488 in Portland, 800-452-5687 elsewhere) can give you campsite availability information. In addition, you can get them from the particular park. Hand delivery of applications is discouraged due to limited staff. Instead, send a $20 check or money order, which covers the park fee plus processing to State Park Headquarters. You're limited to three separate residential dates per envelope. It's a good idea to call before submitting a reservation to find out if there are any spaces left. The parks included are as follows:

Coastal locations: Harris Beach near Brookings, Sunset Bay near Coos Bay, Honeyman near Florence, Beachside, Beverly Beach, and South Beach near Newport, Devil's Lake near Lincoln City, Cape Lookout near Tillamook, and Fort Stevens near Astoria.

Inland locations: Cove Palisades near Culver, Detroit Lake near Detroit, Wallowa Lake near Joseph, and Prineville Reservoir near Prineville. Reservations are taken as early as January, so don't delay. Should everything be booked, the 800 number gives advice on non- · reservation sites and campgrounds run by other agencies.

For camping-related agencies such as the U.S. Forest Service and Dept. of Fish and Wildlife, etc., see "Information," following, in this Introduction.

Oregon Whitewater Sampler

Oregon's world-class whitewater rafting proves that the winter rain clouds here have a silver lining. With 90,000 river miles in the state and hundreds of outfitters to choose from, however, neophyte rafters may have the problem of sorting out an embarrassment of riches. To help navigate the tricky currents of brochure jargon and select the experience that's right for you, here's a list of rivers to run and questions to ask before going:

The famous **Rogue River** reaches its whitewater crescendo at the green forested canyons of the Klamath Mountains in southwestern Oregon. Come June through September to see abundant birds and wildlife and avoid the rainy season. This run is characterized by gentle stretches broken up by abrupt and occasionally severe drop-offs as well as swift currents. Water turbulence on the Rogue is often intensified by constricted channels created by huge boulders. At day's end, superlative campsites give repose to savor your adventures.

Despite the dryness and isolation of Oregon's southeast corner, the **Owyhee River** has become a prime destination for whitewater enthusiasts. The reasons include the red-rock canyons, lava flows, and high desert panoramas which line its course. The 53 miles from Rome to the Owyhee Reservoir has only one section of exceptionally heavy rapids, but the many pools of short, intense whitewater alternating with easy drifts make for a well-paced trip. Be careful not to be lulled by stretches of placid water or such eye-catching diversions as a 10-mile gorge lined by 1,000-foot-high walls, because sharp rocks abound along the Owyhee's course. The best times to come are during May and June. Before going, check conditions with the National Weather Service in Portland (tel. 249-0666) because the Owyhee can only be run in high snow-melt years.

The **John Day River** in northeastern Oregon offers an even-flowing current as it winds through unpopulated rangeland and scenic rock formations. Below Clarno, the grade gets steep, creating the most treacherous part of the state's longest river (275 miles). The 157-mile section of the John Day which rafters, canoeists, and kayakers come to experience also has falls near the mouth which require a portage. The special charm of this Columbia tributary is the dearth of company you'll have here even during the river-running seasons of late March to May and then again in November. Just watch out for rattlesnakes along the bank.

Unlike the John Day and the Owyhee rivers, the **Deschutes** rapids aren't totally dependent on snowmelt. As with the Rogue, river runners enjoy superlative conditions even in the driest of years. As a result, it has become the busiest vacation waterway in the state. The 44 miles between Maupin and the Columbia River contain sage-covered grasslands and wild rocky canyons where you might see bald eagles, pronghorns, and other wildlife. If there's a good run of salmon you might also encounter plenty of powerboats too. Expect most of the thrills and spills near the mouth of Oregon's second-longest river (250 miles). Heavy winds might also whip up in the final quarter of the journey. With an average of 310 days of sunshine annually, weather is seldom a problem except for excessively hot summer days.

Two self-published guides offer blow-by-blow descriptions of these and other rivers in the state: *The Soggy Sneakers Guide to Oregon Rivers* (Willamette Kayak/Canoe Club, Box 1062, Corvallis 97330) and *Oregon River Tours* by John Garren (Garren Publishing, 1008 S.W. Comus, Portland 97219). A good selection of in-depth guides focusing on each river individually is available at Andy and Bax (324 S.E. Grand, Portland 97214; tel. 234-7538). Up-to-the-minute conditions can be certified at the National Weather Service in Portland (tel. 249-0666).

Knowing the contours and characteristics of the river you want to float does not alone ensure a good trip. Choosing an outfitter who can meet your "specs" on cost, style, safety, and the degree of your own participation is integral to an enjoyable experience. A good place to begin is by procuring *The Oregon Guides and Packers Directory* (Box 10841, Eugene 97440; tel. 683-9552). This publication's long roster of white-

water raft trip operators lists the address/phone of each company and their itineraries. Should you consult commercial backpacking magazines and newspaper sports and travel sections, chances are that the blurbs might include adjectives like "participatory" (i.e., you paddle and perhaps help set up camp) and "deluxe" (i.e., you don't paddle if you don't want to, fancy equipment, and good eats provided).

However, detailed as these listings may be, they mean little without some follow-up. For example, if "gourmet meals" are advertised, find out what they include. To ensure an intimate wilderness experience, ask about the number of people in a raft and how many rafts on the river at one time. Are there any hidden costs such as camping gear rental or added transfer charges? What is the cancellation policy? Another consideration is the training and experience of the guides. Can he or she be expected to give commentary about history, geology, and local color? You might also want to check about the company's willingness to customize its trips to special interests like photography, bird-watching, or hiking. Finally, a discussion of safety may be facilitated by a knowledge of the system used to classify river rapids:

Approximate Difficulty of Rapids		Skill Level
Class 1	Easy	Beginner
Class 2	Requires Care	Intermediate
Class 3	Difficult	Experienced
Class 4	Very difficult	Highly Skilled
Class 5	Exceedingly Difficult	Expert Crew
Class 6	Unnavigable	Get Life Insurance

The Oregon whitewater enthusiast's cup runneth over, thanks to the state's securing federally designated Wild and Scenic status for thousands of river miles within her boundaries. Oregon's environmental leadership helped create the Wild and Scenic Rivers Act, which now inhibits dam building and regulates land use along more river frontage here than anywhere else in the nation.

ACCOMMODATIONS AND FOOD

FOOD AND DRINK

Oregon's abundance of fresh produce, seafood, and other indigenous ingredients prompted America's apostle of haute cuisine, James Beard, to extol the restaurants and cooking of his home state. In his autobiography, *Delights and Prejudices,* he implies that Oregon strawberries, Seaside peas, Dungeness crab, and other local fare became his standards by which to judge the culinary staples of the world. This horn of plenty is the basis of a regional cuisine emphasizing fresh natural foods cooked lightly to preserve flavor, color, and texture.

Nonetheless, it *is* possible to have a bad meal in this state. In fact, the quality of the cuisine in some remote eastern Oregon towns is a source of self-deprecating humor for the locals. And as many Yankees will tell you, there is no shortage of bland New England-style clam chowder on the Oregon coast.

Still, it's easy to dine well at an affordable price throughout most of the state. This does not have to mean McDonald's, either. Because Oregon abounds in places with genuine ambience and home cooking at a good value, fast-food listings will be kept to a minimum in this book. Budget travelers might want to bring their own food to expensive resort environments.

Also of note are Oregon's liquor laws. Liquor is sold by the bottle in state liquor stores open Monday through Saturday. Beer and wine are also sold in grocery stores and retail outlets. Liquor is sold by the drink in licensed establishments between 7 a.m. and 2:30 a.m. The minimum drinking age is 21.

Throughout Oregon there are stores purveying locally made food products, which make excellent gifts. In both the Portland and Eugene airports, for example, are minimalls selling Oregon jams, smoked salmon, hazelnuts, wines, and similar products. Another related development is the popularity of "microbreweries"—pubs serving their own beers—throughout the Northwest. The trend is so pervasive in Portland that this metropolis is already being touted as "the city that made Milwaukee nervous."

Oregon Cuisine

What will the newcomer to Oregon notice most on his or her plate? It all depends on where you happen to be. From the Basque food in southeastern Oregon to Portland's purveyors of pan-Asian cuisine (restaurants whose menus feature Chinese, Thai, and Vietnamese dishes), you'll be surprised to find no shortage of exotic offerings in a state more famous in the public mind for salmon and jumbo pears. As for humbler fare, jo-jos (refried baked potato spears encased in spices) and marionberry jams, jellies, and pies are the foodstuffs here whose mention is most likely to confound out-of-staters. The marionberry is a small-seeded dark maroon berry whose tarter-than-blackberry taste suits it well for dessert fare, especially marionberry ice cream. Higher up on the food chain, world-class Oregon lamb and the seasonally available, excellent fresh sturgeon, venison, and game birds are other little-known taste treasures here. The frequent use of locally grown herbs, exotic mushrooms, and organic produce in regional restaurants will also catch your taste buds by surprise. In short, while there is not a defined substratum of Northwest cuisine that is quintessentially Oregon, enough uniqueness and variety exist here to satisfy even the most jaded palate.

ACCOMMODATIONS

Cutting Costs

Oregon lodging prices are for the most part significantly lower than those of neighboring California and Washington. Nonetheless, Cascade mountain and coastal resort areas can put a strain on the pocketbook. Fortunately, state park and national forest campgrounds proliferate in these areas, offering low-cost overnight lodgings in attractive settings. As if by design, the highest percentage of Oregon's 200 state parks surround the high-ticket areas, with sites usually priced around $5-10 a night. Most of these have showers. National Forest Service campgrounds usually cost less, with more primitive facilities; many of them seem to be chosen for proximity to swimming holes and/or scenic appeal.

If creature comforts are a priority, RV parks are often available with such amenities as firewood, laundromats, and showers for about the same price as more basic government sites. All you need is a tent. However, private RV campgrounds and their expensive KOA counterparts tend to be crowded with people and vehicles, inhibiting the enjoyment of nature. Government campgrounds charge less and often feature more aesthetic surroundings.

"Off-season" specials are another way to beat the crowds and the costs. For example, one often sees room rates cut in half on the coast during the February storm-watching season. The cost-conscious traveler should also keep in mind that there is no shortage of large condos and vacation homes which rent out to large parties who can split costs.

If you're looking for a romantic spot for that special occasion or just a place to get away from it all, there are many hotels with aesthetic locations as well as a high level of comfort and service. A compendium of these is published every few years by Graphic Arts of Portland, Oregon, and is aptly entitled *Special Places*.

Bed And Breakfast

These bits o' Britain provide a homey alternative to the typical hotel room. Ashland and the coast lead the state in bed and breakfast establishments, but the idea seems to be catching on everywhere. And why not? Whether it's a glass of sherry by a crackling fire to warm up returning Ashland theatergoers, or a huge picture window on a Pacific storm, these retreats can impart that extra-special personal touch to the best the state has to offer.

If a turn-of-the-century Victorian or an old farmhouse doesn't give a B&B an extra measure of warmth, the camaraderie of the guests and the host family usually will. Most B&Bs restrict kids, pets, and smoking in deference to what are often close quarters. Private baths are also sometimes in short supply. Offsetting any potential intrusions on privacy is an included full or continental breakfast, sometimes in bed. And in Oregon, it has become customary to see homemade jams and breads as well as a complimentary glass of a local wine for a nightcap. For complete free listings of B&Bs in Oregon write to the **Oregon Bed and Breakfast Directory** (230 Red Spur Dr., Grants Pass 97527).

MONEY, MEASUREMENTS, AND COMMUNICATIONS

MONEY

Although the prices listed for hotels, meals, and attractions were current at press time, they will undoubtedly increase due to inflation. But while the rates are not absolute, they should nonetheless prove useful in comparing prices between establishments.

In any case, you'll need Uncle George or plastic to make your transactions in Oregon, and foreign currency can be exchanged at most major banks throughout the state. Canadian coins in particular are considered by many merchants as the bane of existence, and they will not accept them. Banks also turn up their noses at Canadian silver, because it costs them more in shipping and handling than it is worth. The major exceptions to this are Hood River businesses that cater to Canadian sailboarders.

But the presidents on your greenbacks aren't the only ones smiling, because Oregon is one of a handful of states in the country that *does not* have a sales tax. Many visitors take advantage of Oregon's generally low prices and lack of sales tax to purchase big-ticket items to take home. While it appears that the people of Oregon might finally enact a sales tax to help make up for a billion-dollar budget deficit created by lowering property taxes, Oregonians have always had a strong aversion to such a levy. In any case, you will find that room taxes vary from about 5-12%, depending on the locale.

MEASUREMENTS

Oregon—like the rest of the U.S.—has been slow to join the world community and adopt the metric system. You may see some aberrations now and then, like a bank sign giving the temperature in Celsius, or perhaps liter-sized containers at the supermarket, but basically Oregon clings to the English system. By 1995-96 however, metric conversions should start to appear on road signs, according to provisions passed by the U.S. Congress. To aid the traveler not familiar with the English system, we have included a conversion chart in the back of the book.

COMMUNICATIONS

Mail

Most post offices open between 7 and 9 a.m., and close between 5 and 6 p.m. In some of the larger cities, you will find main branches open on Saturday. Sometimes drugstores or card shops have a postal substation open on weekends and holidays when the government operations are closed. If it happens to be Sunday and the post office is closed, you can also get stamps from grocery stores and hotels, with little or no markup. Oregon also has many Federal Express, UPS, and other private shipping companies operating across the state to complement government services.

Telephone

Oregon (so far) has only one area code, (503), but with the dramatic increase in the use of fax machines and other high-tech communications equipment, this is bound to change eventually. We have not included the area code on our telephone listings for this reason. For long-distance calls within the state, dial 1 before the seven-digit telephone number. For now, any out-of-state call into Oregon is prefixed by **503.** For directory assistance in Oregon, call 1-555-1212; for Oregon information from out of state, call 1-503-555-1212.

Media

The two largest-circulation dailies in the state come out of the most populous cities, Portland and Eugene. Both the *Oregonian* and the *Eugene Register Guard* have gained a bevy of Pulitzers and other awards. In general, the *Guard* has fewer columns generated by wire services and stringers than does the *Oregonian.* The result is a big-town paper with a charming small-town feel. The *Oregonian*'s "Arts And Entertainment" section each Friday is of special interest to the traveler. The *Oregonian* is distributed statewide, while the *Guard* is carried in newspaper dispensers as far away from Eugene as Coos Bay. The editorial content of each paper is mostly middle of the road, but can be activist on environmental issues. While this last assessment would be challenged by residents of different parts of this politically diverse state, an equal amount of letters to the editor from the extreme right and the extreme left each day indicates a measure of balance.

Portland and Eugene also dominate the broadcast media, serving far-flung rural communities by means of electronic translators. What is especially noteworthy throughout the state is tremendous support of listener-subscriber public TV and radio. Many Oregon-generated shows, news blurbs, and features are carried by out-of-state public radio outlets.

Warm Springs Indian Reservation's KWSO 91.9 FM is a progressive country radio station spiced with elders chanting in the morning and topical discussions of native issues by younger tribemembers.

Even though regional monthlies like *Northwest Travel, Northwest Parks and Wildlife, Sunset, Travelin'*, and *Pacific Northwest* do not have a strictly Oregon focus, there are usually several destination pieces about the state in each edition of these magazines.

Oregon and *Oregon Coast* magazines confine their coverage to subjects closer to home. All the above periodicals can be obtained at newsstands throughout the state.

HEALTH AND HELP

EMERGENCY SERVICES

Throughout Oregon, dial 911 for medical, police, or fire emergencies. Isolated rural areas often have separate numbers for all three, and they're listed under "Information and Services" in each section of this book. Then, too, one may always dial 0 to get the operator. Most hospitals offer a 24-hour emergency room. Oregon's larger cities maintain switchboard referral services as well as hospital-sponsored free advice lines. Remember that medical costs are high here, as in the rest of the U.S; emergency rooms are the most expensive. However, low-cost inoculation and testing for certain infectious diseases is available through the auspices of county health departments in major cities.

HEALTH HAZARDS

Hypothermia
In this part of the country, the neophyte hiker should be alerted to problems with hypothermia—when your body loses more heat than can be recovered and shock ensues. Eighty-five percent of hiking-related fatalities are due to this malady. In fact, the damp chill of the North-west climate poses more of a hypothermia threat than do colder climes, which have low humidity. In other words, it doesn't have to be freezing in order for death from hypothermia to occur; wind and wetness often turn out to be greater risk factors. Remember that a wet human body loses heat 23 times faster than a dry one. Even runners who neglect to dress in layers in the cold fog of western Oregon often contract low-level symptoms during the accelerated cooling-off period following a workout.

The affliction sets in when the core temperature of the body drops to 95°F or below. One of the first signs is a diminished ability to think and act rationally. Speech can become slurred, and uncontrollable shivering usually takes place. Stumbling, memory lapses, and drowsiness also tend to characterize the afflicted. Unless the body temperature can be raised several degrees by a knowledgeable helper, cardiac arrhythmia and/or arrest may occur. Getting out of the wind and rain into a dry, warm environment is essential for survival. This might mean placing the victim into a prewarmed sleeping bag, which can be prepared by having a healthy hiker strip and climb into the bag with his or her endangered partner. Ideally, a groundcloth should be used to insulate the sleeping bag from cold surface temperatures. Internal heat can be generated by feeding the victim high-carbohydrate snacks and hot liquids. Placing wrapped heated objects against the victim's body is also a good way to restore body heat. Be careful not to raise body heat too quickly, which could also cause cardiac problems. If body temperature doesn't drop below 90°, chances for complete recovery are good; with body temperatures between 80° and 90°, victims are more likely to suffer some sort of lasting damage. Most victims won't survive a body temperature below 80°.

Measures you can take to prevent hypothermia include eating a nutritious diet, avoiding overexertion followed by exposure to wet and cold, and dressing warmly in layers of wool and polypropylene. Wool insulates even when wet, and because polypropylene tends to "wick" moisture away from your skin, it makes a good first layer. Gore-Tex and its counterparts like Helly-Tech or other new "miracle" fabrics make

for more comfortable raingear than nylon because they don't become cumbersome and hot in a steady rain. Finally, wear a hat: more radiated heat leaves from the head than from any other part of the body.

Frostbite
This is not generally a major problem until the combined air and windchill temperature falls below 20°F. Outer appendages like fingers and toes are the most susceptible, with the ears and nose running a close second. Frostbite occurs when blood is redirected out of the limbs to warm vital organs in cold weather, and the exposed parts of the face and peripherals cool very rapidly. Mild frostbite is characterized by extremely pale skin with random splotchiness; in more severe cases, the skin will take on a gray, ashen look and feel numb. At the first signs of suspected frostbite, you should gently warm the afflicted area. In more aggravated cases, immerse hands and feet in warm water between 108-113°F. Do not massage or risk further skin damage. Warming frostbitten areas against the skin of another person is suitable for less serious frostbite. The warmth of a campfire cannot help once the skin is discolored. As with hypothermia, it's important to avoid exposing the hands and feet to wind and wetness by dressing properly.

Poison Oak
Neither the best intentions or knowledge from a lifetime in the woods can spare the western Oregon hiker at least one brush with poison oak. In this writer's experience, 90% of the afflicted campers knew to look out for the three shiny leaves, but still woke up the next morning looking like a pepperoni pizza.

Since the plant seems to thrive in hardwood forests, it's always a good idea to wear long pants, shirts, and other covering on excursions to this ecosystem. Major infestations of the plant are seldom encountered in the Coast Range. In the fall, the leaves are tinged with red, giving the appearance of Christmas decorations. Unfortunately, this is one gift that keeps giving long after the holidays. Even when the plant is totally denuded in winter, the toxicity still remains a threat. Whatever the season, fair-skinned people tend to be more prone to severe symptoms.

BOB RACE

Rhus diversiloba, *the infamous poison oak*

Shots are of course the most efficient way of dealing with poison oak symptoms.

When you know that you've been exposed, try to get your clothes off before the toxic resin permeates your garments. Follow up as soon as possible with a cold bath treated with liberal amounts of baking soda or bleach, or a shower with lots of soap. If this doesn't stop the symptoms, cooling the inflamed area with copious applications of aloe vera or calamine lotion, which draws out the contaminants, is another recourse. Clay has been known to be effective in expelling the poison. In emergency situations, cortisone cream might kill a poison oak rash but it's said to take lots of healthy cells along with it, too. Some tree-planters talk about immunities built up by eating poison oak honey and drinking milk from goats who graze on the weed. Health-food stores now sell a poison oak extract which, if taken over time prior to exposure, is said to mollify the symptoms.

Allergies
Even if you come out of the forests unscathed, Willamette Valley-bound travelers during springtime might have to confront another pernicious health hazard: perennial allergic rhinitis. With the world's highest volume of grass seed produced between Salem and Eugene, allergy-susceptible visitors should expect some sneezing and wheezing as well as itchy eyes during the June-July pollination season. In addition to grass seed, the earlier bloom of various ornamentals throughout western Oregon might occasion such discomfort.

As allergy shots are not always practical, antihistamines are often resorted to as a short-term remedy for those passing through. Unfortunately, such side effects as depression and sleepiness have been attributed to them. Late-ly, many Willamette Valley doctors have been prescribing Seldane, an asthma medicine. This prescription drug (available over the counter in Canada) combats allergic reactions without side effects. Many health-food stores offer herbal remedies, but they usually fall short of the quick relief demanded by travelers. Finally, honey from the area of the offending allergen taken regularly several months prior to the allergy season is often mentioned as a folk remedy.

Beaver Fever
Folk remedies just won't do it for that other hiker headache, "beaver fever." Medically known as giardiasis, this syndrome afflicts those who drink water contaminated by *Giardia lamblia* parasites. Even water from cold, clear streams can be infested by this microorganism, which is spread throughout the backcountry by beavers, muskrats, livestock, and other hikers. Boiling water for 20 minutes is the most common prevention to spare you endless hours as king or queen of the throne in the latrine during and after your trip. At higher elevations, it's a good idea to boil water longer. Should that prove inconvenient, try better living through chemistry: apply five drops of chlorine, or preferably iodine, to every quart of water and let it sit for a half hour. Also available are water pumps that filter out *Giardia* and other organisms, but they cost about $20 and up. First-Need is a filter/pump device that costs about $35. Potable water is also achieved by purification pills like Potable Aqua, iodine-based tablets that cost about a nickel each. However, these chemical approaches are less reliable than boiling. Whatever method you choose, avoid major rivers or any creek that runs through a meadow as your source of water if possible.

INFORMATION

Maps

For a full list of books, maps, and pamphlets on Oregon national parks and forests write to: **Pacific Northwest National Parks and Forests Association,** Forest Service/Park Service Outdoor Recreation Information (1018 First Ave., Seattle, WA 98104; tel. 206-442-0170). Another good source of useful information is the **Explorers Map of Oregon,** available at Exclusive Maps, Ltd., (Suite 369, 1430 Willamette St., Eugene 97401; tel. 935-7499; $7.50). This map depicts hot springs, fossil beds, caves, gold-mining areas, remote beaches, wild areas, Indian village sites, artifact sites, abandoned historical places, petroglyph and pictograph locations, gem, mineral, and precious metal sites, stage and immigrant routes, 19th-century fort locations, Indian travel routes and battlegrounds, anomalies and curiosities, and notes on the state's history and prehistory.

Another local mapmaker, **Raven Maps** (34 N. Central, Medford 97501; tel. 773-1436 or 800-237-0798) is esteemed among the cartographic cognoscenti. Based on U.S. Geological Survey maps, these computer-enhanced topographic projections depict vertical relief (by shading) and three-dimensionality. Many of Raven's offerings are large enough to cover a dining-room table, with costs commonly in the $15-20 range. All Raven maps are printed in fade-resistant inks on fine-quality 70-pound paper and are also available in vinyl-laminated versions suitable for framing.

In Portland, the Nature Center, REI, and Andy And Bax are all good sources of maps pertaining to outdoor recreation. The Portland Visitors Association (see "Portland and Vicinity Information") can furnish state highway maps or you can get one mailed directly from the State Tourism Division (tel. 800-547-7842).

ASK US

The following information centers can be called toll free, and each has a wide variety of information available on its respective locale.

Bay Area Chamber of Commerce, 50 E. Central St., Coos Bay, OR 97420; tel. 800-762-6278 inside Oregon, tel. 800-824-8486 outside.

Eugene Springfield Convention and Visitors Bureau, 305 W. Seventh St., Eugene, OR 97401; tel. 800-452-3670 inside Oregon, 800-547-5445 outside.

Gold Beach-Wedderburn Chamber of Commerce, 510 S. Ellensburg St., Gold Beach, OR 97444; tel. 800-452-2334 inside Oregon, 800-542-2334 outside.

Grants Pass Visitor and Convention Bureau, Box 970, 1439 N.E. Sixth, Grants Pass, OR 97526; tel. 800-547-5927.

Lincoln City Chamber of Commerce, Box 787, 3939 N.W. U.S. 101, Lincoln City, OR 97367; tel. 800-452-2151 (inside Oregon only).

Pendleton Chamber of Commerce, Box 1446, 25 S.W. Dorion St., Pendleton, OR 97801; tel. 800-452-9403 inside Oregon, 800-547-8911 outside.

Southern Oregon Reservation Center, Box 477, Ashland, OR 97522; tel. 800-533-1311 inside Oregon, 800-547-8052 outside.

Seaside Chamber of Commerce, Box 7, 7 N. Roosevelt St., Seaside, OR 97138; tel. 800-444-6740 (inside Oregon only).

Accommodations And Chambers Of Commerce

The **Oregon Tourism Division** (775 Summer St. NE, Salem 97310; tel. toll-free inside Oregon 800-547-7842 or outside Oregon 800-233-3306) will send you a full list of local chambers of commerce and tourist information offices upon request. They also feature many well-produced free pamphlets on different regions, seasons, and activities. Especially recommended are their winter/fall activities booklets and regional loop tour brochures. The **Oregon Motor Hotel Association** (12724 S.E. Stark St., Portland 97233; tel. 255-5135) has a good set of lodging listings across the state.

The following information centers can be reached by toll-free numbers, and they have a wide variety of information available on their respective locales.

Finally, one all-inclusive number merits special mention. **Overnight Success** (tel. 800-365-6343, open daily 8 a.m.-11 p.m.) is a free service that lists 2,000 lodgings. Info is available on motels, hotels, resorts, condos, bed and breakfasts, ranches, inns, and RV parks. Callers state their destination, accommodation features desired, and price range. Then the computer does the rest, and will give the phone numbers of properties that match the specifications.

Camping And Hiking

The **Oregon Guides and Packers Association** (Box 10841, Eugene 97440; tel. 683-9552) has the scoop on outfitting just about any kind of adventure you can imagine. Whether you want to pack llamas into the Kalmiopsis Wilderness, shoot the rapids of Hell's Canyon, or take to the Cascades on horseback, you'll find a listing here for something interesting to do in Oregon.

Oregon State Parks (in Portland and out-of-state tel. 238-7488, rest of Oregon 800-452-5687, Mon.-Fri., 8-4:30) provides info on campsite availability and other recreation information. Remember that while campsite reservations can't be made through the center, they can be canceled there. For info about subjects other than availability, call 378-6305. The **National Forest Service** (tel. 800-283-CAMP, Mon.-Fri. 9-6 Sat.-Sun. 9-2) has a nationwide reservation and information center. There is a

reservation fee in addition to regular campground fees ($6 for reserving family sites, $10 for reserving group sites). Campsites can be booked up to 120 days in advance for single family sites and 360 days in advance for group sites. Campgrounds in the Willamette, Umpqua, and Suislaw national forests are Oregon's bailiwicks covered in this program.

The State Highways Division completed a state camping guide in 1992. It includes state parks system, Forest Service, and BLM sites. All of the campgrounds are indicated on an accompanying map, and the free directory lists user fees and the kinds of facilities available.

The **Oregon Parks and Recreation Division** (525 Trade St., Salem 97310; tel. 378-6305), the **U.S. Bureau of Land Management** (Box 2965, Portland 97232; tel. 231-6273), and the **U.S. Forest Service** (Box 3623, 319 S.W. Pine St., Portland 97208; tel. 326-3651) have free information and maps on specific recreation areas and preserves under their respective auspices. Hikers can benefit from *An Oregonian's Trail Sourcebook,* published by the Oregon Student Public Interest Research Group, or OSPIRG (1536 S.E. 11th, Portland 97214; tel. 231-4181).

Skiers can benefit from info put out by the **Pacific Northwest Ski Association** (Box 34481, Kirkland, WA 98083; tel. 206-822-1770).

In northeast Portland the state-sponsored **Nature of Oregon Information Center** (800 N.E. Oregon St., Suite 177, Portland 97232; tel. 731-4444) makes available the gamut of publications having to do with Oregon outdoors. Much of this is free thanks to the departments of forestry, agriculture, wildlife, tourism, state parks, etc.; U.S. Geological Survey, Forest Service, and BLM maps, as well as reprints of research papers done by various agencies, are on sale also. A TRIS computer station rounds out the treasure trove of information available here Mon.-Fri. 10 a.m-5 p.m.

Locating this important information resource isn't easy for those unfamiliar with Portland. At the end of an obscure street, the center sits a few blocks due east from the Oregon Convention Center and south of Lloyd Center on the bottom floor of a nine-floor state office building. To get there from I-5 driving north, take exit 302A (Coliseum/Broadway/Weidler), go right on Weidler, right on Martin Luther King Blvd., and then left on Oregon Street. Driving south on I-5, take the Coliseum/City Center exit and veer left toward Vancouver. Turn left on Weidler, right on Martin Luther King Blvd., and then left on Oregon Street.

The **Pacific Crest Trail Association** (Box 2514, Lynwood, WA 98036) publishes an eight-page bimonthly newsletter. The 2,638-mile Pacific Crest Trail runs from Canada to Mexico, traversing Oregon along the Cascades at high elevations. Such scenic access routes and off-shoots as the Eagle Creek Trail in the Columbia Gorge and Ramona Falls on the lower slopes of Mt. Hood beckon further exploration. The free publication has articles about events along the trail as well as accounts of trips taken on it.

The **Oregon Coast Charterboat Association** (Box 494, Newport 97365) has a resource guide which helps in selecting a charterboat and skipper, and deciding when to fish and what to bring. It also lists which outfits do sightseeing and whalewatching charters.

Fishing And Hunting

If you are interested in fishing, contact the **Oregon Department of Fish and Wildlife** (506 S.W. Mill St., Box 59, Portland 97207; tel. 229-5403). Nonresident fishing licenses are $4 (for one day), $18.50 (10 days), or $30 (year). The cost for a one-year license for residents is $14.75 for adults, $5.75 for ages 14-17. Halibut, salmon, or steelhead licenses run an additional $5.50 for every 10 fish caught, 40-salmon/steelhead annual limit.

Anglers can dial (800) ASK-FISH to keep up-to-date on Beaver State fishing conditions. Callers with touch-tone phones can choose from a varied menu of recorded information, including data on campgrounds, wheelchair access, and important state regulations.

Hunting licenses are available at the same address (hunting tel. 229-5222). A nonresident license is $100.50, deer tags are $75.50, and elk tags are $165.50. Game tags are needed prior to the first day of hunting season. Apply early, since availability is limited.

WHAT TO TAKE

Without belaboring commonsensical considerations, a few comments are in order regarding the proper apparel for Oregon's rainforest-to-desert diversity.

To begin, remember that this region places a premium on practical and informal dress. A predilection for the outdoors as well as a lack of pretense explain the relative dearth of ties and haute couture even in somewhat formal urban settings.

The Old West is still alive and well east of the Cascades. In the Oregon desert regions, boots are like a second skin. This isn't so much tradition as good sense. It's always advisable to wear boots around horses and when walking in desertlike areas. Durable footwear certainly makes being stepped on or bitten less annoying.

Another concern in the desert is keeping cool. Carry water and wear a shade hat in summer. Cowboy hats work exceptionally well and are in vogue in this region. To avoid dehydration, Gatorade, 7-Up, or good old H_2O might be your best recourse; it's even better than salt tablets or beer for restoring evaporated sodium rates because alcohol depletes the body's water by accelerating perspiration and elimination.

Whether it's the subzero temperatures of the desert melting you or the western Oregon mist cutting through your clothes, spare yourself needless discomfort by being prepared. Despite goose down's superior insulating qualities when dry, it's almost useless when wet because it clumps up and no longer traps air. The synthetic down imitators insulate well and do much better than down when wet but have a stiffness that bothers active wearers. Nonetheless, given the pervasiveness of moisture here, coats with Thinsulate and/or synthetic fleece are becoming more popular than down. A good test of the garment's suitability for vigorous movement is to put it on and quickly raise your fist to your shoulder in an arm-flexing motion. In a better-quality parka, you shouldn't feel insulation material restricting motion at your elbow.

Finally, a word for those who find the lightweight lofting and warming qualities of down hard to kick. These days Eddie Bauer, a well-known Northwest outfitter, has married Gore-Tex to down, so you have a waterproof shell covering a warm insulation layer. Recommended down care for diehards is nothing more than throwing the garment in the washer with powdered detergent, then drying it with sneakers to beat the pockets of down into shape. Do this twice a year to maintain the loft.

GETTING THERE AND GETTING AROUND

TOURS

While not for everybody, group travel is the fastest-growing aspect of a fast-growing industry. Those inclined to "do" Oregon by package tour can recline in the air-conditioned comfort of a Mercedes-like motorcoach as it rolls past the many-splendored landscapes of Oregon. A knowledgeable guide gives you the scoop on what you're seeing in addition to building your anticipation for cliffside coastal grandeur, a jetboat ride on the Rogue, or a play at Ashland's Shakespeare Festival. Sound idyllic? If so, touring Oregon by motorcoach could well be the mode of travel for you.

Many of these packages may seem spendy, but if you compare the price of meals, lodgings, and other services to what you'd pay independently, it's a good dollar value for the upscale traveler. In addition to volume discounts, the tour companies provide the services of a guide to spare you the hassles associated with the logistics and practicalities of travel.

Despite the togetherness that comes from sharing a positive experience with others, younger folks can sometimes feel alienated from the predominantly older clientele and/or constraints imposed by a schedule. On the other hand, there is no better way to survey Oregon in style with a limited amount of time.

OREGON HIGHWAYS

TO DAYTON

12

WALLA WALLA

WASHINGTON
OREGON

BOARDMAN

ARLINGTON

PENDLETON

11

WALLOWA

3

HELLS
CANYON
NAT'L
RECREATION
AREA

IDAHO

82

19

206

JOHN DAY
FOSSIL
BEDS
NAT'L
MONUMENT

CONDON

395

LA GRANDE

ENTERPRISE

82

JOSEPH

218

FOSSIL

19

JOHN DAY
FOSSIL BEDS
NAT'L
MONUMENT

BAKER

TO
GRANGEVILLE

95

JOHN DAY
FOSSIL BEDS
NAT'L MONUMENT

84

30

TO

SNAKE RIVER

26

JOHN DAY RIVER

JOHN DAY

26

ONTARIO

20

95

TO BOISE

20

BURNS

395

95

55

84

HARNEY LAKE

MALHEUR
LAKE

MALHEUR
NAT'L WILDLIFE
REFUGE

78

LAKE
ABERT

FRENCHGLEN

205

OREGON
IDAHO

PLUSH

HART MT.
NAT'L REFUGE

95

LAKEVIEW

140

BLIZZARD GAP
(ELEV. 6,131 ft.)

395

TO ALTURAS

OREGON
NEVADA

TO WINNEMUCCA

© MOON PUBLICATIONS, INC.

The advantages of Oregon tour travel are made manifest by looking at the packages of **Tauck Tours** (11 Wilton Rd., Westport, CT 06880; tel. 203-226-6911) and **Maupintour** (1515 St. Andrews Dr., Lawrence, KS 66046; tel. 800-255-6162). Despite differences in accommodations, routing, and attractions, both companies' itineraries feature a loop from Portland, taking in the best of the coast, the Willamette Valley, a jetboat trip on the Rogue River, a Shakespeare play in Ashland, Crater Lake, and a Cascades Mountain resort as well as the Columbia River Gorge. Along the way, four- and five-star hotels and restaurants give you the luxurious repose to savor your experiences. To book a tour or request additional information, contact the companies or see a travel agent.

Tour season in Oregon begins in late May and can run till the end of September. Before or after that, you're playing dice with the weather. In general, during tour season, be prepared for warm and pleasant days all over the state, morning coastal fog, and cool mountain nights.

BY AIR

It is a simple enough matter getting to and getting around Oregon by air. If there is a break in the weather, the views are breathtaking. The main point of entry is Portland International Airport (PDX), which is serviced by 16 airlines. Your travel agent can help you find the best current bargains, and a good weekly overview of airfares is printed in the Sunday travel section of the *Oregonian*. While good coast-to-coast deals are starting to increase, unfortunately most airlines still consider the state's Portland hub more of a business than a tourist destination and haven't lowered their fares accordingly. As such, flights from California and other West Coast locations are comparatively high priced. If you have booked and want to reconfirm or have a question, you can call the airlines on their 800 numbers.

Horizon Air, tel. (800) 547-9308, the commuter-league farm club of Alaska Airlines, connects with a half-dozen smaller airfields in the state. Horizon operates commuter prop planes with from 10 to 40 seats. If you are sensitive to loud noises and pressure change, ask for

AIRLINES	
Alaska Airlines	800-426-0333
American	800-433-7300
America West	800-247-5692
Continental	800-525-0280
Delta	800-221-1212
Eastern	800-327-8376
Horizon	800-547-9308
Morris	800-444-5660
Northwest	800-225-2525
Piedmont	800-251-5720
Southwest	800-531-5601
Sunworld	800-722-4111
TWA	800-892-4141
United	800-241-6522
USAir	800-428-4322

earplugs when you check in for your boarding pass. Bend/Redmond, Eugene/Springfield, Klamath Falls, Medford, North Bend/Coos Bay, and Salem all enjoy Horizon service. United Express (tel. 800-241-6522) also serves several smaller Oregon markets.

If your final destination is Astoria, Baker, La Grande, Newport, or Pendleton, many private flying outfits connect with these five municipal airports. Just check the yellow pages or the PDX information booth on the first floor.

Finally, the entry of Morris Air Service (tel. 800-444-5660) into Portland's array of domestic carriers warrants special attention. Imagine Supersaver-like fares for flights on Boeing 747s to such far-flung ports of call as Cancun, Orlando, and Anchorage, as well as to Seattle and a half-dozen California cities, with no advance booking requirements! While there are not a lot of frills, you'd be hard-pressed to beat Morris's fares.

BY TRAIN

Amtrak

If the massive increase in Oregon ridership is any indication, the region built by the iron horse is having a second fling with rail travel. For that matter, Amtrak's expanded service nationwide is starting to ease the stigma of the U.S. being the only major country in the world without a well-developed rail line.

Some routes are so popular that getting a sleeper on the Coast Starlight, for example, requires reservations 5-11 months in advance any time of the year. Those who take this route northbound from California will see why when the train crosses into Oregon. After riding all night from the San Francisco Bay Area, passengers wake up to sunrise over alpine lakes and the snowcapped Cascades. As the tracks take you higher, you can see thousands of treetops in the foreground of dramatic peaks, especially if you're on the right-hand side of the car. From Cascade Summit, you head down into Eugene along the beautiful McKenzie River. Commentary over the loudspeaker and on the complimentary handbills enhances your sense of place.

Routes out of Portland on the Pioneer and the Empire Builder show off the Columbia River Gorge to good advantage, in ultramodern, bilevel Superliner Coaches. The Empire Builder goes on the Washington side of the river, enabling you to get a full cross section of Oregon's waterfalls and mountains, while the Pioneer retraces the paths of Lewis and Clark and the Oregon Trail migrants (paralleling I-84 for much of the way). The Pioneer continues from orchard country in the Cascade foothills to eastern Oregon's drier topography.

The trains on these routes are Superliners. These bilevel trains are replete with such people spaces as full-service dining cars and sight-

seers' lounges. The wraparound windows in these cars and a smooth ride are conducive to passenger interaction. While food is expensive and selection limited, it's appetizing enough to eat should your own supplies give out.

Trains are usually more expensive than buses, but cheaper than planes. However, as with buses, special airfares occasionally undercut Amtrak. Kids 2-11 travel half fare; children under two ride free. There are other discounts for groups, seniors, the disabled, and students. The company also advertises special holiday packages. The best buy for extended rail travel is a program called All Aboard America, which is operational year-round. For info and reservations, call (800) 872-7245, or obtain Amtrak's local station number through directory assistance.

Amtrak Fun
A nice introduction to Amtrak is the special Eugene-to-Klamath Falls roundtrip accompanied by a Forest Service interpreter. Trains leave Eugene daily at 5:41 p.m., running Sunday through Friday. As the train begins its 110-mile, 4,500-foot ascent to Cascade Summit near Odell Lake, head to the left side of the observation car. This way you'll face east, toward the most scenic snowcapped peaks. As you climb up and out of the Willamette Valley, you pass from rural farms and timber communities through forest-fire burns and alpine vistas until the final downhill leg, which passes one of the largest lakes in Oregon—Klamath Lake. En route, Native American lore, pioneer history, forest management, and remarks about wildlife enhance the mile-by-mile commentary. The next morning, the Coast Starlight leaves Klamath Falls at 7:02 a.m. and arrives in Eugene at 11:16 a.m. One-way coach fare on this run is $43. A limited number of roundtrip excursion fares are offered daily for $65, which is $21 off the regular roundtrip ticket.

Other Trains
If the mystique of a lonely train whistle and vintage rail cars appeals to you, the following trips should avail some golden moments. The **Mt. Hood Railroad** (110 Railroad Ave., Hood River 97031; tel. 386-3556) was originally built in 1906 to bring lumber out of the Mt. Hood National Forest to Hood River mills. But since 1988 it

has been carrying passengers in restored early-1900s coaches through the scenic Hood River Valley to Parkdale. The "blossom tours" in April are particularly popular, as the trains wind through colorful apple and pear orchards on their way up the valley. The chance to snap a photo of the classic train backdrop by Mt. Hood, buy fall fruit direct from the farmer at the Parkdale station, and explore the national historic landmark depot at Hood River is another highlight. The 49-mile, four-hour roundtrip (adults $17, seniors $15, ages 12 and under $12) departs Hood River at 10 a.m. and gives you an hour to stretch your legs and shop in Parkdale before retracing its route and returning at 2:30 p.m. A 17-mile, two-hour roundtrip to Odell (adults $10, seniors $8, ages 12 and under $6) leaves Hood River at 3 and returns at 5 p.m. Trains run Wednesday to Friday (Parkdale run only) and weekends (both trips) during the fruit blossom season from early April through early June. Thereafter until September 2, the trains run Tuesday to Sunday, both trips every day. From mid-September until the end of the month the spring schedule applies. From early October through late November both runs go on weekends. Take exit 63 off I-84 to get to the station or walk down from the Hood River Hotel on Oak Street.

The **Crooked River Dinner Train** (O'Neil Road, Redmond 97756; tel. 388-1966 after March) shows off the broad vistas of central Oregon's high desert as well as the state's indigenous delicacies and local wines. The 2½-hour, 38-mile route through the Ochoco River Valley goes from Redmond to Prineville, offering reserved brunches and dinners as well as family excursions from mid-June. The elegantly appointed turn-of-the-century interior of this train goes well with the Old West terrain. Friday and Saturday night dinner excursions ($45.50 per person) depart at 6:30 p.m. from the caboose ticket booth a quarter mile east of ORE 97 on O'Neil Road. Dinner entree choices include breast of chicken, prime rib, fillet of chinook, and pasta primavera. Sunday brunch trips leave at 9:30 a.m. and cost $30.50. Brunch entrees include Spanish omelette, quiche Lorraine, and fruit crepes. The Saturday family excursion leaves at 10 a.m. and costs $13.50 for adults, $10.50 for seniors, and $8 for kids 2-15. Board

a half hour prior to departure for each itinerary. (See "U.S. 26: Prineville To Sumpter" for Sumpter Valley Railroad info.)

BY BUS

Greyhound
Greyhound and its offshoots have regular connections to most population centers in Oregon. "Its offshoots" refers to the slew of smaller companies created in the wake of deregulation and Greyhound cost-cutting. In terms of the consumer experience, all this means is that you might have a bus with a different paint job that uses Greyhound terminals and fare structures. Raz, Valley Retriever, Red Ball, and other smaller companies operate on former Greyhound routes and have information on their schedules available from Greyhound personnel. If present trends continue, Greyhound will soon be operating mostly along I-5 in western Oregon. For an update on local carrier service write to the State Tourism Division (775 Sumner St., Salem 97310) for the Oregon passenger services pamphlet.

Since routes are continually being dropped and added it's imperative to call the local Greyhound info number to supplement any printed schedule. The lack of terminals in remote locations is another reason to plan your bus trip carefully.

As for comfort, a ride on a Greyhound is good news and bad news. First, the good news: on the West Coast, buses are usually no more than 10 years old, which means you can enjoy footrests, reclinable seats, and air-conditioning. The majority of folks will also appreciate the fact that there's no smoking permitted on Greyhound while in Oregon. And, should the bus on your route fill up, rest assured that the company will put another bus into service. In fact, this extra departure will often run as an express instead of a local, assuming there's a preponderance of passengers with a common destination.

The bad news is not that bad. Too much air-conditioning in summer and too much heat in winter can be dealt with by dressing accordingly. The unappetizing fare in many of the terminals can be avoided by bringing your own food.

The ticket prices, while usually twice the cost of driving, are still not out of line. Even though a special airline fare might occasionally undercut the bus on longer interstate routes, for the most part the 'Hound costs but a fraction of most air tickets. Consider too that half-fare discounts are available to kids 5-11 and to the disabled traveling with an attendant. Another potential discount is the **Ameripass.** At press time, unlimited travel for a week is $189, for 15 days $249, and for 30 days $349. It's cost-effective only if you're doing lots of travel in a short time. Also keep an eye out for various promotions which feature low-cost long-distance travel, particularly during the summer. The Ameripass and promotional fares are honored by most of the Greyhound franchises, but all connections should be clarified upon purchase.

A few hints about seating will suffice to ensure a smooth trip. The first and last seats on the bus can be a boon or a bane to your traveling comfort depending on your needs. If a footrest and the ability to recline your seat are important, avoid these locations. The front seats are generally the only seats that lack footrests, and the back ones don't recline. Worse yet, restrooms are in the rear of the coach, which inevitably results in an unpleasant odor on longer trips for those seated close by. Despite these shortcomings, the views out the front windshield are the best to be had, and the back row of three seats offers the most stretching room. For more information, call Greyhound at 243-2323. or toll free (800) 531-5332.

Green Tortoise

One commonly hears the Green Tortoise (Green Tortoise Alternative Travel, Box 24459, San Francisco, CA 94127; tel. 800-227-4766) referred to as "the hippie bus." Lest this conjure a seedy anachronism from the '60s, an update is in order. While the Tortoise is not exactly the Orient Express of two-lane blacktop, this mode of travel comes as close to a hotel on wheels as exists in this country. First, imagine a recycled Greyhound with the seats taken out. In their place are foam-rubber mattresses on elevated platforms behind a lounge area in the front of the bus. The chairs and tables here are converted to another sleeping area at night. Just bring your sleeping bag.

In Oregon, the fare is usually about 30% less than Greyhound's and might include such amenities as a stop for a home-cooked meal ($3.50

extra) and a soak in a hot spring. Passengers also have the option to pool money for groceries or eat at the restaurants near Tortoise stops. The clientele are a diverse group with surprisingly many Europeans and Australians. It's a rare Tortoise trip that doesn't turn into a party, although alcohol is prohibited. You can also bring your favorite cassettes to listen to on the Tortoise stereo. Another way Tortoise differs from Greyhound is in its policy of stopping at any freeway exit to pick up or drop off passengers (who are charged an extra $5 for this service). Kids shorter than four feet nine inches travel free with an adult. Always reserve trips in advance.

In Oregon, the Tortoise only travels I-5 between Portland and Ashland. Also, remember that you pay the driver on departure with cash, traveler's checks, or money order. No personal checks or credit cards are accepted. Southbound departures leave Sunday and Thursday (and Tuesday or Friday June 1-October 1), with the exception of the Ashland bus into California (see "Ashland and Vicinity"). Northbound travel happens Tuesday or Saturday (and Thursday or Sunday June 1-October 1).

BY CAR

The automobile remains the vehicle of choice for exploring the state. Oregon is blessed with good roads and light traffic on many thoroughfares. Consider that 141,000 miles of roads and 2.3 million registered cars works out to about 16 cars per mile. But before you jam down on the accelerator, keep in mind that the Man is equipped with the latest in radar technology and sometimes lies in wait out in the middle of nowhere.

Technically, you can only open up to 65 mph on sections of I-5 and I-84. The rest of the roads in the state have a 55 mph maximum speed limit. However, most people here seem to cruise at 5-10 miles above the speed limit and usually appear successful in avoiding trouble with the law.

Nowadays Oregon roads are often depicted in TV automobile commercials—the inviting places replete with mountains majesty or cliffside coastal grandeur. In short, welcome to Car Country, where toll roads are the exception, the traffic is light, and the pavement is in generally good condition.

While the roads are beautiful and largely unfettered by rush-hour bottlenecks, the motorist must be sensitive to the nuances of the weather. Frequent cloudbursts can cause cars to wildly hydroplane all over the road, thick palls of fog that hang over the Willamette Valley can cause multicar pileups, and the icy mountain roads of the Cascades and eastern Oregon also claim their share of victims. From late fall to early spring, expect snow on the Cascade mountain passes and I-5 through the Siskiyous; snow tires and/or chains are often required. Those who foolishly venture forth illegally and get stuck or caught are summarily issued steep fines. Another thing to remember in the winter Cascades is your **snow park permit.** Without the daily sticker or season pass in your left-hand window, a car left in a snow park area will also receive a hefty ticket. This permit is essentially a duty levied by the state to pay for the upkeep of parking and rest areas in the mountains. Pick these up at the local DMV (Department of Motor Vehicles) for a few bucks prior to setting out. They apply to travel November 15 through April 15.

Another consideration for drivers is the fact that the road signs found throughout the state are sometimes less than explicit. Whether it's a turn sign coming up a half mile after the fact or directional markers obscured from view, this state seems to have more than its share of unwanted surprises for motorists.

Finally, keep in mind that in winter, the roads are bound to be covered with sand and gravel in places because the state does not use salts or other chemicals to melt snow and ice. The ground-up pumice from nearby lava deposits comes in many colors and provides great traction, but it sure can scratch up the paint on your car if you tailgate. Also, give oncoming trucks a wide berth to avoid the sandblasting likely to follow in their wake.

Gas is readily available on the main western routes but finding it can be a little trickier proposition on the more remote east side, especially after 5 p.m. Oregon's small-town gas stations are disappearing all over the state due to legislation mandating costly replacements of old gas tanks, which are prone to seepage. In other words, fill up before you leave the city. Another thing to remember is that Oregon is one of the few states which do not have self-service gasoline outlets. This is partial-

ly responsible for the state having among the highest gas prices in the country. Another reason is the gas tax levied to help pay for Oregon's roads.

Renting a car is no problem, assuming you have a credit card. The rental chains (Avis, Budget, Dollar, National, and Thrifty) have outlets in Portland and many other population centers. You can also flip through the yellow pages and try to save some bucks with an independent operator. But while *you* may not care about the way the Rent-a-Dents and Ugly Duckling Rent-a-Cars look, they're not the vehicles of choice to impress your date. Another thing to consider is that the major chains have more service centers to assist you in the event of any mechanical problems. And while it costs a little more, it is always a good idea to make certain that you're adequately insured.

BY BICYCLE

If you like to pedal on your own two wheels, the good news is that Oregon is user-friendly to bicyclists. With special bike routes in cities like Eugene, Medford, and Portland, Oregon has given the right of way to cyclists. In the wake of the oil shocks of the 1970s, the Oregon Legislature allocated one percent of the state highways budget to develop bike lanes and encourage energy-saving bicyclists. In addition to establishing routes throughout the state with these funds, many special parks were developed with bicycle and foot access specifically in mind. For example, minutes away from Eugene's downtown is the Willamette River Greenway bikepath system, which winds through a string of parks. Oxygen-rich air from the vegetation and the peaceful gurgling of the Willamette make a pleasant change from the fumes and roar of traffic. A decent biker could easily beat a car across town during rush hour using the bicycle network.

A similar respect has been granted to the cyclist on the open road. According to the Oregon *Motor Vehicles Handbook,* a bicycle has the right of way, which means that cars and trucks are not supposed to run you off the road. Nonetheless, remember that there are always motorists whose concepts of etiquette vis-à-vis bikers were formulated elsewhere. Play it safe out there: wear a helmet and reflective cloth-

Oregon is user-friendly to bicyclists.

ing, keep close to the right of the road, and always use a light at night. While most of the drivers will give you a wide berth and slow down if necessary in tight spots, rush hours, traffic patterns, and circumstance can change that.

The *Oregon Bicycling Guide,* distributed by the Oregon Department of Transportation (State Highways Division, Salem 97310), is a good pamphlet to have around to help plan a bike trip. This publication includes statewide maps of bike trails and routing suggestions as well as listings for rental/repair shops and bike touring groups. Be aware that transporting your own machine cross-country can sometimes be a problem, as every carrier has its own set of rules and regulations. Check with the bus, train, or plane company to make sure that you are within the allowable parameters.

Fortunately, there are some companies that offer pre-planned group bicycle trips, with everything from the bicycle to the meals and lodging included. **Tour Oregon Style** (Box 987, Oregon City 97045; tel. 655-2831) has a deluxe seven-day coastal bicycle trip that traverses spectacular U.S. 101. All you have to do is pedal; they take care of the rest. The cost is $299 per person, and a small discount is given to groups. **Bicycle Adventures** (Dept. K, Box 7875, Olympia, WA 98507; tel. 206-786-0989) offers a longer Oregon/Washington package.

THE OREGON COAST
INTRODUCTION

The Oregon coast is one of those blessed corners of the earth where you come upon a little piece of paradise wherever you go. The south coast is a world apart, with a landscape dominated by dense evergreen forest parting to reveal black-sand beaches and exceptional rock formations. One often gets the feeling here that sheep and cattle outnumber people.

The central coast is a land of superlatives, boasting such features as the largest ocean-front dunes in the world, the highest coastal viewpoint accessible by car, and the only mainland sea lion rookery located in the lower 48 states. In addition, *The Guinness Book of World Records* recognizes Oregon's other coastal claims to fame, like the smallest navigable harbor and the shortest river in the world.

The north coast can be billed as "the real end of the Oregon Trail." Although that famous frontier wagon road ends inland, the pioneering spirit that it connotes is on display here by the sea. Lewis and Clark, John Jacob Astor, and the legions of settlers who conquered the wilderness are commemorated in the landmark buildings

and historical placards of Astoria, the oldest U.S. city west of Missouri. In like measure, many of the works in north coast galleries draw inspiration from these same historical antecedents.

While each part of the coast possesses a distinct regional flavor, together they have one thing in common. Whether it's virgin beachfront, a lofty promontory, or simply a cozy bed and breakfast, each section of Oregon's seascape will leave you hungering for more.

THE LAND

The Oregon coast includes 362 miles of rain-forest, sand dunes, high-rise basalt headlands, and tidal pools showcasing marine worlds in miniature. This scenery is broken up by over a dozen major rivers, which flow past mountain barriers to the sea. The estuaries of these rivers offer resting places for migratory waterfowl as well as a thoroughfare for spawning fish. They cut through the Klamath Mountains in the southern quarter of the region and bisect parts of the

the view from Cascade Head: a picture-perfect slice of the Oregon coast

Coast Range in the north.

Of the two ranges, the Klamaths are much older, dating back 225 million years. By contrast, the Coast Range, beginning near Coos Bay, emerged from the sea between 20 and 50 million years ago. The mountains of each of these coastal cordilleras rarely exceed several thousand feet in elevation. The uplifts that created both the Klamaths and the Coast Range also left black-sand beaches and offshore volcanic plugs, as well as headlands made of erosion-resistant basalt.

A look at the globe offers a bird's-eye view of this dramatic meeting of rock and tide: the 6,000 miles of water lying between Oregon and Japan are largely unfettered by archipelagoes and reefs—the longest stretch of open ocean on earth. This impression of remoteness and isolation is compounded by the fact that Cape Blanco stands as the westernmost point in the contiguous United States. Finally, this extraordi-

nary region is roughly equidistant from the equator and the north pole. It all adds up to a complex interplay of climatic and geologic forces which have orchestrated nature on a grand scale.

CLIMATE

Coastal rain or shine begins with the Japanese current. This offshore system of tepid water evaporates up into billowy cloud masses which are blown inland by the Pacific westerlies. If these clouds don't drop their moisture over the water or on the shoreline, chances are good that the Coast Range's lower temperatures will create condensation and rain. This translates into a 166-inch annual maritime rainfall, with as much as 150 inches over the mountains.

But generalized regional precipitation totals tell only part of the story. Brookings, with a yearly average of almost 74 inches, and Tillamook, with 94 inches, demonstrate the south-to-north variance. Halfway up the coast, Coos Bay's rainfall totals hover around the 60-inch mark. If this sounds foreboding, remember that almost all of these totals are racked up during the winter months. Keep in mind, too, that in the midst of this gloom, midwinter dry spells with 60°-plus temperatures commonly occur. These respites also serve to thaw coastal habitués used to temperatures in the 40s . . . not that they need it! With infrequent freezes and rarely recorded snowfall, Old Man Winter definitely pulls his punches here. In fact, Coos Bay is often touted as having the mildest (in terms of absence of extremes) year-round climate in the United States.

Here's a little tip for those looking to take advantage of midwinter lulls in the gray wetness which hangs over much of western Oregon. Should you be inland during a rainy spell, keep an eye on satellite photos on TV or in the paper. By the time a major storm reaches the interior, there is often a respite between fronts at the coast. By anticipating the approach of a "blue hole," you can time your visit to coincide with the arrival of nice weather, short-lived as it may be.

In general, count on good weather for traveling mid-April through mid-September, with a preponderance of daytime highs in the 60s. Within this period, there might be enough June gloom to dismay travelers used to simmering southland beaches, but storm-watching is an acquired taste. An added plus is that when summertime inversions drive the temperature readings up east of the Coast Range, the heat will draw cooler maritime air to the shore. While the mountains often lock in these welcome fronts, it can sometimes cause coastal fog and overcast conditions to linger. Nonetheless, respite from the characteristic morning fog banks in summer is often only minutes away upriver on one of the many tidal estuaries.

Finally, newcomers to the region should remember that the icy temperatures of the coastal waters (40-45°) make the beaches more valued for beachcombing than for swimming. Ironically, 20-30 miles offshore, the warming effects of the Kuroshio current create subtropical conditions.

FLORA AND FAUNA

Sandwiched between the mountains and the sea are predominantly mixed conifer forests of Douglas fir, spruce, cedar, and hemlock. Due to the construction industry's penchant for Douglas fir, which they replant assiduously, this tree predominates. The conifers are broken up by pockets of alder, oak, swamp maple, and myrtle trees. A largely edible understory of thimbleberry, salmonberry, blackberry, and salal are interspersed among the ferns and mosses that carpet the forest floor. Apart from Brookings's Azalea Festival and Florence's Rhododendron Festival, coastbound travelers come to take in such horticultural highlights as the insect-eating Darlingtonia plant and the myrtle tree, said to be native only to the Holy Land and southern Oregon. Serious botanists might search out the pine mushroom, exclusive to the Oregon dunes and Japan, or probe the Kalmiopsis Wilderness near the south coast, habitat to many rare plants.

Such eclecticism is paralleled in the animal kingdom. Consider, for example, the nutria and the boomer. The nutria was brought to Oregon in the 1930s from South America to be raised for its fur. After numerous escapes, this furry rodent was able to breed in the wild and establish a niche in the woodlands of the Coast Range. The boomer is another distinctive resident of this ecosystem. Similar in appearance to a beaver (minus the flat tail), the predilection of this primitive rat species for eating Douglas fir seedlings has made it the scourge of the timber industry. Currently an open season encourages hunting of both these varmints.

Other coastal critters include muskrat, raccoon, Roosevelt elk, black-tailed deer, bald eagles, and an impressive array of anadromous fish, shore birds, and migratory waterfowl. Regional estuaries and the Oregon dunes are the

rhododendrons,
another coastal treat

best places to take in this wildlife show. Another distinctive resident of coastal forests is the giant Pacific salamander. This stout, mottled creature grows to a length of more than one foot and is said to produce doglike yelping and snapping sounds. Sightings are rare, but hikers occasionally encounter them around stagnant pools in the Kalmiopsis.

HISTORY

Native Peoples

No one knows when the first inhabitants took up residence on the Oregon coast. An archaeological dig site at Yaquina Head yielded implements 4,000-5,000 years old, the oldest yet found on the coast. But the sea level rose significantly before that time, inundating earlier remains. Willamette Valley archaeological sites dating back 8,000 to 10,000 years and an Applegate Valley (southern Oregon) excavation that unearthed projectile points 10,000 years old hint that Oregon's western edge has hosted our species for longer than the tools found at Yaquina Head would indicate.

What is clear is that by the time the white explorers and settlers came here, Indian culture was a patchwork of languages and cultural traits as diverse as the topography. Most native coastal communities typically included a dozen or more small bands linked by a common dialect. These bands or villages consisted of perhaps an extended family in one or two houses, or a larger grouping under a headman. The linguistic and life-style divisions between native communities were maintained by mountains, an ocean too rough for canoes, and other geographic barriers.

In the aftermath of the Rogue Indian wars in the 1850s, the Chetco, Coquille, Coos, Umpqua, Siuslaw, Alsea, Yaquina, Nestucca, and Tillamook peoples were grouped together with the Rogue River tribes and forced to live on the 1.1-million-acre Siletz Reservation, and so the culture and heritage of many indigenous peoples were lost forever. More tragic than the watering down of cultural distinctiveness was the huge mortality rate resulting from natives being "removed" to the Siletz Reservation and to another small encampment, the Grande Ronde, im-

mediately to the northeast.

Over the years, whatever wealth the Siletz tribes had left was stripped as a result of the United States not honoring a multitude of treaties. The final indignity came in 1951 with the termination of the Siletz Reservation. The divestiture of tribal status meant the loss of health services, educational support, tax exemptions, and other benefits. Predictably, the transition to becoming "first-class citizens" brought about alcoholism and despair for the unprepared natives. In 1977, Senator Mark Hatfield and Congressman Les AuCoin helped push a bill through Congress for tribal restoration. This has resulted in the tribe getting the wherewithal to flourish economically in everything from logging and construction projects to such enterprises as the Smokehouse in Depoe Bay (see "Depoe Bay"). The latter endeavor has been accompanied by an interest in the old ways and a renewed sense of pride in native identity.

The Coming Of The White Man

In 1542, Juan Rodríguez Cabrilho sailed into what is now southern Oregon waters. Sixty years later, Sebastiáno Vizcaíno came to the same area, but he also failed to lay claim for the armada. A succession of Spanish, English, American, and Russian explorers followed in search of whales, sea otter and beaver pelts, and hides for the tallow trade. But the major impetus for exploring this coast was the quest for the mythic Northwest Passage—a sea route connecting the Pacific with the Atlantic. While written histories vary as to the exact dates and locations of these excursions, hundreds of shipwrecks remain as evidence of the exploratory zeal of past centuries. At the northern edge of this rock-studded graveyard for ancient mariners, the fur-trading center of Astoria was established in 1811. Several decades later, gold mining near the Rogue River drew more settlers to the south coast. It was a later gold rush, however, that had the greatest implications for the development of the region.

In 1849, the influx of prospectors into California's Sierra Nevada occasioned a housing boom in San Francisco, port of entry to the goldfields. The demand for Coast Range timber and foodstuffs from Oregon's inland agricultural valleys caused downriver Pacific ports like Astoria and Newport to flourish. As a result, the coastline of California's friendly neighbor to the north was able to develop the necessary economic base for it to prosper and endure.

The exploitation of coastal resources was so successful that Governor Oswald West had to spearhead legislation restricting beachfront development in 1913. This set the tone for future preservationist measures in the state. Today, Oregon has more state parks than anyplace else in America, with the majority of these located on the coast.

WHALEWATCHING

Whalewatching trips serve each part of the coast from December into the early spring. Wherever and whenever you go, dress warmly, take precautions against seasickness, and expect to get wet if you go out on deck. By land or by sea, early morning hours are best because winds cause whitecaps later in the day. This inconvenience can be made up for the instant you see one of these benign monsters come up for air. The sight of a mammal as long as a Greyhound bus breaking water has a way of emptying the mind of mundane concerns. Wreathed in seaweed and sporting barnacles and other parasites on its back, a 40-foot-long, 40-ton California gray whale would look more like the hull of a ship were it not for its sadly expressive eyes.

Further empathy might be engendered upon learning of these mammals' humanlike propensities. Some whale birthings have been observed, for example, which included the help of whale "midwives" pushing mama above the surface of the water so that baby could be born into the air. If "air-born" whales seem implausible, consider that according to recent research, whale language could be the most sophisticated in the animal kingdom.

Though the latter tendencies might endear these cetaceans to some people, it is their homing instinct that makes it possible to enjoy whalewatching on the Oregon coast. Coastal headlands and beaches provide excellent vantage points from which to spy on the 12,000-mile roundtrip December-to-May migration of the California gray whale, particularly in midwinter.

This yearly pilgrimage ranges between Baja and the Arctic, the longest migratory movement by land or sea of any animal. Along the way, the whales search for tiny shrimplike amphipods, their major food during this time. The southward migration along the Oregon coast lasts until early February, although the migration peaks the last week in December. Whales migrating northward can be sighted off Oregon from March through May. Some locals swear that many whales have foresaken migration to take up permanent residency in Oregon waters in recent years.

The following listing gives a cross section of excursions from each part of the coast. Booking info is also available from local Greenpeace chapters in Portland, Eugene, and other major cities. Greenpeace, in conjunction with Newport's **Marine Science Center,** has helped stimulate whalewatching awareness. The Marine Science Center is an extension of Oregon State University, which supplies trained volunteers to staff vantage points 10 a.m.-1 p.m. each day, Dec. 26-Jan. 1. Look for the big sign that says Whalewatching Spoken Here. For additional info, contact Hatfield Marine Science Center, Newport 97365; tel. 867-3011, ext. 226. On the envelope write "Attention: Whales" and include a self-addressed, stamped envelope. You'll receive a list of charter operators as well as background information.

By Land
Cape Arago State Park, west of Coos Bay, has a promontory with a commanding view of the ocean that is excellent for whalewatching.

The Reedsport Chamber of Commerce, located where ORE 38 and U.S. 101 intersect, offers directions to the whalewatching platform across the road from the **Umpqua Lighthouse** in Winchester Bay. The two-tiered platform overlooks the Umpqua River estuary, where whales are often sighted. Seven placards here describe whale habits and habitat. Two jetties provide reference points for directing the observer's gaze.

Rockwork, a pullout just north of the Sea Lion Caves, offers a magnificent view of Heceta Head, as well as frequent spottings of whales, sea lions, and an assortment of seabirds.

(top) air over Broken Top;
(bottom) A mountain biker in his element near Grants Pass (photos by Christopher Scott Murray)

(top) The Penthouse, Chambers Lakes (Peter Hawkins);
(bottom) Caveman Bridge frames sunset colors on the Rogue River, Grants Pass (Christopher Scott Murra

Three miles south of Yachats, immediately after Devil's Churn, there is a sign for **Cape Perpetua Drive.** Follow the steep and windy road up the highest coastal drive in Oregon to the parking lot on top of Cape Perpetua. From there, take the quarter-mile hike on the famous **Trail of the Whispering Spruce** to the old Coast Guard lookout. On a clear day, you can see 150 miles north, south, and west. If there are whales out there, this is one of the best places to spot them. In 1988, Cape Perpetua led all other sites in total sightings. Nearby is **Cape Perpetua Visitor Center,** where you can whalewatch and stay dry behind picture windows. Locals say that sightings of these leviathans can occur any time of year. This has been the case since the mid-'80s between Cape Perpetua and Otter Crest.

At **Depoe Bay,** in addition to the natural blowholes in the lava rock that shoot up a 30- to 50-foot fountain of water when the tide is right, the lucky visitor is often treated to the sight of whales coming up for air just offshore.

Cape Meares State Park lies 10 miles west of Tillamook on a headland that features a lighthouse built in 1896, as well as great views. If you happen to get rained out, take a look at the Octopus Tree, a Sitka spruce of gargantuan proportions located a short walk away from the parking lot.

By Sea

Dick's Sporthaven Marina (16372 Lower Harbor Rd., Box 2215, Harbor 97415; tel. 469-3301) offers two-hour trips beginning in January that cost $25. Reservations necessary.

Betty Kay Charters (Box 5020, Charleston 97420; tel. 888-9021) features three-hour trips on weekends December through January and during part of the spring. Depending upon the size of the boat, the cost ranges from $15-20. Reservations are essential. **Bob's Sport Fishing** (7960 Kingfisher Rd., Box 5457, Charleston, 97420; tel. 888-4241) hosts three- to four-hour trips in December and January for $20. Reservations required, five-person minimum, and discounts for seniors and kids. **Charleston Charters** (Box 5032, Charleston 97420; tel. 888-4846) runs three-hour trips for $15, beginning in December. Reservations recommended.

Cape Perpetua Charters (839 S.E. Bay Blvd., Newport 97365; tel. 265-7777) has daily two-hour trips for $15 beginning in mid-December, depending upon weather and the number of passengers. **South Beach Charters** (Box 1446, Newport 97365; tel. 867-7200) operates two-hour trips daily from mid-December to May for $16, reservations required. **Newport Tradewinds** (653 S.W. Bay Blvd., Newport 97365; tel. 265-2101) offers two-hour trips December through June for $18, three-hour trips are $27 per person with kids under five floating for free. **Newport Sportfishing** (1000 S.E. Bay Blvd., Newport 97365; tel. 265-7558) runs daily two-hour trips departing at 10 a.m. and 1 p.m. from mid-December through May. Adult fare is $25, children $12.50; reservations are recommended.

Oregon Natural Resources Council from Portland (Attn: Michael Carigan, 522 S.W. Fifth Ave., Suite 1050, Portland 97204; tel. 223-4012 or 800-827-9001) or from Eugene (1161 Lincoln St., Eugene 97401; tel. 344-0675) is a coalition of 90 conservation organizations that has put together a series of two-hour trips. Beginning in mid-December and continuing each weekend (Saturday and Sunday) on through mid-April, these charters depart from Newport at 10 a.m. and 1 p.m. The cost is $20 for adults, $15 for children 12 and under. A naturalist gives an informative and entertaining presentation before sailing. Advanced registration is required.

Dockside Charters, near the Coast Guard station (Box 1308, Depoe Bay 97341; tel. 765-2545 or 800-733-8915), has hourly trips daily, year-round depending upon sightings. Cost is $8 per person, $6 for kids under 12; please call ahead. **Allyn's Tradewinds Ocean Sportfishing** (on U.S. 101 at north end of the Depoe Bay bridge; tel. 763-2345) features one-hour trips that cost $8, $6 for kids 7-12, with kids under six free. **Oregon Museum of Science and Industry** (4015 S.W. Canyon Rd., Portland 97221; tel. 222-2828) offers two-hour tours departing from Depoe Bay, depending upon availability of boats, weather, and number of people. A naturalist is on hand to give a presentation. Cost is $18.50, reservations required.

By Air

The **Astoria Flight Center** offers a 40-minute flight in a Cessna 150 for $40. Two or three people can charter a Cessna 172 for $65. Departures are from the Port Astoria airport in War-

Beachcombers should take advantage of Hug Point State Park at low tide.

renton. Call 861-1222 for information.

Aurora Aviation (tel. 222-1754 in Portland or 678-1217 in Aurora) offers charters from Aurora, south of Portland, at $89 an hour (minimum of three passengers) or $260 an hour (minimum of six passengers). Flying time to the coast is approximately 45 minutes.

McKenzie Flying Service in Eugene (tel. 688-0971) has whalewatching flights that begin and end in Newport, with departures also from Eugene or North Bend. Hourly rates, excluding flight time to the coast, are $65 per person in a Cessna 172, $47 in the C-206, $73 in the C-182, and $105 in the C-340.

BEACHCOMBING

The Beach: Contours And Character

For most Oregon visitors who travel west of the Coast Range, life is a beach. Despite Pacific temperatures cold enough to render swimming an at-your-own-risk activity, the cliffside ocean vistas, wildlife, and beachcombing make the coast the state's number-one attraction. With rare exception, all beaches in Oregon below mean high tide are owned by the public. These beaches are generally separated by basaltic headlands, volcanic plugs which remain after wind and sea erosion have worn away the softer surrounding earth.

Black sand, high in iron and other metals, is common on the coast, particularly south of Coos Bay. There was also enough gold in the black sands to spur a flurry of gold-mining activity on the south coast 130 years ago. These days, mining companies are eyeing the shelf off the south coast for possible exploitation of ilmenite, magnetite, chromite, zircon, garnet, gold, and platinum. Scientists have known for decades of the placer deposits of heavy minerals washed ashore on prehistoric beaches thousands of years ago when ocean levels were much lower. These beach sands now lie submerged. A study based on Rogue River and Cape Blanco offshore sands has indicated a significant presence of precious metals there.

Speaking of sand, the Oregon coast has 40 miles of dunes (about 32,000 acres), the largest oceanfront collection in North America. Some hills top out at several hundred feet high. Oregon's Sahara is located between Coos Bay and Florence. Many coastal travelers will notice European beach grass covering the sand wherever they go. Originally planted to inhibit dune growth, the beach grass has solidified into a ridge behind the shoreline, which blocks the windblown sand from replenishing the rest of the beach. In some places, highways are in danger of being engulfed by the dunes.

Throughout your coastal travels, you'll notice names like Oswald West, Samuel Boardman, and Henry B. Van Duzer adorning the names of state parks and highways. These state government officials were the prime movers in preserving the land, building the highways, and establishing the state park system.

Flotsam And Jetsam

Among the first things a newcomer to the Oregon coast notices are the huge piles of driftwood on the beach. Closer inspection usually reveals other treasures. Beachcombers particularly value agates and Japanese glass fishing floats. The volume and variety of flotsam and jetsam here come courtesy of the region's unique geography. Much of the driftwood, for instance, originates from logging operations located upriver on the many waterways which empty into the Pacific. In addition, storms, floods, rockslides, and erosion uproot many trees which eventually wash up on shore.

The Japanese fishing floats are swept into Oregon waters when the Kuroshio current takes a southerly turn. These balls of ornate green and blue glass sometimes require over a decade to reach the Oregon coast after breaking free from fishnets thousands of miles across the sea. In addition to driftwood and floats, shells, coral, sand dollars, starfish, and other seaborne trophies can be best culled from the intertidal zone on south coast beaches. Unfortunately, the more settled and accessible north coast has slimmer pickin's due to the larger population of resident beachcombers and the higher visitor influx. March is the best time to find floats, especially after two-day storms from the northwest, west-southwest, or due west. December to April are the best months to find agates, jaspers, petrified wood, and a variety of fossils. At that time, the gravel bars covered by sand in summer are exposed. Clamming in the tidal flats and crabbing in the estuaries are also popular, but check carefully for conditions.

Consult a tidal chart any time you anticipate an extended beachcombing excursion. Half a dozen people perish here yearly from being washed off a beach, jetty, or outcropping. Tide charts are usually available from chambers of commerce as well as from sport and bait shops.

While you may not always come across a 100-foot-long kelp or a message in a bottle, you'll probably find beachcombing on the Oregon coast to be its own reward.

PRACTICALITIES

Accommodations

Coastal accommodations run the gamut from humble fishing lodges to bona fide five-star resorts. In between are condominiums rented as guest rooms, bed and breakfasts, and conventional motels. Air conditioning is a rarity in these establishments, as is direct access to the beach. The latter is due to the strict land-use statutes against building on the beach. Getting to the beach, however, seldom involves more than a five-minute walk. Rates tend to be much lower in the winter, with special weekend-getaway packages quite common during the February storm-watching season. Rather than give several seasonal rate changes, coastal accommodations listings will instead indicate a range.

Food

Oregon coast cuisine boasts such delicacies as Dungeness crab, razor clams, Yaquina Bay oysters and bay shrimp, as well as world-famous salmon.

Let's start with the bay shrimp as an appetizer. While a hasty visual appraisal of an Oregon shrimp cocktail might prompt an unfavorable comparison to the larger Gulf prawns, these savory morsels prove that good things come in small packages. Expect them to be in season during August. Another coveted crustacean is the Dungeness crab. The firm texture of this species in peak season (March or October) has been compared to that of Maine lobster.

Speaking of which, those used to *Homarus americanus* from the East Coast will be disappointed by the oversized crayfish passed off as lobster on some menus. Nevertheless, the freshwater "crawdads" here are exported all over the world. Oregon's Yaquina Bay oysters are also considered gourmet fare. If you want them fresh, avoid the summer months and wait until the weather is cooler. Razor clams are another indigenous shellfish which for many are an acquired taste. Once you get past their rubbery consistency, however, you might enjoy this local favorite. Local mussels and albacore tuna near the end of July are also worth a try.

Spring chinook salmon (May) from the Rogue River estuary seems to be a "can't miss" item for almost everyone. While red snapper would normally also merit such an assessment, this is not always the case in Oregon, due largely to a case of mistaken identity. In contrast to the red snapper found on southern and eastern menus, this Pacific version is a bottomfish. The brown widow rockfish and its several counterparts which receive the red snapper designation out here have a similar consistency, but more of a fishy taste than their East Coast cousin.

Nightlife
With the exception of the **Salishan Jazz Party** and an occasional big-name rock band playing in Bandon or Newport, there are only taverns and lounges for those interested in stepping out after dark. Taverns sell beer, often cheaply, and are frequented by the locals. Hard liquor, beer, wine, and live music characterize the lounges. Outside of happy hours, prices are much higher than elsewhere, and when many of the bartenders in these establishments pour, they seem to miss the glass. Nonetheless, a picture window on the Pacific or some other pleasant feature can make up for a multitude of sins.

Information
All manner of information is available from the **Oregon Coast Association** (Box 620, Newport 97365; tel. 265-2611, or from Washington, Idaho, Utah, Nevada, and California 800-29-COAST). *Oregon Coast* magazine (Box 18000, Florence 97439-1030) is an excellent bimonthly about life on Oregon's western edge. It is sold all over the state.

Bus Service
The Oregon coast enjoys **Greyhound** service along the length of U.S. 101. Buses leave Portland twice daily, linking up with the coast at Lincoln City and heading south to Brookings. Stops en route include Lincoln City, Newport, Florence, Reedsport, Coos Bay, Bandon, Port Orford, Gold Beach, and Brookings. The 10-hour trip from Portland to Brookings sees few terminals (i.e., you are let out on the street), but that's a small inconvenience for the chance to enjoy this scenic drive. The stretch between Gold Beach and Brookings offers the best views from a bus window. The north and central parts of U.S. 101 do not lack for viewpoints, however, and although going by bike or car affords more flexibility, bus travel has its own advantages, the major one being that it frees you from driving in order to take in the views. Then, too, a bus window affords a greater field of vision with an elevated carriage and wide windows.

The trick to successfully negotiating U.S. 101 along Oregon's coast can be summed up in two words: slow down.

In addition to Greyhound's trunk route from Portland, coast-bound travelers can hook up to U.S. 101 several other ways. From the Willamette Valley, **Valley Retriever,** a Greyhound subcontractor, runs a Corvallis-to-Newport bus which makes three roundtrips daily. Farther south, **Raz,** another 'Hound franchise, rolls along an especially scenic and comfortable coastal route—ORE 126 from Eugene to Florence, and eventually down to Coos Bay. Small bus companies run between Coquille and Roseburg and along ORE 199 from Grants Pass to Crescent City, California, a short distance from the Oregon state line.

Those desirous of reaching the north coast from points inland can take advantage of the Portland-Seaside-Astoria loop. Once on the north coast, Greyhound service is replaced by other alternatives. Local public transportation goes from Tillamook to Astoria, but no public transportation links Tillamook and Lincoln City.

Driving U.S. 101

The motorist heading up the coast from California should keep in mind that no vehicular routes access the population centers of Oregon's interior for the first 150 miles of U.S. 101, with the exception of ORE 199 which runs from Crescent City, California, to Grants Pass. One characteristic of U.S. 101 is heavy summer traffic; you'll have a better chance of passing a slow-moving log truck or a lumbering Winnebago on the four-lane main drag of many coastal cities than on the two lanes of U.S. 101. In any case, be prepared to modify your schedule to accommodate the breathtaking scenery surrounding the road. Also, save time and money by stocking up on groceries and filling up on gas inland before encountering the higher prices endemic to the coast's tourist economy. It also pays to be careful of log trucks doing twice the speed limit on circuitous coastal access roads, as well as bicycles attempting to share hairpin turns with large vehicles. Beach loops are

often less traveled and offer some good scenery. Finally, keep in mind that the majority of the communities on the coast are "strip towns" along U.S. 101. As such, their simple layout usually renders maps of them unnecessary.

By Bicycle

While not for everybody, biking the Oregon coast is the surest way to get on intimate terms with this spectacular region. Before going, get a free copy of *The Oregon Coast Bike Route Map* (Dept. of Transportation, Salem 97310, or from coastal info centers and chambers of commerce). This brochure features strip maps of the route, noting services from Astoria to the California border. With info on campsites, hostels, bike-repair facilities, temperatures, and wind speed, this pamphlet does everything but map the ruts in the road.

By Foot

The **Oregon Coastal Trail** goes 360 miles through some of the most beautiful landscape anywhere. At this writing, about 60% of the trail is completed. The north portion of the trail is in the best condition, while the central and southern sections are still in the process of development. A free map and directory are available by writing the Oregon State Parks and Recreation Department (525 Trade St., Salem 97310; tel. 378-5012) and requesting the *Oregon Coast Trail Guide*. This pamphlet makes it clear where this trail crosses open beaches, forested headlands, the shoulder of 101, and even city streets in some coastal villages.

By Air

Despite a dozen airports on the coast, only the North Bend field near Coos Bay enjoys commercial service. **Horizon,** an offshoot of Alaska Airlines, flies in from Eugene and Portland daily. They fly to these same cities, with occasional through-flights to Seattle and isolated stopovers in Salem.

BROOKINGS AND VICINITY

If you cross the state line on U.S. 101 in early summer, the welcome mat of Easter lily blossoms often lines the way into Oregon's gateway city of Brookings (population 3,400). While the lilies may not carpet these roadsides so extravagantly during the rest of the year, the coast-bound traveler can still look forward to being greeted by mild temperatures and colorful bouquets, even in winter. Enough 60° days occur during February in this south coast "banana belt" town that over 50 species of flowering plants thrive here, along with retirees, sportsmen, and beachcombers. With two gorgeous state parks virtually part of the city and world-class salmon and steelhead fishing nearby, only the lavish winter rainfall that often exceeds 80 inches a year can cool the ardor of local outdoor enthusiasts.

Brookings sits on a coastal plain overlooking the Pacific. The ocean and the Klamath Mountains east of town are linked up by the Chetco River. This river drains part of the near-by **Siskiyou National Forest** and the **Kalmiopsis Wilderness,** renowned for their rare flowers and trees and for possessing some of the wildest country in the United States. Quite fittingly, the Kalmiopsis area is named for the flowering plant that grows nowhere else on earth. This area enjoys strict federal protection, safeguarding the northernmost stand of giant redwoods as well as the coveted Port Orford cedar. The latter species of strong but pliable lumber can fetch $10,000 for a single tree.

But you don't have to trek miles into the backcountry to enjoy the natural beauty of Brookings and vicinity. Just make your way past the somewhat honky-tonk main drag to **Samuel Boardman State Park** north of town, where 11 of the most scenic miles of the Oregon coast await you. Or for a total escape, head down to the harbor to enjoy some of the safest offshore navigation conditions in the region. In short, Brookings is the perfect place to launch an adventure by land or by sea.

BROOKINGS TO PORT ORFORD

HISTORY

What is now the shopping hub of rural Curry County started out as a factory town for the Brookings Box Company in 1914. In the years that followed, lumber, fishing, and tourism became established. If we omit the speculation that the offshore waters here were visited by Cabrilho (in 1542) and the English explorer Sir Francis Drake (in 1579), the local event with the most historical significance was the Japanese bombing incident in 1942. On September 9 of that year, a Japanese air raid scorched the treetops of nearby Mt. Emily in what the Brookings Chamber of Commerce calls the only wartime air bombing mission against the U.S. mainland.

Ironically, this frightful episode had two positive outgrowths of enduring significance. First, it sounded the death knell of a secessionist uprising comprised of southern Oregonians and northern Californians. During the '30s, these people wanted to break off from the Union to set up the self-sufficient agrarian state of Jefferson (see

Harris Beach

"Southern Oregon"). Secondly, the bombing encouraged the local lily industry to expand in an effort to make up for the imminent cutoff of Japanese flowers. Today, the area produces 90% of the world's Easter lily crop.

SIGHTS

Chetco Valley Historical Society Museum

This museum (5461 Museum Rd., Brookings 97415; tel. 469-6651) is in an older red-and-white house built on a hill overlooking U.S. 101 two miles south of the Chetco River. Open Tues.-Sat. 2-6, Sun. noon-6. From November to mid-May hours are Fri.-Sun. 9-5. Admission is free, but donations are always welcome. The structure dates back to the mid-1800s and was used as a stagecoach way station and trading post before Lincoln was president.

Even if you are not one for museums, several exhibits here stand apart from the traditional collections of pioneer wedding dresses, Indian baskets, and spinning wheels. These include a small trunk which came around Cape Horn in 1706, a patchwork quilt dating back to 1844, and an Indian dugout canoe. Should these fail to inspire, an iron casting of a woman's face might do the trick—especially in light of the speculation that this relic was left by an early undocumented landing on the Oregon coast, perhaps by Sir Francis Drake. Drake has been commonly suggested because of the mask's likeness to Queen Elizabeth.

The **World Champion Cypress Tree** is located on the hill near the museum. The 99-foot-tall tree has a trunk circumference of more than 27 feet, and has been home to a pair of owls for years.

Quail Prairie Lookout

If you've always romanticized mountain fire lookout stations but have never seen an operating one, visit the Quail Prairie Lookout, 17 air miles northeast of Brookings. This is one of the few remaining outposts still staffed each summer during the fire season. As negotiating the Forest Service roads just west of the Kalmiopsis Wilderness can be tricky, get exact directions to 3,000-foot Quail Prairie Mountain from the Chetco Ranger Station in Brookings.

HIKES AND BEACHCOMBING

Harris Beach State Park

You're driving north along the first 20 miles of scenic U.S. 101 in Oregon, but instead of stopping to take out the camera, you're asking yourself, "So where's the Oregon coast?" It's easy to have second thoughts after a half-hour drive through the "Twilight Zone" of small-town America, with only a few fleeting glimpses of the ocean. And then, at the northern limits of Brookings (across from the State Information Center on U.S. 101), you find your lost picture postcard at Harris Beach State Park. One look at the 24 miles of rock and tide visible from the parking-lot promontory should quell any mis-givings. The effect can be described as Gibral-tar-like and then some.

Besides stunning views, this state park of-fers many incoming travelers from California their first chance to actually walk on the beach in Oregon. You can begin directly west of the park's campground, where a sandy beach strewn with boulders often becomes flooded with intertidal life and driftwood. The early morn-ing hours, as the waves crash through a small tunnel in a massive rock onto the shoreline, are the best time to look for sponges, umbrella crabs, solitary corals, and starfish. Offshore, Goat Island, Oregon's largest seabird rookery, dispatches squadrons of cormorants, pelicans, and other waterfowl who divebomb the incoming waves for food.

In addition to beachcombing, you can picnic at tables above the parking lot, loll about in the shallow waters of nearby Harris Creek, or cast the tidewaters for perch.

Mill Beach is the southernmost part of the Harris Beach area. Locals prefer the beach ac-cess from downtown, which is easy to miss. To get there, drive toward the ocean on Center Street in downtown Brookings, make a right at the plywood mill, and stop next to a small ball-park. An unimproved road leads to a hillock from which trails take you down to a beach full of driftwood. Residents say that Japanese fishing floats occasionally roll up onto the beach after a storm.

The Kalmiopsis Wilderness/Vulcan Lake

The lure of untrammeled wilderness attracts in-trepid hikers to the Kalmiopsis, despite sum-mer's blazing heat and winter's torrential rains here. In addition to enjoying the isolation of Ore-gon's largest (180,000 acres) and probably least-visited wilderness, they come to take in the pink rhododendronlike blooms of *Kalmiopsis leachiana* in June and other rare flowers. The area is also home to such economically valued species as Port Orford cedar and *Cannabis sati-va*. The illicit weed is the leading cash crop in the state, and its vigilant protection by growers might inspire extra care for those hiking here during the late fall harvest season.

In any case, the Forest Service prohibits plant collection *of any kind* to preserve the region's special botanical populations. These include the insect-eating Darlingtonia plant and the Brewer's weeping spruce. The forest canopy is composed largely of the more common Douglas fir, canyon live oak, madrone, and chinquapin. Stark peaks top this red-rock forest, whose un-derstory is choked with blueberry, manzanita, and dense chaparral. Many of the Kalmiopsis species survived the glacial epoch because the glaciers from that era left the area untouched. This, combined with the fact that the area was an ancient offshore island, has enabled the re-gion's singular ecosystem to maintain its in-tegrity through the millennia. You'd think that federal protection, remoteness, and climatic ex-tremes would ensure a sanguine outlook for this ice-age forest, but an active debate still rages over the validity of some logging claims.

Even if you don't have the slightest intention of hiking the Kalmiopsis, the scenic drive through the **Chetco Valley** is worth it. From Brookings, turn off U.S. 101 at the north end of the Chetco River Bridge, follow County Rds. 784 and 1736 along the Chetco River for six miles, and then turn right and follow County Rd. 1909 to its end. Here, a one-mile-long trail leads to **Vulcan Lake** at the foot of Vulcan Peak, the major jumping-off point for trails into the wilderness. Hikers should watch out for the three shiny leaves of poison oak, as well as for rattlesnakes, which are nu-merous here. Black bears also populate the area, but their lack of contact with humans makes them more shy than their Cascade counterparts.

Streams here in the water-deficient Kalmiop-sis are often too warm to quench a thirst. This high temperature can be better appreciated at one of the preserve's many secluded swimming holes.

Here's what to expect on the way to Vulcan Lake. Road 1909 takes off up the mountains past Pollywog Butte and Red Mountain Prairie. The open patches in the Douglas fir reveal a kaleidoscope of Pacific Ocean views and panoramas of the Chetco Valley and the Big Craggies. For the botanist in search of rare plants, however, the real show is on the trail. No matter how expert you might consider your-self, bring along a good plant guide to help you identify the many exotic species here. On the final leg of the hike, sadler oak, manzanita, Jeffrey pine, white pine, and azalea precede the sharp descent to the lake. Despite steep spots, the walk from County Rd. 1909 to Vulcan Lake is not a difficult one.

If you backtrack from the lake to Spur 260 on the trail, you can make the steep ascent over talus slopes and brush to Vulcan Peak. At the top, from an old lookout, a view of Kalmiopsis treetops and the coast awaits.

PRACTICALITIES

Camping

Campers should pick up a **Siskiyou Forest Service** map and literature on fishing at the ranger station in town (see "Information and Services" below). In addition to printed matter about Siskiyou and Kalmiopsis trails for hikers, the rangers there can tell you where to find some good fishing holes on the nearby Chetco River, noted for its good fall salmon runs and winter steelhead.

Harris Beach State Park, two miles north of town on U.S. 101 (1655 Hwy. 101, Brookings 97415; tel. 469-2021; $15-17), is open all year, but reservations are definitely necessary in the summer. There are 66 tent sites, 85 trailer/motor-home sites (up to 50 feet long), and a special camping area for hikers and bicyclists. Picnic tables and firegrills are provided. Flush toilets, electricity, piped-in water, sewer hookups, sanitary service, showers, firewood, and a laundromat are also available. Whalewatching is particularly good here in January and May.

Loeb State Park is eight miles northeast of Brookings on North Bank Road along the Chetco River. For info call 469-2021 or write c/o Harris Beach State Park. The park is open mid-April to late October, but camping is allowed only during the summer; no reservations necessary. The rate is $15-17 per night, with 53 sites for trailers/motor homes (50 feet maximum), as well as a special campground for bicyclists and hikers. Electricity, piped water, and picnic tables are provided; flush toilets and firewood are available. The campground is located in a secluded myrtlewood grove on the east bank of the Chetco River. This grove is the largest collection of old growth of this species in the state, which imparts a special fragrance to the campsite. Close by is one of the northernmost stands of coastal redwoods. When the south coast is foggy and cold on summer mornings, it's often warm and dry in upriver locations such as this one.

Beyond Loeb State Park is the more primitive **Little Redwood Campround,** which for the price can't be beat. To get there, go one-half mile south of Brookings on U.S. 101 to County Rd. 784, then go northeast for seven miles. At Forest Service Rd. 376 turn northeast and drive six miles to the campground. Contact **Chetco Ranger District,** (Box 730, Brookings 97415; tel. 469-2196) for information. Open late May to mid-September, no reservations necessary. Bargain priced at $4 per night per family, there are 16 sites for tents, trailers, or motor homes (16 feet maximum). Picnic tables and grills are on-site; pit toilets and firewood available. Though it lacks showers and other amenities, Little Redwood is located on the main access route to the Kalmiopsis Wilderness, 20 miles away, and is a good spot for fishing during the winter steelhead run.

Accommodations

While Brookings's campgrounds seem preferable for taking best advantage of the natural splendor just outside of town, you can always get a roof over your head here, but reserve ahead in summer.

The turn-of-the-century contours of the recently restored **Historical Chetco Inn** (417 Fern St., Brookings 97415; tel. 469-9984) showcase the aesthetic sensibilities of famed California architect Bernard Maybeck. The "historical" prefix of the Chetco Inn is also justified by its location on part of the site of the Brookings Box Company. If this matters little to you, perhaps the knowledge that the Inn is the most reasonably priced lodging in town ($27-47) might make a difference. Sitting on a hill in back of the Shell station, the hotel overlooks the town and is close to a shopping center and restaurants.

Holmes Sea Cove Bed and Breakfast (17350 Holmes Dr., Brookings 97415; tel. 469-3025; $80-95), is a year-round retreat located two miles north of Brookings (turn onto Dawson Rd. from U.S. 101). Replete with lushly landscaped grounds and continental breakfast in bed, the Holmeses offer two bedrooms on the lower level of their home and a guesthouse. Below is a private park with picnic tables along a creek by a beach.

Across the street from one another are the **Brookings Best Western Inn** (1153 Chetco, Box N 39, Brookings 97415; tel. 469-2173) and the **Pacific Sunset Inn** (1144 Chetco, Brookings 97415; tel. 469-2144). Farther down Chetco Avenue (also known as U.S. 101) is **Spindrift Motor Inn** (1215 Chetco, Brookings 97415; tel. 469-5345). These all run around $55 during the spring and summer and average $10 less in the winter. What you get for your money is a clean garden-variety motel and, for more money, an ocean view.

Surrounded by water on three sides, the **Chetco River Inn** (21202 High Prairie Rd., Brookings 97415; tel. 800-327-2688; $75-85) is a more intimate alternative. Located just 16 miles from Brookings on the periphery of the Kalmiopsis, it's easy to feel as if you're in your own private forest. Its location near prime fishing river frontage makes this place especially popular during the steelhead season on the Chetco. In addition to an included gourmet breakfast, picnic lunches and dinners are available upon request. The welcome mat here is laid out in the form of thick oriental carpets partially covering floors of green and black marble. Tasteful antiques also decorate this reasonably priced first-class lodging.

Food

In addition to a profusion of down-home eateries, Brookings also has some intriguing ethnic dining alternatives. At the north end of town in a small building which gives the appearance of a drive-in is **Rubio's** (1136 Chetco; tel. 469-4919), one of the better Mexican places along U.S. 101. This will be apparent upon tasting the house salsa and the chiles rellenos. The house specialty, seafood à la Rubio, throws together prawns, ling cod, and scallops in a butter, garlic, wine, and jalapeño sauce.

If you're interested in stretching a dollar and don't mind stretching your stomach, try **Mama's** (703 Chetco; tel. 469-7611), located close to the Greyhound stop. This is the quintessential Italian bistro complete with a five-foot-tall Mama to heap your plate with copious quantities of northern and southern Italian cuisine. The fettuccine Alfredo is excellent, and the homemade ravioli with meatballs should sate even the hungriest hiker.

In contrast to the tight parking lot outside, the interior of **Pickle Barrel Sandwich and Seafood Company** gives the feeling of space in which to stretch your legs and relax. The early logging camp decor is supplemented by period photos. Interesting sandwich combinations for lunch and seafood specialties for dinner are reasonably priced and tasty. Try the Garbage Grinder.

Events

The **Beachcomber's Festival,** held every March, features exhibits, demonstrations, and slide shows as well as an art competition for the best works wrought from indigenous materials like driftwood, agates, and other beachcomber treasures.

The **Azalea Festival** is an unforgettable floral fantasia that takes place each Memorial Day weekend. Among the activities are a parade, flower display and crafts fair, a five-kilometer run, seafood luncheon, and beef barbecue. Much of the activity revolves around Azalea State Park. This WPA-built enclave features 20-foot-high azaleas (several hundred years old) and hand-hewn myrtlewood picnic tables. Wild cherry and crabapple blooms, wild strawberry blossoms, and purple and red violets round out the bouquet. Butterflies, bees, and birds all seem to concur with locals that this array smells sweetest around graduation time in mid-June.

Easter in July celebrates the blooming of the Easter lilies on July 1. Brookings holds this event in conjunction with nearby Smith River, California, where many of the festivities are conducted.

Shopping

Of the many stores on the Oregon coast purveying items made of myrtlewood, a local hardwood famed for its fine grain and durability, **Stateline Myrtlewood** (14377 U.S. 101 South, located 25 feet from the California border, open 8:30-5:30 every day except Thanksgiving, Christmas, and New Year's Day; tel. 469-2307) and its parent store, **The House Of Myrtlewood** (Box 457, Coos Bay 97420; tel. 267-7804), both deserve special mention. Factory tours and an array of quality items ranging from

Samuel Boardman State Park, the first leg of the "fabulous 50 miles"

cranberry candy to smoked salmon complement the myrtlewood clocks, bowls, and other handicrafts. Best of all, the friendly staff at both of these stores will gladly answer any questions as well as volunteer all manner of helpful information.

Information And Services

The **post office** (711 Spruce St., Brookings 97415; tel. 469-2318) is open Mon.-Fri. 9-5. **Greyhound** (tel. 469-3326) stops daily at the corner of Cottage and Pacific.

Wondering about offshore **weather** conditions? The Coast Guard hotline (tel. 469-2242) has the answers. For some fun in the sun, cruise down Easy Street to **Bud Cross City Park** for some **tennis** or a dip in the **outdoor pool.**

The **laundramat** [*sic*] is located within the Brookings Harbor Shopping Center and is open daily 7 a.m -11 p.m.

Before you embark on the country's longest (341 miles) designated scenic highway, U.S. 101, stop off at the **Oregon State Department of Economic Development** just north of town (1630 U.S. 101, Brookings 97415; tel. 469-4117). The facility is open May-Nov.; Mon., Wed., Fri 9-5; Tues.,Thurs. 8-6. For additional information pertinent to Brookings and environs, backtrack from the state facility to the south side of the bridge. Here you'll find the town's **chamber of commerce** (97949 Shopping Center Rd., Box 940, Brookings 97415; tel. 469-3181).\

Recreational information, including forest and trail maps, is available at the **Chetco Ranger Station** (555 Fifth St., Brookings 97415; tel. 469-2196). The station's advisories include info on the Siskiyou National Forest and the Kalmiopsis Wilderness. It's open Mon.-Fri. 7:30-4:30 but is closed on holidays.

Tours

Strahm's Lilies Farm (15723 Oceanview Dr., Brookings 97415; tel. 469-3885) offers self-guided tours free of charge 8:30 a.m.-6 p.m. from late June to Labor Day. To get there, turn off of U.S. 101 about a mile south of the Chetco Bridge onto Benham Lane, which curves south onto Ocean View Drive. Look for signs that lead to the greenhouses. The Strahms' friendly presence and their literature should pave the way for a memorable walk down the garden path.

Fishing

Fishing on the Chetco was once one of southern Oregon's best-kept secrets. The word has gotten out about the river's October run of huge chinook as well as a superlative influx of winter steelhead. And should river traffic ever become too heavy, the late-summer ocean salmon season out of Brookings may be the best in the Northwest.

Five-hour salmon and bottom-fishing trips may be arranged through **Leo's Sporthaven Marina** (Box 2215, Harbor 97415; tel. 469-3301).

NORTH TO GOLD BEACH

The stretch of highway from Brookings to Port Orford is known as the "fabulous fifty miles." Some consider the section of coastline between Brookings and Gold Beach to be the most scenic in Oregon—and one of the most dramatic meetings of rock and tide in the world. The offshore rock formations and winding roadbed hundreds of feet above the surf invite comparison to Europe's Amalfi Drive. This sobriquet is perhaps most apt in the first dozen miles north of Brookings, known as **Samuel H. Boardman State Park.** Of the 11 named viewpoints that have been cut into the highway's shoulder here, the following are especially recommended (all viewpoints are marked by signs on the west side of U.S. 101 and are listed in order of appearance).

House Rock

House Rock was the site of a WW II air-raid sentry tower that sits hundreds of feet above whitecaps pounding the rock-strewn beaches. To the north, you'll see one of the highest cliffs on the coast, Cape Sebastian. A steep, circuitous trail lined with salal (a tart blueberry) goes down to the water. The path begins behind the Samuel Boardman monument on the west end of the parking lot. The sign to the highest viewpoint in Boardman Park is easy to miss, but look for the turnout which precedes House Rock, called Cape Ferrelo (for Cabrilho's navigator, who sailed up much of the west coast in 1543).

Thomas Creek Bridge

The highest bridge in Oregon (345 feet above the water), as well as the highest north of San Francisco, Thomas Creek Bridge has been used for many TV commercials. A parking lot at the south end of the bridge marks a trailhead down. Do not take the path you see closest to the bridge because it's too steep. At the south end of the lot, the true trail eventually leads down to a view of the bridge on one side and miles of coast on the other. The offshore rock formations here are especially interesting.

A few miles down the highway, the **Natural Bridges Cove** sign seems to front just a forested parking lot. However, the paved walkway at the south end of the lot leads to a spectacular over-

look. Below, several rock archways frame an azure cove. This feature was created by the entrance and exit of a sea cave collapsing. A steep trail through giant ferns and towering Sitka spruce and Douglas fir winds down for a closer look. Thimbleberries (a sweet but seedy raspberry) are sometimes plentiful. Here as in similar forests on the south coast, it's important to stay on the trail. The rainforestlike biome is exceptionally fragile, and the soil erodes easily when the delicate vegetation is damaged.

Natural Bridge's counterpart is near the north end of Boardman Park. A short walk down the hillside trail leads you to the **Arch Rocks** viewpoint to see an immense boomerang-shaped basalt archway about a quarter mile offshore. This site has picnic tables within view of the monolith.

Cape Sebastian

Beyond Boardman Park and seven miles south of Gold Beach is Cape Sebastian. This spec-

Natural Bridges south of Gold Beach

tacular windswept headland was named by Sebastián Vizcaíno, who plied offshore waters here for Spain in 1602 along with Manuel de Alguilar. At least 700 feet above the sea, Cape Sebastian is possibly the highest south coast overlook reachable by paved public road. On a clear day, visibility extends nearly 50 miles in either direction. A trail zigzags through beautiful springtime wildflowers down the south side of the cape for about two miles until it reaches the sea. In April and May, Pacific paintbrush, Douglas iris, orchids, and snow queen usher you along. In addition, Cape Sebastian supports a population of large-headed goldfields, a summer-blooming, daisylike yellow flower found only in coastal Curry County.

GOLD BEACH/ ROGUE RIVER ESTUARY

Despite the name "Gold Beach," this town is one part of the coast where the action is definitely away from the ocean. To lure people from Oregon's superlative ocean shores, the nearby Rogue River estuary has been bestowed with many blessings. First, it was the gold-laden black sands which were mined in the 1850s and '60s. While this era gave Gold Beach its name, the arrival of Robert Hume, later known as the "Salmon King of the Rogue," had greater historical significance. By the turn of the century, Hume's canneries had established the river's image as a leading salmon and steelhead stream, a reputation which was later enhanced by the writings of Zane Grey (Rogue River Feud). Over the years, Herbert Hoover, Winston Churchill, Ginger Rogers (who has a home on the Rogue), Clark Gable, Jack London, and Jimmy Carter have come here to try their luck. During the last several decades, whitewater rafting and jetboat tours focusing on the abundant wildlife, scenic beauty, and fascinating lore of the region have hooked other sectors of the traveling public.

Today, Gold Beach is a town of 1,500 and the Curry County seat. Besides serving as the south coast tourism hub, a pulp mill and commercial fishing industry make up the local economy here. The seasonal nature of many local businesses creates serious wintertime unemployment. This fact, combined with torrential rains, drastically reduces the population of Gold Beach from Thanksgiving until spring. Thereafter, the wildflowers and warm weather transform this town into a vacation mecca.

SIGHTS

Driving through town on U.S. 101, just before the road gives way to the bridge, the harbor comes into view on the left. Salmon trawlers, jetboats, pelicans, and seals bobbing up and down will be there to greet you. Across the Oscar Patterson Bridge is **Wedderburn**, a baby sister to Gold Beach. Named for the Scottish birthplace of Robert Hume, its major claim to fame is that it's the home port of the Mailboat, which has been playing postman to upriver residents on the Rogue since 1895.

At the **Curry County Historical Museum** (920 S. Ellensburg, Gold Beach 97444; tel. 247-6113), the local historical society has assembled a small collection of exhibits on Indian and pioneer life, mining in the region's golden age, logging, fishing, and agriculture. It's located at the county fairgrounds at the south edge of town. Particularly interesting are a realistic reconstruction of a miner's cabin, vintage photos, and Indian petroglyphs. Open May 15-Sept. 30, Mon.-Sun. 1-5 p.m.; Oct. 11-May 15, Fri.-Sat. noon-4 p.m. Admission is free.

Jetboat Trips

The best way to take in the mighty Rogue is on a jetboat ride from Gold Beach harbor. Several different companies run this trip, but they all provide comparable service and prices. It's a relaxing and interesting look at the varied flora and fauna along the estuary as well as the changing moods of the river. Most of the estimated 50,000 people per year who "do" the

Rogue in this way take the 64-mile roundtrip cruise. This and the more adventurous 104-mile cruise offer a sumptuous lunch at a secluded fishing lodge for an additional charge. The pilots/commentators usually have grown up on the river, and their evocations of the diverse ecosystems and Indian and gold-mining history adds greatly to your enjoyment. Bears, otters, and beavers may be sighted en route, and fishermen will generally hold up "a big one" to show off. Ospreys, snowy egrets, eagles, mergansers, and kingfishers are also seen with regularity in this stopover for migratory waterfowl.

In the first part of the journey, idyllic riverside retreats dot the hillsides, breaking up stands of fir and hemlock. Myrtle, madrone, and impressive springtime wildflower groupings also vary the landscape. Both the 32- and 52-mile trips focus on the section of the Rogue protected by the government as a Wild and Scenic River. Only the longer trips take you into the pristine Rogue Wilderness, an area that motor launches from Grants Pass also do not reach. The 13 miles of this wilderness you see from the boat has canyon walls rising 1,500 feet above you. Geologists say that this part of the Klamaths is composed of ancient islands and sea floor that collided with North America. To deal with the rapids upstream, smaller, faster boats are used that are able to skim over the boulders with just six inches of water between hull and rock surface.

Remember that chill and fog near the mouth of the estuary are replaced by much warmer conditions upstream. These tour outfits have wool blankets available on cold days as well as complimentary hot beverages. Also keep in mind that the upriver lodges can be booked for overnight stays and your trip may be resumed the following day.

Located just south of the bridge over the Rogue, west of U.S. 101, is **Jerry's Rogue River Jetboats** (Box 1011, Gold Beach 97444; tel. 247-4571 or 800-451-3645). This heavily patronized company runs trips from May through October. They offer a 64-mile roundtrip and a 104-mile roundtrip, both stopping at Paradise Bar Lodge near Blossom Bar rapids, the turnaround point for the shorter trip. The shorter trip (adults pay $25, children 4-11 pay $10) takes six hours and departs daily at 8:30 a.m. and 2:30 p.m., July 1 through Labor Day. The 104-mile whitewater trip (adults $50, ages 4-11 $20) leaves daily at 8 a.m. and noon, May to Oct. Inquire about other itineraries that may be available. An 80-mile whitewater tour, a one-hour lower Rogue cruise, and an hour-long bay cruise are among those offered on a "sometimes" basis. Jerry's is noted for personable, well-informed guides.

Rogue River Mailboats (Box 1165, Gold Beach 97444; tel. 247-7033, 247-6225, or 800-458-3511) is located a quarter mile upstream from the north end of the Rogue River bridge. The rates, trips, and times parallel Jerry's offerings with a couple exceptions: only one 104-mile trip is scheduled daily (8 a.m.), and an 80-

cruising the Rogue River, jetboat style

mile ride is offered (adults $32, ages 4-11 $12), leaving daily at 8 a.m. and 2:30 p.m., July 1 through Labor Day. Besides human cargo, this boat also carries mail sacks, ensuring a warm welcome in upriver locations.

Court's Whitewater Jetboat Trips (Box 1045, Gold Beach 97444; tel. 247-4571, 247-6504, or 800-367-5787), which leaves from Jot's Resort at the north end of the Rogue River bridge, west of U.S. 101, has packages similar to the others but gives more of a discount to kids. On the 64-mile trips, ages 5-12 go for $10, and kids under five go for free. On the 104-mile trip, ages 6-12 go for $20, and those under five go for free. Court's pioneered the first whitewater trips here almost 30 years ago.

Beach Access/Auto Tour

Two miles south of Gold Beach there's easy access to a nice beach at **Hunter Creek.** The creek is just off the highway and marked by a sign. From Hunter's Creek you can pick up Hunter's Creek Rd., which loops north through the forest, finally following the course of the Rogue back into town. The three-hour drive goes past interpretive markers explaining "our national forest, land of many uses," and is mapped out in a free pamphlet available at the Gold Beach Ranger Station. This map shows locations of several picnic areas and campgrounds.

Other roads less traveled include the old coast highway, which you can pick up across from Cape Sebastian State Park; the Shasta Costa Rd. paralleling the Rogue from Gold Beach to Galice; and an unpaved road into the Rogue Wilderness from Agness (a town upriver on the Rogue) to Powers. Despite most of these routes being paved (except the last one), they are all narrow, winding, and not suitable for trailers or motor homes. Maps and directions to these back roads can be obtained from the Gold Beach Ranger Station.

RECREATION

Local Activities

The **Curry County Fair** (920 S. Ellensburg, Gold Beach 97444) usually takes place the second week of August. Highlights include Ore-

gon's largest flower show and a lamb barbecue. Contact the chamber of commerce for more information. The chamber can also fill you in on the exact times for the **jetboat races** that take place July Fourth weekend. People line the river for the event.

To get to **Indian Creek Trail Rides** (Box 194 Wedderburn, 97491; tel. 247-7704), follow Jerry's Flat Rd. one-half mile. Ride along the Rogue on well-trained mounts (one hour $12, two hours $20, family and groups $10 per person). **Gold Beach Summer Theater** (Box 1324, Gold Beach 97444, or contact the chamber of commerce for the season schedule) is a June-to-late-August tradition that used to attract young thespians from all over the state due to its connection with Willamette University. While this is no longer the case, there is no shortage of local talent who plan to continue the modern eclectic repertoire of light comedy and serious drama.

Tours

The Rogue-Pacific Interpretive Center (510 Colvin St., Gold Beach 97444; tel. 247-2732) is a block off U.S. 101 behind the courthouse. This environmental education center offers guided trips which include tidepools, Indian and pioneer sites, coastal forests, and boat charters. They also have free demonstrations on fishing and Indian life and slide shows on natural history. There are special kids' programs on whales, seals, and seashore and forest life. Call them for course descriptions and times.

Outdoor Pursuits

Curry County's only golf course, **Cedar Bend** (Box 1234, Gold Beach 97444) is located in nearby **Ophir.** Eleven miles north of Gold Beach, pick up Ophir Rd. off U.S. 101. Follow it to Squaw Valley Rd., turn right at the Old Ophir Store and continue until you see the links. It costs $9 for nine holes, $12 for 18 holes.

Well-known **fishing guides** Bill McNair and Denny Hughson can be contacted through Jerry's Jetboats (see above). Most lodgings can also set you up with a guide. For fishing and camping advice and equipment, try the **Rogue Outdoor Store** (560 N. Ellensburg, Gold Beach 97444; tel. 247-7142).

The 40-mile **Rogue River Trail** offers lodge-to-lodge hiking, which means you need little

the Schrader Old Growth
Trail near Gold Beach

more in your pack than the essentials. The lodges here are comfortably rustic, serve home-style food in copious portions, and run between $40 and $75. They are also comfortably spaced, so extended hiking is seldom a necessity.

Before you go, please check with the Gold Beach Ranger Station on trail conditions and specific directions to the trailhead. Pick up the western end of the trail 35 miles east of Gold Beach, about one-half mile from Foster Bar, a popular boat landing (see "Rogue River Camp-sites" below). Park there and walk east and north on the paved road until you see signs on the left marking the Rogue River Trail. Go in spring before the hot weather and enjoy yellow Siskiyou iris and fragrant wild azaleas. The trail ends at Graves Creek, 27 miles northwest of Grants Pass. Be careful of rattlesnakes on the trail. Contact the chamber of commerce for more information on the upriver lodges.

In the spring, wildflower enthusiasts should ask at the ranger station (see "Information and Services" following) for directions to the **Buzzard's Roost Trail.** The mile-long path to the top of this 1,000-foot bluff overlooking the Illinois River lets the hiker enjoy calypso orchids, shooting stars, trillium, and a reddish purple iris unique to this area.

Odds And Ends

The more sedentary nature lover can enjoy watching a sunset over cocktails at the **Beach House Lounge** (1432 S. Ellensburg, Gold Beach 97444; tel. 247-6626). The huge wall-length window looks out on a wild meadow, beyond which the surf breaks on a dark-sand beach. This is also the place to come and rock out later in the evening.

Prehistoric Gardens (tel. 332-4463) unfortunately stands out like a sore thumb on the otherwise unspoiled stretch of U.S. 101, 15 miles north of Gold Beach. Imagine a group of dinosaurs built to exact scale amid giant ferns and towering evergreens. While the setting may be appropriate to the display, the reverse is not true unless you're a kid. Still, the explanatory signs and obvious hard work and care of the concessioner are easy for anyone to appreciate. Open daily 8 a.m. to dusk, admission $3.50 for adults, students 12-18 $3, children 5-11 $2.

PRACTICALITIES

Accommodations

As with most coastal cities, there is no shortage of places to stay along the main drag, Ellensburg Street (a.k.a. U.S. 101). In fact, Gold Beach offers the largest number and widest range of accommodations on the south coast, with intimate lodges overlooking the Rogue as popular as the oceanfront motels. A discount of 20% or more on rooms is usually available during the winter here when 80 to 90 inches of rain can fall.

The cheapest place in town is probably the **Oregon Trail Lodge** (550 N. Ellensburg, Box 721, Gold Beach 97444; tel. 242-6030). For about 35 bucks you get sanitized Motel 6-type accommodations with room to spare. The **River Bridge Inn** (1010 Jerry's Flat Rd., Gold Beach 97444; tel. 247-4533 or 800-759-4533) has modern, comfy river view rooms for $55-80. Kitchenettes are available, as are spa suites.

Ireland's Rustic Lodge (1120 S. Ellensburg, Gold Beach 97444; tel. 247-7718) was started by two women who used to bring meals to the rooms. While this is no longer the case here, the touch of home has not been lost. Many of the rooms have fireplaces, knotty-pine interiors, and distinctive decor. Best of all, the grounds are lovingly landscaped with pine trees, flowers, and ocean views. A sandy beach is a short stroll to the west. There are 27 motel units, nine old but well-kept cabins, and cottages which sleep eight each. The rates are $40-61.

Located on the Rogue River's north bank, **Jot's Resort** (94360 Wedderburn Loop, Box J, Wedderburn 97491; tel. 247-6676 or 800-FOR-JOTS) can host a full vacation in one compound featuring pool and spa, sports shop, private dock, rental boats, and an excellent restaurant across the street. The rooms here are at a premium in summer when the motorcoach tours come through. The rates are as follows: $65 for standard view rooms, riverfront condos big enough for six people at $145 and $165. The Rod 'n' Reel across the street features evening entertainment with low-stakes blackjack, a country music duo, and a Big Band dance on weekends.

Tu Tu Tun (96530 N. Bank; tel. 247-6664) resort (open May 1-Nov. 1) emphasizes the tranquility of an evergreen coastal forest on prime river frontage. The latter actually makes you forget that Gold Beach and U.S. 101 are only seven miles away. This feeling of blissful remoteness is reinforced by the absence of phones and TV. As you sit on your patio overlooking the water, only the sounds of an occasional passing boat may intrude upon your Rogue River reverie. A heated pool and other recreational facilities, the lodge's beautifully appointed interiors, and gourmet meals served family style are other appeals of this acclaimed retreat. Tu Tu Tun has earned four-star and four-diamond awards for excellence.

Spring is the best time to be here, because much of the traveling public is still at home and the wildflowers are in their glory. Pink rhododendrons, native to Oregon, blossom at the edge of the forest in May. While autumn is also beautiful, business meetings in September and October necessitate that bookings be made well in advance for stays after Labor Day. The rates range from $108 to $189.

Rogue River Campsites

Campsites east of town along the Rogue and off U.S. 101 en route to Port Orford provide wonderful spots to bed down for the night. Those taking the road along the Rogue should be alert for oncoming log trucks, raft transport vehicles, and other wide-body vehicles

Foster Bar (Siskiyou National Forest, Gold Beach Ranger Station, Box 548, 1225 S. Ellensburg, Gold Beach 97444; tel. 247-6651) campground is located 30 miles east of Gold Beach on the south bank of the Rogue. Take Jerry's Flat Rd. east for 30 miles to the turnoff for Agness. Turn right on Illahe Agness Rd. and drive three miles to camp. There are 10 sites for tents and RVs. Picnic tables and fire rings are provided. Pit toilets and firewood are also available, but there is no drinking water. No reservations are necessary and the fee is $2 per night. The site is open March to late September. This is a popular spot from which to embark on an eight-mile inner tube ride to Agness. The rapids are dangerous, so wear a life jacket. You are also within walking distance of the trailhead of the Rogue River Trail (see "Recreation" above).

Lobster Creek Campground (contact the Forest Service at address above; tel. 247-7922) is nine miles up Jerry's Flat Rd., along the Rogue's south bank. This free campground is open year-round and has five camping sites, picnic tables, fishing, and flush toilets, but there is no drinking water. Ask the Forest Service for directions to the recently established old-growth trail nearby. It is a gentle one-mile walk through a rare and majestic ecosystem which is under siege in other forests throughout the state.

Oceanside Campgrounds

Honeybear Campground (Box 97, 134161 Ophir Rd., Ophir 97464; tel. 247-2765 or 800-

822-4444, ext. 00) is nine miles north of Gold Beach on U.S. 101 (then two miles north on Ophir Rd.), but could just as well be in the Black Forest. The owners have built a large rathskeller with a dance floor. Six nights a week during the summer, there are dances here with traditional German music. Locals praise the Honeybear's on-site delicatessen for its homemade German sausage. There are 20 tent and RV sites, picnic tables, flush toilets, hot showers, firewood, a laundromat, and ocean views for $10-15. It's open May to October.

Arizona Beach Campground (Box 621, Gold Beach 97444; tel. 332-6491) is a combination motel and campground close by a beach with lots of driftwood. It has 31 tent sites, motel rooms, and almost a hundred RV spaces. You can camp on the beach, in an adjoining meadow, or back in the woods by a tiny stream for $10-15. All the amenities are here, 15 miles north of Gold Beach on U.S. 101, but the closely spaced sites lack privacy. Nonetheless, there are few better places for kids, due to the creek running though the site and the proximity of the Prehistoric Gardens (see "Recreation," above). It's open all year.

Food

You can't eat scenery, but Gold Beach restaurants charge you for it anyway. Still, this is one place where the oceanfront and riverside views are often worth it. Then, too, there's always the option of cheaper restaurants away from port. Spring chinook salmon, blackberry pie, and other indigenous specialties taste good anywhere.

The Golden Egg (710 S. Ellensburg, Gold Beach; tel. 247-7528) at last count offered 27 omelette combinations. Try their Western omelette (bacon, onion, green pepper, and cheese) for $4.75. In addition, pancakes and waffles round out the breakfast menu. Sandwiches and burgers are featured at lunch, with moderately priced steak and seafood the bill of fare at night.

As you enter the **Rod 'n' Reel** (on the north end of the Rogue River bridge across from Jot's

Resort, Wedderburn; tel. 247-6823), you'll read a sign that says, "You're a stranger here but once." The food and attractiveness of the restaurant as well as the congeniality of the Powers family and their staff make it so. Breakfast, lunch, and dinner are served here. Lunch is an especially popular meal, due in part to the restaurant's proximity to the jetboat docks. The more important reasons include the grilled crab or shrimp sandwiches with melted cheese ($5.95, real yummy), some of the best salmon (baked, broiled, or poached for $8.50) you've ever tasted, an ample salad bar, and excellent pies, notably the blackberry and strawberry rhubarb. Dinner features fresh seafood and many Italian-accented dishes.

Information And Services

The **Gold Beach Chamber of Commerce** (510 Ellensburg, Gold Beach 97444; tel. 247-7526 or 800-452-2334 in Oregon, 800-542-2334 outside) is open Mon.-Fri. 9-5 and Sat.-Sun. 10-4. They'll send you a good, comprehensive information folder upon request. The Gold Beach **Ranger District office** (1225 S. Ellensburg, Gold Beach 97444; tel. 247-6651) offers a free packet on camping and recreation in the district. It's open Mon.-Fri. 7:30-5. The **post office** (Moore St., Gold Beach 97444; tel. 247-7610) is open Mon.-Fri 8:30-5:30.

The **Greyhound** station (310 Colvin St., Gold Beach 97444; tel. 247-7246) is a terminal case as far as the health hazards of nicotine are concerned. Across the street is a modern building housing the public library. Comfy armchairs here would make this a perfect alternative waiting room to Greyhound, except for the lack of restrooms. Open Mon.-Thurs. 10-8, Fri.-Sat. 10-6. **Stonsell's Coin-Op Laundry** is located on U.S. 101 near Eighth Street.

Curry General Hospital (220 E. Fourth, Gold Beach 97444; tel. 247-6621) is the only hospital in the county. It coordinates the "Mercy Flight," an air taxi service to Medford, should there be any cases it can't handle.

PORT ORFORD AND VICINITY

As you come up U.S. 101 into Port Orford, it's hard to ignore an immense rock promontory fronting the shoreline. Battle Rock was the focus of a conflict between the local Indians and the first landing party of white settlers in 1851. When Captain William Tichenor observed the hostility of the natives onshore, he put nine men ashore on the rock due to its suitability as a battle position. These men defended this outpost long enough for Tichenor to return with reinforcements to carry the day. From such inauspicious beginnings, "Port Awferd," as the locals call it, established itself as the first townsite on the south coast. Shortly thereafter, the town became the site of the first fort established on the coast during the Rogue Indian Wars. This conflict started when gold miners and settlers came into Indian lands. As a result of the clashes, hundreds of local natives were sent to the Siletz Reservation near Lincoln City in 1856.

Besides Indian conflicts, Port Orford has other claims to fame. By a quirk of geography, it is both the most westerly incorporated city in the contiguous U.S. and the center of the country, if you include Hawaii. What's more, *Forbes* magazine dubbed Port Orford the "sleeper" of the Oregon coast, ready to be awakened due to its "knockout" view, despite the fact that it's the rainiest burg on the coast—108 inches annually.

Impressive as some of these geographical calling cards may sound, they have not conferred any great prosperity on the region. Commercial fishing and cedar logging join tourism as the leading revenue producers. Lately, many other eclectic cottage industries have sprung up to supplement the boom/bust, resource-based economy. The outskirts of Port Orford host such diverse undertakings as an escargot-breeding farm, llama and sheep ranches, a goat-milk dairy, and commercial berry growers, as well as plots of land devoted to Christmas trees and exotic herbs. In addition, divers harvest sea urchins to supply the Japanese with a popular aphrodisiac and seafood delicacy.

SIGHTS

Humbug Mountain

Some people will tell you that Humbug Mountain (six miles south of Port Orford on U.S. 101) is the highest mountain rising directly off the Oregon shoreline. Since the criteria for such a distinction varies as much as the tides, let's just say it's a special place. Once the site of native vision quests, today Humbug Mountain's shadow falls upon an Eden-like campground surrounded by myrtles, alders, and maples. Just north is a breezy black-sand beach. A three-mile trail to the top of Humbug will reward the hardy hiker with impressive vistas to the south of Nesika Beach and a chance to see rhododendrons 15 to 20 feet high. The name Humbug derives from the gold miners who were drawn here in the 1850s by tales of gold in the black sands. These stories, of course, proved to be just "humbug." Perhaps more reliable is the Indian legend which says that if the top of the mountain can be seen, the weather will be good.

Battle Rock State Park

Port Orford has an ocean view from downtown that is arguably the most scenic of any city on the coast. A waterfront stroll lets you appreciate the cliffs and offshore seastacks as well as the unique sight of commercial fishing boats being lowered by crane into the harbor. (The harbor is unprotected from southerly winds so boats can't be safely moored on the water.) Here too is the previously mentioned Battle Rock in its own state park. If you can make your way through driftwood and blackberry bushes surrounding its base, you can take the short trail to the top for a heightened perspective on the rockbound coast which parallels the town. You'll also notice the east-west orientation of the harbor. Once you get to the top of the rock, don't think that the battle is necessarily over. Bracing winds will often chill you, and high tides can sometimes render this huge coastal extension an island. The rock is also the focus of a **Fourth of July Jubilee Celebration** which reenacts the historic battle described above.

Downtown Walking Tour

A brochure from the information kiosk in the parking lot opposite Battle Rock details *Port Orford's History in Its Architecture* and introduces you to homes from the last century in a nice 15-minute walk. Also at the kiosk you can find out about the famed fishing in the Elk and Sixes rivers north of town. Scuba divers can make inquiries at the info desk about the many protected coves with water temperatures as high as 50°—which is warm for Oregon's Pacific—and underwater visibility ranging from 10-50 feet in summer.

The Heads

Another shoreline scene worth taking in is located up W. Ninth St. at what the locals call "The Heads," featuring a striking panorama from north to south at Port Orford Head State Park, just a short hike away from the parking lot. If you go down the cement trail to the tip of a blustery headland, you look south to the mouth of Port Orford's harbor. To the north, many small rocks fill the water, along with boats trolling for salmon or checking crab pots. On clear days it's said that visibility extends from Cape Blanco to Humbug Mountain.

Cape Blanco State Park, Hughes House

Eleven miles north of Port Orford on U.S. 101 is Cape Blanco, perhaps the westernmost point of land in the contiguous U.S. (although Californians and Washingtonians beg to differ). Whether or not it rates the nod, the remote appendages of this place will give you the feeling of being at the edge of the continent. From the vantage of Cape Blanco, dark mountains sit behind you and forest almost abuts tidewater. Driftwood and 100-foot-long bull kelp on slivers of black-sand beach fan out from both sides of this earthy red bluff 245 feet above the ocean. Somehow, the Spaniards who sailed past it in 1603 viewed the cape as having a "blanco," white, color. It's been theorized that perhaps they were referring to the fossilized shells on the front of the cliff.

Atop the headland is the oldest and highest lighthouse in continuous use in Oregon. This beacon still uses the same French-made lens that was originally installed in 1870, blinking out a signal every 30 seconds to points 20 miles out at sea. Over the years a number of shipwrecks have occurred on the reefs near Cape Blanco. During WW II, Japanese submarines used the beacon as an orientation mark to aim planes loaded with incendiary bombs at the Coast Range. This effort to start forest fires was motivated by the existence of Port Orford cedar trees here, which were used to construct planes. Due to the perennial dampness, the results were negligible.

The vegetation on the state park road down to the beach will attest to the severity of winter storms in the area. One-hundred-mile-per-hour gales (the record winds were clocked at 184 mph) and horizontal sheets of rain have given some of the usually massive Sitka spruces the appearance of bonsai trees. An understory of salmonberry and bracken fern help evoke the look of a southeast Alaska forest.

PORT ORFORD TO COOS BAY / NORTH BEND

TO REEDSPORT

GOLDEN & SILVER FALLS S.P.

MILLICOMA MYRTLE GROVE S.P.

OREGON DUNES NAT'L REC. AREA

NORTH BEND

ALLEGANY

COOS RIVER

SUNSET BAY S.P.
SHORE ACRES S.P.
COOS BAY
CHARLESTON

CAPE ARAGO S.P.
SOUTH SLOUGH ESTUARINE SANCTUARY

COQUILLE

BULLARDS BEACH S.P.
BANDON

EAST FORK COQUILLE R.

COQUILLE R.

TO ROSEBURG

101

COQUILLE MYRTLE GROVE S.P.

42

SOUTH FORK

POWERS

CAPE BLANCO S.P.

TO GOLD BEACH

POWERS

TO AGNES

PORT ORFORD

PACIFIC OCEAN

0   10mi
0   10km

© MOON PUBLICATIONS, INC.

*the coast south
of Port Orford*

Near Cape Blanco on a side road along the Sixes River is the **Hughes House,** a restored Victorian home built in 1898 for rancher and county commissioner Patrick Hughes. Owned and operated by the state of Oregon, the house serves as a museum and repository of antique furnishings. The Hughes House is open May 1- Sept. 30, Thurs.-Sat and Mon. 10-5, Sun. noon-5.

Activities

Beachcombing for agates and fishing floats on nearby south coast beaches and searching for the lost Port Orford meteorite in the surrounding foothills typify the adventures available in the area. The meteorite was found in the 1860s by a government geologist, who estimated its weight at 22,000 tons. Unfortunately, he was unable to relocate the meteorite when he returned for another look.

Those in search of more conventional pursuits are advised to drive out 14th or 18th streets to **Garrison Lake.** Boating, waterskiing, and trout fishing are available here. Nearby **Buffington Memorial City Park,** west of U.S. 101, has a dock for fishing or swimming on the lake, plus playing fields, tennis courts, picnic areas, hiking trails, and a horse arena. North of the lake, look for agates on **Paradise Point Beach.** Garrison Lake State Wayside offers access to coastal dunes.

Stone Butte Stables (46509 U.S. 101 South, Langlois 97450; tel. 348-2525) lets you ride into

the sunset over Coast Range foothills ushered along by views of the Pacific and abundant wildlife. During early summer, the fields on Stone Butte are covered with wild irises and daisies. Later, purple foxglove and huckleberries proliferate. The rates are $12 for one hour, $15 for 1 1/2 hours, and $20 for the two-hour ride. It's open May to Sept., 10 a.m.-6 p.m. Look for the stables on the hillside eight miles north of Port Orford.

Between Port Orford and Bandon (just south of Langlois) is Floras Lake, which is becoming a mecca for coastal sailboarding. For more info, contact **Floras Lake Windsurfing School** (Box 1591, Bandon 97411; tel. 347-9205).

PRACTICALITIES

Accommodations

Port Orford is the kind of place where a room with a view will not break your budget. The **Shoreline Motel** (Box 426, Port Orford 97465; tel. 332-2903) is across the highway from Battle Rock, has an outstanding view, and offers clean rooms for not much more than $35. **Gwendolyn's Bed and Breakfast** (735 U.S. 101, Port Orford 97465; tel. 332-4373) is a purple gingerbread house out of the 1920s replete with period furniture and three bedrooms with brass beds. At $45-65 for a room with a shared bath, the rates are little more than you'd pay for a cut-rate motel. The owner makes a famous salmon-and-crab pie. Close by are the Golden Owl Deli and the Greyhound stop.

The **Seacrest Motel** (Box C; tel. 332-3040) features views of coastal cliffs and a garden from a quiet hillside on the east side of the highway. The rates are $30-40 for a single and $40-55 for a double. **Home-by-the-Sea** (Box 606, Port Orford 97465; tel. 332-2855) includes a full breakfast in a rate of $75. The dramatic hillside view of Battle Rock seascape makes for excellent stormwatching here.

Campgrounds

Humbug Mountain State Park (six miles south of Port Orford; tel. 332-6774) features 80 tent sites and 30 sites for trailers and motor homes, and wind-protected sites reserved for hikers and bikers at a buck a night. Flush toilets, showers, picnic tables, water, firewood, and a laundromat are available. The park is open April to October; $15-17. **Cape Blanco State Park** (Box 299, Sixes 97476; tel. 332-2971) can be reached by driving four miles north of Port Orford on U.S. 101, then heading northwest on the park road which continues five miles beyond to the campground. It features 58 sites for tents, trailers, and motor homes, as well as hiker/biker sites for $2 a night; picnic tables, water, showers,

and a laundromat are available. No reservations are necessary, and a $15-17 fee is charged mid-April to late September.

Food

While an inexpensive burger or BLT is easy to come by in Port Orford, you'll have to pay for fine dining. Fortunately, "view" restaurants come in all price ranges. The **Wheelhouse Restaurant** (521 Jefferson St., Port Orford; tel. 332-4605) enjoys a location in Battle Rock Park and has low prices. Before 8 a.m., eggs, hash browns, toast, and bacon or ham go for $3.95. Later, such dishes as burgers, clam fritters, homemade soups, and pies are also available. The **Golden Owl Deli** (755 U.S. 101, Port Orford; tel. 332-6592) works well for lunch, featuring diverse sandwiches, or for a late breakfast if you like lox and bagels. It is known for its large sandwiches, smoked salmon, excellent coffee, and fine collection of Oregon wines. Try their submarine of turkey, ham, two cheeses, lettuce, and tomato for $4.95 (whole) or $2.99 (half). This restaurant adjoins a deli counter where you can provision a hike or a picnic.

The **Truculent Oyster** (236 Sixth St., Port Orford; tel. 332-4461) at the south end of town has the nautical atmosphere and fresh fish that one would expect in an Oregon coast seafood

THE SEA OTTERS OF CAPE BLANCO

Down on the beach below Cape Blanco, you might see the furry heads of sea otters peering out from above the whitecaps about 200 yards offshore. The progenitors of this colony were transported here courtesy of the Atomic Energy Commission in 1970. At that time, a planned bomb test in the Aleutians compelled the AEC to move 95 of these animals to this area. In addition to Cape Blanco, they've been sighted south of Port Orford.

Between 1775 and 1823, over 100,000 sea otters were killed for their pelts, many along the Oregon coast. They became the trappings of royalty, selling in Paris for as much as $1,000 apiece. After sea otters were declared extinct south of the Aleutians in 1911, they became a protected species.

Early accounts of the plunder of the sea otter should have brought about their protection long be-

fore the 20th century. An early 19th-century Spanish journal described the colony off of Monterey, California as playful and intelligent. It detailed how a typical otter would dive hundreds of feet down to pull an abalone off a rock; would reemerge on the surface on its back, shell in paw; and then, using its stomach for a table, would crack the shell open with a rock.

In addition to the Spanish chronicler's fascination with otter dining behavior, he noted another similarity to *Homo sapiens* when mama sea otter was observed putting baby in a cradle of kelp. The account went on to describe the mother's reaction upon returning with breakfast and finding her baby missing: she emitted humanlike cries for days on end, eventually starving herself to death.

restaurant, but also features mild Mexican entrees like El Camerone—shrimp, chili, and cheese in a tortilla. Such specialties as oysters sautéed with vegetables and steamer clams run around $8. The house-cut steaks are also very good. The **Peg Leg Saloon** in the same building draws locals here en masse on weekends.

Across the street, **Whale Cove** (U.S. 101 at Battle Rock Beach, Port Orford; tel. 325-7575) has a fantastic ocean view and, it says, "the only master chef on the Oregon coast south of Salishan." The food lives up to the hype. With such local ingredients as mushrooms, berries, game meats, and seafood, the chef fashions entrees that are light and flavorful. The soufflés and too-rich desserts might add a few notches to your belt and some extra bucks to the bill, but

they're worth it. The champagne Sunday brunch (10:30-2:30) is highly recommended. The restaurant closes Tuesday in summer and Tuesday and Wednesday during the winter. After your meal, stop by the **Roaring Sea Gallery** adjacent to the restaurant.

Information And Services

Begin your travels here at **Battle Rock Information Center** on the west side of U.S. 101 (tel. 332-8055). The people here are especially friendly and helpful. The **post office** (Jackson and Seventh, Port Orford 97465; tel. 332-4251) is open 8:30-5:30. The fact that **Greyhound** (1034 Oregon St., Port Orford 97465; tel. 332-1885) is located at the Port Orford Motel means you needn't worry about hours since there's always a clerk on duty.

BANDON AND VICINITY

In contrast to the glitzy tourist trappings of some of the larger coastal towns, Bandon-by-the-Sea is characterized by the style and grace of an earlier era. The glory that was Bandon is alive and well in Old Town, a picturesque collection of shops, galleries, restaurants, and historical memorabilia. A converted Coast Guard station houses the Coquille River Museum, whose placards tell the stories behind the scenes in this restored neighborhood.

The museum's exhibits also detail other aspects of the heritage of this quiet port city near the Coquille River. While logging, fishing, dairy products, and the harvest of cranberries have been the traditional mainstays of the local economy, in the early part of the century Bandon also enjoyed a brief tourism boom. In addition to being a summer retreat from the heat of the Willamette Valley, it was a port of call for thousands of San Francisco-to-Seattle steamship passengers. This era inspired such touristic venues as the Silver Spray dance hall and a natatorium housing a saltwater swimming pool.

The golden age which began with the advent of large-scale steamship traffic in 1900 came to an abrupt end following a devastating fire in 1936. The blaze was started by the easily ignitable gorse weed, imported from Ireland (as was the town's name) in the mid-1800s.

Dramatic descriptions of the townspeople fighting the flames with their backs to the sea earned the incident a citation as one of the top ten news stories of the year.

The facelift given Old Town decades later and the subsequent tourist influx conjured for many the image of the mythical phoenix rising from its ashes to fly again. On the wings of the recovery, Bandon has established itself as a town rooted in the past with its eyes on the future.

Today Bandon is a curious mixture of provincial backwater, destination resort, and new-age artist colony. Backpack-toting travelers from all over the world have been flocking to this town of 3,000 in recent years because of its beaches, its cultural and recreational pursuits, and its European-style hostelry. They coexist happily with the large population of retirees, award-winning artisans, and locals who seem to have cornered the market on late-model pickups with gun racks.

SIGHTS

One of the most appealing things about Bandon is that most of its attractions are within walking distance of each other. In addition, on the periphery of town are a varied array of things to see and do.

West Coast Game Park

Six miles south of Bandon is the West Coast Game Park (Box 1330, Bandon 97411; tel. 347-3106), the self-proclaimed largest wild-animal petting park in America. There are 450 animals, including tiger cubs, chimps, camels, zebras, bison, and two snow leopards. Along with these exotics you'll also encounter such indigenous species as elk, bears, raccoons, and cougars. Even if you're not with a child, the opportunity to pet a pup, a cub, or a kit can bring out the kid in you. The park is open year-round but call during winter because of restricted hours of operation. Regular hours are 9:30 a.m.-dusk in summer, and 9:30-4:30 in other seasons. Adult tickets cost $5, and children get in for $2.75.

Coquille River Museum

Also known as the Bandon Historical Society Museum (south end of West First St. in the old Coast Guard building; tel. 347-2164), this museum first traces the history of the Coquille Indian tribe and its forebears. The chronology continues with the steamers and the railroads that brought in white settlers. One room is devoted to Bandon's unofficial standing as the "Cranberry Capital of Oregon." Black-and-white blowups showing women stooping over in the bogs to harvest the ripe berries are captioned with such *bon mots* as this one from an overseer: "I had 25 women picking for me, and I knew every one by her fanny." Color photos spanning five decades of cranberry festival princesses also adorn the walls.

Another room traces "Bandon's Resort Years, 1900-1931," when the town was called the "Playground of the Pacific." The most compelling exhibits in the museum deal with the fires of 1914 and 1936. Open Tues.-Sun., the museum is often closed January and February. If the museum is closed, call 347-9525 and a tour can usually be arranged. Admission is $1 for adults; children are admitted free.

Bandon Driftwood Museum, Old Town

Old town is four blocks of shops and cafes squeezed in between the boat basin and the highway. Another exposition is Bandon Driftwood Museum, a collection of natural sculptures from gnarly root balls to whole tree trunks.

It is housed at Big Wheel Farm Supply store on First St. in Old Town, across from the boat basin. The hours are Mon.-Fri. 9-5:30; Sat. 9-5; Sun. 11-5.

Preservation buffs should check out Masonic Hall (Second and Alabama), one of the few buildings to have survived both Bandon blazes. A photo in the museum shows the same building and surrounding structures on Alabama St. (then called Atwater) circa 1914. The photo depicts boardwalks leading to a woolen mill, old storefronts, a theater, and the Bandon Popular Hotel and Restaurant, outside which a horse and buggy await. This contrasts greatly with the contemporary scene. Today the Minute Cafe and a parking lot sit on the same spot as some of the structures in the photo. Nonetheless, a turn-of-the-century charm still pervades the architecture and ambience of the neighborhood. Housed within many of the Old Town shops and galleries are artisans pursuing such time-honored professions as glassblowing, leathercraft, and pottery.

Say "Cheese!"

The **Bandon Cheddar Cheese Plant** (on U.S. 101 just north of Old Town, Bandon 97411; tel. 800-548-8961) is the second-largest cheese factory in Oregon. The famous taste and texture of the Bandon Bar (an eight-ounce hunk) are the results of hand-cheddaring by a master cheesemaker. You can watch the process through a window in the gift store and sample the results, including fresh, squeaky cheese curds, every day of the week except Sunday, 8-5. Their jalapeño cheese is a pepper lover's delight.

Old Town Boat Basin

Walk off your cheese samples at the newly refurbished boat basin just north of Old Town. While strolling the docks here, you can watch locals land salmon, steelhead, and Dungeness crab. The commercial fleet steams into the Coquille River's estuary with holds full of salmon, tuna, or whitefish.

The Beach Loop

Seeing as how U.S. 101 follows an inland path for more than 50 miles between Coos Bay and Port Orford, you'll want to leave the highway in

Bandon and take the Beach Loop above the oceanfront on a bluff. There are several access roads which lead to Beach Loop Drive, each about one-quarter mile from each other. Most of the traffic seems to head west on First St. along the Coquille. Another popular approach is from 11th St., which heads toward Coquille Point. On the beach itself are rock formations with such evocative names as Elephant Rock, Garden of the Gods, and Cat and Kittens Rocks. The most eye-catching of all is **Face Rock,** Bandon's answer to New Hampshire's Old Man of the Mountain. This basalt monolith resembles the face of a woman looking at the sky. Indian legends say that she was a maiden frozen by an evil sea spirit. The whole grouping of seastacks looks like a surrealist chess set cast upon the waters. Look for the Face Rock turnout a quarter mile south of Coquille Point on the Beach Loop.

Despite this array, the beach is surprisingly deserted. Perhaps this is due to the long, steep trails up from the water along other parts of the beach. In any case, this dearth of people can make for great beachcombing. Agates, driftwood, and tidepools full of starfish and anemones are commonly encountered here, along with birdwatching opportunities galore. Elephant Rock has a reputation as the Parthenon of puffins, while murres, oystercatchers, and other species proliferate on the other offshore formations in varying concentrations.

The Bird Man Of Bandon

In the movie *The Birdman of Alcatraz,* Burt Lancaster portrays an embittered convict who copes with his confinement by caring for birds. Dan Deuel is Bandon's bird man, a Vietnam veteran with shattered limbs who takes in injured sea lions, raptors, and shorebirds brought to him by beachcombers and government agencies. If you are interested in animal rehabilitation and Dan isn't too busy (call 347-3882 to check), you can get a life-affirming look at his flock-on-the-mend. Particularly interesting are several resident owls. Sometimes there aren't too many critters to look at since they are released back into the wild after being nurtured back to health, but Dan's wealth of knowledge about his charges is always edifying. The bird man's lair can be found by taking the Beach Loop and turning off at Gables Motel on Coquille Point. Dan's cliffside home is easy to spot since its adjoining yard is filled with pens housing the "patients." This heroic operation is largely self-sustaining, so please leave donations.

ACTIVITIES

Bandon Storm-watchers (Box 1693, Bandon 97411; tel. 347-2144 or 347-7246 or 347-2779) is a group that coordinates activities and natural history seminars out of the Bandon Com-

Bandon Ocean Wayside

munity Center. The center is located near Beach Loop Dr. just north of the Face Rock viewing area. On Saturday afternoons Jan. through April, show up just before 3 p.m. for meetings.

Birdwatchers flock to the **Bandon National Wildlife Refuge** (a.k.a. the Bandon Marsh), especially in the fall to take in what may be the prime birding site on the coast. Bar-tailed godwits and Mongolian plovers often join the usual assemblage of migrating shorebirds during October. Access is via unmarked trails off River Rd., bordering the Coquille River east of Bandon.

Bandon Beach Loop Stables (tel. 347-9242) is located four miles south of Old Town, just past Crooked Creek State Park. They rent horses by the hour ($10), day, or week for beach trail rides, with lessons available to beginners. In addition, kids can enjoy 15 minutes on a pony for $2 here. Fishing guides and gear can be arranged through **Bandon Bait Shop** (First and Alabama, Bandon 97411; tel. 347-3905), across from the boat basin. Clamming and crabbing info can also be procured from the youth hostel.

Just off the south end of Beach Loop Dr., **Bradley Lake** has good trout fishing and a boat ramp. It is protected from ocean winds by high dunes.

Winter River Books and Gallery (170 Second St., Bandon; tel. 347-4111) has crystals, objets d'art, and an interesting selection of self-help books. A fine and wide-ranging assortment of travel titles, photo essays, fiction, and tapes also makes this the best bookstore on the south coast.

PRACTICALITIES

Accommodations
The expression "You can't go wrong" applies for price, view, cleanliness, and whatever else you're looking for in this town. Bandon bills itself as America's Storm-watching Capital, and special packages are often available October until March.

Bed And Breakfast
Cliff Harbor Guest House (Box 769, Beach Loop Rd., Bandon 97411; tel. 347-3956) is acclaimed by seasoned travelers as the premiere B&B on the southern Oregon coast. From May to November, reservations should be made two to three months in advance. Casually elegant, this retreat boasts a suite with sitting room, a full breakfast, and a self-contained studio with a spectacular ocean view to the west and to the north for $125 per day in the peak summer season. The off-season rate is $95

Sea Star American Youth Hostel
The youth hostel listed in the Bandon Accom-

BANDON ACCOMMODATIONS

Bandon Beach Motel, 1110 11th St. S.W., tel. 347-4430, $40-65, ocean view, restaurant, pets.

Bandon Wayside, ORE 42 S., tel. 347-3421, $28-40, restaurant, pets.

Caprice Motel, Route 1, Box 530, tel. 347-4494, $35-65, kitchenettes, pets, near restaurants and shops.

Inn at Face Rock, 3255 Beach Loop Rd., tel. 347-9441, $55-105, full-service resort, golf, stables.

La Kris Motel, U.S. 101 and 9th St., tel. 347-3610, $30-58, wheelchair access, restaurant, lounge.

Lamplighter Motel, 40 North Ave., tel. 347-4477, $30-60, kitchenettes, pets.

Sea Star American Youth Hostel, 375 2nd St., tel. 347-9632, $10-13, ocean view, kitchenettes, laundry, board games, 10-15 minutes of chores required daily.

Sea Star Guesthouse, 370 1st St., tel. 347-9632, $60-100, restaurant, laundry. This is an extension of the hostel with nicer rooms facing the ocean and no chores.

Sunset Ocean Front Resort, 1755 Beach Loop Rd., tel. 347-2453, $40-195, wheelchair access, wood-paneled rooms, family suites, ocean views, restaurant, lounge.

Windermere, 3250 Beach Loop Rd., tel. 347-3710, $50-85, ocean view, quiet, kitchenettes.

*the lighthouse at
Bullards Beach*

modations chart is the only such facility on the coast. Along with the amenities previously described, this property has skylights, a natural wood interior, a wood stove, and a harbor-view courtyard. Private, couple, and family rooms are available.

Campgrounds
Bullard's Beach State Park (Box 25, Bandon 97411; tel. 347-2209) is a great place to spend the night, fish, crab, bike, fly a kite, or picnic. The park has about 100 campsites with some hiker/biker spaces. To get there, drive north of town on U.S. 101 for about a mile; just past the bridge on the west side of the highway is the park entrance. The beach itself is reached via a scenic two-mile drive paralleling the Coquille River. There are campsites by the river. Electricity, picnic tables, and fire grills are provided. You'll also find a store, a cafe, a laundromat, an inviting sandy beach, and hiking trails. The fee for camping at Bullard's Beach along the Coquille is $15-17 a night.

A side road going out to the north jetty takes you to the octagonal **Coquille Lighthouse,** built in 1896. It was abandoned in 1939 but has been refurbished and is open in summer, 12-5, for inspection. Etchings of ships that made it across Bandon's treacherous bar, and those that didn't, greet you as you enter.

Food
Bandon has quite a few restaurants which serve up specialty dishes that break the mold while not breaking your budget. **Wheelhouse Seafood Grill** (First and Chicago, Bandon; tel. 347-7933) deep-fries their fish (they also grill and broil) with a beer batter that doesn't mask the taste of the food. **Andrea's Old Town Cafe** (160 Baltimore, Bandon; tel. 347-2111) features such items as the restaurateur's home-raised lamb as well as fresh-caught local ling cod with Andrea's own tomato feta sauce. Count on Andrea's for something special for breakfast, lunch, and dinner.

International flavors predominate at the **Sea Star Coffeehouse** (375 Second St., Bandon; tel. 347-9533), with European breakfast plates, croissants, pita sandwiches, fruit dessert crepes, soups, salads, and espresso drinks. As with Andrea's, a premium is placed on fresh local ingredients in a dinner menu which changes to conform to the seasonal catch or harvest.

Bandon Boatworks (South Jetty Rd., Bandon; tel. 347-2111) has fresh seafood and steaks for lunch and dinner. For a dinner appetizer, try their squid in the chef's secret-recipe batter. Other predinner delectables include the cranberry bread and a sumptuous salad bar. The Boatworks has views of the Coquille Lighthouse and an intimate lounge with entertainment. A change of pace here is Sunday brunch and Mexican food (dinner only). The restaurant is closed Monday and goes into winter hibernation during January and February.

South of downtown, **Lord Bennett's** (1695 Beach Loop Dr.; tel. 347-FOOD) cliffside aerie looks out over the breakers in what is easily Bandon's most dramatic restaurant view. Lunch and dinner here do justice to these surroundings with elegantly rendered seafood dishes.

Entertainment

Bandon has several theater groups and a well-regarded 350-seat performance center, **Harbor Hall** (325 Second St., Bandon 97411; tel. 347-4404). Arlo Guthrie, Doc Watson, Jerry Jeff Walker, Bo Diddley, Taj Mahal, and Riders in the Sky have appeared here, along with a local professional repertory group, Encore Presenters. In addition to light comedy and musicals, Encore also presents InsomniACTs, an after-dinner late-night theater with mime, blackout skits, reader theater, dances, etc. The programs of Encore and the other theater groups can be found through the daily paper, *Western World*, and the chamber of commerce.

Less posh, but equally as dynamic as Harbor Hall/Encore Presenters, is the Breuer Building's (First St. in Old Town) **Whimsical University of Bandon.** This is a loose (in more ways than one) gathering of artists, writers, craftspeople, and actors who generate a constant flow of outrageous art shows, performance pieces, and poetry readings.

For nightlife, **Lloyd's Lounge** and the **Pastime Tavern** are side by side on Second Street. Lloyd's sells hard liquor and has weekend bands and dancing as well as low-stakes blackjack. The Pastime features Rainier beer on tap at 60 cents a glass and 80 cents a pint, as well as a good jukebox.

CRANBERRIES

From the vantage point of U.S. 101 between Port Orford and ten miles north of Bandon, you'll notice what appears to be reddish-tinged ground in flood-irrigated fields. If you get close, you'll see cranberries, small evergreens that creep along the ground and send out runners that take root. Along the runners, upright branches six to eight inches long are formed, on which pink flowers and fruits develop. These berries are cultivated in bogs to satisfy their tremendous need for water and to protect them against insects and winter cold. Bandon leads Oregon in this crop, with an output ranking third in the nation. Oregon berries are often used in juice production by Ocean Spray because of their deep red pigment and high vitamin-C content.

It is possible to arrange a visit to see some of these bogs. The most interesting time is during the late autumn harvest. Write the **Cranberry Growers Alliance** (P.O. Box 1737, Bandon 97411) for more information on when and where to watch the harvest. A sweeter encounter can be found at **Cranberry Sweets** (First and Chicago Streets, Bandon 97411). Herein are confections ranging from cranberry fudge to cranberry truffles. Sugar fans will be glad to know it's open seven days a week, 9-5.

Oregon bogs were producing wild cranberries when Lewis and Clark first traded with the Indians for them in 1805. Shortly thereafter, cultivated bogs were developed in Massachusetts, which like Oregon has acid soils with lots of organic materials conducive to berry production. By the California gold rush of 1849, East Coast growing and harvesting techniques had transformed Bandon's marshes into commercial cranberry bogs. In the years to come, much of the modern equipment for harvesting these bogs was developed in Bandon. Wet-picking, for instance, is facilitated by the water reel, which is rotated to create eddies on the bog to shake berries off the vines. After they float to the surface, the cranberries are pushed by long booms toward a submerged hopper. They are then conveyor-belted onto trucks. Walking through the bogs without trampling the berries is made possible by fastening wooden platforms with short pegs to the soles of boots.

Without such innovations, Thanksgiving dinner wouldn't be the same. In order to bring the enormous annual volume of cranberries to the dinner table for the holidays, all these harvesting techniques as well as processing and packaging technology are called into play. Coincidentally, Bandon's berries often join turkeys from the Northwest's leading poultry farms in the Willamette Valley and southern Oregon for that traditional November repast.

Events

The biggest weekend for Bandonians comes in mid-to-late October when the **Cranberry Festival** brings the whole town together in a parade, crafts fair, and the Bandon High Cranberry Bowl—in which the local footballers take on traditional rival Coquille High.

During the Christmas holiday season, the merchants of Old Town and fisherfolk deck their stores and boats with white lights in the traditional **Festival of Lights.** Particularly striking is the Coquille Lighthouse lit up like a Christmas tree.

On Memorial Day, the Bandon Storm-watchers organize the annual **Wine and Seafood Festival.** On the same weekend, competitors in the sandcastle contest create amazing sculptures out of sand, water, and imagination. This takes place on the beach off Beach Loop Dr. at Seabird Lane. Construction starts at 9 a.m.; judging is at 1 p.m. Call 347-9616 for more information. A fish fry is the big event of Bandon's **Fourth of July.** Later, at dusk, fireworks are launched across the Coquillle to burst above the river.

Fishing

In summer, anglers come to southern Oregon for salmon and bottomfish. Bandon is midway between such fishing meccas as the Elk and Sixes rivers (25 miles south near Port Orford) and the Millicoma River (25 miles north near Coos Bay). The southerly rivers have salmon in November and December. The Millicoma and Bandon's own Coquille River have steelhead October to March.

Information And Services

The **Bandon Chamber of Commerce** (Second and Chicago, Bandon 97411; tel. 347-9616) has an authoritative 63-page guide and a large annotated pictographic map of the town. The **post office** (one block east of U.S. 101, Bandon 97411, tel. 347-3406) is open Mon.-Fri 9-5. **Greyhound** (Bandon Book and Frame, 610 Second St., Bandon 97411; tel. 347-3324) is only one block from the hostel. It's open Mon.-Sat. 9-5:30. A public transit van (tel. 347-4131) is available 10 a.m.-4 p.m.; call for additional information. *The Western World* (1185 Baltimore St., Box 248, Bandon 97411; tel. 347-2423) is a useful compendium of cultural/recre-

ational goings-on here. **Southern Coos General Hospital** (640 W. Fourth, Bandon, 97411; tel. 347-2426) features an ocean view that in itself is therapeutic, as well as an emergency room and facilities for coronary/respiratory care.

NORTH FROM BANDON

You can escape the tedium of U.S. 101's inland route to Coos Bay by taking the Seven Devils Beach route a few miles north of Bandon. This road will eventually get you to Coos Bay by way of Charleston, a fishing village which sits closer to the ocean than its larger neighbors to the east of U.S. 101. En route, beaches, state parks, and an estuarine preserve make the drive interesting. The sights detailed in this chapter are expanded upon in "The Bay Area," which follows.

Whisky Run

The first beach encountered is Whisky Run, whose ore-bearing sands spread gold fever down the south coast in the early 1850s. As many as 2,000 miners worked here (and are to blame for the original misspelling) until a storm washed away the deposit. Other forms of beachcombing at Whisky Run and on the beaches to the north are still thriving, however. Agate-hunting, after a season of winter storms, and clamming make these solitary shorelines ideal places to forget the cares of the world. The only reminder of humankind is a life-affirming one. The sight of a wind-energy farm's pinwheels above the beach is evidence of the continuing effort to find alternatives to fossil fuels. Enough energy is generated here to supply several hundred Oregon homes.

South Slough Estuarine Preserve

From the beaches, the road climbs northeastward toward the South Slough Estuarine Preserve, whose visitor-center displays and trails can make an hour pass profitably. The center looks out over several estuarine arms of Coos Bay, the largest harbor between San Francisco Bay and the Columbia River. These vital wetlands nurture a vast web of life which is detailed by the placards captioning the center's exhibits. The coastal ecosystem is presented by the "10-

minute trail" in back of the visitor center. The various conifers and the understory are clearly labeled along the gently sloping half-mile loop. Branch trails lead down toward the water for an up-close view of the estuary itself. Down by the slough, you may see elks grazing in marshy meadows and bald eagles circling above, while *Homo sapiens* harvest oysters and shrimp in these waters of life.

Charleston

From South Slough, you drive four miles on Seven Devils Rd. into the little town of Charleston, which makes few pretensions of being anything other than what it really is—the third-largest commercial fishing port on the Oregon coast. Four processing plants here can or cold-pack tuna, salmon, crab, oysters, shrimp, and other kinds of seafood. The town might occasionally smell of fish, but the few restaurants and lodgings here are good dollar values. Moreover, a post office, a laundromat, and a visitor info center are all conveniently crammed together on the main street, the Cape Arago Highway (ORE 240).

Sunset Bay, Shore Acres, And Cape Arago State Parks

A portion of this road heads south and west of Charleston to some of the most idyllic beaches and interesting state parks on the coast. Pick up this stretch of highway close by the junction of Seven Devils Road. Among the several beaches on the road to Cape Arago, **Sunset Bay State Park** is the big attraction. This is because its sheltered shallow cove is warm and calm enough for swimming, a rarity in the Pacific north of Santa Barbara, California. In addition to swimmers, divers, surfers, and boaters, many people come here to watch the sunset. Near the park is one of three golf courses within a 10-mile radius. A four-mile cliffside trail from Sunset Beach south is the best way to appreciate the seastacks and islands between here and Cape Arago.

Less than a mile south at **Shore Acres State Park,** the grandeur of nature is complemented by the hand of man. The park is set on the grounds of a lumber magnate's turn-of-the-century estate. Formal Oriental gardens here are in themselves compelling attractions, but the headland's rim is more dramatic. White-caps appear to hang suspended upon contact with the rock embankments at the base of Shore Acres' sandstone cliffs. The orange, brown, and buff strata of these escarpments heighten the visual effect.

Although the original Simpson mansion burned to the ground in 1921, the grounds are still kept up by the state, which was ceded the land by the family. A restored gardener's cottage with antique furnishings sits in back of the gardens. It is open for exhibition Dec. 9-31, with music, entertainment, and refreshments. The history of the Simpsons is really the history of the Coos Bay/Charleston/North Bend area and is captioned beneath period photos in the observation tower and in a small enclosure at the west end of the floral displays. Also in the gardens, note the copper egret sculptures and the greenhouse for rare plants from warmer climes.

A few miles south is **Cape Arago State Park**. Locals have made much of the fact that it was a possible landing site of the English explorer Sir Francis Drake in 1579 and have put a plaque here commemorating same. Such speculation is not just confined to this part of the south coast. At any rate, beachcombers can make their own discoveries in the tidal pools which abound here. (For more information on Cape Arago, see "The Bay Area," following.)

THE BAY AREA: COOS BAY, CHARLESTON, NORTH BEND

The towns around the harbor of Coos Bay refer to themselves collectively as the "Bay Area." In contrast to their namesake in California, the Oregon version is not exactly the Athens of the state. Nonetheless, the visitor will be impressed by the area's beautiful beaches (including the largest oceanfront dunes in North America), as well as scenic and historic state parks. Because much of this natural beauty is on the periphery of the industrialized core of the Bay Area, it's easy to miss. All the motorist sees entering Coos Bay/North Bend on U.S. 101 are the dockside lumber mills and foreign vessels anchored at the world's largest lumber port.

The historical antecedents for this scene were laid over a century ago when the region's mills supplied lumber to a gold rush-era housing boom in San Francisco. Heading up this effort was Simpson's lumber company, and later on, the family shipping concern. By the turn of the century, Simpson ships were hauling lumber to 11 nations. Also during that time, companies such as Weyerhaeuser were building their mills by the Union Pacific tracks here.

Today, the Bay Area is in transition along with other western Oregon towns dependent upon timber. The region's wealth of diversions and what is probably the mildest weather of any major city in Oregon is being promoted to draw tourists and retirees, and to recruit new businesses.

SIGHTS

Along The Coast

To many people, an estuary is just a place where you get stuck in the mud. More often than not, however, the interface of fresh water and salt water represents one of the richest ecosystems on earth, capable of producing five times more plant material than a cornfield of comparable size while supporting great numbers of fish and wildlife. The south slough of Coos Bay is the largest such web of life on the Oregon coast. **The South Slough Estuarine Preserve Visitor Center** (off Cape Arago High-

way on Seven Devils Rd. in Charleston; tel. 888-5558) will help you coordinate a canoe trip through the estuary and offers guided hikes as well. Paralleling the drive to the visitor center is the **estuary study trail,** the first of a large network of pathways you'll encounter here. The center is open daily in summer 8:30-4:30. In the off-season, it operates Mon.-Fri. 8:30-4:30, Sept.-May. The admission is free.

The jewel of the previously detailed "tremendous trio" of Oregon state parks about 12 miles southwest of Coos Bay is **Shore Acres.** This former estate of Louis J. Simpson began as a summer home and grew into a three-story mansion complete with an indoor heated swimming pool and large ballroom. Originally a Christmas present to his wife, Shore Acres became the showplace of the Oregon coast, with formal and Japanese gardens eventually added to the 743-acre estate. After a 1921 fire, a second smaller (two stories high and 224 feet long) incarnation of Simpson's "shack by the beach" was built. This was acquired by the state in 1942 after it fell into disrepair. Because of the cost of upkeep, the latter had to be razed, but the gardens have been maintained. The international botanical bounty culled by Simpson clipper ships and schooners is still in its glory, complemented by award-winning roses, rhododendrons, and azaleas. It's open year-round till dusk, with a dollar fee charged for vehicles only in summer and on holiday weekends.

When there's a storm, it's not uncommon to feel the spray atop the 75-foot promontory at Shore Acres. And when conditions are calm, be sure to look for sea lions along this part of the coast.

Coos County Museum

The Coos County Museum is close to the Conde McCullough Bridge, one of several distinctive 1930s-era high-wire acts by Oregon's master bridgebuilder. The museum houses more than the usual bric-a-brac from earlier eras, thanks largely to the region's heritage as a shipping center. A turn-of-the-century Regina music box,

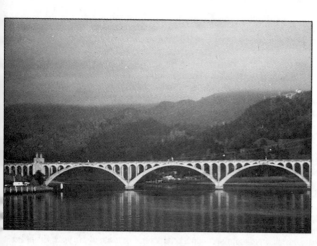

The Oregon coast is dotted with distinctive bridges.

a piano shipped around the Horn, miniature boat models, and a jade Chinese plaque, as well as Coos Indian beadwork/artifacts make this collection especially memorable. In summer, the museum is open Tues.-Sat. 10-4, Sun. 1-4. From Oct. till Memorial Day, it's open Tues.-Sat. 10-4. The admission is 50 cents, 25 cents for ages 12 and under. Outside the museum, old-time logging equipment and a 1920s steam train are also worth a look. Close by is a tourist information center.

Seaman's Center

From North Bend, head south into Coos Bay. The route follows unending dockside detritus of mills and foreign cargo ships, giving no hint where one city ends and the other begins. Park your car near the intersection of U.S. 101 and the Coos Bay/Charleston turnoff. This is the center of town. Southbound travelers will notice a storefront on the right-hand side of the street with an orange model pagoda in the window. Seaman's Center (171 N. Broadway, Coos Bay 97420) is a cafe/club where old salts mingle with foreign sailors and anyone else interested in a wealth of sea lore and camaraderie. Model ships made by retired seamen, oddities from the back alleys of Oriental ports, as well as coins and curios from the harbor cities of the world fill this treasure chest of maritime memorabilia. What's more, matey, your ears will be filled with some scintillating sagas. Since this center is

also operated by an evangelical group, you might also hear the Gospel. The center is open every day after 5 p.m. when ships are in port. There is no admission fee. Across the street is a tourist information center.

The Harbor: Milling Around

Due to the decline in the supply of lumber and the subsequent mill closures, the Weyerhaeuser and other forest-product facility tours are currently not operating. But it's still fun to watch the ships docking and the portside wood-chip piles growing by dozens of feet overnight. Wood chips are Oregon's number-one forest-product export. What had been considered surfeit slivers can now be made into a low-grade paper with the addition of chemicals during processing aboard the Japanese factory ships in the harbor. What's left onshore is often enough "hog fuel"to provide sufficient BTUs to heat a mill. Given the return on these chips, locals call these piles the "million-dollar view." Another roadside perspective on the mills is the sight of "log broncs." These short, powerful boats are highly maneuverable. The broncs evoke the "little engine that could" as they move the floating logjams from the millpond to the conveyors into the mill.

House Of Myrtlewood

To see something closer to a finished product, take the House of Myrtlewood (located just off U.S. 101 at the south end of town, Box 457,

Coos Bay, 97420; tel. 267-7804) factory tour. Myrtlewood carving is an Oregon folk art with a long history.

In 1869, the golden spike marking the completion of the nation's first transcontinental railroad was driven into a highly polished myrtlewood tie. Novelist Jack London was so taken by the beauty of the wood's swirling grain that he ordered an entire suite of furniture. Hudson's Bay trappers used myrtlewood leaves to brew tea as a remedy for chills.

During the Depression years, the city of North Bend issued myrtlewood coins after the only bank in town failed. The coins ranged from 50 cents to $10 and are still redeemable—though they are worth far more as collector items. The House of Myrtlewood tour shows you how an uncut myrtlewood log gets fashioned into bowls, clocks, tables, and other utensils. No admission is charged for this 25-minute guided run through a working factory. After you're done, the store itself is a delight, with Oregon gourmet foods and crafts supplementing the quality woodwork.

Museums

The **Coos Art Museum** (235 Anderson Ave., Coos Bay 97420; tel. 267-3901) is the Oregon coast's only art museum, featuring paintings by Robert Rauschenberg, Larry Rivers, and Romare Bearden. Don't miss the Prefontaine Room on the second floor of the museum. Photos and videos of this native-son world-class runner bear out his credo of "I want to make something beautiful when I run." It's open Tues.-Fri. 11 a.m.-5 p.m., and on weekends 12-4.

Just south of here is the *Marshfield Sun Printing Museum* (1049 N. Front St., Coos Bay, 97420; tel. 269-1363) at the junction of Front St. and U.S. 101. This newspaper was in operation from 1891 to 1944. In 1944, Marshfield became Coos Bay. From an old print shop on the first floor, proceed upstairs to vintage photos of early Marshfield and exhibits on printing and newspaper history. It's open June-Aug., Mon., Wed., and Fri., 1-4, and the last Sunday of each month (except December). There is no charge.

Golden And Silver Falls State Park

Twenty-five miles northeast of Coos Bay in the Coast Range is Golden and Silver Falls State

Park. Two spectacular waterfalls are showcased in this little-known gem of a park. Getting there involves driving east of Coos Bay along the Coos River, crossing to its north bank, and continuing along the Millicoma River through the community of Allegany. To find your way from Coos Bay, look for the Allegany/Eastside exit off U.S. 101. Beyond Allegany, continue up the East Fork of the Millicoma River to its junction with Glenn Creek, which ultimately leads to the park. The narrow windy roads make this trip unsuitable for a wide-body vehicle. Ignore signs indicating that the bridge is out because the access is always passable.

You can reach each waterfall by way of two half-mile trails. Both 200-foot cataracts lie about a mile apart from one another, and although both are about the same height, each has a distinct character. For most of the year, Silver Falls is more visually arresting because it flows in a near semicircle around a knob near its top. During or just after the winter rains, however, the thunderous sound of Golden Falls makes it the more awe-inspiring of the two. Along the trails, look for the beautifully delicate maidenhair fern. En route, **Millicoma Myrtle Grove State Park** makes a fine prelude or appendix to a tour of the House of Myrtlewood Factory.

Oyster lovers might want to visit **Quallman's** (4898 Crown Point Rd., Charleston; tel 888-3145). Just look for the signs on the north side of the Charleston Bridge on the east side of the highway. It's open Mon.-Sat. 8:30-5:30 and has fresh high-quality oysters for sale.

RECREATION AND EVENTS

There are two public golf courses in the Bay Area. One, the **Sunset Bay Golf Course** (11001 Cape Arago Hwy., Charleston 97420; tel. 888-9301) is a nine-holer and has been described as "one of the most interesting courses anywhere" by *Golf Oregon* magazine. The other is the 18-hole **Kentuck Golf Course** (Kentuck Inlet, North Bend 97459; tel. 756-4464).

Fishing charters, bay cruises, whalewatching, and the like can be arranged through **Charleston Charters** (Box 5457, Charleston 97420; tel. 888-4846); please call in advance.

The bulk of the Bay Area's special events fall in July and August. The first event of note in summer is the **Oregon Coast Music Festival** (Box 663, Coos Bay 97420; tel. 269-4150) in mid-July. Coos Bay is the most common performance venue of these south coast classical, jazz, and folk concerts. Tickets cost $8, $6 for seniors.

In late August, the everpresent blackberry is celebrated with the **Blackberry Arts Festival.** Food and winetasting booths and street artists fill the downtown. Picking the fruit itself can best be enjoyed just south of Charleston on the Cape Arago Highway (but everyone has his own secret patch). Avoid picking near roads, as exhaust fumes and the possibility of herbicides sprayed along the road shoulder could mean unhealthy residues on (or in) the berries. Both the Himalaya blackberry and the Pacific blackberry (or dewberry) are found here. The latter is the only native Oregon blackberry, while the Himalaya variety took root in the wild after originally being a cultivated plant brought from Europe. The Himalaya's hooked thorns, heavy canes, and large leaves distinguish it from the dewberry's slender stems and diminished leaf presence. Both can be enjoyed midsummer to midfall.

In mid-September, perhaps the best-known Bay Area personality of this century, Steve Prefontaine, is honored with a 10-km race. Prefontaine was a world-class runner whose gutsy style of running and record performances made him a major sports personality until his death at 24 years of age in 1974. Many top-flight runners pay homage by taking part in the race. For more information on this and the previous listings, contact the chamber of commerce (see "Information and Services," below).

The major airport on the south coast hosts North Bend's **Air Show** (1321-D Airport Way, North Bend 97459; tel. 756-1723) at the beginning of August. The show itself occurs between noon and 3 p.m., but the festival gets off the ground with a pancake feed at 8 a.m.

PRACTICALITIES

Accommodations

Some people take umbrage at the fact that many accommodations here face industrial sites. Nevertheless, there is no shortage of low-cost places at which to stay, and noise is seldom a problem.

Over in Charleston is a lodging within walking distance of fishing, charter boats, clamming, and dock crabbing. **Capt. John's Motel** (8061 Kingfisher Dr., Charleston 97420; tel. 888-4041) is clean, quiet, and has some units with kitchenettes. Close by is a special fish/shellfish-cleaning station and, with any luck, your dinner. Staying in Charleston also puts you close to state parks and within easy reach of laundry and postal services, as well as offering temperatures that are warmer than Coos Bay in winter and cooler in summer. The rates run $30-50 in summer and $25-45 in winter; reserve well in advance for July and August.

Situated at a high elevation out of the coastal wind and fog is the aptly named **Highland's Bed And Breakfast** (608 Ridge Rd., North Bend 97459; tel. 756-0300). The glass-and-cedar home has a huge deck which overlooks meadows, a river, and thousands of acres of the Coast Range. Breakfast on the deck is as much a feast for the palate as it is for the eyes. A few miles from U.S. 101 and nearby sand dunes, beaches, and fine restaurants, Highland's still gives the feeling of being serenely remote. All rooms have antique furniture and private baths (one with a whirlpool tub). There is also an adjoining kitchen, and a family room with satellite TV and library. The rates are $63-90.

Another area bed and breakfast, **Coos Bay Manor** (955 S. Fifth St., Coos Bay 97420; tel. 269-1224), offers the luxury of a renovated Georgian-style mansion for around $60. Large rooms with baths and feather beds, as well as homemade blackberry cobbler accompanying an excellent breakfast, also recommend this spot.

A spendier alternative is the **Coos Bay Red Lion** (1313 Bayshore Dr., Coos Bay 97459; tel 267-4141). Red Lion is a luxury chain in the West, and in terms of creature comforts, they're hard to beat. Large rooms with immense beds, thick pile carpet, and everything else in the way of little extras are characteristic of these units. The Coos Bay Red Lion is also distinguished by having one of the best restaurants in town, a lounge with quality entertainment, and a happy hour with complimentary hors d'oeuvres. The rates range between $70-90.

Campgrounds

Cape Arago (south of Charleston; tel. 888-5353) has a county park with a few hiker/biker sites with beautiful views at no charge. Even though crowds at **Sunset Bay State Park** (for reservations write 13030 Cape Arago Hwy., Coos Bay 97420; tel. 888-5353) can make it seem like a trailer park in midsummer, the proximity of Oregon's only major swimming beach on the ocean keeps occupants of the 108 tent sites and 29 trailer sites here happy. There are also a laundromat and showers. Sites are $8, RVs $10.

The first campsites encountered south of Charleston on the Cape Arago Highway are at **Bastendorff Beach County Park** (tel. 888-5353). For $7, 25 tent sites and 30 trailer sites enjoy drinking water, wood stoves, flush toilets, and hot showers (for an extra two bits). Fishing and hiking are the recreational attractions. Like the previously mentioned campgrounds on the Cape Arago Highway, it's open all year.

Food

Oregon's Bay Area abounds in places where your nutritional needs can be met, if not in fine style then at least at the right price. There is no shortage of seafood places along this part of the coast, but you'll find the freshest, cheapest maritime morsels close to where they're caught. **The Sea Basket** (Charleston Boat Basin, Charleston 97420; tel. 888-5711) typifies the good seafood, fast service, and relatively low prices in these parts. Oysters are especially tasty in this restaurant, with two noted breeding farms close by. This and other fish dinners (halibut, scallops, prawns, etc.) with potatoes or rice and salad usually don't run you more than $7. The fluorescent glare above the cafeteria-style tables frequented by fishermen in work-blackened denims may not count much for atmosphere, but you'll leave satisfied.

The Portside (opposite Captain John's Motel, Charleston Boat Basin, Charleston 97420; tel. 888-5544) close by has won Silver Spoon Awards from the Diners Club the past three years. Fine dining in Charleston might seem a contradiction in terms, but the chance to select your own lobsters and crabs out of a tank, along with the sight of the fleet unloading other dinners just outside the door, would whet the appetite of any gourmet. Reserve ahead for the Friday night all-you-can-eat seafood buffet at a low price.

Even though the **Blue Heron Bistro** (110 W. Commercial, Coos Bay 97420; tel. 267-3933) is located in the heart of downtown Coos Bay, it evokes dining experiences in the San Francisco Bay Area or some other place far from this logging port. This impression can come from opening the door to the restaurant, or opening the menu. The restaurant's tile floors, newspapers on library-style posts, and international posters adorning the walls are in keeping with a European-influenced bill of fare. The extensive menu's eclectic array ranges from Greek salad to Cajun-style blackened fish and emphasizes the freshest ingredients and a creative interpretation whenever possible. An impressive list of microbrews and imports as well as Oregon, California, and European wines will complement whatever dish you order. Expensive, I hear the reader thinking, but it's not really. For not appreciably more money than you'd pay for a high ticket at Denny's, you can enjoy an oasis of refinement in "Timbertown, U.S.A."

The dining room at the **Coos Bay Red Lion** (tel. 267-4141, ext. 305) offers extra-thick cuts of prime rib and flambé items prepared tableside which are as much a treat to look at as to taste. This restaurant is an "in" place to eat out when there's a special occasion here, so make reservations.

Information And Services

With over 16,000 people, the Bay Area is the population hub of the coast. As such, it has a large array of services available. **Coos Bay Chamber of Commerce** (50 E. Central, Coos Bay 97420; tel. 260-0215 or 800-762-6278) is five blocks west from U.S. 101 off Commercial Avenue. It's open Mon.-Fri. 9 a.m.-7 p.m., weekends 10-4. From Sept. to May hours are Mon.-Sat. 9-5 (closed on Sunday).

North Bend's **information center** is just south of the harbor bridge (138 Sherman Ave., North Bend 97459; tel. 756-4613). It's open Mon.-Fri. 8:30-5, Sat. 10-3, and Sun. 10-4. From Labor Day to Memorial Day the center is not open on weekends. Another information resource is the **Oregon State Parks** office (115 S. Fifth, Coos Bay 97420; tel. 269-9410).

To get out of town, head to the Tioga Hotel's **Greyhound** depot (tel. 267-6517). The terminal is open Mon.-Fri. 7-4:30, Sat. 7-3, and Sun. 7-8 a.m. If Greyhound doesn't fit into your plans, consider the **North Bend Airport** (1321-D Airport Way, North Bend 97459). Horizon (tel. 756-2170) flies to or from Eugene and Portland almost every day of the week, and on occasion, to Salem and Seattle. To get to the airport, follow the signs on the road between Charleston and North Bend.

Within the city the Shuttle (tel. 267-4521) offers low-cost transport and scenic/historical tours. There is no set schedule but it's on call 24 hours. Roundtrip within the city can be had for $5, and the fare to Shore Acres one way is $7.

The Coos Bay Public Library (525 W. Anderson, Coos Bay, 97420; tel 267-1101) is open Mon.-Thurs. 1-4, Fri. 10-5, and Sat. 12-5. For **medical emergencies,** Tel-Med (1775 Thompson Rd., Coos Bay 97420; tel. 269-2313) and the ambulance (tel. 269-1151) will get help fast. Help Line (tel. 269-5910) gives referrals. In what's considered a "big city" on the Oregon coast, you might occasionally need the **police** (tel. 269-1151). The **post office** (Fourth and Golden, Coos Bay 97420; tel. 267-4514) is open Mon.-Fri. 8:30-5.

REEDSPORT/WINCHESTER BAY

If you're about to go fishing or coming back from a dunes hike, you'll appreciate a hot meal and a clean low-priced motel room in Reedsport. Otherwise this town of several thousand people might seem like a strange mirage of cut-rate motels, taverns, and burger joints in the midst of the Oregon Dunes NRA.

It evolved because of the site's proximity to the Umpqua River. Jedediah Smith explored this country in the 1820s after the Hudson's Bay Company's Peter Skene Ogden theorized that the Umpqua River might be the fabled Northwest Passage. Even though it wasn't, this river is still one of the great fishing streams of the state. Zane Grey avoided writing about it, lavishing the publicity instead upon the Rogue to divert people from his favorite steelhead spots. At any rate, Winchester Bay's Salmon Harbor Marina has given the whole area new life in recent years, following hard times precipitated by the decline in timber revenues. Salmon Harbor sits at the mouth of the Umpqua, one of the largest rivers between San Francisco Bay and the Columbia.

SIGHTS

Just south of Winchester Bay is **Umpqua Lighthouse State Park.** Even though the 1893 lighthouse isn't open to the public, there's a county museum (tel. 440-4500) there with marine and timber exhibits, open May through Sept., Wed.-Sat. 10-5, Sun. 1-5.

Close by the Dunes NRA Headquarters on U.S. 101 south of Reedsport is ORE 38, which takes you inland to Curtin and I-5. Oregon's "foremost motorcycle road" (according to Harley-Davidson) goes through pastoral countryside along the Umpqua on a well-maintained highway. One highlight is the **Dean Creek Elk Preserve** just outside of Reedsport. There are about 55 Roosevelt elk here, the largest species of this animal in the world. They graze the preserve's marshy pastures in full view of the highway. Farther east are a number of historical placards by landmarks in the one-time shipping center of **Scotsburg.** Cargo ships from this town supplied San Francisco markets with meat, milk, and produce between 1856 and the early 20th century.

PRACTICALITIES

Accommodations
Bargain rooms are easy to find in Reedsport off U.S. 101, but forget about ambience and seclusion. For the latter, check out the small towns close by.

Of the half-dozen motels that sit off of U.S. 101 in Reedsport, the **Fir Grove Motel** (2178 Winchester Ave., Reedsport 97467; tel. 271-4848) is slightly less expensive, but comparable in comfort to the other lodgings. The rooms go for $34 for a single, $42 for a double, and about $10 less on each rate in winter.

Umpqua River
Lighthouse

For about the same money, the **Winchester Bay Motel** (Fourth and Broadway, Winchester Bay 97467; tel. 271-4871) puts you next to the water. Reserve ahead of time in fishing season.

A few miles north of Reedsport in **Gardiner** is another lodging alternative with more character than motel row for not significantly more money. **The Gardiner Guest House** (401 Front, Box 222, Gardiner 97441; tel. 271-4005) is located in a cute, tranquil, paper-mill town which sits close by the confluence of the Smith and Umpqua rivers. The 1883 home was built by local bigwig and State Senator Albert Reed, for whom Reedsport was named. The recently remodeled home still has the Victorian feel, without lacking in modern comforts. Choose between a room with the facility down the hall for $35 ($45 peak season), or a view room with private bath for $55 ($65 peak). A large home-cooked breakfast is included in the rates.

Gardiner was created in the wake of a shipwreck. The *Bostonian* (owned by Mr. Gardiner) was dashed against the rocks at the mouth of the Umpqua in 1856 and from its remnants the first wooden structure in this area was built. It was soon joined by other white-painted homes and facilities for a port on the Umpqua. While this "white city by the sea" declined in importance when the highway elevated Reedsport to regional hub status, the homes still bear the same color scheme from the earlier era.

Food

Reedsport is not the culinary center of the coast. However, there are some intriguing alternatives in surrounding Dune Country.

Ten miles south of Reedsport is a fisherman's friend, the **Stable Cafe** (at the corner of Eighth and Park, Lakeside 97449; tel. 759-3322). Generous breakfast portions at a good price in an old-time homey atmosphere attract a following to this little diner on the shores of Ten Mile Lakes.

Up the road in Winchester Bay, lunch and dinner at the **Seafood Grotto** also offer the touch of home. This family restaurant relies on the local fleet to supply the ingredients for homemade cioppino, clam chowder, and what might be the best grilled salmon in Dune Country. The menu has a range of prices and selections to suit a variety of budgets and appetites.

If you're looking for something to do after dinner in Winchester Bay, check out the dance floor, table tennis, billiards, and insipid video games at the **Oasis Lounge** (Eighth and Clearlake St.; tel. 271-9976). There's a decent 24-hour restaurant on the premises. As for Reedsport, locals praise the **Windjammer** (1280 Highway Ave.; tel. 271-5415) for its seafood and salad bar. Try an overstuffed omelette for breakfast if you're hungry. In addition, the ship models crafted by the owner's son are something to see.

Charters

Winchester Bay has what is probably the cheapest deep-sea-fishing outfitter in Oregon. **Main Charters** (Fourth and Beach streets, Winchester Bay 97496; tel. 271-3800) charges around $30 for a full day of salmon or bottom fishing. Call the day before for reservations.

Information And Services

The Reedsport Chamber of Commerce **infor-** mation kiosk (tel. 271-3352) is located at the junction of U.S. 101 and ORE 38 just north of the NRA Visitor Center. It's open 10-5 every day, but don't expect lots of help. The Forest Service personnel at the **Oregon Dunes NRA Visitor Center** just south on U.S. 101 (855 Highway Ave., Reedsport 97467; tel. 271-3611) should fill in any gaps. They maintain office hours Mon.-Fri 8-4:30, weekends 10-5:30. From Labor Day to Memorial Day there are no weekend hours.

DUNE COUNTRY: NORTH TO FLORENCE

Even though the 47 miles of U.S. 101 between Coos Bay and Florence doesn't overlook the ocean, your eyes will be drawn westward every few minutes. After all, it's not every day that you can see mountains of shifting sand that have swallowed up a giant conifer forest. The largest and most extensive oceanfront dunes in the world are found in this national recreation area. Halfway between Coos Bay and Florence in Reedsport is Oregon Dunes NRA headquarters. This town of 5,000 people and the nearby fishing village of Winchester Bay have carved out tourist identities as refueling and supply depots for excursions into Oregon's Sahara-by-the-Sea.

These forays can take several forms. While joyriding in noisy dune buggies and other off-road vehicles doesn't lack for devotees, the best way to appreciate the interface of ecosystems is on foot. Dunes exceeding 500 feet in height, wetland breeding grounds for animals and waterfowl, evergreen forests, and deserted beaches can be encountered in a march to the sea. En route you might also come upon the nearly extinct silver spot butterfly and the insect-eating Darlingtonia plant.

But most of your attention will probably be focused upon the dunes themselves. How did they come to be in a coastal topography otherwise dominated by rocky bluffs? A combination of factors created this landscape over the past 12,000 years, but the principal agents of dune creation have been the Coos, Siuslaw, and Umpqua rivers. The sand and sediment transported to the sea by these waterways are deposited by waves on the flat shallow beaches. Prevailing westerlies move the particulate matter exposed by the tide eastward up to several yards per year.

Ancient forests lie beneath these dunes, a fact occasionally proven by hikers as they stumble upon the top of an exposed snag. The cross section of sandswept woodlands seen from U.S. 101 demonstrates that this inundation is still occurring. Nonetheless, the motorist will have the impression that the trees are winning the battle, as the dunes are only intermittently visible from the road. A further inhibition to appreciating the range and size of Oregon's dunes is the limited or obscured access from U.S. 101.

The Forest Service personnel at the Dunes NRA Visitor Center in Reedsport can direct you to the best points of entry as well as supply info on camping and hiking in this remarkable landform. One tip you're bound to hear is that the

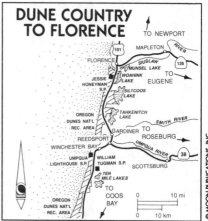

DUNE COUNTRY TO FLORENCE

highest dunes can be reached from secluded trails and campsites south of Reedsport. If your interests extend to fishing, boating, and water-skiing, however, **Ten Mile Lakes** and other freshwater paradises encountered en route from Coos Bay (and later on, north of Florence) might divert you from playing in the sand. Many of these lakes were formed when advancing dunes trapped upland streams. Oceangoing anglers can enjoy the coast's saltwater sportfishing capital, Winchester Bay, six miles south of Reedsport.

The Dunes NRA is home to over 400 species of wildlife, but the only dangerous animal within this ecosystem is possibly the American teenager. This species migrates here during summer vacation to enact puberty rites or auditory assaults with boom boxes. Extreme caution is advised in parking lots or within earshot of dune buggies.

SIGHTS

Begin your travels at the visitor center (855 Highway Ave., Reedsport 97467; tel. 271-3611) where U.S. 101 intersects ORE 38. In addition to the info on hiking, camping, and recreation, the Siuslaw Forest Service personnel are very helpful. Next door is a Reedsport tourism info kiosk which can complete an orientation.

Dune Access

The most spectacular dunes landscape can be found nine miles south of the visitor center at **Umpqua Dunes** (at North Eel Campground near Lakeside). After you emerge from a quarter-mile hike through coastal evergreen forest, you'll be greeted by dunes 300 to 400 feet high. It's said that dunes near here can approach 500 feet high and a mile long after a windblown buildup. In any case, be it mountain or mole-hill, the view here is most photogenic. Since a regular trail through the dunes is impossible to maintain, you should only expect to find wooden posts spaced at irregular intervals west of the dunes to guide you to the beach.

Honeyman State Park, 10 miles south of Florence, also has a spectacular dunescape and then some. Come here in May when the rhododendrons bloom along the short, sinuous road heading to the parking lot. A minute's walk west of the lot brings you to a 150-foot-high dune overlooking Cleawox Lake. From the top of this dune, look westward across several miles of sand, marsh, and remnants of forest at the blue Pacific.

Due to the fact that they are difficult to see from the highway, the most commonly asked question in the visitor center is "Where are the dunes?" To answer it for everybody, the National Forest Service opened an overlook about halfway between Reedsport and Florence south of Carter Lake at the point where the dunes

The dunes stretch for nearly 50 miles along U.S. 101 between Coos Bay and Florence.

come closest to U.S. 101. In addition to four levels of railing-enclosed platforms connected by wooden walkways, there are trails down to the sand. It's only about a quarter mile to the dunes and, thereafter, a mile through sand and wetlands to the beach.

You can hike a loop beginning where the sand gives way to willows. Bear right en route to the beach. Once there, walk south 1½ miles. A wooden post marks where the trail resumes. It then traverses a footbridge going through trees onto sand, completing the loop. If you go in February, this loop has great birdwatching potential.

HIKING

A hike through the dunes lets you star in your own *Lawrence of Arabia* flick and moonwalk in the earthbound Seas of Tranquility. The soundtrack can be provided by the 247 species of birds here—along with your heartbeat—as you scale these elephantine anthills. Deserted beaches and secret swimming holes are among the many rewards of the journey.

Getting Oriented

In order to ensure a bon voyage, it's important to understand this terrain. To begin, carry plenty of water and dress in layers because of hot spots in dune valleys and ocean breezes at higher elevations. Expect cool summers and wet, mild winters. While rainfall here can average over 70 inches a year (with 75% of it falling March-November), a string of dry, 50-60° days in February is not uncommon. Another surprise is summertime morning fog, brought in by hot weather inland. These fogs, together with the inevitable confusion caused by dunes that don't look much different from each other, make a compass necessary. The lack of defined trails also compels such measures as marking your return route in the sand with a stick. Binoculars help with visual orientation, not to mention the birdwatching opportunities galore. Finally, there are always the sounds of traffic and surf to help you determine the eastern and western extents of this bailiwick.

Prior to setting out, write for or pick up the *Hiking Trails Recreation Opportunity Guide* from the Siuslaw National Forest Service, Oregon

Dunes National Recreation Area. This and their other publications will correct the superficial impression that the dunes are just a domain for all-terrain vehicles and campgrounds for day-hikers.

Tahkenitch/Three Mile Lake Trails Loop

Hiking Trails documents several well-laid-out trails to overnight destinations far from vehicular vibrations, where you may come upon wildlife ranging from black bears to tundra swans. One such overnight excursion is the Tahkenitch/Three Mile Lake Trails Loop, a six-mile jaunt through wind-sculpted dunes and varied vegetation broken up by lakes, creeks, and a forest. The trail begins at the Tahkenitch Lake campground. To get there, drive seven miles north of Reedsport on U.S. 101 and 100 yards west on Forest Service Road 1090. Tahkenitch means "Many Arms," which the Salish Indians conjured from the starfishlike extensions of this lake. After a quarter mile of walking, the path splits, with the right fork going to Tahkenitch Dunes. Instead, head west to Three Mile Lake, several miles distant. Past the junction of the two trailheads look for rhododendrons blooming in early June and huckleberries to munch on in late August. Thereafter, the trail to Three Mile Lake alternates between spruce forest with ferns and sorrel and marshy areas with yellow skunk cabbage. The path culminates in a hillock above the lake with the dunes on the right. After a good night's sleep in the sand, continue west through low-lying marshes, shore pines, and small dunes. Once you hit the beach, continue north until you meet the Tahkenitch Dunes Trail close by the mouth of Tahkenitch Creek. From here head east across the dunes, following the marker posts back.

RECREATION

Riding across the dunes into the sunset on a trusty steed sounds like a fantasy, but you can do it, too, thanks to **C&M Stables** (90241 U.S. 101, Florence 97439; tel. 997-7540). Rates work out to $20 per person for trips of from one to two hours (with discounts for larger parties). The stables are open daily Memorial Day through Labor Day. They operate Wed.-Sun. the rest of the year. With beach rides, dune trail excursions and sunset trips, there's something for everybody. Call for specific times and reservations.

Another option for those who fear to tread is **Dunes Frontier** (83960 U.S. 101, Florence, 97439; tel. 997-3544). This company rents vehicles for travel in specially designated areas within the Dunes NRA. Odysseys, small one-person dune buggies, go for $25 per hour and a $50 deposit. You must be strapped in with a helmet, stay within the marked territory, and be especially careful going uphill. If you lose power on an incline, it's possible to roll over when turning around to go back down. The 20-person dune buggy rides cost $5 for adults, $2.50 for children 6-10 years old, and kids under five ride for free. A four-seater goes for $45 per hour. Protective goggles are provided, along with a driver. Go in the morning when the sand tends to be blowing around less.

The **Dune Mushers Mail Run** is a noncompetitive endurance dogsled run held in March of each year. This is the world's longest organized dry-land run for dogsled teams. It goes most of the length of the dunes, from Horsefall Beach in the south, ending in Florence. Call 269-0215 for more information.

CAMPGROUNDS

North Eel Creek
Set along Eel Creek near Eel Lake and Ten Mile Lakes is North Eel Creek Campground. The area boasts superlative hiking and aquatic sports as well as a fisherman's favorite, **The Stable Cafe** (on neighboring Lakeside's Main St. close to Ten Mile Lakes), if your breakfast rations run low. The camp is open June to late September at $8 per night with no reservations necessary. Picnic tables, firegrills, piped water, and flush and pit toilets service the 52 tent sites and RV spaces. It is near several other campgrounds 10 miles south of Reedsport.

Tahkenitch Landing
Another Forest Service campground close to trails and water sports is Tahkenitch Landing, seven miles north of Reedsport. There are 15 sites for tents or motor homes up to 22 feet long. This place is somewhat primitive, with pit toilets and no drinking water, but the price ($2 a night) and proximity to all the amenities at nearby Tahkenitch Lake Campground make it a can't-lose proposition. The camp overlooks the lake on an open piece of land with picnic tables. For more information on North Eel and Tahkenitch Landing campgrounds, contact **Oregon Dunes Recreation Area** (855 Highway Ave., Reedsport 97467; tel. 271-3611).

Nearby State Parks
Umpqua Lighthouse and **William A. Tugman** state parks (Box 94, Winchester Bay 97467; tel. 271-4118) are five and eight miles south of Reedsport respectively, in the heart of dune country. The Umpqua beacon, which bears the name of the river whose mouth it illuminates, is a light in the forest for campers who like fishing, boating, swimming, and hiking. Trails from here lead to the highest dunes in the U.S. (elevation 545 feet), west of Clear Lake. From mid-April to late October, 41 tent sites and 22 trailer sites go for $8 per night. Firewood, flush toilets, a laundromat, picnic tables, electricity, and piped water are on-site facilities.

Tugman is a larger campground with 115 sites and a similar range of creature comforts, price, and recreation. It sits on the west shore of Eel Lake east of U.S. 101 across from where the dunes reach their widest extent, two miles to the sea.

FLORENCE AND VICINITY

"Location, location, and location." This tenet of business success also explains the growing appeal of Florence for retirees and vacationers. Many people who could afford to live almost anywhere choose to do so here between the Dunes NRA and some of the most beautiful headlands on U.S. 101. The fact that Florence is also situated halfway up Oregon's coastal route and a little over an hour's drive from shopping and culture in Eugene has made it a major beachhead of vacation-home development in the region. A mild climate, a modern health-care facility, and lower housing prices than would be encountered elsewhere in a comparable setting also explain the influx.

Florence began shortly after the California gold rush of 1849 put a premium on the lumber and produce upriver from the Siuslaw River estuary here. Several decades later, the town's name was inspired by a remnant from a shipwreck which floated ashore, bearing the ship's nom de guerre, Florence. The townspeople either recognized an omen when they saw it or just figured they couldn't come up with anything better.

SIGHTS

Easy access to beach and dunes is offered by South Jetty Rd. just south of the Siuslaw River Bridge and Florence proper. While birdwatching opportunities abound in the marshy lakes en route to the beach at all times of the year, the chance to see tundra swans here November to January is a special treat. The six-foot wingspan of this majestic bird is best appreciated with binoculars, and waterproof boots are a must for comfortable hiking in the area.

Siuslaw River Bridge
If first and last impressions are enduring, Florence is truly blessed. As you enter the city from the south, a graceful bridge over the Siuslaw greets you. Shortly after you leave city limits to the north, U.S. 101 climbs to dizzying heights above the ocean.

The Siuslaw River Bridge is perhaps the most impressive of Conde McCullough's WPA-built spans. The Egyptian obelisks and art deco styling characteristic of other McCullough designs are complemented by the views to the west of the sand dunes. To the east, the riverside panorama of Florence's Old Town beckons further investigation. Prior to making the turnoff several blocks beyond U.S. 101, you can stop at the chamber of commerce on the highway. Old Town itself is a pleasant restoration, with all manner of shops and restaurants along the river. The absence of car traffic is conducive to a pleasant walk after lunch there. One place to stop if you're looking for regional titles is **Old Town Books** (1340 Bay St., Florence; tel. 997-6205). The friendly staff here will also gladly direct you to local attractions and answer any questions you might have about the region.

Museums
To fill in the missing captions on the original town site and get some notion of Indian and pioneer life, return to the highway for the **Siuslaw Pioneer Museum** (85294 U.S. 101, Florence 97439; tel. 997-7884). You'll find it on the south side of the Siuslaw River on the west side of the highway in a converted church. Open year-round 10-4 every day except Monday, the usual array of artifacts is accompanied by an account of how the U.S. government double-crossed the Siuslaw tribe, who sold their land to the feds and never received the promised recompense.

Another museum in town is the **American Museum of Fly Fishing** (280 Napal St., Florence 97439; tel 997-6102). Located three blocks north of the Old Town waterfront, thousands of fishing flies are attractively framed here. Next to the tufts of feathers and hair are fish paintings and lifelike wooden amphibian sculptures. This palace of Poseidon is open 10-5 daily with an admission charge of $2.50 for adults; kids under 16 get in free.

Indian Forest
Four miles outside of town is the Indian Forest

(88493 U.S. 101, Florence 97439; tel. 997-3677). When you see a totem pole on the right-hand side of the road, pull into this exhibit of Native American dwellings. A Navajo hogan, an Ojibwa wigwam, a Sioux tipi, and other dwellings are on display here. A kitschy plastic horse and a herd of real buffalo gaze forlornly over this assemblage. It's open daily June to August 8 a.m. to dusk. In May, September, and October, the exhibit is open 10-4. The admission is $3, half that for kids below 18; under-fives get in free.

Fifteen miles east of Florence in the Mapleton area are several cascades on Kentucky Creek and the North Fork of the Smith River. Known collectively as **Kentucky Falls,** they are set in an old-growth forest on a trail kept up by the Mapleton Ranger Station of the U.S. Forest Service (10692 ORE 126, Mapleton 97453; tel. 268-4473). Contact this office for exact directions or refer to the "Eugene" section for an in-depth discussion.

Darlingtonia Wayside

Several miles up the road from Florence in an area noted for dune access and freshwater lakes is the Darlingtonia Wayside. In a sylvan grove of spruce and alder are a series of wooden platforms that guide you through a bog overlooking the carnivorous Darlingtonia plants, which are shaped like serpent heads. Known alternatively as the pitcher plant, cobra orchid, or cobra lily, the sweet smell the plant produces invites insects to crawl into the top of the Darlingtonia's serpentlike extension.

Once inside, thin transparent "windows" allow light to shine inside the leaf, confusing the bug as to where the exit is. As the insect crawls around in search of an escape, downward-pointing hairs within the enclosure inhibit its movement to freedom. Eventually, the tired-out bug falls to the bottom of the stem, where it is digested. The plant needs the nutrients from the trapped insects to compensate for the lack of sustenance supplied by its small root system. If you still have an appetite after witnessing this carnage, you might want to enjoy lunch at one of the shaded picnic tables here.

Sea Lion Caves

Ten miles north of Florence, you'll have an op-portunity to descend into a sea cave to observe the only mainland rookery of the Steller's sea lion in the lower 48. Sea Lion Caves (91560 U.S. 101, Florence; tel. 547-3111) is home to several hundred of this species. These animals occupy the cave during the fall and winter, which are thus the prime visitation times. The Steller's sea lions you'll see at those times are cows, yearlings, and immature bulls. Otherwise, go a quarter mile past the concession entrance to the "rockwork" turnout, where the herd can often be witnessed on the rocky ledges several hundred feet below. Many people snap the picturesque **Heceta Head Lighthouse** across the cove to the north from the turnout. It's said that this is the most photographed beacon in the United States.

Enter Sea Lion Caves through the gift shop on U.S. 101. To the right, tickets can be purchased 9 a.m.-7 p.m. in summer and 9-4 in winter for $5. Kids 6-15 get in for $3, and those under five enter free. A steep downhill walk reveals stunning perspectives of the coastal cliffs as well as several kinds of gulls and cormorants which nest here. The final leg of the descent is facilitated by an elevator. After disembarking the lift into America's largest sea cave, look for the sea lions to the left from behind a partition. You'll also note a set of stairs on the right. These lead up to a view of Heceta Head Lighthouse through an opening in the cave. Flash photography is forbidden in the cave, so bring high-speed film if you wish to take pictures inside.

The Steller's sea lions were referred to as *lobos marinos* (sea wolves) in early Spanish mariners' accounts of their 16th-century West Coast voyages, and their doglike yelps might explain why. You'll notice several shades of color in the herd, which has to do with the progressive lightening of their coats with age. Males can sometimes weigh over a ton and dominate the scene here with macho posturings to scare off rivals for harems of as many as two dozen cows. Their protection as an endangered species enrages many fishermen, who claim that the sea lions take a significant bite out of fishing revenues by preying on salmon. In any case, the sight of these huge sea mammals close-up in the cavernous enclaves of their natural habitat should not be missed . . . despite an odor that can be likened to sweat-soaked sneakers.

PRACTICALITIES

Accommodations

As in Reedsport, there are budget motels on the main drag here, but to experience the coast fully, try one of the romantic getaways between Florence and Yachats.

Campgrounds

Camping here offers recreational opportunities comparable to those at the Dunes NRA, with more varied scenery.

Carl G. Washburne State Park (c/o The Campground, Florence 97439; tel. 238-7488) is popular with Oregonians due to its proximity to beaches, tidepools, Sea Lion Caves, and elk. The eight tent sites and 58 RV sites have such modern conveniences as showers, a laundromat, electricity, and piped water. It's located 14 miles north of Florence on U.S. 101 (several miles past Sea Lion Caves), then one mile west on a park road. The fee is $15-17, $2 for hiker and biker spaces, and it's open all year.

Heceta Head Lighthouse is within state park boundaries, but closed to the public. According to some accounts, Heceta was the first European to set foot in Oregon (in 1774). Beyond Heceta Head is a trail down to the beach at adjoining **Devil's Elbow State Park.** Be conscious of tides here if you climb along the rocks ad-

joining the beach en route to the top of Heceta Head. Near these campgrounds, Devil's Elbow Tunnel on U.S. 101 is a 600-foot cut through solid mountain.

An ideal place to escape from the summertime coastal crowds is the **North Fork of the Siuslaw** campground (write Siuslaw Forest, Mapleton Ranger District, Mapleton 97453; tel. 268-4473). Chances are you'll see mostly locals here—if anybody. From Florence follow ORE 126 about 15 miles to Mapleton and the junction with ORE 36. The latter road will take you 13 miles to County Route 5070. Then it's a short drive to the riverside campsite, (or you can drive the North Fork Siuslaw River Road from Florence 14½ miles). The fee is $4 between July and early September. Sheltered picnic tables, fire pits, and crawdads in the river are other reasons to come.

Close by is the **Pawn Old Growth Trail,** a half-mile pathway through several-hundred-year-old Douglas fir and hemlock. The trailhead, located at the confluence of the North Fork of the Siuslaw and Taylor's Creek, is a good place to see salmon spawning in the fall and observe water ouzels (also called "dippers"). It follows the creek and offers interpretive placards along the way.

By the way, nearby ORE 36 makes an interesting access road back to the Willamette Valley if you're not in a hurry. Its circuitous route pass-

---

FLORENCE ACCOMMODATIONS

Americana Motel, 3829 U.S. 101, tel. 997-7115, $44-49, kitchenettes, covered pool.

Driftwood Shores, 88416 1st Ave., tel. 997-8263, (800) 422-5091, $60-150, restaurant, lounge, indoor pool and spa, all rooms have ocean view.

Gull Haven on the Sea, 94770 U.S. 101, (16 miles north of town), tel. 547-3583, $35-70, sandy beach, seclusion, pets, private bath, kitchen privileges, midweek discounts available, reserve early.

Johnson House Bed and Breakfast, 216 Maple St., tel. 997-8000, $55-70, antiques in an old Victorian a block from the bayfront, full breakfast, afternoon tea, down comforters.

Le Chateau Motel, 1084 U.S. 101, tel. 997-3481, $35-55, restaurant, pool, wheelchair access, laundromat.

Money Saver Motel, 170 U.S. 101, tel. 997-7131, $32-65, off-season discounts available, adjacent to Old Town.

Park Motel, 85034 U.S. 101 South, tel. 997-2634, $39-49, restaurant, pets, kitchenettes.

Silver Sands Motel, 1449 U.S. 101 North, tel. 997-3459, $35-55.

es through Deadwood and ends up in the Junction City area.

Food

A famous Zen master once said, "If you can make a cup of tea right, you can do anything." The same aphorism seems to apply to clam chowder in coastal restaurants, if three Florence eateries are any indication.

The local **Mo's** (1436 Bay St., Old Town Florence; tel. 997-2185) is the largest outlet of this famed Oregon chowderhouse, and its fresh fish, fast service, and fair prices make it this neighborhood's most popular restaurant. Highly recommended are the dozen baked oysters (seasonal availability) served with salad, chowder, or homemade bread for $8.95. Even if you don't eat here, you might want to stock up on Mo's clam chowder base packaged to go.

The Bridgewater Seafood Restaurant and Oyster Bar (129 Bay St., Old Town Florence; tel. 997-9405) features exotic clam chowder with Indonesian clams, in keeping with a Banana Republic decor, and the only "fine dining" in Old Town. Of course, this also means the highest prices on the waterfront ($2.75 for a cup of chowder), but to be fair, you're getting what you pay for and then some. The Bridgewater was the recipient of a "People's Choice Award" for the best clam chowder in town several years back. Besides that, if you don't like it, the chowder's free. Fresh fish, often with a Cajun flair, is the star of a menu whose lunch entrees average around $6.50, twice that for dinner. A lower-priced option exists on Wednesdays, winter through early spring, with the all-you-can-eat seafood dinner buffet for $9.95.

Another chowder feted by the People's Choice Award as well as a 1990 *Oregon Coast* magazine poll is the creamy clam-filled concoction made by **The Blue Hen** (1675 U.S. 101, Florence; tel. 997-3907) at the north end of town. Fourteen finely chopped items go into this orange-specked beige soup. However, as the name and the sign out front imply, chicken is the mainstay of this small cafe operating out of a home on the highway. As at Mo's, you may be asked to share your table with the interesting cross section of travelers drawn to this Oregon coastal hub. It's open Mon.-Sat. 8 a.m.-8 p.m. You'll enjoy dining on the outdoor deck in summer.

Up the road a few miles, it's a safe bet that you'll find the chowder and whatever else is ordered to your liking. That's because **The Windward Inn** (3757 U.S. 101, Florence; tel. 997-8243) is one of the better restaurants in the state. Without belaboring the critical acclaim and kudos, let's just say it's good enough to make believers out of even jaded guidebook writers. Fresh-cut flowers, skylights, a wood-paneled interior, and four separate dining rooms set the stage for an imaginative and extensive menu. For the budget-conscious, the bistro dinners are lighter meals that might forestall your wallet losing too much

Devil's Elbow State Park north of Florence

MO'S

Several decades ago Mo Niemi started up a humble fish shanty on the Newport bayfront. Locals extolled her tasty and reasonably priced seafood, especially the clam chowder. Knowledge became more widespread during the filming of *Never Give an Inch,* starring Paul Newman and Henry Fonda. Restaurant scenes from this movie (based on Ken Kesey's *Sometimes a Great Notion*) were filmed here, and the stars soon became restaurant devotees. Over the years other luminaries ranging from Robert Kennedy to Bruce Springsteen joined the club. Soon outlets at Coos Bay, Florence, Lincoln City, and Otter Rock opened up, along with an annex to handle the overflow in Newport. Menus are pretty much standard in each restaurant, with fresh fish, clam chowder, and burgers the main bill of fare. Long benches around the kind of tables you'd find in a logging camp cookhouse impart an air of informality to what has become an institution on the Oregon coast.

weight here. A chicken-and-veal sausage known as *boudin blanc* ($8.50) also makes for an excellent lower-priced alternative to a full dinner. If you're into a full splurge, go with the fresh mussels broiled on the half shell with Oregon hazelnuts, Oregon peppered bacon, and Tillamook cheddar cheese ($14.75).

After dinner, have dessert at either of **BJ's Ice Cream Parlor**'s two locations (2930 U.S. 101 or 1441 Bay St., Florence; tel. 997-7286). BJ's churns out 48 flavors famous all over Oregon. Full fountain service, ice cream cakes, cheesecakes, gourmet frozen yogurt, and pies complement the cones and cups.

Driving east on ORE 126 en route to Eugene from the coast lets you follow the Siuslaw past isolated farms and lush forests topped by clearcut ridges. Shortly after leaving Florence, you come to **Mapleton**. Set at the base of the Coast Range, it's one of the rainiest burgs in the whole state. It also has two restaurants which'll evoke remembrances of things past.

The Alpha Bit Crafts Cafe (10780 ORE 126, Mapleton; 268-4311) is only 11 miles outside of Florence, but it exists in a different time and space. Started by a commune in the nearby town of Deadwood, the restaurant serves a varied menu of good ol' American food and vegetarian fare (try the grainburger) at reasonable prices. The preparations frequently include produce grown on Alpha Farm, and the 25-cent coffee puts the higher-priced coastal brews to shame. Also don't miss the home-baked cakes and pies, and the December 1991 *Life* magazine article about the commune, available upon request. Finally, the unusual local crafts and fine selection of books make Alpha Bit the cultural center of Mapleton.

A mile or two down ORE 126 is the **Gingerbread Village** (12300 ORE 126, Mapleton; tel. 268-4713). This is the kind of place your parents might have taken you when you were a kid . . . you know, a greasy spoon without the grease, serving simple, wholesome meals. While the food here is good enough to get you to Eugene, the gingerbread is unforgettable. Order it warm so the vanilla ice cream on top melts down decadently. Getting this dish to go costs a quarter more ($1.25), but the "boat" it comes in carries a disproportionately larger serving.

Events And Recreation

During the third week of May, Florence celebrates the **Rhododendron Festival,** coinciding with the bloom of these flowers which proliferate in the area. A parade, boat and slug races, a carnival, a flower show, and a five-kilometer "rhody's run" highlight the festivities. Contact the chamber of commerce for more info.

On July 4 at 2 p.m., the **National Stilt Walking Championship** starts at the corner of Maple and Bay streets in Old Town.

Ocean Dunes Golf Links (3315 Munsel Lake Rd., Florence 97439; tel. 997-3232) lets you tee off with sand dunes as a backdrop. The manicured 18-hole course has a driving range, a full pro shop, and equipment rentals on-site. A new course, **Sand Pines Golf Course,** (1050 35th St.; tel. 800-497-1937), opened to the public in April 1993. Greens fees are $35 at this Scottish links-style course, which could well be Oregon's answer to Pebble Beach.

The Harbor Theatre (1368 Bay, Old Town Florence; tel. 997-3361) charges $4 for first-run movies with discounts for seniors and kids. The showtime is 7 p.m.

Sternwheeler trips on the Siuslaw started up in 1992. The 65-foot *Westward Ho* (tel. 268-4017) docks nine miles east of U.S. 101 on ORE 126 and can be boarded there for morning tours. In the afternoon, the boat departs from the docks at Old Town. Some itineraries focus on timber-industry history (including a mill tour) in addition to the succession of historic sites along the Siuslaw between Florence and Mapleton. A morning roundtrip (9-11 a.m.) includes a light breakfast and costs $10. One-hour trips depart the Old Town dock on the hour from 2 to 5 p.m; $8 per person. Paddlewheelers along the Siuslaw were part of the two-day Eugene-to-Florence pilgrimage a century ago.

The old **stagecoach road** still exists. To find it, drive on Oregon 126 through Mapleton, avoiding the turnoff to Eugene. Instead, continue straight onto ORE 36 toward Swiss Home. In about five miles from the junction of ORE 126 and ORE 36, you'll come to an unmarked bridge over the river. Cross it and turn left at the dead end two blocks down. This one-lane stage road is unsuitable for RVs, but it certainly enables car travelers to bounce on down memory lane. It is a circuitous route crossing a number of one-lane bridges over the Siuslaw. About half of the route is gravel, but it's well-maintained. An overhanging rock, which was blasted away to give clearance to stagecoaches, is an eye-catching remnant here of bygone days. This 15-minute detour returns to ORE 126 at Richardson Bridge.

Huckleberry picking is another attraction just outside of town. Some prime pickin's are found about five miles north of Florence at the Sutton Creek Trail, which begins in the campground with the same name that's just off of U.S. 101. During late summer or fall, these berries flourish below the dense canopy of shorepine here. Rhododendrons bloom in profusion mid-May to early June. In addition to these delights, you can hike through the dunes here, which are broken up by several freshwater lakes. The Forest Service in Reedsport can answer your questions about the huckleberries and the trails here.

Information And Services

The **Florence Chamber of Commerce** (270 U.S. 101, Florence 97439; tel. 997-3128) is three blocks north of the Siuslaw River Bridge; open 9-5. Close by the junction of ORE 126 and U.S. 101 is the library. **Peace Harbor Hospital** (400 Ninth St., Florence 97439; tel. 997-3128) is open 24 hours. A dozen specialists are represented, along with an emergency room. The **post office** (770 Maple St., Florence 97439; tel. 997-2533) is open Mon.-Fri. 8-5. **Greyhound** (2107 U.S. 101, Florence 97439; tel. 997-8782) is open Mon.-Fri. 9-5, Sat. 9-1.

YACHATS AND VICINITY

Yachats (when "ya-hots," you're hot) is an Alsea Indian word which means "at the foot of the mountain," which aptly describes this resort town of 575 people in the shadow of Cape Perpetua. While the native campfires are gone now, ceremonial clamshell middens have been found on area beaches. More importantly, the legacy of the Alsea will live on forever as long as people come here to gaze in wonder at sunsets and at the fury of winter storms.

SIGHTS

Cape Perpetua

The most notable sight near Yachats, indeed on the whole central coast, is the view from 800-foot-high Cape Perpetua. Oregon's highest paved public road this close to the shoreline affords 150 miles of north-to-south visibility from the top of the headland. On a clear day, you can also see 37 miles out to sea. Prior to hiking the trail or driving to the top of Cape Perpetua, stop off at the **Siuslaw Forest Visitor Center** (mile marker 188.5, U.S. 101; tel. 547-3289) on the east side of the highway. A picture window framing a bird's-eye view of rockbound coast along with exhibits on forestry and marinelife begin your orientation to the region here. The center is open 10-5 daily, except Christmas. Personnel at the desk have maps and pamphlets about such trails as Cook's Ridge, Riggin' Slinger, and Giant Spruce, as well as directions for the auto tour to the summit. In addition, they can point the way to tidepools and berry patches.

The awe-inspiring four-mile Saint Perpetua Trail to the cape's summit is of moderate difficulty. En route, placards explain the role of wind, erosion, and fire in forest succession in this mixed-conifer ecosystem. Historic events, such as the naming of the cape by England's Captain Cook on Saint Perpetua's Day in 1778 and the devastating Columbus Day storm of 1962, are also documented.

At the crest of Cape Perpetua the **Trail of the Whispering Spruce** begins, a quarter-mile loop through the grounds of a former WW II

Coast Guard lookout built by the Civilian Conservation Corps in 1933. The southern views from the crest take in the highway and headlands as far as Coos Bay. Halfway along the path, you'll come to a WPA-built rock lean-to that makes a lofty perch for whalewatching. Beyond this ridgetop aerie the curtain of trees parts to reveal fantastic views of the shoreline between Yachats and Lincoln City as far north as Cape Foulweather.

The two-mile drive up the cape is complicated by a not-so-prominent sign on U.S. 101 indicating the turnoff, and a junction in the road midway to the summit which can lead the unsuspecting on a wild ride in the opposite direction. To begin your auto ascent, drive a hundred yards north on U.S. 101 from the visitor center and look for the steep winding spur road on the right. As you climb, you'll notice numbered roadside markers annotated with explanations about forest ecology. Halfway up, you'll come to a Y in the road. Take a hard left and follow the road another mile to the top of Cape Perpetua. If you miss the left turn here and go straight ahead, you'll soon find yourself on a 22-mile paved-over logging route to Yachats. Despite distant shorelines and mountaintops on the horizon, the butchered forests along this blacktopped "cat" trail and signposts bearing

Forest Service rationalizations for same might leave you more worried than inspired. Recent clearcuts on the opposite side of this headland facing Yachats have prompted many disgruntled locals to refer to Cape Perpetua as "Cape Clearcut."

State Parks, Coastal Waysides

Between Heceta Head and Yachats, state parks and viewpoints abound with attractions. There's so much to see here that keeping your eyes on the road in this heavily traveled section becomes a challenge.

On the way to Cape Perpetua, **Neptune State Park** has a beautiful beach and is near the 9,300-acre **Cummin's Creek Wilderness** east of U.S. 101. Scenic shorelines can also be found to the south of the cape at **Muriel O. Ponsler** and **Stonesfield Beach** waysides. Close by, there's a chance to explore tidepools and sometimes observe harbor seals at **Strawberry Hill.** The **Cape Perpetua Visitor Center** is open 9 a.m.-5 p.m. in summer with twice-daily guided walks to give the visitor info about old growth, the plants, the animals, and the tidepools (reachable by a trail heading west from the parking lot).

Just north from the junction of the Cape Perpetua road and U.S. 101 is **Devil's Churn.** Here, the tides have cut a deep fissure in a basalt embankment on the shore. While watching the whitewater torrents in this foaming cistern, beware of "sneaker waves," particularly if you venture beyond the boundaries of the **Trail of the Restless Waters.** The highlights here are the spouting horns where sea water is funneled between rocks and explodes into spray. All along this stretch of the coast, many trees appear to be leaning away from the ocean as if bent by storms. This illusion is caused by salt-laden westerlies drying out and killing the buds on the exposed side of the tree, leaving growth only on the leeward branches.

On the south bank of the Yachats River is a short but beautiful beach loop off U.S. 101. The roadbed sits astride the landscaped grounds of beach houses and a foamy sea. Tidepools and blowholes on the bank by the river's mouth are a special treat. Ocean Dr. along the opposite bank will also guide you to where the river meets the sea. It loops around wave-battered **Yachats**

State Park and heads north along the ocean, where it becomes Marine Drive. After going through a residential community, it eventually takes an easterly turn to reconnect with U.S. 101. In town the **Little Log Church Museum** (Third and Pontiac) sits a few blocks from U.S. 101. Clothing and tools from pioneer days and a working pump organ are on display along with period furnishings. The hours of operation are variable, so check the chamber of commerce.

PRACTICALITIES

Accommodations

Yachats-area lodgings take full advantage of the dramatic setting in a town they call "the Gem of the Oregon coast." For the ultimate in seclusion, **Oregon House** (94288 U.S. 101, Yachats 97498; tel. 547-3329), nine miles south of Yachats, overlooks the Pacific from a high cliff. Seven suites with private baths and kitchens, some with fireplaces, as well as one bed-and-breakfast room take advantage of forested walking trails to the beach and a glass-enclosed whalewatching tower. Except in the case of the B&B room, there is an additional charge for full breakfasts. This is the kind of place that is especially cost-effective for groups, with a unit for four at $46 and more spacious units with kitchen, fireplace, dining room, etc., for larger parties costing $66. Ask the hotel proprietors about oceanfront grottoes between here and Sea Lion Caves.

A little closer to Yachats at the beginning of the beach loop (on the south bank of the Yachats River and west of U.S. 101) are the **Shamrock Lodgettes** (Box 219, Yachats 97498; tel. 547-3312). Shamrock's beautiful parklike landscape frames a selection of individual log cabins or more conventional rooms. Stone fireplaces, in-room movies, and ocean or bay views all contribute to a relaxed get-away-from-it-all feeling. The sauna and Jacuzzi on the premises also enhance the "mellowing-out" process, which'll begin as soon as you set foot here. The much-requested cabins range between $64 and $90, while other units start at $50 and go up to $70—a small price for peace of mind.

For those looking for a budget place close to the center of town with some of the comforts of home, try **Rock Park Cottages** on W. Second (tel. 547-3214/343-4382), two blocks from the chamber of commerce and a stone's throw from Yachats State Park. Consisting of five cabins right on the beach, Rock Park has to be considered one of the better bargains on the coast. Should weather keep you inside, the wood-paneled walls hold bookshelves with reading matter and board games, and the kitchens are equipped with dishes. The price can be negotiated for multinight stays, but seems to average around $40 per night for a double, 10 dollars less in winter.

The **Fireside Motel** (U.S. 101, Box 313, Yachats 97498; tel. 547-3636) and the elegant **Adobe Resort** (see "Food" following) both overlook Smelt Sands Beach. If you appreciate all services in one compound, from dining room to gift shop, the Adobe ($60-70) gets the nod, but for slightly less money ($40-70) the Fireside's smallish rooms have more than enough amenities. In addition to ocean views, many of the rooms also have such extras as refrigerators and fireplaces. Perhaps the most appreciated little touch is the guidebook the management has put together for guest use. It can point the way to some of the area's natural attractions, including Smelt Sands and Cape Perpetua.

Campgrounds

Set along Cape Creek in the **Cape Perpetua Scenic Area** (Cape Perpetua Visitor Center, Box 274 Yachats 97498; tel. 563-3211), the Forest Service campground here has 37 sites for tents, trailers, or motor homes up to 22 feet long. Picnic tables and firegrills are provided. Flush toilets, piped water, and sanitary services are available, no reservations are necessary, and the $8-12 fee applies mid-May to late September. The Forest Service rangers put on slide-illustrated campfire talks here and at Tillicum Beach during summer months.

Just south, **Neptune State Park** has several dollar-a-night beachfront hiker/biker sites, and four miles south you can turn east off U.S. 101 and follow Forest Service Rd. 56 to get to **Ten Mile Creek.** With no reservations and no fee, this small secluded campground has four sites for tents and small RVs. You'll find firegrills, picnic tables, primitive sanitary facilities, but no piped water. It's just 15 minutes off the highway, but feels more remote.

Several miles down Ten Mile Creek is **Rock Creek** (c/o Siuslaw Forest, Waldport Ranger District, Waldport 97394; tel. 563-3211) For $6 a night you get a small out-of-the-way campground a quarter mile from the ocean. Most of the 16 sites are for tents, but a few accommodate small RVs. Firegrills and picnic tables provided; flush toilets and piped water are available.

If you're on a budget, try **Lanham Bike Camp,** which involves a hike in from Rock Creek but doesn't charge a fee. There's everything you need to make it through the night at the 10 primitive sites here, but bring your own water. Each place is open all year and doesn't require reservations.

Food

The eight restaurants in town are able to satisfy a variety of tastes and budgets. Right on the main highway **Yachats Coffee Merchants** (220 U.S. 101, Yachats; tel. 547-3100) combines reasonable prices, home-smoked meats, fresh seafood, and an array of potent coffee drinks and home-baked items. Try the alderwood-smoked Oregon chicken ($6.45) for dinner or the captain's platter of fish, shrimp, scallops, and oysters ($9.95)—only if you're *really* hungry.

Almost right across the street is **La Serre** (Second and Beach, Yachats; tel. 547-3420). A bright skylit restaurant with lots of plants creates an appropriate setting for cuisine that eschews deep-fat frying and is heavy on the whole wheat. This may not suggest gourmet continental fare, but somehow La Serre pulls it off. With entrees running the gamut from strawberry-ricotta crepes to charbroiled steaks, the menu manages to please the brie-and-chablis set as well as the health-conscious. It's not cheap, but hey, live a little!

The **Yankee Clipper** (125 Ocean Dr., Yachats; tel. 547-4004) is a tiny but charming sandwich shop overlooking the Yachats River estuary. Fresh ingredients and care go into soup and sandwich creations (try the shrimp melt) ideal for a lunch in the $5 range. Blustery days pack 'em in here for hot coffee, homemade desserts, and the angry beauty of the river meeting the sea.

Another place for a light bite and a long cup of coffee is the **New Morning Coffee House and Bookstore** (U.S. 101 and Fourth St., Yachats;

tel. 547-3848). Set on a hillside just west of U.S. 101, it gives the appearance of an old beach house with modern architectural flourishes. You can sit downstairs near the bustling espresso counter or upstairs in the extravagantly windowed bookstore. On sunny days, kick back on the outside deck the restaurant shares with the **Back Porch Gallery** (paintings, sculpture, weaving, pottery, porcelain dolls). Wherever you plop down, continental breakfast, homemade bread, and desserts ensure a happy landing.

Elaborate picnic fare is available from the **Yachats Crab and Chowder House** (131 U.S. 101, Yachats; tel. 547-4132) "To Go shop" including fresh half crab and garlic bread, rock cod and halibut fish and chips, as well as assorted breads, meats, and cheeses.

On a hill overlooking Smelt Sands Beach is the glass-enclosed **Adobe Resort** (155 U.S. 101, Yachats; tel. 547-3141), with its semicircular dining room. The setting is a great place to start the day for breakfast or end it with a romantic evening repast. Adobe breakfasts have eye-opening flair, as demonstrated by cream-cheese pancakes and intriguing variations on French toast and omelettes. Later in the day, the somewhat pricey fare here includes imaginative dishes like Oregon shrimp Sonora style (shrimp, onions, chilies, sour cream, and melted cheeses wrapped in a tortilla), and fettuccine in a garlic cream sauce with assorted shellfish. After dinner take a drink up to the Crow's Nest Lounge. Make reservations ahead of time in this acclaimed dining room on the north end of town.

Events
During the Yachats **smelt fry** held the second week of July, up to 700 pounds of this sardine-like fish are served on the grounds of Yachats School. Yachats is one of the few (perhaps the only) places in the world blessed with a run of oceangoing smelt. Information is available from the chamber of commerce.

The **Yachats Kite Festival** falls in November when the winds really kick up. Shamrock Lodgettes proprietor Robert Oxley has all the info. Contact him via the hotel or at Box 364, Yachats 97498.

Information And Services
The **Yachats Chamber of Commerce** (Box 174, Yachats 97498; tel. 547-3530) has a central location on the highway (right across from the Coffee Merchants) and a loquacious staff. Ask them about fishing, rockhounding, birdwatching, and beachcombing in the area. Next door, **On the Rise** bakery offers grainy goodies to take with you on these journeys. The **Greyhound** stop is also in the parking lot of the bakery/chamber of commerce/food market complex. The Yachats **post office** (Yachats 97498) is right behind La Serre.

WALDPORT AND VICINITY

Originally a stronghold of the Alsea Indians, Waldport also has had incarnations as a gold rush town and lumber port. In addition, a decade ago it gained an unseemly notoriety for being a hotbed of environmental activism. When locals rallied against the spraying of dioxin-based defoliants in Coast Range forests, Waldport attracted national media attention. These chemicals were used by the lumber industry to eliminate blackberries, vine maples, and other vegetation that impede the growth of the Douglas fir. When the defoliants were linked to abnormally high numbers of birth defects and miscarriages, citizens rallied successfully for a government ban on the toxins.

This otherwise quiet town, whose name in German means "Forest Port," is today possessed of more mundane distinctions. A chamber of commerce flier touts Waldport's livability, suggesting that the town's "relative obscurity" has spared it the fate of more crowded tourist towns. This may also be explained by a nondescript main drag that gives no hint of surrounding beaches and prime fishing spots. For those passing through, the town provides a low-cost alternative to the name destinations; in Waldport you won't have to fight for a parking spot or make reservations months in advance.

ACTIVITIES

Waldport's recreational raison d'être is fishing. World-class clamming and Dungeness crabbing in Alsea Bay and the Alsea River's famous salmon, steelhead, and cutthroat trout runs account for a high percentage of visits to the area.

The **Alsea Bridge Historical Information Center** (Alsea Bridge; tel. 563-2133) in Waldport is open Wed.-Sun. 9 a.m.-4 p.m. Displays about transportation methods along the central coast since the 1800s and info on the Alsea tribe are worth a quick stop. Admission is free.

Seal Rock State Park, four miles north of town, attracts beachcombers and agate-hunters as well as folks who come to explore the tidepools and observe the seals on offshore rocks. The Park's name derives from a seal-shaped rock in the cluster of interesting formations in the tidewater.

Seven miles east of Waldport are the nine square miles of **Drift Creek Wilderness.** Within this area are stands of old-growth forest. Here you can see hemlocks hundreds of years old. These trees are the "climax forest" in the Douglas fir ecosystem. They seldom reach old-growth status since the timber industry tends to replant only fir seedlings after logging operations. There is also perhaps the largest population of spotted owls in the state here. Steep ridges and their drainages as well as small meadows make up the topography. The trailhead closest to Waldport is the **Harris Ranch Trail,** which descends 1,200 feet in two miles to a meadow near Drift Creek. The wilderness is administered by the Siuslaw National Forest— Waldport Ranger Station (tel. 563-3211), which can supply specific directions to the different trailheads into this increasingly rare ecosystem (see "Information and Services"). The local access to Harris Ranch and Horse Creek trails leaves ORE 34 at the Alsea River crossing seven miles east of Waldport.

PRACTICALITIES

Accommodations

"Cottage" is a word often heard between Yachats and Waldport. It may be a duplex or self-contained cabin-type lodging, generally by a beach. The price ranges between $30 and $65 for units with kitchen facilities, fireplaces, and oceanfront locations. Cottages with all of the above include **Deane's Oceanside Lodge** (8800 S.W. U.S. 101, Waldport 97374; tel. 547-3321), **Terry-a-While Motel** (7160 S.W. U.S. 101, Waldport 97374; tel. 563-3377), **Sea Stones Cottages** (6317 S.W. U.S. 101, Waldport 97374; tel. 547-3118), the **Edgewater Cottages** (3978 S.W. U.S. 101, Waldport, 97374; tel. 563-2240), and **Cape Cod Cottages** (4150 S.W. U.S. 101, Waldport 97374; tel. 563-2106).

Camping

Two premium campgrounds sit about four miles south of Waldport on U.S. 101 along the beach. **Beachside State Park** (reserve at Box 1350, Newport 97365; tel. 563-3023) is located near a half mile of beach not far from Alsea Bay and Alsea River. This is a paradise for rock fishermen, surfcasters, clammers, and crabbers. For $11-12 a night from mid-April to mid-October, there are 60 tent sites and 20 sites for RVs up to 30 feet long. With all the amenities, including a laundromat and hot showers, Beachside fills fast, so reserve early.

A half mile down U.S. 101, the Forest Service has comparable site offerings at **Tillicum Beach.** Set right along the ocean, the campground is open all year and doesn't require reservations. For $7 a night you have the full range of creature comforts plus ranger campfire programs in summer. Forest Service roads from here access Coast Range fishing streams, which are detailed in a Forest Service map. You'll also appreciate the strip of vegetation blocking the cool evening winds that whip up off the ocean here.

Should Beachside and Tillicum be filled to overflowing, you might want to set up a base camp in the Coast Range along ORE 34—especially if you have fishing or hiking in the Drift Creek Wilderness in mind. Just go east of Waldport 17 miles on ORE 34 to **Blackberry Campground** (Siuslaw National Forest, Alsea Ranger District, Alsea, 97324; tel. 487-5811). There are 33 sites open May-Sept. for tents and RVs, most of them on the river. A boat ramp, flush toilets, and piped water are on-site. The Kozy Kove Kafe (see "Food") is eight miles away.

Food

Forget fine dining in Waldport. This is an eat 'n' run town. Unless you want to drive to Yachats, **Bumps 'n' Grinds** (225 Maple St., Waldport; tel. 563-5769) is the only place in the area for gourmet coffee. They also have bakery specialties, lunch (chicken enchiladas are good), and Alsea Bay views off the deck. For lunch and dinner, **At'sa Pizza** (Seastrand Mall, Waldport; tel. 563-3232) is a favorite with the locals. Premium ingredients go into their pizza, calzone, and pasta dishes. The homemade garlic rolls and "grinders" (submarine or hero sandwiches) are great for picnics, and like everything else here are moderately priced. There is also an outlet in Newport (tel. 265-6000).

At the south end of Waldport across from the Visitor Information Center is another local franchise. Like **Leroy's Blue Whale** in Yachats (tel. 547-3397), the Waldport branch of this restaurant (tel. 563-3445) is located right on U.S. 101. These self-described "family restaurants" can be counted on for low prices and a varied menu of American food. Culinary flourishes are limited to seafood dishes such as squid rings and prawns sautéed in wine and butter. These places stay open in January when many of the other eateries in nearby Yachats close early or suspend operation for the month.

Also at the south end of town on U.S. 101 is **Moby Dick's Waldport Seafoods** (tel. 563-HOOK). If you're holed up in a cottage with a kitchen or camping, you'll appreciate fresh fish at a good price. The cooked crab here is exceptional, attesting to Waldport's status as a leading Dungeness crab fishery, and the smoked fish also makes a great to-go snack.

If you're interested in a unique dining experience, follow ORE 34 along the Alsea River for nine miles to a most unlikely site for a good restaurant. Attached to a trailer court and convenience store is the **Kozy Kove Kafe** (9464 ORE 34, Tidewater 97390; tel. 528-3251 or 800-388-KOVE). The dining room and lounge float on a bed of logs by a riverbank and are well placed to observe Australian black swans, elk, salmon jumping in September, and other wildlife. Breakfasts are hearty, and lunch and dinner focus on fresh seafood and steak. Clam chowder and strawberry shortcake are recommended accompaniments. There are also Mexican (try the "fajitas with the flame") and Italian entrees to add spice to this retreat from the ordinary.

Information And Services

At the south end of Waldport on the west side of U.S. 101 is the **Visitor Information Center** (tel. 563-2133). It's open 9-4 daily during summer. The **Siuslaw National Forest—Waldport Ranger Station** (Waldport Ranger District, Waldport 97374; tel. 563-3211) can provide information on area camping and hiking. A **post office** (Waldport 97374; tel. 563-3011) can be found on ORE 34, one block east of U.S. 101. Close by on ORE 34 is the **public library**, which is open Mon.-Fri. 1-4:30, Sat. 11-2. ORE 34 itself is a scenic 60-mile access road to Corvallis.

Gene-O's Guide Service (Box 43, Waldport 97374; tel. 563-3171) calls on 35 years of experience to help you reel in salmon and steelhead. **Crestview Hills Golf Course** (1680 Crestline Dr., Waldport 97374; tel. 563-3020) has nine holes and a pro shop a mile south of town.

The **Greyhound** stop is at the Waldport Pharmacy, across from the junction of ORE 34 and U.S. 101.

NEWPORT AND VICINITY

The discovery of a tiny sweet-tasting oyster in Yaquina Bay during the 1860s was the first major impetus to growth and settlement in Newport. These tasty morsels which delighted diners in San Francisco and at New York's Waldorf-Astoria Hotel are almost gone now, but their port of embarkation is still bustling with activity. New factories to process surimi (a fish paste popular in Japan) and whiting are expected to provide hundreds of jobs here, and a state-of-the-art aquarium will bring in the tourist dollar. The shops, galleries, and restaurants along Newport's historic bayfront, together with the Performing Arts Center and quieter charm of Nye Beach, keep up a tourism tradition that goes back over a century. Today, Newport boasts more oceanfront hotel rooms than any place between San Francisco and Seattle, except perhaps for Lincoln City. This can make for traffic jams on holiday weekends, but it's a small price to pay for proximity to some of the coast's best agate-hunting beaches, cultural programs, and restaurants.

SIGHTS

Sea Gulch Trail

In addition to the diverse appeals of Newport, the area is also distinguished by a handful of attractions that skirt the line between the tasteful and the tawdry. This tightrope is skillfully walked at **Sea Gulch** (along U.S. 101; tel. 563-2727), a collection of chainsaw sculptures on the east side of the highway five miles north of Waldport. The creator of these red cedar Rodins has a light touch with his sawblades as well as a cartoonist's flair in his art. Western and fantasy themes are humorously hacked out on the quarter-mile Sea Gulch Trail, where anthropomorphic bears and bigfoot vie for attention with cowboys, gnomes, Rip Van Winkle, and Mother Goose. It's open daily 8 a.m.-7 p.m. in winter, and closes an hour or two later in summer. The admission is $3.50, with discounts for seniors and kids.

Mark O. Hatfield Marine Science Center

Just prior to crossing the bridge into downtown Newport, head east on the road that parallels the bay to the Hatfield Marine Science Center (Marine Science Drive, Newport 97365; tel. 867-0100). At the door to greet you is an octopus in an open tank pointing the way to oceanography exhibits and a "hands on" area where you can experience the feel of starfish, anemones, and other sea creatures. The back hallway has educational dioramas and there's a theater showing marine-science films throughout the day. If you proceed left from the octopus tank, you'll see tanks with different sea ecosystems. Beyond the walls of the museum, the center's Seataugua program offers field trips each August (check with the front desk for details). Admission is free and it's open daily 10 a.m.-6 p.m. in summer and daily 10 a.m.-4 p.m the rest of the year. This facility is a low-key but interesting alternative to the Oregon Coast Aquarium, which is located less than a mile south.

The Oregon Coast Aquarium

The Oregon Coast Aquarium (2820 S.E. Ferry Rd., Box 2000, Newport 97305; tel. 867-3474) features 40,000 square feet of galleries devoted to wetland communities, near-shore and marine ecosystems, and an environmental center. A whale theater and four acres of sea lions, sea otters, tidepools, undersea caves, and the largest walk-through seabird aviary in the Americas also grace this facility. Of the 200 species of Pacific Northwest fish, birds, and mammals on display here, don't miss the sea otters, spotted ratfish, wolf eels, leopard sharks, lion's mane jellyfish, and the tufted puffins. The younger set will be especially fascinated by the sea cave (with simulated wave action), which houses a resident octopus.

The research facilities of the nearby Hatfield Marine Science Center effectively complement the educational concerns of the Coast Aquarium. While the new facility's raison d'être is public outreach, it's more low-key than the "high-viz" floating zoos commonly associated with other aquariums. In other words, the interpretive placards, videos, and tape presentations are more essential to the experience here than at your typical undersea peep show.

Yaquina Bay Harbor, Newport: very much a working neighborhood

In addition to leaving here with a heightened understanding of the coast biome, you might also come away with something from the museum shop's first-rate collection of regional books and oceanographic tomes or perhaps some crystals or gemstones. The Ferry Slip Cafe is also on-site, emphasizing such Oregon fare as Tillamook dairy products, seasonal fruits, and seafood. The aquarium is open 10 a.m.-4:30 p.m. October-May, 9 a.m.-6 p.m. the rest of the year. Prices are $7 for adults, $5 for students, $3 for kids 4-12, and those under four get in free. To get there going north on U.S. 101, turn right on 32nd St. just before the Yaquina Bay Bridge and follow Ferry Slip Rd. to the parking lot.

Lincoln County
Historical Society Museum

After crossing the bridge, a half-hour stop at the Lincoln County Historical Society Museum (545 S.W. Ninth St., Newport 97365; tel. 265-7509) is recommended. It's located a half block east of the chamber of commerce on U.S. 101. The logging, farming, and maritime exhibits (particularly Newport shipwrecks) are interesting, but the Siletz Indian baskets and other Indian artifacts steal the show.

The museum flier on coast historical sights details the hardships of inadequate housing, insufficient food, and poor medical facilities which plagued the diverse tribes that made up the Confederated Siletz Indian Reservation. These dozen tribes were defeated during the Rogue Indian Wars and other conflicts of the 1850s. In 1856, 2,000 of these coastal natives were marched to a north coast reservation site. En route, they were sometimes forced to stand shivering in freezing rain until the tide moved out, permitting them to cross a beach. It's no wonder that at the end of one year their numbers had dwindled to 600.

The museum is open Tues.-Sun. Hours are 10 a.m-5 p.m., June-Sept.; 11 a.m.-4 p.m. Oct.-May. Admission is free. Just north of the log cabin that houses the Lincoln County collection is the **Burrows House**. This is part of the museum and has the same hours, but focuses exclusively on pioneer life. Antique buffs will especially enjoy these exhibits.

The Bayfront

The bayfront is easy to miss. After crossing the Yaquina Bay Bridge, look for the green marker pointing east at the intersection of U.S. 101 and Hubert St. Several right turns take you down the hill to Bay Blvd., the bayfront's main drag. Forget about parking anywhere here unless you arrive early. Spots close by the boulevard can often be found, however, along the hillside access route to downtown, Canyon Way. Just curb your wheels to inhibit rolling. One of the first things that'll strike you about the bayfront is that it's a working neighborhood. The cries of fishmongers purveying wharfside walkaway cocktails and the smells of fish-packing plants and canneries fill the air as you stroll the boulevard. On the waterfront, you can watch fishermen step off charter boats with their salmon catch and head to Jack's for canning, or observe vessels laden with everything from wood products to whalewatchers out in the bay.

The facilities of Oregon's second-largest fishing port eventually give way to restaurants, shops, and galleries. **Ripley's Believe It or Not! The Waxworks,** and **The Undersea Gardens** are worth a look should the other appeals of Newport pall.

Yaquina Bay State Park
While it's difficult to get a bad meal on the bayfront and there is no shortage of true objets d'art sold here, sooner or later you'll want respite from crowds and commercialism. Relief is just a boat ride away, with at least a dozen reputable fishing charter and whalewatching excursion operators here to serve you. Landlubbers are advised to drive under the bridge to Yaquina Bay State Park for sweeping sea and bay views. There's also the old **Yaquina Bay Lighthouse** (tel. 867-8451), built in 1871 and abandoned three years later. It seems materials intended for lighthouse construction at Otter Crest were mistakenly delivered to this location, which proved to be a poor site. The restored Yaquina Bay beacon, replete with period furniture, is open daily noon-5 p.m. between Memorial Day and Labor Day; the rest of the year it's just open weekends. The chance to hear about the ghost here is alone worth the modest price of admission (50 cents).

Better yet, pick up a reprint of the first written account (1899) of the ghost story at the Lincoln County Museum (see above), then round out your perspective with the century-old pictures on the lighthouse walls, which will convey the bleakness of the treeless, windswept cliff where this lighthouse was erected. This is important because the spit-and-polish facade of the restoration surrounded by stands of coastal pines would be an inappropriate setting for a ghost story. Without ruining the tale for you, let's just say that if you stand outside the lighthouse on a dark, windy night and hear a maiden's wail, don't linger.

Finally, Yaquina Bay State Park is a good place to have a picnic, or you can descend the trails to the beach and dig for razor clams.

Nye Beach
Another breather from the rampant commercialism on the bayfront and along U.S. 101's business district is Nye Beach. Located a mile north from the bayfront on the western side of U.S. 101 (look for signs on the highway), this one-time favorite retreat for wealthy Portlanders has undergone a revival. Rough times and rougher weather had reduced luxurious beach houses here to a cluster of weatherbeaten shacks until a new performing arts center went up several years back. On the heels of the development of this first-rate cultural facility, the conversion of a 1910 hotel into a kind of literary hostel (see "Practicalities") encouraged other restorations. Culture vultures, beach lovers, and people-watchers will want to come to Nye Beach soon, before the shadows of nearby resort hotels grow larger.

Agate Hunting
Agate hunting after winter storms is a passion here. Prior to the ice ages, metals, oxides, and silicates were fused together to create the type of quartz. Red, amber, and blue tones sometimes form stripes or spots on these rocks. The best place to find these treasures is on the beach north of Hotel Newport, appropriately called **Agate Beach.** The beach north of Seal Rock as well as area estuaries and streambeds are also worth a look Oct.-May. Procure the free pamphlet *Agates: Their Formation and How to Hunt for Them* from the chamber of commerce before setting out.

Toledo And Sights North
Aficionados of antiquities can head six miles east of town on ORE 20 to Toledo, where "junque" shops abound. This small town's fortunes have risen and fallen with the timber cut. At one time, the world's largest spruce mill was here. In fact, all of the spruce wood for Howard Hughes's *Spruce Goose* (most of the Spruce Goose is actually Wisconsin birch) was shipped from the Toledo mill. In the era of big timber's swan song, dealers of collectibles have sprouted up to take advantage of coastbound traffic

from the Willamette Valley. Most of the antique shops are located on Main Street.

North of Newport is **Yaquina Head Light-house** (turn west at Welton's Townhouse). It is Oregon's tallest and second-oldest lighthouse (1873) still in active service, but it's closed to the public. However, the **Yaquina Head Out-standing Natural Area** is open during daylight hours, with an observation deck providing views of seals, sea lions, and shorebirds. Of late, this look-out has also had whale sightings throughout the summer. Low tide reveals sea stars, purple urchins, anemones, and hermit crabs. Tools dat-ing back 5,000 years have been unearthed at Yaquina Head. Many were made from elk and deer antler and bone as well as stone. Clam and mussel shells from middens in the area evidence a diet rich in shellfish for the area's ancient in-habitants.

Beaches north of town include **Agate Beach,** famed for its gemstone-hunting opportunities, **Moolack Beach,** a favorite with kite flyers, and **Beverly Beach,** where 20-million-year-old fos-sils have been found in the sandstone cliffs above the shore. Beverly Beach also attracts waders, unique for Oregon's chilly waters. Off-shore sandbars temper the waves and the weather so it's not as rough nor as cold as many coastal locales.

ACTIVITIES

Sampling Local Fare

Despite the high cost of such local delicacies as Yaquina oysters and Oregon wines, these gourmet treats needn't set you back much if you visit some of Newport's tasting rooms. On the road to Toledo about eight miles east of the bayfront, the **Oregon Oyster Company** (6878 Bay Rd.; tel. 265-3078) is the only remaining commercial outlet of Yaquina Bay oysters, on sale 9 a.m.-4 p.m. daily. Visitors are welcome to observe the farming and processing of these succulent shellfish. Before you leave, try the smoked oysters on a stick. Wash your oysters down with a bayfront bacchanal, courtesy of the tasting room at **Alpine Vineyard** (818 S.W. Bay Blvd.; tel. 265-6843), open from mid-June to mid-September.

Fishing Charters

Charter companies here are numerous. In ad-dition to the whalewatching charters (average cost $15 for a two-hour trip) listed in this chap-ter's introduction, salmon and bottom fishing average $30-40 for a four-to-five-hour run. Some local outfits include **Sea Gull Charters** (343 S.W. Bay Blvd.; tel. 265-7441), **Newport Sport-fishing at the Embarcadero Dock** (1000 S.E. Bay Blvd.; tel. 265-7558), and **Newport Tradewinds** (653 S.W. Bay Blvd.; tel. 265-2101). Sea Gull and Tradewinds also offer whalewatching at $14-18 per person.

Natural Highs By The Sea

For those who prefer to take matters into their own hands, the **clamming** and **Dungeness crabbing** are superlative in Yaquina Bay. If you haven't done this before, a local tackle shop will rent crabpots or rings and offer instruction. The best time to dig clams is at an extremely low tide. Tide tables are available from the chamber of commerce and many local businesses.

And if you're the kind who just likes to watch, **Yaquina Birders and Naturalists** (tel. 265-2965) welcomes newcomers on its free weekly hikes. This group sponsors monthly outings on the third weekend of the month except during July and August. To really get down, rent diving equipment ($50) and get tips from **Deep Sea John's** (South Jetty Rd.; tel. 867-3742). John can direct you to sheltered coves north of Depoe Bay. Whalewatching and scenic flights can be negotiated with **Bertea Aviation** (tel. 867-7767) at Newport Airport, three miles south of the Yaquina Bay Bridge.

Sports

Swimming and **tennis** enthusiasts are not served only by resort facilities. The city of New-port operates an indoor swimming pool at N.W. 12th St., (tel. 265-7770). In addition, you can raise a racquet at six public outdoor tennis courts and several privately owned indoor courts. The public courts are located at N.E. Fourth and Benton streets and Bay Creek Rd., one block north of the public swimming pool. While its name might evoke visions of that other course on the 17-mile Drive between Monterey and Carmel, the **Agate Beach Golf Course** (just north of Newport on U.S. 101; tel. 265-7331) is more on the order of a nine-hole pitch-and-putt course. True devotees can go 17 miles north to **Salishan Lodge** (tel. 764-3632) to play an 18-hole award-winning course set in the foothills of the Coast Range. The greens fee ranges between $25 and $38, depending on the time of year, and club rental is $15. Keep in mind that this is a Scottish links course where the roughs are really rough.

The Arts
The **Newport Performing Arts Center** (777 W. Olive; tel. 265-9231), the coast's largest, hosts local and national entertainment in the 400-seat Alice Silverman Theatre and the smaller Studio Theatre. At the same address is the **Oregon Coast Council for the Arts,** which puts out a free monthly newsletter and has ticket info on the previously mentioned venues, as well as the **Newport Visual Arts Center** (239 N.W. Beach Dr.; tel. 265-5123). If you care to take in a flick, **Newport Cinema** (5836 North Coast Hwy.) and **Midway Theatre** (453 South Coast Hwy.; tel. 265-2111) will do the trick.

PRACTICALITIES

Accommodations
The cliché "something for everybody" might literally be the case as far as places to stay in Newport go. A vast network of accommodations can be found in every price range here. Here's one worthy of special mention:

The **Sylvia Beach Hotel** (267 N.W. Cliff; tel. 265-5428) combines the camaraderie of a hostel with the intimate charm of a bed and breakfast. Built in the era when the Corvallis-to-Yaquina Bay train and seven-seater Studebaker touring cars from Portland ferried the newly wed and the nearly dead to Nye Beach, this hostelry was considered the height of luxury. Known as the Cliff House and later on as the Gilmore Hotel, even a "Honeymoon Capitol of Oregon" sobriquet could not forestall it eventually being overshadowed by newer, more elaborate resorts.

Its rebirth as the Sylvia Beach Hotel was expedited by a national historic landmark designation and a literary theme that has attracted an enthusiastic following. The 20 guest rooms

have been named after different authors and furnished with decor evocative of each respective literary legacy. The Edgar Allen Poe Room, for instance, has a pendulum guillotine blade, stuffed ravens, and who knows what else, given Poe's recurring theme of cementing family relations. The Tennessee Williams Room sets the stage with a ceiling fan, a glass menagerie, and mosquito netting, while the Agatha Christie Room drops such clues as shoes underneath the curtains and capsules marked poison in the medicine cabinet.

The Sylvia Beach would be just another cute idea were it not for an imaginative innkeeper who even facilitates guest interactions. This often comes to pass over highly acclaimed nouvelle cuisine in the oceanfront restaurant, **Tables of Content,** thanks to a game called Two Truths and a Lie. Guests seated at long tables regale each other with several stories, the object being to distinguish which one is true. If this doesn't break the ice, there's hot wine served in the library at 10 p.m., which often leads to conversations far into the night.

Most of the rooms run $60-85, with oceanfront suites featuring a fireplace and deck going for $130. All these rates include a full breakfast and reflect double occupancy. Single patrons pay $10 less. The fact that no smoking, pets, young children, or radios are allowed on the premises should also be mentioned. And if you're looking for a budget room, Sylvia Beach features dormitory bunk beds for $20 per night. Even if you don't stay here, you're invited to come by for a look at unoccupied rooms whose doors are always left open for this purpose. If nothing else, have a meal at the Tables of Content. There's a nice view of the breakers, good company, and not overly spendy Northwest cuisine.

To get there, turn off U.S. 101 on N.W. Third and follow it down to the beach, where N.W. Third and Cliff streets meet. Then, look for a large four-story dark green wooden structure with a red roof on a bluff above the surf.

Campgrounds
Sites at **South Beach** (Box 1350, Newport 97365; tel. 867-4715) and **Beverly Beach** (Star Route North, Box 684, Newport 97365; tel. 265-7655) state parks could well be the most popular places to stay of their kind on the Oregon

NEWPORT ACCOMMODATIONS

B.W. Windjammer Hallmark Resort, 744 S.W. Elizabeth, tel. 265-8853, $75-105, wheelchair access, ocean view, restaurant/lounge, fireplaces, pets, kitchenettes.

City Center Motel, 538 S.W. Coast Highway 101, tel. 265-7381, $26-44, pets, kitchenettes.

El Rancho Motel, 1435 N. Coast Highway 101, tel. 265-5192, $37-40, pets, kitchenettes, near playground.

Embarcadero Resort Hotel, 1000 S.E. Bay Blvd., tel. 265-8521, $66-162, bay view, laundry, restaurant/lounge, covered pool, kitchenettes.

The Hotel Newport, 3019 N. Coast Highway 101, tel. 265-9411, $64-94, wheelchair access, ocean view, pool, restaurant/lounge, nonsmoking rooms, live entertainment.

Little Creek Cove, 3641 N.W. Oceanview Dr., tel. 265-8587, $72-85, ocean view, fireplaces, kitchenettes.

Money Saver Motel, 861 S.W. Coast Highway 101, tel. 265-2277, $30-65, kitchenettes, laundry, nonsmoking rooms.

Moolack Shores Motel, 8835 N. Coast Highway 101, tel. 265-2326, $75-99, wheelchair access, ocean view, fireplaces, kitchenettes, small and secluded.

Newport Motor Inn, 1311 N. Coast Highway 101, tel. 265-8516, $37-40, pets, nonsmoking rooms, restaurant/lounge.

Park Motel, 1106 S.W. 9th St., tel. 265-2234, $40-65, kitchenettes.

Penny Saver Motel, 710 N. Coast Highway 101, tel. 265-6631, $32-46, kitchenettes, nonsmoking rooms, complimentary continental breakfast.

Puerto Nuevo Inn, 544 S.W. Coast Highway 101, tel. 265-5767, $40-100, wheelchair access, nonsmoking rooms, complimentary continental breakfast.

Sands Motor Lodge, 206 N. Coast Highway 101, tel. 265-5321, $28-40, kitchenettes, pets, nonsmoking rooms, laundry.

Shilo Inn, 536 S.W. Elizabeth, tel. 265-7701, $80-132, wheelchair access, ocean view, pets, covered pool, laundry, restaurant/lounge, complimentary continental breakfast.

Surf 'n' Sand Motel, 8143 N. Coast Highway 101, tel. 265-2215, $54-87, ocean view, fireplaces, pets, kitchenettes.

Sylvia Beach Hotel, 267 N.W. Cliff St., tel. 265-5428, $55-125, wheelchair access, ocean view, pool, restaurant/lounge, nonsmoking rooms.

Tides Inn, 715 S.W. Bay St., tel. 265-7202, $35-100, ocean view, pets, kitchenettes.

Val-U Inn Motel, 531 S.W. Fall St., tel. 265-6203, $40-115, wheelchair access, ocean view, laundry, restaurant/lounge, nonsmoking rooms, complimentary continental breakfast.

Viking's Cottages, 729 N.W. Coast St., tel. 265-2477, $50-85, ocean view, fireplaces, pets, kitchenettes.

Waves Motel, 820 N.W. Coast Highway 101, tel. 265-4661, $39-75, ocean view, nonsmoking rooms, complimentary continental breakfast.

Whaler Motel, 155 S.W. Elizabeth, tel. 265-9261, $73-89, wheelchair access, ocean view, pets, kitchenettes, nonsmoking rooms, complimentary continental breakfast.

Willers Motel, 754 S.W. Coast Highway 101, tel. 265-2241, $36-75, wheelchair access, ocean view, laundry, nonsmoking rooms.

coast. The absence of other camping in the area and the special features of each campground explain their appeal.

Beverly Beach's 152 tent sites, 127 RV spaces, and hiker/biker campground ($2) are set seven miles north of Newport on the east side of the highway in a mossy glade. Across the road is a tunnel leading to a beach. **Devil's Punchbowl** and **Otter Crest** are one and two miles up the highway, respectively. All the amenities, including a cafe, are provided for $15-17 per night, and they're open all year.

South Beach State Park is located two miles south of town along the beach, with opportunities for fishing, agate hunting, and hiking. It has the full range of creature comforts, including a laundromat. It's open mid-April to late October at $15-17 per night (hiker and biker spaces $2).

Food

This is a town for serious eaters—folks who know good food and don't mind paying a tad more for it. It's also the kind of place where there are wharfside vendors as well as fast-food joints and a 24-hour Safeway (220 U.S. 101; tel. 265-2930) to do it on the cheap. Since you'll probably be spending most of your time at either Nye Beach or the bayfront, eateries in those neighborhoods highlight this section.

The bayfront is where Mohava Niemi, a Siletz Indian, opened the original **Mo's** (622 S.W. Bay Blvd.; tel. 263-9411) several decades ago. When word got out about the good food and low prices, Mo's small homey place soon had more business than it could handle. In response to the overflow, **Mo's Annex** (tel. 265-7512) was created across the street. While both establishments feature such favorites as oyster stew and peanut butter cream pie, the Annex bay window has the nicer view. Other ways to enjoy quality and quantity here include prime rib specials ($13.95 on Saturday) and an all-you-can-eat seafood buffet held the last Friday of every month ($6.95).

Champagne Sunday brunch overlooking the bay at the **Embarcadero** dining room (1000 S.E. Bay Blvd.; tel. 265-8521) lets you fill up on all the breakfast entrees, fresh seafood, and bubbly you can handle for $12.95. This is a good deal in what is otherwise a high-ticket restaurant. Reservations are recommended between 10 a.m. and 2 p.m.

Another fancy but flexibly priced alternative is a place which earned the *Pacific Northwest* magazine best seafood award, **Canyon Way Bookstore and Restaurant** (1216 S.W. Canyon Way; tel. 265-8319). Instead of going the haute cuisine route (if you must, the famous baked Yaquina Bay oysters cost $14.95), the budget-conscious might prefer to feast on homemade quiche and croissants from the carryout shop after browsing the wide-ranging selection of travel titles in the front room bookstore. These can be savored with a cup of espresso. In addition to the bakery selections in the carryout shop, there is other low-priced luncheon fare. In the evening, early dinners (available 5-6 p.m. only) for $8.95 almost halve the later menu prices for the same order, and smaller but still substantial "light dinners" go for $9.95. You'll also appreciate little extras such as an extensive wine and beer list, outdoor patio dining, and works by local artists adorning Canyon Way's walls.

The **Whale's Tale** (452 S.W. Bay Blvd.; tel. 265-8660) is another bayfront restaurant that has great food at all meals, but is more cost-effective at breakfast and lunch. Eggs Newport ($7) will keep you going all day: local Oregon shrimp and two poached eggs on an English muffin topped with béarnaise sauce and accompanied with home fries. The poppyseed pancakes are also first-rate.

Night owls will be grateful for the **Pip Tide's Restaurant and Lounge** (8365 S.W. Bay Blvd.; tel. 265-7797). Besides a 24-hour restaurant, they have low-stakes blackjack tables and live rock 'n' roll bands.

Also on N.W. Beach Dr. is the **Chowder Bowl** (728 N.W. Beach Dr., Nye Beach; tel. 265-7477), with another location on the bayfront (434 S.W. Bay Blvd.; 265-5575); their clam chowder ($2.50) or salad bar with chowder and garlic bread ($4.95) are favorites with hikers and coast route bikers. But the best deal of all for the trencherperson is the Tuesday night all-you-can-eat fish and chips with salad bar for $9.95. The chowder is also touted as the best in the West by locals.

Next door, the **Sand Bar** is a loud and crowded hangout for friendly fisherfolk. Up and over a block to the east is the prominent Italian-flag facade of **Don Petrie's Italian Food Company** (613 N.W. Third, Nye Beach; tel. 265-3663). This place evokes San Francisco's North Beach pasta houses, offering filling manicotti and fettuccine dinners for $6-9. Try the specialty of the house, seafood lasagna. The pesto at this restaurant adds much to certain dishes.

Events

The biggest bash here is the **Newport Seafood and Wine Festival,** which presents these palate pleasers, along with music and crafts, at the Newport Marina at South Beach (across Yaquina Bay from the bayfront). A huge tent joins the exhibition hall wherein festival goers wash down delights from the deep with Oregon vintages. The second event of note is **Loyalty Days and Sea Fair** in early May, focusing on sailboat races, a chicken feed, and a parade. Call the chamber for updates.

Outside of town, the **Siletz Powwow** takes place on the second weekend of August. It brings together tribes from all over the Northwest to nearby Siletz for a celebration of the reenfranchisement of the Siletz tribe and reservation. Crafts, food, and traditional dancing spice up this event. Siletz can be reached via ORE 20 (Bay Rd.), which will take you to Toledo. At the crossroads, follow ORE 229 eight miles to Siletz. Contact the Siletz Smokehouse (see "Depoe Bay") for more details.

Information And Services

The Newport Chamber of Commerce (S.W. U.S. 101, Newport 97365; tel. 800-263-7844) has lots of literature available. The *Comprehensive Guide to Services* is the most helpful pamphlet of its kind made available by coastal cities. A booklet on agate hunting is also recommended. The office is open daily 8:30-5, except Nov.-Jan., when there are no weekend hours.

Greyhound (956 W. 10th St.; tel. 265-2253) handles 'Hound service along U.S. 101 and the **Valley Retriever** (tel. 265-2253) feeder line service from the Willamette Valley along U.S. 20.

Given the size of this city, there's more likelihood of calling the city **police** (tel. 265-5352) than in many other coastal locales. Other useful numbers might include **Pacific Communities Hospital** (tel. 265-2244) and the **ambulance** service (tel. 265-3175). The Coast Guard **weather** phone is tel. 265-5511. The **library** (35 N.W. Nye St.; tel. 265-2153) is open Mon.-Thurs. 10 a.m.-8 p.m., Fri.-Sat. 1-6, and Sun. 1-4. The **post office** (310 S.W. Second St., Newport 97365; tel. 265-5542) is open Mon.-Fri. 8:30-5.

NORTH TO DEPOE BAY

The expanse of flat beaches and sandstone bluffs north of Newport takes on a more dramatic aspect after you leave the highway at the Otter Crest Loop six miles south of Depoe Bay.

Devil's Punchbowl

At the swirling waters of **Devil's Punchbowl,** an urnlike sandstone formation has been sculpted by centuries of tidewater flooding what had been a cave until the roof collapsed. The inexorable process continues today, thanks to the ebb and flow of the Pacific through two openings in the wall of the cauldron. The state park viewpoint sits at a low elevation above the spectacle, giving you a ringside seat on this frothy confrontation between rock and tide. When the water recedes, you can see purple sea urchins and starfish in the **Marine Gardens** tidepools 100 feet to the north.

To the south of the Punchbowl vantage point are picnic tables and a wooden walkway down to the beach. In the parking lot in back of the overlook is a Mo's outlet where a seat occupied by "The Boss" himself, Bruce Springsteen, on June 11, 1987, is enshrined. Enjoy the cuisine that made this Oregon coast chain an institution, then go several doors down to the Otter Rock Cafe and have the marionberry coffeecake for dessert. By the way, we vote Otter Rock's chowder the best on the coast.

Farther along the loop is the **Inn at Otter Crest,** a pricey condo resort whose **Flying Dutchman** dining room (tel. 765-2111) faces 453-foot **Cape Foulweather** (also known as Otter Crest) to the north. Classical cuisine is served here at dinnertime, and more reasonably priced sandwiches and salads can be enjoyed at lunch. The restaurant's bluffside aerie makes a great place to watch the sunset or look for whales.

The visibility from atop the cape can extend down to Yaquina Head on a clear day. The view north is another photographer's fantasy of headlands, coves, and offshore monoliths. Bronze plaques in the parking lot tell of Captain Cook naming the 500-foot-high headland during a bout with storm-tossed seas in 1778. Comic relief from the coast's parade of historical plaques comes with a tablet bearing the inscription, "On this site in 1897, nothing happened."

The Lookout gift shop on the north side of the promontory is a good place to get Japanese fishing floats for a few bucks or take advantage of the telescopes by the entrances.

From the Otter Crest parking lot, continue north on the loop, whose dips and turns bring the view from the cape into sharper focus. Shortly after this road-less-traveled terminates, U.S. 101 takes you past **Whale Cove.** The tranquility of the calendar-photo-come-to-life here is deceptive. During Prohibition, bootleggers used the rocky crescent-shaped shoreline as a clandestine port. More recently, a court decision allowing property owners to restrict access to Whale Cove threatens to undermine public ownership of other Oregon beaches.

DEPOE BAY AND VICINITY

William Least Heat Moon in *Blue Highways* characterized Depoe Bay thusly: "Depoe Bay used to be a picturesque fishing village; now it was just picturesque. The fish houses, but for one seasonal anomaly, were gone, the fleet gone, and in their stead had come sport fishing boats and souvenir ashtray and T-shirt shops."

To be fair, tourists have always come here since the establishment of the town. In fact, for all intents and purposes, the town didn't really exist until the completion of the Roosevelt Highway (U.S. 101) in 1927, which opened the area up to car travelers. Prior to that time, the area had been mainly occupied by a few members of the Siletz Reservation. One of the group worked at the U.S. Army depot and called himself Charlie Depot. The town was named after him, eventually taking on the current spelling.

Depoe Bay also took on another incarnation as part of the so-called Twenty Miracle Miles. This bit of hype originally denoted the attractive stretch of rockbound coast near Depoe Bay north to the broad beaches of Lincoln City. Nowadays, the only thing miraculous about the region is that dozens of gift shops selling the exact same merchandise next door to each other survive year after year.

SIGHTS

Depoe Bay is situated along a truly beautiful coastline which cannot be fully appreciated from an automobile. An especially nice perspective is offered alongside the **Channel House Bed and Breakfast** at the west end of Ellingson Street. Just go left up this road where U.S. 101 passes the Channel Book Shop (see "Activities and Events" following).

As you drive over the bridge in town look down to your right to see the world's smallest navigable harbor. This distinction is announced by a sign citing the *Guinness Book of World Records* claim to fame (a tactic repeated later in Lincoln City with its "world's shortest river"). Despite the hype, the boat basin here is unique because it's a harbor within a harbor. This topography is the result of

wave action cutting into the basalt over eons until a 50-foot passageway leading to a six-acre inland lagoon was created. In addition to whale-watching, folks congregate on the bridge between the ocean and the harbor to watch boats maneuver into the enclosure. A blowhole can also be enjoyed from this vantage point when there is sufficient tide.

North of town is **Boiler Bay,** so named because of the boiler remaining from the 1910 wreck of the *Marhoffer,* visible at low tide. This bay is a favorite spot for rock fishing and whalewatching.

PRACTICALITIES

Accommodations
Depoe Bay lodgings require advance reservations on weekends and holidays.

OTTER ROCK TO ROCKAWAY BEACH

(preceding page) the Rogue River Gorge along Hwy. 12 (Christopher Scott Murray);
(this page, top) the Columbia River near the community of Hood River;
(this page, bottom) along the Siletz River, Lincoln County (photos by Warren Weber)

DEPOE BAY ACCOMMODATIONS

Arch Rock Motel, Box 21, Depoe Bay, tel. 765-2560, $28-40, ocean view, pets, kitchenettes.

Beachcombers Haven, 7045 Glen Ave., Gleneden Beach, tel. 764-2252, $35-60, oceanfront, fireplaces, laundry.

Budget Motel, Box 66, Depoe Bay, tel. 765-2287, $35-60, ocean view, pets, sundeck, cable, TV/Showtime.

Channel House Bed & Breakfast, Box 56, Depoe Bay, tel. 765-2140, $55-140, oceanfront, fireplaces, Country Inn with Jacuzzi, full breakfast included.

Four Winds Motel, Box 423, Depoe Bay, tel. 765-2793, $28-45, ocean view, pets, free coffee.

Holiday Surf Lodge, Box 9, Depoe Bay, tel. 765-2133, $37-60, ocean view, motel and cabin units, health club, laundry.

Ocean West Motel, Box 414, Depoe Bay, tel. 765-2789, $28-35, ocean view, pets.

Surfrider Oceanfront Resort, Box 219, Depoe Bay, tel. 764-2311, $50-70, oceanfront, lounge, covered pool, sauna, and Jacuzzi.

Whale Cove Inn, SRS Box 1-X, Depoe Bay, tel. 765-2255, $55-115, ocean view, rest/lounge, Jacuzzi.

Food

The following restaurants represent a cross section of the old reliables in the region.

For unpretentious all-American diner food at low prices try the **Whale Watch Cafe** (221 S.W. U.S. 101, Depoe Bay; tel. 763-2623). This cafe juts out over the ocean channel leading to the harbor, making for a great view. This is fortunate because with one grill in this mom-and-pop operation, service is slow. It's also worth waiting for, particularly at breakfast. The pancakes and the Denver omelette are recommended.

The **Chowderbowl** (U.S. 101, Depoe Bay; tel. 765-2300) serves the same tasty chowder as the Newport outlets. A salad bar, oyster and crab specials, and moderate prices are also here in this reprise of the Newport restaurant.

Two miles south of Depoe Bay is a dining room in the **Whale Cove Inn** (Star Route South, Box 1-X, Depoe Bay; tel. 765-2255) which is everything you could want in a restaurant in this part of the state. If fresh fish innovatively prepared at reasonable prices and a romantic sea coast view don't put a twinkle in your eye, perhaps the Friday night rib special and cozy lounge next-door will. Little touches like binoculars at your table and the friendliest waitresses on the coast also rate a thumbs-up.

The local favorite in Depoe Bay is the **Sea Hag** (5757 U.S. 101, Depoe Bay; tel. 261-7901). Their seafood hors d'oeuvres (fried whitefish, scallops, oysters, smoked tuna, and boiled baby shrimp) give ample testimony to their claim of "seafood so fresh the ocean hasn't missed it yet." Another popular dish is salmon stuffed with crab and shrimp, baked in wine and herb butter. A lavish salad bar, a Friday night all-you-can-eat seafood buffet, and a recipe for clam chowder fêted by the *New York Times* has also generated good word of mouth.

Two other restaurants north of the bridge also get good reports from locals. **Oceans Apart** (177 N.W. U.S. 101; tel. 765-2513) and **Tidal Raves** (279 N.W. U.S. 101; tel. 765-2995) boast the best views in town and a casual ambience. The resemblance ends there. Tidal Raves is open for lunch and dinner with tasty food at moderate prices. In addition to fresh fish and other seafood dishes like beer-battered prawns and oyster spinach bisque, the restaurants' pasta specialties are uniformly excellent. The Pasta Rave features crab, shrimp, ling cod, snapper, and more on a bed of linguine in Alfredo sauce.

Oceans Apart serves breakfast and lunch with a Hawaiian flair at a fraction of what would be charged in the islands. Consider such entrees as Paka Paka Keoni (sautéed red snapper with coconut topped with macadamia nuts) and the Island Boy's Dream (Portuguese sausage, two eggs, and rice or potatoes). Less adventuresome types can find salmon, Yaquina Bay oysters, a crab-broil sandwich, and the like. Whatever your tastes, you'll appreciate the hang-loose yet attentive waitstaff.

Finally, the **Siletz Tribal Smokehouse** (272 U.S. 101 South, Box 1004, Depoe Bay; tel. 765-2286 or 800-828-4269) at the south end of town should not be missed. In addition to native objets d' art, the fresh smoked salmon and smoked tuna ($12-13 a pound) are of exceptional quality. You can sample these traditional native delicacies prepared several different ways (try the honey-smoked fish) from the tray on the counter. Canned and vacuum-packed fish are also available for purchase. This is a good place to find out more about the Siletz tribe's August powwow (or call 800-922-1399). When you're done here, take your gourmet treats (which incidentally go well with Oregon microbrews) and drive two miles south on U.S. 101 to Rocky Creek Wayside near Whale Cove. This has to be the coast's best ocean view with picnic tables.

ACTIVITIES AND EVENTS

Book Browsing
The largest used-book emporium on the Oregon coast is the **Channel Book Shop** (tel. 765-2352), located just south of the bridge, across from the chamber of commerce. The store's five rooms of romance novels, Westerns, travel books, and varied esoterica also function as the citadel of higher learning in Depoe Bay. In the front of the store, pick up the free map of used-book shops on the Oregon coast.

Charters
With the ocean minutes from port here, catching a salmon or seeing a whale is possible as soon as you leave the harbor. On the way back into port you might see the **spouting horns**, 50-foot "geysers" of sea water that shoot through fissures in basalt when the tide is high. Charters are also popular because of reasonable prices. Fishing trips average around $35 for a five-hour run, and whalewatching excursions run $5-7 per person per hour. Some companies are **Dockside Charters** (Box 1308, Depoe Bay 97341; tel. 765-2545), **Deep Sea Trollers** (Box 513, Depoe Bay 97341; tel. 765-2705), and **Depoe Bay Sportfishing** (Box 388, Depoe Bay 97341; tel. 765-2382). **Sunset Scenic Flights** (Box 427, Gleneden Beach 97388; tel. 764-3304) is located at Gleneden Beach Airport a half mile southwest of Salishan Resort midway to Lincoln City. Whalewatching and scenic coastline flights of variable lengths depart from hangar number seven.

Events
The **Depoe Bay Salmon Bake** takes place on the third Saturday of September at Fogarty

the narrow inlet to Depoe Bay, the world's smallest navigable harbor

Creek State Park just north of town on U.S. 101. Fresh ocean fish are caught and cooked on the beach Indian style on alder stakes over an open fire and served with all the trimmings ($18 per person). The **Fleet of Flowers** happens each Memorial Day in the harbor to honor those lost at sea. Over 20,000 people come to witness a blanket of blossoms cast upon the waters. The **Salishan Jazz Party** is a more refined incarnation of the late, great Otter Crest Jazz Festival, where oldies but goodies used to join new-wave musicians of note. The Salishan fête takes place on a weekend in April or early May; call Salishan Lodge (tel. 800-452-2300) and ask for Ginger Baehr to get details.

Information And Services
Depoe Bay Chamber of Commerce (Box 21, Depoe Bay 97341; tel. 765-2889) offers a lot of printed matter about the town as well as the central coast in general. What's really special about their office is a tranquil back patio overlooking the boat harbor where you can sit and recover from the shop-until-you-drop ambience along U.S. 101.

The **laundramat** [*sic*] is open 24 hours in the rear lower level of Mall 101 at the north end of town. Also at the north end of town is the **post office** (Depoe Bay 97341) next to the U.S. Bank. The Coast Guard **weather service** (tel. 765-2122) can be contacted around the clock.

NORTH TO LINCOLN CITY

Salishan Lodge
Seven miles south of Lincoln City on the east side of U.S. 101 is a sign advertising the Salishan Lodge (tel. 800-452-2300). Named for a widespread native tongue in the Oregon territory, this resort is one of a dozen properties in the nation that consistently receives a five-star as well as a five-diamond rating.

Even if you don't stay here, the grounds and facilities are worth a look. The art gallery is free and features the best Oregon artists (also check out master woodcarver Leroy Setziol's bas-relief panels in the Dining Room). The forested trails behind the golf course (rated among the top 75 in the United States) showcase the rainforested foothills of the Coast Range. A breezeway behind the lobby displays interesting native artifacts and fossils, and the beautifully landscaped grounds look down on Siletz Bay in the distance.

Understated elegance and respect for natural surroundings are encountered at every turn —no high-rise schlocky beach architecture or neon signs here. This low-key approach at top-drawer prices ($149-220 in summer) attracts well-heeled nature lovers, corporate expense-account clientele, folks enjoying a special occasion, and serious golfers. You'll also find Mom 'n' Pop from Anywhere, U.S.A., and seminar attendees on winter weekend specials at half the summertime rates.

Despite the fact that the resort does not have oceanfront views or rooms appreciably larger or more ornate than those at many other places, the occupancy rate is high year-round. From attractive cedar-shaked self-contained units in the upper level of the complex to the smaller luxury motel rooms overlooking the golf course, you'll find nicely appointed interiors in earth colors with no trace of Naugahyde in sight.

In addition to the recreational and aesthetic appeals of the resort, the **Dining Room** is also responsible for Salishan's lofty reputation. Consistently touted as one of the top three restaurants in the state, it has become famous for its creative interpretations of seasonal Northwest delicacies and a 20,000-bottle wine cellar. The latter is open for tours, as are the grounds, whose plantlife is described by pamphlets available at the front desk. Fliers on area nature trails, art, and other topics are also available.

Salishan celebrated its 25th anniversary in 1990. The essence of its enduring popularity is perhaps best expressed in the words George Bernard Shaw used to describe another palace of poshness: "This is the way God would have done it if only he had the money."

Crafthouses
Just past Salishan on Immonen Rd., **Alder House II** is a glassblowing operation open to the public. The variety of shapes and colors produced are fascinating aspects of this ancient craft which the artisans here will explain to you. Alder House is open Tues.-Sun. 10 a.m.-5 p.m. A few hundred yards up the road is **Mossy Creek Pottery.** The large windows enable you to watch the proprietors at work, if you're lucky

enough to arrive during their irregular working hours. The high-quality creations of both craft houses are on sale at bargain prices. The road to these establishments is indicated by signs on U.S. 101.

Sometimes A Great Notion

Back on the coast route to Lincoln City, you'll come to the turnoff for ORE 229 along the Siletz River. If you drive down the north side of the river for a few miles, you'll note a Victorian house on the opposite shore that's built to last. A huge porch once fronted the riverbank, heavily reinforced against the elements. This was taken down in the decade following the movie version of Ken Kesey's *Sometimes a Great Notion*, but it lives on in the first pages of the novel.

The 1971 film, *Sometimes A Great Notion,* (which was renamed *Never Give A Inch,* when it was shown on TV) starred Paul Newman, Lee Remick, Henry Fonda, and Michael Sarrazin. The plot concerns the never-say-die spirit of an antiunion timber baron, his not-always-supportive family, and life in the mythical Coast Range logging community of Wakonda. Much of this movie was shot in this area, with cafe scenes taking place at Mo's on Newport's bayfront.

Drift Creek Covered Bridge

Closer to Lincoln City is another U.S. 101 turnoff, Drift Creek Road, which leads 2½ miles to the oldest covered bridge in Oregon. Oregon features 53 such structures (as late as 1934, there were over 300 before they fell into disrepair). They were built to inhibit the effects of moisture upon the wooden planks and to keep horses from spooking when crossing over water.

LINCOLN CITY AND VICINITY

The Lincoln City area encompasses five towns that banded together for reasons of apportionment and mutual business interests. What "business" means in this case is tourism in its worst conceivable form. In a state known for its appreciation of growth limits and the need for urban planning, Lincoln City's seven miles of shell shacks and "For Sale/Zoned Commercial" signs are an anathema. As if seeking revenge, Mother Nature has visited erosion problems on the sandstone bluffs upon which sit some Lincoln City hotels, condos, and business establishments.

Ironically, the city is also home to the recreation mecca of **Devil's Lake State Park,** a gem without equal among coastal freshwater playgrounds. In addition, prime kite-flying, mushroom-hunting, and birdwatching venues have also resisted the encroachment of civilization.

SIGHTS

Around Town

The **D River Wayside** is a state park property where you can watch what locals claim is the "world's shortest river" flow into the ocean. It traverses a 440-foot path from Devil's Lake and, despite its unspectacular appearance, was a cause célèbre when *Guinness* threatened to withdraw the D's claim to fame in favor of a Montana waterway. Local schoolkids rallied to its defense with an amended measurement, and perhaps the D's title will be restored. Another controversy surfaced when Kyllo's (see "Food" below) began building its new restaurant over the river's estuary in 1991. In addition to seeing D River flow from "D" Lake into "D" ocean, the beach here is great for kite-flying. The river itself is the point from which the street numbers of the city begin.

In commemoration of the establishment of Lincoln City, a 14-foot bronze statue was donated to the city by an Illinois sculptress. *The Lank Lawyer Reading in His Saddle While His Horse Grazes* originally occupied a city park (Governor Hatfield and actor Raymond Massey came for the dedication). Today the impressive statue is off in a nondescript lot at N.E. 22nd and Quay Ave. (look for the sign on U.S. 101 near the Dairy Queen pointing the way).

With ORE 18 connecting Lincoln City to the Yamhill County wine country, it's not surprising to find several tasting rooms in town to pique your taste buds. **Honeywood Winery** (30 S.E. U.S. 101, Lincoln City 97367; tel. 994-2755) sits across from the D River; try the blackberry wine from Oregon's oldest continuously operating winery. **Oak Knoll Winery** (3521 S.W. U.S. 101, Lincoln City 97367; tel. 996-3221) presents its own varietals (try the 1985 Pinot Noir) along with award winners from other Oregon vintners. The hosts can help you plan a wine-country foray, and they sell cases at bulk discounts. **Chateau Benoit,** found in the Quality Factory Village on Devil's Lake Rd. at the south end of town, also has a place at which to sample some excellent Pinots.

East On ORE 18
Heading east of Lincoln City on ORE 18 takes you on a road framed by the giant fir stands of the Van Duzer corridor. Just prior to heading over this pass through the Coast Range you cross the 45th parallel (it's just outside of Lincoln City by the Devil's Lake Golf Course on U.S. 101, before its junction with ORE 18, indicated by a sign on the highway). At this point you are halfway between the equator and the north pole (every degree of latitude is 66 miles).

About a dozen miles east of town is the **Van Duzer Forest Wayside,** a prime spot on the Salmon River for a picnic. The site used to be a

post office on an old stagecoach route. ORE 18 continues on through the Coast Range until the greenery of the tall firs gives way to drier orchard country wherein a major percentage of the world's filberts are grown. Roadside stands selling walnuts, cherries, and other crops dot the highway. You'll also see antique stores and tasting rooms as you ease into Yamhill Valley wine country (see "Day-Trips From Portland").

PRACTICALITIES

Accommodations
Outside of Portland and Eugene, there aren't any cities in Oregon to rival Lincoln City for sheer volume of creature comforts. There are 1,800 hotel rooms here, and many face the ocean or are close to a beach. The most reasonably priced lodgings, however, are on the noisy main drag in this strip town to end all coastal strip towns. But no matter where you go, you're never far from the madding crowd.

Campgrounds
Several wilderness retreats are worth noting in

OREGON'S CIVIL WAR CONNECTION

Despite the haphazard patterns of growth here, the choice of Abraham Lincoln's name for the city was not made arbitrarily. Shortly after Oregon gained territorial status, Honest Abe was nominated as its first secretary. Even though he declined the nomination, his name was affixed to this north coast county in 1867. And when five smaller coastal communities decided to consolidate in 1965, the choice of the appellation "Lincoln City" was lent impetus by both the centennials of his passing and of the Civil War's conclusion.

This was also in keeping with Oregon's long-standing tradition of assigning Civil War-era place names to cities and counties. And why not? The major players in America's domestic theater of war had their first curtain calls out west. General George Pickett of Pickett's Charge fame at Gettysburg, General Edward Baker, who distinguished himself at the Battle of Balls Bluff in Maryland; Generals Phil Sheridan and William Tecumseh Sherman, whose marches across the Shenandoah Valley and Georgia were Confederate nightmares; General George McClellan,

who preceded Ulysses S. Grant as head of the Union Army; and Generals George Crook and Phil Kearney all served in Oregon. The Southern side was represented at Fort Vancouver near Portland with General Robert E. Lee and the "eyes and ears of the Confederacy," Jeb Stuart.

Primarily, these men were involved in protecting the Oregon Trail settlers, gold-mining areas, and trading posts from Indians. When the Civil War drew these men east, the area was left unprotected and incurred much damage. In 1981, Oregon symbolically and unsuccessfully lobbied for a $1.3 million reparation for the losses due to the lack of federal protection. In any case, the aforementioned Civil War generals' presence is still remembered in the names of the Oregon towns of Sheridan, Baker, and Grants Pass, as well as Crook and Sherman counties. Oregon's entry into the Union helped break a tie in Congress on the vote to abolish slavery. It's altogether fitting then that there would be a city named for the Great Emancipator, Abraham Lincoln.

LINCOLN CITY ACCOMMODATIONS

Anchor Motel and Lodge, 4417 S.W. U.S. 101, tel. 996-3810, $25-55, pets, kitchenettes, nonsmoking rooms, cable.

Bay West Motel, 1116 S.W. 51st St., tel. 996-3549, $45-80, kitchenettes, fireplaces, cable, river view, ocean view.

Beachfront Motel, 3313 N.W. Inlet Ave., tel. 994-2324, $48-68, pets, kitchenettes, wheelchair access, fireplaces, ocean view.

Blue Heron Landing Motel/Marina, 4006 W. Devils Lake Rd., tel. 994-4708, $50-105, pets, kitchenettes, cable, nonsmoking rooms, river/lake view.

Brey's Oceanview Bed and Breakfast Inn, 3725 N.W. Keel, tel. 994-7123, $55-80, wheelchair access, fireplace, cable, tennis, ocean view.

Budget Inn Motel, 1713 N.W. 21st., tel. 994-5281, $36-46, pets, nonsmoking rooms.

Captain Cook's Motel, 2626 N.E. U.S. 101, tel. 994-2522, $30-40, pets.

Char Lu Ocean Front Motel, 1605 N.W. Harbor, tel. 994-9529, $40-70, pets, kitchenettes, cable, nonsmoking rooms, ocean view.

City Center Motel, 1014 N.E. U.S. 101, tel. 994-2612, $30-40, pets, kitchenettes, cable.

Coho Inn, 1635 N.W. Harbor Ave., tel. 996-3684, $62-92, pets, kitchenettes, fireplaces, cable, ocean view.

Edgecliff Motel, 3733 S. U.S. 101, tel. 996-2055, $40-80, wheelchair access, fireplaces, cable nonsmoking rooms, pets, ocean view.

Ester Lee Motel, 3803 S.W. U.S. 101, tel. 996-3606, $45-90, wheelchair access, fireplaces, ocean view.

D Sands Motel, 171 S.W. U.S. 101, tel. 994-5244, $80-110, wheelchair access, covered pool, cable, nonsmoking rooms, ocean view.

Inn at Spanish Head, 4009 S. U.S. 101, tel. 996-2161, $92-139, wheelchair access, pool, restaurant/lounge, nonsmoking rooms, laundry, ocean view.

Lincoln Lodge Ocean Front Motel, 2735 N.W. Inlet Ave., tel. 994-5007, $50-70, kitchenettes, fireplaces, cable, ocean view.

Lincoln Shores Motel, 136 N.E. U.S. 101, tel. 994-8155, $40-90, wheelchair access, fireplaces, cable, nonsmoking rooms, ocean view.

Nendels Cozy Cove, 515 N.W. Inlet Ave., tel. 994-2950, $46-115, wheelchair access, pool, fireplaces, complimentary continental breakfast, ocean view.

Nordic Motel, 2133 N.W. Inlet Ave., tel. 994-8145, $59-79, kitchenettes, wheelchair access, fireplaces, covered pool.

Ocean Terrace Motel, 4229 S.W. Beach Highway 101, tel. 996-3623, $40-90, wheelchair access, pool, restaurant/lounge, nonsmoking rooms, cable, ocean view.

Palmer House Bed and Breakfast, 646 N.W. Inlet, tel. 994-7932, $75-95, fireplaces, cable, nonsmoking rooms, ocean view.

Red Carpet Inn, 2645 N.W. Inlet Ave., tel. 994-2134, $50-60, pets, fireplaces, covered pool, cable, nonsmoking rooms, ocean view.

Sailor Jack Ocean Front Motel, 1035 N.W. Harbor Ave., tel. 994-3696, $50-60, pets, wheelchair access, fireplaces, nonsmoking rooms, complimentary continental breakfast, ocean view.

LINCOLN CITY ACCOMMODATIONS (CONT.)

Sandcastle Beachfront Motel, 3417 S.W. Anchor Ave., tel. 996-3613, $53-90, kitchenettes, fireplaces, cable, ocean view.

Sea Echo Motel, 3510 N.E. U.S. 101, tel. 994-2575, $30-47, pets, kitchenettes, cable, ocean view.

Seagull Beach-Front Motel, 1511 N.W. Harbor Ave., tel. 994-2948, $55-120, pets, kitchenettes, wheelchair access, nonsmoking rooms, ocean view.

Sea Gypsy Motel, 145 N.W. Inlet Ave., tel. 996-5266, $50-100, wheelchair access, covered pool, cable, nonsmoking rooms.

Sea Horse Oceanfront Motel, 2039 N.W. Harbor Dr., tel. 994-2101, $50-95, pets, kitchenettes, fireplaces, covered pool, cable, ocean view, nonsmoking rooms

Shilo Inn, 1501 N.W. 40th St., tel. 994-3655, $50-102, pets, wheelchair access, covered pool, restaurant/lounge, nonsmoking rooms, laundry, ocean view.

Siletz Bay Inn, 861 S.W. 51st St., tel. 996-3996, $35-145, wheelchair access, fireplaces, cable, ocean view.

Surftides Beach Resort, 2945 N.W. Jetty, tel. 994-2191, $50-95, wheelchair access, covered pool, restaurant/lounge, live entertainment, ocean view.

Westshore Oceanfront Motel, 3127 S. Anchor Ave., tel. 996-2001, $55-69, pets, kitchenettes, fireplaces, cable, ocean view.

---

the Lincoln City area. One remote escape is at the previously mentioned **Van Duzer Wayside** on ORE 18. A dozen primitive hiker/biker sites (free) sit in a beautiful forest near the Salmon River.

More free rustic sites can be found about eight miles north of town and just south of Neskowin. To get there, just look for the "Scenic Drive" sign east of U.S. 101 and follow County Rd. 12 for four miles. From there, travel about 100 yards west on Forest Service Rd. 12131 and you'll see the campground set along **Neskowin Creek.** To find out about the trails in the surrounding rainforest, call or write the Siuslaw National Forest (Hebo 97121; tel. 392-3161). The campground is open mid-April to mid-October—bring your own water or water-purification kit. The nearby scenic drive continues up into an area of huge trees captioned by Forest Service placards explaining the ecology.

More elaborate camping is available at **Devil's Lake State Park** (write to reserve at 1542 N.E. Sixth, Lincoln City 97367; tel. 994-2002). Sixty-eight tent sites and 32 RV sites are serviced with all the amenities, including showers, a cafe, and a laundromat. The fee is $15-17 per night ($2 for hiker and biker spaces) mid-April to late October. This campground is just off U.S. 101 at the northeast end of town.

Food

Lincoln City offers surprisingly many cost-effective and palate-pleasing dining options.

The best smoked fish in these parts can be had at **Barnacle Bill's Seafood Store** (2174 U.S. 101; tel. 994-3022). The smoked sturgeon here is half the price it is on the East Coast, and although it's not thin-sliced in the style of New York delis, it has a more delicate flavor. Look for a little storefront on the east side of the highway in the middle of town. Another place to graze is the **Safeway** at the northern edge of town in the Lincoln Plaza Mall. Stock up here, too, before heading north on the Three Capes Loop en route to Tillamook.

Mo's (860 S.W. 51st St.; tel. 996-2535), as usual, can be counted on for good clam chowder and full fish dinners in the $6-9 range. You'll find more of the same north of town off U.S. 101 at **Dory Cove Restaurant** (5819 Ogan Rd.; tel. 994-5180) near Road's End State Park. The prices are a little higher than at Mo's, but the range of broiled seafood entrees and cheeseburger fantasies make this place the favorite with locals. Another Lincoln City hot spot is **Kyllo's** (2733 N.W. Hwy. 101; tel. 994-3179), specializing in broiled, sautéed, and baked seafood rather than fried items, plus excellent homemade desserts. The latter can be washed down by Oregon microbrews and wines. The waiting line here usually extends out the door, regardless of weather. Kyllo's will soon open a new location on the D River.

A place that appeals to everybody is the **Otis Cafe** (Otis Junction on ORE 18, Otis; tel. 494-2813), whose innovative variations on American road food have been warmly embraced by everyone from local loggers to yuppies stopping off on the drive between Portland and the coast. Breakfast in this small, unpretentious cafe five miles northeast of Lincoln City is such an institution that long waits on the porch are the rule on weekend mornings. The reasons why include the thick-crusted molasses bread that comes with many orders, buttermilk waffles, and their legendary hash browns under melted Rogue Valley white cheddar ($4.35). A half portion for one dollar less is the equivalent of all-you-can-eat fare, so walk the beach at Neskowin before tackling the unabridged version. Large portions, low prices, and a culinary touch that turns pork chops and rhubarb pie into epicurean delights are also in full evidence at lunch and dinner (Thurs.-Sun. till 9 p.m.).

The **Bay House** (5911 S.W. U.S. 101, Lincoln City; tel. 996-3222) is a place food critics have described as "intimate" and "elegant." You might also add "expensive." Dinners can run over $30 a person, but the poached salmon, sumptuous salads with mounds of sweet bay shrimp, topped off by the impossible creamy lemon-almond cheesecake and a Siletz Bay view, might actually be worth it, especially at sunset.

The reasonable prices at Salishan Lodge's **Sun Room** are a welcome surprise. This casual restaurant might be less elaborate than Salishan's five-star Dining Room, but its Northwest cuisine comes from the same kitchen. Breakfast, lunch, and dinner are served here overlooking the golf course, and you don't have to dress up or make reservations.

A good cup of coffee can be had at **Cap'n Bean's Espresso By the Sea** (128 S.E. U.S. 101; tel. 994-7743). This Portland-based chain also has a wide variety of pastry and dessert items. It's located across from D River State Park on the north side of town. The **Lighthouse Brew Pub** (4157 U.S. 101 North; tel. 994-7238) is a welcome rehash of the McMenamin formula so successful in the Willamette Valley. Just look for a lighthouse replica in a parking lot on the north side of U.S. 101 across from McDonald's. Pizza bread, burgers, sandwiches, and chili can be washed down by McMenamin's own ales or some other quality brew, as well as hard cider and wine.

Cafe Roma Bookstore and Coffeehouse (1437 N.W. U.S. 101; tel. 994-6616) brings an air of refinement to Lincoln City. Fresh home-baked pastries and desserts, fresh-roasted gourmet coffees and espresso drinks, as well as a collection of interesting books make this a wonderful retreat on a cold or drizzly day.

Hershey's Place (815 S.W. 51st St.; tel. 996-9966), where Siletz Bay meets the ocean, offers a varied menu with such nightly dinner specials as blackened redfish, baked oysters, and homemade lasagna averaging about $11. Low-cholesterol dishes are available for all three meals, compounding the impression of something for everyone. There's plenty to feast your eyes on, too, with a telescope available to focus on the multitude of seals, as well as eagles and over a hundred other species of birds.

Kernville Steak and Seafood House (186 Siletz Hwy, Kernville; tel. 994-6200) looks out on the river and surrounding hills through huge picture windows. Blue heron and deer are frequent dinner companions here, but the real attractions are the half-dozen nightly seafood specials (all in the $12-15 range) which often showcase fresh-caught shellfish. The other heavy hitters on the menu include prime rib and chicken and dumplings. You might couple your visit here with a look at the *Sometimes a Great Notion* film location (see "Depoe Bay"). In any event, finding this dinner house is tricky because its inconspicuous facade on the south side of the river displays no sign.

Events And Activities
The **Cascade Head Music Festival** (Box 145, Otis 97368; tel. 994-5999) is another Oregon kulturfest that brings together world-class artists in an informal setting. Prior to 1992, the jazz and classical offerings of this event were presented in the intimate setting of the Otis Firehall. Now the indoor tennis courts of the Surftides Resort (2945 N.W. Jetty Ave., Lincoln City) will host the event. In addition to better acoustics,

more seats, and improved amenities, such renowned artists as the jazz vocalist Nancy King will continue to typify the roster of guest artists. Concerts take place on June weekends and cost around $15 per performance.

Several Lincoln City beaches have interesting **tidepools** to explore. Some of the best places in town are north of **Roads End State Park** and at S.W. 11th St. (Canyon Drive Park). There are also intertidal life zones at N.W. 15th St. and at 32nd. A few miles north of Lincoln City (off U.S. 101) on the north bank of the Salmon River estuary is another set of pools to visit. Just follow Three Rocks Rd. (see "Neskowin Hiking," below). Public telescopes at S.W. 51st St. let you watch a colony of seals offshore.

Lincoln City calls itself the kite capital of the world, pointing to its position midway between the pole and the equator, which gives the area predictable wind patterns. The spring **Kite Festival** takes place Mother's Day weekend; the fall festival is held the last weekend in September. The event is famous for giant spin socks, some as long as 150 feet. The exact time depends on when the winds are right at the D River Wayside, site of the contest. Call 994-3070 or (800) 452-2151 (in Oregon) for more information. When you come by the D River Wayside, go across U.S. 101 to **Catch The Wind Kites** (tel. 994-9500) for a shop that's bound to set your spirits soaring.

Devil's Lake is the recreation center of Lincoln City. In addition to sailboarding and hydroplaning, eight species of fish can be caught here. There's also good birdwatching at this lake, which Indians said held a sea monster that gobbled up unwary visitors. Devil's Lake Golf and Racquet Club and picnic tables grace the lake's shores, along with boat-launching facilities. Of the five points of access, East Devil's Lake Rd. off U.S. 101 northeast of town is the best, offering a scenic route around the lake. Mountain bikes, canoes, and paddleboats can be rented at the **Blue Heron** (4006 W. Devil's Lake Rd., Lincoln City 97367; tel. 994-4708) and sailboard rigs from **Windsurfing Oregon** (4933 S.W. U.S. 101, Lincoln City 97367; tel. 996-3157) are also available for those who want to experience the lake more intimately. Also ask the visitor and convention bureau about the Blues Festival held at Devil's Lake each fall.

The **North Lincoln City Historical Museum** (1512 S.E. U.S. 101) has 2,000 items, including old-time logging machinery, homesteading tools, and exhibits on fishing, military life, and Indian history. Check out the early fashion mannequins and a WW II mine that was washed ashore. It's open Wed.-Sun. noon-4 p.m.; admission is free.

Tennis players can enjoy the public outdoor courts at N.W. 28th. If the weather is bad, play indoors at **Neptune Courts** (tel. 994-8442) and at the **Surftides** (2943 N.W. Jetty Rd., Lincoln City 97367; tel. 994-2191). These are about half the price of **Salishan** (tel. 764-3633), which averages about $15 per person for about a 75-minute set. Another alternative is Salishan's early-morning or late-night rate of $7 per person (for more information see "North to Lincoln City" under "Depoe Bay"). An outdoor court goes for $10.

Golfers can choose between two nine-hole courses at Neskowin (tel. 392-4120 and 342-2377) 12 miles north of Lincoln City or the 18 holes at the Devil's Lake Club. The small condo and beach house community of Neskowin also has **riding stables** (48490 Hawk Rd., Neskowin 97149; tel. 392-3277) and a scenic beach to explore. **Proposal Rock,** a high forested butte, sits impressively in Neskowin's tidewater, inviting an assault. Unfortunately, the thick underbrush and undeveloped trails impede in-depth exploration, but the slopes here still have some great hideouts.

At the **Lincoln City Community Pool** (tel. 994-5208), you can swim for $1.50 and shower for 75 cents, and the **Bijou Theatre** (1624 N.E.101; tel. 994-8255) has first-run movies.

Information And Services

The **Lincoln City Chamber of Commerce** (3939 N.W. U.S. 101, Lincoln City 97367; tel. 994-3070 or 800-452-2151 in Oregon) is open Mon.-Fri. 9-5 and on weekends 10-4. The **Lincoln City Visitor and Convention Bureau** (801 S.W. U.S. 101; tel. 994-8228 or 800-452-2151) is apt to be more helpful, however. Ask for info on the town's impressive collection of antique and used-book shops. The factory-outlet mall (Quality Factory Village) located between Salishan and Lincoln City off U.S. 101 is worth a gander too, if only for Chateau Benoit's tasting

Old growth forest characterizes the flora in the Cascade Head Scenic Research Area near Neskowin.

LINCOLN CITY VISITOR AND CONVENTION BUREAU

room/espresso shop and steals on London Fog raincoats and American Tourister luggage. The **Traveler's Convenience Center** (660 S.E. U.S. 101) a mile south of the D River has a coin laundry. The **Greyhound** station (316 S.E. U.S. 101; tel. 994-8418) sits behind a bowling alley and is open 9-7. The public **library** can be reached at tel. 996-2277, and the **post office** (Lincoln City 97367; tel. 994-2128) is two blocks east of U.S. 101 on E. Devil's Lake Road. It's open Mon.-Fri. 8:30-5.

NESKOWIN HIKING

The tiny family-oriented vacation town of Neskowin (rhymes with "let's go in") has a quiet appeal based on a beautiful beach and two golf courses in the shadow of 1,500-foot-high Cascade Head. When you drive in off of U.S. 101, a deli, a post office, and the **Hawk Creek Cafe** greet you. Behind this small complex are the moderately priced **Proposal Rock Inn** and the **Neskowin Resort**. In addition, the excellent Raku Grill Restaurant sits at the end of this complex, with original art creations of the owners adorning the walls. There are few more beautiful restaurants on the coast. As for the food, let's just say life imitates art whenever taste is concerned here. In deference to the prevailing feeling in Neskowin regarding publicity, it would be inappropriate to elaborate further upon creature comforts. Let's just say you come here

more for what's outside your room than what's inside.

Cascade Head Scenic Research Area

The previous statement is made manifest two miles south of town along the Cascade Head and Hart's Cove trails. The trails fall within the Cascade Head Scenic Research Area, the only region so designated in the United States. It was set aside by Congress in 1974, thanks to the efforts of the Nature Conservancy, and is today a mecca for 6,000 hikers annually. Rain-forested pathways and wildflowered meadows give way to dramatic ocean views on Cascade Head and the Harts Cove trails. The trailheads can be reached on Forest Service Rd. 1861 (also called Cascade Head Rd.), an old gravel road west of U.S. 101. Three miles down, there's a fork to a viewpoint where you should bear left. Three-quarters of a mile farther downhill on 1861, begin the hike to Cascade Head by a large Nature Conservancy sign and a highway guardrail.

The first part of the trail runs through arching red alder treetops and 250-year-old Sitka spruces with five-foot diameters. The understory of mosses and ferns is nourished by 100-inch rainfalls. In addition, a mind-boggling array of mushrooms comes out in the fall. Above the woods is a grassy hillside at the top of which you can look south over the mouth of the Salmon River, clear down to Siletz Bay (and sometimes to Cape Foulweather). This climb shouldn't take much more than 20 minutes. To the north you can see Cape Lookout. From this 1,300-foot perch, you can descend the long slope west toward the 500-foot-high **Pinnacle,** the headland's westernmost thrust. The Pinnacle is fenced off to protect endangered plants and species. The Forest Service and Nature Conservancy fear the onslaught of hiking boots obliterating several rare wildflowers common only to here and Cape Lookout. Originally, these barriers were built by farmers to keep their stock from going over the cliffs.

Indians purposely burned areas around Cascade Head to provide "browse" for deer and to reduce the possibility of larger, uncontrollable blazes. These manmade alterations were complemented by the inherent dryness of south-facing slopes that receive increased exposure to sun. In contrast to these grasslands, the northern part of the headland is the domain of giant spruces and firs because it catches the brunt of the 100-inch yearly rainfalls and lingering fogs.

Less than two miles from the Pinnacle is **Three Rocks Road.** En route you descend steep meadows and lose 800 feet in elevation, which might make the hike back a less-than-appealing proposition. The access to Three Rocks Rd. is several miles south of Forest Service Rd. 1861 on U.S. 101. A midsummer trip to the area is enhanced by purple foxglove blooms breaking up the white yarrow, Queen Anne's lace, and daisies. So beautiful are these blooms, you might want to hike Cascade Head from Three Rocks Rd. in the spring. To drive to the Three Rocks Rd. trailhead, go two miles through a rural residential community to Savage Road, go up the hill about a mile, passing the Ridge Road entrance to Sitka Center (see below). As you head down the hill you'll come to a curve on the shoulder, which is a parking lot big enough for a half-dozen cars. Beyond it is the trailhead, marked with a Nature Conservancy sign and a brochure box. Another option is to take the six-mile trail from the parking lot near the junction of Three Rocks Road.

Around these parts, many will tell you that Cascade Head is the highest promontory on the Oregon coast rising directly off the shoreline. This is true as long as you accept the figure of 1,770 feet as its height. Because a height of just over 1,500 feet is just as often reported for Cascade Head, the south coast's 1,756-foot Humbug Mountain might get the nod. The north coast's Neahkahnie Mountain is also mentioned for its 1,700-plus-foot elevation. One thing is for certain: the silliness of such statistical preoccupations is immediately evident when you're surrounded by the grandeur of any of these headlands.

Hart's Cove

To the right of the Cascade Head trailhead on Forest Service Rd. 1861 is the beginning of the trail to Hart's Cove. This five-mile hilly loop can have plenty of mud, so boots are recommended as you tromp through the rainforest. You'll emerge on an oceanfront meadow overlooking Hart's Cove, where the barking of sea lions might greet you. For more info on these trails, write to **Hebo Ranger District** (c/o Siuslaw National Forest, Hebo 97122; tel. 392-3161).

Sitka Center For Art And Ecology

The region in the shadow of Cascade Head can be explored in even greater depth thanks to the Sitka Center for Art and Ecology (Box 65, Otis 97368; tel. 994-5485). From June through August, classes are offered in art and nature as an expression of the strong relationship between the two. Experts in everything from local plant communities to Siletz Indian baskets conduct outdoor workshops on the grounds of Cascade Head Ranch. Classes can last from a couple of days to a week, and fees vary as well. For complete info, write for a brochure or call the Sitka Center office between 10 a.m. and 5 p.m. during the period of instruction, or noon-4 p.m. other times of the year.

THE THREE CAPES LOOP

The Three Capes Loop, a 35-mile byway off U.S. 101 between Neskowin and Tillamook, is considered by many to be the preeminent scenic area on the north coast. While the beauty of Capes Kiwanda, Lookout, and Meares justifies leaving the main highway, it would be a mistake to think of this drive as a thrill-a-minute detour on the order of the south coast's Boardman Park or the central coast's Otter Crest Loop. Instead of fronting the ocean, the road connecting the Capes winds mostly through dairy country, small beach towns, and second-growth forest. What's special here are the three capes themselves, and unless you get out of the car and walk on the trails, you'll miss the aesthetic appeals and the distinctiveness of each headland's ecosystem. The wave-battered bluffs of Cape Kiwanda, the precipitous overlooks along the Cape Lookout Highway, and the bizarre octopus tree at Cape Meares are the perfect antidotes to the strip towns along U.S. 101.

SIGHTS

U.S. 101 north from Neskowin passes through pastoral settings befitting Tillamook County's nickname, "the Land of Cheese, Trees, and Ocean Breeze." If you've tasted Tillamook cheddar and Tillamook ice cream, touted by the *New York Times* as superior to Häagen-Dazs, chances are the mere sight of the cows grazing the lush grasses here will have you salivating. After thoughts of cheese, the realities of trees and ocean breeze will begin to take form on the Three Capes scenic drive turnoff about eight miles north of Neskowin.

Cape Kiwanda And Haystack Rock
Assuming you're not diverted by what some people consider to be the best fishing stream in the state, the **Nestucca River** (noted for chinook and coho salmon and steelhead), the next object of your prolonged gaze will be Haystack Rock. The sight of this 327-foot seastack a half mile offshore in Nestucca Bay will greet you after you make your way through tiny Pacific City. Your attention will probably then shift to

the sandstone escarpment of Cape Kiwanda just to the north of the beach, especially if seas are rough. In storm-tossed waters, this cape is the undisputed king of rock and roll if you go by coffee-table books and calendar photos. While other north coast sandstone promontories have been reduced to sandy beaches by the pounding surf, it's been theorized that Kiwanda has endured thanks to the buffer of Haystack Rock. In any case, hang-gliding aficionados are glad that the cape is here. They scale its shoulder by climbing over hundreds of feet of deep sand in order to set themselves aloft off the north face.

Most people will probably be content just to look up the coast from here at the knockout view of Cape Lookout or south at the unique spectacle of American fishing dories being launched into the ocean off the beach. The latter practice has been a tradition since the 1920s after commercial fishermen took these flat-bottomed boats out to sea when gill-netting was banned on the Nestucca River.

Cape Kiwanda is the undisputed king of rock 'n' roll.

These days outboard motors have replaced oar power, enabling the dories to get 50 miles out to sea from the Pacific City shoreline. If you come here around 6 a.m., you can watch them taking off. The fleet's late afternoon return attracts a crowd which comes to see the dorymen skidding their crafts as far up on the beach as possible to the boat trailers. Other people meet the dories to buy salmon and tuna direct. In addition, this beach is besieged by surfers, who enjoy some of the longest waves on the Oregon coast. Other invasions are seen just north of Cape Kiwanda, where squadrons of dune buggies play king of the mountain outside the town of Sandlake.

Cape Lookout

While the appeals of Cape Kiwanda might be missed by the uninitiated or the sedentary, Cape Lookout can be appreciated by a glance out your car window on the way up to the cape or from beachside picnic tables at the state park in its shadow. However, the two-mile walk out to the tip of the cape should be attempted by anyone in reasonable health. Even if you settle for a mere 15-minute stroll down the trailhead, you'll be able to look southward beyond Haystack Rock to Cascade Head. Giant spruces, western red cedars, and hemlocks surround the gently hilly trail to the tip of the cape. Halfway to the overlook, there are views north to Cape Meares over the Netarts sandspit. A bevy of wildflowers and birds can further enhance your march to the westernmost edge of this headland. Clear days in early April find hordes of whalewatchers scanning the horizon from atop this 500-foot cliff.

The Cape Lookout trail is marked only by a sign on the highway that says, rather cryptically, Wildlife Viewing Area. Such understatement is ironic, given the esteem in which this pathway is held by Oregonians. What the views from Capes Sebastian and Perpetua are to the south and central coasts, the overlooks here are to the northern part of the region. But even if you're not able to make this pilgrimage, the views along the highway to Cape Meares and south to Cascade Head are exhilarating. After a 10-minute drive past the Wildlife Viewing Area, follow the signs to Cape Lookout State Park fronting the beach. A trail beginning at the registration booth even-

Cape Meares in a benign mood

OREGON TOURISM DIVISION

tually leads to a ridge above the ocean. Another trail heads north through a variety of estuarine habitats along a five-mile sandspit separating Netarts Bay from the Pacific. The former is a popular site for clammers and crabbers.

The road between Netarts and Cape Meares heads into the pricey beach-house community of Oceanside. Many of the homes are built into the cliff overlooking the ocean, Sausalito-style. This motif reaches its apex atop Maxwell Point. From the **House on the Hill** parking lot (see "Accommodations" following), you can peer several hundred feet down at **Three Arch Rocks Wildlife Refuge,** part-time home to one of the continent's largest and most varied collections of birds. A herd of sea lions also populates this trio of sea stacks from time to time.

Cape Meares

With stunning views, picnic tables, a lighthouse, and a uniquely contorted tree a short walk from the parking lot, Cape Meares State Park is the most user-friendly site on the Three Capes Loop. The park was named for English navigator John Meares, who mapped many points along this coast in a 1788 voyage. The famed octopus tree is less than a quarter mile up a forested hill. The tentacle-like extensions of this Sitka spruce have also been compared to the arms of a candelabra. Another writer likened this tree to a gargantuan spider in a near-fetal position. The 10-foot diameter of its base supports five-foot-thick trunks, each of which by itself is large enough to be a single tree. An Indian legend about the spruce contends that it was shaped this way so that the branches could hold the canoes of a chief's dead family. Supposedly, the bodies were buried near the tree. This was a traditional practice among the tribes of the area, who referred to species formed thusly as "council trees." Scientists have propounded several theories for the cause of its unusual shape, including everything from wind and weather, to insects damaging the spruce when it was young.

Beyond the tree you can look back at Oceanside and Three Arch Rocks Refuge. The sweep of Pacific shore and offshore monoliths makes a fitting finale to your sojourn along the Three Capes Loop, but be sure to also stroll the short paved trail down to the lighthouse, which begins at the parking lot and provides dramatic views of an offshore wildlife refuge, Cape Meares Rocks. Bring binoculars to see tufted puffins, pelagic cormorants, seals, and sea lions.

The restored interior of this 1890 lighthouse is open May-Sept., Thurs.-Mon. 11 a.m.-6 p.m. This beacon was replaced as a functioning light in 1963 by the automated facility located behind it. The free tour is occasionally staffed by volunteers who might tell you about how the lighthouse was built here by mistake, and perhaps offer a peek into the prismatic Fresnel lenses. Before leaving the park, be sure to hike 200 yards east of the parking lot into the woods for a look at a giant Sitka spruce. Another giant Sitka is situated in the woods near the park's entrance.

PRACTICALITIES

Accommodations
The best deal in the area, if you're fortunate enough to get a reservation, is the **House on the Hill** (Box 187, Oceanside 97134; tel. 842-3060), located on previously described Maxwell Point. For $65-100 you get the seclusion and cliffside ocean grandeur of this headland. Such a location for this price is an incredible bargain.

Campgrounds
Campsites along the loop might offer greater proximity to the capes as well as increased cost-effectiveness for a protracted stay compared to a room at a motel. Two campgrounds between Cape Meares and Cape Lookout offer centralized locations, great views, and more than the usual run of campground creature comforts.

Cape Lookout State Park (13000 Whiskey Creek Rd., West Tillamook 97141; tel. 842-4981 or 800-452-5687 in Oregon) has 197 tent sites and 53 trailer sites, as well as special camps for hikers and bikers. Showers, flush toilets, and a laundromat are available here. Reservations are required, so enclose a $14 deposit, desired dates, and desired specs for your site. Overnight fees from May to early October are $15-17 (off-season rates are $3 less). Hiker and biker spaces are also available for $2 per night.

Happy Camp (Box 52, Netarts 97143, tel. 842-4012) is a few miles away in Netarts. Stop in at the Schooner Restaurant (see listing below) along the Netarts spit just off the highway for complete directions. There are 30 tent sites and 40 RV sites. All the amenities are available at $15 a night. Reservations are accepted and it's open all year.

Food
A decent selection of roadside stands, moderately priced local hangouts, and fine dining are available along the Three Capes scenic drive. **Wee Willies Restaurant** (6300 Whiskey Creek Rd., Netarts; tel. 842-6869) has home-baked goodies and grilled-crab-and-Tillamook-cheddar-cheese sandwiches. You can also get chili dogs, hot dogs, burgers, and the like. It's located a few miles north from Cape Lookout State Park. Just look for a drive-in secluded among the trees on the west side of the highway.

As you come to the end of Netarts spit after driving the highway from Cape Lookout State Park, you'll see a turnout west of the road with two wide-body mobile homes attached to each other. There is no indication that this is the **Schooner Restaurant and Lounge** (tel. 842-4988) until you come to a sign at the far end of the turnout. The Schooner caters most of the year to a lot of fixed-income retirees, as the restaurant's 1950s-style prices attest. In addition to run-of-the-mill diner food, there are local fish specialties (try the oyster burger, $3.75), home-made soup, and homemade bread pudding and carrot cake for dessert. Fresh cinnamon rolls and the cook's own biscuits and gravy are deliciously filling for breakfast. Gourmet it ain't, but geographically speaking, it's the best restaurant to be found for miles.

If hanging plants, a piano, and Nestucca River frontage don't make you feel at home, the apple pie and other wholesome fare at the **Riverhouse** (34450 Brooten Rd., Pacific City; tel. 965-6722) probably will. The seafood crepes, burgers, and open-face sandwich combinations are the perfect pick-me-ups after a morning of fishing or beachcombing along the Nestucca River estuary. Your bill should run around $6 for lunch and twice that for dinner (try the steamer clams simmered in vermouth). Weekends feature the eclectic offerings of live musicians on Saturday night and a wonderful Sunday brunch. Come early, as seating is limited in this small 11-table restaurant. Close by, at the **Grateful Bread Bakery** (34085 Brooten Rd., Pacific City), the challah, carrot cake, and other homemade baked goods deserve special mention.

At first, the weatherbeaten cedar shakes outside **Roseanna's Cafe** (Pacific St., Oceanside; tel. 842-7351) might lead you to expect an old general store, as indeed it was decades ago. Once inside, however, the lace curtains, fresh flowers, and shocking pink tablecloths leave little doubt that this place takes its new identity seriously. From an elevated perch above the breakers here, you'll be treated to expertly prepared steak and seafood followed by sumptuous desserts. Dishes centered on local oysters and fresh salmon are the specialties frequently touted by the staff. The menu is suprisingly extensive, as is the wine list, but be forewarned—the bills can be high at Roseanna's, so you might just prefer to come for a dessert such as blackberry cobbler ($4.50) and watch the waves over a long cup of coffee.

Anchor Tavern (Pacific St., Oceanside; tel. 842-2041) is the only alternative for food by the beach. It's basic microwaved bar fare, but by the second beer you might not care.

TILLAMOOK AND VICINITY

Without much sun or surf, what could possibly draw enough visitors to Tillamook to make it one of the top three tourism attractions (according to a state survey) in Oregon? Superficially speaking, a tour of a cheese factory in a town flanked by Tillamook Bay mudflats and rain-soaked dairy country shouldn't pull in over 750,000 tourists a year. But as anyone who has driven to Tillamook via the Three Capes Loop, or past Neahkahnie Mountain on U.S. 101 can attest, those tasty morsels of jack and cheddar provide the perfect complement to the surrounding region's scenic beauty.

Aesthetic and gastronomic appeals notwithstanding, Captain Robert Gray was merely looking for safe harbor when he pulled into the area of present-day Garibaldi, just north of Tillamook, in 1788. Some historians cite this as the first American landing on Oregon soil. In any case, the region—whose name in Indian parlance means "Land of many waters"—has been written up in several other footnotes of history. Shortly after the turn of the 19th century, Tillamook Bay's sandspit was the site of a popular resort known as Bay Ocean. Over the years, changes in ocean currents due to contruction of a new jetty caused the sandspit to wash away and by 1953 nothing remained of the three-story hotel, natatorium, cabins, and private homes here. As any old-timer on the coast will tell you, "Woe betide those who build their castles on the sand." However, many people still choose to construct houses on unstable Oregon sandspits.

In 1933 the Tillamook Burn devastated forests in the Coast Range east of town in what was the worst disaster in the state's history. The blazes raged for four weeks, reducing massive acreage of old growth to rows of charred stumps. Fires in 1939 and 1945 further ravaged the area, leaving a total of 355,000 acres destroyed after the three blazes. Seedlings planted by a community reforestation effort in the years that followed have produced an impressive stand of trees in these forests today.

A decade after the burn, the Tillamook blimp hangars, the two largest wooden structures ever built, according to *Guinness,* went up south of town. The hangars were built partially in response to a Japanese submarine firing on Fort Stevens in Astoria. Of the five stations on the Pacific coast, the Tillamook blimp guard patrolled the waters from northern California to the San Juan Islands and escorted ships into Puget Sound. Until 1946, when the blimps were decommissioned, naval presence here created a boomtown. Bars and businesses flourished and civilian jobs were easy to come by. After the war years, Tillamook County returned to the economic trinity of "trees, cheese, and ocean breeze" which has sustained the region to the present day.

Tillamook's namesake lighthouse is actually visible between Cannon Beach and Seaside.

OREGON TOURISM DIVISION

SIGHTS

Local Bounty

The traveler heading north toward Tillamook on U.S. 101 encounters sights which might prove even more compelling than the ever-popular cheese factory. Start with a field of artichokes, a crop not usually seen in the United States outside of California. Eleven miles south of Tillamook on U.S. 101, near Beaver Road in Hebo, is a fruit stand purveying the locally grown 'chokes as well as an astounding variety of herbs, perennials, and fruit. The cherries, marionberries, blackberries, and plums are also recommended, as are the homemade fruit jams. Even if you're not hungry, **Bear Creek Artichokes** (tel. 398-5411; for information write 1604 Fifth St., Tillamook 97141) displays the creations of an enterprising horticulturist who'll be glad to share gardening tips with passersby.

Munson Creek Falls

Four miles north of the fruit stand on U.S. 101 is a one-mile access road to the highest waterfall in the Oregon Coast Range. Munson Creek Falls drops 266 feet over mossy cliffs surrounded by an old-growth forest. A roadside marker on the east side of the highway just past the Pleasant Valley sign directs you up a steep road past a cluster of homes. A very narrow, bumpy dirt road then takes you to the parking lot at the base of the falls. A trail from the middle of the lot provides a good view with a minimum of exertion. This is a spectacle in all seasons, but come in winter when the falls pour down with greater fury.

The Blimp Hangar Museum

Farther north on U.S. 101, you'll see huge barn-like buildings east of the highway. The Blimp Hangar Museum (4000 Blimp Blvd., Tillamook; tel. 842-2413) is housed here in the huge (1,080 feet long, 300 feet wide, 195 feet high) hangars of the decommissioned Tillamook Naval Air Station. The chance to look inside a structure big enough to hold a dozen football fields and a 20-story building is justification enough to pull off the highway. You can learn about the big role the blimps played during wartime as well as how they are used today. The modern blimps you might see in the hangar are leased by airborne advertising companies and Aerolift, an enterprise which develops dirigibles to gather up timber from remote logging sites. The museum is open 10 a.m.-6 p.m. daily in summer and on weekends only the rest of the year. Admission is $2 adults, $1 children 6-12.

While all kinds of blimp stories abound in Tillamook bars, only one wartime encounter has been documented. Recently declassified records confirm that blimps were involved in the sinking of what was believed to be two Japanese submarines off Cape Meares. In late May 1943, two of the high-flying craft, assisted by U.S. Navy subchasers and destroyers, dropped several depth charges on the submarines, which are still lying on the ocean floor.

Tillamook County Pioneer Museum

West of the highway in the heart of downtown, Tillamook County Pioneer Museum (2106 Second St., Tillamook 97141; tel. 842-4553) is famous for its taxidermic exhibits as well as memorabilia from pioneer households. Particularly intriguing are hunks of beeswax with odd inscriptions recovered from near Neahkahnie Mountain (see "Cannon Beach"). It's open Mon.-Sat. 8:30-5, and Sun. noon-5 from April through September. In winter, the museum is closed Mondays but the rest of the schedule remains the same. Admission is a dollar, $5 for families, and half price for those 12-17 years of age.

Tillamook Cheese Factory

The Tillamook Cheese Factory (4175 U.S. 101 North, Tillamook 97141; tel. 842-4481) welcomes visitors with an imposing parking-lot reproduction of the *Morning Star,* the ship that once transported locally made butter and cheese and now adorns the label of every Tillamook product. The quaint vessel symbolizing Tillamook cheesemaking's humble beginnings stands in stark contrast to the technology and sophistication that go into making this world-famous gourmet product today.

Inside the plant, a self-guided tour follows the movement of curds and whey to the "cheddaring table." Whey is drained from the curds, which are then cut and folded. These processes are coordinated by white-uniformed workers in a stadium-sized factory. As you look down on the antiseptic scene from the glassed-in observation area, it's hard to imagine this as the birthplace of many a pizza and grilled-cheese sandwich. If you can bring yourself to taste a few samples, however, the operation-room ambience will quickly be forgotten.

User-friendly informational placards and historical displays also inject a human touch to the proceedings. They recount Tillamook Valley's dairy history from 1851, when settlers began importing cows. The problem then was how to ship the milk to San Francisco and Portland. Even though salting butter to preserve it created some export revenue, there remained for ships the difficulty of negotiating the treacherous Tillamook bar. In 1894, Peter McIntosh introduced techniques here to make cheddar cheese, whose long shelf life enabled it to be transported overland.

In the early 1900s, the Tillamook County Creamery Association absorbed smaller operations and the modern plant opened in 1949. Today, Tillamook churns out tens of millions of pounds of cheese annually, including Monterey jack, Swiss, and multiple variations of their famous cheddar. Pepperoni, butter, cheese soup, milk, and other products are also available at the ice-cream counter, gift shops, and deli. The Tillamook Cheese Factory and visitor center is open daily from 8 a.m.-8 p.m. in summer and closes at 6 p.m. in winter.

PRACTICALITIES

Accommodations

Tillamook County has plenty of garden-variety places to stay. Especially deserving of mention are the bargain rates at the **Idle Nook Motel** (41 N.W. 20th, Rockaway Beach; tel. 355-2007). Situated across from Karla's Krabs on the way to beautiful Rockaway Beach, you can choose between rooms with kitchenettes, oceanfront location, and a variety of other "specs" for $22-32 during the winter months.

Food

While not always the height of haute cusine, Tillamook restaurant fare can at least draw on the local bounty from the sea and surrounding farm country. Dungeness crab, bay shrimp,

clams, and oysters are indigenous to the area and a burgeoning number of wine and gourmet outlets throughout Tillamook County provide alternatives to the high-priced deli at the end of the creamery tour.

The **Blue Heron French Cheese Factory** (2001 Blue Heron Dr.; tel. 842-8281) offers samples of its brie and Camembert cheese, picnic fixin's for sale, and wine tasting from leading Oregon vineyards. Lunchtime sandwiches can be supplemented by locally raised and cured meat from **D's Sausage Factory** (tel. 842-2622), located down the road in between the Blue Heron and the Tillamook Cheese Factory on the west side of U.S. 101.

The **Muddy Waters Coffee** company (1904 Third St.; tel. 841-1400) makes the daily grind that much better for Tillamook folks and travelers in search of a decent cup.

North of downtown on U.S. 101, **La Casa Medello** (1160 U.S. 101 North; tel. 842-5786) serves lunch and dinner daily, primarily Mexican food geared to American palates at good prices. Full dinners with large portions and a low grease factor go for around $7.

If you're in town for the evening, dinner at **Hadley House** (2203 Third St.; tel. 842-2101) culls fresh ingredients from the Pacific and the pasture. Moderate prices and a pleasant staff also recommend this local favorite across from the courthouse.

Your Tillamook County gourmet tour continues 25 miles north in **Garibaldi**, where **Miller's Seafood Market** (tel. 322-0355) sits on the left-hand side of U.S. 101. Fresh salmon, ling cod, and bottomfish are the specialties here. Garibaldi is a fish-processing center, so Miller's selection is both low-priced and fresh.

North of Garibaldi on U.S. 101 is the resort town of **Rockaway.** A walk along the seven miles of sandy beach here could well provide your only respite from 50 miles of inland towns between Tillamook and Neahkahnie Mountain. Another reason to hit the brakes in Rockaway is **Karla's Krabs** (2010 U.S. 101 North, Rockaway; tel. 355-2362). Karla's roadside snack shack exterior in no way suggests that this place catered former Governor Neil Goldschmidt's inaugural or is one of the concessionaires at Portland Trailblazers games in Memorial Coliseum. However, while prices on the menu here bespeak such wallet-stretching influences, the smoked fish delicacies in the display case are worth any asking price. It's hard to resist such exotic offerings as snapper jerky smoked in a honey glaze, alderwood-smoked halibut and prawns, or the extra-large Willapa Bay smoked oysters. Picnickers in a less experimental mood might ask for a serving of Karla's mainstays—chinook salmon and smoked sturgeon. Karla's also does a great job with a light-battered fish and chips.

After eating your way up the coast, what could be more fitting than to wash it all down with a local wine? The **Nehalem** (pronounced "Knee-hail-em") **Bay Winery** (34965 ORE 53, Nehalem; tel. 368-5300) produces varietal wines as well as fruit and berry wines (Pinot Noir, gewürtztraminer, and blackberry). Tour the winery and picnic on the grounds 10 a.m.-5 p.m. daily. To get there, look for an ORE 53 sign on U.S. 101 and follow it to the winery.

Shortly before leaving Tillamook County, gourmets pull off into the little hamlet of Manzanita. When adjacent coastal areas are fogbound, Manzanita Beach usually enjoys sunshine due to the shelter of Neahkahnie Mountain. Its single main drag, Laneda Avenue, is home to the **Blue Sky Cafe** (154 Laneda Ave.; tel. 368-5712) and **Jarboe's,** across the street, two of the better restaurants on the Oregon coast. Blue Sky takes vegetables from its own gardens and shellfish from Tillamook Bay to create such memorable dishes as pan-fried Cajun-style oysters rolled in spices and toasted pecans as well as a variety of sumptuous dinner salads. Chicken Santa Fe and filet mignon wrapped in bacon and several other entrees are noteworthy despite their lack of local flavor. Jarboe's offers Old World cuisine literally a stone's throw away from the Pacific.

Should you decide to stay the night in Manzanita, call Julianne Johnson at 368-7304 (or write in advance to **Manzanita Oceanfront Retreat,** P.O. Box 116 Manzanita, 97130) to book a night by the sea. You have a choice of rooms with shared bath for $40, or more expensive self-contained oceanfront units.

Recreation

Along with birdwatching, crabbing, and salmon fishing in Tillamook Bay and angling in the area rivers, the Tillamook State Forest holds lots of other recreational opportunities. From a distance, the forest seems like a tree plantation, but hidden waterfalls, old railroad trestles left over from the days of logging trains, and moss-covered oaks in the Salmonberry River Canyon will convince you otherwise. Birdwatchers and mushroom pickers can easily penetrate this thicket thanks to 1,000 miles of maintained roads and old railroad grades. Two challenging trails off ORE 6, **King Mountain** (25 miles east of Tillamook) and **Elk Mountain** (28 miles east of Tillamook), let you traverse lands affected by the Tillamook Burn and enjoy scenic views. A pamphlet entitled *Tillamook Forest Trails* is put out by the State Forestry Dept. (Tillamook District, 4907 E. Third St., Tillamook; tel. 842-2543). Birdwatchers come to Tillamook Bay June to November to sight pelicans, sandpipers, tufted puffins, blue herons, and a variety of shorebirds. Prime time is before high tide.

Camping

Kilchis County Park (tel. 842-8662) has cheap ($5) but primitive sites near a river with good steelhead and salmon fishing. To get there, go up Kilchis River Rd. about 10 miles northeast of Tillamook. The park is closed September through May.

Information And Services

The **Tillamook County Chamber of Commerce** (3705 U.S. 101 North, Tillamook 97191; tel. 842-7525) is located across the parking lot from the cheese factory. It's open Mon.-Fri. 9-5, Sat. 1-5, Sun. 11-2, mid-June through September.

The **post office** (2200 First St., Tillamook 97191) is open Mon.-Fri. 8:30-5.

The **RAZ Beach Bus** goes from Tillamook to Portland, picking up at Sixth and Main at 10 a.m. Inquire at the Jiffy Market (604 Main St.; tel. 842-5848) for details. The cost should be around $10. For local transportation between Tillamook and Seaside, call or write **Salt Water Shuttle Transit and Charter Service** (Nehalem 97131; tel. 368-6711). Special stops are indicated on their schedule, featuring such diverse locations as the Tillamook Cheese Factory, Oswald West State Park, and Arch Cape. The drivers also respond to flag stops at unmarked locations where it's safe to pull over.

Other useful numbers include the **Tillamook Crisis and Resource Center** (tel. 842-9486), **Tillamook Ambulance** (tel. 842-4444), the county **sheriff** (tel. 842-2561), and the **Alderbrook Golf Course** (Idaville Rd., tel. 842-6413). The latter is located north of town and charges a $12 greens fee. Good regional titles can be found at **Rainy Day Books** (2015 Second St.; tel. 842-7766).

Events

The **Tillamook County Fair** takes place the second week of August and represents more than three-quarters of a century of tradition. Call the chamber of commerce for more information. The **Dairy Festival** takes place throughout June with rodeos, parades, and evocations of the Swiss-German roots of the region's settlers. Lederhosen, polka bands, sausages, and thousands of cheese-crazed tourists make this a lively celebration of the end of a long rainy season.

CANNON BEACH AND VICINITY

John Steinbeck in *Travels With Charlie* bemoaned how present-day Carmel, California, would be eschewed by the very people who gave the town the appealing sobriquet of "artist colony." This same thing could well happen to the Carmel of the Oregon coast, Cannon Beach, unless the growth which began in 1980 is slowed. Within a decade, the number of motel rooms here has doubled, as has the number of visitors on a busy weekend (which now averages 10,000-12,000).

Nonetheless, the broad stretch of beach highlighted by the impressive promontory Haystack Rock still provides a contemplative experience, although you might have to walk a couple of miles from your parking place to get to it. And if you're patient and resourceful enough to find a space for your wheels, the finest gallery-hopping, crafts, and shopping on the coast await. The city is zoned in such a way as to keep it small enough for strolling, and a location far removed from U.S. 101 spares it the kind of blight seen on the main drags of other coastal tourist towns.

The hamlet got its name when a cannon from the wrecked U.S.S. *Shark* washed ashore south of the current city limits in 1846. The *Shark* had met its end in the waves of the treacherous Columbia bar while monitoring a territorial dispute with a contingent of English merchant ships.

In 1873, stagecoach-and-railroad tycoon Ben Holladay helped create the first coastal tourist mecca, Seaside, while ignoring its attractive neighbor in the shadow of Haystack Rock. In the 20th century, Cannon Beach evolved into a bohemian alternative to the hustle and bustle of the more robust resort scene to the north. Before

the recent era of development, this place was a quaint backwater attracting laid-back artists, summer-home residents, and the overflow from pricier digs in Seaside. Today, the low-key charm and atmosphere conducive to artistic expression are threatened by a massive visitor influx and price increases. While such vital signs as a first-rate theater, a good bookstore, and fine restaurants are still in ample evidence in Cannon Beach, your view of them from the other side of the street might be blocked by a convoy of Winnebagos.

SIGHTS

Neahkahnie Mountain, Oswald West State Park

South of Cannon Beach, north of Manzanita, is Neahkahnie Mountain. The coast highway traces part of the mountain's outlines 700 feet above the Pacific. Nowhere along U.S. 101 is the roadbed so high above an ocean view; and soaring another thousand feet above you on the other side of the highway is the peak named for the Tillamook tribe's fire spirit. Nonetheless, keep your eyes on the road until you've parked your car. The area is full of hikers and occasionally, at daybreak or dusk, Roosevelt elk and black-tailed deer.

Scenic turnoffs abound, but take the half-mile trail from the main parking lot at Oswald West State Park (look for signs) to **Short Sands Beach.** This lot is on the east side of the road, where the trail winds down under a culvert beneath the highway. From Short Sands Beach you can pick up the three-mile old-growth-lined Cape Falcon Trail to the highway, or you might want just to linger at Smuggler's Cove. Spruce, hemlock, and cedar rainforests crowd the secluded shoreline and it's easy to believe local legends of Spanish pirates burying a treasure along this coast. One legend had the crew of a shipwrecked Manila galleon salvaging its cargo of gold and beeswax (a popular commodity in trade with the Orient) by burying it in the side of the mountain. To deter Indians from the site, the Spanish pirates killed a black man and buried him on top of the cargo. While this account taken from native histories has never been substantiated, a piece of crudely inscribed beeswax retrieved from the Neahkahnie region (on display at Tillamook's Pioneer Museum) keeps speculation alive.

In any case, there is real treasure here today for all who venture into this realm. We have Governor Oswald West's 1913 beach bill to thank for Oregon's virgin shoreline. And a 1967 amendment to West's bill additionally protected the dry-sand area of the beach (from the high-tide line to the vegetation line). The spirit of the legislation is honored with the **Matt Kramer Memorial.** Kramer was a reporter whose detailed coverage of the 1967 legislative proceedings produced a groundswell of public support for the bill.

Your return to the highway via the **Cape Falcon Trail** takes you back to a point north of where you parked your car. Die-hard hikers can now elect to trek the **Neahkahnie Summit Trail.** Look for the trailhead just north of the viewpoint honoring Oswald West, marked by a small sign across the highway. It's several miles of steep, and at times narrow, trail to the top. The summit offers stunning views north to Tillamook Head and south to Cape Meares. In the spring, thimbleberry, wild onion, and foxglove thrive, along with other flora. On the way back, retrace your steps or descend the southern route on a one-mile trail. This trail is located 2½ miles south of the Short Sands parking area in Oswald West State Park almost directly across from an old golf course. The trailhead is located up a rocky dirt road a mile from U.S. 101.

Entering Cannon Beach
Several miles up from Oswald West State Park's main parking lot is **Arch Cape Tunnel,** cut right into the mountain. This marks the end of the state park but not the beauty. On the way into Cannon Beach, views of **Hug Point State Park** and pristine beaches will have you lacing up your hiking boots again. Two miles south of the downtown area, park at **Tolovana Beach Wayside.** Picnic and restroom facilities aren't the only reasons to come here. This is an excellent base from which to walk south three miles to Hug Point (so named because wagons had to dash between the waves hugging the point to get around) or north two miles past Haystack Rock into town. If you are going to Hug Point, you'll appreciate how the knot of beachgoers thins out south of Tolovana. Time your trek to coincide with low tide, when all manner of marine-life in tidal pools will be exposed. At low tide, you'll also see remains of an 800-foot-long, Model-T-sized road blasted into the base of Hug Point, an early precursor to U.S. 101. The cliffs at Hug Point are gouged with caves and crevasses which also invite exploring.

Heading into town on foot from Tolovana is a good idea on holiday weekends, when there's a dearth of parking spaces. As you head north, **Haystack Rock** will loom larger. This is the third-highest coastal monolith in the world, measuring 235 feet in height. Flanking the mountain are two rock formations known as **The Needles.**

the view from
Neahkahnie Mountain,
overlooking the spot of
an as-yet-undiscovered
treasure supposedly
hidden by the crew of a
wrecked Spanish galleon

OREGON TOURISM DIVISION

These skinny spires had two other counterparts at the turn of the century, which were gradually leveled by weathering and erosion. Old-timers will tell you that a trail to the top of Haystack was dynamited by the government to keep people off this bird rookery and away from the intertidal life at its base. It also reduced the number of intrepid hikers trapped on the rock at high tide.

Today the area is designated an Oregon island national wildlife refuge and has wilderness status. During the summer, the **Haystack Rock Awareness Program** sponsors free interpretive programs here and evening programs in Cannon Beach; check the chamber of commerce for details. While these talks are interesting, the beach will also speak to you with its own distinctive voices. Don't miss the cacophony of shorebirds at sunset and the winter phenomenon of "singing sands" created by wind blowing over the beach.

The Beach Loop Into Town
Driving into town along the beach loop which branches off U.S 101, you'll pass such destination resorts as the Tolovana Inn, the Surfsand, and the Surfview. Thereafter, the town which greets you is more like Cape Cod and Carmel than any other town on the Oregon coast. Wood shingles and understated earth colors dominate the architecture of tastefully rendered galleries, bookstores, and bistros. Throngs of walkers along Hemlock St., the main drag, also distinguish this burg from the typical

coastal strip town whose heart and soul have been pierced by U.S. 101. You have to go clear to the north end of Cannon Beach to find a gas station, and even then you're liable to bypass its stone-cottage facade.

Klootchy Creek And Saddle Mountain
From the north end of town, it's not far to the junction of U.S. 101 and U.S. 26. The latter goes 80 miles east to Portland, but many coastal travelers just travel two miles on U.S. 26 to visit Klootchy Creek Park. In an old-growth spruce and fir forest here you'll find the **world's tallest Sitka spruce.** Standing 216 feet high and 52 feet in circumference, it's believed to be over seven centuries old. To find the tree, look for signs on the north side of the highway shortly after leaving Cannon Beach.

Another reason to head east from Cannon Beach is the hike up 3,283-foot **Saddle Mountain.** To get to the trailhead, take U.S. 26 for 15 miles and turn left on the prominently indicated Saddle Mountain Road. Although it's paved, this road is not suitable for RVs or wide-bodied vehicles. After seven twisting miles, you'll come to the trailhead of the highest peak in this part of the Coast Range. The trail is steep, gaining over 1,600 feet in three miles, and takes over four hours roundtrip, but is worth the effort.

On a clear day, hikers can see some 50 miles of the Oregon and Washington coastlines, including the Columbia River. Also possible are spectacular views of Mt. Rainier, Mt. St. Helens, Mt. Hood, and unfortunately, miles of clearcuts. If you go between May and August you'll be treated to a wildflower display that is nationally famous among botanists. On the upper part of the three-mile trail to the top, species from Alaska and Canada which pushed south during the last ice age thrive. The cool, moist climate here keeps them from dying out as they did at lower elevations. Some early blooms include pink coast fawn lily, monkey flower, wild rose, wood violet, bleeding heart, oxalis, Indian paintbrush, and trillium. There are around 2,000 species of flora in all. There are also deer, elk, and black bear in the surrounding forests.

Down U.S. 26 about one mile west of Elsie you can visit **Camp 18 Logging Museum** (Box 195, Seaside 97138; tel. 755-2476). Here, the chance to look at steam donkeys and other antique logging equipment breaks up the long drive to Portland. A restaurant serving American road food in a large log building might also add to your respite here. Family-style seating, specials catering to lumberjack appetites, and a gift shop purveying Northwest books and crafts are additional enticements.

Jewell Meadow Wildlife Area

Farther east down U.S. 26, however, is the best place of all to see wildlife. Each fall and winter Roosevelt elk come to the Jewell Meadow Wildlife area. Elk-hunting season is in November, so come before October at dawn or dusk for the best viewing times. Black-tailed deer might show up in the spring and summer. To get there, take U.S. 26 to the Jewell junction (about 20 miles east of Cannon Beach) then head north on an unmarked state road for nine miles to **Jewell.** Turn west and drive one mile on ORE 202 to parking spaces in close proximity to elk on Fishhawk Creek. If there are no elk in the first parking area or at headquarters, go on to the third lot and viewpoint. Three miles west is 100-foot-high Fishhawk Falls at Lee Wooden County Park. For more info, call 755-0204.

Ecola State Park

Ecola State Park is just north of the Cannon Beach townsite. Thick conifer forests line the access road to Ecola Point. This forested cliff has many trails which lead down to the water. The view south takes in Haystack Rock and the overlapping peaks of the Coast Range extending to Neahkahnie Mountain. Out to sea, the sight of sea lions basking on surf-drenched rocks (mid-April through July) or migrating gray whales (March) and orcas (May) are seasonal highlights. From Ecola Point, trails lead north to horseshoe-shaped **Indian Beach,** a favorite with surfers. Some prefer to drive there as a prelude to hiking up Tillamook Head, considered by Lewis and Clark to be the region's most beautiful viewpoint (see "Following Lewis and Clark" under "Seaside and Vicinity" following).

The name Ecola means "whale" in Chinook jargon and was first used as a place-name by William Clark, referring to a creek in the area. Lewis and Clark journals note a 105-foot beached whale found somewhere within present-day Ecola Park's southern border, Crescent Beach. This general area represents the southernmost extent of Lewis and Clark's Oregon coastal travels.

From Ecola Point, the historic **Tillamook Rock Lighthouse** sits a mile northwest out to sea. This beacon was operative from 1881 to 1957, despite sustained 100-mile-per-hour gales that frequently pushed seas up and over the 130-foot height of the light. Today it serves as a depository for cremated human remains.

During summer weekends and other high usage times, there is a $3 admission fee at the park.

Les Shirley Park

A city park worth visiting is Les Shirley Park. In addition to being the probable location of the whale carcass observed by Lewis and Clark, this place has interpretive signs to explain the interaction of ocean and fresh water that occurs in Ecola Creek estuary. To reach the park after leaving town on the beach loop to U.S. 101, turn left on Fifth St. at the foot of the hill. Pass the sign for Ecola State Park; Les Shirley Park is a few more blocks ahead.

PRACTICALITIES

Camping

Nehalem Bay State Park (write: 8300 Third St., Nehalem 97130; tel. 368-5943), about 15 miles south of Cannon Beach, offers varied recreation and lots of camping spots. Sand-

*the view from
Ecola Point summit*

wiched between the bay and a six-mile ocean-front strip are 292 sites going for $15-17, plus some bargain biker/hiker sites ($2) and hot showers. Boating, crabbing, and windsurfing in the bay are popular here. Close by is the town of **Manzanita,** where wealthy Portlanders summer. Park amenities include a laundromat, flush toilets, and piped water. No reservations are necessary (but it can get crowded during summer so reserve during July and Aug.), and it's open mid-April to late October.

At **Oswald West State Park** (write: 8300 Third St., Nehalem 97130; tel. 368-5943 or 238-7488) you walk a half mile from a parking lot to campsites in a grove of old-growth conifers backdropped by high cliffs. In addition to Short Sands Beach, Smuggler's Cove, and the previously detailed hiking options, surfing and tide-pooling can be enjoyed nearby. The State Parks Division supplies wheelbarrows to cart your gear from the parking lot to 36 primitive campsites. Here camping is allowed mid-May to October and costs $9 a night.

Accommodations

If you're not willing to make stormwatching an acquired taste, do not reserve Cannon Beach lodgings from mid-January through early March. During this time much of the annual rainfall total of 80 inches is recorded. Should high room rates or crowds on weekends other times of the year be a deterrent, remember that Cannon Beach is only an hour and a half from Portland, perfect for a day-trip.

A nice oceanfront family-style lodge is the **Sea Sprite** (write for brochure to Box 66, Tolo-vana Park 97145; tel. 436-2266). With a beach-front location just south of Haystack Rock, plus kitchens, TV, and spectacular views, it's not surprising that this place commands $55-120 rates during the regular season. What *is* surprising is the off-season discount of 50% of these rates, Oct.-May, Sunday through Thursday. These family-style beach cabins are a throwback to the Oregon coast of an earlier era. Inside you'll find such homey touches as fireplaces, games, books, periodicals, and rockers. Outside you have flowers, picnic tables, and the best of Cannon Beach shopping and beachcombing in close proximity. Two cabins are for two people, one cabin holds six, a two-bedroom cottage holds eight, and a couple lodgings sleep five people each. To get there take the Beach Loop (Hemlock St.) south of town and turn west at Nebesna Street. If the Sea Sprite is filled up, the same management will steer you to the **Hearthstone Inn** (Hemlock and Jackson streets; tel. 436-2266; $75-85), which also features off-season specials.

Two moderately priced motels close to town but far enough from traffic for peace and quiet are the **Blue Gull** (632 Hemlock St.; tel. 436-2714) and **McBee Motel** (888 S. Hemlock St.; tel. 436-2569). But for somewhat more money than the $40-75 you'd pay at these places, you can get the intimacy and flavor of a bed and breakfast. In Cannon Beach the two-bedroom **Tern Inn** (3663 S. Hemlock; tel. 436-1528) is close enough to the beach for good views. Private baths, private entrances, and full breakfasts with home-baked goodies go for as low as $75 a night. Reserve a month in advance.

The **Cannon Beach Hotel** (1116 Hemlock St.; tel. 436-1392) is a 1910 converted loggers' boardinghouse with 30 rooms and a small cafe and restaurant on the premises. Full breakfasts are included in the $50- to $105-per-night rates, and lunch and dinner can be enjoyed here apart from the lodging package. Reserve a week in advance.

Food

As you might expect, eating out can get expensive here. However, there are some some ways to beat the costs and if you can't, there are a few justifiable splurges.

The **Mariner Market** (139 N. Hemlock St.; tel. 436-2412) is an antique-filled grocery that's fully stocked with fresh meat, fruit, and vegetables. The Mariner's prices beat the tab at several other markets in town and it's open 9 a.m.-9.p.m. Before you leave, check out the antique grocery paraphernalia, old-time bottles and containers, and the jewelry and crystal shop upstairs. A locally made, no-brand-name smoked beef jerky available at the checkout counter makes for an awesome hiking snack.

The **Lazy Susan Cafe** (126 N. Hemlock St.; tel. 436-2816) is set back from Hemlock Street in Coaster Square. Just look for Coaster Theater (108 N. Hemlock St.) on the west side of the street and go beyond it into the mall. This is *the* place in town for breakfast and lunch. Homemade muffins, eggs Benedict, and the best coffee in town can fuel up or finish off an early morning beach walk. Homemade soups and sandwiches are the bill of fare at lunch. With prices not going too much beyond $5 for a good-sized meal, the lines can be long on weekend mornings.

Morris' Fireside Restaurant (207 N. Hemlock; tel. 436-2917) is an attractive log building where moderately priced steak and seafood are featured along with "logger" breakfasts. Portions are large and so is the selection. Try the crab-and-cheese sandwich for lunch and the fresh seafood special for dinner.

Mo's at Tolovana (3400 S. Hemlock), formerly Daggatt's, sits next to Tolovana Park and boasts a restaurant site once selected by *Pacific Northwest* magazine as having "the most romantic view on the Oregon coast." Add this to Mo's reliable formula of fresh fish and rich clam chowder at reasonable prices and you can't miss.

Several afterthoughts deserving of serious consideration are the chocolate-covered shortbread at **Cannon Beach Cookie Company** (239 N. Hemlock; tel. 436-2832) and the espresso drinks and ice cream across the street at **Osburn's Ice Creamery** (240 N. Hemlock; tel. 436-1470). The latter is adjacent to **Osburn's Deli** (tel. 436-2234), featuring $4.25 sandwiches that can make a meal for two. Summertime specials on local produce, and people-watching from old classroom chairs on Osburn's porch, are Cannon Beach traditions. At night **Bill's Tavern** (188 N. Hemlock St.; tel. 436-

Short Sands Beach at Oswald West State Park

2202) is nightlife in Cannon Beach. The wood stove, pool table, and dart board create a friendly ambience and the joint jumps on weekends with live rock bands. Should your interests be more sedentary, a nice selection of burgers and microbrews will help you make it through the night.

If you're hiking along the beach or in the Coast Range south of town, the **Arch Cape Deli** (six miles south of Cannon Beach where Ocean Rd. meets U.S. 101) is a good place to provision a picnic, enjoy homemade soup, or just have cookies washed down by excellent coffee.

Shopping And Galleries
Most of the Cannon Beach galleries and shops are on Hemlock Street. At the north end of town **White Bird Gallery**'s (tel. 436-2681) varied arts and crafts are worth a special look. Also on the northern part of Hemlock is a fine kite store, **Once Upon A Breeze** (tel. 436-1112). In the middle of the block is **Cannon Beach Book Company** (tel. 436-1301), one of the best bookstores on the coast. This is the place to pick up regional titles or a good novel for that rainy weekend.

The Great Northwest Shoe Swap
Designer kites, Japanese glass fishing floats, berry jams, myrtlewood bowls, and objets d'art culled from galleries are among the gift-shopping treasures typically found on the Oregon coast. But in 1991, a unique event added a new wrinkle to the scene. It all started when a cargo of Nike athletic shoes washed up on north coast beaches, the result of the wreck of an Asian ship. The Japanese current swept the shoes down from the north Pacific to be deposited on Clatsop County beaches. Before long, beachcombers here were forming "shoe swap" clubs to match up sizes and styles in pairs. With extensive washing, these shoes were almost good as new, or at least good enough to sell for less than the $50-120 asking price at conventional outlets. From Cannon Beach north, the flotsam footwear was advertised on laundromat bulletin boards, in community newspapers, and by hawkers on the street. Nike, Beaverton's multibillion-dollar shoemaker, did nothing to spoil this party, rev-

eling instead in the publicity generated by the incident. Oceanographers are currently studying the shipwrecked shoes to bolster their understanding of ocean currents.

Events
The half-dozen other **sandcastle contests** which take place on the Oregon coast are given nary a mention in this book, so much do they pale in comparison to the Cannon Beach event. Approaching its third decade, this is the state's first and most prestigious competition of its kind. Tens of thousands of spectators show up to watch 1,000-plus competitors fashion their creations with the aid of buckets, shovels, and squirt guns. This event is free to spectators, but entrants pay a fee. Recent winners included Egyptian pyramids and a gigantic sea turtle. The event usually coincides with the lowest-tide Saturday in late May. Call 436-2623 to find out the exact date of this collapsible art show, which takes place a mile north of Haystack Rock. Building begins in the early morning; judging starts at noon.

The **Author Series** features notable regional writers reading from their works in spring and fall. Dates and locations are posted around town, or contact the chamber of commerce for additional information.

The **Stormy Weather Festival** in November brings out local artists, musicians, and their creations. Call the chamber of commerce for details. December heralds the annual **Dickens Festival**. Each Friday and Saturday Dec. 1-16, local thespians don traditional Victorian costumes and perform a Dickensian Christmas play at the Coaster Theater (108 N. Hemlock; tel. 436-1242). Other related events such as teas and lamp-lighting ceremonies usher in the holiday season with a Dickensian or Victorian motif.

The Coaster Theater (for information or reservations write Box 643, Cannon Beach 97110) also features summer plays as well as local and out-of-town shows in winter.

Getting There
In addition to the bus company that operates between Tillamook and Seaside (see "Tillamook" above), there is a free Cannon shoppers' shuttle that runs 9 a.m.-6 p.m. daily. The

schedule is available at the chamber of commerce. If you're driving north on U.S. 101, there's a choice of four entrances to the beach loop to take you into town. The most practical choice is the first one, Tolovana Park, which is connected to the Coast Highway by Warren Road. From Tolovana Park you follow the Beach Loop (part of the old Oregon Coast Highway and also known as U.S. 101 Alternate) north into the downtown core. Along the way, gorgeous views of Haystack Rock and surfside lodging line the route. As the resort ambience gives way to shops, galleries, and restaurants, this beach loop is referred to as Hemlock St., the main drag of Cannon Beach.

Information And Services

The **Cannon Beach Chamber of Commerce** (Box 64, 201 E. Second, Cannon Beach 97110; tel. 436-2623) is open Mon.-Sat. 11 a.m.-5 p.m., Sun. 11 a.m.-4 p.m., and is occasionally closed on winter weekends. The **post office** (155 N. Hemlock, Cannon Beach 97110; tel. 436-2822) is open Mon.-Fri. 9-5. Artists and writers congregate in Cannon Beach for one- or two-week courses in the **Haystack Program for the Arts.** Call the arts office (tel. 464-4812) of Portland State University for more details. **Sandpiper Medical Walk-in Clinic** (171 N. Larch; tel. 436-1142) offers quality medical care for the whole family and minor emergency services. It's located in Sandpiper Square behind the stores on the main drag.

SEASIDE AND VICINITY

Seaside is the quintessential family beach resort. The beach is long and flat, protected from ocean tides by scenic headlands; lifeguards are on duty weekends. In addition, Seaside has beachside playground equipment and the only West Coast boardwalk north of Santa Cruz, California. Atlantic City it's not, thank goodness, but the carny motif of the Jersey Shore is evoked by the cotton candy, Ferris wheel, arcades, and abundance of tourist facilities. South of town the presence of clammers and waders in the shallows and surfers negotiating the swells also recalls the liveliness of a southern California or Atlantic Ocean littoral instead of the remote peacefulness of many Oregon beaches. East Coast visitors often liken Cannon Beach to Provincetown, and Seaside to Coney Island—prior to their declines.

Located in the shadow of majestic Tillamook Head at the mouth of the Necanicum River, Seaside has attracted tourists since the early 1870s, when transportation magnate Ben Holladay sensed the potential of a hotel near the water. Train service from Portland helped realize that potential. Prior to being the first coastal resort in the state, Seaside's fame as the end of the Lewis and Clark Trail made it a national landmark. The dynamic duo came here in the winter of 1805-06 and set about boiling seawater nonstop for seven weeks to produce four bushels of salt for the trip back east.

In recent years, the town has become more than just a retreat for Portland families. Oregon's apostle of haute cuisine, the late James Beard, used to hold a celebrated cooking class here each summer. This opened the door for writers' retreats, art classes, and business conventions. If these occasions or a family outing should bring you to Seaside, you'll enjoy the spirit of fun—just be prepared to swallow hard when you see the bill.

SIGHTS

Downtown Seaside

Sightseeing in Seaside means walking the **Prom.** This two-mile-long boardwalk, extending from V St. to 12th Ave., was constructed in 1921 to replace the rotten planks from an older walk and protect ocean properties from the waves. Beaches along the way offer vantages from which to contemplate the sand, surf, and massive contours of 1,200-foot-high Tillamook Head. Along the Prom is the **Turnaround,** a small traffic circle framing a placard proclaiming this point the end of the trail for Lewis and Clark. Eight blocks south of here between Beach Dr. and the Prom is a replica of the Lewis and Clark salt cairn. Running east from the Turnaround, Broadway—Seaside's central traffic artery—goes a half mile to U.S. 101 (Roosevelt) through a mind-numbing array of arcades, game rooms, gift shops, taverns, and a carousel.

If you tire of having a good time on Broadway,

make your way to **Seaside Historical Museum** (570 Necanicum Dr.; tel. 738-7065), whose Clatsop Indian artifacts will impart more of a sense of history than anything else in town. It's open daily 10:30 a.m.-4:30 p.m.; admission is $1 for adults, 50 cents for children.

Just because you're downtown doesn't mean you can't enjoy some of nature's bounty—anglers can reel in trout, salmon, and steelhead from the Necanicum River right in the center of downtown.

Following Lewis And Clark
Just south of Seaside you can walk in the footsteps of Lewis and Clark to **Tillamook Head.** In January 1806, on a quest for a beached whale, Clark found the promontory. He was moved enough by the view to later write about it in his journal:

I beheld the grandest and most pleasing prospect which my eyes ever surveyed. Immediately in front of us is the ocean breaking in fury. To this boisterous scene the Columbia with its tributaries and studded on both sides with the Chinook and Clatsop villages forms a charming contrast, while beneath our feet are stretched the rich prairies.

Prior to setting out, arrange to have a friend drive down to **Indian Beach** to pick you up at the end of this seven-mile, three-hour pilgrimage. Or you can be picked up another mile south at the Ecola Point parking lot. To get to the trailhead, drive south of Seaside out Avenue U (Beach St.) past the golf course to Edgewood St., until you reach the parking lot at the end of the road. Nearby is an area known as **The Cove,** frequented by surfers and fishermen. As you head up the forested trail on the north side of Tillamook Head you can look back over the Seaside townsite. In about 20 minutes, you'll be looking down at the ocean from cliffs 1,000 feet above. Several hours later, you'll hike down onto Indian Beach, arriving near the restrooms.

PRACTICALITIES

Whatever your price range, you'll have to reserve ahead for a room in Seaside during the summer and spring break (This holiday in Oregon takes place from the third week in March to the beginning of April and brings out high school cruisers en masse.) If you do, chances are you'll be able to find the specs you're looking for, given the area's array of lodgings; if you don't, come prepared to camp.

Bed And Breakfast
One option especially worth considering in the so-called Sunset Empire is a stay at a bed and breakfast. In Seaside, the **Boarding House** (208 N. Holladay Dr; tel. 738-9055) overlooks the Necanicum River. The 1898 Victorian features fir tongue-and-groove walls and beamed ceilings.

Frederic Remington's depiction of Lewis and Clark meeting an Indian

SEASIDE BED AND BREAKFAST

10th Avenue Inn Bed and Breakfast, 125 10th Ave., tel. 738-0643, $60-80, cable TV, meals available, nonsmoking rooms, ocean view.

Gilbert Inn Bed and Breakfast, 341 Beach Dr., tel. 738-9770, $70-125, meals available, fireplace, nonsmoking rooms, ocean view.

Riverside Inn Bed and Breakfast, 430 S. Holladay Dr., tel. 738-8254, $45-85, wheelchair access, meals available, river view.

Summer House Bed and Breakfast, 1221 N. Franklin, tel. 738-5740, $55-75, cable TV, fireplace, meals available, nonsmoking rooms.

The Boarding House Bed and Breakfast, 208 N. Holladay Dr., tel. 738-9055, $65-100, cable TV, meals available, fireplace, nonsmoking rooms, river view.

Walker House Bed and Breakfast, 811 1st Ave., tel. 738-5520, $60-70, cable TV, meals available, laundry, nonsmoking rooms.

All rooms have private baths and go for $55-95 a night. Reserve two weeks in advance in summer. The **Riverside Inn** (430 S. Holladay Dr.; tel. 738-8254) has separate four-room cottages overlooking the river, with double occupancy rates ranging $45-80. Private baths, homemade breakfast, and special discount rates Sun.-Thurs. for stays of three days or more are available October through June. During peak season, be sure to reserve a room a month in advance.

Gaston's Beachside Bed and Breakfast (Corner of I Ave. and the Prom; tel. 738-8320) is the best deal on the Prom. This two-room 1906 home charges $35-65 including a full breakfast. Guests share a bath. **Chocolates For Breakfast** (606 N. Holladay; tel. 738-3622) is a 1921 house with double occupancy rates of $45-65. A river view, chocolate hazelnut croissants for breakfast, and an artsy motif make this place a winner.

Budget Accomodations
If you're in need of a budget room here, the **Holladay Motel** (426 S. Holladay Dr.; tel. 738-3690) and the **Mariner** (429 S. Holladay; same tel. as above) offer rooms with facilities down the hall in the $35 range. They share the same management and use of a pool.

Camping
Saddle Mountain and Klootchy Creek parks (see "Cannon Beach" above), due east of Cannon Beach on U.S. 26 (the Sunset Highway), make great camping spots.

Klootchy Creek Park (Clatsop County Parks, Astoria 97103; tel. 325-2631), home of the giant spruce, is 300 yards off U.S. 26. It has nine primitive sites that go for $6 a night. You're paying for proximity to the tree, the beaches, and the civilized haunts of two nearby coastal cities as well as fishing (trout, steelhead, salmon) on the banks of the Necanicum River.

Saddle Mountain State Park (Cannon Beach 97110; tel. 861-1671) also has nine primitive sites with flush toilets and firewood available. Open from mid-April to late October, these campsites make good alternatives to beachfront parks on cloudy days. Sites go for $9 a night. No reservations are necessary at either campground.

On Tillamook Head north of Ecola State Park, there's a primitive campground, accessible to backpackers or all-terrain cyclists, a third of the way up the head from Indian Beach (the Cannon Beach side). It can be approached by using an abandoned logging road which runs parallel to the hiking trail from Indian Beach.

Food
While a stroll down Broadway might have you thinking that cotton candy, corn dogs, and saltwater taffy are the staples of Seaside cuisine, there are several eateries here which can satisfy taste and nutrition as well as the broad-based clientele of this beach town. For breakfast, the **Pig'n Pancake**'s (323 Broadway; tel. 738-7243) Swedish pancakes and crab-n-cheese omelette are tops. Don't be put off by its superficial ap-

SEASIDE ACCOMMODATIONS

Ambassador by the Sea, 40 Ave. U, tel. 738-6382, $50-130, cable TV, kitchenettes, laundry, pool, nonsmoking rooms, ocean view.

Best Western Ocean View Resort, 414 N. Prom, tel. 738-3334, $80-230, wheelchair access, kitchenettes, fireplace, covered pool, laundry, nonsmoking rooms, complimentary continental breakfast, ocean view.

Coast River Inn, 800 S. Holladay Dr., tel. 738-8474, $40-75, wheelchair access, cable TV, kitchenettes, laundry, nonsmoking rooms.

Colonial Motor Inn, 1120 N. Holladay Dr., tel. 738-6295, $55-85, cable TV, laundry, nonsmoking rooms, river view.

Country River Inn, 1020 N. Holladay Dr., tel. 738-8049, $40-75, wheelchair access, cable TV, restaurant, nonsmoking rooms, river view.

Del Mar Motel, 210 N. Downing, tel. 738-7622, $30-50, cable TV, pets, kitchenettes, restaurant/lounge, laundry.

Driftwood Motel, 815 N. Holladay Dr., tel. 738-5597, $50-75, small 10-unit property with a laundry.

Hillcrest Inn, 118 N. Columbia, tel. 738-6273, $40-85, wheelchair access, cable TV, kitchenettes, laundry, nonsmoking rooms.

Hi-Tide Motel, 30 Ave. G, tel. 738-8414, $60-125, cable TV, kitchenettes, pool, covered pool, nonsmoking rooms, ocean view.

Huntley Inn, 441 2nd Ave., tel. 738-9581, $66-77, wheelchair access, cable TV, kitchenettes, covered pool, river view.

Inn on the Prom, 361 S. Prom, tel. 738-5241, $55-125, kitchenettes, fireplace, nonsmoking rooms, ocean view.

Lanai Condos Motel, 3140 Sunset Blvd., tel. 738-6343, $80-95, cable TV, kitchenettes, pool, ocean view.

Mariner Holladay Motel, 429 S. Holladay Dr., tel. 738-3690, $35-70, wheelchair access, cable TV, pool, pets, kitchenettes, nonsmoking rooms.

Ocean Vista Motel, 241 Ave. U, tel. 738-7473, $61-81, cable TV, pets, kitchenettes.

Oceanfront Motel, 50 1st Ave., tel. 738-5661, $62-82, wheelchair access, ocean view.

River View Inn, 555 Ave. G, tel. 738-0670, $45-75, wheelchair access, cable TV, kitchenettes, nonsmoking rooms, river view.

Royale Motel, 531 Ave. A, tel. 738-9541, $40-65, wheelchair access, river view.

Seaside Beach Club, 561 S. Prom, tel. 738-7113, $135-145, wheelchair access, cable TV, kitchenettes, laundry, nonsmoking rooms, ocean view.

Seashore Resort, 60 N. Prom, tel. 738-6368, $68-84, covered pool, ocean view.

Shilo Inn-Oceanfront, 30 N. Prom, tel. 738-9571, $95-182 cable TV, kitchenettes, fireplace, covered pool, laundry, restaurant/lounge, nonsmoking rooms, ocean view.

Shilo Inn Seaside, East 900 S. Holladay Dr., tel. 738-0549, $90-105, wheelchair access, cable TV, kitchenettes, covered pool, laundry, nonsmoking rooms, complimentary continental breakfast.

Sundowner Motor Inn, 125 Ocean Way, tel. 738-8301, $50-90, wheelchair access, cable TV, pets, kitchenettes, covered pool.

Tides Motel, 2316 Beach Dr., tel. 738-6317, $50-110, cable TV, kitchenettes, pool, nonsmoking rooms, ocean view.

Tradewinds Motel, 1022 N. Prom, tel. 738-9468, $50-65, pets, kitchenettes, ocean view.

White Caps Motel, 120 9th Ave., tel. 738-5371, $60-150, pets, kitchenettes, laundry, ocean view.

pearance. Although it looks like just another chain on the main drag, you can count on this place for three meals every day of the week. **Dooger's** (505 Broadway, Seaside; tel. 738-3773), a chain with an outlet in Cannon Beach (1321 N. Hemlock; tel. 431-2225), has won acclaim for its clam chowder. Local clams and oysters, fresh Dungeness crab legs, sautéed shrimp, and marionberry cobbler are also the bases of Dooger's do-good reputation. **Cafe Espresso** (600 Broadway; tel. 738-6169) has coffee drinks, breakfast fare, and views of the Necanicum River. Another plus is its proximity to outdoor concerts on the public square.

Equidistant from Seaside and Cannon Beach is an eatery that has been a roadside institution since 1938. The **Crab Broiler** (junction of U.S. 101 and U.S. 26, Cannon Beach; tel. 738-5313). has many dishes based around crab and cheese, so how can you go wrong? Mexican flavors predominate at **Christiano's** (412 Broadway, Seaside; tel. 738-5058). Along with chiles rellenos and huevos rancheros, such seafood dishes as Mexican prawns (*mucho* garlic!) and Halibut Ixtapa spice up the menu. Complement it with a margarita, Mexican beer, or for dessert, a plate of the south-of-the-border custard, flan. There's also an outlet in Astoria (144 11th St., Astoria; tel. 325-1816).

Should the taste of weak coffee and the ambience of Seaside on a holiday weekend pall, try the **Pacific City Bakery and Cafe** (601 Pacific Way, Gearhart; tel. 738-0245). Gearhart is an appealing out-of-the-way place just north of Seaside, a half mile west of U.S. 101. This is the area where famed food writer James Beard was raised. Beard himself would probably give Pacific City's croissants five stars, so flaky and buttery are these breakfasttime mainstays here. They take center stage again at lunch, providing the foundations for delectable sandwich fillings. Particularly recommended is the smoked salmon and cream cheese with thin-sliced red onion on croissant. Pasta and seafood dishes as well as crepes also pop up at lunch- and dinnertime in the surprisingly urbane little cafe.

Events And Recreation

Seaside predates any other town on the Oregon coast as a place built with good times in mind. A zoo and racetrack were among Sea-

side's first structures. Today, the town hosts the likes of the **Miss Oregon Scholarship Pageant** in July at the Civic Center and the **World Cup Kite Competition** (for stunt kite flyers) at the Turnaround in October. Contact the chamber of commerce for information on these events.

The story of Lewis and Clark has always been an integral part of Seaside lore. Lately it is also the focus of the town's major summer event, the **Lewis and Clark Pageant** (783 First Ave.; tel. 738-0817 or 800-444-6740). The pageant's staged "Journey to the Pacific" takes place in Broadway Park on the east side of town along the banks of Neawanna Creek, and tells the story from the time the expedition started in 1803 near St. Louis, Missouri, to its arrival in 1805 at Fort Clatsop. Showtime is 8 p.m. Thurs.-Sat. and 2 p.m. Sunday, July 29 through Aug. 22. Tickets are $7.50 for adults, $6.00 for seniors, and $4.50 for students ages 8-16; kids under eight get in free.

Fishermen don't only come to Seaside for the Necanicum River's steelhead, trout, and salmon. **Carnahan Park** on Cullaby Lake north of Seaside has crappies, bluegills, perch, catfish, and largemouth bass. Just west of Cullaby, **Sunset Lake** adds trout to the list. Boating, swimming, and water sports add to the appeal of Cullaby Lake.

Golfers can escape to public courses south of Seaside (451 Avenue U; tel. 738-5261) and north in the small town of **Gearhart** (Gearhart-by-the-Sea Resort, Marion St.; tel. 738-5248). Greens fees are $7 for Seaside's nine holes and $14 for Gearhart's 18-hole course. Gearhart also boasts a quieter beach than Seaside and a bowling alley (Evergreen Lanes, west side of U.S. 101 just north of the road to downtown) that reportedly serves the best hamburgers and homemade pie around.

Despite the lifeguard stand, don't swim in Seaside unless you're used to the North Sea. Instead, head to **Sunset Pool** (1140 E. Broadway, Seaside; tel. 738-3311). Fees are $2 for adults, with discounts for children and seniors. Hours vary greatly, so call in advance.

The Turnaround is the starting point and finishing line for such famed races as the eight-mile **Across-the-Sand** beach run and the **Hood-to-Coast Relay,** in mid- and late August, respectively. At the end of each February, the highly regarded **Trail's End Marathon** loops partway to Astoria and back to the Turn-around. Check with the chamber of commerce for details.

Tennis players will find free courts in **Cannon Beach City Park** (Second Ave. and Spruce St.) with coin-operated lights. In Seaside, the **high school** (1901 N. Holladay Dr.) and **Broadway School** (1120 Broadway) have free courts with lights. There are also free public courts in Gearhart.

The surfing venues north of Tillamook Head, Indian Basin, and near Short Sands Beach in Oswald West State Park can be enjoyed with surfboard and equipment rentals from **Clean-line Surf Shop** (719 First Ave., Seaside; tel. 738-7888). Boogie boards and surfboards go for $12.50, wetsuits, boots, and flippers cost $15, or you can spend $25 for the complete package.

Two area bike shops with rentals are **Mike's Bike Shop** (248 N. Spruce St., Cannon Beach; tel. 436-1266) and **Prom Bike Shop** (622 12th Ave., Seaside; tel. 738-8251). Rental fees at these places run $3-6 per hour. Mike's special-izes in mountain bikes, which can be returned at a Warrenton outlet.

Birdwatchers revel in **Necanicum Estuary Park** (1900 block of N. Holladay across the street from Seaside High School). Local stu-dents have built a viewing platform, stairs to the beach, a boardwalk, and interpretive signs. Great blue and green herons and numerous migratory species flock to the grassy marshes and slow tidal waters near the mouth of the Necanicum River. Occasionally, Roosevelt elk, black-tailed deer, river otters, beavers, minks, and muskrats can also be sighted.

Information And Services

The **Seaside Chamber of Commerce** (7 Roosevelt, Seaside 97138; tel. 738-6391 or 800-444-6740 in Oregon) is open from May to mid-Sept., Mon.-Fri. 8 a.m.-6 p.m., Sat. 10-4 , and Sun. noon-4. In the off-season, the hours are Mon.-Fri. 9-5, Sat. 10-3, and Sun. noon-3. **Greyhound (RAZ)** (9325 S. Holladay Dr., tel. 738-4121) has service to Portland and a bus which goes to Astoria at 9 a.m. daily.

A **laundromat** is located on 57 N. Holladay St. near First Avenue. It's open daily 6 a.m.-11 p.m. The **police** (1090 S. Roosevelt Dr.; tel. 738-6311) are there to help you in the event of trouble. The **post office** (300 Avenue A, Sea-side 97138; tel. 738-5462) is open Mon.-Fri. 8:30-5. **Providence Seaside Hospital** (725 S. Wahanna Rd.; tel. 738-8463) has 24-hour ser-vice and an emergency room.

(this page, top) thrill-seekers on the Rogue River near Grants Pass (Christopher Scott Murray);
(this page, bottom) ship hull, Clatsop County (Oregon Tourism Division/Peter Iredale);
(following page) the Foley River Trail in the Three Sisters Wilderness (Christopher Scott Murray)

ASTORIA AND VICINITY

Many coastal travelers are aware of Astoria's legacy as the oldest permanent U.S. settlement west of the Mississippi, whose glory days are kept alive by museums, historical exhibits, and Victorian homes. This often creates the expectation of a Williamsburg of the West, where the portrayal of heritage is a focal point of the local identity. The reality of modern-day Astoria is more accurately captured in a locally popular bumper sticker which defiantly proclaims, We Ain't Quaint! This city of 10,000 people is still rooted in a resource-based economy whose logging, fishing, and canneries are in decline. The preserved pioneer past and attractive historic homes may soften these rough edges, but not enough to let anyone mistake Astoria for a tourist town.

A maritime flavor dominates the local scene, with old salts filling many a smoky barroom with stories of ships that didn't make it past the waves and weather of the Columbia bar. Where the River of the West meets the ocean offshore here could well be the biggest widow-maker on the high seas, earning it the title, Graveyard of the Pacific.

Another striking aspect of the town is the pervasiveness of such Scandinavian traditions as public steam baths, *lutfisk*, and *smorrebrod* platters. Nonetheless, Hollywood has chosen Astoria's picturesque neighborhoods to simulate the all-American city on at least a half-dozen occasions. Given its rich history, this is altogether fitting.

HISTORY

The Clatsop Indians lived in this area for thousands of years before Astoria's written history began. The region was first chronicled by Heceta, a Spanish explorer who sailed near the Columbia's mouth but failed to enter. American presence on the Columbia began with Captain Robert Gray's discovery of the river in 1792, which he christened after his fur-trading ship. Thereafter, Lewis and Clark's famous expedition of 1803-1806, with its winter encampment at Fort Clatsop south of present-day Astoria, in-corporated the Pacific Northwest as part of a new nation. In 1811, John Jacob Astor's agents built Fort Astoria—the first settlement west of the Mississippi. Despite temporary occupation by the British between 1813 and 1818, the fort and a shaky American presence were able to hold on until settlers came to farm the region during the Oregon Trail era of the 1840s.

From that time until the 1900s, emigrants of Scandinavian descent predominated. Commerce grew with the export of lumber and foodstuffs to gold rush-era San Francisco and the Far East. Shipwrecks became commonplace on the treacherous Columbia River bar despite Captain Flavel's pilot service in the 1850s. Later, Fort Stevens was built during the Civil War to guard against a Confederate naval incursion. Salmon canneries became the basis of Astoria's economy during the 1870s, helping it grow into Oregon's second-largest city—and a notorious shanghaiing port. Over the ensuing decades, logging, fishing, and shipbuilding coaxed the population here up to 20,000 by WW II.

Near the end of the war, a Japanese submarine's shelling of Fort Stevens made it the only fortification on American soil to have sustained an attack in a world war (this fact is disputed by two locations in California). After the war, the region's fortunes rose and fell with the resource-based economy. In a 1966 attempt to supplement that economy with tourism, the State Highway Division built the 4.1-mile **Astoria Bridge,** connecting Oregon and Washington (according to *Guinness,* the world's longest three-span, continuous through-trusses bridge). The bridge provided the final link in 1,625-mile-long U.S. 101. The modern era has also been characterized by the development of world-class museums and artful Victorian restorations.

Unfortunately, preserving Astoria's glory days could not make up for the closing of the canneries and the decline of logging and fishing. Moves to make Astoria a major port of entry for Japanese cars and to begin large-scale tourist enterprises on the waterfront have been suggested as a means to improve the economic climate here. Whether or not Astoria's ship ever comes in, let's hope the unpretentious charm of this hillside city by the sea will not be lost in the process.

THE LAND

The view from **Astor Column** on Coxcomb Hill (for directions see "Museums and Miscellany" following) orients you to the city and the north coast. To the north, note the freighters docked on the edge of Astoria's cityscape and the Astoria (to Megler, Washington) Bridge spanning the Columbia. Across Baker Bay to the northwest, on the Washington side of the six-mile channel that Robert Gray entered in 1792, is Cape Disappointment. Looking over Young's Bay south and west of Astoria, the Clatsop Plains extend to Tillamook Head. Although the 1840s settlers had no luck farming these sand traps, the relative flatness of the terrain lent itself to the building of the region's first road, which U.S. 101 now parallels. The beaches west of the road contribute 95% of the state's harvest of razor clams. Farther south, the plains give way to a dense area of settlement around Seaside. Tillamook Head, the coast's northernmost headland, then defines a valley cut by the Necanicum River. Fair-weather views reveal Saddle Mountain southeast of this lowland. Clear visibility also treats you to panoramas of Mt. St. Helens and Mt. Hood on the far eastern horizon. A visit to the information booth on top of the hill (open from Memorial Day to the second week of Sep-

tember) and a look at the annotated bronze relief map of the north coast should precede climbing the steps to the top of the column. The map is found on the entry walkway and notes the distances and directions to such landmarks as Mt. Rainer, Mt. St. Helens, Tillamook Head, and Saddle Mountain.

SIGHTS

Flavel House

Begin your walking tour at the Flavel House (441 Eighth St., Astoria 97103; tel. 325-2203) on the corner of Eighth and Duane, a right turn off Marine Dr., which is an extension of ORE 30. This splendid Queen Anne-style Victorian mansion was built by George Flavel, whose guiding of vessels across the Columbia bar made him Oregon's first steamship captain and Astoria's earliest millionaire. The home's intricate woodwork, period furnishings, and art, along with its extravagantly rendered gables, cornices, and porches, rank it with the Carson Mansion in Eureka, California, as a Victorian showplace. From its fourth-story cupola, Captain Flavel could watch his own sailing fleet, and it's said that his wife would keep the light going in this perch when the captain was bringing in a ship. The 14-foot ceilings, Persian rugs, and an international array of tiles are upstaged only by the fireplaces in every room framed in exotic hardwoods. Known locally as "the house with the red roof," it has withstood more than a century of

one of Astoria's
many well-preserved
Victorian homes

storms off the Columbia River estuary. This landmark for incoming ships is now the foremost monument to Astoria's golden age as the leading port in the Northwest.

Flavel House is open daily May to Sept., 10 a.m.-5 p.m., and charges $3 for adults, $2.50 for seniors, and $1 for children 6-12. The admission price includes any two of the three museums operated by the Clatsop County Historical Society (see "Museums and Miscellany" following). Close by is **Shallen Winery** (1598 Duane St.; tel. 325-5978), where you can quench a thirst by sampling this vineyard's specialty fruit wines.

Walking Tour

In addition to the Flavel House, Astoria is home to dozens of beautifully preserved 19th-century and early-20th-century houses. A walking tour of many of them is laid out in a guidebook written by a local historian and available for $2. After the Flavel House tour, however, most people seem content to forego the purchase and let the architectural scenery do the talking. Just start walking south on Eighth St. and turn on Franklin Avenue. Continue east to 11th St., then detour south a block on 11th St. to Grand Ave., east on Grand, north on 12th St., and back to Franklin, continuing your eastward trek. Walk to 17th St., then south again to Grand, double back on Grand two blocks to 15th St., then walk north on 15th to Exchange St. and east on Exchange to 17th, where you'll be just two blocks from the Columbia River Maritime Museum. The route will take you past 74 historical buildings and sites.

Doorways Of Astoria

The ornate doorways of Astoria weave Victorian nuance and other architectural sensibilities together well enough to merit a special look, particularly at the following addresses: 1243 Franklin Ave., 1509 Franklin Ave., 1555 Franklin Ave., 1 Second St., 10 Sixth St., 130 Bond St., and 441 Eighth Street. Walkers will also take note that the streets here are alphabetical.

MUSEUMS AND MISCELLANY

The above walking tour makes for a very full morning. If you get an early start, however, you'll still have time to visit several other Astoria landmarks. Among these, Fort Clatsop, Fort Stevens, Astoria Column, and the Maritime Museum are must-see attractions.

Astoria Column

Astoria Column is located a short distance from Marine Dr. down 16th Street. You'll go through the southeast residential part of the city before beginning the drive up Coxcomb Hill Road. It's also accessible by city bus (See "Information and Services" following). Once atop this 595-foot summit, walk the 166 steps up the 125-foot tower. A frieze depicting major historical events adorns the column's exterior but the real attraction is the view of the surrounding countryside. This column was a joint project of the Great Northern Railroad and the descendants of John Jacob Astor to commemorate a 1926 cross-country rail excursion.

Fire Fighters Museum

Back on Marine Drive is the Uppertown Fire Fighters Museum (30th and Marine Dr.; tel. 325-2203). This exposition contains hand-pulled, horse-drawn, and motorized fire-fighting vehicles in service from 1877 to 1921. In addition, fire-fighting memorabilia and equipment from this period are exhibited, supplemented by photos and information about Astoria's major blazes. The museum is operated by the Clatsop County Historical Society and has hours and admission similar to the Flavel House's.

Heritage Museum

The Clatsop County Historical Society also operates the Heritage Museum (1618 Exchange St., Astoria 97103; tel. 325-2203). Several galleries with antiquities, tools, and old photographs depict various aspects of life in Clatsop County. Gallery One deals with the natural history, geology, native American artifacts, early immigrants and settlers in the region, and important natural events. Gallery Two portrays the development of commerce in such enterprises as fishing, fish packing, logging, and lumber. Gallery Three concentrates on the 22 ethnic groups who came to Clatsop County in search of a better life. The hours and admission here are the same as those of the Flavel House.

Fort Clatsop

To reach Fort Clatsop National Memorial (Route 3 Box 604FC, Astoria 97103; tel. 861-2471), site of the Lewis and Clark encampment, from Marine Dr. head west across Youngs Bay, taking care to stay in the right lane to avoid getting sidetracked by alternate U.S. 101. Lewis and Clark crossed this bay en route to the Fort Clatsop site after their original encampment on the Washington side proved too exposed to the elements. On the other side of the bay look for signs for the Fort Clatsop turnoff a quarter mile past the Fort Stevens State Park sign. Then turn left off the Coast Highway and follow the direction markers. This memorial sits six miles south of Astoria and three miles east of U.S. 101 on the Lewis and Clark River. Although the expedition's story is nicely narrated here with displays, artifacts, slides, and films every day except Christmas, summertime "living history" reenactments are the main reason to come. The winter of 1805-06 put a premium on wilderness survival skills, some of which are exhibited here by rangers in costume, 9 a.m.-5:30 p.m. daily, Memorial Day to Labor Day. You can see the tanning of hides, making of buckskin clothing and moccasins, and the molding of tallow candles and lead bullets. In addition, visitors may occasionally participate in the construction of a dugout canoe or try their luck at starting a fire by striking flint on steel.

Despite the discomfort, a visit on a cold, wet wintry day is an opportunity to better understand the travails of Lewis and Clark. This group consisted of 30 people including one black, one Indian, and a baby, all of whom spent the winter of 1805-06 here. The dynamic duo and party camped near the mouth of the Columbia River in November 1805 and wrote, "Ocian view! O! The joy!" The fort was built a month later and named for the Clatsop tribe. The party remained at this site for 106 days and began its trek east on March 23.

The hands-on experiences complement the following permanent features of Fort Clatsop: a log replica of the original fort (site of living history exhibits); a well-equipped visitor center (check for botanical walks on the bulletin board here); a beautifully landscaped picnic area; and trails that lead from the visitor center to the fort, to the canoe landing, and to a spring used by the

expedition in 1805-06. Admission is $1 for visitors ages 17-61, all others free, and the ticket is good for seven days. The maximum charge is $3 per family. Gates to the memorial are open 8 a.m.-8 p.m. during the summer season and 8 a.m.-5 p.m. the rest of the year. Admission is free on winter weekends.

Fort Stevens

From Fort Clatsop, retrace the route back to U.S. 101 and the sign pointing the way to Fort Stevens (Fort Stevens Historic Area, Hammond 97121; tel. 861-2000). This Civil War-vintage outpost is situated 10 miles west of Astoria, 15 miles northwest of Seaside, on the northwest corner of the coast. To get there, drive through Warrenton en route to Pacific Dr. in Hammond, which leads to the Fort Stevens Historic Area and Military Museum. The fort was established shortly before the Confederates surrendered at Appomattox on April 9, 1865.

Its creation was not the only outgrowth of the Civil War on the West Coast. The year before, Lincoln had created the city of Port Angeles, Washington, for "lighthouse purposes." Given the subsequent creation of Fort Stevens shortly thereafter, it's a safe assumption that "lighthouse purposes" also meant being on the lookout for Confederate ships and the British, whom the Union feared would ally themselves with the South. This seems more credible when you consider that the last shots of the war were fired by the *Shenandoah* on a fleet of Yankee whalers in the Bering Strait. The June 5, 1865, shelling occurred after the surrender because the Confederate skipper was unaware of the Appomattox treaty, signed two months before.

Though Fort Stevens was spared in the Civil War it sustained an attack in another conflict. On June 21, 1942, a Japanese submarine fired 17 shells on Battery Russell (massive gun emplacements), making it the only U.S. fortification in the 48 states to be bombed by a foreign power since the War of 1812. No damage was incurred and the Army didn't return fire. Shortly after WW II, the fort was deactivated and all armaments were removed.

Today, the site features a memorial rose garden, old photos, weapons exhibits, and maps, as well as seven different batteries and other structures left over from almost a century of service.

Exploring some of the gun batteries and climbing to the nearby commander's station for a scenic view of the Columbia River and South Jetty are popular visitor activities. During the summer months, guided tours of the underground Battery Mishler ($1.50) and a narrated tour of the Fort's 37 acres on a two-ton U.S. Army truck ($2.50) are also available. The summer programs include Civil War reenactments and archaeological digs; consult the visitor center for schedules. The fort's hours are 10 a.m.-6 p.m., Memorial Day to Labor Day, and Wed.-Sun 10 a.m.-4 p.m. during the rest of the year. Except for the tours, admission is free.

Eight miles of bike trails (See "Sports and Recreation" following, for info on rentals) link the historic area to the rest of the park and provide access to Battery Russell and the 1906 wreck of the British schooner *Peter Iredale* (more remnants of the ship are displayed at the Maritime Museum). You can also bike to the campground one mile south of the Military Museum.

Parking is available at one of four lots about a mile apart from one another at the foot of the dunes. The beach runs north to the Columbia River, where excellent surf fishing, birdwatching,

and a view of the mouth of the river await. South of the campground (east of the *Peter Iredale*) there's a self-guided nature trail around part of the two-mile shoreline of **Coffenberry Lake.** The lake also has two swimming beaches with bathhouses and fishing for trout and perch.

Columbia River Maritime Museum
About a half mile east of downtown Astoria, near the foot of 17th St. on the north side of Marine Dr. (U.S. 30), the Columbia River Maritime Museum (1792 Marine Dr.; tel. 326-2323) is hard to miss. The roof of the 37,000-square-foot museum simulates the curvature of a wave, and a gigantic 25,000-pound anchor from the U.S. battleship *Indiana* is also hard to ignore. This eye-catching facade is more than matched by what's inside. Even if the Columbia River could talk, it would be hard-pressed to surpass the eloquence of this museum's historical displays. The eras when Indian canoes plied the Columbia, Lewis and Clark camped on its shores, and dramatic shipwrecks occurred on its bar are recounted with scale models and miniatures of ships and paintings. The chance to peer through a periscope, man the bridge of a WW II destroyer, and enter a Columbia River sternwheeler pilothouse imparts a hands-on aspect to your experience here. Scrimshaw, fishing and cannery artifacts, and sea charts dating as far back as 1587 also highlight your visit.

At the end of your journey through maritime history, tour the 128-foot lightship *Columbia*. This vessel served as a floating lighthouse, marking the entrance to the mouth of the river and helping many ships navigate the dangerous waters. It was replaced in 1979 by an unmanned, 42-foot-high navigational buoy after almost three decades of service. The museum is open 9:30 a.m-5 p.m. and closed only on Thanksgiving and Christmas Day. Adults are $4, seniors $3, under 18 $2, and children under six get in free.

Twilight Eagle Sanctuary
Six miles northeast of Astoria in the Burnside area is the new Twilight Eagle Sanctuary (for more info write the Twilight Eagle Sanctuary, c/o Oregon Eagle Federation, 5873 Estate Dr., Klamath Falls 97601). The 15-acre parcel here hosts 50 eagles during the winter. In addition,

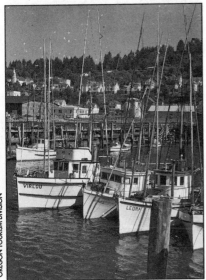

OREGON TOURISM DIVISION

fishing boats at Astoria Dock

there are ducks, Canada geese, wrens, songbirds, and on occasion, tundra swans. To get there, drive six miles east of town on U.S. 30 and turn left at Burnside. Another left a half mile later will take you to the viewing platform.

SPORTS AND RECREATION

Fishing
More than any other industry, commercial fishing has dominated Astoria throughout its history. Salmon canneries lined the waterfront at the turn of the century. Albacore and longline shark fishing put dinner on the table in the '30s and '40s. In the modern era, commercial fishing has turned to sole, rockfish, flounder, and less-well-known bottom fish. If it's not enough to watch these commercial operations from the dock, **Tiki-Fleet** (897 Pacific St., Hammond 97121, next to the coin laundry; tel. 861-1201) and **Thunderbird Charters** (tel. 325-7990) will show you where to drop your line for salmon, sturgeon, and bottom fish. Given the retail price of fresh salmon, you could theoretically pay for a charter trip by landing a single fish. Sports anglers can fish for salmon in either salt or fresh water (depending on time of year) or go after trout, bass, catfish, steelhead, and sturgeon in freshwater lakes, streams, and rivers. Ling cod, rockfish, surf perch, or other bottomfish can be pursued at sea, off jetties, or along ocean beaches.

Astoria Flight Center
Another way to avoid being landlocked is the Astoria Flight Center (tel. 861-1222). One person is charged $40, groups of two or three are charged $65, for a 40-minute flight. See the whalewatching section in this chapter's introduction for information on similar options along the coast.

Oregon Coast Trail
More down-to-earth pursuits can be found along the Oregon Coast Trail. It extends from Fort Stevens Park to the area around Three Capes Lookout. The first stretch extends south along the beach for 14 miles to Gearhart. It's a flat, easy walk, and your journey could well be highlighted by a sighting of the endangered silverspot butterfly. It now frequents just six sites, in-

cluding four in Oregon, with Clatsop County being one of them. The endangered status of this species protects it under law, and has stopped developers from building resorts on coastal meadows and dunes north of Gearhart. Look for a small orange butterfly with silvery spots on the undersides of its wings. You also might encounter cars on the beach. This section of shoreline is inexplicably the longest stretch of coastline open to motor vehicles in Oregon. Call the State Parks and Recreation Division for an up-to-date report on trail conditions before starting out (tel. 800-452-5687).

Tapiola Pool, Tennis Courts
Outdoor recreationists will also appreciate Tapiola Pool (901 W. Marine Dr., tel. 323-7027), and tennis courts at three locations: 36th and Leif Erickson; 785 Alameda (the gray school); and Sixth and Niagara. The latter facility is lit until 10 p.m. More courts with lights can be found in Warrenton at the corner of Second and Alder streets.

Bike Rentals
Bike rentals are conveniently located next to Fort Stevens State Park Historic Area (316 Russell Dr., Hammond; tel. 861-0937). Ten-speeds, mountain bikes, and youth bikes may be rented by the day or by the hour.

Auto Tour
An auto tape tour of the coast is available through **Blue Sky Publications** (P.O. Box 4227, Salem 97302; tel. 362-3403). Cassettes include Astoria to Lincoln City and Lincoln City to Brookings, each of which sells for $20. While the commentary sounds like wooden ad copy at times, these high-fidelity tapes have some good information. Other locales covered by the company include Portland and the Columbia Gorge.

PRACTICALITIES

As with the rest of the north coast, bed and breakfasts are the best way to go. This kind of lodging is all the more appealing in Astoria, with its picturesque hills framing Victorian neighborhoods. Homes of merchants, politicians, sea captains, and salmon canners number among Astoria's bed and breakfast offerings.

Fort Columbia Hostel

If a B&B is out of your budget range, try the Fort Columbia AYH Hostel (tel. 206-777-8755) across the river in Chinook, Washington. Despite the typically low youth hostel rates, this is more than just another no-frills crash pad for backpackers. The rustic former Army hospital on a hill above the Columbia has rocking chairs and couches on a long porch, and a fire going on chilly evenings to bring together naturalists, historians, ornithologists, and beachcombers in homey communion. Outdoor barbecue pits on beautiful grounds become gathering spots on warm summer nights. Any misgivings you might have about dormitory-style rooms in a military infirmary are also tempered by 11-foot, tin-tile ceilings evocative of the turn of the century. One private room is available for couples. Reservations are not necessary in this well-kept secret.

To get there, cross the Astoria Bridge ($1.50 toll), go two miles west on U.S. 101, and look for signs to Fort Columbia State Park. A Pacific Transit bus goes there for 50 cents from the Greyhound station (364 Ninth St.) several times a day. Call before you go because the hostel closes for some months during the winter; however, the manager says the hostel will open to accommodate reservations. Regular hours are 5 p.m.-9 a.m., June to mid-Sept. As with other AYH hostels, some chores are required.

Bed And Breakfast

Franklin Street Bed and Breakfast (1140 Franklin St., Astoria 97103; tel. 325-4314) is an elegant turn-of-the-century Victorian. Five rooms with private baths and queen beds can accommodate 14 people here. It's within walking distance of downtown and a continental breakfast is included in the rates ($68-115 a night, double occupancy). Minimum two-night stay on weekends and advance reservations, 10 days in advance, have become necessary due to the popularity of this place.

The **Rosebriar Inn** (636 14th St., Astoria 97103; tel. 325-7427) is located on a quiet neighborhood street near the Maritime Museum. For $48-98 nightly (double occupancy) you have a choice of three rooms with baths or seven without (facilities down the hall). In this spacious former convent, a full breakfast on a family-style dining table is also included. Reserve a week and a half in advance during summer.

Camping

With 260 tent sites, 343 RV sites, and a special area for walk-in campers and bicyclists, **Fort Stevens State Park** (Hammond 94121; tel. 861-1671) is the largest camping facility in the state. In addition to the usual amenities you'll find a laundromat and playground. To get there from Astoria, cross the Klaskanine River west on Hwy. 30 and take the Hammond exit four miles to the park. Five miles of ocean frontage and three miles of Columbia River frontage, as well as several small lakes here, make this *the* place on the north coast for water sports. Add the park's amenities and other natural attractions and you have the perfect base camp from which to take advantage of the region. Just be sure to avoid spring break (around March 20 to April 1) if you wish to be spared the rites of spring enacted here by Oregon teenagers. Reservations are accepted here and a $15-17 fee is charged. The state park is open year-round.

Food

If you like good food with a minimum of expense and pretense you've come to the right place. But first, several retail outlets are deserving of mention.

The freshest produce in town is available Tues.-Sat. 9-5:30 at **Columbia Farmers Market** (Sixth and Bond; Astoria, tel. 325-4045). Just look for a ramshackle yellow house one block off Marine Drive.

As you come into Astoria from the east after crossing the bridge on Marine Dr. (U.S. 30), you'll see a nondescript storefront on the left among the bars and bait shops. Little would you suspect that one of Oregon's most esteemed purveyors of gourmet smoked fish conducts business here. **Josephson's Smokehouse** (106 Marine Dr., Astoria; tel. 325-2190) produces a Scandinavian cold-smoked salmon without dyes or preservatives, so it is seldom sold through retail outlets. Instead, Josephson's caters to mail-order clientele (to order: P.O. Box 412, Astoria 97103) and fine restaurants which serve the product upon arrival. You can buy direct at a cheaper (but not cheap) price than the mail-order rates. Pickled salmon, salmon jerky, *former home of Miss Nellie Wilson and parrot*

sturgeon caviar, and a variety of alder-smoked and canned fish are also sold here.

Oregon's number-one retail chain, **Fred Meyer** (1451 U.S. 101, Warrenton; tel. 861-3003) has a deli that stocks salads, meats, cheeses, French bread, and other takeout items. This store is also known for good deals on clothes, camping equipment, and hardware.

Underneath the Astoria Bridge near the water, **Cafe Uniontown** (218 W. Marine Dr.; tel. 323-8708) offers a taste of Astoria with fresh seafood, Finnish breads, and a dessert called Swedish cream—a mousselike concoction topped with blackberries. Carnivores and pasta-lovers needn't go hungry either, with a varied menu featuring prime rib and fettuccine alfredo. Check out the 1907-vintage bar in the restaurant's lounge, where weekend songfests can end your evening on a high note. Nearby **Pacific Rim** (229 W. Marine Dr., Astoria; tel. 325-4481) can satisfy your hankerin' for pizza and burgers better and more cheaply than any other place in town. In addition, the low-priced and tasty Italian entrees at this drab cafe might also make you forget seafood temporarily.

If you can't, try the fish and chips at the **Ship Inn** (1 Second St.; tel. 325-0033). A state travel magazine selected this restaurant as the best pub in Oregon, and another regional publication gave it awards for seafood and business lunches. Even if you're not very hungry, you can always enjoy its scenic waterfront location while snacking on English cheeses, Cornish pasties, and imported brews. Jazz and bluegrass also provide conviviality here.

The **Columbian Cafe** (1114 Marine Dr.; tel. 325-2233) is where the meatless '60s meet '90s Northwest cuisine. The good selection of entrees and fresh catch of the day are all expertly prepared and moderately priced. The chef here is also famous for Uriah's St. Diablo jelly, which comes in garlic, jalapeño, and red-pepper flavors. These jellies are available here and sold throughout the state. You may also enjoy the free-flowing political repartee with the staff and regulars in this cramped but friendly place. Next door, the **Border Town Bar** does justice to its name with hefty helpings wrapped up in flour tortillas.

Events

The biggest event in town is the **Astoria Scandinavian Festival** (Box 754, Astoria 97103; tel. 325-6311), which takes place the weekend of June 21, Friday through Sunday. Local Danes, Finns, Icelanders, Norwegians, and Swedes come together to celebrate their heritage. Costumed participants dance around a flowered midsummer pole (a fertility rite), burn a bonfire to destroy evil spirits, and have tugs-of-war pitting Scandinavian nationalities against each other. Food, dancing, crafts, and a parade bring the whole town out to Astoria High School on West Marine Drive just off ORE 202. Admission is $5 for adults and $1 for children 6-12.

Another fête that might prove enjoyable is the **Great Astoria Crab Feed and Seafood Festival,** held the last weekend in April. Seafood, cookery, wines, crafts, a carnival, and a traditional crab dinner are featured. Admission is $3 for adults, $2 for seniors, and $1 for children 6-12; call 325-6311 for more information.

The chamber of commerce offers a **Victorian homes tour** the second weekend in August. They also coordinate the **Astoria Regatta** in conjunction with this event.

Cultural stimulation can be found on 10th St. at **Parnassus Books** (234 10th St.; tel. 325-1363) and the **Ricciardi Gallery** (108 10th St.; tel. 325-5420). Around the corner from the bookstore is **Michael's Antiques and Art Gallery** (1007 Marine Dr.; tel. 325-2350).

Theater
Those interested in a melodrama with historic antecedents might enjoy *Shanghaied,* which is based on Astoria's dubious distinction as a notorious shanghai port during the late 1800s. A local theater troupe, the **Astor Street Opry Co.,** has shows Thurs.-Sat. nights, mid-July through mid-August. Performances begin at 8 p.m. in the lobby of the John Jacob Astor Apartments, a renovated 1920s hotel at 14th and Commercial St. in Astoria. Tickets can be purchased at Paperback Traffic (1015 Commercial St.; tel. 325-4642) for $5-10 or at the box office, which opens at 7 p.m. Chase scenes, bar fights, and a liberal sprinkling of Scandinavian jokes will have you laughing, in between applauding the hero and booing the villain.

Information And Services
With 10,000 people, Astoria is the largest city and media hub of the north coast. The local newspaper, the *Daily Astorian,* is sold around town and is worth a look if only to get the editorial slant of Steve Forrester. This former Washington correspondent's witty commentary on events local, regional, and national pulls no punches.

Throughout the north coast KMUN (91.9 FM Astoria and Seaside, 89.5 in Cannon Beach) is a public radio station with community-based programming that is especially diverse. Classical, jazz, rock, and folk music, public affairs, radio drama, literature readings and children's bedtime stories, and NPR news will keep your dial glued to this frequency.

The **Astoria Chamber of Commerce** (111 W. Maine Dr.; tel. 800-535-3637 or 325-6311) will send you a free guidebook (write: P.O. Box 176, Astoria 97103) to all the sites as well as maps, motel listings, and other visitor information. The facility itself also has generic north coast and southwest Washington materials. It's open daily 8 a.m.-8 p.m.; Oct.-April hours are Mon.-Fri. 8-5.

To get around town take **TBR Transit** (Greyhound terminal, 364 Ninth St. at Duane St.; tel. 325-3524). A full city loop is made every hour Mon.-Sat. 6:30 a.m.-7:15 p.m. The fare is 50 cents.

To get out of town, **Greyhound,** whose service is through RAZ (364 Ninth St.; tel. 325-5641), has morning and evening service to Portland. There's an Astoria-to-Seaside run which leaves at 7:30 p.m.

The **post office** (Astoria 97103; tel. 325-2141) is located in the Federal Building at Eighth and Commercial. It's open Mon.-Fri. 8:30 a.m.-5 p.m.

Other useful numbers include the **county sheriff** (tel. 225-2061), the **Coast Guard** and **airport** at Warrenton (tel. 861-2242), and **Columbia Memorial Hospital** (2111 Exchange St.; tel. 325-4321).

ANN IONG

PORTLAND AND VICINITY

In shadows cast by 100-year-old trees and buildings, the new Northwest is taking shape in Portland, Oregon. Here amid greenery seldom seen in an urban environment, high-tech business ventures, a full cultural calendar, and an activist community are carving out a vibrant image. A latticework of bridges over the Willamette River adds a distinctive profile, while parks, malls, and other people spaces give Portland a heart and a soul. The overall effect is more European than American, where the urban core is equal parts marketplace, cultural forum, and working metropolis.

Such a happy medium is the result of progressive planning and a fortunate birthright. Patterns of growth in this one-time Indian encampment at the confluence of the Willamette and Columbia rivers were initially shaped by the practical Midwestern values of Oregon Trail pioneers as well as by the sophistication of New England merchants. Rather than the boom-bust development which characterized Seattle and gold-rush San Francisco, Portland was designed to be user-friendly over the long haul. During the modern era, such utopian refinements as the most advanced and extensive mass-tran-

sit systems in the U.S. and an urban plan which places strict limitations on the height of buildings and the space between them were added. In this vein, aesthetically pleasing and historic architecture has been spared during Portland's last decades of growth.

Another blessing is Portland's auspicious location. Even though it sits 110 miles from the Pacific Ocean on the Columbia River, the city's port handles among the largest overall tonnage of foreign waterborne cargo on the West Coast. On the export side, the timber, grain, and produce of eastern Oregon, the Columbia Gorge, and the Willamette Valley frequently depart Portland for Pacific Rim countries. In addition to this commerce on the Columbia, battleships, ocean liners, and other vessels go into dry dock here for repair and renovation.

Portland's waterways are her lifeblood in other ways. Mt. Hood's Bull Run watershed supplies some of the purest drinking water anywhere in the U.S., and the printing, textile, papermaking, and high-tech industries place a premium on Portland's clean-running aqueous arteries. Cheap and abundant power from the Willamette and Columbia rivers' hydro projects has also provided an incentive for many other industries to locate here.

The traveler will appreciate Portland's proximity to rural retreats. With scenic Columbia Gorge and year-round skiing on Mt. Hood to the east, and the Carmel of the Oregon Coast, Cannon Beach, to the west, relief from urban stress is little more than an hour away. Other nearby getaways include the wine country and the historic sites of Champoeg and Oregon City. Closer to home, Forest Park is the largest urban wilderness in the country. Washington Park's Japanese and Rose gardens are other internationally renowned places of beauty and contemplation.

The cultural offerings in this city of 437,319 are noteworthy for their scope and excellence. Whether it's the wine, cheese, and camaraderie on first-Thursday-of-the-month gallery walks or the smorgasbord of live theater and state-of-the-art concert halls, Portland's music mavens and culture vultures enjoy a full table. In like measure, bibliophiles revel in one of the world's largest bookstores, Powell's, as well as many other outlets for rare editions. The Portland Symphony Orchestra under the baton of James De Priest has also gained an international reputation through its compact-disc recordings and world travels. As for popular music, top rock acts regularly hit Portland, while the local pub scene showcases many fine blues and jazz players.

On a smaller scale, readings by local literati Ursula Le Guin and Jean Auel, or equally prominent visiting authors, are a treat for Portland's book lovers. The flame of knowledge is kept burning by Portland's museums. Such arcane exhibition halls as the Portland Police Museum and the American Advertising Museum complement the Oregon Museum of Science and Industry and the Washington Park Zoo. Adding to this array are more movie screens, radio stations, and bookstores than in any American city of comparable size.

Nonetheless, there are faint rumblings of trouble in River City. In recent years, Portland has not been exempt from the urban ills of gang warfare, escalating real estate prices, and a sizable homeless population. Locals will tell you that rush-hour traffic jams on the Banfield Expressway (I-84), the Sunset Highway (ORE 26), and the "Terwilliger Curves" portion of I-5 get worse each year. This is due to the fact that greater Portland's population doubled from 704,000 in 1950 to 1,403,000 in 1991 and is still climbing. Despite these problems, Portland's quality of life is still frequently touted by surveys and media as being unsurpassed by few, if any, major American cities. *Newsweek* picked it as one of 10 hot spots for the 1990s, and Allied and United Van Lines said it was the most moved-to destination in the country in 1989. As such, the era of "small is beautiful" may soon be a thing of the past here. Come now and see Portland in its Golden Age.

EARLY HISTORY

Sauvie Island, northwest of the current city limits, was the site of an Indian village whose name inspired William Clark to christen the nearby river the Willamette in 1805. Two decades later, England's establishment of Fort Vancouver across the Columbia brought French trappers into the area, some of whom retired around what would eventually become Portland. The city was formally born when two New Englanders, Pettygrove from Portland, Maine, and Lovejoy from Boston, Massachusetts, flipped a coin at a dinner party to decide who would give a name to a 640-acre claim they co-owned. The state-of-Mainer won and decided in the winter of 1844-45 to name it after his birthplace. The original claim is located in the vicinity of Southwest Front Street.

The trade which grew up along the Willamette River and the so-called plank road south of the city enabled Willamette Valley produce and lumber from the interior to find an outlet to the sea at Portland's Columbia River port. Portland was thus able to make the transition from a sleepy village referred to as Stumptown to the major trade center and population vortex in the state. The single event which contributed to the emergence of Portland as Oregon's leading city, however, was the Lewis and Clark Exposition in 1905. Two to three million people attended this centennial celebration of the famed expedition, establishing the city in the minds of the American business community as the gateway to the Orient as well as paving the way for significant population growth in the years following the fair. By 1910, a metropolis of almost a quarter million

PORTLAND AND VICINITY

© MOON PUBLICATIONS, INC.

people had grown up at the confluence of the Columbia and Willamette rivers, almost tripling the town's population over a period of five years.

Moreover, the years between 1905 and 1912 saw the substantial expansion of railroads, farming, and livestock raising east of the Cascades, in part attributable to the growth of the Rose City as a commerical hub. The shift of America's timber industry from the Great Lakes states to the northwest also occurred during this era. In response to this deluge of commodities, new wharves and factories were built at the northern end of the Willamette Valley. On the grounds of the original exposition site, northwest Portland became a center of housing and commerce. Not surprisingly, city fathers have hopes for a bicentennial celebration of the Lewis and Clark expedition in 2005 to once again showcase the town in a beneficial way.

ECONOMY

A Harris poll at the end of 1991 ranked Portland the fifth-best city in the country in which to locate a business. The CEOs polled in this survey probably recognized the fact that Portland is at a geographical crossroads with economic destiny. With a leading seaport, I-84 and three transcontinental railroads linking the city to the east, and I-5 providing connections north and south, Portland is perfectly located to take advantage of Pacific Rim trade as well as stateside business opportunities. Also facilitating the flow of commerce are 21 weekly flights heading to Tokyo, Seoul, Nagoya, Taipei, and Bangkok.

GETTING ORIENTED: PORTLAND NEIGHBORHOODS

Portland's revival picked up steam in the 1970s, turning a city mostly known for rain, roses, and run-down buildings into a showplace of eye-catching art and architecture. Included in this legacy were the renovation of the historic Old Town neighborhood and Pioneer Courthouse Square, as well as a law requiring that one percent of construction costs go toward public art projects.

Before getting started on your travels, here are a few things worth keeping in mind. Most Portlanders sleep east of the Willamette River. The business district, shopping areas, museums, and theaters west of the Willamette can be easily reached from east-of-the-river residential areas by mass transit. Buses and light rail are preferable to cars because of streets closed to traffic and the dearth of parking in the city. Once you're downtown, Portland's compact beauty invites strolling. In addition to parks, galleries, and shops which engage the eye, city blocks are half the size (200 feet) of those in most other cities. And the downtown landscape is basically flat, which lets you log miles on foot relatively painlessly. So ditch your car, put on your walking shoes, and ride the bus to its point of origin, **Transit Mall,** on Fifth and Sixth avenues. This strip of 11 blocks is banned to vehicular traffic other than Tri-Met buses. Bus and light-rail travel is free throughout much of downtown (see "Mass Transit Buses and Light Rail" under "Getting There and Getting Around" in the "Practicalities" section following).

Finding Your Way
Before you start muddling your way through downtown, look for some folks wearing green baseball caps and jackets and navy-blue pants. They are part of the **Portland Guides** (tel. 295-0912) program and serve as walking information centers.

If you cannot find one, the following observations will help you get the lay of the land. The line of demarcation between north and south in addresses is Burnside St.; between east and west it's the Willamette River. These give a reference point for the address prefixes southwest, southeast, north, northwest, and northeast.

Another useful thing to keep in mind is that avenues run north-south and streets run east-west. Many street names on one side of the river continue across to the other. A series of 12 bridges connect east to west. Almost every downtown address will carry a southwest or northwest prefix.

Other aids to orientation include the fact that Front Ave. is the road nearest the Willamette River downtown and Water Ave. is the nearest on the east side. Thereafter, numbered avenues begin.

The city's major thoroughfares are Grand Ave., Martin Luther King Jr. Blvd. (formerly Union Avenue), Sandy Blvd., U.S. 26, and S.E. 82nd Street. Expect most streets downtown to run one way, alternating with the next going in the opposite direction. Streets in the Northwest District are named alphabetically (e.g., Burnside, Couch, on through Wilson.) Ankeny St. precedes Burnside, but by definition is in the Southwest District. The only exceptions to this ordering system are Roosevelt and Seed streets, which are substituted for the "X" and "Y" streets, respectively.

Finally, addresses increase by 100 each block, beginning at the Willamette River for avenues and Burnside for streets.

A convenient part of town for the traveler to take care of essentials is the Hollywood District north of 42nd. A mini-mall off N.E. 42nd and Hancock features a bank, a laundromat, and an excellent coffee shop, **Sweet Indulgences** (1925 N.E. 42nd Ave.; tel. 249-0686). Across the street is a post office subcontractor who has weekend hours when the "official" post office outlets are closed.

EXPOSE YOURSELF TO ART

The following introduction to Portland neighborhoods is intended to give an idea of how the city is laid out. Obviously, you can't do all of this tour in one day, so slow down and savor each part of town. After reading the capsule descriptions of sights in the walking tour, you can find out the hours, costs, and other details in the sections which follow. The bus stops of the most far-reaching and cost-effective inner-city transportation system in the nation (according to the American Transit Association) feature brick-inlaid promenades and glass-canopied pavilions garlanded with floral displays. But the aesthetics don't stop there. These waiting areas have so many ornate statues and fountains that former Portland Mayor Bud Clark exhorts you to "expose yourself to art" here. A famous poster depicts hiz' honor flashing the female nude statue *Kvinneakt* (on Fifth Avenue between S.W. Washington and S.W. Stark), underscored by the aforementioned invitation.

Portland Building

The best-known statue in the city is Raymond Kaskey's ***Portlandia,*** which ranks right behind the Statue of Liberty as the nation's largest copper sculpture. Located outside Michael Graves's postmodern Portland Building (S.W. Fifth Ave. between S.W. Main and S.W. Madison), the golden-hued female figure holding a trident recreates the Lady of Commerce on the state seal. Locals refer to it as "Queen Kong," and sometimes practical jokers from Portland State University will dangle a giant yo-yo from her outstretched finger. Inside the Portland Building on the second floor is the **Metropolitan Center for Public Art** (1120 S.W. Fifth Ave.,

Portlandia *beckons passersby.*

PORTLAND DOWNTOWN

Room 1023; tel. 796-5111), where you can pick up a brochure annotating a walking tour of the city's murals, fountains, sculptures, and other art forms.

More graphic evocations of the region are rendered by the 16th-century **petroglyphs** etched into Columbia River basalt at City Hall across Madison St. from City Hall on Fourth Ave. (east courtyard, behind 1220 S.W. Fifth Ave.) and the simulated cascades at **Ira's Fountain.** To get to the fountain, walk down S.W. Fourth Avenue to S.W. Third and Clay streets (in front of Civic Center). From the block-long fountain complex, retrace your steps back down Fourth to Yamhill Street. If you turn left on Yamhill and go west a block, the Northwest motif is maintained by small bronzed beavers, bears, ducks, and sea lions congregating near a series of pools around the Pioneer Courthouse.

Pioneer Courthouse Square

You are now on the north side of Pioneer Courthouse (555 S.W. Yamhill), the oldest public building in the state, constructed between 1869 and 1873. The classic contours of this gray granite structure contrast with the blue-tiled, mauve-and-beige tuxedo-patterned facade you saw at the Portland Building. On the first floor of the Hall of Justice is a post office with historic photos on the wall. Period furniture and brass lamps line the hallways on the way to the Ninth Circuit Court of Appeals, located upstairs in room 204. If court is not in session, ask a security guard to let you in to see the Victorian courtroom between 8:30 a.m. and 5 p.m. weekdays.

One block west, outside the front door of the building, is **Pioneer Courthouse Square** (bordered by Yamhill, Morrison, Sixth Ave., and Broadway), the cultural vortex of the city. On the south side of the square is *Allow Me,* a life-sized statue of a businessman with an umbrella hailing a cab. Also within the amphitheaterlike confines of the square is **Powell's Travel Bookstore** (701 S.W. Sixth Ave., at S.W. Yamhill St.; tel. 228-1108). Here you can rent the 80-minute narrated *Portland Downtown Discovery Walk* and a tape player for around $10. It traces 90 historic sites within a 20-block radius, complete with sound effects, interviews with local experts, and digressions on architectural subjects.

Diagonally across the square is a 25-foot col-

All roads lead to Pioneer Courthouse Square.

TED LONG ISHIKAWA

umn known as the **weather machine.** Every day at noon the forecast is delivered by one of three creatures—a dragon if it's stormy, a blue heron in overcast weather, or a sun figure. As if that's not enough, the machine also emits a small cloud accompanied by a fanfare while colored lights display temperature and air quality. The red-bricked square in summer hosts jazz, folk, and other types of music every Tuesday through Thursday from noon till 1 p.m. at the **Peanut Butter and Jam.** On warm spring and summer nights the music and crowds return, augmented by symphony-goers departing just up Broadway. The Birkenstocks and Gore-Tex of casual Northwest attire mingle easily with business suits here.

Should you tire of people-watching, inspect the bricks on the square, each of which bears the name of one of the 50,000 donors who anted up $15-30 for the privilege. From the northeast corner of the square gaze up at the white-brick and terra-cotta clock tower of the Jackson Tower on S.W. Yamhill and Broadway, and over at the copper sheathing of the Guild Theater building on Ninth and Salmon to experience the glory that was Portland in the early part of this century.

The South Park Blocks And Cultural Attractions

Paralleling Broadway and the square to the west are the South Park Blocks, created in 1842 and comprising a 25-block spread between Park and Fifth avenues. Come here in the fall and you can sense Portland's New England heritage. One-hundred-year-old elm trees with their bright yellow leaves line a series of small parks down the middle of Park Avenue. These sentinels tower above cast-iron benches, bronze statues, and neatly trimmed grass fronting the **Portland Art Museum** and the **Oregon Historical Society.** Be sure to check out the murals portraying Lewis and Clark, Sacajawea, fur traders, and Oregon Trail pioneers on the south and west walls of the Historical Center on Main Street. **Portland State University** is at the south end of the Park Blocks. Sandwiched in between the Park Blocks and Broadway is the heart of the theater district, with the **Performing Arts Center, Schnitzer Hall,** and several smaller theaters nearby. On S.W. Salmon St. and Park Ave., note the four Simon Benson (see "Hotel Dining Rooms" under "Practicalities" following) drinking fountains. In the same block is the Italianesque Shemanski Fountain with its *Rebecca*

At the Well statue. Several years ago, the city increased the number of brighter period-style lampposts here to make it more inviting after dark. To further help the neighborhood realize its potential, there are plans to forge mass-transit links to the Greyhound/Amtrak terminals at Union Station. This would provide easy access to heritage-rich neighborhoods and Waterfront Park on the banks of the Willamette.

DOWN BY THE RIVERSIDE

Old Town And Skidmore

The tile-roofed clock of the **Union Station** on N.W. Sixth Ave. has been a beacon since 1890 when passenger trains first rolled into the redbrick terminal. If you walk southeast from Union Station, you pass through **Chinatown,** a compact area of restaurants and exotic Oriental grocery stores. In 1890 Portland had the largest Chinatown on the West Coast. The gargoyled gate at Fourth Ave. and Burnside is always good for a photograph. Notice that the male statue is on the right with a ball under his foot, while the female has a cub under her paw. In spring, the cherry blossoms on Fifth and Davis become the highlight of Chinatown. Overlapping this neighborhood are the museums, galleries, restaurants, and shops of **Old Town.** Many of the buildings here date from the 1880s, despite the fact that Portland's beginnings stretch four

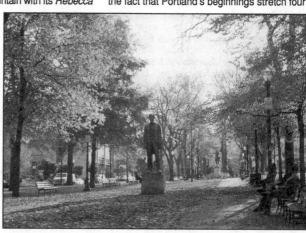

fall foliage at the south park blocks

the China Gate

decades earlier. This is because an 1872 fire razed much of what was then the commercial district. Cast-iron buildings with Italianate flourishes went up in the wake of the fire. While a large number of these foundry facades were torn down in the 1940s to make way for a Willamette River bridge and a waterfront freeway, a few (more than in any other place in the U.S. except New York City's Soho district) survive in Old Town and the adjoining **Skidmore Historic District.** Old Town runs predominantly north of West Burnside between Front and Fourth avenues.

Skidmore spills over just south of Burnside. These neighborhoods are adorned with antique street signs, newly touched-up "old brick," and lots of iron and brass. Despite this ambience, the sights and sounds of traffic and panhandlers on W. Burnside might intrude upon your reveries of 19th-century Portland. Nonetheless, these street people would fit right into the historical fabric of a century ago, when shanghaied seamen and unemployed loggers were commonplace here. In fact, the term *skid row* is said to have originated in Portland or Seattle. This expression came from the "skid roads," paths on which logs were slid downhill to waterfront mills. After logging booms went bust, lumberjacks and other folks down on their luck would hit the skids in these parts of town. If you're not careful in the Old Town/Skidmore districts after sunset, you too might end up "history."

Just south of Burnside near the Burnside Bridge is the **Skidmore Fountain** (S.W. First Ave. and S.W. Ankeny St.), named for a man who intended that it provide refreshment for "horses, men, and dogs." Just south of the fountain, read the Ankeny Block placard on the wall for a good, concise description of Portland's architectural evolution. Despite the spouts and animal troughs, the 1888 bronze-and-granite fountain is purely decorative. It does serve, however, as a portal to **Saturday Market** (108 W. Burnside; tel. 222-6072) and to **Waterfront Park,** a mile-long oasis of greenery along the Willamette. At the north end of Waterfront Park are granite boulders with inscriptions pertaining to the history and contributions of Japanese-Americans in the Northwest. Ranked as the largest continuously operating open-air handicrafts market in the United States, Saturday Market is an outdoor potlatch of homegrown edibles, arts, crafts, and excellent street performers. The market takes place every Saturday and Sunday from April through Christmas in the shadow of the Burnside Bridge. On Saturdays the hours are 10 a.m.-5 p.m.; on Sundays the market operates 11 a.m.-4:30 p.m.

The 26 food booths here are a street-grunter's delight. Particularly recommended are Cajun shrimp, elephant ears (deep-fried whole-wheat slabs immersed in butter, cinnamon, and sugar), the soul food at **My Brother's Place** ("If my sauce don't send you, you have nowhere to

Food and local color are found at Yamhill Market.

go"), and the seafood crepes at **Nutritious Delicious Crepes.** The handicrafts range from exquisite woodwork (at reasonable prices) and feather jewelry to homemade fire-starter kits and juggling toys. What's astonishing is the high quality that's been maintained here for over two decades.

Across S.W. First Ave. and cobblestoned **Ankeny Square** is the **New Market Theater,** constructed in 1872 as a theater and produce market. Today it houses inexpensive restaurants and boutiques in a three-tiered atrium. Public restrooms are upstairs in the southeast corner of the building.

Two blocks south the **Failing Building** (235 S.W. First Ave. and Oak St.) typifies the influences and use of cast iron so popular during the 1880s. Today it houses McCormick and Schmick's restaurant. Writer Gideon Bosker asserts that you can trace the evolution of American architectural style on a stroll through Portland. This is easy to believe if you turn left on S.W. Oak and S.W First, then left again on S.W. Front Ave. to a prime location of elegant restorations. Prior to Portland's era of expressways and bridge building, this whole neighborhood was filled with cast-iron facades and Italianate architecture.

Waterfront Park And
Yamhill Historic District
From the Skidmore District, head east to Waterfront Park. En route to **RiverPlace,** an attractive area of restaurants, specialty shops, and boating facilities, you'll pass joggers and the **Salmon Street Springs Fountain.** This is often the centerpiece for one of Portland's many festivals and provides a refreshing shower on a hot day. The fountain water's ebb and flow is meant to evoke the rhythms of the city. Tom McCall Waterfront Park is named for the governor credited with helping to reclaim Oregon's rivers. In the early 1970s it replaced Harbor Drive, a freeway that impeded access to the scenic Willamette River.

From the waterfront meander through the **Yamhill Historic District** back to the intersection of S.W. Fifth and Washington.

THE PARK AND ENVIRONS

Washington Park
From Fifth and Washington board the colorfully painted Tri-Met bus line #63/Zoo/OMSI (Washington Park). The route includes **Washington Park**—the hillside home of the **Rose Garden,** the **Japanese Garden,** and the **Washington Park Zoo.** In addition, there's the **Oregon Museum of Science and Industry Annex,** a historic carousel, the **Western Forestry Center,** the **Hoyt Arboretum,** and nearby, the **Pittock Mansion** (see "Museums and Miscellany" following). Clear days can feature views of Mt. Hood and other Cascade peaks from some of

WASHINGTON PARK

MACLEAY PARK

PITTOCK MANSION

N.W. PITTOCK

PITTOCK ACRES PARK

MONTE VISTA TER.

N.W. BEUHLA VISTA TER.

N.W. HERMOSA BLVD.

N.W. IMPERIAL

N.W. MAYWOOD DR.

TO N.W. 23rd AVE.

N.W. SANTANITA TER.

W. BURNSIDE ST.

S.W. TICHNER

N.W. IRVING

S.W. CHAMPLAIN DR.

S.W. KINGSTON

S.W. PARKSIDE

S.W. MARCONI

S.W. WRIGHT

LEWIS AND CLARK MONUMENT

S.W. PARK PL.

BARNES RD.

S.W. HAMPSHIRE

S.W. RUTLAND TER.

S.W. MURRAY LN.

S.W. VIEW

S.W. BENNINGTON

S.W. FAIRVIEW

JAPANESE GARDENS

INTERNATIONAL ROSE TEST GARDEN

S.W. CANYON RD.

S.W. CASCADE

S.W. CASCADE

WASHINGTON

S.W. EVERGREEN LN.

FAIRVIEW BLVD.

HOYT ARBORETUM

PARK

26

KINGSTON

TO INTERSTATE 405

VIETNAM VETERANS MEMORIAL

WORLD FORESTRY CENTER

S.W. KNIGHTS BLVD.

S.W. CANYON RD.

MUSEUM OF SCIENCE AND INDUSTRY ANNEX

ZOOLOGICAL GARDENS AND ZOO

26

| 0 | 0.2 mi |
| 0 | 0.2 km |

these Washington Park aeries. To the rear of Pittock Mansion, you can see Mt. Rainier over 150 miles away on the northeast horizon when the conditions are right.

Northwest District

You can then head a mile downhill on foot or by bus to the Northwest District (north of Burnside between N.W. 18th and N.W. 27th avenues). In the heart of the neighborhood, N.W. 23rd St., Victorian homes have been remodeled into boutiques to join stylish shopping arcades, bookstores, restaurants, and theaters. If you continue north for another mile, you'll see **Forest Park** looming over industrial northwest Portland, the largest park within a city in the United States.

The Pearl

Moving east down Burnside you come to a neighborhood which is affectionately referred to as the Pearl (north of Burnside to Marshall, N.W. Eighth Ave. to N.W. 15th Ave.). Here, old warehouses have been turned into art galleries and antique showrooms. The soon-to-be renovated North Park Blocks, vintage trolleys, and a Union Station train museum will add more polish to the Pearl in the next few years. First-Thursday-of-the-month gallery walks feature a catered "open house" at these establishments. On the southern fringe of the Pearl, **Powell's Books** (see "Entertainment" following) is on 10th Ave. and Burnside.

At this point, you've surveyed enough of downtown Portland to get a feel for what goes on west of the Willamette. There are other Portlands worth visiting on the other side of the river. Here are three excursions by mass transit which offer a gourmet taste of this realm:

LLOYD CENTER

Go to any Gresham-bound MAX (Metropolitan Area Express) station in downtown Portland (pick-up points include Skidmore Fountain-Ankeny Square, and N.W. First Avenue and Davis St. in Old Town). Purchase "one-two" zone tickets and head to Lloyd Center. This mall was the world's largest shopping center in 1960 and today boasts over a hundred retail

outlets, a newly domed ice-skating rink, **Lloyd Ice Pavilion** (tel. 282-2511), and the largest theater in the city (**Lloyd Cinemas,** 4510 N.E. Multnomah; tel. 248-6938), with 10 screens and a futuristic neon interior. Nearby there is also the **Holladay Market** where **Coffee People** (1200 N.E. Broadway; tel. 284-4359) serves up some of the city's best coffee. In the same building, shops selling deli items, baked goods, produce, meat and fish, Mexican food, and pizza make this a favorite eat-'n'-run outlet. Despite these attractions, the journey might be better than the destination. The MAX route goes over the Steel Bridge, from which there are great views of the city and river traffic and the spires of the convention center.

Hawthorne District

Hop a #5 Hawthorne Tri-Met bus from S.W. Fifth Transit Mall or from Union Station. This neighborhood (from S.E. 17th to S.E. 55th avenues along Hawthorne Blvd.) recalls the hip gourmet ghettos of Berkeley, California, and Cambridge, Massachusetts. Stores purveying records, fine coffees, secondhand clothing, antiques, crafts, and books join cafes and galleries along Hawthorne Boulevard.

A dense concentration of these establishments can be found between 32nd and 39th avenues. Beyond the Hawthorne District looms **Mt. Tabor.** This extinct volcano has drive-up views of Mt. Hood, the downtown, and the lower Willamette Valley. If you don't have a car, a #15 Mt. Tabor bus will get you close enough to hike the trail to these panoramas.

SELLWOOD

Antique hunters will be drawn from downtown to Sellwood in the southeast of Portland. Once a separate city, it annexed itself to Portland in 1890. To get there from downtown, take bus #65. Over 30 antique stores are spread along 12 blocks straddling a cliff above the Willamette River. As with the Hawthorne District, many of the stores open after 11 a.m. Most Sellwood stores are closed Sunday and Monday. At mealtime, the **Sellwood House** (7937 S.E. 13th Ave.; tel. 230-9040) serves home-cooked food with gourmet flair and reasonable prices.

MUSEUMS AND MISCELLANY

Washington Park,
International Rose Test Gardens
If you're not on a bus you can get here the following ways: follow U.S. 26 west and look for signs, or go west on Burnside a mile beyond N.W. 23rd Ave., turn right on N.W. Barnes Rd., and then make another right turn on N.W. Irving and follow the signs.

The Rose City's welcome mat is out at this four-acre garden overlooking downtown. With more than 400 species it's the largest rose test garden in the country. The blossoms are at their peak in June, commemorated by the Rose Festival (see "Events" following), but even if you're down to the last rose of summer, there's always the view of the city backdropped by (if you're lucky) Mt. Hood. The best vantage point for the latter is the east end of the garden along the Queen's Walk, where the names of the festival beauty-contest winners are enshrined (since 1907).

If you enter from the parking lot west of the restrooms near the center of the garden, look for the rose labeled "Fragrant Cloud" to the left of the walkway at the beginning of the row. As its name suggests, this is *the* place to stop and smell the roses. On the right-hand side of the walk is the all-star lineup of award winners. This floral fantasia can be enjoyed from dawn to dusk at no charge. And while I promised you a rose garden, leave the roses behind, because the fine for picking flowers here runs a steep $250 per rose.

Japanese Gardens
From the Rose Garden head west up the steps that go past the parking lot and tennis courts on the way to the Japanese Gardens (off Kingston Ave. in Washington Park; tel. 223-4070). You can walk up the short but steep road that leads to the Japanese Gardens, or hop the free open-air shuttle that climbs up the hill every 10 minutes or so. The Japanese Gardens so moved the Japanese ambassador in 1988 that he pronounced it the most beautiful and authentic landscape of its kind outside Japan. Ponds and bridges, sand and stone, April cherry blossoms, and a snowcapped Fujiyama-like peak in the distance help East meet West here. This is always an island of tranquility, but connoisseurs will tell you to come during the fall-foliage peak in October. Many people in Japan feel these gardens are at their best when it's raining. In any case, it's open daily in summer 10 a.m.-6 p.m. and thereafter, Sept. 16-April 4, it's open daily 10-4. The gardens are closed on Thanksgiving, Christmas, and New Year's Day. Admission is $3.50 for adults, $2 for students and seniors; under age three gets in free.

Washington Park Zoo
After the Japanese Gardens, you can catch the Zooliner train, which goes four miles to the zoo. The train costs $2 for ages 12-64 (discounts for seniors) and runs 10:30 a.m. to 6:15 p.m. at 40-minute intervals. Figure on 35 minutes for a roundtrip. The ride itself is worth your time if only because the Zooliner is a 30-year-old steam engine. But that's not all. The forested ridge defining the route features 112 species of birds, 62 kinds of mammals, and hundreds of plants. During a brief stopover, you may see the five major mountain peaks of the Cascade Range: Rainier, St. Helens, Adams, Hood, and Jefferson. The train may not run when the weather is rainy or attendance is low.

The zoo (4001 S.W. Canyon Rd.; tel. 226-1561) itself predates the Rose Garden (1887 versus 1917) and it exerts almost as ubiquitous a presence within the city. This is evident from a huge elephant prominently painted on a building near the Burnside Bridge and an array of zoo animals depicted on the multicolored bus #63. The city is justly proud of the zoo's award-winning elephant-breeding program and the nation's largest chimpanzee exhibit. Also noteworthy are a colony of Humboldt penguins from Peru and an Alaskan tundra exhibit featuring grizzlies, wolves, and musk-oxen. The latter exhibit is supplemented by polar bears swimming in pools of simulated Arctic ice. Whenever possible, animals are kept in enclosures here which recreate their natural habitats. The most recent example is the African Grasslands exhibit, which houses impalas, zebras, giraffes, and a black rhinoceros. You also shouldn't miss the zoo's **Elephant Museum**, which takes a lighthearted look at pachyderms. Along with the elephant jokes, elephants in literature and art are depicted with dioramas and masks. A look at the ivory trade injects a somber note into the proceedings. The exhibit is completed by the zoo's collection of the world's largest and most prolific herd of captive Asian elephants. In this vein, it should be mentioned that the zoo also specializes in breeding rare and endangered species, such as orangutans and red pandas.

There are several food service outlets at the zoo. The major restaurant is the Africafe, which offers a good selection of moderately priced cafeteria food. The chance to dine overlooking a glassed-in aviary is the big attraction here, however.

Compounding the impression that it's all happenin' at the zoo are the free concerts in the amphitheater on Wednesday (jazz) and Thursday (bluegrass) nights for nine weeks during summer. Contact the zoo for information on times and the schedule of performers.

The zoo is open May through October each day 9:30 a.m.-5:30 p.m. The rest of the year, it's open daily 9:30 a.m.-4 p.m. Admission is $5 for adults, $3.50 for seniors, and $3 for kids 3-11 years old. Since many of the animals are nocturnal, it's usually best to get to the zoo early in the morning. But if you go late in the day on the second Tuesday of every month, you can enjoy the zoo at a reduced price.

Oregon Museum Of Science And Industry Annex

Across the street from the zoo entrance is the Oregon Museum of Science and Industry Annex

(4015 S.W. Canyon Road, Washington Park; tel. 222-2828) or "OMSI." Your time is best spent at the new OMSI facility on the Willamette River (see below).

World Forestry Center

Just over from OMSI Annex is the World Forestry Center (4033 S.W. Canyon Rd.; tel. 228-1367), which offers exhibits on the natural processes of trees, the types of forests in the world, fighting forest fires, silviculture, and timber-industry activities. Also featured is the Jessup Wood Collection, within which are displayed examples from the 505 trees native to North America. Dioramas, films, and mechanized exhibits are complemented here by lectures, shows, and special events. The center's most well known (and after five minutes, most boring) attraction is a 70-foot talking tree. It's open daily 9 a.m.-6 p.m. in summer, in winter daily 10-5 p.m (closed Christmas Day). Admission is $3; seniors and students get in for half price.

On the grounds is a classic carousel (one free ride with Forestry Center admission ticket), operating only during dry seasons, and a steam engine that began hauling logs in the Coast Range in 1909. Also, don't miss the unique wooden items sold in the gift shop.

Pittock Mansion

Up the hill from the zoo/OMSI/Forestry Center complex, where Washington Park meets Forest

Pittock Mansion

Park, is the Pittock Mansion (tel. 823-4469). Situated at nearly the highest point in the west hills, 1,000 feet above sea level, this French Renaissance mansion completed in 1914 also stands above the rest of the grand edifices in the city for other reasons. *Oregonian* founder Henry Pittock spared little expense in furnishing his 22-room shack with such accoutrements as modern showers with multiple shower heads, a central vacuum-cleaning system, room-to-room telephones, and a Turkish smoking room. The antique furniture, access to Forest Park trails, and fair-weather views of the Cascades also make this place a fixture on many itineraries. Lunch and afternoon tea are available in the Gate Lodge, the former caretaker's cottage behind the mansion. Tea is served at 11:30 a.m., 1 p.m., and 2:30 p.m. For $8 you get turkey sandwiches with scones, jam, and fruit (reservations required). Regular tours are conducted (1-5 p.m.) daily except Sunday, and the grounds are open to the public until dark. The mansion is especially nice to visit when it's bedecked in Christmas finery. Admission is $3 for adults, $2.50 for seniors, and $1 for youngsters ages 6-18. Mass-transit access from downtown is provided by bus #77 to N.W. Barnes and Burnside St., at which point you'll have to walk the steep half mile up Pittock Avenue.

The Park Blocks

The **Oregon Historical Center** (1230 S.W. Park Ave.; tel. 222-1741) unfurls a pageant of Oregon's patrimony with artifacts, paintings, historical documents, and vintage photos. A permanent display on the second floor focuses on naval and overland explorers, Indians, and the growth of Oregon communities. Exhibits here include ship models by early coastal mariners, pioneer crafts and tools, and an original 1845 covered wagon. Mundane items like early bicycles, snow skis, and fashions move the time machine into the 20th century. The first floor hosts revolving exhibits. The Trails of Oregon exposition on the first floor uses Oregon Trail wagons as a metaphor for all the ways people came west and why. The upper floors house a library and photo collection which is open to the public. The center's hours are Tues-Sat. 10 a.m.-5 p.m., Sun. noon-5 p.m., closed Mondays. The museum's $3 charge also allows patrons to use the photo archives (a real treat) and library.

Across the street, the **Portland Art Museum** (1219 S.W. Park Ave.; tel. 226-2811) can complete a perspective on the Northwest coastal Indians. The masks and totem poles displayed here are not merely ornamental but are intimate parts of tribal ritual. The totem animals represent archetypal presences in native belief systems and are rendered with loving detail. Northwest themes are also breathtakingly displayed in the following works: Albert Bierstadt's historic painting of Mt. Hood (European and American Collection), the raven sculpture and Lelooska's totem pole (Axel Rasmussen Collection of Northwest Coast Native Art), and the Wasco horn bowl (Elizabeth Cole Butler Collection of Native Art).

Other permanent collections include prehistoric Chinese artifacts, tribal art of Cameroon, and contemporary sculpture and painting from around the world. The latter exhibit is housed in a room just to the left of the information desk and showcases the techno-wizardry and "smart art" embraced by current tastes. Traditionalists can revel in the museum's collection of works by Picasso, Monet, Degas, Calder, Brancusi, Stella, and Renoir. (Perhaps the two most touted acquisitions of the museum are Monet's painting, *Water Lilies,* and Brancusi's sculpture, *The Muse.*) In addition, you can have lunch at the **Ron Paul Cafe** here and listen to jazz Wednesday evenings.

Hours can vary so check *Willamette Week* listings or call the museum. Current hours are Tues.-Fri. 1-7 p.m. (Thursday till 9:30 p.m.), weekends noon to 5 p.m. Admission is $3 for adults, $1.50 for seniors, and 50 cents for students. Go on the first Thursday of the month between 4 and 9 p.m. for free admission. Also take advantage of the film series put on by the Museum's Northwest Film and Video Center (tel. 221-1156). The series features classic and eclectic flicks.

Cowboys Then And Now

Take a ride to Cowboys Then and Now (729 N.E. Oregon St.; tel. 731-3200) museum for an educational and entertaining perspective on the symbol of the American West. Predictably, the primary exhibits in this exposition funded by the Oregon Beef Council and Cattlemen's Heritage

Foundation focus on the history of men and women struggling to raise the stock that helped feed and clothe a nation. The dominant display is a 50-foot time line tracing the beef industry from its inception when Christopher Columbus introduced cattle to North America in 1494.

In a related exhibit, just push a button and a talking cowboy mannequin standing next to a restored chuck wagon will chew the fat with you for a while. To further help you feel at home on the range, a western landscape mural backdrops the cowpokes. Among other Western artworks here are paintings by E.B. Quigley and Charles Russell.

Despite an area of 2,000 square feet, this small museum manages to convey 400 years of cowboy history quite well. Treatment of such arcane subjects as cowboy poets, buckaroo music, movie stars, nonwhite cowboys (including Blacks and Mexicans) and a "horn to hoof" exhibit pointing out that over half of each steer slaughtered goes for nonmeat products (e.g., footballs, baseballs, pharmaceuticals, asphalt, and marshmallows) helps debunk some stereotypic notions. The saddle collection is also noteworthy. Located three blocks from the Oregon Convention Center at Oregon Square, it's open Wed.-Fri. 11 a.m.-5 p.m. and Sat.-Sun. noon-5 p.m. No beef about the price, admission is free.

Oregon Museum Of Science And Industry
OMSI (1945 S.E. Water Ave.; tel. 797-4000) is a hands-on interactive museum where you can pilot a ship from its bridge, gain insight on cardiology from a walk through a giant heart, or coordinate the Gemini space capsule's movements from Mission Control. The showcase of OMSI's new 18 1/2-acre campus, however, is the Omnimax theater (adults $6.50, seniors $5.50, and children $4). Here you can be transported into such exotic locales as a volcano or space through the medium of 70-mm film projected onto a four-story-high domed screen. Incredibly vivid acoustics help complete the "you are there" effect in what may be the most intense audiovisual experience ever created. Astronomy and laser shows at the Murdock Sky Theater (adults $4, seniors $3.50, and children $3) and six exhibit halls containing interactive displays make OMSI the perfect entree into the world of science and technology for all ages and levels of

sophistication. Particularly enjoyable is the "Nature's Fury" exhibit where visitors can sit inside an earthquake room and feel the simulated effects of a tremor. Trekkies will relish the opportunity to see the bridge of the starship *Enterprise,* assuming that this popular exhibit isn't on loan to some other institution.

The museum is open seven days a week. Winter hours are Sat.-Wed. 9:30-5:30, Thurs.-Fri. 9:30-9; closed on Christmas. Summer hours from Memorial Day to Labor Day are Sat.-Wed. 9:30-7, Thurs.-Fri 9:30-9. General admission to OMSI exhibits is adults $6.50, seniors $5.50, and children $4. A dining area with a river-view outdoor patio offers sandwiches, salads, pizza, espresso, and other simple, tasty fare. A gift shop selling glow-in-the-dark star maps, kaleidoscopes, and other quality educational toys is also worth a look.

To get there from I-5, take the exit onto Water Avenue. From the Marquam Bridge, take exit 300-B. From I-405 and the Hawthorne Bridge, look for brown signs next to the highway directional markers. Tri-Met's #6 bus will pick people up downtown on S.W. Salmon and Fifth Ave. and drop them off in front of OMSI. This bus can also be caught at the Oregon Convention Center MAX station.

Riverside Museums
The **American Advertising Museum** (9 N.W. Second Ave.; tel. 226-0000) could just as easily be called the Museum of Modern Americana. Housed in the former Erickson Saloon Building (dating back to the 1890s), the displays trace the early history of advertising up through the best campaigns of all time. Everything from Burma-Shave billboards to Will Vinton's California Raisins guide your journey through this visual and auditory feast. Hours are Wed.-Sat. 11-5, Sun. noon-5. The admission is $1.50, under 12 free. Around the corner is **La Patisserie** (208 N.W. Couch; tel. 248-9898), a second-floor walk-up coffeehouse whose windows overlook Old Town, one of the best people-watching neighborhoods in the city. You can also enjoy a tasty and sumptuous breakfast for little more than $5 here.

The **World's First 24-Hour Coin Operated Art Gallery** (219 Ankeny) can be found near Second Ave., two blocks south of Burnside

Street. The bizarre storefront features the World's Cheapest Psychic and the Church of Elvis. Drop a quarter into this vending machine to hear the King from beyond the grave, get "psychic counseling" (as well as "three predictions" and "past-life regressions"), and immerse yourself in various other forms of "erratica." Across the street, the seafood aromas of **Dan and Louis Oyster Bar** (208 S.W. Ankeny; tel. 227-5906) and an odd mix of characters from nearby missions and Saturday Market can add to the ambience.

Farther east is the **Oregon Maritime Center and Museum** (113 S.W. Front Ave.; tel. 224-7724). The Waterfront Park location is appropriate, given the Willamette River docking facilities which used to be here. Handmade ship models, Spanish pieces of eight, sternwheelers, and navigational instruments fill this little monument to Portland shipping tradition. Also, don't miss the sea stories told by the "watchstanders." At any given time, a couple of members of the crew will be on deck, eager to share their stories. Also, the new restored sternwheeler here is a floating museum of interest. It was the last remaining steam-powered sternwheel tug in any major harbor in the world when it was retired in 1981. The hours in summer are Tues., Thurs., Fri., Sat. 11-4, Sun. noon-5. In winter, it's open Fri., Sat. 11-4, Sun. noon-5. The admission is $2 for adults, 25 cents for seniors and students, free for kids under eight.

The **Police Historical Museum** (111 S.W. Second Ave.; tel. 963-0191) makes the history of law enforcement and the Portland Police Department an entertaining, if kitschy, excursion into the annals of crime control. An outdated display on drugs and their slang names, a homemade-weapons exhibit (including jerry-built but nonetheless efficient guns fabricated in prison) join uniforms, badges, and old jail cells in this arcane assemblage. The museum is located in the Justice Center Building on the 16th floor, room 1682. It's open Tues.-Fri. 10 a.m.-3 p.m. and is free. Just up from the Justice Center on S.W. Fourth and Main, check out the bronze elk. Set in a fountain which had been a trough for horses and pioneers, it now serves as the city's most aesthetic traffic divider.

A fast-disappearing aspect of Americana is

represented by the vintage carousels on display at the **Carousel Museum** (330 N.E. Holladay; tel. 235-2252). Primal memories can be evoked in adults and passed on to their kids here when visiting the largest collection of its kind in the country. The museum is located near the Seventh Avenue MAX station and the admission is $1, free for children six and under.

Old Churches
Lovers of interesting churches can take in the Old Church (1882) and the Korean Church, both rich in Victorian nuance, by heading west on Clay St. en route to U.S. 26.

BEYOND DOWNTOWN

The Grotto (N.E. 85th and N.E. Sandy Blvd.; tel. 254-7371) is a Catholic shrine whose hand-hewn cavern surrounded by lushly landscaped grounds can induce a profound sense of peace, no matter the religious orientation of the visitor. Within the ivy-covered fern-lined grotto is an impressive marble pieta. Outside the 30- by 50-foot enclosure, old-growth firs tower over the 110-foot cliff housing the shrine. Roses, camellias, rhododendrons and azaleas, and a cliffside view of the Columbia River also make this worth the 20-minute pilgrimage from downtown Portland (take Tri-Met bus #12). It's open daily 9 a.m. to dusk and the admission is free.

Sauvie Island
At the confluence of the Willamette and Columbia rivers is the rural enclave of Sauvie Island. Swimming, U-pick farms (raspberries, pumpkins, strawberries, and apples), and birdwatching on the Pacific Flyway (eagles, great blue herons, geese, and sandhill cranes) are some of the activities that can be enjoyed a scant 20 minutes from downtown (take I-5 north to the Fremont Bridge, then cross the bridge and look for signs to U.S. 30 northwest to St. Helens, Linnton, and Sauvie Island). In addition, anglers come to Sauvie's lakes and sloughs for panfish and bass and the Columbia side's sand beaches (check out **Walton Beach** at the end of N.W. Reeder Rd. for swimming) for sturgeon, salmon, and steelhead; bikers come for the 12-mile biking

bookworm paradise

loop, and wildlife aficionados come to the northern half to sight red foxes and black-tailed deer.

The more sedate can enjoy fall foliage and the **James Y. Bybee House** (Howell Park Rd., Sauvie Island; tel. 621-3344). This 1858 farm was built by Oregon Trail pioneers and is furnished with pieces from that period. If you're not edified by reading Sauvie Island's written history dating back to Lewis and Clark, the Bybee House also features an orchard with 115 species of apples brought by the pioneers and a collection of old farming implements. The house is open June-Labor Day, Wed.-Sun. noon-5 p.m. There is no admission charge here, although Sauvie's $2.50-a-day parking fee might destroy the island-out-of-time ambience. The island is open for day use 4 a.m.-10 p.m.

Crystal Springs Rhododendron Garden

To the south of the city near the **Reed College** campus (distinguished for producing the highest number of Rhodes Scholars in the United States) is the Crystal Springs Rhododendron Garden (S.E. 28th Ave. at Woodstock Blvd.; tel. 796-5193). Come in April and May to see 600 varieties of rhodies as well as azaleas on seven acres broken up by an island on a spring-fed lake. Even without the 2,500 species of flowers here, birdwatching and fall foliage encourage a visit. An interpretive sign overlooking the lake provides information about the habitat and diet of commonly seen waterfowl and aquatic birds

here. From March till Labor Day a $2 admission fee is charged on weekends and holidays. Otherwise, it's free. To get there, take the #19 Woodstock bus (on the Beaver line) and get off at the Reed College entrance. From there, ask any student to point the way.

ENTERTAINMENT

Book Lovers' Portland

While Portland lacks the population base of larger cities, Portlanders buy more books per capita than people in most other parts of the country. In bookstore sales per household Portland ranks ahead of New York City, the largest volume market in the U.S. Here's a random overview of some bibliophilic haunts here:

Powell's Books (1005 W. Burnside; tel. 228-4651) is a Portland institution. Over a million new and used books are housed in a labyrinth of hallways which take up a city block. A helpful staff and maps of the stacks help locate whatever you might be looking for in 50 sections ranging from automobiles to Zen. To make it even more appealing, there is the **Ann Hughes Coffee Room** (tel. 228-4651) at the west side of the store, which sells espresso drinks, pastries, salads, soups, and snacks. The *New York Times* and other papers on library-style posts and the chance to look over prospective book purchases while sipping coffee makes Ann Hughes (and

Powell's) a bastion of civilization in a neighborhood dominated by old warehouses and a brewery. Free parking in a special garage on the side of the store and authors reading their works several nights a week compound this impression.

You'll find an on-site coffeehouse and author readings at **Conant and Conant Booksellers** (S.W. 10th; tel. 241-7726). This family operation is noteworthy for its community activism and multicultural orientation. If you find yourself along the waterfront, check out **Book Port at RiverPlace** (write: 315 S.W. Montgomery, Suite 340; tel. 228-2665). Although the place is relatively small, the selection is outstanding and the staff extremely helpful. Other noteworthy bibliophilic haunts include the offbeat **Catbird Seat Bookstore** (913 S.W. Broadway; tel. 222-5817), with a good selection of self-help titles, and **Rich's Cigar Store** (801 S.W. Alder St.; tel. 228-1700; and 706 N.W. 23rd; tel. 227-6907), which stocks out-of-town newspapers and magazines from around the world. Finally, Hawthorne Blvd. (from 19th to 43rd avenues) features the highest concentration of used-book stores anywhere in town.

Readings And Lectures

Of the many literary events going on in this city, Literuption and Portland Arts and Lectures are the most well-known events on the circuit. **Literuption** (at Masonic Temple on the South Park Blocks; tel. 223-7692) features several dozen Northwest writers doing readings, as well as bookstore booths. Lectures run 10 a.m.-6 p.m. on a weekend in March.

Portland Arts and Lectures (Schnitzer Hall, 1037 S.W. Broadway; tel. 241-0543) provides a forum for prominent literati, scientists, and other intelligentsia in a half-dozen presentations autumn through winter. The series ($60) is usually sold out, but single tickets ($15) are sometimes available. Call 248-4496 for more information.

Theater

Portland's concentration of first-rate theater as well as opera, dance, and other kinds of stage productions is fast becoming one of the West Coast's worst-kept secrets. With equal doses of tradition and eclectic dynamism, the curtain rises on the most diverse schedule to hit the footlights in any city of comparable size.

Headquarters for much of this activity is the **Portland Center for the Performing Arts** (1111 S.W. Broadway; tel. 248-4496). Four stages grace this facility: 3,000-seat **Civic Auditorium**, 2,776-seat **Arlene Schnitzer Hall**, 900-seat **Intermediate Theater**, and 350-seat **Dolores Winningstad Theater.** Each theater has features suited to different kinds of productions. The Schnitzer Hall is a sumptuously restored 1928 vaudeville-and-movie house. The Winningstad is a high-tech Shakespearean courtyard theater with wraparound balconies. The Intermediate is the crown jewel here, with elegant cherry paneling, teal velour upholstery, and a stage as large as the seating area. Civic Auditorium at Third and Clay is designed to accommodate larger audiences. On the way to the stage, the aisles are pitched at such an incline that ladies should think twice about wearing high heels. While lacking the aesthetic flair of the other theaters, the acoustics and vantages of the stage here are top-notch.

These venues host performances by the Oregon Symphony Orchestra, Portland Opera, Portland Youth Philharmonic, the Oregon Shakespeare Festival, Portland Center Stage, Ballet Oregon, West Coast Chamber Orchestra, Oregon Repertory Singers, Portland Gay Men's Chorus, and Pacific Ballet Theater. Rock, classical, jazz, and country music artists also concertize here. Ticket prices run $10-55, with frequent discounts for seniors and students. You can usually expect to pay around $25 for most events. The free one-hour **tours** of the Schnitzer Concert Hall (Wed., Sat. 11 a.m.-1 p.m.) are a good intro to Portland's leading cultural center. Tours leave from the lobby of the New Theatre buildings on S.W. Broadway and Main.

The following cross section of theater groups charts the way to a memorable evening. The **Portland Center Stage—Oregon Shakespeare Festival** (c/o Portland Center for the Performing Arts, 1111 S.W. Broadway; tel. 248-6309) is the outreach of the Ashland company whose Shakespeare series is the most esteemed of its kind in the country. Portland's Shakespeare season features five plays running from November through April. Thus, Shakespeare aficionados can look forward to a different play each month to provide a wintertime counterpart to Ashland's spring, summer, and fall offerings. Ticket prices run $16-22; students and seniors pay $7 on the day of the show.

Mainstream fare is the rule at the **Portland Repertory Theater** (25 S.W. Salmon St.; tel. 224-4491). Along with such American classics as *Bus Stop,* the curtain also rises on Noel Coward-type English comedies. Located downtown in the World Trade Center, near the waterfront, the Rep's convenient underground parking and technologically sophisticated, intimate 230-seat theater pack 'em in with near sellouts each season. The curtain times are Tues. and Sat. at 8 p.m., Sun. at 2 p.m. and 7 p.m. Half-price tickets are available a half hour before performances.

Due to a funding crunch (as of this writing), Portland's oldest theater company is not functioning. When it's revived, expect children's theater, comedies, and Broadway musicals at **Portland Civic Theater** (1530 S.W. Yamhill; tel. 226-3048). *The Fantasticks, Hair,* and an annual rendition of *Peter Pan* at Christmas typify the productions. Ticket prices range $13-15 for the Thurs.-Sun. performances.

Artists Repertory Theater (Wilson Center YWCA, 1111 S.W. 10th Ave.; tel. 242-2400) is a company run by actors whose presentations run the gamut from the classics to modern. This is an Oregon version of high-quality off-Broadway theater.

The **Oregon Stage Company** (17705 N.W. Springville Rd.; tel. 690-7325) presents a highly regarded theater series at the Rock Creek campus of Portland Community College. Expect serious drama, contemporary comedy, and occasional musical productions.

Firehouse Theatre (1436 S.W. Montgomery; tel. 241-4902) specializes in multicultural presentations and experimental theater. This intimate hall also houses the offices of the Portland Theatre Alliance, which can help with discount tickets (see below).

For curtain times of all of the above and smaller community-based troupes consult *Willamette Week* (see "Media" under "Information and Services" in the "Practicalities" section following). **The Portland Theatre Alliance** at the Firehouse Theater has recently announced walk-up windows in the **Galleria** mini-mall (S.W. Morrison at 10th, just west of Pioneer Courthouse Square), offering half-price tickets to live local theater the day of the show. Thursday through Sunday, tickets are available for 90% of local shows. There are typically 10 to 12 shows from which to choose. Monday through Wednesday, tickets are available for any show that hasn't been sold out. Occasionally, there are even tickets to the Portland Opera. This outlet is open Thurs.-Sat. noon-6, Sun. noon-5.

Other places to get your cultural fix include **Portland Opera** (1516 S.W. Alder St.; tel. 241-1407) and the **Oregon Ballet Theater** (1119 S.W. Park Ave., Civic Auditorium; tel. 227-6867). Opera tickets range $18-36 (discounts to dress rehearsals for seniors and students) and ballet admission is $9-30. Finally, the **Oregon Symphony** takes the stage September to June with classical, pops, Sunday matinees, and children's concerts. The matinees are the least expensive ($4-6) of the shows, which otherwise range $8-28. Students and seniors may purchase half-price tickets one hour before a classical concert.

the Intermediate Theater at the Portland Center for the Performing Arts

Galleries

Gallery hopping on the first Thursday of every month facilitates an introduction to Portland's artistic community. More than 30 gallery owners coordinate show openings, and many offer complimentary refreshments. A free shuttle bus connects gallery districts that evening. The bus has 12 stops and begins its route from S.W. First and Taylor at 6:30 p.m., continuing into the night (the time of the last run varies depending on season; consult *The Downtowner* weekly, which sponsors the service, for the exact schedule). The Pearl District is a good place to start. Here, warehouses have been converted to artists' lofts and a large concentration of display spaces (see "The Pearl" under "The Park and Environs" above).

Nightlife

Music and laughs, they're all here in the Rose City, but in varying degrees. To put it more bluntly, jazz is hot, comedy is usually not. In any case, whether it's cooling your heels or dancing up a storm, there's no shortage of night spots. Portland's major comedy club, the **Last Laugh** (426 N.W. Sixth Ave.; tel. 295-2844), might suffer from poor acoustics and a lack of intimacy if you sit in the back, but the talent is there; besides, it's just about the only game in town. Hours are 6 p.m.-12:30 a.m. daily. Cover charges are $5.50 Sun.-Thurs., $8 Fri., Sat. At this writing, the Last Laugh was considering a move to a suburban venue sometime in 1993.

The major competition for laughs is **Club Max** (310 S.W. Lincoln; tel. 221-0450) at the Red Lion Inn—Downtown. National headliners and regional acts, a good PA system and lighting, as well as good views of the stage, make up for its hard-to-find location. Shows take place Friday and Saturday. There's a cover charge of $5.

Jazz, Blues, And Rock

Portland is a prime venue on the West Coast circuit for practitioners of these quintessentially American musical art forms. Several jazz and blues festivals each summer are well attended, and you can manage to get an earful on any given night of the week in Portland night spots all year long. Nationally known bluesman Robert Cray and his locally popular former sidekick Curtis Salgado were weaned on the Port-

land club circuit, which occasionally hosts the icons of the Delta, Chicago, and Texas-style variations of this music. Performers like James Cotton and Queen Ida have appeared at the **Rose City Blues Festival** (tel. 282-0555) in early July in Waterfront Park (admission free, but donations go to Oregon Food Bank).

The **Rock 'N' Rose** concert series happens at the beginning of September. Tickets go on sale at Ticketmaster outlets in late June for this Rose Garden amphitheater homage to some of the best rock acts around. Ticket proceeds help pay for the Washington Park Concert series in late August, which features bluegrass, classical, and other musical genres.

The jazz scene here boasts Russian-born pianist Andres Kitaev, the nationally known pianist Tom Grant, and the venerable Mel Brown Sextet with Leroy Vinnegar. You also might appreciate the large number of places in town where jazz is served up with dinner. *Willamette Week* listings and fliers on telephone poles and billboards let you know who's playing and where; also check out *Blues Notes*, a local publication available at bookstores and elsewhere about town. The Friday *Oregonian* features an "Arts and Entertainment" section which also helps you plan your evening out. But the best source of all for jazz information is **Jazz Hotline** (tel. 222-5003). For rock, a free publication, *Live Music*, available in retail outlets, is recommended.

Reggae, blues, and rock lovers can enjoy a variety of local and nationally known artists at these clubs: **Key Largo** (31 N.W. First; tel. 223-9919), which is open Mon.-Fri. 11:30 a.m.-2:30 a.m. and has a $2-8 cover charge; **Roseland** (8 N.W. Sixth Ave.; tel. 227-0071), and the **Dandelion Pub** (31 N.W. 23rd Pl.; tel. 223-0099), both of which are open nightly. Another bastion of blues and boogie is the **White Eagle** (836 N. Russell; tel. 282-6810), a dimly lit former biker bar which, despite its location in an industrial area near freeway interchanges, manages to book some of the best acts in the city. Out in Gresham, the **M&M Lounge** (137 N. Main St.; tel. 665-2626) often hosts Portland's premier blues guitarist, Jim Mesi. These places may be smoky or sweaty, but are unsurpassed for live acts and the chance to kick up your heels. In like measure, devotees look to the **La Luna Theater** (221 S.E. Ninth Ave.; tel. 235-

0027), **Melodyland** (615 W. Alder; tel. 232-2759), and the new-wave clubs **Satyricon** (125 N.W. Sixth Ave.; tel. 243-2380) and the **X-Ray Cafe** (210 W. Burnside; tel. 721-0115) for inspiration. Blues freaks enjoy **Bojangles** (2229 S.E. Hawthorne; tel. 233-1201) for live music Thur.-Sat. and on Monday nights. Next door, **Cafe Lena's** Tuesday night poetry readings and Beat coffeehouse ambience offers an attitude adjustment. Also in the Hawthorne neighborhood, **Mark's Hawthorne Pub** (3518 S.E. Hawthorne Blvd.; tel. 233-1178) offers pool, pinball, video poker, microbrews, and blues, folk, and pop acts. **Belmont Inn** (3357 S.E. Belmont St.) gives new-wave a chance to break the blues-jazz monopoly east of the river.

The **Portland Art Museum** (1219 S.W. Park Ave.; tel. 226-2811) features top-flight jazz and blues in their museum after-hours concerts. Musicians set up stage in the sculpture court each Wednesday 5:30-7:30 p.m. Admission is $3.50.

Jazz with Italian-flavored cuisine is presented at **Parchman Farm** (1204 S.E. Clay; tel. 235-7831) 8 p.m.-1 a.m. nightly. This club is in the Ladd's Addition neighborhood, just off Hawthorne Boulevard.

The "in place to be out" is **Brasserie Montmartre** (626 S.W. Park Ave.; tel. 224-5552). Hours for music are 8 p.m.-1 a.m. nightly. Live local jazz is accompanied by magicians and your own artistic creations (crayons supplied free of charge). While much of the menu here has a nouvelle French flair and prices reflecting same, you can get a great burger and lighter entrees here if you're on a budget. Food is served till 4:30 a.m. A high-ceilinged Paris-in-the-'30s decor makes an appropriate backdrop to this classy spot.

DJ's (4420 S.E. 39th; tel. 771-0742) is the home away from home of local favorites the Mel Brown Sextet with Leroy Vinnegar. And every Sunday, 3:30-7:30 p.m., there's a jam of other Portland jazz musicians which is broadcast over local radio station KMHD-FM, 89.1 on your dial. In recent years it's been the premier club for local jazz acts as well as the only Portland club to book nationally known acts on a regular basis, including Jim Hall, Herb Ellis, Wynton Marsalis, and Harry Connick, Jr.

Jazz de Opus, next door to La Patisserie, has great bar food and a steady stream of quali-ty players. Jazz lovers should also check the *Oregonian* and *Willamette Week* for who's playing at such hotels as the Benson, the RiverPlace Alexis, the Vintage Plaza, and the Heathman.

Finally, the **Mt. Hood Festival of Jazz** (Box 696, Gresham 97030; tel. 666-3810) is *the* event of the year for local jazz lovers as well as connoisseurs from all over the world. Lou Rawls, Count Basie, Stan Getz, Ella Fitzgerald, Wynton Marsalis, and Grover Washington, Jr. have graced this event, which takes place the first weekend of August at Mt. Hood Community College in Gresham. Two nine-hour concert days make up the schedule. Tickets go for around $20 per day and local dining spots cater the affair. Those on a budget should bring a picnic. To get there, take I-84 to the Wood Village/Gresham exit and follow the signs to the community college.

Cinema

In addition to the previously mentioned Art Museum series (1510 N.E. Multnomah; tel. 248-6938) and the 10-screen Lloyd Cinemas, Portland offers a wide variety of theaters and an equally diverse choice of cinematic experiences. On the top floor of Lloyd Center, the **Lloyd Mall Cinemas** (tel. 335-3756) give further diversity to this neighborhood's offerings.

The **Movie House** (1220 S.W. Taylor; tel. 222-4595) offers wine, cheese (card tables and chess upstairs), and art flicks. And at **Mission Theater and Pub** (1624 N.W. Glisan St.; tel. 223-4031) you can settle into old couches with your pint of microbrew, a burger, or a thick sandwich, to watch old Marx Brothers and 1940s classic movies for $1 (and newer flicks, too). It's more a tavern than a movie house, but by the second or third mug, you won't care. It's open 5 p.m. to midnight. The McMenamin brothers also combine film, beer, and food at the **Bagdad Theatre and Pub** (3710 S.E. Hawthorne; tel. 230-0895) and the **Power Station** (2126 S.W. Halsey St.; tel. 669-8754). These places tend to focus on recent hit movies. Adults only except for Sunday matinees at the Bagdad.

The marble staircase of **KOIN Center Cinema** (S.W. Third at Clay, tel. 243-3515) leads to six screens showing art films and high-quality Hollywood releases. **Cinema 21** (616 N.W. 21st. Ave.; tel. 223-4515) is an old auditorium in the artsy Northwest District showing foreign, experimental, and new-wave movies, as well as documentaries, cult favorites, and revivals.

The art deco **Fox Theater** (833 S.W. Broadway; tel. 248-6986) showcases first-run films. Proximity to Pioneer Courthouse Square and the Park Blocks can make parking difficult, but the lovingly rendered Roaring Twenties motif makes it worth the extra effort. The admission is $5. Another well-preserved screen gem is the **Roseway Theater** (7229 S.W. Sandy Blvd.; tel. 281-5173), featuring modern films as well as musicals of the '40s and '50s and a real pipe organ. Another oldie but goody is the **Hollywood Theatre** (N.E. 41st and Sandy Blvd.; tel. 248-6977). Enter beneath art deco obelisks to enjoy fading first-run flicks for $1.50.

Finally, the **Broadway Metroplex** (1000 Broadway; tel. 248-6960) combines a downtown location, plush interiors, quality munchies (featuring an outlet of highly regarded Starbuck's coffee), along with several screens showing first-run movies.

Miscellaneous Hangouts

Portland's diverse communities congregate in brewpubs, discos, fern bars, and cabarets.

The **Dakota Cafe** (239 S.W. Broadway; tel. 241-4151) has something for everybody. Disco and R&B recorded music as well as a house band provide background for a yuppie/Bohemian mix. It's open Mon.-Fri. 6:30 p.m.-2:30 a.m., Sat.-Sun. 8 a.m.-2:30 a.m.

Produce Row Cafe (204 S.E. Oak St.; tel. 232-8355) has dozens of beers on tap for a buck a glass and 200 bottled domestic and imported beers. Huge sandwiches are also a good value, and one feeds two people. The cafe straddles the warehouses beneath Martin Luther King Jr. Blvd. and is open Mon.-Fri. 11 a.m.-1 a.m., Sat. noon-1 a.m., and Sun. 2 p.m.-midnight.

Along with such popular microbrews as Blue Heron Ale and Grant's Ale, brewpubs have earned Portland a good reputation for quality beers and ales. Brewpubs are generally small, friendly beer bars built around custom-made house ales. Food is served and minors are allowed in until after the dinner hour. Portland's preeminent brewpubmeisters are the McMenamin brothers. The **Mission Theater and Pub** (1624 S.W. Glison; tel. 223-4021), the **Hills-**

dale Brewery and Public House (1505 S.W. Sunset Blvd.; tel. 246-3938), and the **Fulton Pub and Brewery** (1618 S.W. Nebraska St.; tel. 246-9530) are joined by other McMenamin establishments in Portland, Hillsboro, Gresham, Eugene, and Lincoln City. Such unusual brews as raspberry-flavored Ruby Tuesday, Terminator, Hammerhead, and Mars Bar ales have given this brewpub chain a dedicated following. Food offerings are centered on well-prepared finger food and appetizers.

The **Goose Hollow Inn** (1927 S.W. Jefferson St.; tel. 228-2010) is a popular neighborhood tavern that reflects the personality of the owner, Portland politico Bud Clark. The repartee can be fast and furious here unless it's Sunday, when blues or jazz fills the room 5-9 p.m. However, the management does advertise "quality tunes at a volume you can converse to." With combination sandwiches ranging from $3 to $6.50 (the best Reuben in town), homemade soup, and the Goose Hollow Famous Potato Salad, there probably won't be much talking anyway. The **Lotus Card Room and Cafe** (932 S.W. Third; tel. 227-6185) is a hipster hangout with a singles bar in the front room, a cafe and two pool tables occupying a middle salon, and a disco in the rear of the building. Each day at 4:30 p.m. people come for the happy-hour special, when some of the best appetizers in town (notably the fried calamari and onion rings) go for $1.95 apiece.

RECREATION

Spectator Sports

Portland is a town more for athletes than devotees of spectator sports. Nonetheless, the two stadia in the Rose City draw huge crowds.

In the case of **Memorial Coliseum** (1401 N. Wheeler; tel. 235-8771), this is entirely understandable given the success of the **Portland Trail Blazers,** who nearly won the National Basketball Association championships in 1991 and '92. Although the NBA season here is a near sellout, you can occasionally procure ticket-broker offerings through the *Oregonian* classifieds or from scalpers beyond a two-block radius of the Coliseum. For general info, contact **Portland Trail Blazer Customer Service** (700 N.E. Multnomah, Suite 600, Portland 97232). In several years, the Coliseum (the NBA's second-smallest stadium) will be replaced by a larger arena. Currently, prices range from $9.50 to $150 per game with many price gradations between these ticket classes. It's also worth checking the Coliseum box office, or better yet (less waiting), Ticketmaster outlets such as the Portland Repertory Theatre (25 S.W. Salmon; tel. 224-4491). For open seats, chances are you'll find some single seats, but it's doubtful you'll find two next to each other. If you do get into a game, be sure to enjoy the smoked-salmon sandwiches created by the Karla's Krabs of Oregon coastal fame (but sold under a different name). The **Winter Hawks** hockey team of the Western Hockey League also plays at the Coliseum.

Mention should also be made of the **Portland Beavers,** an AAA farm team that plays baseball in **Civic Stadium** (1844 S.W. Morrison; tel. 248-4345). Tickets are $3-5.

Murrary Kemp Greyhound Park (N.W. 223rd and Glisan St., Box 9, Fairview 97024; tel. 667-7700) is the only place to see greyhound racing on the West Coast. It's located southeast of Portland near Gresham. The **Multnomah Kennel Club**'s glass-enclosed facility offers beautiful views of Cascade peaks and excellent dining facilities along with pari-mutuel wagering. Evening post time is 7:30 p.m., matinee post time is 1 p.m. The season runs from May through September. The best way to get here is by MAX. Ride it to the Gresham City Hall or Central Station, then board the Tri-Met #82 Eastman bus directly to the track. While the bus isn't free, the driver will give you a free pass to the races.

The sport of kings is on display at **Portland Meadows** (1001 N. Schneer Rd.; tel. 284-9144), Friday through Sunday. A glass-enclosed grandstand with complete food service ensures comfort October-April.

Hiking

Portland has more urban wilderness than any other city in the country, and as whole books have been written about these retreats, we will have to confine ourselves to just a few hikes and refer the reader to the **Portland Audubon Society Bookstore** (5151 N.W. Cornell Rd.; tel. 292-6855), which has maps of more than 200 urban wildlife habitat sites in Portland, and

A Pedestrian's Portland by Karen and Terry Whitehill (Mountaineers Books, $10.95). The book outlines 40 walks in greater Portland, which the authors divide into six areas.

Without doubt, the part of Portland most conducive to a walk on the wild side is up in the hills behind the Northwest neighborhood. The largest urban wilderness in the world, **Forest Park** is accessible off I-5 (heading north) by taking the Fremont Bridge into northwest Portland and making a left onto Nicolai Street. Turn left off Nicolai onto 27th St. and follow it to Thurman Street. Make a right on Thurman and follow it to its end to reach the portal of Forest Park. The paved walkway at the edge of the wilderness has numerous sidetrails to forested hillsides. Despite scenic beauty, the smells and sounds of Portland's industrial northern extremity can occasionally pierce the tranquility here. Thus, weekends and holidays are recommended for excursions into this preserve. Nonetheless, what other city has a park in which bear, elk, deer, and cougar have been sighted? What other city park has old-growth trees and wild scenic areas?

A scenic adjunct is **MacLeay Park,** which can be reached via the Forest Park route and a turnoff onto Upshur Rd. (instead of Thurman), following it to its end. The Audubon Society Headquarters and bookstore is located near the trailhead. The gentle uphill trail here follows a deep gully paralleling a creek.

Another way to reach MacLeay and Forest parks is via the 14-mile **Wildwood Trail,** which heads north through the Hoyt Arboretum and Pittock Acres before plunging downhill into the parklands below. The trail begins on Canyon Rd. near the zoo, OMSI, and Forestry Center. Or, you can drive to the **Arboretum Visitor Center** (4000 S.W. Fairview Blvd.; open 10-4 p.m. daily) or the Pittock Mansion to begin your descent into MacLeay and Forest parks.

The arboretum is the gem of the Wildwood Trail and covers 214 acres and seven miles of trails, including a one-mile tour through one of the country's largest collections of conifers. On Saturdays and Sundays Oct.-April at 2 p.m., guided tours highlight foliage season. Prime time to come is during the **Fall Festival of Color** weekend around October 20. Events begin at 9:30 a.m. with a guided one-mile loop (for independents, a comprehensive trail map is available for 50 cents) through more than two dozen species of deciduous trees.

The Wildwood Trail is part of a proposed larger network of trails to loop the city. This was originally the brainchild of the Olmsted brothers (of Yosemite Valley and Central Park fame) at the turn of the century. Their proposed 40-mile loop concept has expanded to a 140-mile matrix. Now the goal is to complete a hiking/biking path connecting parks along the Columbia, Sandy, and Willamette rivers. To find out more, contact the **40 Mile Loop Land Trust** (tel. 241-9105) or pick up a map of the loop at Powell's Travel Bookstore at Pioneer Courthouse Square (tel. 228-1108).

On the other end of town, another potential component of the loop beckons urban walkers in search of rural pleasures. Snaking along the east bank of the Willamette River between the Sellwood and Ross Island bridges, the **Oak Bottoms Wildlife Park** is a birdwatcher's paradise. Great blue and green herons find this wetland a prime habitat. In winter, a dozen species of waterfowl can be found. Summertime residents include warblers, orioles, swallows, and woodpeckers. Whenever you go, look for wood ducks joining such permanent denizens as beavers and muskrats.

A ridge along Sellwood Blvd. frames Oak Bottoms and offers good views. You can hike into it at the north end of Sellwood Park at S.W. Seventh Ave. and Sellwood Blvd. The parking lot at the 5000 block of S.E. Milwaukie Blvd. also offers access. After you descend, a loop trail encircles the wetlands, paralleling the bluff on the east side and following the railroad tracks to the west.

Sports

Tennis courts, cycling paths, and lakes for swimming and sailing abound in Portland parks (Portland Parks, 1120 S.W. Fifth Ave., Room 502; tel. 796-5193). Free swimming pools can also be located by calling this number.

Runners enjoy numerous events, including the well-regarded **Portland Marathon** and the **Cascade Runoff**. To find out about these and other events call the **Runner's Hotline** (tel. 223-7867). The **Oregon Runner's Club** (Box 549, Beaverton 97025-0549; tel. 626-2348) is the second-largest club in the country and is glad to recommend the best places to run.

Bipeds in less of a hurry can pick up a free annotated walker's map at Powell's to supplement the one outlined in "Portland Neighborhoods" above. Bikers can procure the *From Here to There by Bike* map at many bookstores in town. *Best Bike Rides Around Portland* (Church and Wisengate Giraffe Works) is the road atlas for local pedal pushers. If you can't find it at Powell's, write the **Bicycle Commuter Service** (4438 S.E. Belmont St., Portland 97215) for ordering info. The 1992 update focuses on rides outside the city into places like the wine country and the Columbia Gorge, supplementing such local favorites as Sauvie Island and Skyline Boulevard. New provisions to let bicycles on selected Tri-Met bus routes (bike racks are on board, with $5 passes available at Pioneer Square) will help you get out of the armchair and onto the road. Cyclists looking for organized 30- to 100-mile rides at a touring pace should hook up with the **Portland Wheelmen Touring Club Hotline** (tel. 282-PWTC).

As for golfers, 20 18-hole courses are within 20 miles of the city, but only half are public. Two of the best are: **Heron Lakes** (3500 Victory Blvd.; tel. 289-1818), designed by Robert Trent Jones and 15 minutes from downtown; and **Eastmoreland Golf Course** (24225 S.E. Bybee Blvd.; tel. 775-2900). This also has a driving range and the course is near the Crystal Springs Rhododendron Garden. Greens fees average about $13 for 18 holes on public courses in Portland. Golfers looking to play just nine holes should keep in mind that the public courses will allow them to reserve a tee time only one day in advance. Those who want to play 18 holes can reserve earlier, giving them the preferred starting slots.

U-pick And Farmer's Markets

The *Tri-County Farm Fresh Produce Guide* (tel. 324-4990) lists dozens of U-pick outlets and farm-fresh fruit stands in the Clackamas (Washington), and Multnomah county area. Addresses, phone numbers, hours, and maps are available in this free guide. Pick one up at Powell's Travel at Pioneer Square or at the main store. The best months to find produce items are also annotated in the guide. The **Ripe and Ready**

The sternwheeler Columbia Gorge cruises Portland Harbor and the Columbia River.

Hotline (tel. 226-4112) can further help you locate outlets.

Here are several Portland-area markets: **Portland Farmer's Market** (Albers Mill parking lot, 1200 N.W. Front Ave.; tel. 231-2880), **Beaverton Farmer's Market** (S.W. Farmington Rd., between Hall Blvd. and Betts St.; tel. 643-5345), and **Saturday Market** (see "Down By The Riverside" above). These markets operate on weekends, usually from 8 a.m. till 1 p.m., through October.

Finding the Portland market can be difficult. The easiest way is to get on Front St. and head north till your view of the sky is blocked by the Broadway Bridge. Then look for the Alber's Mill building, with its name emblazoned near the top of the edifice.

EVENTS

The **Portland Rose Festival** (tel. 228-9411) has been the major wingding here for nine decades. The Rose Queen and her court (chosen from local high school entrants), sailors and prostitutes, and floats in several parades clog Portland's traffic arteries during this 24-day citywide celebration each June. Air shows, a hot-air balloon classic, the Indy World Series car race, and a traditional rose show round out the big doin's. The flier available at the visitor and convention bureau has more information.

The key to enjoying festival events is avoiding traffic and parking hassles. A $3 Tri-Met pass is good for unlimited rides on MAX or the bus all day long, for the passholder and up to three kids, six and under. As for traffic, be especially wary of the waterfront. Such festival features as food booths and carnival rides in Tom McCall Park, as well as military ship displays on the Willamette, draw crowds reminiscent of lemmings to the sea.

Two of the more colorful offshoots of the June fête are the Grand Floral Parade and the Festival of Flowers at Pioneer Courthouse Square. In the latter event, all manner of colorful blossoms fill the square to overflowing. This bouquet is on display during the first week of the several-week celebration. As for the Grand Floral Parade, this usually begins the Saturday following the opening of the festival. The floats combine the beauty of flowers with high-tech wizardry in aesthetically whimsical creations. You can reserve seats in the Coliseum for around $10, but save your money and station yourself on an upper floor along the parade route. Any lofty perch is sufficient for taking in all the hoopla, drill teams, Rose Queen, and equestrian demonstrations. This procession is the second-largest all-floral parade in the United States. The parade and the flower display prove that in Rose Festivals, as in life, the best things are free.

Also in June (through mid-July) is **Chamber Music Northwest** (Reed College Commons, 3203 S.E. Woodstock Ave.; tel. 229-6400), presenting concerts nightly except Sunday. Music begins at 8 p.m. and people picnic beforehand. Enjoy strawberry shortcake at intermission. Tickets to this nationally acclaimed series cost $9 for adults and $7.50 for ages 7-14. Other concerts in this event take place at the beautiful campus of a private school, Catlin Gabel. To get there, take U.S. 26 west, get off at exit 217 (Barnes Rd./Hospital), turn right at the end of the off-ramp, and right onto Barnes Rd., then follow the signs to the school. It's located next to St. Vincent's Hospital, just off Barnes Road.

In July, the **Multnomah County Fair** (Portland Expo Center; tel. 285-7756) attracts the likes of Johnny Cash, prize bulls, and agricultural exhibits. A carnival midway and food concessions are also fixtures at this event.

An August festival, **The Bite** (Tom McCall Waterfront Park; tel. 248-0600), lets you sample local culinary specialties of Portland restaurants, with the proceeds going to the Special Olympics. Live music is also featured.

Early September's **Artquake** (tel. 227-2787) takes place in the Center for the Performing Arts and the Park Blocks for three days. Entry fees are negligible (outdoor events free, indoor events $2) to this collage of music, theater, dance, food, crafts, and visual arts.

The **Wintering-In Festival** at Howell Territorial Park (Sauvie Island; tel. 222-1741) happens near the autumnal equinox. Enjoy fresh farm produce, crafts, and music at the restored pioneer homestead (see "Sauvie Island" above).

In October, watch the salmon spawn at Oxbow Park in the Sandy River Gorge outside Gresham. Old-growth walks, an eight-km run, and a barbecue as well as arts and crafts round out this fête. To get there from downtown, take I-84 east to the Wood Village exit. Turn south on Division and east on Oxbow Parkway, then follow the signs to Oxbow Park. There's a $3 parking fee. Call 248-5050 for more information. An-

glers are kept busy here with spawning runs of coho, fall and spring Chinook, and winter and summer steelhead.

The day after Thanksgiving, a Christmas tree is lit in Pioneer Square and a skating rink installed. Skate rentals are available and a small admission is charged. The best Christmas lights display is on Peacock Lane in southeast Portland; check at the visitor and convention bureau for more details.

Tours

In a guide for independent travelers a listing of tours may seem out of place, but sometimes there are organized outings that provide insights unavailable elsewhere.

One such perspective is provided by a harbor cruise on a sternwheeler. This mode of transport opened up the Willamette a century ago, and the 599-passenger *Columbia Gorge* (tel. 223-3928) today enables you to appreciate the fascinating and otherwise inaccessible (to pedestrians) Swan Island dry-dock facilities. Cruise to within 100 feet of the world's largest dry dock, which is actually a huge floating tank made of hollow pontoons filled with an amount of river water proportional to the weight of the vessel. When a ship goes into dry dock, the dock sinks and tugs push the ship into place. The dock master then raises the dock by pumping water out over the course of 90 minutes. Most tours spend 15 minutes here, leaving the bulk of the two-hour itinerary to sightsee the river traffic, seven of the city's 12 bridges, grain terminals, and other facets of this busy port. In addition, there are beautiful views of the skyline. Shipyard sophisticates might want to remember that cruise ships hit the docks here for repairs in May and September, Alaskan oil tankers in summer, and military ships year-round.

During winter, less traffic from pleasure craft makes possible unobstructed views, and evening tours feature the spectacle of lights switching on for the night crews. Box lunches and dinners are available on some trips. Basic tours cost $10.95.

The *Columbia Gorge* departs Waterfront Park (S.W. Front and S.W. Stark, north of the Morrison Bridge) October to mid-June, Fri.-Sun. There are often morning and afternoon cruises, but times and itineraries change, so call ahead (tel. 223-3928) for reservations.

Another riverside perspective is available courtesy of the **Willamette Shore Trolley** (2511 S.W. Moody St.; tel. 222-2226), an authentic 1913-vintage streetcar. The 30-mile roundtrip journey between Portland and southern suburb Lake Oswego lets you enjoy lush forest and parklands on the west bank of the Willamette which would otherwise be inaccessible. The east bank of the river is clearly visible, as are many interesting homes. At this writing, the trolley operates only on weekends March 7-Dec. 31, but more extensive use is planned. Call ahead for updates and reservations.

The enclosed heated cars are best appreciated during winter, a season when the leaves are off the trees so views are unobstructed. Begin your journey at the station on the corner of S.W. Moody Ave. and Sheridan St., under the Marquam Bridge. Prices range from $15 for a family of three to $22 for a family of six. Single fares go for $5-7. A vintage trolley runs at Christmastime in other parts of the city as an adjunct to existing mass transit. Call Tri-Met for details.

Plans are also underway to connect Riverplace to Union Station with a trolley line.

Close by Powell's Bookstore is a touring opportunity of special interest on a hot day. The **Blitz-Weinhard Brewery** (1133 W. Burnside St.; tel. 222-4351) offers free tours every half hour. This is the oldest continuously operating brewery in the U.S. Just register at the reception desk. The highlight of the brewery tour is of course the tasting room.

Finally, there is **Gray Line of Portland** (Box 17306, 21320 N. Suttle, Portland 97217; tel. 285-9845). Gray Line in most cities runs competent tours with experienced drivers. Portland's outfit is no exception. In addition to day-trips to such locales as Mt. Hood, the coast, and the Columbia River Gorge, three- and seven-hour city tours depart April through late October at 9 a.m. from major hotels (call ahead to reserve space). The city itineraries concentrate heavily on Washington Park and the scenic West Hills and cost $26 for the full-day trip and $15 for the several-hour loop (half price for children under 12).

PRACTICALITIES

ACCOMMODATIONS

Portland poses no problem for those seeking a reasonably priced overnight. An AYH hostel, a traditional city-center landmark, a well-kept standard motel just over the bridge from the urban core, and a bed and breakfast give the bargain hunter a choice of excellent accommodations at half the price of comparable digs in San Francisco.

Some Surprises

The **Portland AYH Hostel** (3031 S.E. Hawthorne Blvd.; tel. 236-3380) is the least-expensive ($12 members, $15 nonmembers) and one of the best-located places to stay in Portland. It's situated in amongst the restaurants and shops of the Hawthorne neighborhoods and on the bus line (from downtown take bus #5 to 31st Ave.; from the airport take #12, then transfer to #5). Kitchen privileges and restaurants serving tasty, inexpensive, nutritious food a few blocks away also recommend it. Make reservations for this large, rambling white hostelry in summer due to the influx of folks from other countries. A spacious screened-in back porch provides a cool place to sleep in July and August. It should also be mentioned that a day-use fee of $3 is invoked and some chores are required. At presstime, Hostelling International announced the April 1, 1994 opening of a 100-bed hostel in a historic building on the corner of S.W. 11th Ave. and Washington Street. An international coffee house, guest kitchen, and 100 more beds will be added to the hostel in the next several years.

Adjunct services for hostel guests and other members of the traveling public are provided by **Hostelling International** (1520 S.E. 37th Ave., Portland 97214; tel. 235-9493). Guidebooks and a variety of day packs are sold here, free pamphlets are available, and resource people are on hand to provide assistance. Hostelling International also organizes van tours of the region, as well as recreational activities like skiing and whitewater rafting. The goods and services here are very reasonably priced.

Despite a moderate price, the **Mallory Hotel** (729 S.W. 15th Ave. at Yamhill, Portland 97295; tel. 223-6311 or 800-228-8657), at first glance suggests a luxury lodging, with a lobby boasting ornate plaster, crystal chandeliers, and an elegant, skylit interior. The dining room's marble pillars and chandeliers sustain the four-star facade along with the elaborate jungle motif of the Driftwood Room Lounge. A location not far from the boutiques of the Northwest district and the Center for the Performing Arts also recommends it. With an address like this, the Mallory's free parking is also especially appreciated. Only the rather plain rooms might justify low prices of around $47 for a single and $52 for a double. And if you're lucky enough to score one of the king-sized suites for $90, you'll probably walk away shaking your head in disbelief at this lodging value. The staff members, who've been there for years, are efficient but more curt than courteous. A sister hotel, the **Imperial** (400 S.W. Broadway; tel. 800-452-2323), is another good value in a comparable price range.

Hojo's Inn (3939 N.E. Hancock; tel. 288-6891 or 800-524-9999) sits tucked away off Sandy Blvd. in Portland's Hollywood district. This motel (formerly the Jade Tree) recently became part of the Howard Johnson's chain, an East Coast outfit known for supplying the basics and then some at affordable prices. Proximity to restaurants, movies, shopping, and the bus line (15 minutes from downtown) comes along with clean, large, well-appointed rooms which range $34-51.

The best B&B in the city, the opulent **Portland's White House Bed and Breakfast** (1914 N.E. 22nd, Portland 97212; tel. 287-7131), gives you the presidential treatment. Located just off Broadway near an avenue of shops and restaurants, only 5-10 minutes from Lloyd Center and downtown, this lovingly restored 1912 lumber baron's mansion has rates ranging from $72 to $104, double occupancy. The innkeeper's baked scones and other goodies at breakfast and tea, together with the complimentary sherry nightcap, impart the touch of home.

PORTLAND ACCOMMODATIONS

NORTH

Best Western Inn at the Meadows, 1215 N. Hayden, Meadows Dr., tel. 286-9600, $70-145, cable, pets, restaurant/lounge, weight room, nonsmoking rooms, complimentary continental breakfast.

Budget Value Viking Motel, 6701 N. Interstate Ave., tel. 285-6687, $38-42, cable, pets, kitchenettes, fireplace, pool, laundry, nonsmoking rooms.

Delta Inn, 9930 N. Interstate Ave., tel. 289-1800, $50-60, cable, pets, kitchenettes, laundry, nonsmoking rooms.

Friendship Inn Sands Motel, 3801 N. Interstate Ave., tel. 287-2601, $35-40, cable, pets, nonsmoking rooms.

John Palmer House, 4314 N. Mississippi, tel. 284-5893, $50-85, restaurant/lounge.

Mel's Motor Inn, 5205 N. Interstate Ave., tel. 285-2556, $35-45, cable, pets, kitchenettes.

Palms Motel, 3801 N. Interstate Ave., tel. 287-5788, $35-45, cable, pets.

Red Lion Hotel, Jantzen Beach, 909 N. Hayden Island Dr., tel. 283-4466, $125-160, cable, pets, restaurant, lounge, pool, live entertainment, river view.

Red Lion Inn Coliseum, 1225 N. Thunderbird Way, tel. 235-8311, $76-83, cable, pets, restaurant/lounge, nonsmoking rooms, river view.

Westerner Motel, 4333 N. Interstate Ave., tel. 281-0097, $35-45, cable, pets.

NORTHEAST

Ara-Bell Motel, 11324 N.E. Sandy Blvd., tel. 252-6059, $27-40, cable, kitchenettes, laundry, nonsmoking rooms.

Best Western Fortniter Motel, 4911 N.E. 82nd Ave., tel. 255-9771, $50-60, cable, kitchenettes, nonsmoking rooms, complimentary continental breakfast.

Best Western Kings Way Inn, 420 N.E. Holladay St., tel. 233-6331, $65-80, cable, restaurant, laundry, nonsmoking rooms.

Cabana Motel, 1707 N.E. 82nd Ave., tel. 252-0224, $35-40, cable, kitchenettes, laundry, nonsmoking rooms.

Cameo Motel, 4111 N.E. 82nd Ave., tel. 288-5981, $35, cable, kitchenettes, laundry, nonsmoking rooms.

Capri Motel, 1530 N.E. 82nd Ave., tel. 253-1151, $35-45, cable, kitchenettes, complimentary continental breakfast.

Carriage Inn, 2025 N.W. Northrop, tel. 224-0543, $40-50, cable, pets, kitchenettes, laundry.

Chumaree Inn, 8247 N.E. Sandy Blvd., tel. 256-4111, $50-100, cable, pool, restaurant/lounge, laundry, nonsmoking rooms.

City Center Motel, 3800 N.E. Sandy Blvd., tel. 287-1107, $35-40, cable, pets, nonsmoking rooms, complimentary continental breakfast.

Comfort Inn Lloyd Center, 431 N.E. Multnomah, tel. 233-7933, $60-85, cable, covered pool, nonsmoking rooms, complimentary continental breakfast.

Days Inn Hotel, 11550 N.E. Airport Way, tel. 252-3200, $70-85, cable, restaurant/lounge, pool, laundry, nonsmoking rooms, complimentary continental breakfast.

Dune Motel, 1525 N.E. 37th Ave., tel. 288-6751, $35-45, cable, pool, nonsmoking rooms, complimentary continental breakfast.

Econo Lodge Airport, 9520 N.E. Sandy Blvd., tel. 252-6666, $45-75, cable, restaurant.

Execulodge, Convention Center, 1021 N.E. Grand Ave., tel. 235-8433, $54-108, cable, restaurant/lounge, weight room, live entertainment, nonsmoking rooms.

Hojo Inn, 3939 N.E. Hancock, tel. 288-6891, $35-60, cable, pets, nonsmoking rooms.

PORTLAND ACCOMMODATIONS (CONT.)

Holiday Motel, 8050 N.E. Union Ave., tel. 285-3661, $35-45, cable, pets.

Midtown Motel, 1415 N.E. Sandy Blvd., tel. 234-0316, $22-29, cable, nonsmoking rooms, complimentary continental breakfast.

Best Western Pony Soldier Inn, 9901 N.E. Sandy Blvd., tel. 256-1504, $65-75, cable, kitchenettes, restaurant/lounge, pool, weight room, laundry, nonsmoking rooms, complimentary continental breakfast.

Portland Super 8 Motel, 11011 N.E. Holman, tel. 257-8988, $55, cable, pets, laundry, nonsmoking rooms.

Shilo Inn Lloyd Center, 1506 N.E. 2nd Ave., tel. 231-7665, $50-60, cable, pets, laundry, nonsmoking rooms, complimentary continental breakfast.

Shilo Inn, Portland Airport, 3828 N.E. 82nd Ave., tel. 256-2550, $45-60, cable, pets, kitchenettes, pool, laundry, nonsmoking rooms.

States Motel, 2620 N.E. 82nd Ave., tel. 255-0103, $32, cable, kitchenettes, pool, covered pool, weight room.

Travelodge Hotel, 1441 N.E. 2nd Ave., tel. 233-2401, $65-90, cable, restaurant/lounge, pool, nonsmoking rooms.

SOUTHEAST

Aaron Motel, 2724 S.E. 82nd Ave., tel. 771-6460, $28-45, basic.

Del Rancho Motel, 7622 S.E. 82nd Ave., tel. 777-3806, $32-49, cable, kitchenettes.

Best Value Inn, 3310 S.E. 82nd Ave., tel. 777-4786, $30-40, cable, pets, nonsmoking rooms.

Camaree Inn, 4512 S.E. 82nd Ave., tel. 774-8876, $35-50, cable, nonsmoking rooms, complimentary continental breakfast.

Cascade Motel, 10308 S.E. 82nd Ave., tel. 775-1571, $38-45, cable, pets, kitchenettes.

Chestnut Tree Inn, 9699 S.E. Stark, tel. 255-4444, $40, cable, kitchenettes, nonsmoking rooms.

Unicorn Inn Motel, 3040 S.E. 82nd Ave., tel. 774-1176, $40-50, cable, kitchenettes, nonsmoking rooms.

SOUTHWEST

Cypress Inn, Downtown Portland, 809 S.W. King, tel. 226-6288, $50-80, cable, kitchenettes, laundry, nonsmoking rooms, complimentary continental breakfast.

Downtown Value Inn, 415 S.W. Montgomery Ave., tel. 226-4751, $35-45, cable, pets, laundry, nonsmoking rooms.

Imperial Hotel, 400 S.W. Broadway, tel. 228-7221, $60-75, cable, restaurant/lounge, nonsmoking rooms, riverside view.

Mark Spencer Hotel, 409 S.W. 11th Ave., tel. 224-3293, $55-70, kitchenettes, laundry, nonsmoking rooms.

Nendels Inn, 9900 S.W. Broadway, tel. 228-2251, $55-85, cable, restaurant/lounge, pool, weight room, nonsmoking rooms.

Portland Inn, 1414 S.W. 6th Ave., tel. 221-1611, $70-80, cable, restaurant/lounge, pool, weight room, live entertainment, nonsmoking rooms.

Portland Rose Motel, 8920 S.W. Barbur Blvd., tel. 244-0107, $35, cable, pets, kitchenettes, laundry.

Ranch Inn Motel, 10138 S.W. Barbur Blvd., tel. 246-3375, $30-40, cable, pets, kitchenettes.

Riverside Inn, 50 S.W. Morrison, tel. 221-0711, $60-90, cable, restaurant/lounge, nonsmoking rooms, riverside view.

Saharan 4th Ave. Motel, 1889 S.W. 4th Ave., tel. 226-7646, $30-40, pets, kitchenettes.

Sixth Avenue Motel, 2221 S.W. 6th Ave., tel. 226-2979, $40-50, cable, pets, nonsmoking rooms.

St. Francis Hotel, 1110 S.W. 11th Ave., tel. 223-2161, $33, laundry.

The Greenwood Inn, 10700 S.W. Allen Blvd., tel. 643-7444, $85, kitchenettes, fireplace, restaurant/lounge, pool, weight room, live entertainment, nonsmoking rooms.

Eclectic Lodging Choices

For those who enjoy rural serenity within commuting distance of downtown, there's camping in **Milo McIver State Park** (24101 South Entrance Rd., Estacada 97013; tel. 630-7150). Set on the banks of the Clackamas River (five miles northwest of Estacada), you're 25 miles from downtown Portland, but this retreat seems farther away. To get there, take I-84 east to I-205 south and follow the exit to ORE 224/Estacada. The road forks right at the town of Carver to go 10 miles to the campground. There are 44 hookup sites, flush toilets, showers, firewood, and a laundromat here, as well as fishing for winter steelhead and late-fall salmon. Other recreation includes hiking and horse trails and a boat ramp. Mount Hood ski slopes are an hour east of the park. Bagby Hot Springs and the trail to it through an old-growth forest are other attractions within an hour's drive off ORE 224. Campground fees are $9 per night with no reservations, and it's open year-round.

Finally, if your funds are low and you just need a place to bed down for the night that is hygienic and safe, try **Warner Pacific College dormitories.** The college rents out dorm rooms June 15 to Sept. 1 for $5 a night. The campus is in the 2200 block of S.E. 68th St. and asks advance reservations by phone (tel. 775-4366). Overnight guests must supply their own bedding on otherwise bare mattresses. In addition, they request no smoking, drinking, or pets in their dorms, which are separated by sex.

FOOD

Portland's renaissance has resulted in the highest number of restaurants per capita of any city in the country. Perhaps more impressive is the fact that you can have a singular dining experience for much less than you'd pay for a gourmet outing in either Seattle or San Francisco. Even the traditionally overpriced bland food served in many hotel dining rooms can often turn out to be affordable and tasty here. Also noteworthy are local chains of ethnic fast food, pan-Asian cuisine, a profusion of microbreweries, and innovative purveyors of Northwest cuisine. The following cross section leaves many upscale restaurants to such dining guides as *Portland's*

Best Places (Sasquatch Press) and *Pacific Northwest* magazine (see the general Introduction). What's left are places with personality and a sense of fun geared to the budget of the average traveler.

Ethnic Eateries

While not for the faint of palate, the dim sum at **Fong Chong** (301 N.W. Fourth; tel. 220-0235) is one of the more exotic low-cost dining adventures in the city. It all begins at 11 a.m. every day, when carts of steaming Cantonese delicacies come whooshing down the aisles. Even if the mumbled explanations of the barely bilingual staff don't translate, the array of crepes and buns stuffed with chicken, shrimp, pork, and other fillings are so varied and cost so little (averaging about $1.70 per plate) that you can't miss. After 3 p.m. the restaurant reverts to unadventurous Cantonese fare off the menu. The adjoining Oriental grocery, however, is always fascinating.

Across the bridge to the northeast, near Lloyd Center, **Saigon Kitchen** (835 N.E. Broadway; tel. 281-3669) improves upon Fong Chong's functional decor and replicates the bountiful servings and reasonable prices. Although Vietnamese flavors predominate, Thai dishes like beef in coconut juice and basil leaves and ginger chicken spice up the menu. Dinner combination plates in the $8-10 range might include such uncommon specialties as squid or tropical fish in garlic sauce or charcoal chicken with lettuce, mint, cilantro, rice papers, and peanut sauce. And don't overlook the fried squid in garlic sauce. This restaurant has always been the darling of Portland's alternative weeklies, who rightfully extol its spring rolls (called *cha gio* in Vietnamese). A serving of three of these at lunch comes to your table all chopped up and ready for dipping into the restaurant's hot-sweet fish sauce—a wonderful light meal in the $4 range.

Chang's Mongolian Grill (1 S.W. Third Ave., tel. 243-2700; 2700 N.W. 18th Ave., tel. 645-7718; and N.E. 23rd Ave., tel. 253-3535) is based on an intriguing concept which can best be described as Chinese-style burritos cooked to order. Each outlet of the chain features a colorful Genghis Khan mural backdropping a stagestruck chef cooking your hand-picked ingredients on a large domed grill. Mooshu pancakes with plum sauce and other condiments are stacked tableside for you to wrap the just-cooked fixin's, and you can return to the grill for as much fresh veggies, thin-sliced raw meats, and fish as you like. Pickled cabbage, soup, and tea come with the meal. All-you-can-eat lunches cost $5 and dinners cost $7.50.

Two other pan-Asian restaurants worth checking out are **Xien Hong** (5314 N.E. Sandy Blvd.; tel. 288-2743) and **Yen Ha** (6820 N.E. Sandy Blvd.; tel. 287-3698). Though predominantly Vietnamese, Chinese and Thai influences often assert themselves in the cuisine of each kitchen. Extensive menus, low prices, and high quality distinguish both restaurants. Xien Hong's soups ($4) are meals in themselves and Yen Ha's meat dishes are particularly noteworthy. Xien Hong's late-night hours are especially appreciated on the east side of the Willamette River, where most restaurants close by 10 p.m. In any case, Portland's large Vietnamese community has graced the Rose City with some of the best purveyors of this cuisine outside Saigon, so sayeth *New Yorker* food philosopher Calvin Trillin.

The **Bangkok Kitchen** (2534 S.E. Belmont; tel. 236-7349) is the kind of place Portlanders have up their sleeve to catch visiting Thai-food aficionados by surprise. No one would ever guess that this storefront neighborhood diner specializes in such exotic sauces as Nuuc Mann (hot-sweet fish sauce) and a peanut-and-chili-pepper blend that'll make you cry out in pain and ecstasy at the same time. As you might have guessed, don't specify "hot" here unless you're still on novocaine after a dental appointment. With a minimum of caution, however, you can enjoy one of the best restaurant values in Oregon.

A small northern Indian restaurant on the corner of 11th Ave. and S.W. Morrison has become the talk of Portland's cost-conscious gourmets. The $5.95 buffet lunch at **India House** (1038 S.W. Morrison St.; tel. 274-1017) lets you load up your plate with a variety of vegetable curries, samosas (triangular potato pastries with flaky crust), tandoori chicken, basmati rice, and salads.

Indian food connoisseurs will tell you that this cuisine is distinguished by the diner's being able to taste a number of individual spices in one dish, a quality in ample evidence in many India House specialties. You'll even notice this fanfare

of flavors in a kind of bread served here. Naan is an unleavened bread cooked in a tandoor oven, a superhot barbecue pit lined with clay. The toasty texture and slight mesquite aftertaste come through with your first bites, and thereafter, the complexities of other flavors assert themselves. The Keema naan, for example, is redolent with cumin and mustard seed, beneath flecks of lamb and butter on top. You can cool your tongue off with the Darjeeling tea and rice pudding for dessert, well-chosen accompaniments to finish off this budget banquet.

A good way to judge a Mexican restaurant is by its chiles rellenos. If a place can make this popular dish with a light, crisp batter so as not to mute the taste of the chile pepper and melted cheese, chances are it can pull off the whole enchilada in fine style. **Chez Jose** (8502 S.W. Terwilliger Blvd.; tel. 244-0007) passes this test and probably meets any other standard you might use to judge a Mexican restaurant. You'll also appreciate such touches as being asked if you prefer your order hot or mild, as well as the use of Oregon's famous Tillamook cheddar along with the traditional Monterey jack in many recipes. Best of all, a sumptuous combination plate here can feed two people for $7.50. For a few bucks more you can order a serving of Mexican chocolate ice cream with a cinnamon aftertaste that recalls the flavor of hot chocolate south of the border. Another branch of Chez Jose is located at N.E. 22nd and Broadway.

Maya's Tacqueria (1000 S.W. Morrison; tel. 226-1946) offers well-rendered Mexican fast food ranging from chiles rellenos to chicken mole enchiladas. The Mexican beer and refrescos and the best array of salsas in Portland also make this elaborate taco stand seem closer to the Guadalajara marketplace than to Pioneer Courthouse Square. On warm days, sit outside to watch passersby and admire the Mexican-style murals. **Santa Fe Tacqueria** (831 N.W. 23rd Ave.; tel. 226-0406) is Maya's outlet in the stylish Northwest barrio.

South-of-the-border flavors are also served up at **Macheesmo Mouse** (723 S.W. Salmon St., tel. 228-3491; 811 N.W. 23rd Ave., tel. 274-0500; 3500 S.E. Hawthorne Blvd., tel. 232-5688; 1200 N.E. Broadway, tel. 249-0002), but with a cooking style that's heart-smart and nutritious. Many items list calorie count and come with brown rice and whole-grain tortillas. Thanks to fresh salsa and the Cajun flavors of the restaurant's own Boss Sauce, healthy fast food never tasted so good.

A few blocks off N.E. Burnside you'll find the best Tex-Mex food in the city. Behind the hole-in-the-wall facade of a neighborhood beer joint, **Esparza's Cafe** (2725 S.E. Ankeny St.; tel. 234-7909) welcomes you with mahogany booths and a "Back in the Saddle Again" decor. Begin your meal here with nachos—shreds of stringy chicken under melted cheese and slivers of jalapeño, all of which appear to have been proportioned and positioned on each individual chip to maximize flavor. While other *antojitos* (traditional appetizers and snacks) demonstrate similar flair, it's the brisket in chile colorado sauce, scrambled huevos rancheros, and diced nopalito cactus lightly dusted with cornmeal that'll evoke El Paso-Juarez for those who have been there. If you haven't, forgo Otis and Aretha on the jukebox for a norteño polka to accompany Esparza's flavors of the *frontera*.

The original nuevo-wavo Mexican identity of **Casa U-Betcha** (612 N.W. 21st St., tel. 227-3887, and 1700 N.E. Broadway, tel. 282-4554) has now been replaced by an eclectic Southwestern sensibility. But this restaurant is not only about food. The high-viz cartoon wackiness of the original northwest Portland outlet has also changed to an even gaudier art nouveau motif. Splashy multicolored tile floors sit below an azure ceiling that could have been inspired by a velvet Elvis painting in the Casa on Broadway. The things that haven't changed, however, are excellent appetizers (try the duck confit salad and camarones Mazatlan, a pan-seared shrimp), intriguing variations on salsa (including corn, apple, and mint salsas), and large portions. Many appetizers alone could make a meal here, and the entrees, though superficially spendy for a Latin restaurant ($10-14), can comfortably sate two people. Afterwards, Broadway Books, located next door to the northeast outlet, offers interesting selected fiction and arcane bargain titles to peruse.

Other new ethnic food arrivals in Broadway's smorgasbord of dining possibilities include Casa U-Betcha's oriental offshoot, **Noodlehead**, located next door to its parent restaurant; and

Papparazzi (2015 NE Broadway; tel. 281-7701), whose pizzas are heavy on ingredients like goat cheese and sun-dried tomatoes. As with most places on Broadway, Papparazzi has a no reservation policy, so avoid peak dining hours.

Across the street and two blocks west at **Ron Paul's** (N.E. Broadway and 15th) light entrees, creative salads, and famous desserts are often inspired by international cuisines and made with local ingredients. This upscale deli is the best place in the city for a gourmet meal under $10.

The truly famished will enjoy the inexpensive, all-you-can-eat luncheon buffet at the two-restaurant complex shared by the **Monte Carlo** and **Lido** (1016 Belmont; tel. 238-7627). Lasagna, chicken, and all kinds of salads and pastas find their way onto this spread. Excellent pizza and thick minestrone soup are highlighted at dinner.

Another place for pizza is the **Bridgeport Brew Pub** (1313 N.W. Marshall St.; tel. 241-7179). The malt-based pizza crust and out-of-this-world toppings (olives, chorizo, yellow peppers, and eggplant) washed down by the brewery's handmade Blue Heron Ale make a tough combination to beat. Nonetheless, **Escape From New York** (913 S.W. Alder St., tel. 226-4129; and 622 N.W. 23rd Ave., tel. 227-5423) is frequently touted as the best by-the-slice operation in town.

At the edge of Old Town is a Portland institution. *Joie de vivre* is in the air when you step into **Alexis** (215 W. Burnside, tel. 224-8577), but it's not just the retsina, Greek music, and folk dancing that keep people coming back. This is the best Greek food in Oregon. Appetizers like calamari or saganaki (fried cheese) might start your meal here. You can spend an evening just ordering appetizers and enjoying the crusty bread, but it would be a shame to forgo such entrees as the moussaka and oregano chicken. On weekends this moderately priced taverna features belly dancing and an atmosphere that'll bring out the Zorba in anyone.

Eye-openers

Although lunch is also served at the **Bijou Cafe** (132 S.W. Third Ave.; tel. 222-3187), it has built its reputation on breakfast. While fried cinnamon bread and red snapper hash are morning mainstays in this airy cafe, ordinary breakfast food like scrambled eggs, hash browns, muffins, and oatmeal are done perfectly here with the freshest and most nutritious ingredients. As for the latter, Bijou patrons appreciate the restaurant's emphasis on organic produce and wholegrain products for no more than it would cost to eat at a highway truck stop.

Zefiro's (500 N.W. 21st Ave; tel. 226-3394) national media attention in the likes of *GOURMET* magazine usually focuses on its innovative Mediterranean-accented dishes at lunch and dinner. You'll have a better chance of getting a seat however at breakfast. Begin with the fresh-squeezed Granny Smith apple juice or coffee served in a soup bowl. The latter is the perfect accompaniment to warm pear brioche pudding or a pumpkin and pecan muffin.

The four-course, Jewish-style Sunday brunch has helped establish **Bread and Ink** (3610 S.E. Hawthorne; tel. 239-4756) as *the* gathering place in the Hawthorne neighborhood. The white-washed walls with lots of windows create a convivial atmosphere for lox, borscht, cheese blintzes, and other delicacies. If this is not the way you choose to start the day, there's always an assortment of homemade breads and imaginative omelettes to sustain you. Later on in the week, lunchtime diners line up for a massive burger topped with Gruyère cheese and Bermuda onion.

Portland's most famous breakfast haunt is the **Original Pancake House** (8600 S.W. Barbur Blvd.; tel. 246-9007). This Wed.-Sat. operation has spawned many imitations, but the Original is still the greatest. If you're without a car, take bus #38 from downtown. The restaurant opens at 7 a.m., but be there early on weekends. Latecomers should bring a book because waits for seating can be excruciatingly long. Once at the table, the famous apple pancake is a Frisbee-sized cinnamon-laced delight for the growing boy or girl. Lighter appetites can choose from among 20 other varieties priced between $4 and $6.50.

At the **Cadillac Cafe** (914 N.E. Broadway; tel. 287-4750), if the Fleetwood-fin-shaped logo and shocking-pink color scheme don't wake you up in the morning, the first-rate breakfast will. The thematic continuity of the restaurant's decor,

along with fresh flowers and clean architectural lines, bespeak the same attention to detail that greets northeast neighborhood breakfastgoers and lunchtime devotees of the menu's expertly prepared "comfort food." Here, you'll find a light omelette batter that doesn't overwhelm the taste of the ingredients inside and perfectly done hash browns. On Sundays, we recommend an early arrival to get a seat for Henry's North American (sweet Italian sausage scrambled with eggs, spinach, and Swiss cheese) and other specialties. At lunch, such sandwich standbys as tuna melt and ham and Swiss might even be better than the way mom used to do it.

The **Hawthorne Cafe** (3354 S.E. Hawthorne; tel. 232-4982) carries the banner for a neighborhood long known for its Bohemian feel and ethnic flair. Therefore, it shouldn't be surprising that this restaurant serves up hearty breakfasts and lunches whose nutritional concerns are reminiscent of the '60s—but with the tastiness of Mediterranean cuisine. The latter comes courtesy of such garnishes as the restaurant's homemade hummus and strips of seasoned lamb known as "gyro." Moderate prices and cozy mini-dining rooms also make this place a winner.

Food Fetishes

With legions of joggers and bikers as well as a leading naturopathic college and chiropractic school, Portland is known for its health-conscious population. The five stores of **Nature's Northwest** add to this reputation. In addition to an incredible array of produce and natural food products, Nature's flagship outlet on 24th and Fremont and the new mega-store on 30th and Division boast a selection of takeout gourmet items, many of which have a decidedly "un-gourmet" price. The 24th Street store's upstairs dining room and Division Street's Sante Restaurant (3000 Division St. Portland, tel. 233-4340) let you partake of this bounty in pleasant surroundings. Dinner is served at Sante every night except Monday and brunch is served till 3 p.m. on weekends. This is a chance to enjoy some of the best Northwest cuisine in the city in a price range between $3.95 and $11.95.

Chuck Hinton's **Rib Express** (3328 N.E. Killingsworth, Portland) is a takeout counter serving downhome hickory-smoked barbecue at a good price. Pork and beef ribs as well as chicken are doused in Chuck's own special sauce, which is the talk of the neighborhood. The sweet-potato pie is excellent for dessert.

Despite the fact that Oregonians often describe **Rose's** as an East Coast-style delicatessen, New York deli mavens will find themselves searching high and low for knishes, kasha, and other standard fare of Jewish soul food. Nonetheless, the tradition of overstuffed sandwiches ($6-9) is taken to a new level here. In a town where, more often than not, they cut the corned beef with the grain instead of against it, the quality meats piled high on fresh rye (and other breads) will make the most jaded East Coast transplant sit up and take notice. One sandwich feeds two here (try the Reuben), and if you're still hungry, there're always the football-sized pastries in the display case for dessert. And regardless of how you feel afterward, order some rum balls to go. For hikers going to or from Washington and Forest parks, the West Hills outlet (315 N.W. 23rd Ave.; tel. 227-5181) is recommended; en route or returning from the Columbia River Gorge, the restaurant at the Menlo Park Shopping Center (12329 N.E. Glisan St.; tel. 224-6545) is closest; coast-bound travelers should put on the brakes at the Rose's in the Beaverton Town Square (tel. 643-4287).

If you're looking for good, no-nonsense sustenance try **Hamburger Mary's** (840 S.W. Park Ave.; tel. 223-0900). Thick burgers with salad fixin's on a whole-wheat bun are the specialty, but many come here for great coffee and the chance to create an omelette from two dozen possible ingredients. Stuffed baked potatoes and old movies screened in the adjoining bar are two other highlights. If it's sunny, you can sit outside this crowded hole-in-the-wall. Inside, a quirky decor—which can best be described as '60s flea-market chic—with lots of plants, and prices as comforting as the good ol' American food, await.

Old Wives' Tales (1300 E. Burnside; tel. 238-1470) is a restaurant whose wholesome multiethnic vegetarian cuisine demonstrates that "moderately priced and nutritious" doesn't have to mean boring. The addition of chicken and fresh seafood, along with beer, wine, and espresso, to the offerings of this onetime "health food" restaurant has enabled it to make the transition to the epicurean tastes of the '90s. The best salad bar in town, famous Hungarian mushroom soup, fresh seafood hash, and cozy backroom booths are other reasons to come.

As you approach **Rimsky-Korsakoffee House** (707 S.E. 12th Ave.; tel. 232-2640), the old red house gives no indications (not even a hand-lettered sign bearing its name!) that this is Portland's favorite artsy hangout and coffeehouse. Only the lines extending out the door on a crowded weekend might convey that the place is something special. Folks come for mocha fudge cake washed down by espresso drinks, live classical music, as well as people and ideas in creative ferment. The atmosphere of a refined house party reigns here 7 p.m.-midnight on weekdays and 7 p.m.-1 a.m. on weekends. Expect a surprise in the upstairs bathroom.

The **Ringside** (2165 W. Burnside; tel. 223-1513) offers a menu of predominantly meat and potatoes, and its decor of hunting trophies and faded boxing photos seems out of a Hemingway novel. The only concessions to current culinary fashion here are a few chicken and fish dishes, and the restaurant definitely stands on tradition when it forgoes the heart-smart use of leaner beef. The customers, many of whom eat their dinner in the red glare of the restaurant's crowed bar, maintain that a less marbled steak would have no flavor. No matter where you stand on the issue, you can always count on a well-prepared red-meat repast here. Be that as it may, it's the lightly battered yet crisp onion rings that enabled the restaurant to make a name for itself. In addition to the plump Walla Walla sweets with a hint of spice, the baked potatoes here are also a highlight.

Hotel Dining Rooms

The two most venerated hostelries in Portland are the **Heathman** (S.W. Broadway at Salmon St.; tel. 241-4100) and the **Benson Hotel** (S.W. Broadway and Oak St.; tel. 228-2000). In like measure, their dining rooms enjoy a reputation for serving some of the finest cuisine in the region. As in most establishments of this ilk, dinner can be on the spendy side, but this doesn't mean you have to totally deny yourself the opportunity to break bread in these hallowed halls.

THEO ROMMEL

the Benson Hotel

In contrast to dinner, where checks can exceed $40 per person, breakfast at the Benson's London Grill is not appreciably more expensive than many places in town, and the few extra bucks are worth it. The experience begins the moment you step into the hotel. The Russian walnut lining the Benson lobby, together with the marble fireplace and staircase, bespeak the glory that was Simon Benson's Portland in 1916. Benson's legacy also includes the Columbia Gorge Hotel and Scenic Highway as well as dozens of ornate drinking fountains he put up around the city (to promote a teetotaling outlook).

Downstairs from the Benson lobby, the chandeliered and mahogany-paneled **London Grill** continues Simon Benson's traditions of excellence. Whether it's the open-face shrimp omelette with goat cheese and herbs or the vegetable frittata, the scrumptious food, first-rate service, and plush surroundings give a taste of Portland at its best. Better yet, it shouldn't run you too much more than $7. For a little more than twice that price, try the Sunday brunch here. This Portland tradition lets you enjoy three meals in one, with items ranging from standard breakfast fare to spicy Chinese noodles, braised veal tips, and sushi. It's all good, but save some room for the chocolate petits fours.

Across the street, amid the indoor greenery of the posh Vintage Plaza hotel, **Pazzo** (422 S.W. Broadway; tel. 228-1515), serves inexpensive continental breakfast fare with a flair. Along with cornmeal scones, foccacia and other bakery delights, there's a sumptuous fruit salad and robust Italian-style coffee.

The Heathman Hotel's interior also exudes the understated Old World elegance of the Benson, with generous use of teak paneling and marble. However, the prices in its trendy **Heathman Restaurant** (extolled by the late James Beard) will appeal more to the expense-account traveler than to explorers on a budget. Nonetheless, low-priced ($2.50-$2.95), tasty soups and rolls are served in the lounge during lunch. Afterward, in the wood-paneled lobby, Heathman elegance can also be experienced at afternoon tea, 2-4:30 p.m. Ten teas from around the world, finger sandwiches, scones, pasties, strawberries, and chocolates are served on English bone china in what has become a Portland tradition (reservations appreciated). If you're interested in a late lunch, for $11.95 you can get cucumber-and-bay-shrimp sandwiches, salmon canapes, and ham-and-cheddar rolls, along with pound cake, shortbread, and all the other traditional teatime accompaniments.

The **Heathman Bakery and Pub** (901 S.W. Salmon St.; tel. 227-5700) also serves Northwest cuisine in the style of its parent restaurant, but at a fraction of the cost (the restaurant is also called B. Moloch, after the caricaturist whose work adorns the walls). The specialty here is gourmet pizza, but pasta-seafood concoctions and dishes boasting such local ingredients as hazelnuts, chevre, Oregon lamb, game pâté, and homemade sausage, as well as the in-house Widmer microbrew, are also parts of the restaurant's identity. Lest this sound like the kind of place where only yups come to sup, a $6-10 price range and an informal atmosphere are guaranteed not to scare you away. You can go the takeout route here or have a server bring the food to your table after you place your order at the counter. And if you're willing to stand in line long enough, it's possible to get some of the best bread in the city at a low price when the Heathman Bakery has $1/loaf specials.

Finally, if you have a reason to splurge, try **Alexander's** (921 S.W. Sixth Ave.; tel. 226-1611) on the 23rd floor of the Portland Hilton. Even though the tab for two is occasionally equivalent to the price of a decent motel room, views of the snowcapped Cascades backdropping Portland's cityscape and the exquisite presentation of the food here can render material concerns irrelevant. As for what to order, consult the personable maitre d', Joseph, for special insights into what's good that evening. While the entrees skillfully walk a tightrope between nouvelle and traditional, the desserts can only be described as sinfully decadent.

Seafood
Jake's Famous Crawfish (901 S.W. 12th St.; tel. 226-1419) is not just famous for those lobsterlike denizens of the Oregon freshwater deep. It is also renowned for the widest-ranging seafood menu in the Northwest and one of the most extensive Oregon wine lists. The largest privately owned fine art collection in the region also graces the mahogany-paneled confines of Jake's. But when all is said and done, it's the local crawfish (available May through September) that put the restaurant's name up in lights. Other specialties include clam chowder, smoked salmon and sturgeon, steamed butter clams, spring chinook salmon, and bouillabaisse. You can also get a good steak here. For the best luck, order one of the two dozen or so specials off the "fresh sheet." Whatever you decide on, leave room for chocolate-truffle cake. Getting reserved seating in this 100-year-old landmark is often difficult, but not enough to deter dozens of reservationless people who might wait over an hour for an opening. A cost-effective way to enjoy Jake's cuisine minus the wait is to partake at Jake's Backstage Restaurant located in the lobby of the Performing Arts Center. Open 6-8 p.m. each evening, this dinner buffet includes such popular Jake's dishes as cedar plank salmon, au gratin potatoes and truffle cake. Vegetarian selections are also available. The full buffet is $9.95 with a dessert-only alternative.

McCormick and Schmick's (235 S.W. First Ave.; tel. 224-7527) has venerable roots—it's the offspring of century-old Jake's restaurant, and enjoys a location in the historic Failing Building from the same era—but this popular seafood emporium definitely has new ideas when it comes to food preparation and presentation.

THE GOVERNOR

Food aficionados, history buffs, and downtown explorers will all find something to appreciate at the newly renovated **Governor Hotel** (S.W. 10th St. at Alder, tel. 503-224-3400 or 800-554-3456). Built in 1909 in response to the city's decade of exponential growth, the old Governor has emerged from a $16 million facelift none the worse for its appropriation of the Princeton Building next door (a former Elks Temple and now the hotel's west wing), new rooftop balconies, and in-room fax machines.

The hotel's sparkling terra-cotta facade encloses an oasis of old Portland: inside, high ceilings, arts-and-crafts-style furnishings, and the lobby's landmark sepiatoned mural depicting scenes from the Lewis and Clark Expedition all contribute to the turn-of-the-century sense of taste, proportion, and sanity. Even if your budget won't stretch to include a night or two at the Governor (rooms begin at $105 and top out with the $500 Governor or Presidential suites), stop by the **Celilo Lounge** in the lobby for a drink (live music nightly, usually jazz) or a meal of regionally inspired fare prepared by executive chef George Poston. The Sunday brunch, at $14.50 a plate, is especially recommended. Afterward, wander across the street to the Galleria with its cluster of first-rate shops, including Made in Oregon and the Fossil Cartel.

Managed by the same folks who run Salishan Lodge, the state's consistently rated five-star hotel, and the Skamania Lodge across the Columbia River from Cascade Locks, the meticulously tended Governor is listed in the National Register of Historic Places.

Consider such M&S bargain bar items as pesto prawns and mahimahi with mango chutney. Among the appetizers, a platter of Oregon, Washington, Canadian, and Californian oysters and a garlicky chanterelle sauté also evidence a deliciously creative approach. Add the above to an entree on the order of baked halibut with brie and crab and a dessertlike marsala custard and chances are you'll never consider going to any other Portland fish place except this one.

Salty's on the Columbia (3839 N.E. Marine Dr.; tel. 288-4444) is a great choice for Columbia Gorge-bound travelers. The river frontage and fish-on-ice displays which greet you here set the mood for a seafood feast. Bills can run high, so save this one for an occasion. Many fresh specials supplement the menu, which offers such imaginative dishes as a Caesar salad garnished with bits of blackened smoked salmon. Rich desserts and a nautical-theme bar well stocked with Northwest microbrews also recommend this place. If it's warm, the outdoor seating above the river is a special treat. When you emerge from the restaurant, fair-weather views of Mt. Hood can provide the finishing touch to your dining pleasure.

INFORMATION AND SERVICES

Portland's visitor-information resources are far-reaching and extensive. Begin at **Portland Convention and Visitors Center** (26 S.W. Salmon St.; tel. 222-2223). This facility, open 8:30 a.m.-5 p.m., sits across Front Ave. from Waterfront Park's beautiful fountain. In addition to knowledgeable personnel, P.C.V. has the most complete collection of printed traveler-information pamphlets in the state. While Portland is naturally the focus of most of these publications, materials about every part of the state fill the racks here. The best free **maps** of the city are available nearby from Powell's at Pioneer Square and from Hertz on the corner of S.W. Sixth Ave. and Salmon (tel. 249-5727). A free copy of *The Offbeat Tourist Guide to the Wild & Wacky Side of Portland, Oregon* can be obtained by sending a SASE to **Wacky Map** (Box 4966, Portland 97208). Attention is given to such attractions as the X-Ray Cafe's extensive velvet painting collection (see **Jazz, Blues, and**

Rock above), the old Corno's Store billboard (a huge, multicolored depiction of produce), and the 24-inch-diameter Mills End Park (located on a median strip on Front St.), which is the world's smallest city park.

A local events **hotline** (tel. 233-4444) can supplement the media sources identified below to update you on what's going on, where, and at what time. Other useful numbers include a **Crisis Line** (tel. 223-6161), **Women's Crisis Lines** (tel. 235-5333), **Men's Resource Center** (tel. 235-3433), **Drug Counseling and Intervention** (tel. 320-9654), **Health Help Center** (tel. 288-5995), and the **Aging Services Division** (tel. 248-3464).

The hours of the main **post office** (715 N.W. Hoyt St., Portland 97208; tel. 294-2124) are Mon.-Fri. 8:30 a.m.-8 p.m. and Sat. 8:30 a.m.-5 p.m.

The **Multnomah County Library** has 15 branches throughout the city with books, films, records, and at some branches, videos available for borrowing. The central branch (801 S.W. 10th Ave.; tel. 223-7201) is a top-notch research facility with a newspaper and periodical section that's well organized and voluminous.

Media

The *Oregonian* (1320 S.W. Broadway; tel. 221-8327), Portland's only daily, is joined by 16 alternative or community papers which circulate around the city. The *Oregonian's* "Arts and Entertainment" section comes out each Friday.

Most useful to the traveler are *Willamette Week* (2 N.W. Second Ave.; tel. 243-2122) and two sister publications, the *Downtowner* and *This Week* (6960 S.W. Sandburg St., Tigard; tel. 620-4140). All are free at commercial outlets throughout the city and suburbs.

Willamette Week comes out each Wednesday and has the premier entertainment listings in the city, and also news, reviews, and comment about a wide range of subjects relevant to visitors. Restaurants, artistic and theatrical presentations, sports, and the local political scuttlebutt are often dealt with in an irreverent, sometimes sardonic, tone.

The *Downtowner* also has extensive listings, as well as some reviews and articles, but is more mainstream in its criticisms and listings. Read *This Week* for Marilyn McFarlane's "Northwest Discoveries" column, which is probably the best weekly travel commentary in the state.

As for radio, Portland's 29 radio stations have something for everybody. Noteworthy on the AM band are a preponderance of call-in talk shows. The FM band concentrates more on music, though several listener-subscriber stations do their part to revive the grand old art of conversation with interviews and news commentary. KBOO (90.7 FM) features eclectic community-based programming. KOPB (91.5 FM) offers classical music and National Public Radio news shows.

GETTING THERE AND GETTING AROUND

By Car

Portland sits on or near the routes of Interstates 5, 405, 205, and 84. I-5 runs from Seattle to San Diego and I-84 goes east to Salt Lake City. I-405 circles downtown Portland to the west and south. I-205 bypasses the city to the east. U.S. 26 heads west to Cannon Beach and east to the Cascades.

The parking situation in Portland has its good news and bad news. First the bad news. Even though parking meters and day parking proliferate in the city, it's often hard to find an empty spot. The good news is that many of the parking garages accept merchant validation stamps (on the garage receipt) for free parking. As for parking on the street, parking is free from 6 p.m. to 8 a.m. on weekdays and all day Sunday.

Information on car rentals can be found in the general Introduction. A reliable cab company is **Broadway Taxi** (tel. 227-1234). Cabs charge $2 upon pick-up and each additional mile is $1.50. A trip from the airport to downtown runs about $23. It can be difficult to hail a cab here, so it's best to give them a call or catch one in front of a hotel.

By Bus And Train

The **Greyhound** bus station (550 N.W. Sixth Ave.; tel. 243-2323) has storage lockers available for 75 cents a day.

The **Green Tortoise** (616 S.W. College St.; tel. 225-0310) goes to Seattle Tuesday and Saturday (and Thursday and Sunday June 1-Oct. 1) at 4 p.m. for $15 and to San Francisco at 12:30 p.m. Sunday and Thursday (plus Tuesday and

Friday June 1-Oct. 1) for $59. Departures are from the University Deli on Sixth and College across from the Cheerful Tortoise. Eugene departures cost $10 and leave the same day as the San Francisco runs.

Amtrak runs Coast Starlight trains north and south and Pioneer and Empire Builder routes east and west along the Columbia. Trains depart for Seattle at 8 a.m., 2:30 p.m., and 5:30 p.m. The trip takes four hours and costs $30 oneway. Trains depart for San Francisco at 3:05 p.m., arriving at 8:50 a.m. the next day. One-way fare is $135. Trains depart for Salt Lake City at 10:15 a.m., arriving at 5:40 a.m. the next day. For reservations, call 800-USA-RAIL. Several Portland city buses (nos. 31-35, 54, or 56-59) will take you to Amtrak. Pick up any one of them at the downtown transit mall.

By Air

Portland International Airport (general information, tel. 231-5000, ext. 411) is a modern facility served by 16 major airlines. Delta uses PDX as a West Coast hub. Short hops in the Northwest are served by Horizon and United Express. For more information on airlines and rental companies here, consult the general Introduction.

Buses from downtown run 5 a.m.-12:30 a.m., and leave from S.W. Sixth Ave. and Main Street. From the airport, buses depart every 15 minutes, 5:30 a.m.-11:30 p.m. Catch #12 outside the baggage claim. It arrives downtown 40 minutes later via Sandy Blvd.

Other ways of getting to town include free hotel courtesy shuttles and the RAZ Downtowner (tel. 246-3301), which stops at the Greyhound station as well as many hotels en route for $7.

To drive to the city, if you follow the signs to downtown they first go to I-205, then I-84, which brings you to the Willamette River. Take the Morrison Street Bridge across the river to downtown.

Perhaps the most unusual feature of PDX is its affordable high-quality concession shops, including such Oregon mainstays as Powell's Books, City Kids toy store (high-quality American and imported playthings), Nike, the Real Mother Goose (a combination gallery and crafts store purveying woodwork, jewelry, and singular art pieces), Oregon Mountain Community (camping gear), Van Duyn Chocolates, Made In Oregon (Northwest gourmet food, crafts, books, etc.), and Norm

Thompson (the Northwest's answer to L.L. Bean), plus a restaurant where you can get dishes à la Jake's and Timberline Lodge. You'll be glad to know that each store must keep its prices identical to those at downtown outlets. As *Oregonian* writer David Sarasohn put it, "This is the image we want to show the rest of the world. Literate yet playful, athletic but epicurean, and on all occasions wearing natural fibers."

Finally, storage facilities at PDX include lockers (C and D concourses) that charge 50 cents a day, and D.J.'s Baggage Service (across the hall from Continental and American baggage claims; tel. 281-9464), with nightly rates starting at $2 a suitcase. It should be mentioned that lockers can accommodate only smaller items.

Mass-transit Buses And Light Rail

Begin your orientation to the Tri-Met bus system at Pioneer Square. Here, the Tri-Met office (1 Pioneer Courthouse Square, 701 S.W. Sixth Ave.; tel. 233-3511) is open 9-5 p.m. weekdays. Information can be obtained from Tri-Met drivers, hotel front desks and concierges, or any branch of Willamette Savings. Or, you can call these numbers: recorded information for call-a-bus (tel. 231-3197), all-night information (tel. 231-3196), special needs transportation (tel. 238-4952, Mon.-Fri. 8:30 a.m.-4:30 p.m.), and bicycle commuter service (tel. 233-0564). Fares range from 95 cents (basic fare) to $1.25 (long trips), and all-day tickets cost $3.25. Seniors ride anywhere for 45 cents. These fares also apply to MAX, the light-rail train which does not make as many stops. MAX runs every 15 minutes. To ride it to its easternmost extremity, Gresham, takes 45 minutes and costs $1.25 each way. Buy tickets from machines at MAX stations before boarding. Tri-Met buses require exact change and you can purchase tickets at the Tri-Met office or aboard the area bus.

Passengers in the downtown area can ride free anywhere in "Fareless Square." This 300-square-block area is defined by I-405 to the south, N.W. Hoyt St. to the north, and the Willamette River to the east. Thirty-one shelters (color-coded by their region) make up Transit Mall. Southbound buses pick up passengers on S.W. Fifth Ave.; northbound travelers board on S.W. Sixth Avenue.

A one-day pass is a good way to get oriented to Portland and environs. Purchase one at Tri-Met service centers (or some credit unions, banks, and supermarkets like Safeway and Albertson's) or at "Tri-Met Central" beneath Pioneer Courthouse Square. In addition, bus drivers can issue a transfer good for all day and all zones, which is the equivalent of a one-day pass. Between Tri-Mets' 74 lines and MAX, you can ride from Gresham in the east to Hillsboro in the west and from Vancouver, Washington, in the north to Wilsonville and Oregon City to the south. From the downtown core, the popular northeast part of town is accessible via these lines: #8 Irvington, #9 Broadway, #10 N.E. 33rd, and #12 Sandy Blvd., which turns around at the airport. Two lines are your keys to northwest Portland: #13 to Montgomery Park (or farther north to MacLeay and Forest parks) and #17, which travels all the way to Sauvie Island. As for other parts of town, remember that bus lines numbered in the 70s are crosstown lines—you can't pick these up at the Transit Mall downtown, but they link various neighborhoods and cut across many of the lines downtown.

The first step in setting up your own personalized mass-transit tour is picking up a schedule at one of the Tri-Met service centers or bus-information racks scattered around town. For the ultimate aid in figuring where you want to go and when, pay $2.50 for a complete Tri-Met guide, which includes a map (or you can purchase the map alone for $1), schedules, and the lowdown on attractions in various neighborhoods.

DAY-TRIPS FROM PORTLAND

THE WINE COUNTRY

Although the vinifera grape thrives throughout the interior valleys of western Oregon from the Columbia River to the California border, the so-called wine country is popularly conceived of as just those vineyards west and southwest of Portland. This is where the rich soil and long, warm, gentle growing season have created conditions which sustain the largest concentration of vineyards in the Northwest. The slow-cooling fall days engender a complexity in the regional product by inhibiting high sugar concentrations while maintaining the natural acidity of the grape. In summer, Oregon's northern latitude makes for long sunny days without excessive heat, a condition which bodes well for the harvest. These factors conspire to produce wines delicate in flavor, low in alcohol, and crisp in finish, despite a tendency toward fruitiness.

A free monthly publication, *Oregon Wine* (Oregon Wine Press, 644 S.E. 20th Ave., Portland 97214), is available in retail outlets throughout western Oregon and can help plan a foray to vineyards throughout the state. In addition, wine and restaurant reports and vintner interviews provide useful information.

With this publication and a preponderance of other literature about wine, it's easy to be overwhelmed. As such, the following wine country ramble concentrates on what most people are looking for—the pick of the harvest. In Oregon that means Yamhill County Pinot Noir.

More often than not, tasting rooms in Oregon are no-frills makeshift affairs, but that can impart a personal touch which is sometimes lacking with slicker promotion-oriented wineries. Oregon vintners are quick to explain this lack of glitz by saying that they prefer to put their money into the product. After a day along the trails of the Pinot Noir, you'll happily drink to that!

Getting Started
Before you go, pick up a *Discover Oregon Wineries* pamphlet at the Portland Convention and Visitors Center (Salmon St. across from Waterfront Park) or by contacting the **Oregon Winegrowers Association** (Box 6590, Portland 97228-6590; tel. 233-2377). This pamphlet includes directions to the state's vineyards, their hours of operation, and a description of each location's offerings.

ESCAPE TO WASHINGTON COUNTY

First, the Oregon Trail led pioneers to the Willamette Valley, a land "where crops never failed." Getting the crops to markets and to Columbia River ports via Portland, however, necessitated another frontier thoroughfare, the Tualatin Plank Road. Today, a different sort of promised land has grown up around the Plank Road: Washington County. Given the million-dollar deals cut in high-tech boardrooms, and the Nike headquarters here, the region between Portland and the Coast Range summit may be more aptly termed "Oregon's tomorrow country."

But equally prominent is the county's identity as a retreat from Portland's urban stress. Despite a population glut around Beaverton, most of the county is decidedly rural. You can enjoy a bucolic bacchanal ten minutes from downtown Beaverton (**Ponzi Vineyards,** Vandermost Rd., Beaverton; tel. 628-1227); hike Coast Range trails one-half hour away (con-

tact the **Tillamook State Forest Office** in Forest Grove; tel. 357-8005); or follow a primrose path through botanical displays and U-pick farms (contact the **Washington County Visitor's Association,** 5075 Griffiths Dr., Suite 120, Beaverton; tel. 544-5555 or 800-537-3149). Other Washington County escapes include the 10-mile bike trail around manmade Hagg Lake (seven miles southwest of Forest Grove; tel. 359-5732) and a scenic loop drive marked with signs and annotated by a folder available from the Washington County Visitor's Association.

As anyone who has toured Washington County's award-winning wineries or enjoyed its rural splendor can tell you, the time to visit "tomorrow country" is today. To avoid rush-hour traffic on the Sunset Highway (ORE 26), follow Burnside St. and Barnes Rd. out of downtown along a beautiful winding route through the West Hills across the county line.

YAMHILL COUNTY VINEYARDS

Yamhill County wineries and tasting rooms generally are open May-Oct., 11 a.m.-5 p.m. Those that do not have these hours can usually be visited around Thanksgiving, when there is an open house in the region. In any case, it's always a good idea to call in advance to confirm hours and other details. Blue-and-white signs on 99W and its offshoots help point the way to such pantheons of pinot as Rex Hill, Veritas, Knudsen Erath, Sokol Blosser, Yamhill Valley, and Amity. All these places have tasting rooms open to the public and accommodate visitors for more of the year than many of their counterparts.

On The Trail Of Pinot Noir

If you look at a globe, you'll notice that U.S. 99W west of Portland shares a latitude in common with the great wine-making regions of the world. While Oregon's Yamhill County (located on the northern cusp of the Willamette Valley) is not yet the Loire Valley of France, its early-ripening grapes, notably the Pinot Noir and chardonnay, regularly vie with the world's best in international competitions. This began in 1975, when an Oregon Pinot Noir beat out dozens of French burgundies. The state also gained attention for its truth-in-labeling law, which mandates that the varietal grape named on the bottle must be

90% of the pulp used to make the wine in question; other states require just 75%.

Good wine and good food go together, which explains the creation of some surprisingly sophisticated restaurants and bed and breakfasts in this very rural area. Yamhill wine touring has also become popular due to the fact that downtown Portland sits a mere 30 to 40 miles away from the greatest concentration of wineries. Just take I-5 south of the city and go west on U.S. 99W, and within 45 minutes you'll find yourself in the midst of filbert orchards and grapestakes. In terms of distance, this might evoke wine-touring routes from San Francisco to the Napa and Sonoma valleys, but the similarity ends there. Don't expect tours of Oregon wineries, and on-site restaurants are seldom seen—nor is there the weekend traffic of Yamhill's California counterparts.

Yamhill County Bacchanal

Your Yamhill County bacchanal starts two miles east of Newberg where **Veritas** (31190 N.E. Veritas Lane, Newberg 97132; tel. 538-0666) and **Rex Hill Vineyards** (30835 U.S. 99W, Newberg 97132; tel. 538-0666) flank the road. Each winery highlights pinot noir, chardonnay, and riesling. Veritas's 1988 white riesling won the Governor's Trophy as the best wine in the state in 1989. While the Veritas tasting room has a beautiful view of Newberg backdropped by the Red Hills of Dundee, Rex Hill has the more elegant facilities and features Pinot Gris, a wine not produced in the U.S. outside of Oregon. Also try the '85 and '88 Pinot Noirs and ask about Rex Hill's many other recent award-winning varietals, notably the '88 and '89 chardonnays. Hours at Rex Hill are 11-5 daily, April-December. In winter, it's open Fri.-Sun. 11-5 p.m., Feb.-March. Veritas is open June-Aug., 11-5 p.m. daily. On cool days, you'll appreciate the fireplace here.

Oregon's best-known and greatest-producing winery (35,000 cases annually) is **Knudsen Erath** (17000 N.E. Knudsen Lane, Dundee 97115; tel. 538-3318). Its wood-paneled tasting room sits high in the Red Hills of Dundee, where it commands an imposing view of local vineyards and the Willamette Valley. To get there, go two miles north from the center of Dundee until you see a blue state highway sign marking the turnoff near the junction of U.S. 99W and Ninth Street. Ninth St. turns into Worden Hill Rd., a thoroughfare destined to be lauded as the glory road of Oregon wine, given the legacy of Knudsen Erath. Appropriately, the road looks out over vistas dominated by grapevines. The winery's 1987 Pinot Noir vintages have garnered medals in competitions all over

Yamhill County wine country

OREGON STATE HIGHWAYS DIVISION

the world. The tasting room is open 10-6 p.m. daily in summer, 11-5 p.m. Oct. 15-May 15, and offers cabernet sauvignon, gewürztraminer, chardonnay, and riesling. Beautiful picnic sites also attract visitors here.

The intersection of Sokol Blosser Lane and U.S. 99W sits about two miles west of Dundee. Sokol Blosser Lane leads to a winery of the same name. In addition to its 1988 Pinot Noir, the **Sokol Blosser** '87 Redland chardonnay is especially recommended at the tasting room. The latter is open daily May-Oct., 10:30 a.m.-5:30 p.m. Nov.-Apr., the hours are 11 a.m.-5 p.m. Free tours of the vineyard are given every hour and an array of Oregon gourmet food products is on sale here. Sokol Blosser's manicured fields framed by white oaks and madrone make a pleasing view from the tasting-room picture window.

You'll find that the **Yamhill Valley Vineyards** (Oldville Rd., off ORE 18; tel. 843-3100) tasting room is set amid an oak grove on a 9,300-acre estate and features a balcony overlooking the vineyard. This winery's first release, an '83 Pinot Noir, first distinguished itself at a 1985 tasting of French and Oregon vintages held in New York City. This wine was also selected as the best vintage wine in Oregon at the 1990 state fair. Yamhill's 1988 Willamette Valley estate-bottled chardonnay took a silver medal there. Riesling and gewürztraminer are also available for tasting May-Dec., Tues.-Sun. 11 a.m.-5 p.m; Jan.-Apr., weekends only 11 a.m.-5 p.m.

Another Yamhill County winery that distinguished itself at the 1990 state fair was **Amity Vineyards** (18150 Amity Vineyards Rd. S.E., Amity 97101; tel. 835-2362). Its 1985 Pinot Noir, Willamette Valley Winemaker's Reserve, took a gold medal, and the 1989 dry riesling took a silver. A 1989 gewürztraminer from Amity took a bronze in this competition. If you like sweet wines, a late-harvest botrytised riesling here makes an excellent dessert wine or nightcap. Two unique vintages round out the winery's offerings. If you prefer a red wine that is less robust, a light fruity Pinot called Nouveau is produced by Amity. In 1990, they also released the state's first certified organic wines. So as not to imply that other wines aren't safe, they refrain from labeling it as such, instead calling this chem-

ical-free Pinot "eco-wine." The tasting room is open noon-5 p.m. daily, June-Oct.; noon-5 weekends only, Nov.-May. It's closed Dec. 24-Jan 31.

Amity wines are also featured at the **Lawrence Gallery** (tel. 843-3787), nine miles southwest of McMinnville on ORE 18. There are also 30 other Oregon wines available for tasting here, as well as the work of a multitude of Oregon artists and craftspeople. Upstairs is the elegant Augustine's restaurant.

Food, Lodging, And Events

McMinnville might be 35 miles south of Portland, but make reservations here in advance to dine at one of the best Italian restaurants in the state, **Nick's Italian Cafe** (521 Third St.; tel. 434-4471). The low-key atmosphere of McMinnville's downtown might at first make you wonder about such an assessment, but any trepidations will be quickly dispelled by the aromas of Nick's hearty fare and a wine list which is both extensive and distinctive. As a host to many wine-country functions, Nick is privy to special releases found nowhere else. The latter are fitting accompaniments to such unique culinary interpretations as lasagna with pine nuts, local mushrooms, and dried tomatoes. Green vegetarian spinach ravioli with parmesan, and minestrone with pesto are other favorites. The less adventurous will be pleased by the restaurant's famous grilled salmon as well as pastries and desserts made on the premises. A five-course, fixed-price dinner goes for $25 and is highly recommended. Dinner is not served on Monday.

Should you care to extend your stay in the wine country, there is no shortage of bed and breakfasts to accommodate you. Before leaving Portland, consult *Oregon Wine* for a hostelry that can meet your specs.

The Mattey House (10221 N.E. Mattey Lane, McMinnville 97128; tel. 434-5058) is one lodging that combines Old World charm, proximity to wineries, and a breakfast second to none. Set in the middle of wheat fields and orchards at the edge of McMinnville, this 1892 Victorian mansion with big windows looks inviting at the end of a day of wine touring. While some of the rooms may be small or lack private baths, individual phones, or TV, you can't beat the Mattey House for coziness and refinement. Antique furnishings, period wallpapers, and old photographs set the mood for afternoon wine and cheese in the living room. A breakfast of homemade breads and jellies, made with fruits and berries from the innkeeper's own orchard, and smoked salmon and scrambled eggs get your Yamhill bacchanal off to a great start. This fusion of viniculture and Victoriana goes for $60-70 a night. To get there, turn off U.S. 99W between McMinnville and La Fayette onto Mattey Lane and drive until you get to a large oak tree near the house.

Of all the events in the Yamhill wine country and its counterparts, no fête can boast the world-class status of the **Annual International Pinot Noir Celebration** (International Pinot Noir Celebration, Box 1310, McMinnville 97128; tel. 472-8964). More than 50 American and international pinot noir producers are on hand for symposiums, tastings, and winery tours. Meals prepared by internationally known chefs are also a highlight. The three-day event takes place at the end of July on the Linfield College campus in McMinnville. While the cost of registration ($350) is prohibitive for many, tickets to the final tasting can be purchased separately for $30. This epicurean delight takes place on the last day and features a tasting of more than 50 esteemed vintages from around the world.

Also in the McMinnville area, in 1995 there will be a museum of aviation centered on the "Spruce Goose," newly acquired from its previous digs in California. This is a homecoming of sorts for the immense Hughes aircraft, as some of the plane's wood was milled in the Coast Range.

While harvest festivals, concerts, and other events effectively complement tasting and touring, a drive through the region from mid-September into early October could well offer the biggest treat for the senses. At this time, the sight of multihued grape leaves creates a festive fall feeling, while intoxicating aromas of fermentation fill the air.

A HISTORY LOOP TOUR

Champoeg State Park

Below Yamhill County, just southeast of Newberg on ORE 219, is Champoeg (pronounced "sham-poo-ee" or "cham-poo-ee-eck"), often touted as the birthplace of Oregon. The name means "Field of Roots" in Chinook, referring to the camas

coveted by native Americans who boiled it to accompany the traditional salmon feast.

Champoeg State Park commemorates the site of the 1843 vote to break free from British and Hudson's Bay Company rule and establish a pro-American provisional government in the Oregon country. To get there from Portland, drive south on I-5 until you see signs for exit 278. This exit directs you to a rural route which goes five miles to the park visitor center (tel. 678-1251). The 568-acre park is equidistant from Portland and Salem along the Willamette River.

The visitor center has exhibits detailing how the Calapooya Indians, explorers, French Canadian fur traders, and American settlers lived in the Willamette Valley. It's open every day 9-5, and there is no admission charge. The grounds also have several historic buildings. Adjacent to the visitor center is the Manson Barn, built in 1862. The Old Butteville jail (1850) and one-room schoolhouse have also been moved to Champoeg to help evoke frontier life. Just west of the park entrance is a replica of the 1852 house of pioneer Robert Newell (tel. 678-5537). Particularly interesting is the second floor, which showcases Indian artifacts and a collection of inaugural gowns worn by the wives of Oregon governors. The house is open Feb.-Nov., Wed.-Sun. noon-5. Admission is $1.50 for adults, 50 cents for children. The **Pioneer Mother's Museum** replicates the dwellings in the Willamette Valley circa 1850. A collection of guns and muskets from 1775-1850 is also displayed. Admission is 75 cents.

During July, Thurs.-Sun., the **Champoeg Historical Pageant** (Box 4567, Salem 97302; tel. 245-3922) traces Oregon life from settlement to statehood. The spirited drama entitled *Story of Old Oregon* unfolds at the state park on a set decorated with tepees, pioneer cabins, and a turreted fort; many of the key events depicted actually occurred here. The show starts at 7:30 p.m., but get there at 6:30 to picnic and enjoy the warm-up entertainment. A dinner is available for $4.25 if you didn't bring your own. Also recommended is a blanket, because evenings are often cool here. Tickets are available on-site and cost $8 for adults, $6 for seniors, and $5 for children ages 5-16.

French Prairie Loop

Before leaving Champoeg State Park, pick up a brochure at the visitor center outlining the French

Prairie Loop, a 40-mile byway for car and bicycle touring. History buffs, thrift shoppers and antique aficionados will enjoy the chance to indulge their passions on this drive. French-Canadian trappers settled here in the 1820s and '30s to help the Hudson's Bay Company establish a presence in the Willamette Valley. During the 1849 California gold rush, wheat and produce from this area were shipped to granaries and warehouses in the area of present-day Portland and on to San Francisco.

Churches and buildings dating back to the 19th century have earned **St. Paul,** one of the towns on the loop (ORE 219), National Historic District status. The Northwest's oldest Catholic church, St. Paul's (circa 1846—some parishioners claim ancestral links with the French-Canadian trappers, who were Oregon's first permanent white settlers), is in the process of a million-dollar reconstruction as the result of a March 26, 1993 earthquake (see "Land" in the general Introduction). The church is being rebuilt with its original bricks and will be reinforced with concrete.

On the east side of the loop, **Aurora** (at the junction of ORE 219 and U.S. 99) also enjoys NHD status. Oregon's legacy as a haven for utopian communities began here with a Prussian immigrant, Dr. William Keil. He started up a communal colony for Oregon Trail pioneers, naming the town which grew out of it after his daughter. The Aurora colony fused Christian fundamentalism with collectivist principles, garnering distinction for its thriving farms and the excellence of its handicrafts. Despite Aurora's early success, a smallpox epidemic in 1862 and the coming of the railroad (which undermined Willamette River trade in the next decade) provided the catalysts for the town's demise. Keil himself died in 1877, and the struggling colony disbanded a few years later.

The Old Aurora Colony Museum (tel. 678-5754) consists of five buildings, including two of the colony's homesteads, the communal wash house, and the farm equipment shed. Admission is $2.50 for adults and $1 for children; children under six are admitted free. The entry fee admits you to a slide show explaining the history of the colony and a tour of five historic buildings. Each time of year has different hours of operation. Call for times. Old tool buffs will particularly enjoy the guided tour. Other items of interest include a musical instrument collection and a recording left

The 1843 conference at Champoeg marked the beginning of American rule in Oregon Country (from a mural in the state capitol).

over from the colony band, as well as quilts and an herb garden. After the tour, you can take an Aurora walking tour (ask for the free pamphlet) of 33 structures close to the museum to increase your understanding of the site's historical context.

The museum is easily located by turning east as you enter town. After one block, you'll see the Old Aurora Colony Museum, housed in a former ox barn. The past also lives on in Aurora thanks to two-dozen clapboard and Victorian houses, as well as 18 antique shops, all clustered along U.S. 99E.

OREGON CITY

History
Farther north from Canby on U.S. 99E, the road attractively parallels the Willamette River. Jagged rock bluffs on one side of the highway contrast with the smooth-flowing river framed

by stately cottonwood and poplar trees. More variety is added by islands in the channel and the broad expanse of 40-foot **Willamette Falls** in Oregon City. As the terminus of the Oregon Trail and the only seat of American power in the territory until 1852, this town is the site of many firsts. Leading off the list is Oregon City's status as the first incorporated city west of the Rockies. Other claims to fame include the West's first mint, paper mill, and newspaper, and the world's first long-distance electric power transmission system. The Oregon territorial capital also was the site of the state's first Protestant church and Masonic lodge.

Ironically, a representative of British interests in Oregon country is credited with starting up Oregon City. John McLoughlin, the Canadian-born chief factor of the Hudson's Bay Company, encouraged French-Canadian trappers to cross the Columbia River from Fort Vancouver and settle here in the northern Willamette Valley, inspiring the name French Prairie. To further the development of this British beachhead, McLoughlin built a flour mill near Willamette Falls in 1832. He moved down to Oregon City himself in the 1840s and became an ardent supporter of American settlers who wanted Oregon to be independent of England and part of the United States.

McLoughlin's flour mill was the precedent for other uses of waterpower here. It also helped attract pioneers who came over the Cascades via the Barlow Road extension of the Oregon Trail. As a result, Oregon City became a manufacturing center. Its river port thrived due to Willamette Falls impeding the movement of merchant ships farther south on the river. Although the development of the railroad and the city of Portland diminished the city's importance, its glory days live on today thanks to National Historic District status. Buildings which date back to the mid-19th century exemplify Queen Anne, Federal, and Italianate architectural styles.

Sights

Heading north on U.S. 99E from Willamette Falls, look for the Tumwater turnoff on the east side of the highway for the **Clackamas County Historical Society Museum** (211 Tumwater Dr., Oregon City; tel. 655-5574). Looking back at the falls from the elevated perspective of the

museum parking lot is a fitting prelude to the exhibits in the collection. The latter is amply recounted with diaries, artifacts, and historic photos on the second floor of the building. Prior to seeing these items, you'll encounter a time line which correlates world events over thousands of years to the geologic, political, and social growth of Oregon. This imparts a larger perspective to what you'll see in the exhibit hall. Signposts for your journey through the ages here include Indian baskets and arrowheads, a horse-drawn carriage, and the world's first kidney dialysis machine (invented locally). The county collection serves as a valuable complement to the End of the Trail Visitor Center and historic homes just north of here. The admission is $3 for adults, with discounts for kids, seniors, and families. Hours are Mon.-Fri. 10 a.m.-5 p.m.; Sat., Sun., and holidays 1-5 p.m.

Ten minutes north on U.S. 99E you'll come to a somewhat-the-worse-for-wear rendition of the old territorial capital city. To re-experience the glory that was 19th-century Oregon City take a right turn off U.S. 99E (McLoughlin Blvd.) onto Seventh St. and follow it to the base of the cliff. At Seventh and Railroad streets, you'll see an immense gray elevator which scales the 90-foot escarpment (operates Mon.-Sat. 7 a.m.-7 p.m., free of charge) backdropping the lower section of town. Take a left-hand turn when you exit the elevator, and a few minutes' stroll northeast along the clifftop will have you peering across a street at the backyard of an Oregon City landmark.

The **McLoughlin House** (713 Center St.; tel. 656-5146) between Seventh and Eighth streets is an impressive clapboard-style home of the Father of Oregon. To spare it flood damage, the building was moved from its original site near the river to this location. Behind it are steps leading back to the lower section of town. The admission ($2.50 for adults, discounts for seniors and kids) may seem a tad steep to view an unexciting collection of original and period furnishings, but the docent's ghost stories and historical insights can make it all come alive. In addition, the grounds are lovingly landscaped with rhododendrons, azaleas, and roses. The building is open Tues.-Sat. 10 a.m.-4 p.m., Sun. 1-4 p.m., closed on holidays and during January.

If you walk a block east to Washington Street

and then a quarter mile north, you'll come to the **End of the Oregon Trail Visitor Center** (500 Washington St.; tel. 657-9336). The terminus of the famous frontier thoroughfare is also claimed by The Dalles in the Columbia River Gorge. The Barlow Road, a spur of the original trail, traversed the Cascades (from The Dalles) to arrive here, forming the basis of Oregon City's claim. The latter distinction is the basis of the exposition housed in the basement of the library and senior center. Here displays, artifacts, and pictures of covered wagons and trail-weary migrants articulate the pilgrimage to the Willamette Valley promised land. Video productions provide more background on native American culture, the missionary influx, as well as the incursion of trappers and settlers. Pamphlets with five walking tour itineraries are available here for 75 cents. Admission for adults is $2, $1.50 for seniors and children under 12. Hours are Tues.-Sat. 10 a.m.-4 p.m., Sun. 11-4. The center is closed in January.

Behind the building and across the parking lot is the turn-of-the-century **Stevens-Crawford House** (603 Sixth St.; tel. 655-2866), an adjunct of the Clackamas County Historical Society Museum. Hours are Tues.-Sat. 10 a.m.-4 p.m., Sun. 1-4 p.m. Admission is $1.50 for adults (discounts for seniors and kids) or free with your receipt from the Historical Society Tumwater Street Museum. The exhibits here allow you to imagine yourself experiencing Oregon City as an early settler might have: cooking on a wood stove, canning fruits and vegetables, riding streetcars, etc.

A new large-scale interpretive center will be completed in 1995, two years after the state formally initiates its celebration of the 150th anniversary of the Great Migration of 1843. In the interim, there'll be information booths at the end of the trail on the same site at Abernethy Green. Organizers have selected an area often identified as the end of the Barlow Road section of the Trail to set up these facilities. To find them, just follow Washington St. north to its intersection with Abernethy Rd. or ask one of the locals for directions to Kelly Field. Those heading south on I-205 from Portland can locate this site by looking for three connected buildings in the shape of giant covered wagons on the side of the highway.

When the new center is completed, visitors will first enter a gallery filled with artifacts from pio-

neer days displayed in a period setting. The first building will also feature storytellers dressed in period clothing. The second gallery will showcase a 17-minute presentation on the Oregon Trail. A gift shop and three-dimensional model of the End of the Oregon Trail will occupy the third building. The admission charge hadn't been set at press time but is expected to be around $4.

Pageantry And Environmental Awareness
Another way to take in the history of Oregon City and the Oregon Trail is at the pageant held Tues.-Sat at 8 p.m. at Clackamas Community College, from mid-July through the beginning of August. Tickets are $7.50 with discounts for seniors, children, and families at certain shows. Fridays and Saturdays, an Indian-style salmon feed ($6.50) starts at 6 p.m., followed by a free pioneer-history talk at 7 p.m. Call 657-0588 for reservations (not required) for the show. To get there, take exit 10 off I-205 and follow ORE 213 south almost three miles to Clackamas Community College.

But that's not all that's happening on the campus. **John Inskeep Environmental Learning Center** (Clackamas Community College, 19600 South Molalla Ave., Oregon City 97045; tel. 657-6958, ext. 351) is pioneering efforts of a different sort. The 80-acre environmental-study area showcases alternative technologies and recycling against a backdrop of ponds, trails, and wildlife. Exhibits on aquaculture, birds of prey, and wetlands are included in this environmental education center's portrayal of Oregon's ecosystems. The exhibits are supplemented by one of the largest telescopes in the Northwest. Tours and interpretive programs are available at the center on Sunday afternoons. While there's no admission charge, donations are requested. Hours are 9 a.m.-dusk daily.

The center has a special outreach program in February. From 3-4:30 p.m. every Saturday during the month, learn about beavers, spring chinook salmon, herons, waterfowl, and wildlife on the center's 37-foot *Envirotrekker*. This vessel is moored in Oregon City's sportcraft boat marina. For more info, call 657-6958, ext. 2351, Tues.-Sat., or consult the *Oregonian*'s "Arts and Entertainment" listings on Friday during February. Adjacent to the Inskeep Environmental Learning Center is the **Home Orchard Society Arboretum,** displaying Oregon's array of fruit-bearing plants.

Food And Lodging

Even though Portland restaurants are 15 minutes away via I-205 and I-84, for good food and an atmosphere in keeping with Oregon City's heritage, try the **Fellows House** (416 S. McLoughlin Blvd; tel. 656-2089), a restaurant in a restored 1867 ship captain's home. Between 7 a.m. and 3 p.m., enjoy hearty breakfast fare and such lunchtime sandwich creations as Dungeness crab with melted cheddar, avocado, onion, tomato, and lettuce topped by the inn's special sauce on fresh sourdough bread.

THE COLUMBIA RIVER GORGE

Portlanders with only a day to show out-of-towners what Oregon is all about often head east to the Columbia Gorge. In the 70 miles between Troutdale and The Dalles, the state's pioneer history, rainforest-to-desert diversity, orchard country, and hydropower extolled in Woody Guthrie's "Roll On Columbia" paint a mural-come-to-life of the Oregon experience. The majesty of the river, together with dozens of waterfalls coming off the huge basalt cliffs, provide the kind of scenery inadequately enshrined in calendar art and coffee-table books.

HISTORY

Artifacts and petroglyphs found in the Columbia Gorge date human presence there back 10,000 years. Further historical perspective is lent by the fossilized remains of mastodons, camels, and ancient horses unearthed near The Dalles. The advent of the white man began with the arrival of the American Navy's Captain Gray in 1792. His ship, the *Columbia Rediviva,* was the inspiration for the name of the river. Prior to this time, British mariners Cook (in 1778) and Vancouver (in 1792) navigated past the river's five-mile mouth at Astoria but failed to note it, probably because of bad weather. All of these explorers were motivated by a desire to find a sea route connecting the Atlantic and the Pacific. Upon hearing of Gray's voyage of discovery, Vancouver dispatched Admiral Broughton to establish a British presence on the river. Broughton proceeded to name Mounts Hood, Adams, and Rainier after British naval officers on his excursion

Multnomah Falls in the Columbia River Gorge, America's second highest cascade

Engineer Samuel Lancaster emulated the dry masonry techniques of Charlemagne's legions.

up the Columbia. The next major incursion was that of Lewis and Clark (in 1805) who, despite coming by land from the east, were also drawn here in part by the search for the Northwest Passage.

Their journals described "great quantities of salmon" and "a large number of Indians" along the river. It's a good bet that the native population they observed included not just the local residents, because the shores of the Columbia have traditionally hosted gatherings of tribes. As a result, an intermingling of cultures took place, which might have been manifested in a Gorge tribesman wearing a Yurok (California) headband, Kwakiutl (British Columbia) sandals, and a Hudson's Bay Company blanket. Even their Chinook dialect became saturated with French and English expressions.

The subsequent decades saw further erosion of the Indian culture. The coming of the trappers during the first part of the 19th century, the missionaries in the 1830s, and the Oregon Trail migrants in the 1840s brought infectious diseases and depleted the salmon as well as other resources in the Columbia Gorge. Steamship transport in the 1850s and the completion of the Union Pacific tracks several decades later facilitated future incursions into this sacred Indian domain.

Lancaster's Vision

The modern era began with the building of the Columbia Gorge Scenic Highway in 1913. When the project was finished several years later, it was the only paved road in the Northwest, as well as the first designated scenic highway in the country. It was financed by Sam Hill, heir to a railroad fortune, who wanted to build a road to his Maryhill estate on the Washington side of the river. Backed by prominent Portland citizens such as lumber magnate Simon Benson, the project also attracted the support of a national group called the Good Roads Committee. Hill recruited engineer Samuel Lancaster for the task and took him abroad to study the classic roads of Europe. Such inspirations as Bingen-on-the-Rhine in Germany and the Axenstrasse in Switzerland are reflected in the hairpin turns and scenic overlooks of Lancaster's road. Other touches included the dry-masonry (without mortar) building techniques of Charlemagne's legions, Florentine viaducts, ornate tunnels, and stone benches. Much of the route was beveled into the steep basalt cliffs in order to highlight a view on every curve.

During the highway's construction, civic groups and convict labor joined road crews to give form to Lancaster's vision. Once completed, it became a tradition for middle-class families from Portland to pile into the Model T for Sunday drives on the Columbia Gorge Scenic Highway. By the '30s, the 73.8-mile thoroughfare became so crowded that a state study called for a speedier route. Interstate 84 was the result several decades later. While the riverside route of the interstate didn't lack for aesthetic appeal, Lancaster

THE MYTHIC LEGACY OF THE COLUMBIA GORGE

Modern-day history books include Lewis and Clark and the Oregon Trail pioneers in their writings about the Columbia River Gorge. Future tomes on the region will add Woody Guthrie, D.B. Cooper, and perhaps Bigfoot to the Who's Who of area notables. While their relationship with the only sea-level cleft in the Cascades was transitory, each of these gorge travelers has carved out a permanent niche in the psychic landscape of the Pacific Northwest.

Perhaps the most tangible remnants of this legacy are the 26 tunes penned by Woody Guthrie here during one month in the spring of 1941. He had been hired by the federal government (for $266.60) to write a song to help sell the public on the Bonneville Dam's goal of harnessing the river for irrigation, flood control, and cheap electricity. Out of this effort came such standards as "Roll on Columbia" ("your power is turning our darkness to dawn") and "Pastures of Plenty." Considering his forebears in the Columbia Gorge, it's altogether fitting that the folksinger laureate of our country reached his creative peak in this storied landscape.

Despite Guthrie's predominant themes of social justice and environmental grandeur, a song about the heist of the century might have been forthcoming had this troubadour been writing after November 24, 1971. On that day, D.B. Cooper bailed out of a Boeing 727 over southwestern Washington with $200,000 in cash—the result of the world's first successful airplane hijacking/extortion. It all began when someone calling himself Dan Cooper (later misidentified to a UPI reporter as "D.B." by the F.B.I.) commandeered a Portland-to-Seattle flight by handing the stewardess a note about a bomb he said would explode unless he received a large sum of money and some parachutes. To underscore his threat, he opened his briefcase to reveal a foreboding network of wires and sticks. After his request was complied with at the Seattle airport, the flight headed back toward the Oregon border, where he jumped out of the plane and into history. He also might have jumped into the Columbia River if a small portion of the money recovered along its banks in 1980 is any indication. Some years later, a diver found what he claimed was Cooper's parachute not far from this site. In any case, the derring-do of this modern-day Jesse James was the high-tech equivalent of a stage robbery committed at a full gallop. With only unconfirmed sightings of the mysterious Mr. Cooper over the last two decades, all that remains of this crime is the poetic justice of its Old West backdrop to stir imagination and wonder.

Another secret the Columbia Gorge might share if it could talk would be the whereabouts of the abominable snowman, a.k.a. Bigfoot or Sasquatch. Indian tribes of the region regarded this creature as a fact of life and celebrated its presence in art and ritual. Whether it exists outside the mind or not, the King Kong of the Northwest forests has attracted to the region everyone from hunters and academics to curiosity seekers and National Enquirer reporters. Although the notion of a half-man, half-ape eluding human capture seems implausible at first, a brief look at some of the evidence might convince you otherwise. As recently as the winter of 1991, reports from a remote area of the Blue Mountains (whose chief drainage is the Columbia River) spoke of more than 60 miles of tracks left in the snow by a large five-toed creature. Scientists on the scene were of the opinion that the pattern of the prints and the gait could not have been fake. A similar conclusion was reached in 1982 about a plaster cast of footprints taken from the same mountain range. A Washington State University professor detected humanlike whorls on the toe portions of the prints, which he said showed that the tracks had

ANNIE LONG

to have been made by a large hominid. Reports and evidence of actual encounters abound in the annals of the Northwest, compelling the U.S. Army Corps of Engineers to list it as an indigenous species, accompanied by a detailed anatomical description. Skamania County, whose southern border is the Columbia River shoreline, declared the harming of these creatures a gross misdemeanor punishable by a year in jail and a thousand-dollar fine.

The unwavering belief of Bigfoot adherents among the scientific community and the native insistence that it's a living entity has naturally met with skepticism. No matter what you believe, it's not inconceivable that a creature somewhat like ourselves could avoid detection for so long, given the recent discoveries of primitive tribes in the Amazon and in the Philippines.

In any case, Bigfoot, Woody Guthrie, and D.B. Cooper all possess a mythic aura that will last as long as people gather round the campfire to sing songs and tell stories. And in the flickering firelight, there might be a shadow or an echo of someone or something that'll give you pause. It's all happened many times before here in the Columbia River Gorge.

would have been appalled to see the ensuing neglect and desecration of the old road. Today only one-third of his route remains intact, with the rest consigned to gravel pits and garbage dumps, or simply abandoned. Both state and federal governments have earmarked millions to restore the road to its former glory by the year 2000. The Columbia Gorge National Scenic Area Act passed by Congress in 1986 also made provisions for bicyclists, pedestrians, and people in wheelchairs. Thus, the road which started the American love affair with motor touring could well be breaking new ground by the 21st century.

A Dam Site Better
Tapping the hydropower potential of the river stimulated Roosevelt to initiate the Bonneville Dam and power project in the '30s. This was the first of many dams on the river, and the undertaking yielded benefits immediately. Besides employing thousands during the Depression, the WPA project supplied cheap power to Kaiser's shipyards and Boeing Aviation during World War II. Another Bonneville by-product was the creation of a 370-mile navigable channel from the Pacific Ocean to Idaho, enhancing commerce at the port of Portland. In the decades that followed, aluminum plants and other industries dependent on cheap power came to the Northwest, thanks to Columbia's hydropower. Today the river generates 80% of the region's kilowatts.

Roll On Columbia
The blessings conferred upon the Northwest by the river extend beyond the Columbia's usefulness as an artery of transport and commerce, a major salmon and sturgeon fishery, a source of irrigation water for the surrounding orchard country, and the generator of electricity for the western United States. The scenic beauty of the waterway and the gorge it occupies have forever drawn admirers of Mother Nature's handiwork. In recent years this influx has increased exponentially due to the popularity of sailboarding and other forms of outdoor recreation.

To ensure that the Gorge doesn't become loved to death or overdeveloped, the government created the Columbia Gorge Scenic Area in 1986, an experiment in preserving nature's beauty as well as the region's livelihood. Since there's not enough land for a national park, given the river valley's steep contours filled to the brim with 50,000 residents, this alternative environmental jurisdiction was instituted to monitor growth. Many residents fear that the federal government's Columbia Gorge Commission will put a damper on business expansion in the areas outside the dozen small towns here. Already, restrictions on recreation and controversies over Indian fishing rights have caused the commission to lock horns with the quintessential dilemma facing Oregon and the whole Northwest: the fact that one person's conservation is very often another's unemployment.

THE LAND

As the only sea-level break in the Cascade Mountains, a range extending from western Canada into California, the Columbia River flows

1,214 miles from its source in British Columbia to its mouth at Astoria. In so doing, it carries a quarter-million cubic feet of water per second to the Pacific. This is 10 times the flow of the Colorado, but to motorists driving east from Portland, the river appears placid. Now only Woody Guthrie songs and old photos in Columbia Gorge museums and roadside cafes hint at the river's force before the dams reduced the whitewater to what often seems like a hybrid sailboarding pond cum shipping canal. While the four hydroelectric projects along the waterway turned darkness to dawn, the Columbia in an earlier incarnation strutted its stuff in a manner more befitting the second-largest and most powerful river on the continent. The power of waterfalls located near Cascade Locks and The Dalles motivated their selection as dam sites, and before damming, much of the mile-wide channel of the Columbia in through the Gorge was too rough for the safe passage of commercial vessels. But even if we were able to gaze upon a Columbia flowing from the mountains to the sea unimpeded by dams or shipping locks, it couldn't begin to approximate what transpired here after dozens of Ice Age inundations.

Missoula Floods
About 15,000 years ago near the end of the Pleistocene Epoch, an ice lobe from Canada backed up the water of a lake in the area of present-day Idaho and Montana. When the lake waters rose high enough to breach and wash away the dam, 500 cubic miles of water powered across eastern Washington into Oregon. This cycle was repeated at least 40 and possibly 100 times or more over a period of several thousand years. Flood waters were 1,000 feet deep where The Dalles is today; they crested almost 750 feet high at Crown Point and covered the Portland area under 400 feet of glacial runoff. These so-called Missoula Floods scoured away the valley walls, changing the V-shape of the river valley to its present U-shape, and forming cliffs and waterfalls on the Oregon side of the waterway.

Diverse Bioregions
The resulting contours of the Gorge have formed a conduit for weather systems east and west of the Cascades. The meteorological mix of air masses has created a high concentration of amazingly diverse microclimates between Portland and The Dalles. Consider that only 50 miles separate temperate rainforests at Bonneville (75-inch average annual precipitation) from the arid grasslands at Celilo (12-inch average annual precipitation). Several thousands of feet between the highest and lowest elevations in the Gorge also help define one of the greatest

ranges of plant habitats per square mile to be found anywhere in the world. In Oneonta Gorge alone there are 12 plant species found nowhere else. *Wildflowers of the Columbia,* by Russ Jolley, published by the Oregon Historical Society Press, identifies 744 of the area's more than 800 species of flowering shrubs and wildflowers. The region's combination of sun and shade, heat and cold, moisture and dryness, humus soil and rock, as well as the juxtaposition of grassland and forest, can provide a textbook introduction to most of the bioregions of the American Northwest.

THE COLUMBIA GORGE
SCENIC HIGHWAY

With a near-total absence of hotels as well as places to camp and eat, the most spectacular section of the Columbia River Scenic Highway is best treated as a day-trip. Beyond Multnomah Falls, creature comforts abound in nearby Cascade Locks and Hood River.

The Columbia Gorge takes on a different aspect when you depart I-84 and enter the Columbia River Scenic Highway (ORE 30) at exit 22 at Corbett, 15 miles from downtown Portland. It's possible to get on the Scenic Highway earlier in Troutdale, but you are away from the

Columbia River. Thus, ignore the first signs for the Scenic Highway you'll see on I-84. Pull off instead at the **Royal Chinook Inn** (2605 N.E. Corbett Hill Rd., Corbett 97019; tel. 695-2297) for a look at vintage photos from the era before the dams tamed the torrents and before motorists were able to speed through the region at 65 miles per hour. The Royal Chinook's walls are festooned with shots of Indian fishermen clustered around Celilo Falls (currently The Dalles Dam), Model Ts in the foreground of a waterfall, and other poignant images from days gone by. This is also the only restaurant to get a bite for the next 12 miles of the scenic drive, until Multnomah Falls. Their specialty is fresh local salmon. Better yet, get their smoked salmon to go at $12.95 a pound.

From the cafe wend your way to the top of the hill. If you bear left and follow the signs for Crown Point and Multnomah Falls, you'll soon experience America's first auto-tour route in all its glory. (If you take the road marked Larch Mountain instead, you'll go 14 miles to an overlook featuring views of the snowcapped Cascades, gorgeous beargrass blossoms in June, picnic tables, and trailheads to the Gorge below.)

Vista House
Vista House at Crown Point, 725 feet above the Columbia, was built in 1917 as a visitor center in

© MOON PUBLICATIONS, INC.

honor of the highway's completion. The outside observation deck up the steps from the main floor showcases 30 miles of the Columbia River Gorge. Samuel Lancaster is paid homage with a plaque outside Vista House which aptly describes his routing as possessed of "poetry and drama." Photos of the various stages of the road's construction are on display in the main rotunda, as are wildflower cuttings to study. Downstairs is a bookshop and wallboard of printed materials about the Gorge past and present. Hours are 10 a.m.-6 p.m. daily, April through October.

Waterfalls

From Vista House, the next 11 miles feature a waterfall a mile, the largest concentration of high waterfalls in the United States. The highest here are Multnomah at 620 feet (the second-highest waterfall in the contiguous 48 states) and Latourell at 249 feet. While all of the cataracts are beautiful and distinctive, the three most majestic falls are, by Lancaster's design, the most visible and accessible from the road. These include the two just mentioned as well as Wahkeena Falls.

Latourell Falls is the first of the big three seen by motorists. A paved 150-yard trail takes you down to Latourell's base, where the shade and cooling spray create a microclimate for fleabane, a delicate bluish member of the aster family, and other flowers normally common to alpine biomes. The filmy tendrils of water against the columnar basalt formations on the cliffs make Latourell a favorite with photographers. Foragers appreciate maidenhair fern and thimbleberries, but hopefully not enough to ever denude the slope. Another trailhead begins in the middle of the parking lot and climbs around and above the falls, though bushes obscure the overhang from which the water descends. You'll probably be more inclined to stop after 50 yards and take in the distant perspective of Latourell from across the canyon.

Wahkeena Falls, whose name means "Most Beautiful," is a 242-foot series of cascades which descends in staircase fashion to the parking lot. To the right of the small footbridge abutting the road is the beginning of the two-mile **Perdition Trail.** This steep path affords views of both Wahkeenah and Multnomah falls. Higher up are

SAVING COLUMBIA RIVER SALMON

With the endangered-species designation of the Snake River sockeye salmon in 1992, what promises to be the most far-reaching attempt to reverse the destruction of salmon habitat is being considered. No longer would the Columbia River's flow be regulated solely in the interests of hydroelectric power, shipping, and irrigation. Instead, Oregon's eight dams on the river would release water at appropriate junctures to help speed young sockeye and other species on their journey to the sea. This way the smolt pilgrimage will last the two weeks it used to take prior to the advent of the dams. Currently, a fish born in an Idaho tributary must skirt the turbine blades and other structural impediments at Bonneville and its counterparts as part of a two-month 900-mile obstacle course to the Pacific. Other salmon-saving measures recommended by the Northwest Tribal Council, federal agencies, utilities, and state governments in the Columbia drainage include transporting fish around Bonneville by barge, predation control, and reduced catch limits. The price tag for all of this could exceed a billion dollars, with utility ratepayers, supermarket shoppers, and farmers feeling the bite well into the next century.

The benefits, however, seem worth it. One study suggests that 60,000 jobs and a billion dollars in annual personal income hang in the balance for Northwest commercial fishermen. But the real bottom line may be better appreciated from the perspective of the Northwest native people. They consider the salmon the totem animal of the inland watershed and its well-being is tantamount to the health of the environment. Considering that the numbers of spawning Columbia River salmon are 20% of their former glory and that several varieties are classified threatened or endangered species (legally mandating salmon-saving measures), it's clear that this vital part of the ecosystem could disappear unless drastic action is taken. To let it be completely destroyed would inflict long-term damage on the region's resource-based economy as well as being a philosophical departure from the pioneering tradition that has resulted in Oregon's bottle bill, urban greenways, land-use laws, and coastal protection.

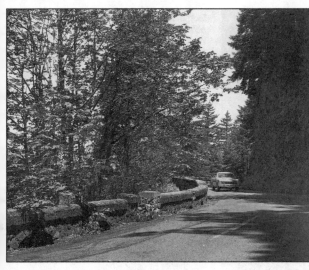

The Columbia Gorge
Scenic Highway was the
first paved highway
in the Northwest.

panoramic vistas of the Columbia River and
Gorge. This trail is especially striking in October,
when the cottonwoods and the bigleaf and vine
maples sport colorful fall foliage. Hikers should
also be on the lookout for poison oak, which
grows below the 800-foot level in the Gorge. A
picnic area is north of the Scenic Highway
across from the falls. At this writing, the wooden
staircase to the upper level of this trail has not
been replaced after the fires of October 1991.
See the Angel's Rest hike at the end of this section if you're looking to hit the trail on the Scenic
Highway.

Multnomah Falls pours down from the
heights with an authority worthy of the prominent
Indian chief for whom it is named. The half-mile-
long uphill trail to the bridge should be attempted by anyone capable of a small amount of exertion. Here you can bathe in the cool mists of
the upper falls and appreciate the power of Multnomah's billowy flumes. The more intrepid can
reach the top of the falls and beyond, but the
view from the parking lot should be edifying.
Placards detailing forest canopies and their un-
derstories at different elevations and other aspects of the ecosystem are on display in the
first 100 yards of the trail.

Look for the image of an Indian maiden's face
on the rock behind the falls. Legend has it that
she threw herself over the falls as a sacrifice to
head off an epidemic. Now when the breeze
blows through the water, a silvery stream separates from the upper falls, framing the maiden's
form as a token of the spirits' acceptance of her
gesture.

The falls area also has a snack bar as well as
Multnomah Falls Lodge (tel. 695-2376). This
magnificent structure was built in 1925 and is
today operated by a private concessioner under
the supervision of the U.S. Forest Service. A
cheery solarium adjacent to a high-ceilinged
dining room built from native wood and stone
makes a casually elegant setting to begin or
end a day of hiking. WPA-commissioned paintings of the Cascades and Columbia Gorge
scenes and a menu with such indigenous fare as
grilled fresh rainbow trout with two eggs and
Caesar salad with smoked salmon also effectively articulate the surroundings.

Up From The Ashes—Angel's Rest Hike
In early October 1991, massive fires engulfed
portions of the Mt. Hood National Forest off the
Scenic Highway. At the time, it was feared that
massive erosion from the devastation of the
trees and the understory would do in the network
of trails in and around the route of the waterfalls. Thankfully, a year after the holocaust, only

OREGON TOURISM DIVISION

Oneonta Gorge is a cool, moist, and green enclave just down the road from Multnomah Falls.

one trail, the Perdition, is still out of service on its upper levels.

For a good perspective on the fire as well as a great view of the gorge between Portland and Bonneville, Angel's Rest Trail #415 is recommended. To get there off I-84 take eastbound exit 28 and follow the exit road a quarter mile to its junction with the Scenic Highway. At this point hang a sharp right as if you were going to head up the hill toward Crown Point, but pull over into the gravel parking area on the north side of the highway instead. The trailhead is on the south side of ORE 30. The steep 2.3-mile path to the top of this rocky outcropping gains 1,600 feet and takes you from an unburned forest through vigorous new brush growth beneath live evergreens with singed bark. This gives way to charred conifers as you near the summit. Scientists hope these snags and new openings in the forest can breed more biodiversity in the ecosystem. At any rate, the lack of foliage on the branches of burnt trees has opened new vistas of the Columbia Gorge below.

Recreation
Several activities merit special mention in the

Gorge. Reasonably priced "flightseeing" is available in a four-seat Cessna from the Troutdale airport. Marvin Woidyla offers a Mt. St. Helens excursion which loops back over the Gorge, taking in the Bonneville Dam and the waterfalls close up. Reserve by calling 666-2660 and expect to pay around $30 a person.

Swimming is safe at historic and scenic **Rooster Rock State Park** (exit 25 off of I-84 near Troutdale). On summer weekends a dollar parking charge is leveled on each car. West of the parking area is the monolith for which the park is named. Lewis and Clark labeled the cucumber-shaped promontory on November 2, 1805. Playing fields and a gazebo front a sandy beach on the banks of the Columbia here. The water in the roped-in swimming area is shallow but refreshing. A mile or so east is the only nude beach officially sanctioned by the state of Oregon. Prior to going, sailboarders might want to call 695-2220 for info on wind conditions and weather at Rooster Rock.

Information And Services
For travelers not coming into the Gorge via I-84 along the river, the **Columbia Gorge Ranger Station** (31520 S.E. Woodard Rd., Troutdale 97060; tel. 695-2276) has maps and information on trail locations and recreation opportunities. The ranger station can be reached by taking ORE 30 off of I-84 at the Troutdale exit. Though this road at first veers from the river, it eventually connects with the Scenic Highway.

For visitor information of all kinds, the **Gorge Information Service** (tel. 800-222-8611 in Oregon, 800-222-8660 outside of Oregon) has the answers.

Vista House at Crown Point State Park on the Columbia River Scenic Highway east of Troutdale and west of Multnomah Falls (Box 204, Corbett 97019; tel. 695-2230) offers visitors a "Columbia Gorge Sights and Services" pamphlet, a regional map, and a handbill reviewing the geologic evolution of the Columbia Gorge. Vista House is open April-Oct.,10-6 daily.

The **Multnomah Falls Information Center** (Box 68, Bridalveil 97019; tel. 695-2376) has a ranger on duty to recommend campgrounds and hikes. You might ask personnel here about such nearby jaunts as Oneonta Gorge (a mile east of Multnomah Falls) as well as Eagle Creek

Locals call Vista House the "million dollar restroom."

Trail and the Pacific Crest Trail outside of Cascade Locks (see "Hiking and Camping" in "Cascade Locks" folowing). The center's hours are daily 9-5, June-September. Thereafter, hours vary greatly so call ahead.

A Portland-based group, **Friends of the Columbia Gorge** (Box 40820, Portland 97240-0820; tel. 241-3762) offers "Columbia River Gorge Guided Tour" tapes and a map for $21.95. This group also sponsors a free guided hike on weekends in the middle of June; walks are geared to different levels of exertion.

In 1995, the **Gorge Discovery Center** (for info write Box 998, The Dalles 97058; tel. 246-8600) will open. This facility will focus on the plant communities, geology, and native American presence in the gorge. The building site is on a bluff three miles west of The Dalles, overlooking the Columbia River, and will provide a staging area for everything from native American ceremonies to historical pageants.

CASCADE LOCKS

The sleepy appearance of modern-day Cascade Locks belies its historical significance. The town is perched on a small bluff between the river and I-84, and its services and creature comforts are mostly confined to its main drag, Wa Na Pa Street. Before the shipping locks which inspired the burg's utilitarian name were constructed in 1896 to help steamboats navigate around hazardous rapids here, boats had to be portaged overland.

Two events which took place outside the city limits, however, gained the town a permanent place in history books. The first of these claims to fame may not have existed at all, but many reputable scientists now believe that an ancient natural bridge once spanned the Columbia's mile-wide channel. According to native oral histories, this formation was destroyed by lava flows from the eruption of two nearby volcanoes. What are believed to be geologic remnants of this event lie just upstream from a modern structure called the Bridge of the Gods in honor of the Indian landmark. The span was raised in 1938 to compensate for a heightened river level due to the Bonneville Dam.

The second event, the construction of the Bonneville Dam in the late '30s, inaugurated boom times in Cascade Locks. Thousands of workers patronized its businesses and set up temporary residence in the area. The dam created 48-mile Lake Bonneville, which submerged the shipping locks. Today you can see Indian dip-net fishermen by the 1896 locks site in the town's riverfront Marine Park.

Boom times are gone now, but this little town with a dazzling river view and down-to-earth people is a refreshing change of pace from the big city to the west as well as the burgeoning tourist scene and industrial parks of her neighbors to the east. Reasonably priced food and lodging, a historical museum, the Bonneville Dam, and sternwheeler tours together with superlative hiking trails nearby also make for a nice stopover, as long as you don't come during winter. Most of the 75-inch annual precipitation falls at that time, along with ice storms and gale-force winds. Two funnel clouds were even sighted outside of town during the Columbus Day

storm of 1962. Such violent weather is not completely devoid of benefits, however. The rains fostered the growth of massive Douglas firs near here which led to a once-thriving timber industry. Nowadays, the winds account for the Columbia Gorge's status as the sailboarding capital of the world, and the tourist economy's ripple effects are starting to be felt in Cascade Locks.

SIGHTS

Bonneville Dam

The Bonneville Dam (write: Public Information, U.S. Army Corps of Engineers, Box 2946, Portland 97208) can be reached via exit 40 off I-84. The signs lead you under the interstate through a tunnel to the site of the complex, Bradford Island. En route to the visitor center you drive over a retractable bridge above the modern shipping locks. On the other side are the powerhouse and turbine room. Downriver is the second-largest exposed monolith in the world (Gibraltar is first). This 848-foot lava promontory abutting the shoreline is known as **Beacon Rock**. Beyond the generating facilities is a bridge, underneath which is the manmade fish-diversion canal. These fishways cause back eddies and guide the salmon, shad, steelhead, and other species past turbine blades. You'll want to stop for a brief look at the spillways of the 500-foot-wide Bonneville Dam, especially if they're open. While Bonneville isn't anywhere near the largest or the most powerful dam on the river, it was the first project on the leading hydroelectric waterway in the world. Along with its potential for generating 40% of America's power needs, the Columbia's storage of irrigation water and its dam-related recreation sites make the river the most valuable resource in the Northwest—too valuable to be diverted for drinking water in southern California, despite pleas from Los Angeles politicians.

Benefits notwithstanding, the downside of damming is graphically illustrated by the sight of Indian fishermen enacting a weary pantomime of their forefathers by the Bonneville spillways. The **visitor center** (tel. 374-8820) is open 9-5 year round. Ask the Army Corps of Engineers personnel at the reception desk about tours of the power-generating facilities and about public campgrounds, boat ramps, swimming, and picnicking areas. The reception area has exhibits on dam operations, pioneer and navigation history on the Columbia, and fish migration. A long elevator ride will take you down to the fish-viewing windows, where the sight of lamprey eels—which accompany the mid-May and mid-September salmon runs— and the fish-counting procedures are particularly fascinating. The fish-counting practice helps determine catch limits on the popular species. Outside the facility there's access to an overlook above the fish ladders. A walkway back to the parking lot is decorated with gorgeous roses from spring into fall.

Retrace your route back to the mainland from Bradford Island and turn right, following the signs to the fish hatchery. This facility is open every day 7:30 a.m.-5 p.m. Come during spawning season (May or September) to see the salmon making their way upriver. At this time head to the west end of the hatchery, where steps will lead you down to a series of canals and holding pens. So great is the zeal of these fish to spawn that they occasionally leap more that a foot out of the water here.

The salmon and trout ponds and the floral displays are worth your attention at certain times of the year, but the sturgeon pools to the rear of the visitor center are always something to see. Biologists say that the Columbia River white sturgeon, with bony plates instead of scales, has remained unchanged for 200 million years. These sleek black fish can grow as large as 18 feet and weigh 1,200 pounds. More often than not, however, a big one is lucky to reach half that size. Despite being the largest freshwater species in North America, this river-bottom scavenger was largely ignored until the gourmet feeding frenzy of the last two decades put a premium on domestic sources of caviar. When *New York Times* columnist Craig Claiborne pronounced the Columbia's product superior to that of the Caspian Sea, its notoriety was established. In addition, fresh-cooked Columbia River sturgeon is a specialty in the finest dining rooms in the state. The Bonneville Dam visitor center and fish hatchery are both free of charge.

The Marine Park
Down by the river is the Cascades Locks Marine Park. The highway exit for it is about halfway up Wa Na Pa St. going east. Just follow the signs. Here the sternwheeler *Columbia Gorge* (Box 307, Cascade Locks 97014; tel. 374-8427) makes it possible to ride up the river in the style of a century ago. River legends and scenic splendor accompany you on a two-hour narrated cruise. This 145-foot, 330-ton replica carries 599 passengers on three decks. From October through May, the sternwheeler is docked near downtown Portland and cruises the Willamette; from mid-June to the last week of September, riverfront Marine Park is the home port.

The current schedule has three cruises per day. At 10 a.m., the cruise focuses on Lewis and Clark; at 12:30 p.m. the Oregon Trail is highlighted; and at 3 p.m. turn-of-the-century entertainment is featured. No reservations are needed. The cost is $9.95 for adults, $5 ages 4-12, and children under four are free. Outdoor and indoor seating and a snack bar ensure a comfortable ride.

In addition to its regular runs, such events as Sternwheeler Days, sunset cruises, Father's Day brunches and dinners, a Fourth of July dinner trip to Portland, and a senior barbecue with western entertainment are scheduled. During the Christmas holidays, the sternwheeler takes part in the Christmas Boats Lights Parade on the Columbia River. Write or call the sternwheeler office for more information about all of the above as well as the new weekend dinner cruises and Labor Day Sunset Dance Cruise (with '50s music). Reservations are needed for all of these special trips. Port of Cascade Locks also houses the ticket office as well as an information center and gift shop, which sells an excellent local hiking trails map for $1.25. Historical photos of early sternwheelers and 50-cent showers for hikers also make this facility particularly worthwhile.

About a quarter mile west of the visitor center, **Cascade Locks Historical Museum** (Box 307, Cascade Locks 97014; tel. 374-8535) is housed in an old lockkeeper's residence and exhibits Indian artifacts and pioneer memorabilia. Information about the fish wheel, a paddlewheel-like contraption that conveyor-belted salmon out of the river and into a pen is especially fascinating.

BARGES

There once was a little girl who lived in Portland and whose bedroom window looked out over the Columbia River. She loved to watch the boats going up and down the waterway, especially the big barges at night. She spent a lot of time looking out of her window, because she was a very sick little girl. She always wondered where the boats were going and what kind of adventures they would have during their voyages, and she'd dream of going along with them some day. Sadly, she passed away from leukemia at the tender age of ten. But before she departed, she left behind a little song that she made up while watching the barges ply the river. Her friends taught the song to their music teacher, who was able to teach it to other teachers in the school district. "Barges" quickly caught on and spread across the Northwest and to points beyond. Soon the Girl Scouts of America picked up on the song and made learning it an integral part of achieving a Mariner's Badge.

Nowadays, children on opposite sides of the globe in Europe and Japan sing it. "Barges" is a very special gift for the rest of us that shows us how to see the world through children's eyes.

arr. by Ted Long Ishikawa

2. Out of my window looking in the night, I can see the barges flickering light
Starboard glows green and port is glowing red, you can see them flickering far ahead
Barges I would like to go with you, I would like to sail the ocean blue
Barges are there treasures in your hold, do you fight with pirates brave and bold

This diabolical device was perfected in Oregon in the early 20th century and was so successful at denuding the Columbia of fish that it was outlawed. June through September it's open Mon.-Wed. noon-5, and Thurs.-Sun. 10-5. In May it's open weekends 10-5. Outside the museum is the diminutive *Oregon Pony,* the first steam locomotive on the Pacific coast: its maiden voyage dates back to 1862.

Hikes

Since the **Eagle Creek Trail** is highly recommended by a lot of people, try to avoid peak-use times like summer weekends. This trail begins at Eagle Creek Campground (see "Camping" below) and goes 14 miles to Wahtum Lake, where it intersects the Pacific Crest Trail. Along the trail are seven waterfalls, one of which features a perspective from behind the cascade itself. Ideally, this is a two-day backpack, but if you prefer a day-trip, consider Eagle Creek Trail #440 to Punchbowl Falls. It can be reached from the Eagle Creek Campground via exit 41 off I-84. The four-mile roundtrip to the falls is an easy hike. If you can, come in February when tourists are scarce and stream flow is high.

From Punchbowl Falls continue 1.5 miles to High Bridge. Tall trees, spring wildflowers, basalt outcroppings, and nice views into Eagle Creek's whitewater cleft make the journey almost as compelling as the destination. High Bridge is 80 feet above this particularly beautiful section of the creek. The trail continues on the other side of the gorge several more miles to Tunnel Falls, where you can walk through a tunnel behind the falls.

Wildflowers spring up in April and linger on into August in the higher elevations. To locate such Columbia Gorge endemics as Oregon Fleabane and Howell's daisy, bring along Russ Jolley's *Wildflowers of the Columbia.* Many of these one-of-a-kinds are species left over from a previous glacial period that have adapted here because of the shade and moistness of the south side of the Gorge. Almost two-dozen varieties of fern, trillium, beargrass, yellow arnica, penstemon, monkeyflower, and devil's club are among the more common species here. This hike is 13 miles roundtrip and is best undertaken on a weekday in spring to catch the blooms and avoid the crowds.

As a prelude to hiking Eagle Creek or one of the several other trails in the area, you might want to wander an informative interpretive loop of less than a mile. Just cross the footbridge on the approach road, the Eagle Creek Trailhead, to the other side of the river. After crossing the bridge, follow the markers which describe the region's mixed-conifer forest at various elevations. At trail's end, you might want to take on the steep two-mile trail to Wauna Point. While not as visually arresting as other area jaunts, the view of the Columbia River and its Gorge at the summit makes the effort worthwhile.

PRACTICALITIES

Accommodations

This town of 820 people features several reasonably priced hotels. Throughout the Columbia Gorge there is a five percent room tax. Canadian travelers frequenting the region here can find some of the best exchange rates between the border and Reno.

The best lodging bargain in the Gorge may be the **Scandian Motor Lodge** (Box 217, Cascade Locks 97014; tel. 374-8417). A room with a queen bed is usually around $43-48, depending on the time of year and the number of people. A two-bed room averages $5 more. Rooms with a sauna go for $5 more than the two-bed rooms. The units boast a warm Scandinavian decor with wood paneling, air-conditioning, and a restaurant and lounge, as well as an adjacent laundromat. This retreat fills fast in summer.

Bed And Breakfast

West of Cascade Locks, the only place to stay on the waterfall route of the Scenic Highway is in keeping with its setting. **Bridal Veil Bed and Breakfast** (Bridalveil 97010; tel. 695-2333 or 284-8901 from Portland) is a homey country inn with a knotty pine interior, antique quilts, historical photos, and the kind of furniture you used to find in grandma's house. Queen beds, breakfast out on the front porch, and the nearby trails and waterfalls of the Scenic Highway make this worth the $60 rate. Incredibly, this place is only 30 minutes from Portland. From Cascade Locks, backtrack on I-84 then take exit 35,

Punch Bowl Falls empties into Eagle Creek and is accessible from Eagle Creek Campground.

Scenic Highway/Ainsworth Park (past the Bonneville Dam exit). It's near Bridalveil Falls State Park on the Scenic Highway. This makes an ideal fall getaway amid a riot of color.

Camping
Camping par excellence is close by town. While the **Eagle Creek Campground** (Columbia Gorge Ranger District, tel. 695-2276, or write Mt. Hood National Forest, 31520 S.E. Wooded Rd., Troutdale 97060) can be noisy and crowded, it's an ideal base camp for hiking. There are sites for tents and RVs up to 22 feet long, with picnic tables, firegrills, flush toilets, sanitary services, and firewood available. It's located between Bonneville Dam and Cascade Locks off I-84 and is open mid-May to October. The fee is $5. At the seven-mile point of the Eagle Creek Trail (see "Hiking" above) there's a primitive free campground, but it fills up on summer weekends.

Herman Horse Camp (write Mt. Hood National Forest, Troutdale 97060; tel. 695-2276) is only one-half mile east of Cascade Locks, near the Pacific Crest Trail. It's a half mile from Herman Creek and is one of three campgrounds in the area. A full array of services including a laundromat, a store, a cafe, and showers are nearby, supplementing the seven tent and RV sites. Piped water, firegrills, picnic tables, and stock-handling facilities are also welcome additions here. It's open mid-May to Oct., with no reservations or fee required. **Cascade Locks Marine Park** (Box 307, Cascade Locks 97014; tel. 374-8619) has campsites available close by the center of town. The museum and sternwheeler are in the complex, as are tennis courts. Whatever amenities are not available on-site are within walking distance. It's open all year and the fee is $7.

Food
Forget health food and haute cuisine until you get to Hood River. In Cascade Locks, you get downhome country cookin'—and lots of it—at a decent price.

The **Charburger** (714 Wa Na Pa St., Box 366, Cascade Locks; tel. 374-8477) is located near the Bridge of the Gods at the beginning of town. This is a great place if you're on the go and don't want to spend a fortune for a quick bite. In addition to an extensive salad bar and a bakery, there is a cafeteria line specializing in "home-baked" (and it tastes that way) chicken, omelettes cooked to order, and other wholesome but unexotic dishes. Prices for a meal seldom exceed $5. Other features include a takeout window and a Sunday brunch. The restaurant's outlet in Hood River (4100 Westcliff, Hood River; tel. 386-3101) is also located at the west end of that town.

The **Cascade Inn**, (in front of the Scandian Motor Lodge; see "Accommodations" above; tel. 374-8340) is a neighborhood meat-and-potatoes kind of place where a luncheon crowd of loggers, tradesmen, and secretaries wolf down such overstuffed sandwiches as the Millworker—two beef patties, cheese, bacon, lettuce, tomato, onions, mayonnaise, and relish on a bun. This might not be a "heart-smart" alternative, but you'll leave feeling full and the space inside your wallet should not decrease substantially either. There's a lounge next door.

Information And Services
In addition to the previously mentioned Marine Park Visitors Center, the **Cascade Locks Tourism Committee** (Box 355, Cascade Locks 97014; tel. 374-8619, ask for Tahoma) can provide help in planning your visit.

Cascade Locks is served by **Greyhound** and the **Amtrak** Pioneer. Amtrak can arrange for riders in Portland to be transported to Cascade Locks by an 11 a.m. train in time to catch the 12:30 p.m. sailing of the sternwheeler and to return to Portland by a late-afternoon westbound train. The **state police** can be reached at tel. (800) 452-8573.

HOOD RIVER AND VICINITY

In the past, Hood River was known to the traveling public primarily as the start of a scenic drive through the orchard country beneath the snowcapped backdrop of Mt. Hood, Oregon's highest peak. Since the early '80s however, well-heeled adherents of sailboarding have transformed this town into a Malibu-in-the-making. Instead of the traditional dependence on cherries, apples, peaches, and pears, Hood River now rakes in up to $25 million annually from the invasion of "boardheads." A good percentage of this subculture tends to be yuppies able to "drop out" here for extended periods to the tune of $50-100 a day for basic creature comforts (according to a University of Oregon study).

The abundance of civilized amenities in the midst of spectacular surroundings complements ideal conditions for this sport. The fury of the winds derives from the heat of the eastern desert drawing in the westerlies. The confining contours of the Gorge dam up these air masses and precipitate their gusty release. Because prime time to "catch a blow" is midday, this is also the best time to find a parking spot downtown. The notion that affluent young people in bathing garb would rescue Hood River from cutbacks at Jantzen apparel, Diamond fruit packers, and other economic mainstays seems the stuff of fantasy—like riding the wind on the great River of the West. City center features an unnaturally high concentration of ethnic eateries, sports-equipment shops, and boutiques for a town of 4,500 people. The main thoroughfare, Oak Street (which becomes Cascade Street as you head west) is set on a plateau between the riverfront marine park to the north and streets running up the Cascade foothills to the south. New brick facades dress up old storefronts, and attire on the order of multihued wetsuits and sandals predominates.

The scenic highlights of Hood River are the orchards during the end of the April Blossom Festival and the leaves here during color season in October. To view the area in its totality, drive to the end of town on Oak St. and bear right on ORE 35 till you see the sign for **Panorama Point** one mile up the road. Vistas here afford a distant perspective on the orchards below Mt. Hood.

SIGHTS

Columbia Gorge Hotel
To ease the culture shock of going from the Scenic Highway and the sternwheeler to the brave new world of sailboarding in Hood River, stop first at the Columbia Gorge Hotel (4000 West Cliff Dr., Hood River 97031; local tel. 386-5566, elsewhere 800-345-1921). Take exit 62 off of I-84 to get there. The hotel is a lovingly preserved memento to the jazz age of the Roaring Twenties, when it was graced by visits from Rudolph Valentino, Clara Bow, and the big bands. Built by lumber magnate Simon Benson (who was also a patron of the Scenic Highway) in 1921, the grounds feature a 207-foot waterfall and the neo-Moorish outlines of a hotel nicknamed the "Waldorf of the West." Glittering chandeliers in the lobby, large wing chairs

around the fireplace, and fresh-cut bouquets in the dining room bespeak the refinement of an earlier era.

Rates here are high (expect to spend $135-175 a night during peak season, although winter rates are close to half that), but a more romantic retreat would be hard to come by. Spacious rooms with heavy wooden beams, brass beds, fluffed-up pillows, and period furniture clearly demonstrate what was meant by the "good ol' days."

The dining room looks east at the Columbia rolling toward the hotel from out of the mountains and west toward alpenglow from the sunsets. Selected in 1990 as the "Number One Restau-

BOB RACE

Hood River has become the sailboarding capital of the world.

rant in Oregon" by *Pacific Northwest* magazine, the hotel's fare draws heavily on nature's bounty. Local mushrooms, fruits, and wild game as well as Columbia River salmon and sturgeon are featured prominently here. There is also the "world famous farm breakfast." Imagine four courses running the gamut of American breakfast food served with such theatrical flourishes as "honey from the sky"—Hood River Valley apple blossom honey poured from a height of several feet above the table onto hot, fresh-baked biscuits. As they say at the hotel, "You don't just get a choice, you get it all."

Hood River Museum

To learn the history of the region, drive back to the junction of Oak St. and ORE 35, then cross I-84 toward the river. At the intersection turn left and follow the signs to Marina Park and the Hood River Museum (tel. 386-6772). To get there off I-84, take exit 64 and follow the signs. Exhibits here trace life in the Hood River Valley from prehistoric times to the founding of the first pioneer settlement in 1854. Thereafter, the area's development as a renowned fruit-growing center is emphasized. Native American stone artifacts, beadwork and basketry, pioneer quilts, and a Victorian parlor set the time machine in motion. The contributions of the local Finnish and Japanese communities, and WW I memorabilia introduce the first half of the 20th century. Photos and implements related to fruit harvesting and packing methods round out the historical collections on the first floor. Upstairs, antique logging equipment, dolls, and remnants of a presentation by local schoolchildren for the Lewis and Clark Exposition in 1905 are on display. At the center of the museum is an attractive open-air courtyard planted with Columbia Gorge flora. From April to autumn, the museum is open Wed.-Sat. 10-4, Sun. noon-4. Other months, it's open Mon. and Tues. by appointment. Admission is free.

Columbia River Views

Back in town drive up to the offices of United Telephone between Oak and State streets. The lot is restricted to staff vehicles, so park elsewhere and walk to what has to be the most scenic employee parking anywhere. Unimpeded views of the Columbia River, the mouth of the

REBECCA SINGER

the "dry" view of the gorge as seen from Rowena Crest

White Salmon River and its deep gorge, the south face of an extinct volcano, and the western flank of Mt. Adams are all laid out before you.

The last leg of the Columbia River Scenic Highway can be reached by driving 15 minutes east on I-84 to **Mosier**. At the far end of this small town is a sign pointing the way to the final section of Lancaster's artful thoroughfare. While not as spectacular as the earlier route of the waterfalls, this section of ORE 30 still provides a picturesque, restful alternative to the interstate.

Rowena Crest
The highlight of the drive is Rowena Crest. Almost nowhere else can you see both the dry eastern and wetter western faces of the Columbia River Gorge with such clarity and distinction. The dark Columbia River basalt cliffs here are derived from massive lava flows 15 million years ago. The terracing of the region was due to the action of the Missoula Floods upon Columbia Plateau fault scarps. More information on the geology and ecosystem here is available from a free pamphlet in the drop box on the north side of the highway, courtesy of the **Tom McCall Nature Preserve**. This 2,300-acre sanctuary on part of Rowena Crest was created by the Nature Conservancy and has trails on the hillsides that are open to the public.

These cliffs represented the beginning of the last hurdle facing Willamette Valley-bound Oregon Trail pioneers. After Rowena, the Gorge cliffs rose up so high that the pioneers were forced to either build rafts and float the then-hazardous rapids on the river, or to follow the Barlow Trail around the south flank of Mt. Hood.

Today, Tom McCall Nature Preserve is the site of a mid-May pilgrimage by wildflower lovers. Because the preserve lies in the transition zone between the wet west and the dry east, several hundred species and four endemics flourish here. Included in the spring display are yellow wild sunflowers, purple blooms of shooting stars, scarlet Indian paintbrush, and blue-flowered camas. And of course, as with any nature preserve or public park, love the flowers and leave them behind for the next person to enjoy.

South On ORE 35
Contact the Hood River Ranger Station (6780 ORE 35, Parkdale 97041; tel. 352-6002 locally, 666-0701 from Portland) about sightseeing the northeastern flank of Mt. Hood. Offshoots from ORE 35 provide access to such mountain meccas as Lost Lake and Cloud Cap.

The well-known view of **Lost Lake** with Mt. Hood in the background, is a calendar-photo-come-to-life. Located 25 miles south of Hood River, the lake offers hiking trails, camping, a limited number of cabins, fishing, rowboats for rent, and a small store. Autumn huckleberry season is the best time to come. In any event, avoid summer weekends. To get there, take Lost Lake Road from Dee.

Cloud Cap is an 1891 mountaineers' club-house whose historic edifice and magnificent mountain and forest views make it a favorite with sightseers and photographers. Tillie Jane and Cloudcap Saddle campgrounds are located close by, open only during the summer months. Tillie Jane is a good base from which to explore the Cooper Spur area, and its counterpart offers scenic views and unspoiled high-country beauty. Nearby you can access the Timberline Trail (see Mt. Hood). To get there, take ORE 35 to Cooper Spur Road. After passing Cooper Spur Ski Area, follow the signs until coming to Cloud Cap at the end of a gravel-and-dirt road 10 miles from ORE 35.

ACTIVITIES AND RECREATION

Sailboarding

Sailboarding and vineyard-hopping complement nearby Columbia Gorge hiking and auto touring, as well as Mt. Hood skiing. Regarding the latter, the "gorge route" from Portland (I-84 and ORE 35) to Mt. Hood ski slopes is becoming a popular alternative to the more direct ORE 26. Local wags insist that the lighter traffic can save as much as an hour on weekends, not to mention the scenic appeals of this route. While this is hard to believe, the crystal paradise created by iced-over waterfalls off I-84 make it a worthy scenic detour.

As for sailboarding, neophytes, adepts, and their fans congregate around the Hood River Marina (exit 64 off I-84). This complex offers a complete package: swimming beach, picnic shelter, concessions, exercise course, and jogging trail. Another good place to watch sailboarding is Riverfront Park at The Dalles. To get there, take exit 87 off of I-84. Hood River has the highest density of shops in the world geared to this sport. They rent equipment and give lessons. For information about sailboarding, wind, and weather, call 387-WIND (-9463) or pick up a copy of Northwest Sailboard (Box 918, Hood River 97031). This magazine is available all over town.

Winetasting

Two local vineyards offering tasting and tours are the Three Rivers Winery (275 Country Club Rd., Hood River 97031; tel. 386-5433), open Mon.-Sat. 11-5, Sun. 1-5; and the Hood River Vineyard (4693 Westwood Dr., Hood River 97031; tel. 386-7772), open 10-5 daily. The microclimate here is similar to that which produces Germany's Rhine wines. In addition to the rieslings, chardonnays, gewürtzraminers and other white-wine varietals produced here, the area is also famous for fruit wines and award-winning Pinot Noir.

In-town Pursuits

Hood River Golf (1850 Country Club Rd., Hood River 97031; tel. 386-3009) has nine holes and beautiful views of Mt. Hood, Mt. Adams, elk, and geese. It's open daylight to dark. Come in fall if only to see the spectacular foliage.

Two worthwhile shopping stops are Waucoma Bookstore (212 Oak St., Hood River 97031; tel. 386-5353) and the Fruit Tree (4140 Westcliff Dr., Hood River 97031; tel. 386-6688). The bookstore's selection evidences taste and an appreciation of titles relevant to the locale. You can also pick up some gourmet coffee here, listen to beautiful music, or browse through a selection of unique cards and pottery. The Fruit Tree is located on the river side of I-84 on the way to the Columbia Gorge Hotel, across from Charburger, and is the perfect place to find a gift box of Oregon jams, smoked salmon, hazelnuts, and other goodies. They help coordinate shipping right from the store and also have fresh local produce. Try the apple cider. You won't get big discounts on the produce but it's first rate. Sappington Orchards (3187 ORE 35; tel. 386-3357), six miles south of Hood River, lets you buy direct from the grower at a good price from mid-September through mid-December, 9 a.m.-6 p.m. daily.

PRACTICALITIES

Accommodations

It's hard to find a room in spring and summer in Hood River, and the prices reflect it. (By the way, remember to add an eight percent Hood River room tax.)

Just west of town, however, there are two reasonably priced alternatives in the $30-40-a-night range. The Vagabond Lodge (4070 Westcliff Dr.; tel. 386-2992) and the Meredith Gorge Motor Lodge (4300 Westcliff Dr.; tel. 386-1515 or 800-537-5938) have standard motel rooms, many with river views. Proximity to Hood River's **Charburger Restaurant** (4100 Westcliff Dr.; tel. 386-3101) is another plus if you like better-than-average American road food at Cascade Locks (rather than Hood River) prices.

Boardheads interested in extended stays should realize that rental housing goes fast and comes dearly these days. Nonetheless, the **Inn at the Gorge** (1113 Eugene St.; tel. 386-4429) has a deal after the summer ("when the rain in Portland can give the desert air a yank") which offers rates as low as $275 a month. During other seasons, you'll pay $58-72 a day for private baths and a complete kitchen and living area in each unit. In addition to transfers to and from Amtrak and Greyhound, the innkeepers can provide sailboarding instruction. This 1908 Victorian home away from home also includes a large and tasty breakfast every morning and has bicycles on hand for guest use.

The chamber of commerce has a complete listing of the two-dozen other bed and breakfasts in the area which they'll gladly send upon request. Most cost above $60 per day, however, and may soon run higher.

If the notion of a vintage 1910 hotel appeals to you but you're not prepared to pay Columbia Gorge Hotel prices, the **Hood River Hotel** (102 Oak St.; tel. 386-1900) might be your window on the river and on the past. This is not to say that it's cheap, with most of the rooms going for $70-90 (with complimentary continental breakfast), but this graceful rendering of memory lane enjoys river views as well as proximity to downtown dining and shopping. If you miss having TV in your room here, the high-ceilinged oak-paneled first floor with adjoining lounge and dining area provides an inviting place to revive the grand old art of conversation.

Camping

It's best to consult the **Hood River Ranger Station** (6780 ORE 35, Parkdale 97401; tel. 352-6002 local, or tel. 666-0701 in Portland) for Mt. Hood area campgrounds if you can't find a place at some of the following local sites.

Tucker Park (2440 Dee Hwy, Hood River 97301; tel. 386-4477) is a county park campground set along the banks of the Hood River, four miles south of town on ORE 281. Despite a location off the tourist trail, there's a store, cafe, laundromat, and ice machines within one mile. From April through November, five tent and 29 RV sites go for $8 a night, with picnic tables, electricity, piped water, flush toilets, primitive showers, firewood, and a playground.

Viento Park (tel. 235-2205) is eight miles west of Hood River on the river side of I-84. From mid-April to late October you'll pay $7 a night for five tent sites and 58 RV sites. Electricity, picnic tables, and piped water are provided. As with the other Columbia Gorge state parks, no reservations are accepted.

Special events during the Hood River Blossom Festival include an orchard tour aboard the Mt. Hood Railroad.

MT. HOOD RAILROAD

Sunset Campground is located behind the only laundromat on the west end of Cascade St. in Hood River. In addition to laundry facilities, restrooms and showers can be found in the open area planted with trees which serves as the campsite. There are 16 tent spaces and hookups for seven RVs. Sunset is a first-come, first-served facility, but call 386-6098 for more information.

Food

The brie-and-chablis set which blows into town during peak sailboarding season has brought sophisticated tastes and higher prices to Hood River. It's still possible, however, to get a decent meal without paying a fortune. Best of all, there's not a town of this size anywhere else in Oregon with as much consistently good coffee or as many places catering to vegetarians.

You'd never guess it from its minimalist decor, but the local lunchtime favorite in Hood River is the **Coffee Spot** (12 Oak St.; tel. 386-1772). Whether it's a cup of premium brew with a spinach ricotta croissant ($1.60) for breakfast, or such imaginative lunchtime sandwiches as cheese and pesto ($2.85 for an ample half sandwich) or tuna, almonds, and water chestnuts ($2.75 for a half sandwich), you can feast for a pittance at this small delicatessen/coffeehouse. And its "Java Hour," 3-5 p.m. daily, lets you enjoy coffee drinks at half price. Coffee Spot was chosen as the best "business lunch" in a *Pacific Northwest* magazine poll.

Locals swear by **Bette's Place** (at the Oak Mall, 416 Oak St.; tel. 386-1880) for breakfast. This family restaurant also specializes in chicken dumplings every other Sunday; seafood, vegetarian fare, and orders to go are available. It's open every day except Wednesday. **The Mesquitery's** (12th and B streets; tel. 386-2002) wood-smoked and barbecue flavors issue forth a wake-up call to your taste buds at lunch and dinner. Particularly recommended is pollo vaquero ("chicken cowboy-style"), mesquite-grilled chicken doused in rust-colored pico de gallo sauce and rolled up in a taquito. The menu also features ribs and fish in a restaurant where the spice (as well as the price) is always right.

To make your evening an occasion, try **Stone Hedge Inn** (3405 Cascade Dr.; tel. 386-3940). This turn-of-the-century house surrounded by a wooded area and gardens has a warm paneled interior that's conducive to leisurely dining. Even "light" dinners (portions are huge) here can range $13-18, but the elegantly presented steak, lamb, duck, and seafood dishes are the best in town. What everyone talks most about, however, is the selection of delectable desserts. Chocolate cheesecake, and strawberries coated in white and dark chocolate with Grand Marnier are two such memorable confections. Call ahead for reservations and directions to this romantic hideaway at the end of a long, serpentine dirt road. It's open Wed.-Sun. from 5 p.m.

Picnickers are referred to the appetizer and deli section at **Safeway** (419 State St.; tel. 386-1841).

For evening musical entertainment, barbecued burgers, Cajun oysters, and vegetarian munchies washed down by Hood River's award-winning microbrew, Full Sail Ale, head for **White Cap Brew Pub** (506 Columbia St.; tel. 386-2247). Add the panoramic view from the outdoor deck and you have the most laid-back atmosphere in town. Ask about brewery tours and tastings here, too.

Events

The most popular events in Hood River County highlight sailboarding and the seasons of blossom, harvest, and foliage in the orchards.

April 20-21, the **Hood River Blossom Festival** celebrates breathtaking views of the valley's orchards in bloom. Arts and crafts, dinners, and the seasonal opening of the Mt. Hood Railroad (see "Information and Services" below) also can be enjoyed. Contact the Hood River Chamber of Commerce for more details.

The fall counterpart of this fête is the **Hood River Harvest Fest.** On October 20 and 21, the valley welcomes visitors for two days of entertainment, crafts, fresh locally grown produce, and colorful foliage. Admission is free and the apples and pears are ripe. Hood River is the winter pear (d'anjou) capital of the world and produces Bartletts, comice bosc, and other varieties at different times of the year. Cherries, peaches, and apples round out the horn of plenty here. Newton pippin apples are another renowned Hood River product. The 15,000 acres of orchards are still the leading economic factor in the county, with Diamond Packing the leading pear shipper in the United States.

Two premier sailboarding events take place on the Columbia in July. The **Columbia Gorge Pro-Am** is the world's largest slalom sailboarding event and traditionally falls between the second and ninth of July. Peak season is April through September for this sport. **Hood River Windsurfing** (tel. 386-5787) has all the information.

Another sailboarding spectacular happens July 12-15. The **Gorge Cities Blowout** is a 20-mile open-water race from Cascade Locks to Hood River. Call Michael Clark at 667-7778 for details.

Information And Services

The **Hood River Valley Visitors Council** (Port Marina Park, Hood River 97031; tel. 386-2000) has an extensive array of maps and pamphlets about the area. Take exit 64 off of I-84 and follow the signs to get here. Down the road is the **post office** (Hood River 97031).

In addition to **Greyhound** (located at the feed store at the west end of town, across the street from Olivia's) and **Amtrak** Pioneer service (the depot is just below Oak St.), **Hood River Taxi and Transportation** (315 Oak St.; tel. 386-3355) offers in-city taxi service Sun.-Thurs. 7 a.m.-midnight, Sat. 7 a.m.-3 a.m., as well as group van tours. **Hood River County Transit** (1020 Wilson St.; tel. 386-4202) is a

local public bus system.

Club Wet Inc. (Box 697, Hood River 97031; tel. 386-6084) has regular flights between Seattle and Hood River. Call ahead for reservations and ticketing. The average flight time is one hour. Also at the Hood River airport is **Scenic Flites Northwest** (tel. 386-1099 local, or 256-3086 from Portland), which offers a three-quarter-hour Gorge flightsee for $45 per person. To get to the airport, take exit 62 off I-84 onto West Cascade to 13th. Go past the hospital and shopping center, where 12th becomes Tucker Road. Follow the airport signs past the drive-in to the airport.

Hood River Memorial Hospital (13th and May streets; tel. 338-7889) is open 24 hours a day with a physician-staffed emergency room. **Care Corner** (12th and May; tel. 386-1111) offers immediate care for illnesses and injuries. This facility refers more serious cases to Hood River Memorial.

The **Mt. Hood Railroad** (110 Railroad Ave.; tel. 386-3556, ext. 804) has tours in 1910 passenger cars which traverse the scenic 20-mile valley between Mt. Hood and the Columbia River. (See the general Introduction for complete information.)

Public restrooms are located below City Hall on State Street.

THE DALLES

It hits you shortly after leaving Hood River. Scrub oak gives way to sage and the grasslands of eastern Oregon. And then, just as suddenly, you come upon the traffic and acrid air of an urban environment. You've come to The Dalles, a place Lewis and Clark in 1805 called the "Trading Mart of the Northwest." Instead of seeing an Indian potlatch on the Columbia, however, the modern visitor will see 10,000 souls living in the industrial hub of the Gorge. While the cherry orchards and wheat fields south of town and the aluminum plants and timber mills by the river are more what The Dalles is about these days than tourism, a complete perspective on the history of Oregon is impossible without a day-trip here.

Shortly after you enter town on exit 82, stop off at the **Chamber of Commerce** (corner of Second and Portland streets, 404 W. Second St., The Dalles 97058; tel. 296-2233) and pick up their pamphlets, *The Dalles: Historic Gateway to the Columbia Gorge* and *Walking Tours to Historic Homes and Buildings.* Take a gander at the restored Wasco County Courthouse next door, which was moved from its original location. This court presided over much of the country west of the Rockies in the mid-1800s. The following overview in conjunction with these publications can annotate your day-trip here. As the walking tour showcases churches, homes, and government buildings built between 1859 and 1929, let's look at those parts of town whose history dates back before that time. Our itinerary will conform to historical chronology.

Seufert Park

Although the visitor center is at the west end of The Dalles, begin your travels six miles east of town off I-84 on exit 87 with the Seufert Park interpretive center, staging area for the free train which tours The Dalles Dam. (For information on this complex, call 296-9778.) The train and tour take about an hour and run April 14-June 4, Wed.-Sun. 10-5, with the last train departing at 4 p.m. From June 5 to Sept. 3, the hours are 9-6 with the last train departing at 5 p.m. You'll immediately notice that the dam's longest arm runs parallel to, rather than across, the river. This is because the trough through which the Columbia runs here is so narrow that there wouldn't be room for navigation locks, generators, fish ladders, and spillways with a conventional design. In addition to detailing the workings of the world's fourth-largest hydroelectric project, displays and commentary recount the historical importance of this location as a gathering place and gateway for native peoples and pioneer travelers. Just upstream from here was Celilo Falls, where Indians armed with spears and dip-nets pursued salmon for centuries. Although The Dalles Dam ended the fishing frenzy by submerging the falls in 1957, reminders in the form of artifacts and customs recall its spiritual and mercantile significance in the native tradition. Archaeological finds here of objects originating in places as far away as the Great Lakes hint at the draw exerted by this bartering mecca. Photos portraying Indians spreading their 20-foot-long dip-nets from precarious platforms above the falls will also help the imagination.

Finally, you might be treated to this same sight on the Columbia today, albeit with lower water and reduced catch levels. If you can be in this area the first weekend of April, the Visitor Information Bureau can direct you to where the age-old native ritual of welcoming the first salmon upstream takes place. The public is welcome to join the Indians free of charge for salmon cooked over an open fire and served with boiled roots and venison. The Celilo Village is located 12 miles east of The Dalles on a shelf at the foot of a bluff overlooking I-84. Just take the Celilo exit off I-84. Look for the ceremonial lodge located a short distance southwest of the exit. This was the site of the Indian fishing village described by Lewis and Clark. It went into decline with the coming of the dams, particularly the Dalles project.

Not surprisingly, the Seufert Park interpretive center's emphasis is on the coming of the white man. The arrival of Meriwether Lewis and William Clark was the seminal event in defining another role for the river—transportation for westbound travelers in the Oregon country. French voyagers who had passed through at the behest of fur-trapping concerns called these waters near Celilo Falls "La Grande Dalle de la Columbia" ("The Big Trough of the Columbia"). From this point, the river was not considered safely navigable. As time went on, the area and the town became known as The Dalles. Oregon Trail emigrants loaded their wagons onto boats after portaging them overland around La Grande Dalle de la Columbia. These portages were later abetted by the first railroad tracks in Oregon, constructed by the Oregon Steamship Navigation Company. Thus, the region near the modern dam site has been a focal point for Oregon native civilizations as well as for a pioneer transportation and trade route. Today, the dam itself is the northern terminus of the world's largest intertie power system. Several other important landmarks are back on the other end of town.

Rock Fort

To further stimulate your reverie of the early explorers and for the sake of historical chronology, your next stop might be Lewis and Clark's Rock Fort. Coming from the west, take exit 82 and drive a mile to a sign indicating the road (Weber St.) to the port area. Head east a mile and make a right at the UPS building on W. First St. heading east. As you drive past the warehouses, several signs will reassure you that you'll be at the dynamic duo's overnight bivouac shortly. The gravel lot surrounded by big stones overlooking the river stands in contrast to the warehouses and billboards nearby. Unlike the more impressive Rooster Rock, Beacon Rock, and other Lewis and Clark landmarks, this site will call more upon your imagination to ward off the sights, smells, and sounds of the surrounding industrial park.

City Park And Fort Dalles

For another less-than-thrilling walk on hallowed ground, proceed to The Dalles City Park at Sixth and Union streets. Pioneer Ezra Meeker placed a marker on this site in 1906 to commemorate the end of the original Oregon Trail. In 1845 Samuel Barlow opened the first overland route to the Willamette Valley here, extending the initial route. Barlow Road aficionados should pick up the USFS brochure to guide them over much of this pioneer thoroughfare. The **Dalles Visitor and Convention Bureau** (tel. 800-225-3385) puts out a driving-tour pamphlet which also outlines how to traverse the northernmost portions of the route.

In this park you'll also note the Victor Trevitt House. An interesting postscript on this pioneer printer and politico is supplied at the Memaloose rest stop halfway between the Dalles and Hood River on the west side of I-84. Behind the restroom overlooking Memaloose Island on the Columbia is a historical placard mentioning that Trevitt's grave was put on the island among native burial sites at his own request, so high was his esteem for his red brothers. "Memaloose" means "to die" in Chinook, and this island was a death of sorts a half-century ago. At the time, water backed up by the Bonneville Dam submerged this sacred site, reducing it to its current half-acre size. Given the decimation of the Indian population and the salmon runs, this event can be viewed as adding insult to injury.

As the final prelude to the walking tour, visit Fort Dalles (for information write: City of The Dalles Museum Commission, Box 806, The Dalles 97058; tel. 296-4547) at 15th and Garrison streets. Unlike the preceding points of interest, there's an actual structure here housing memorabilia to help evoke the past. The Surgeon's Quarters, dating back to 1856, serves as a museum for armaments, period furniture, and other pioneer items. In 1850, Fort Dalles was established in response to the massacre of missionaries Dr. Marcus and Narcissa Whitman. The Whitmans had attempted to impose the white man's ways on the Indians with unfortunate results. For instance, the natives could not understand the concept of private property and felt that Whitman's whipping of those who inadvertently took what they considered to be communal property was unduly harsh. The last straw occurred when a smallpox vaccine administered by Whitman to Indian and white children killed the native children while the white children were cured. The Indians were further confused and understandably angry when they were told that their offspring's adverse reactions were due to a lack of immunities. Their violent retaliation incited Congress to establish the only military post between Fort Vancouver and the Rockies. The Surgeon's Quarters is the one remaining part of this complex.

Several years later, the establishment of Wasco County in 1859 made The Dalles the seat of a 130,000-square-mile bailiwick stretching from the Cascades to the Rocky Mountains. This was the largest county ever formed in the United States.

Now you're ready to take on the walking tour described in the pamphlet, with an understanding of the rich heritage of this gateway to the Gorge and the Oregon Country.

A box lunch from the **Dobre Deli** (308 E. Fourth St.; tel. 298-8239) is a substantial and cost-effective way to sustain your foray along the path of Lewis and Clark and the Oregon Trail. Call ahead to order their "hearty lunch," consisting of assorted meats (six ounces) and cheeses (three ounces), three slices of bread (wheat, sourdough, dilled rye, or French roll), homemade salad (half pint), and a slice of mousse cake or two cookies. This costs $4.95. For a dollar less, the "petite lunch" serves skimpier appetites. The deli packs each item in resealable plastic or Ziploc bags, ensuring freshness, and provides drinks at a nominal extra charge. For those who elect to stay over, **Williams House Bed and Breakfast** (608 W. Sixth, The Dalles 97058; tel. 296-2882) is highly recommended. In addition to affordable Victorian elegance, the innkeepers can alert you to local attractions.

THE WILLAMETTE VALLEY

This 25- to 40-mile-wide and 120-mile-long fertile river valley bordered by rainforested mountain ranges was the object of Oregon Trail pioneer dreams. Here they found a land where crops never failed, a place which offered a second chance, a stage upon which to play out the most cherished economic, civic, educational, and cultural impulses of civilization. One hundred fifty years after the emigrants' epic march across the continent, diversified agriculture, esteemed universities, and cosmopolitan cities fill the Willamette Valley landscape. Covered bridges and historic homes are also here to remind us of the taming of the frontier.

Horn Of Plenty

Prior to the coming of the white man, the Calapooya Indians had subsisted for centuries on game, berries, camas and wapato tubers, and fish. They had never cultivated the soil or logged, save for burning to provide browse for deer and soils for grasses, roots, and berries. But centuries of setting fire to the valley had cleared the land of a lot of trees and exposed rich alluvial soils ideal for farming.

The first Europeans who came here in the second decade of the 1800s also declined to take advantage of the prime farmland, preferring instead to reap easy money from the fur trade. It fell to the Oregon Trail influx in the mid-19th century to break ground for the present-day agricultural colossus. Today the valley boasts national leadership in everything from berry to prune production. It has carved an identity as the primary source of such specialty crops as English holly, bearded iris, and lily bulbs. Coveted green beans, the highest-yielding sweet corn in the U.S., and domination of world markets in grass seed and hazelnuts compound the impression of pastures of plenty.

But you don't have to go to the farm to experience the Willamette Valley's abundance. It's possible to walk down certain streets in many valley towns during the fall and sample the bounty from pear, plum, and walnut trees as well as blackberry bushes. In the spring, cherry trees in public places provide the snacking treat of choice.

Now, as then, the valley is the population center of Oregon. Eugene and Salem are the state's second- and third-largest cities and the region as a whole accounts for over 60% of the state's residents. Nonetheless, you seldom get the feeling of being in a big metropolis, thanks to bike routes, parks, and land-use planning based on environmental imperatives.

The Willamette River

This progressive orientation is embodied in the history of the Willamette River. After the Willamette served as the transport route for valley produce to Portland en route to gold rush-era San Francisco, prosperity and people coalesced around its shores. By the 1960s, 20 municipalities and over 600 industrial plants along the river had so befouled the waters that Governor Tom McCall described it as an "open sewer." The next decade's Willamette Greenway legislation put $50 million and the efforts of industry toward a cleanup. The results were the first significant salmon spawning runs in 40 years and a spate of riverfront parks and recreation areas.

The coast fork of the river originates south of Cottage Grove; the Middle Fork comes out of the Cascades near Oakridge. They meet each other and the McKenzie River near Eugene. The surrounding valley extends from Cottage Grove to Portland. (Since the northern Willamette Valley is within the orbit of Portland, it is treated in "Portland and Vicinity" above.) Further south, Salem, Corvallis, and Eugene have carved a distinct identity as the Emerald Empire.

SALEM AND VICINITY

The used-car lots and fast-food outlets encountered on the way into Salem off I-5 contrast with the inspiring murals and displays in the capitol building. It's comforting to be reminded in the state house of Oregon's pioneer tradition and proud legacy of progressive legislation. Close by, the tranquil beauty and museums of historic Willamette University also provide a break from the Xerox-copy drabness of a town dominated by gray buildings housing the state's bureaucracies.

HISTORY

The Calapooyan name for the locality of Salem was Chemeketa, or "Place of Rest." Connotations of repose were also captured by the Methodist missionary appellation "Salem." This is an anglicized form of the Arabic *salaam* and the Hebrew *shalom,* meaning "peace." The surrounding croplands along with Willamette River transport and waterpower quickly enabled Salem

a quiet Willamette Valley country lane

BRUCE BUSH

WILLAMETTE VALLEY REGION

TO ASTORIA

TO SEATTLE

TO CANNON BEACH

TO TILLAMOOK

COLUMBIA RIVER

TO HOOD RIVER

VANCOUVER

PORTLAND

BEAVERTON

GRESHAM

TO MT. HOOD

WILSONVILLE

OREGON CITY

CHAMPOEG S.P.

McMINNVILLE

TO LINCOLN CITY

WILLIAMSON S.P.

MAUD

WILLAMETTE MISSION S.P.

BASKETT SLOUGH NAT'L WILDLIFE REFUGE

SALEM

SILVER FALLS S.P.

ANKENY NAT'L WILDLIFE REFUGE

NORTH FORK SANTIAM RIVER

TO BEND

ALBANY

SOUTH FORK SANTIAM RIVER

CORVALLIS

TO NEWPORT

SODAVILLE SPRINGS S.P.

GREEN PETER RESERVOIR

WILLIAM L. FINLEY NAT'L WILDLIFE REFUGE

SWEET HOME

FOSTER RESERVOIR

CASCADIA S.P.

TO BEND

WILLAMETTE RIVER

FERN RIDGE RES.

0   15mi

0   15km

BLUE RIVER

ARMITAGE S.P.

SPRINGFIELD

McKENZIE RIVER

BEN & KAY DORRIS S.P.

VENETA

EUGENE

DEXTER RESERVOIR

FALL CREEK RESERVOIR

TO FLORENCE

LOOKOUT POINT RESERVOIR

COTTAGE GROVE

DORENA RESERVOIR

TO CRATER LAKE

TO ROSEBURG

OAKRIDGE

© MOON PUBLICATIONS, INC.

to become the New Jerusalem envisioned by Oregon Trail pioneers. Over the years, the city forged an economic destiny in government, food processing, light manufacturing, and wood products. Today, it has a population of almost 90,000 people.

Peoples Of The Central Valley

Even if you don't have time for in-depth exploration, you'll probably find the diverse ethnic makeup of the north-central valley fascinating. In the town of **Woodburn** (located eight miles northwest of Mt. Angel), for example, local school classes are taught on a multilingual basis to accommodate the large concentration of Mexican migrants and Russian Old Believers here. The latter fled religious persecution in the 1960s by traveling to Brazil and New Jersey and then to the Willamette Valley. A small museum devoted to their history is located on the grounds of the Mt. Angel Abbey. Down in the town of Mt. Angel, signs in Spanish add further evidence of a rich cultural mix. In addition, many residents proudly point to French-Canadian backgrounds bespeaking their connections to the region's first pioneers.

SIGHTS

Mission Mill Museum

In 1840-41 the site of the Jason Lee House and Parsonage moved from the Willamette River upstream to Mill Creek, laying the foundations for the present-day cityscape. These structures along with the Boon Home were part of a Methodist mission to the Indians. The reconstructed Thomas Kay Woolen Mill dating back to 1889 is also on the four-acre site of what is now called Mission Mill Museum (1313 S.E. Mill St.; tel. 585-7012). The oldest frame house in the Northwest and water turbines converting fleece into wool fabric are interesting, but those with limited time might prefer to come here just to obtain brochures about Salem and vicinity in the reception area in front.

Eight retail shops, a deli, a crafts shop, and a restaurant are also on the grounds. The museum is open daily 10-4:30, except Thanksgiving, Christmas and New Year's Day. To gain admission to the historic houses and the mill, adults pay $5, seniors $4.50, students 12-18 pay $4, and children under six get in free. Tours of the complex begin every hour on the hour, 10-4. To get there from I-5, exit at ORE 22, go west on Mission St. for two miles to the 13th St. overpass, turn north onto 12th St., and go west onto Mill Street.

Willamette University
Across the street from the museum is Willamette University (900 State St.; tel. 370-6300), the oldest institution of higher learning west of the Mississippi. It began as the Oregon Institute in 1843, a school that Methodist missionary Jason

Lee founded to instill Christian values among the settlers. Over the years, Willamette University has turned out its share of Oregon politicos, including longtime senators Mark Hatfield and Bob Packwood.

The campus is one of Salem's many oases of greenery that soften the hard edge of a city dominated by government buildings and nondescript downtown thoroughfares. Campus landscape architecture features a Japanese garden, ornate fountains, and a grove of five sequoias six feet in diameter. This grove, which sits between the state capitol and Collins Hall (home of the science departments), has beside it an

Oregon rock of ages. Found atop Ankeny Hill in Salem, the granite boulder floated down from northeastern Washington on an ice raft during the same Missoula Flood that shaped the Columbia River Gorge 25,000 years ago. This glacial erratic stands as a reminder that the Willamette Valley is largely composed of Lake Missoula sediments. In Collins Hall, crystals and exhibits on Oregon glacial activity join an impressive taxidermic array of Oregon wildlife. There's no admission charge and it's open during university hours.

State Capitol

If visiting the state capitol building (tel. 378-4423) strikes you as the kind of saccharine excursion best reserved for a first-grade class trip, you're in for a pleasant surprise. The marble halls of Oregon government are adorned with attractive murals, paintings, and sculptures of the seminal events in this state's inspiring history. These incidents are given eloquent voice by on-site tour guides whose commentary is sure to fill in any gaps in your understanding of this pioneer saga. The Capitol is located on Court Street between W. Summer and E. Summer streets, just north of the Willamette University campus.

Atop the Capitol dome is a gold-leafed bronze statue of a bearded, axe-wielding pioneer. Massive marble sculptures flank the main entrance— *Covered Wagons* on the west side and *Lewis and Clark by Sacajawea* on the east. Maps of the Oregon Trail and the route of Lewis and Clark are visible on the backs of the statues. The symbolism is sustained after you enter the double glass doors to the rotunda. Your eyes will immediately be drawn to an eight-foot-diameter bronze state seal, set into the floor, which juxtaposes an eagle in flight, a sailing ship, a covered wagon, and forests. The 33 marble steps beyond the cordoned-off emblem lead up to the House and Senate chambers, and symbolize Oregon's place as the 33rd state to enter the Union. Four large murals adorning the rose travertine walls of the rotunda illustrate the settlement and growth of Oregon: Robert Gray sailing into the Columbia estuary in 1792; Lewis and Clark at Celilo Falls in 1805; the first white women to cross the continent being welcomed by Dr. John McLoughlin in 1836; and the first wagon train on the Oregon Trail in 1843. Bronze reliefs and smaller murals sym-

The bearded axe-wielding pioneer stands tall on top of the capitol rotunda.

OREGON DEPT. OF TRANSPORTATION

bolic of Oregon's industries also are here.

Near the ceiling in the Senate and House chambers are friezes depicting an honor roll of people who influenced the growth and settlement of Oregon. Included are Thomas Jefferson, who sanctioned the Lewis and Clark expedition, and Thomas Condon, native son and naturalist extraordinaire. Also among the names are those of six women, headed by Lewis and Clark's interpreter-guide Sacajawea. The biggest surprise in the array might be John Quincy Adams, who determined the southern boundary of Oregon when he was secretary of state. In both legislative chambers look for forestry, agricultural, and fishing symbols woven into the carpets; murals about the coming of statehood are behind the speakers' rostrums.

Among the many architecturally eye-catching features to be found in the Capitol are the rotunda's black marble, the House chamber walls and furnishings of golden oak, black walnut room appointments in the Senate, a walnut-paneled governor's office, and bronze doorknobs inlaid with the state seal throughout the building. All this was paid for with part of the $2 million it took to build the Capitol in 1938.

If you don't want to roam independently, free half-hour building **tours** are given on the hour 9 a.m.-4 p.m. weekdays, and 10 a.m.-3 p.m. Saturdays, with a lunch break on all days from 12 to 1.

A tower at the top of the Capitol dome gives a superlative view of the valley and surrounding Cascade peaks and is worth the 121-step walk from the fourth floor. It's open from Memorial Day to August but is closed off during this time when the temperature reaches 90°. Tours to the top go up during the same weekday building tour hours cited above. On weekends the tower tour hours are Sat. 9:30 a.m.-3:30 p.m., Sun. 12:30-3:30 p.m. Both tours run Memorial Day through August and other times of the year by appointment. Also worth a look in the building is the ongoing exhibit of outstanding Oregon artists in the governor's ceremonial office upstairs. Downstairs is a fine gift shop of Oregon-made crafts, food, and other indigenous items.

State Archives Building
At the entrance to the Capitol Mall on N. Sumner St., another softly arched marble building has become a popular destination, but not just for the purposes of soaking in Oregon's pioneer and political traditions. The luxurious interior decor of the new State Archives building is viewed by Oregonians as a symbol of bureaucratic extravagance in an era of belt-tightening for everyone else. They come here and glare at $127-a-square-yard carpet covering $180-a-square-yard travertine limestone floors, all illuminated by light fixtures costing $5000 apiece.

Overpriced adornments notwithstanding, the quilt of Oregon historical scenes on the second floor and other thematic objets d'art are both aesthetic and inspiring. In this vein, anyone who goes to look at the archives themselves will come away with a special perspective on pioneer history. It's hard not to get chills as you read the scrawled accounts of a meeting of early state leaders, or first-hand descriptions of settler life. Original documents relating to the Oregon Territory as well as the first copy of the state Constitution also highlight this paper trail. It's all summed up quite well by the words below a glass mural of the pioneers in the reception area: "To think we came all that way, risked everything, used our bodies as plows, and arrived here with our lives."

Capitol Grounds
At each end of the Capitol building are parks. Between the capitol and the State Executive Building on the corner of Court and Cottage streets is **Wilson Park.** Lush lawns, a gazebo for concerts, and a wide variety of trees, including sequoia, Port Orford cedar, Asian cedar, blue spruce, mountain ash, dogwood, and incense cedar, invite a picnic. Two large multicolored rose gardens bloom through much of the year to garnish your spread, and a trio of bronze beavers make the perfect lunch companions. Also to the west of the building are the beautiful E.M. Waite Memorial Fountain and a replica of the Liberty Bell. To the east is **Capitol Park,** where you can admire Corinthian columns salvaged from the old capitol (destroyed by fire in 1935) and statues of Dr. John McLoughlin, Reverend Jason Lee, and the circuit rider. The latter honors horseback evangelists to the pioneers during the era of missionary zeal.

The oldest government building in Salem is the **Supreme Court Building** (1147 State St.), dating back to 1914. It's located to the east of the Capitol on the southern half of the block across Waverly St., facing State St. and bounded by 12th Street. The building's facade is white terracotta and the marble interior has tile flooring. Visual highlights include an ornate stairwell and a stained-glass skylight in the third-floor courtroom framing a replica of the Oregon state seal. Above all, don't miss the public restrooms. Tastefully appointed in marble, oak, and tile, these facilities were described in *Oregon* magazine as "doing justice to public needs."

South of the legislative building and the campus are some other places that encourage a step back in time. The historic **Deepwood Estate** (1116 S.E. Mission St.; tel. 363-4825) features tours of an elegant 1894 Queen Anne-style home with gorgeous stained-glass windows and a well-marked nature trail. English formal gardens here evoke a more genteel era, and the Pringle Creek Trail's native flora and the public greenhouse's tropical plants have a timeless appeal. Parking is at 12th and Lee streets near the greenhouse. The Deepwood Estate is open May through September, noon-4:30 p.m. every day except Saturday. Winter hours are Sun., Mon., Wed., Fri. 1-4 p.m., and the grounds are closed on holidays. Admission is $2, with discounts for children and seniors. Sit in Deepwood's pagoda-like gazebo with the scent of boxwood heavy in the air on a spring afternoon and you'll soon forget the hue and cry of political proceedings at the Capitol.

Bush House And Park
Bush House Museum (600 Mission St.; tel. 363-4714) is located in Bush Pasture Park off Mission, High, and Bush streets. This 1877 Victorian, with many original furnishings, is the former home of a pioneer banker and newspaper publisher. Even if you're not big on house tours, the Italian marble fireplaces and elegant walnut-and-mahogany staircase are worth a look. The museum is open Sept.-May, Tues.-Sun. 2-5 p.m., and June-Aug., Tues.-Sun. noon-5 p.m. The last tour begins at 4:30 p.m. Adults pay $1.50, with discounts for students and seniors. The house is part of the 80-acre **Bush Pasture Park.** Besides being a sylvan retreat for picnickers and sports enthusiasts, the park is home to the **Bush Barn Art Center** (write c/o the Bush House Museum; tel. 581-2228). Located next to the Bush House, this center features two galleries with monthly exhibits. On the grounds you'll also find the Bush Conservatory Greenhouse and rose gardens. The Bush Barn hours are Tues.-Fri. 10 a.m.-5 p.m., Sat. 1-5 p.m. The conservatory is open Mon.-Fri. 8 a.m.-4 p.m., Sat. 2-4:30 p.m. Both have free admission.

Gilbert House Children's Museum
If you liked Portland's OMSI and Eugene's WISTEC (Willamette Science and Technology Center), the Gilbert House (116 N.E. Marion St.; tel. 371-3631) should more than sate your inquiring mind or those of your kids. Inspired by A.C. Gilbert, a Salem native whose many inventions included the Gilbert Chemistry Set and the Erector Set, this hands-on exposition takes in art, music, drama, science, and nature. Whether you're designing a card or bookmark in the craft room, putting on a puppet show, or disassembling a parking meter, the outlets for creativity here are adaptable to any mood or mind-set. If you don't have participatory inclinations, you can still enjoy fascinating exhibits like the one dedicated to A.C. Gilbert, whose Olympian athletic exploits and proficiency as a world-class magician were overshadowed by his inventions.

As you might expect, even the gift shop here is a winner. Museum hours are Tues.-Sat. 10 a.m.-5 p.m. and Sun. noon-4 p.m. Admission is $2. To get there, drive to the riverfront between the two ORE 22 bridges. Take the Front St. bypass and enter the riverfront via Court St. on the south or Union St. on the north. Park in the lot just north of the Marion St. bridge.

Honeywood Winery
Of the half-dozen local vintners, Honeywood Winery (501 S.E. 14th St.; tel. 362-4111) is the largest and the most easily reached with a location a block from Mission Mill Village. It also bills itself as Oregon's oldest winery, having begun in 1934. Honeywood produces a full line of fruit (try the blackberry) and varietal wines and offers free tasting Mon.-Fri. 9-5, Sat. 10-3, and Sun. 1-5 p.m., all year long. Tours leave Mon.-Fri. at 10 a.m. and 2 p.m.

The Reed Opera House Mall
At the corner of Court and Liberty is the Reed Opera House Mall. This one-time venue of minstrel shows and other pioneer cultural activities still retains a brick facade and long windows but has new tenants—the boutiques and restaurants of a tastefully rendered shopping mall. After you admire the restoration, which helped this atrium gain admittance to the National Register of Historic Places, peek inside a shop that does justice to the creative traditions of the frontier—**Made In Salem** (189 N.E. Liberty St.; tel. 399-8197). This is a crafts co-op of four dozen local artisans. Creations made from stained glass, Oregon's exotic woods, and many other media are featured, along with artists working on-site. It's open Mon.-Thurs. 10-6, Fri. 10-9, Sun. noon-3.

The Enchanted Forest
Seven miles south of Salem off I-5 on exit 248 is the Enchanted Forest (8462 Enchanted Way, Turner 97392; tel. 363-3060), one man's answer to Walt Disney. An enterprising Oregonian has single-handedly built a false-front western town, a haunted house, and many more attractions. Whether it's the old woman who lived in the shoe, the seven dwarves' cottage, or Alice in Wonderland's rabbit hole, these and other nursery-rhyme, fairy-tale re-creations will get thumbs

up from anyone under 99 years of age. It's open daily 9:30 a.m.-9 p.m., March 15-Sept. 30. Adults pay $4 and ages 3-12 pay $3.50, with admission to the bobsled ride and haunted house each 75 cents extra.

Gardens

Both **Schreiner's Iris Gardens** (3625 N.E. Quinaby Rd., Salem 97303; tel. 393-3232) and **Cooley's Gardens** (11553 N.E. Silverton Rd., Silverton 97381; tel. 873-5463) bill themselves as the world's largest iris growers. Both claims are correct based on different criteria, but the important thing to remember is that from mid-May through the first week of June these are the places to visit to take in the peak blossom seasons. Schreiner's is seven miles north of Salem next to I-5, and Cooley's is on the way to Silver Falls State Park. Both places can be visited 8 a.m.-dusk.

PRACTICALITIES

Accommodations

Coming into town off the interstate you'll see cut-rate motels advertised with loud billboards. Need we say more? If you think so, please consult the accompanying chart.

Food

Salem is blessed with an unusually large amount of Mexican restaurants for a city this size in the Northwest. Many of these establishments boast regional specialties from the state of Jalisco that cater to the large influx of agricultural workers who've come to the Willamette Valley from northwestern Mexico. Some ubiquitous entrees in these places include carne asada and camarones al mojo de ajo. Carne asada is grilled beefsteak, often tough but flavorful. Camarones al mojo de ajo is shrimp coated with garlic and butter. An example of a typically unpretentious but tasty "estilo Jalisco" restaurant is **La Estrellita** (1111 N.W. Edgewater; tel. 362-0522). With a name that translates as "The Little Star," this place shines with the aforementioned specialties as well as such other classics as camarones à la Diabla (shrimp cooked in red sauce with onions and mushrooms) and chile verde (chunks of pork, green pepper, onions, and spices in a green tomatillo sauce). Dinners run about $8 and can be washed down by a dozen different kinds of Mexican beer. La Estrellita's north Salem outlet (3295 N.E. Silverton Rd.; tel. 362-7032) makes it a perfect stopover en route to Silver Falls State Park. Despite a fast-food ambience, this place serves the real stuff.

SALEM ACCOMMODATIONS

Best Western Pacific Highway Inn, 4630 N.E. Portland Rd., tel. 390-3200, $53-62, wheelchair access, cable TV, pool, restaurant/lounge, nonsmoking rooms.

Chumaree Hotel and Convention Center, 3301 N.E. Market St., tel. 370-7888, $65-110, wheelchair access, pets, covered pool, restaurant/lounge, laundry, nonsmoking rooms, live entertainment.

City Center Motel, 510 S.E. Liberty St., tel. 364-0121, $37-45, cable TV, pets, nonsmoking rooms, complimentary continental breakfast.

Execulodge, 200 S.E. Commercial St., tel. 363-4123, $50-75, cable TV, pool, restaurant/lounge.

Salem Grand Motel, 1555 State St., tel. 581-2466, $29-65, wheelchair access, cable TV, pets, pool, nonsmoking rooms, very close to capitol complex and Willamette University.

Salem Super 8 Motel, 1288 N.E. Hawthorne, tel. 370-8888, $45, wheelchair access, pets, covered pool, laundry, nonsmoking rooms.

Shilo Inn, 1855 N.E. Hawthorne, tel. 581-9410, $60-70, cable TV, pets, pool, nonsmoking rooms, complimentary continental breakfast.

State House Bed and Breakfast, 2146 State St., tel. 588-1340, $45-70, cable TV, meals available, laundry, nonsmoking rooms, river view.

Tiki Lodge, 3705 N.E. Market St., tel. 581-4441, $40-55, cable TV, pool, pets, kitchenettes, laundry, restaurant/lounge, nonsmoking rooms.

An ethnic restaurant in a more centralized location is **Dahlia's** (in the Reed Opera House, 189 N.E. Liberty St.; tel. 371-1812). In addition to being convenient to downtown shopping and sightseeing, this restaurant manages to be elegant and informal. The menu ranges from haute cuisine to hamburgers, and while it's spendy for Salem, you're guaranteed to have a good meal in this European-style bistro. This is a good place for an occasion, with plenty of indoor foliage, skylights, and glass to keep things bright, open, and cheery. Dahlia's lunch specials with Mediterranean flair have the secretaries in the government buildings talking.

Another secretarial pool favorite is **Croissant Co. Bakery and Cafe** (190 S.E. High St.; tel. 36-BREAD). They bake the best bread in Salem, and the bagels, croissants, pumpernickel, and sourdough wheat are especially popular. Coffee and lunch are served in the bakery, plus items like pasta salads and ham-and-cheese croissants. Finish things off with scrumptious home-baked cookies. The **Off Center Cafe** (12th and N.E. Center St., 1741 N.E. Center; tel. 362-9245) has a clientele and a vegetarian-influenced menu that appear to have been imported from the hip college eateries of Eugene. In any case, breakfasts (Tues.-Sun.), lunches (Tues.-Fri.), and dinners (Fri.-Sun.) here are tasty and filling. Great coffee, a soda fountain, and scrumptious fruit pies also make this an inexpensive retreat from the ordinary. Coffee-lovers will also take note that the top three leading coffee purveyors in Salem (according to a *Statesman Journal* reader poll) are within a couple of blocks of each other on Court Street. The poll-winning Beanery and the runner-ups Governors Cup and Starbucks also feature an assortment of pastries.

Two places to kill hunger pangs in a hurry are **Los Baez** (12920 N.E. Lancaster Dr., tel. 371-3867; and 2920 S.E. Commercial St., tel. 363-3109) and **North's Chuckwagon** (694 N.E. Lancaster Dr.; tel. 581-7311). Los Baez is the home of the legendary Wally Burrito, more than a meal in itself with chicken, beef, pork, cheese, refried beans, guacamole, and sour cream wrapped in a flour tortilla and topped with green enchilada sauce. It might not be estilo Jalisco, but at $4, it's one of the best deals you'll find north of the border.

North's Chuckwagon is an all-you-can-eat buffet with food that's good and ample enough to attract long-haul truckers. In addition, the prices here are in line with the budget of fixed-income retirees. The fare at lunch is not substantially different from the selection at dinner, but it's a buck cheaper.

If you're looking for a spread with more exotic cuisine, try **Queen of Sheba** (498 N.E. Church St., corner of Church and Marion streets) for an Ethiopian-style lunch buffet. After ladling lentils, spicy stewed beef, or vegetables onto your plate at the steam table, return to your seat and take matters into your own hands—literally. Injera, a spongy sourdough bread, is used to scoop up these fillings (silverware upon request). The pastel-colored latticework canopy and white-washed walls also make this small restaurant seem a continent away from the Meier and Frank parking lot across the street.

When you hear that **Mazzi's** (4250 S.E. Commercial St.; tel. 364-3374) is a chain with other outlets in Eugene, Portland, Anchorage, and Corvallis, you might think it's just another formula pizza joint. The only thing cliché about the restaurant, however, is the red-checkered tablecloths. You immediately sense quality when you sample a handful of Parmesan cheese from the bottle on your table. Instead of the usual heavily salted stale-tasting condiment-from-a-can which passes for cheese, these tasty morsels are as fresh as the hot French bread that accompanies every meal. The best deal for dinner is the $10.95 pasta special—a large salad, minestrone soup, spaghetti, and ravioli, with spumoni ice cream for dessert. Although we know it's not the case, everything here seems homemade from scratch. Except perhaps for a pizza crust that's too doughy, Mazzi's is every traveler's Italian-food fantasy.

Camping

Many of the Salem and vicinity excursions are close to campsites. **Silver Falls State Park** (20024 Silver Falls Hwy., Sublimity 97385; tel. 873-8681) lets campers escape the valley's summertime heat. There are 53 tent sites and nine sites for trailers or motor homes up to 35 feet long. Rates are $15-17. From mid-April to early October this facility operates with electricity, piped water, and picnic tables. Showers, firewood, and a laundromat are available. In addition to hiking, swimming, and biking, there are stables near the park's entrance.

On the way to Breitenbush Hot Springs, **Cleator Bend** (write: Willamette National Forest, ORE 22, Detroit 97360; tel. 854-3366) offers a campground close enough to the Breitenbush Hot Springs Retreat Center and facilities to permit day use there. Nearby, the Breitenbush River has good fishing. There are nine sites for trailers or motor homes up to 16 feet long, as well as picnic tables and firegrills. Fees are $3 a night from mid-May to late September. On Forest Service Rd. 46, you'll pass several other campgrounds between ORE 22 and the retreat center.

Recreation And Activities

Salem's recreational mix belies its reputation for being a town dedicated to legislation and little else. Cultural life revolves around the **Pentacle Theatre** (Box 186, Salem 97303; tel. 364-7121), located five miles west of downtown Salem. From the government buildings, follow the signs marked "ocean beaches" and "Dallas." Signs on the right-hand side of the highway direct you up the hill and to the theater. This large, attractive wooden building hosts an award-winning 10-play season. Those who prefer more active pursuits should head to **Leierer's Outdoor LTD** (934 E. Hylo Rd.; tel. 581-2803). This store offers canoe rentals on the Salem waterfront each weekend. One-day guided Santiam and Willamette river trips are also available. Rafting and kayaking equipment can be rented from **Santiam Whitewater Outfitters** (1595 N.E. Cottage St.; tel. 585-2628). They also provide guide service.

The **Salem Golf Club** (2025 Gold Course Rd.; tel. 363-6652) is one of the best public courses in the state. Another alternative is **Santiam Golf Course** (ORE 22 and Golf Club Rd., Stayton; tel. 764-3485). If you drive 15 minutes east on ORE 22 you can look forward to combining a round of golf with a walk in the country. Low greens fees and a full-service restaurant and bar add to the pleasure.

U-pick farms are a delight from spring through fall in and around Salem. Cherries, strawberries, apples, peaches, plums, and blackberries are some of the bounty available. Early in June, the Salem *Statesman Journal* (tel. 399-6622)

puts out a list of local outlets in the area (what's available where and when) entitled "Oregon Direct Market Association." The *Statesman Journal* is sold throughout the Willamette Valley, central coast, and central Oregon and has a "weekend planner" section with entertainment listings and reviews every Friday. Although these listings focus on Salem, some attention is also given to events throughout the Willamette Valley.

Fruit stands abound as well in the newspaper's U-pick guide. Many concessions, such as **Bauman Farms** (12989 Howell Prairie Rd.; tel. 792-3524) have both self-service harvest as well as over-the-counter sales (over-the-counter price for strawberries is $8 for 10 pounds or 70 cents a pint). In addition, several dozen other agricultural products are available here, ranging from 10 berry varieties to pumpkins. Items such as fresh home-pressed apple cider and holiday gift packs round out the array. To get to Bauman's take U.S. 99E one mile south of Woodburn to Howell Prairie Road. Following the signs, go about a half mile to reach the stand.

The **Oregon State Fair** (2330 N.E. 17th St.; tel. 378-3247) is an annual celebration held in Salem during the 11 days prior to Labor Day. The fair showcases Oregon agriculture, industries, tourist attractions, natural resources, government, and cultural activities. Big-name entertainment, amusement-park rides, an international photography show, and a horticultural exhibit are also included in this blend of carnival and commerce.

The Salem Art Association (see "Bush House And Park" above for address and phone) puts on the **Salem Art Fair and Festival** for several days the third week of July. The event includes 200 artists, performing arts, food, children's activities, a five-km run, an Oregon authors' table, wine and cheese tasting, and art-techniques demonstrations.

Information And Services

The **visitor center** (1313 Mill St.; tel. 581-4325) is in the first building of the Mission Mill complex and has pamphlets and brochures covering Salem and the whole state of Oregon. It's open Mon.-Fri. 9-5.

Salem provides a lot of ways to get in and out of town. The **Greyhound** station (450 N.E. Church St.; tel. 362-2428) is open daily 6:45

a.m.-8:45 p.m. **Amtrak** (13th and Oak streets; tel. 588-1551) sits across from Willamette University. The Salem **airport** (tel. 588-6314) is a few miles east of downtown. Flights to Portland and the coast are provided by **Horizon Airlines** (tel. 800-547-9308). A Salem-to-Portland airport shuttle is run by **Hut Limousine Service** (tel. 362-8059). For short hops to town, there's Salem **Yellow Cab** (tel. 362-2411). Or rent a car at **National** (745 N.E. Liberty St.; tel. 585-4226 or 800-CAR-RENT).

Mass-transit bus service in town means **Cherriotts** (216 High St.; tel. 588-2877). Terminals are in front of the courthouse. Fares range from 25 to 50 cents, depending on the length of your trip, and originate from High Street. Especially appreciated is the Free Zone. Unlimited free rides are permitted within most of the State Capitol Mall as well as to hundreds of downtown shops and restaurants. The zone is defined by the Willamette River on the west, 12th St. on the east, Union to the north, and Mission to the south. Hours of service are Mon.-Fri. 6 a.m.-6:15 p.m. (with buses every half hour during rush hours). On Saturday, they run every hour 7:45 a.m.-6:15 p.m.

The **Green Tortoise** departs Salem/Brooks exit 263 at the Arco Truckstop, going south at 1:45 p.m. and north at 3 p.m. See the general Introduction for info on days of service.

The **post office** (1030 25th St., Salem 97301) is open Mon.-Fri. 8-5. Other useful numbers include the **Salem Hospital Memorial Unit** (tel. 370-5701) and the **Women's Crisis Center** (tel. 399-7722).

DAY-TRIPS FROM SALEM

Silver Falls State Park

If Silver Falls State Park (22024 Silver Falls Hwy., Sublimity 97385; tel. 873-8361) were in California instead of a remote part of the Willamette Valley, it would probably be designated a national park and be flooded with visitor facilities and people year-round. Instead, one of Oregon's largest and most spectacular state parks remains relatively quiet except during the summer. At that time, hordes seeking relief from the valley heat head up to this cool enclave of waterfalls in the foothills of the Cascades, 26 miles northeast of Salem. They come to see 10 major waterfalls 30 to 178 feet in height cascading off canyon walls in a forest filled with old-growth Douglas fir, ferns, and bigleaf and vine maple. The best time to come is during fall foliage season when there are few visitors, just before icy roads and trail closures inhibit travel. The east winds of autumn sometimes make the falls here appear like ice sculptures. In spring, the mid-April blooming of trilliums and yellow wood violets on the canyon bottom is another highlight.

To get there from Salem, drive east on ORE 22 toward Stayton and take the turn toward Sublimity on ORE 214, which heads 10 miles north to the town of Silverton. Here signs divert you east up steep, winding Silver Creek Drive (an extension of ORE 214) above the town. After several miles, this route levels out into gently undulating hills and Christmas tree farms as it loops south. A dearth of signs and a distance that seems longer than the posted 15 miles from town will have you second-guessing these directions until you come to the Silver Falls parking lot. Walk across the bridge over Silver Creek on the east side of the lot, where a trail map located by the restrooms outlines several hiking options. Serious hikers will want to take on the seven-mile **Silver Creek Canyon Trail,** which heads down into a fern-lined basalt gully. The profusion of trees and moisture gives the air a special freshness here, and when the sun hits some of the 10 falls just right you can see rainbows.

The highlight of this 1930s-vintage, Civilian Conservation Corps trail is 177-foot-high **North Falls.** The opportunity to walk behind a waterfall attracts a lot of visitors here who follow the trail through a basalt overhang in a cleft of the cliff. Bikers and horseback riders also enjoy specially designated trails in this 8,300-acre paradise. A $1 per vehicle day-use fee is charged on summer weekends and on holidays. If you're coming from Portland, leave I-5 at Woodburn and follow Rural ORE 214 through Mt. Angel and Silverton to the park.

Mount Angel Abbey And Oktoberfest

Four miles northwest of Silverton off ORE 214 is a retreat of a different sort. High above the rest of the Willamette Valley is the Mt. Angel Abbey (St. Benedict 97373; tel. 845-3066 or 800-365-

5156). The Benedictine abbey sits on a 300-foot hill overlooking cropland and Cascades vistas. From the bluff, look northward at Mt. Hood, Mt. St. Helens, Mt. Adams, and according to locals, Mt. Rainier on exceptionally clear days. Further inspiration can be gained from an ancient manuscript library and the landscaped serenity of the abbey's hilltop quadrangle.

For a meditative retreat, you can stay at the Abbey for $35 per day for lodging and meals ($20 for just the room). While the creature comforts are ascetic, the peace of the surroundings and the beauty of the monks' rituals brought from Switzerland in 1880 will make the cares of the world go away no matter what your spiritual orientation (or lack thereof). Weekend retreats begin Friday at 7:30 p.m. and end on Sunday at 1 p.m. For further information and reservations write Mt. Angel Abbey Retreat House, St. Benedict, or call 845-3317.

Mt. Angel's other claim to fame is **Oktoberfest,** which takes place in mid-September down in the town itself. Over the quarter century of its existence, many hundreds of thousands have come to guzzle brews in the beer garden ($2 admission) and enjoy the oompah-pah of German traditional music. The festival offers monastery tours, stage shows, art displays, yodeling, and street dancing amid beautiful surroundings. The biggest attraction of all, however, is the food. Stuffed cabbage leaves, strudels, and an array of sausages are the stuff of legend in the Willamette Valley. Call 845-9440 for details or write Box 1054, Mt. Angel 97362. Mt. Angel's location an hour south of Portland makes it an excellent day-trip. Just take the Woodburn exit, no. 272. If you're approaching the Abbey from Salem off I-5, take the Chemwa exit and follow the signs.

Bikers relish the foothills and farmland around Mt. Angel, which are nearly devoid of traffic. Fall color is exceptional here, and a varied topography ensures an eventful ride whatever the season. Lowland hop fields and filbert orchards give way to Christmas-tree farms in the hills. On the way up, pumpkin and berry patches also break up the predominantly grassy terrain. This region is also known for its crop of red fescue, a type of grass seed grown almost nowhere else except the northern Willamette Valley.

Nurseries abound in the area as well. If you were to take exit 271 off I-5 near Woodburn (en route to Molalla), a trip to the Wooden Shoe Bulb Company's 17-acre tulip farm in late March and early April would colorfully illustrate Oregon's rites of spring. Just turn right at the flashing yellow light onto Meridian Rd. and go 1½ miles. After making a left on Newman Rd., look for the field ablaze in color on the right. Call 634-2243 for more details.

Breitenbush Hot Springs

Salem residents have traditionally taken to the hills via ORE 22 along the North Santiam River to enjoy the fishing and camping at **Detroit Lake** as well as skiing at Hoodoo Ski Bowl (see "The High Cascades"). Lately, the traffic to the mountains includes those seeking a different kind of renewal. Breitenbush Hot Springs Retreat and Conference Center (Box 758, Detroit 97342; tel. 854-3314 or in Salem, tel. 371-3754) offers mineral-springs baths, trails forested with old growth, as well as a wide variety of programs aimed at healing body, mind, and spirit.

Whether or not new-age bodywork and meditation appeal to you, the peace and beauty of the Breitenbush complex will enchant and edify. Set in the Cascade foothills, this onetime Indian encampment's artesian-flow hot springs have attracted people for healing throughout the ages. The pools, set variously in forest and meadow, have curative effects thanks to 30 freely occurring minerals including the salutary chemical lithium. Music, storytelling, theater, and superb vegetarian cuisine are also part of the experience. Finally, a special sanctuary with a vaulted glass pyramid roof lets you watch the stars or winter storms through the canopy of trees.

The retreat cabins are spartan but sufficient. All have electricity and heat, and most have indoor plumbing. Rates range between $40 and $70 per person (bring your own bedding or pay $7 extra) and include three sumptuous vegetarian meals and use of the facilities and waters during your stay at Breitenbush. Large tents on platforms are also available June-Oct. for $35-40 per person. Day-use fees for hot springs and other facilities are $10 for a full day and $5 for a half-day. Individual meals for daytime visitors are $5, all-you-can-eat, and the food is sure to make converts of those who still think of vegetarian fare as mostly rice and slime. Just bring your own coffee if you're used to one for the road.

Guided (arrange at the reception desk) or individual hikes through an old-growth forest are highly recommended here. This is a good opportunity to see that bird in the headlines, the spotted owl (see "Fauna" in the general Introduction).

To get to Breitenbush from Salem, take ORE 22 to the town of Detroit. Turn at the gas station (the only one in town) onto Forest Service Rd. 46. Drive 10 miles to Cleator Bend Campground. Go 100 feet past the campground and take a right over the bridge across Breitenbush River. Follow the signs, taking every left turn after the bridge, to the Breitenbush parking lot.

Mount Jefferson

After a soak in the pools at Breitenbush, your muscles will be primed to hike up Mt. Jefferson, Oregon's second-highest peak, 10,495 feet

OREGON DEPT. OF TRANSPORTATION

Some of Oregon's finest hikes are found on and around 10,495-foot Mt. Jefferson.

above sea level. This snowcapped symmetrical volcanic cone dominates the Oregon Cascades horizon between Mt. Hood to the north and the Three Sisters to the south. Unlike Mt. Hood, Mt. Jefferson is rarely visible to motorists approaching from the west.

Twelve miles east of Detroit on ORE 22 turn left; follow Forest Service Rd. 2243 (Whitewater Creek Rd.) 7.5 miles to the Whitewater Creek trailhead. Then it's an easy 4.5 mile hike to Jefferson Park. This is the northern base of the mountain and features a plethora of lakes and wildflowers. The alpine meadows here are full of purple and yellow lupine and red Indian paintbrush in July. On the way up, wild strawberries and red huckleberries can provide a delectable snack. For a special experience during the summer, start up the trail after 5 p.m. on the night of a full moon and enjoy this trail bathed in soft lunar light.

Above Jefferson Park, the ascent of the dormant volcano's cone is a precarious endeavor and should only be attempted by the best in the business. You'll reach the bottom of Whitewater Glacier at 7,000 feet. Thereafter, climbing routes steepen to 45° and snow and rock ridges destruct upon touch. Near the top, the rocks aren't solid enough to allow use of ropes or other forms of climbing protection, forcing what climbers refer to as "death moves," particularly because going down is even more dangerous than going up. Even if you head up the more sedate south face you can expect difficulties due to the instability of the final 400 feet of rock on the pinnacle.

Those who elect not to make the ascent may run into other problems. Sometimes the mosquitoes in Jefferson Park are bloodthirsty enough to pierce thick clothing. On occasion, the area is so crowded with day-use visitors and folks moving along the Pacific Crest Trail nearby that this place seems more like a city park than a mountain wilderness. No matter . . . the sight of Mt. Jefferson in alpenglow at sunset or shrouded in moonlight will make you forget the intrusions of man or the elements.

CORVALLIS AND VICINITY

The name Corvallis refers to the city's pastoral setting in the "heart of the valley." But this appellation just tells part of the story. The influence of Oregon State University looms so large here that it might as well be called "College Town, U.S.A." In fact, Cascadia, the quintessential college town in Bernard Malamud's novel *A New Life,* was modeled on Corvallis. Everything from the coffeehouses and used-book stores to the pizza joints and network of biking trails seems to owe its existence to the ivy-covered walls of academe here.

Beyond the campus neighborhood, the vast acreage of Oregon State University's agricultural extension complex contains facilities ranging from lambing barns to experimental forests in the Coast Range. Agriculture and engineering are emphasized in OSU's course offerings, attracting a less flamboyant student body than the more liberal arts oriented University of Oregon in Eugene. As such, the Corvallis institution is sometimes characterized as "Oregon Straight" or "Moo U." Call it what you will, the campus is essential to the economic base of the city, supplying recruits for local companies as well as assistance to agricultural endeavors.

After gazing upon the grass-seed farms surrounding the town or at the sprawling Corvallis division of the electronics industry giant Hewlett Packard, it's evident that OSU is the straw that stirs the drink for this city of 50,000. But it doesn't stop there. The university planted the seeds to create multinational engineering giant CH_2M Hill and the Hatfield Marine Science Center in Newport, as well as establishing fertile ground for other start-ups that have taken root beyond the confines of the Willamette Valley.

Corvallis is not so much a place to sightsee as a place to live. While it lacks a Golden Gate Bridge or a Space Needle, this community was selected as the second-best "micropolitan" city in the country (according to the *Rating Guide to Life in America's Small Cities,* Prometheus Books, 1990) based on environment, economics, education, housing, transportation, sophistication, recreation, public safety, and urban proximity.

Aesthetic beauty, tranquility, and Corvallis's central location in the heart of the valley also recommend it as a base from which to explore the bird sanctuaries, the Coast Range, and nearby historic communities. In town, you'll be struck by the abundance of stately old trees, some dating back to the first pioneers who came here in 1847. Streets with wide bike lanes and scenic routes for cyclists that parallel the Willamette and Mary's rivers also contribute to the feeling of an idyllic time warp here. This is especially the case in summer, when many students leave town.

SIGHTS

Campus And Downtown

In springtime, the daffodil-lined approach to Corvallis on ORE 99W is made even more glorious by the Coast Range and its highest mountain, **Mary's Peak** (4,097 feet), to the west over the hay meadows. Much of the winter, this summit is obscured by rain or fog. Your first stop should be the 500-acre Oregon State campus (follow the signs to Jefferson or Monroe streets; tel. 737-0123), home to 15,200 students. The parklike campus of this 1868 land-grant institution is the hub of activity in town, with a slew of eateries, bookstores, and craft boutiques on its periphery. Cultural activities on campus include lectures, concerts, theater productions, films, and art exhibits. Many are free and open to the public. Get an activities calendar at no cost by writing the Office of University Relations, Oregon State University, Corvallis 97331.

Come to OSU mid-January through mid-March and you can watch ewes giving birth in the lambing barns. To get there from downtown Corvallis, take Harrison St. to 35th and turn left. Continue four blocks and turn right on Campus Way. Look for the white barn just up the road on the right. While the notion of one of these fleecy specimens on a dinner plate might strike visitors here as akin to eating Bambi, OSU research has helped establish Oregon lamb as a gourmet product. Thanks to a diet of nutritious grasses

CORVALLIS

indigenous to Northwest soils, Oregon lambs are larger and richer in flavor than the ever-popular New Zealand product.

The campus also maintains 11,500 acres of woodlands, notably **McDonald Experimental Forest** and **Peavy Arboretum** (entrance eight miles north of Corvallis on U.S. 99W) that feature hiking trails as well as the chance to see the rare Fender's blue butterfly. The latter had been thought extinct for the last 50 years until a habitat was rediscovered here in 1990. This ecosystem serves primarily as a living laboratory for the OSU Forestry Department. (For more information on the campus-managed forests, check the forest research office on campus, tel. 737-4452.)

The university facility to visit is the **Horner Museum** (in the basement of Gill Coliseum on 26th St. off Washington St. and Western Blvd., on the southwest portion of the OSU campus; tel. 754-2951). Taxidermic displays of regional animals, mineral exhibits, and pioneer and Indian artifacts (including sagebrush sandals; see "Fort Rock" in the "Lake County" section) highlight Oregon's oldest and largest state-owned collection of human and natural history. Although the focal point of the exposition is Oregon, the "Other Worlds" exhibits expand the scope of what many refer to as "Oregon's Smithsonian." Hours are Tues.-Fri. 10 a.m.-5 p.m., Sat. 10 a.m.-2 p.m., Sun. 2-5 p.m. Admission is free. Before you leave, pick up the museum's pam-phlets about Oregon history. These can aid you in exploring this part of the Willamette Valley.

The major historic landmark in the city is the **Benton County Courthouse** (near Fourth, Fifth, and Monroe), the oldest functioning courthouse in the state. You can't miss its large white clocktower. Also downtown is the **Corvallis Art Center** (Seventh and Madison streets; tel. 654-1551), located in the renovated 1889 Episcopal church near Central Park. It sells local crafts and hosts weekly lunchtime concerts. Hours are Tues.-Sun. noon-5 p.m.

Houses, Heritage, And Hospitality

Oregon's greatest concentration of historic homes and covered bridges is around Corvallis, making it more than just another college town. In addition to the surrounding heritage-conscious communities, artifact collections and pageantry also liven up the historical landscape of Linn and Benton counties.

Three miles west of Corvallis on ORE 20 is the town of **Philomath,** with the **Benton County Historical Society** (1101 Main St., Philomath 97370; tel. 929-6230). Looms, carriages, printing presses, and other pioneer-history exhibits are mildly diverting here, but the real star is the 1867 Georgian-style brick structure housing the collection. Just look for the imposing building on the right-hand side of the highway on your way to the coast. Hours are Tues.-Sat. 10 a.m.-4:30 p.m., Sun. 1-4:30 p.m. Admission is free.

Oregon State University, Corvallis

Albany

Twelve miles east of Corvallis on ORE 20 is Albany, which has more historic homes than any other city in Oregon. More than 350 Victorian houses here are left over from Albany's golden age, 1849 to the early 20th century, when steamships and railroads exported Willamette Valley produce and flour. Wheat was the primary crop. In 1910, 28 trains departed this former commercial hub daily. The **Albany Visitors Association** (435 W. First Ave., Albany 97321; tel. 926-1517 or 800-526-2256) and an information gazebo (corner of Eighth and Ellsworth streets) have maps and pamphlets about the three historic districts covering 100 blocks here.

Pick up another pamphlet that lays out a self-guided **covered bridge tour**. These canopied crossings protected the wooden trusses from rain, extending the life of the bridges by several decades. By the late '30s, many of the 300 or so covered bridges in the state had fallen into disrepair or were replaced by modern steel and concrete spans. Statewide, 54 remain, with 30 in the Willamette Valley. The Albany Visitors Association pamphlet lays out a tour of eight bridges reachable by a 20- to 30-minute drive from the Albany-Corvallis area. All of these are within an eight-mile radius of **Scio**, a town 13 miles northeast of Albany on ORE 226.

The **Fire Museum** (120 S.E. 34th St.; tel. 967-4302) is another place in town you might want to tour independently. Call the fire department for hours and be sure to check out the 1907 steam-driven, horse-pulled engine. Tree lovers will want to ask at the visitors association or information gazebo for the flier on old plantings around town. These include copper beech, catalpa, elm, and sycamore trees in various gardens, and the old-fashioned rose and herb gardens near the gazebo.

Prime time for a stroll down Albany's memory lane is during the Christmas holiday season. On the second Sunday in December, annual old-fashioned **parlor tours** let you revel in eggnog, snapping fires, and frontier hospitality as a guest at a number of Victorian homes. Visitors are welcomed by hostesses at each home and are permitted to walk through the parlor and other open rooms. Entertainment and homemade refreshments are part of the festivities.

Pick up tickets at the United Presbyterian Church (330 S.W. Fifth Ave.); $7.50 for adults, children under 12 free. On most Fridays and Saturdays in December, a historical district hay-wagon caroling tour (reservations tel. 928-9634) can get you in the holiday spirit. The $3 charge includes hot beverages. Tickets are available at Flinn's Block (222 First Ave.), where tours depart every half hour.

Other organized house tours take place every Sunday in July and August, 1-5 p.m. These are conducted by guides dressed in Gibson-girl costumes. Tours leave in horse-drawn carriages from the gazebo and cost $3 per person. The summer interior tour is held on the last Saturday in July, 11 a.m.-5 p.m. Visitors are invited to walk through the gardens and complete interiors of several homes; background anecdotes are supplied by guides. Old-fashioned quilts and dolls complement the tour, as do many people in turn-of-the-century dress strolling the avenues. Admission is $6 for adults, $4 for seniors and children. At all times of the year, more than a dozen antique shops also lure visitors here. A list of these stores is available at the information gazebo.

Brownsville And Vicinity

When Albany's air is befouled by August field-burning and a pulp mill, a more pristine version of the pioneer experience awaits in Brownsville. Drive south on ORE 99E (or I-5) and take exit 216; ORE 228 will take you five miles east into this small town located between the Calapooia River and the Cascade foothills. This 1846 settlement began to prosper in 1862 with a woolen mill and, shortly thereafter, the coming of the railroad. Today, the **Linn County Historical Museum** (101 Park Ave., Brownsville 97327; tel. 466-3390) is located in a turn-of-the-century train depot flanked by freight cars and a circus train. Inside these structures are displays focusing on the life-style of the area's first settlers (a barbershop, kitchen, post office, etc.), the Calapooya tribe, and local natural history. Kids will especially relish the vintage covered wagon and 50 miniature horse-drawn wagons, sleighs, carriages, and carts. After viewing exhibits, pick up a self-guided tour brochure here Mon.-Sat. 11 a.m.-4 p.m., Sun. 1-5 p.m. May-September. Donations suggested.

The museum also coordinates wagon-ride interludes into the past. Known as **Carriage Me Back Days,** these excursions reenact daily life from days of old. This pageant takes place the third weekend of April. Check here too about tours of the **Moyer House,** an elegant 1881 Italianate home whose high-ceilinged interior features a Carrera marble fireplace, ornate wood trim, hand-painted floral patterns, stencils on the ceilings, and oil-painted outdoor scenes on the upper panels in the bay windows. Come in June to see the strangely twisted wisteria tree on the front lawn in full bloom.

Brownsville and vicinity has other worthwhile attractions. A **pioneer cemetery** on the east end of Kirk St. shelters the grave of the last Calapooya Indian, and some headstones here date to 1846, when Brownsville was established. What ended up being Oregon's third-oldest continuously operating settlement began as a ferry stop on the Calapooia River. A collection of

rocks, Indian arrowheads, and woodcarvings is housed in an interesting stone structure at the **Living Rock Studio** (ORE 228 west of town; tel. 466-5814). The highlight here is the series of colorful Biblical scenes made from translucent stone. Admission is free and hours are Tues.-Sat. 10 a.m.-5 p.m., Sun. 2-5 p.m.

The state's oldest yearly celebration takes place here in June with the **Pioneer Picnic.** Northeast of Brownsville between Sweet Home and Lebanon is the **Council Tree,** a huge Douglas fir that served as the site of the annual gathering of the Calapooyas. This 400-year-old tree can be reached by taking ORE 228 to Sweet Home and heading north a few miles on ORE 20 to Liberty Rd., which goes a mile to the turnout. Northeast of town, the **Quartzville Creek** Recreational corridor has gold panning opportunities. Follow U.S. 20 seven miles and turn left to the access road which goes 27 miles to Quartz Creek. A week's panning here is not like-

WILLAMETTE BIRD SANCTUARIES

The federal government established several bird sanctuaries between Salem and Eugene in the mid-1960s because of the encroachment of urbanization and agriculture on the winter habitat of the dusky Canada goose. This species now comes to **Baskett Slough National Wildlife Refuge** (N.W.R.), west of Salem, **Ankeny N.W.R.,** southwest of the capital, and **Finley N.W.R.,** south of Corvallis, each October after summering in Alaska's Copper River Delta. Refuge ecosystems mesh forest, cropland, and riparian environments to attract hummingbirds, swans, geese, sandhill cranes, ducks, egrets, herons, plovers, sandpipers, hawks and other raptors, wrens, woodpeckers, and dozens of other avian ambassadors. A pamphlet, *Birds of Willamette Valley Refuges,* details the best months to birdwatch, frequency of sightings, and locations of hundreds of kinds of birds. It can be obtained by writing the Refuge Manager, Western Oregon Refuges, 26208 Finley Refuge Rd., Corvallis 97337; tel. 757-7236.

In the interest of maintaining the sanctity of the birds' habitat, the refuges restrict birders by closing some trails in winter; other trails farther from feeding grounds are kept open year-round. While Finley and Baskett N.W.R.s along 99W are more user-friendly to hikers than Ankeny (Ankeny Hill exit, off

I-5, six miles south of Salem, then drive Buena Vista Road through the refuge), it's still advisable to pick up refuge maps in the drop boxes at each locale to find your way.

A hike that can be enjoyed any time of year is Finley N.W.R.'s one-mile **Woodpecker Loop.** A variety of plant communities exists here, due to Calapooyan field-burning followed by pioneer logging and cattle grazing. Its location on the border between the Coast Range and the Willamette Valley also contributes to the diversity. Forests of oak and Douglas fir, and a mixed-deciduous grove combine with marshes to provide a wide range of habitats. Look for the rare pileated woodpecker in the deciduous forest. The loop's trailhead is reached by taking 99W to Refuge Road. Look for the footpath on the right after driving three miles. A drop box has a pamphlet with pictures and information on the birds, wildlife, and plant communities here.

Another trail that's always open is the one-mile **Baskett Butte Loop.** Along with birdwatching, Willamette Valley views can be enjoyed here from an elevated perch. From the junction of ORE 22 and ORE 99W, drive north on 99W almost two miles, turn left onto Colville Road, then drive one mile to the trailhead on the right. The path climbs gently above the Morgan Lake trailhead.

ly to produce a quantity large enough to fill a tooth, but the pleasant surroundings and primal thrill of finding "color" in your pan is sure to get you hooked. The Sweet Home area is famous among rockhounds for petrified wood and agates. Finally, Brownsville and vicinity might evoke a feeling of déjà vu, having provided big-screen backdrops for such recent films as *Isn't It Shocking*, *The Flood*, *The Body*, and *Stand By Me*.

Sweet Home Recreation And Camping
About 14 miles east of Sweet Home off U.S. 20 is **Cascadia State Park** (Box 736, Cascadia 97329; tel. 343-7812), near the banks of the South Santiam River. Rocks here form great swimming holes. A nearby waterfall, a cave with petroglyphs, and a hand pump to draw up mineral water are other appeals. Also on ORE 20 are superlative boating and fishing on Green Peter and Foster Lake reservoirs. No reservations are required for Cascadia's 26 tent sites and trailer spaces. Such amenities as piped water, flush toilets, and firewood are available, and a store is located within a mile. It's open mid-April to late October; $5 a night.

Natural Attractions
West of Corvallis, two spots have drawn seekers of natural beauty and solitude for millennia. Mary's Peak and Alsea Falls are each a short drive from ORE 34, a scenic route to Waldport, which branches off of ORE 20 southwest of Philomath.

Mary's Peak (for information write: Siuslaw National Forest Supervisor's Office, 4077 Research Way, Box 1148, Corvallis 97333; tel. 757-4480) sits about 12 miles southwest of Corvallis. A sign north of the highway points the way to a 10-mile drive to the top of the Coast Range's highest peak. Along the way, pretty cascades, interesting rock outcroppings, and over-the-shoulder views of the Cascades on the eastern horizon intensify your anticipation of this moutaintop Calapooyan vision-quest site. When you get to the parking lot at the end of the road, the view is impressive—but don't stop there. If it's a clear day, take the short walk across the meadows to either of the two summit lookouts for perspectives on Mounts Hood and Jefferson, the Three Sisters to the east, and the Pacific Ocean at the base of the Coast Range to the west.

In the foreground of the Cascades, agricultural plots patchwork the verdant Willamette Valley, site of 83% of Oregon's prime farmland. During August, huge smoke plumes rise off the valley floor, making it look like a war zone. And it is, in a sense. Despite no shots being fired, you're looking at an environmental battleground. The state's 200-million-dollar-a-year grass-seed industry burns the fields here in order to kill off such diseases as ergot and nematodes. The fire also eradicates weeds that compete with rye grass and would otherwise have to be sprayed with herbicides. Field-burning also recycles nutrients back into the soil.

Nonetheless, the respiratory distress inflicted upon valley residents has compelled several serious attempts to ban the practice. When smoke from grass-seed fields was implicated in a 20-car pileup on I-5 in 1989, the anti-burning campaign gained impetus. While farmers have been able to head off opposition by pointing to the agricultural benefits and cost-effectiveness of field-burning, they also have been working with opponents to find alternative uses for the straw. There is optimism on both sides that creating new uses for the excess straw, and expanding existing ones, will eventually eliminate the need to burn the fields. Using the straw to fuel power plants, and to make paper, composition firewood, fiberboard, composting materials, kitty litter, and animal feed are some of the possibilities being considered.

The outlook is not so sanguine for opponents of clearcutting on the flanks of Mary's Peak. The Forest Service claims its hands are tied, despite potential damage to the watershed when erosion on denuded slopes spills into streams. The summit, thanks to being a federally designated botanical area, remains untouched. A biome unique to the Coast Range exists up here, with such flora as alpine phlox, purple lupine, and the blue-green noble fir. Snow, an infrequent visitor to most Coast Range slopes, can often be found here in winter, even at lower elevations. In fact, the road is sometimes impassable without chains from late fall till early spring. A snow-park permit, which costs $2.50, is required for day use, Nov. 15-April 15. Write the Alsea Ranger Station (Box 18591, Alsea 97327) for more info.

CORVALLIS ACCOMMODATIONS

Huntington Manor, 3555 N.W. Harrison Blvd., tel. 753-3735, $55, bed and breakfast, cable TV, fireplace, laundry, nonsmoking rooms.

Jason Inn Motel and Restaurant, 800 N.W. 9th St., tel. 753-7326, $40-85, cable TV, pets, pool, restaurant/lounge, nonsmoking rooms, live entertainment.

Model Motel, 1480 S.W. 3rd St., tel. 752-8756, $20-58, cable TV, pets, kitchenettes, restaurant/lounge, nonsmoking rooms.

Nendels Inn, 1550 N.W. 9th St., tel. 753-9151, $50-60, wheelchair access, cable TV, pool, restaurant/lounge, laundry, nonsmoking rooms.

Shanico Inn, 1113 N.W. 9th St., tel. 754-7474, $47-55, wheelchair access, cable TV, pets, pool, nonsmoking rooms.

The Hanson Country Inn, 795 S.W. Hanson St., tel. 752-2919, $50-60, bed and breakfast, nonsmoking rooms.

Valu-Inn by Nendels, 101 N.W. Van Buren, tel. 752-9601, $40-70, cable TV, pets, restaurant/lounge, nonsmoking rooms.

Farther down ORE 34 is the town of **Alsea.** The adjoining Lobster Valley area drew many countercultural refugees here in the '70s, a portion of whom have remained to become farmers and craftspeople. The work of some of these local artisans, including pottery, baskets, and hand-tied fly-fishing lures, is sold at **Farmer's Kitchen and Herb Garden** (185 W. Main, Alsea 97314; tel. 487-4384). The gardens that surround the rustic dining room here provide herbs and edible flowers for the restaurant. The greenness of the valley surrounded by Coast Range foothills recalled the lower alpine regions of Europe enough to inspire the nickname "Little Scotland."

South of here, a paved-over logging road through the tall timbers of the Coast Range can take you back to the Willamette Valley on a remote scenic byway. Look for a sign that says Alsea Falls, South Fork Road/Monroe. You'll follow the Alsea River much of the way until you come to the sloping parking lot near Alsea Falls on the east side of the road. A short trail leads you to a picturesque cascade, ideal for a picnic. The road continues through once-active logging towns into farming country and the Finley Wildlife Refuge south of Corvallis (see "Willamette Bird Sanctuaries" above). From here, ORE 99W goes north to Corvallis or south to Junction City and Eugene.

PRACTICALITIES

Accommodations
The accommodations chart covers area lodgings, which are pretty much what you'd expect for a midsized Willamette Valley college town—lots of garden-variety motels with an occasional upscale unit for visiting parents of OSU students.

Bed And Breakfast
Bed and breakfasts can provide a dollar-wise alternative to an impersonal hotel room. There are some good choices in the Corvallis area.

Lilla's Bed and Breakfast and Cafe (206 S.W. Seventh Ave., Albany; tel. 928-9437) is a century-old house rich in Victorian nuance. The rates are $45-55 for two, including a full breakfast. Lilla's is also reputed to be a good place to have Sunday brunch or dinner (not included with lodging).

In Corvallis, the **Madison Inn Bed and Breakfast** (660 S.W. Madison Ave., Corvallis 97333; tel. 757-1274) is a 1903 vintage home on the National Register of Historic Places; it's across from Central Park and within walking distance of OSU and downtown. For $50-60 double occupancy, you can enjoy such comforts of home as patchwork quilts, antique furniture, fresh flowers, sitting rooms filled with books, complimentary wine, and breakfast with home-baked goodies. Reserve this one a month in advance.

Camping

Camping in this part of the Willamette Valley can be delightful, especially in late spring and early autumn.

In Corvallis, your best bet from April to late October is **Willamette City Park** (Corvallis Dept. of Parks and Recreation, Box 1083, Corvallis 97339; tel. 757-6918). To get there drive a mile south of the city on ORE 99W, then go a half mile east on S.E. Goodnight Rd. to the park. For $4 a night, you can enjoy one of the 25 sites for tents and RVs serviced by vault toilets, piped water, and a small outdoor kitchen. If you need civilized comforts, a store, cafe, and laundromat are a mile away. Trails to the nearby Willamette River yield birdwatching and fishing opportunities in this 40-acre park.

Food

Just because *Pacific Northwest* magazine in its 1990 restaurant poll mentioned several Corvallis-area eateries as among the elite of the state, don't get the impression that the town is full of prohibitively priced dining spots. The city's Eden-like setting is ideal for picnics, and there's no shortage of places to get good grub no matter what your tastes or budget might be. In addition to the sub shops, Chinese takeout places, and pizza joints opposite the campus, the eat 'n' run for lunch bunch will especially appreciate **Bombs Away Tacqueria** (2527 Monroe St.). This always-filled-to-capacity 65-seat restaurant's walls are lined with colorful murals, and the sidewalk outside is lined with wait-list devotees of finger food made with the freshest ingredients and organic produce. Other reasons for the queue include prices that top out at $5.25 (baby back ribs), as well as microbrews and Oregon wines on tap.

The **Albany Farmer's Market** (Water and Broadalbin streets, Albany) is a short drive from Corvallis. Saturdays 9 a.m.-noon, June through Thanksgiving, enjoy the Willamette Valley's bountiful harvests of corn, fruit, garlic, peppers, or whatever else happens to be in season. There are also cut flowers on sale as well as such regional specialties as the mild-tasting large-cloved elephant garlic, marionberries (a hybrid blackberry with a tart taste developed by Oregon State University), and dried jumbo Brooks prunes. Best of all, you're buying direct from the grower at a fraction of supermarket cost.

Another Albany tradition is **Novak's Hungarian Paprikas** (2835 Santiam Hwy., Albany; tel. 967-9488). Authentic kolbasz (a spicy saus-

late spring in the Willamette Valley, a prime camping time

OREGON DEPT. OF TRANSPORTATION

age), stuffed cabbage, and chicken paprika exemplify the earthy Eastern European fare. Try chocolate cake with apricot preserves for dessert. Lunch and dinner are served Sun.-Fri., dinner only on Saturday, 4 to 9 p.m.

Back in Corvallis, start the day at **Cafe Croissant** (215 S.W. Fifth; tel. 752-5111) with croissants (selected as the best in town by a local publication) or homemade granola. For lunch there's quiche, soups, salads, and lasagna. Fresh vegetables from the owner's garden are a special treat in summer, as is the array of muffins and pastries from the in-house bakery any time of the year.

Another place guaranteed not to go against the grain is the **New Morning Bakery** (231 S.W. Second, tel. 754-1081; and 1870 S.W. Third, tel. 757-1821). Try the honey cinnamon rolls here or choose from over a dozen varieties of cookies. New Morning salads, pasta dishes, and sandwiches can provision a picnic. It's close enough to Riverfront Park on the Willamette for a picnic, which is a good idea given New Morning's limited seating. Take along some Italian flat bread or French bread for your outing. Oregon-made jams, homemade soups, Italian pastry, cheesecake, and other desserts are also available here.

Near Central Park behind the Benton County Courthouse is **Oscar's** (559 Monroe Ave.; tel. 753-7444), another picnic-in-the-park and breakfast favorite of the locals. Design-your-own omelettes can be ordered throughout the day and quiche, salads, and sandwiches are served after 11 a.m.

Perhaps the best place to provision a picnic is **First Alternative Co-op** (1007 S.E. Third; tel. 753-3115), which you'll encounter as you come into town via ORE 99W from the south. The organic-produce section is a marvel, and the largely volunteer staff can give excellent leads on what's happening in the area. Across from the co-op, **Papa's Pizza** is a better-than-average chain. The best pie in town, however, is at **Woodstock's Pizza Parlor** (945 N.W. Kings Blvd.; tel. 752-5151).

Another spot for those who place a premium on wholesome fare is **Nearly Normal** (corner of Monroe and 15th; tel. 753-0791), whose mismatched kitschy decor does justice to its name. Low prices and huge helpings reflect the predominantly student clientele, who savor egg and stir-fry dishes, burritos, and falafels. There's live music on Wednesday, Thursday, and Saturday, and an entertaining waitstaff every day of the week.

Two Corvallis restaurants that were polled as tops in their respective categories were the **Gables** (1121 N.W. Ninth; tel. 752-3364) and **Papagayo's** (550 N.W. Harrison; tel. 757-8188). The Gables is full of students and parents on graduation day enjoying prime rib, fresh seafood, lamb chops, and other traditional standbys. This is the most expensive place in town (though early-bird specials can make things more affordable), but the understated homelike elegance and venerable cuisine make it perfect for an occasion. To get there, follow Harrison to Ninth; the restaurant is located a half mile west of ORE 99W.

Exquisite Mexican paintings and hand-woven tapestries on the walls prepare you for something unique even before you sit down at the table at Papagayo's. The menu itself features weekly specials rarely seen north of the border to complement permanent entrees like enchiladas and chiles rellenos. Whether it's pozole (a stew with hominy, chicken, and pork covered with shredded cabbage, lettuce, and salsa) or black-bean chili, there's always something for the Mexican-food maven with a sense of adventure. Often what might seem innovative here actually draws from the *real* cuisine of Mexico, as opposed to the Tex-Mex-influenced fare found in the majority of U.S. places.

In this vein, Papagayo's uses a delicious Gruyère-like cheese from Chihuahua in their chiles rellenos. This is the way it's done in most of Mexico, where they've never heard of Monterey jack, and after one bite of queso Chihuahua, you'll see why. The mesquite grill, fresh locally grown peppers, and the traditional mole (a chocolate-and-chile sauce over turkey or chicken) served in honor of the Christmas holiday season are also noteworthy. Not only is the food extraordinary, but the portions are sufficiently ample to inspire disbelief at the $10 average dinner tab.

Events

Of the many events in Corvallis, the premier celebration has to be the **Corvallis Fall Festival.** This gathering of exceptional artists and craftspeople is now in its second decade. Nonstop varied entertainment and a block of food concessions, including an Oregon wine garden, backdrop this hotbed of creative ferment 10 a.m.-6 p.m., the last weekend in September. Contact the chamber of commerce for more information about this event which takes place in Central Park (between Sixth and Eighth, Monroe and Madison).

The OSU **basketball** season at Gill Coliseum (26th and Washington; tel. 754-2951) is a favorite wintertime activity here because the Beavers are a perennial Pac-10 championship contender. Tickets begin at $6.50.

On the first full weekend of June, **Lebanon** celebrates its **Strawberry Festival** (for information write: 104 Park St., Lebanon 97355; tel. 258-7164). This town southeast of Albany off ORE 20 has become famous for its annual *Guinness* world-record-sized strawberry shortcake, whose 17,000 pieces are dished out at the climax of the event.

On the third weekend in June, the 100-year-old **Brownsville Pioneer Picnic** features an old-time fiddlers jamboree and a tug-of-war involving large local teams. Also on the agenda are a parade, carnival, crafts fair, foot race, and tour of historic homes (for information see "Linn County Historical Museum" above). The three-day celebration is held near the spot where a ferry plied the Calapooia in 1846, now part of 10-acre Pioneer Park, located off Main St. at the end of Park Avenue. This event begins every morning with a wagon-train breakfast.

Albany's **World Championship Timber Carnival** takes place July 1-4. Contact the visitors association for more information. Admission is $6 for adults and $4 for children to see three days of logging-related competition. While such events as speed-climbing, springboard-chopping, and log-rolling have little place in the increasingly mechanized world of modern timber management, they're still fun to watch.

Information And Services

The **Corvallis Area Chamber of Commerce** (420 N.W. Second, Corvallis 97330; tel. 757-1505) has a driving-tour brochure of the area to supplement this section. Better yet, contact the helpful folks at the **Corvallis Visitor's Information Center** (420 N.W. Second, Corvallis 97330; tel. 757-1544). They can direct you to such locally favorite attractions as a recently renovated covered bridge on the OSU campus and Avery Park Rose Gardens. The latter boasts floral beauty framed by towering redwoods. **Greyhound** and **Valley Retriever** (153 N.W. Fourth; tel. 757-1797) operate every day, with routes north, south, and west to the coastal town of Newport. The **Green Tortoise** departs Corvallis/Lebanon exit 228 behind Vip's restaurant for points north at 2 p.m., or south at 2:30 p.m. (see the general Introduction for the days of service and more info). **Amtrak** is at 110 W. 10th St. in Albany (tel. 928-0885).

The main **post office** (311 S.W. Second, Corvallis 97330) is open 9-5 weekdays. The **Parks and Recreation Department** (tel. 757-6418) can steer you to numerous recreation facilities in and around the area, including an indoor rock-climbing gym, tennis courts, and city parks. **Trysting Tree Golf Course** (ORE 34 and N.E. Electric Rd.; tel. 752-3332) is located across the river from downtown Corvallis. **Good Samaritan Hospital** (3600 Samaritan Dr.; tel. 757-5111) has 24-hour emergency-room service.

To catch up on local events, read the *Corvallis Gazette Times* (Box 368, Corvallis 97339; tel. 753-2641). KOAC (550 on the AM dial) is an excellent public radio station with a top-notch news team and excellent classical music offerings. It serves much of western Oregon and can be picked up in remote coastal and mountain communities.

Corvallis has many fine bookstores. Among them, the **Book Bin** (351 N.W. Jackson, tel. 752-0040; and 2305 Monroe, tel. 753-TEXT) and **Avocet Used Books** (614 S.W. Third) have good selections of regional titles.

EUGENE AND VICINITY

The pioneers who established Eugene's townsite in the mid-1800s were motivated by visions of material prosperity derived from thick forests and good soil for farming. By contrast, many of the modern immigrants over the last few decades haven't come here primarily to get rich. The local job market, even when big timber is booming, is cyclical at best. Instead, a gardenlike setting, good schools, and a recreational and cultural mix unsurpassed by any other city of comparable size explain Eugene's present-day allure.

The Willamette River curves around the northwest quarter of the community and abundant trees and flowers dot the cityscape. From an elevated perch you can see the Coast and Cascade ranges beckoning you to beach and mountain playgrounds little more than an hour away. In town, a world-renowned Bach Festival and other big-time cultural events are showcased in the Hult Center, praised by the *L.A. Times* as having the best acoustics on the West Coast. The University of Oregon campus provides another forum for the best in art and academe, while its Hayward Field track has been the site of the U.S. Olympic Trials several times.

Outdoor gatherings such as Saturday Market and the Oregon Country Fair bring the community together in a potlatch of homegrown edibles, arts, and crafts. You'll also see Eugenians outside, indulging in such local passions as jogging, biking, basketball, and gardening. Less evident to those passing through might be the huge network of environmental organizations and other outlets of political and social activism (Eugene has more human-services organizations per capita than any other city in the United States). The 110,000 people who live in Eugene combine with neighboring Springfield's population of 41,000 to make up the second-largest residential center in the state. Visitors from rural Lane County flock to the Eugene/Springfield area on weekends to shop at Valley River Center, see a movie, attend a convention, or simply go "garage saleing" (this place seems to have more flea markets than just about anywhere!).

Eugene has also earned the reputation as the timber capital of the world. Situated between the Willamette and Siuslaw national forests, the area is the major point of origin for domestic lumber sales. The mill-choked municipality of Springfield may at first seem like Eugene's ugly half-sister, but the traveler can appreciate some good dining spots and city parks there, and the town is also the gateway to the scenic McKenzie River National Recreation Area. In addition to economic fluctuations caused by the timber industry, the region's fortunes rise and fall with the University of Oregon, the single largest employer and a leading recipient of federal grants.

The activities of another economic mainstay, the multimillion-dollar grass-seed industry, contribute to summertime air-quality emergencies with field-burning and allergy-causing pollens. Air pollution, from this source as well as wood

BRUCE BUSH

The Eugene Skinner cabin sits under a canopy of fall foliage at Skinner's Butte.

EUGENE / SPRINGFIELD

TO SALEM

ARMITAGE S.P.

COBURG RD.

5

McKENZIE VIEW DR.

TO MARCOLA

GATEWAY ST.

GAME FARM RD.

McKENZIE RIVER

OLD HILL RD.

HARLOW RD.

2nd ST.

3rd ST.

MARCOLA RD.

105 126

EUGENE-SPRINGFIELD HWY.

105 126

AUTZEN STADIUM

CENTENNIAL BLVD.

BUTTE PARK

WILLAMALANE PARK

MOHAWK BLVD.

EMERY ST.

TEWAY PARK

BANK PARK

ALTON BAKER PARK

5th ST.

7th ST.

14th ST.

McKENZIE WILLAMETTE MEM. HOSPITAL

28th ST.

TO SISTERS

126

SACRED HEART HOSPITAL

99 126

ISLAND PARK

MAIN ST.

32nd ST.

42nd ST.

HILYARD ST.

UNIVERSITY OF OREGON

FRANKLIN BLVD.

SPRINGFIELD

JASPER RD.

AGATE ST.

24th AVE.

HENDRICKS PARK

TO FALL CREEK

AMAZON PARK

30th AVE.

MIDDLE FORK WILLAMETTE RIVER

SOUTH AMAZON PARK

0th AVE.

LANE COMMUNITY COLLEGE

SEAVEY LOOP

COAST FORK

MT. PISGAH

BUFORD RECREATION AREA

FOX HOLLOW RD.

WILLAMETTE RIVER

HULL PARK

EAST SPENCER BUTTE PARK

99

TO ROSEBURG

5

58

TO OAK RIDGE

Evening falls over Spencer's Butte and Eugene.

JUPITA NDEVER

stoves, automobiles, and industrial emissions, constitutes the major noticeable excess in a town noted for a health-conscious, progressive outlook. More often than not, a cleansing rain saves the day here for those with sensitive respiratory systems.

In an era when expressions like "livability" and "quality of life" exist primarily as media buzzwords, these elusive entities have taken tangible form in Eugene, Oregon.

SIGHTS

The two areas of visitor interest are minutes south of the Willamette River. The campus, in Eugene's southeast quadrant, and the downtown (bounded by Fifth and 10th avenues, and Charnelton and High streets) are only a five-minute drive apart from each other. Serious walkers can manage the two-mile distance without trouble.

Skinner's Butte

A good place to get oriented in Eugene, visually as well as historically, is Skinner's Butte. If you look north from most anywhere downtown you'll see this landmark. A beautiful park fronting the Willamette River is located at the butte's northern base. It's reachable by following the Scenic Drive signs to the river via High Street. This riverfront site served as a dock for pioneer sternwheelers and was where founding father

Eugene Skinner ran a ferry service for farmers living north of the river. The town tried to become a major shipping port, but the upper Willamette was uncharted, as well as too shallow and meandering. In addition, sunken logs, gravel bars, and submerged trees and rocks made steamboat navigation difficult. As a result, Ben Holladay's Oregon and California Railroad became Eugene's most effective mode of transport in 1871.

Eugene Skinner, like so many Oregon Trail-era migrants, wanted to take advantage of the federal government's 640-acre land giveaway offer to pioneers, so he staked a claim from the banks of the Willamette to present-day Eighth Ave. and from Monroe St. to the river on Hilyard Street. He built his shelter on Second and Lincoln streets and later opened up Lane County's first trading post here.

By following the Scenic Drive signs from the park or driving north on Lincoln St. (you can also walk up from the south side in 15 minutes), you can get to the top of the butte and enjoy the vantage point from which Eugene Skinner surveyed the landscape in June 1846. Calapooya Indians called this promontory Yapoah, meaning "High Place," and used it for ceremonial dances. While a city of 110,000 people (261,000 in the greater Eugene-Springfield area) has grown up in the once-pristine valley below, you can still see the Cascade and Coast ranges on a clear day, as well as pockets of greenery throughout the city. You can also spot another good reference point in your orientation, **Spencer's Butte,** looming above the southern hills four miles away.

Another historic house in the area is the 1888 **Shelton McMurphey House** (perhaps the inspiration for the name of local author Ken Kesey's main character in *One Flew Over the Cuckoo's Nest)* on the lower south slope of the butte. The aqua-colored Victorian is the most eye-catching of some 2,000 designated historic properties in the city. During the third week of May the interior of this and other landmarks in the east Skinner's Butte neighborhood may be toured (contact the visitors and convention bureau for more information).

Fifth Street Public Market
The past and the present happily coexist a few blocks from the butte's south flank at the Fifth Street Public Market (296 E. Fifth; tel. 484-0383), an old-time feed mill converted into an atrium. This rustic structure houses an impressive collection of crafts boutiques, specialty stores, and restaurants surrounding an open-air courtyard. This courtyard is a favorite haunt of sun worshippers, people-watchers, and street performers.

For a more downhome version of the public market, head to the area near Eighth and Oak streets each Saturday from the first weekend in April until mid-December (when a Christmas Fair at the Lane County Fairgrounds takes over). The **Saturday Market** (Box 427, Eugene 97440; tel. 686-8885) features open-air food and crafts

booths in operation 10 a.m.-5 p.m., accompanied by "new vaudeville" and musical performers. While the latest incarnation of this traditional gathering is not the bargain basement it used to be in the '70s, the good vibes and creative spirit of the community are still in ample evidence. The small farmer's market set up across Eighth Ave. from the crafts area has always been a good place to get fresh inexpensive produce.

Hult Center For The Performing Arts
While you're walking between the two markets, you might look west past the Eugene Hilton and notice another imposing building close by. This is the Hult Center for the Performing Arts (1 Eugene Center; tel. 687-5000 for the box office, tel. 687-5087 for tour information) on Willamette St. between Sixth and Seventh avenues. In addition to its status as a top-flight performance venue, this place is worth a look for aesthetics alone. From the frog and troll statues that greet you at the Sixth Ave. entrance to the high-ceilinged interior bedecked with masks, artistic touches abound.

Hult Center talent is showcased beneath interlocking acoustic panels on the domed ceiling and walls of the 2,500-seat **Silva Concert Hall,** simulating a giant upside-down pastel-colored Easter basket. The **Jacobs Gallery** exhibits local artwork, providing another feast for the eyes. Even the bathroom tile here is done up in a visually pleasing theatrical motif. Free guid-

Saturday Market, a Eugene institution

ed one-hour tours are offered every Thursday and Saturday at 1 p.m. or by special arrangement. Call for reservations or arrange for one at the front desk. The lobby and ticket office are open Mon.-Fri. 11 a.m.-5 p.m., Sat. 11-3, and one hour prior to performances.

Campus

From downtown head a few blocks south to 13th Ave. then east to the University of Oregon campus (visitor information available at Oregon Hall, Agate and 13th; tel. 346-3814), bounded by Franklin Blvd., 11th and 18th avenues, and Alder and Moss streets. With an enrollment around 17,000 students, plus multimillion-dollar federal endowments placing the school in the upper echelon of American university funding, you might be expecting a bureaucratic, impersonal feeling here. Instead, the grounds of the campus are graced by architecturally inviting buildings dating back to the school's creation in the 1870s,

Deady Hall, the oldest building on the U of O campus

as well as 400 varieties of trees. **Deady Hall,** the oldest building on campus, was built in 1876. This bucolic campus has often been selected by Hollywood to portray the ivy-covered halls of academe, most notably in the comedy *Animal House*. The quiet and tranquility of the campus are sustained by a ban on vehicular traffic beyond 13th Ave. and Kincaid Street. You can get a free **campus tour** weekdays 10:30 a.m. and 2:30 p.m. from Oregon Hall. You're better off, however, just picking up the free map and setting your own pace.

If you wander the north part of the U of O complex toward Franklin Blvd., you'll see majestic and rare trees (including a Chinese dawn redwood) dotting the landscape between the schools of law and journalism. Interesting outdoor sculptures also liven up a stroll of the campus.

A must on any campus tour is the **Museum of Art** (next to the main library; tel. 346-3027). The highlight is a second-floor nationally renowned Oriental collection, but the revolving paintings and photography exhibits on the first floor are also usually worthwhile. A secret hideaway on the first floor is a courtyard that could have been taken out of a charming older neighborhood in Paris. You might also stop at the excellent crafts shop to the left of the door as you enter the museum. There's no admission charge to the museum and the hours are Wed.-Sun. noon-5 p.m., Sept.-June. If you're so inclined, call the museum office about free one-hour tours.

Oregon prehistory is showcased in the **Natural History Museum** (1680 E. 15th Ave.; tel. 346-3024), with artifacts from digs in eastern Oregon and bird and mammal fossils from around the state. A portion of Thomas Condon's fossil collection displays the curiosities culled from the earth by the man known as Oregon's first geologist and the discoverer of the John Day Fossil Beds. Other cultures are also the focus of exhibits here. A $1 donation is requested and the hours are Wed.-Sun. 12-5 p.m.

Next to the Museum of Art is the **U of O Library.** On the second floor, the **Oregon Collection** (tel. 346-3468) has books and periodicals about the state in open stacks—a great place to plan trips or learn about the region. The map library on the first floor can also augment the trip-planning process.

PARKS

Hendricks Park

Beyond the campus and downtown, Eugene and vicinity has five parks that rank among its preeminent attractions (other parks are mentioned below in "Activities and Recreation"). About two miles east of the campus on a forested ridgeline is Hendricks Park, home to 850 naturally occurring rhododendrons and azaleas and around 10,000 hybrids. There are several ways to get to the park, the easiest being to turn from Fairmount Blvd. onto Summit Drive. Or take Lane Transit bus #27/Fairmount, disembark at Summit Dr., and hike on up the hill a quarter mile. Two parking lots accommodate cars; one near the picnic area of stoves and tables, the other at the upper entrance on Sunset Boulevard. The rhododendron gardens are in their glory during May, with 15- to 20-foot-high plants in shades of pink, red, yellow, and purple. Even though the display declines by late June, it's always a great place to stroll. Gorgeous views of the city can be enjoyed from the west end of the garden, and tree-shaded footpaths lead to benches located in secluded cul-de-sacs on the hillside.

The Rose Garden

Another floral display is located at the Owens Memorial Rose Garden at the end of Jefferson St., along the banks of the Willamette River. Another way to get there is to walk downriver on the bikepath in back of the Valley River Inn until you get to the footbridge. On the other side of the river are the gardens. Thirty varieties of roses here peak in June and last until fall. Along with 3,000 roses, tremendous old cherry and oak trees also command attention.

Ridgeline Trail

The South Hills Ridgeline Trail is only minutes from downtown Eugene and offers wildlife-watching opportunities (look for deer, tree frogs, garter snakes, and all kinds of birds) and more species of fern than perhaps any other single spot in Oregon. In addition, old-growth Douglas fir and the lovely and increasingly hard-to-find calypso orchid grow here. A pamphlet listing all the trailside flora and fauna and their months of bloom is put out by Eugene Parks and Recreation Cultural Services (22 W. 27th Ave., Eugene 97401; tel. 687-5333). The trail is seldom steep and has some spectacular views of the city through clearings. A spur route leads up to the highest point in Eugene, **Spencer's Butte** (elevation 2,052 feet), via a steep and often muddy trail. (If you like seclusion, however, this route might be preferable to the ones outlined in the next paragraph.) The Ridgeline Trail can be reached from several points, including Dillard Rd.; near the corner of Fox Hollow and Christenson roads; near Willamette and 52nd; off Blanton Rd. near 40th; and the Spencer's Butte parking area (see below).

Spencer's Butte

The Spencer's Butte parking lot is nearby. Just drive south on Willamette St. until you see the signs on the left side of the road. According to one legend, the butte was named after a 19th-century English trapper killed by Indian arrows. The Calapooyans called it "Chamate," meaning "Rattlesnake Mountain." An 1848 account (from Batterns DeGuerre's *Ten Years In Oregon*) of the view from the summit reads as follows:

On one hand was the vast chain of Cascade Mountains, Mt. Hood looming in solitary grandeur far above its fellows; on the other hand was the Umpqua Mountains, and a little farther on, the coast ridge. Between these lay the whole magnificent panorama of the Willamette Valley, with its ribbon streams and carpetlike verdure.

The view today has all of the above but there are some differences. Below the north summit you look down on Eugene/Springfield, with Fern Ridge Reservoir in the northwest toward Junction City. Beyond the reservoir you can sometimes see Mary's Peak. Other Cascade mountains not noted in the previous account but often visible from the butte include Mt. Jefferson, Mt. Washington, the Three Sisters, and Mt. Bachelor. To the southeast, Creswell and the hills around Cottage Grove are visible.

The two main trails to the top vary in difficulty. If you bear left immediately after leaving the parking lot, you'll come to the route known among the locals as The Face. This trail is shorter in distance than its saddleback counterpart, but much steeper and littered with boulders and, sometimes, muddy spots. It can be scaled in 40 minutes by anyone in reasonable health.

The main trail is a straight shot from the parking lot, looping up and around the steep hills. These inclines are broken up by flat stretches. Allow about an hour for the ascent. Signs caution against rattlesnakes, falling limbs, and poison oak, the latter being the most likely problem. The three shiny leaves of the notorious plant can be seen in many places along the trail, particularly on the flanks of the summit. A mixed-conifer forest featuring old-growth Douglas fir with an understory of numerous ferns and wildflowers will usher you along. Die-hard hikers equipped with boots or other durable footwear will enjoy "shooting the butte" in the snow. A snow chute leads you up into a winter wonderland with trails wreathed by old-growth fir dusted with snowflakes.

Mount Pisgah

Mount Pisgah (Friends of Mt. Pisgah, Box 5601, Eugene 97405; tel. 747-3817) features a mile hike to a marvelous viewpoint and an arboretum on the lower slopes. The arboretum (plants and bird lists are often available at the visitor center, open weekends) sponsors such events as a fall fair dedicated to area mushrooms and a spring wildflower show and plant sale (dates vary, so call ahead). Mount Pisgah can be reached by following E. 30th Ave. from Eugene past Lane Community College to the I-5 interchange. Cross the bridge over the freeway, turn left, and take the next right onto Seavey Loop Road. You'll cross the Coast Fork of the Willamette River and then turn left onto a gravel road (look for the Mt. Pisgah signs) which leads to the trailhead; the arboretum is just beyond the parking lot.

The path to the 1,514-foot-high Mt. Pisgah summit has a dearth of trees, enabling hikers to enjoy vistas of the Willamette Valley on the way up. At the top an unforgettable perspective of the valley in the foreground and the Three Sisters and other Cascade peaks in the distance awaits. Installation of a monument is underway on the summit, honoring author Ken Kesey's son and other members of the ill-fated U of O wrestling team who perished in a van accident (Oregon's most celebrated author lives two miles to the

east in **Pleasant Hill**). This memorial consists of a sculpture with a relief map depicting the mountains, rivers, towns, and other landmarks in the Eugene area. Supporting the map are three five-sided bronze columns upon which the geologic history of Oregon over the past 200 million years is portrayed, using images of more than 300 fossil specimens.

Those making the climb in August will find blackberry bushes for browsing along the way. If you're perspiring from the climb, when you're back on the valley floor head south of the trailhead to the adjoining **Buford Recreation Area** for a dip in the cool waters of the Willamette River. The banks of the Coast Fork here also have a great profusion of white oak, blackberry bushes, and poison oak.

ACTIVITIES AND RECREATION

Eugene's identity is rooted in its reputation as "Tracktown, U.S.A.," and also in its superlative Parks and Recreation Department. In 1988, *Money* magazine ranked Eugene the sixth-best place to live in the nation, and *Self* magazine called the city America's best place to work out. Both articles cited Eugene's recreational priorities as positive factors in the rankings. The *Self* article went into depth about the 100 miles of bike paths, backcountry cycling minutes from downtown, and track events.

But wait, there's more. Hiking trails, whitewater rafting, golf courses, and other outdoor pursuits are complemented by more sedate activities like winetasting, scenic drives, and museums. The following listings scratch the surface of this array. More detailed information can be culled from the Eugene/Springfield Convention and Visitors Bureau or Eugene Parks and Recreation (see "Information and Services" below).

Highbrow Haunts

Maude Kerns Art Center (1910 15th Ave.; tel. 345-1571) is near the U of O campus. Set in an old church, this gallery is dedicated to contemporary art of nationally known as well as regionally prominent artists. The center is open Mon.-Sat. 10 a.m.-5 p.m., Sun. 1-5 p.m. Admission is free.

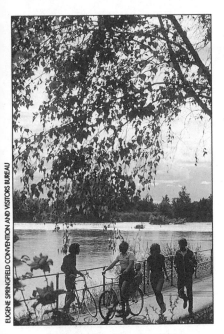

Alton Baker Park offers miles of biking along the Willamette River.

Hinman Vineyards (27012 Briggs Hill Rd.; tel. 345-1945) is a perfect place to spend a summer's afternoon. The winery is 15 miles southwest of downtown and is open noon-5 p.m. daily. Drive west on 11th Ave., turn left on Bertelson Rd., then right on Spencer Creek Road. A left down Briggs Hill Rd. takes you to the tasting room, located on a hillside overlooking a valley.

The Lane County Historical Museum (740 W. 13th Ave.; tel. 687-4239) can be found next to the fairgrounds. Just look for the steam donkey on the front lawn. There are other 19th-century logging vehicles and period rooms, on display. Hours are Tues.-Fri. 10 a.m.-4 p.m., Sat.-Sun. 11-4. Admission is $1, seniors 75 cents, children (under 18) 50 cents.

Water, Water, Everywhere
Alton Baker Park along the Willamette, and the **Millrace Canal,** which parallels the river for three or four miles, provide escapes from Eugene's main downtown thoroughfares. The millrace is easily accessed from the U of O campus by crossing Franklin Boulevard. Rent canoes or kayaks from **EMU Waterworks Company** (1395 Franklin Blvd.; tel. 346-4386), run by U of O students. The rental rates are $3.60 an hour on the millrace, $14 a day off the millrace with a $30 deposit. Hours are Mon.-Fri. 12:30-dusk; Sat.-Sun. 11 a.m.-dusk, March through October. Enter Alton Baker Park below the Ferry Street Bridge. In addition to running and biking paths, there's also **Autzen Stadium,** home football field for the U of O Ducks (and occasionally a venue for rock concerts), and the nearby **Willamette Science and Technology Center** (2300 Leo Harris Parkway; tel. 484-9027). WISTEC's raison d'être is to stimulate scientific understanding and curiosity in everyday life. Permanent exhibits here have an OMSI-like (see Portland "Sights") flavor, and are complemented by a new set of scientifically thematic expositions every three months. The latter have included Chaos, Illusions, Imagery, and Bicycles. WISTEC's hands-on orientation reaches its apex during the summer thanks to these traveling exhibits. Admission is $6 per family, $3 for adults, and $2 for children.

The excellent Lane Service District **Planetarium** is connected to WISTEC. Its 45-minute presentation is highly recommended (call ahead for times). Planetarium admission is $3 for adults, $2.50 for students/seniors, and $1 for children. The WISTEC/Planetarium complex is reached from I-5 by taking I-105 west to the Coburg Rd. exit and following the signs to Autzen Stadium (look for Centennial Blvd. and the Leo Harris Parkway).

Farther west on the Willamette is the **Riverhouse Outdoor Program** office (301 N. Adams St.; tel. 687-5329), headquarters of the Parks Department outdoor program and a roped-off swimming area.

Reservoirs (for information contact the U.S. Army Corps Public Information, Box 2946, Portland 97208-2946) beyond downtown Eugene provide a wide range of recreation. The one closest to town is **Fern Ridge Lake.** Camp, picnic, swim, water-ski, sail, or watch wildlife here. In addition, fishing for crappie, cutthroat trout, largemouth black bass, and catfish is excellent in early spring. This lake was formed when the Long Tom River was dammed in 1941. Its southeast shore was designated a wildlife refuge in 1979. To reach the lake drive 10 miles west of downtown on W. 11th Ave. (ORE 126) toward Veneta, or take Clear Lake Rd. off of ORE 99W. Marinas on the south or north shores are especially coveted by sailboaters and sailboarders. The lake is drained in winter to allow for flood control, but the resulting marsh (and wildlife refuge) hosts tree frogs, newts, ospreys, rare purple martins (in spring), black-tailed deer, red foxes, beavers, muskrats, minks, pond turtles, and great blue herons. The wildlife area is closed to the public January 1-March 15 for the protection of wintering birds. To get there, make a right off ORE 126 onto Territorial Rd. and look for a sign on the right. This section of Territorial Rd. is also part of the Old Applegate Trail, the southern counterpart to the Oregon Trail.

Dorena Reservoir is 30 minutes south of Eugene and has camping, fishing, and boating. The Army Corps dammed the Row River to create the facility, which can be reached by driving south on I-5 or ORE 99 for 20 miles to Cottage Grove. Then head under the bridge below I-5's Cottage Grove exit and pick up Row River Rd. (this goes up into the mountains, so check snow conditions), which goes eight miles east to Dorena Lake. En route, several covered bridges in this area can be visited. In addition, Dorena Reservoir is the gateway to the **Bohemia mining district** (see "Events" below) where there are old abandoned mines. Check the Cottage Grove Pioneer Museum (Birch and H streets; tel. 942-3963) for more information on these attractions or contact the Cottage Grove Chamber of Commerce (710 Row River Rd., Box 487, Cottage Grove 97424; tel. 942-2411). The ranger station in Cottage Grove (tel. 942-5591) has a map of a 70-mile Bohemia driving loop ("Tours of the Golden Past"), as well as updates on snow conditions.

An hour to the east of Fall Creek Reservoir off ORE 126 is **Cougar Reservoir and hot springs.** From Eugene go 42 miles on ORE 126 to the town of Blue River, then four miles down Forest Service Rd. 19 (paved) up to the west side of Cougar Reservoir. The springs can be reached by hiking to the end of a short trail. This trail overlooks a steep drop-off, so be care-

An angler tries his luck at Dorena Lake.

ful. The several pools in this tranquil forest setting can be overcrowded on weekends.

Off The Beaten Track
Along with the well-known hiking areas described above, the nearby Cascade and Coast ranges also have some recently developed hidden gems, thanks, paradoxically, to such extractive industries as logging and gravel. The industrial "cat" trails which once cut swaths through these forests are today maintained (and sometimes paved over) by the Forest Service for access to natural wonders. Two such places are Kentucky Falls and a grove of the tallest trees in the Northwest.

Picturesque **Kentucky Falls** is set in an old-growth forest on the upper slopes of the Coast Range. To get there from downtown Eugene, drive 35 miles west on ORE 126 to the Whiteaker Creek Recreation Area on the south side of the road, approximately six miles west of the Walton Store and post office. The route to Kentucky Falls winds through the clearcut lower slopes of 3,700-foot-high **Roman Nose Mountain** (the highest peak in this part of the Coast Range).

From Whiteaker Creek Recreation Area drive one mile south and make a right turn. Then in another one mile bear left on Dunn Ridge Rd. (Forest Service Rd. 18-8-28). In about seven miles you'll turn left onto a back road to Reedsport (Forest Service Rd. 19-9-13). Several miles later veer right onto Forest Service Rd. 23 and go about one mile to Forest Service Rd. 2300-919. Several miles later, you'll arrive at the Kentucky Falls trailhead, marked by a sign on the left side of the road. An old-growth Douglas-fir forest on gently rolling hills for the first half mile gives way to a steep descent into a lush canyon. The upper falls is visible a little over a mile down the trail. You'll hear the water before you actually get a full cross section of a broad cascade pouring out from over the rim of this green canyon. On your drive back to ORE 126, retrace your route carefully to avoid veering off on a hair-raising spur route to Mapleton.

A chance to see what may be the **Northwest's tallest trees** is possible northeast of **Lowell.** This recently discovered grove's 500-year-old Douglas firs average close to 300 feet in height. The tallest tree has been measured at 322 feet, which places it in the rarefied atmosphere of the giant sequoia. Be sure to take along a forest map from the Lowell Ranger Station (Lowell 97452; tel. 937-2129) or the Forest Service headquarters in Eugene (211 E. Seventh Ave.; tel. 687-6521).

To get there from Eugene, take ORE 58 to Lowell. From Lowell, follow Jasper-Lowell Rd. two miles to the Unity Covered Bridge and turn right onto Big Fall Creek Road. Proceed down Big Fall Creek Rd. for 11 miles, to where it becomes Forest Service Rd. 18. Turn left onto Forest Service Rd. 1817 and continue on for 10 miles until you reach Forest Service Rd. 1806, at which point you will turn left. Go down 1806 for three miles and then turn left onto Forest Service Rd. 427. The trailhead is a half mile down the road on the left-hand side, but park on the right.

Sports Facilities And Outdoor Programs

The U of O and Eugene Parks and Recreation provide the community with a wide-ranging smorgasbord of recreational facilities and programs.

University sport facilities are open to the public year-round for $2 per day. Covered tennis courts and racquetball courts are found on 15th Ave., east of the physical education building. There are also gyms, weight rooms, a swimming pool, and more racquetball courts inside the physical education building. Pick up schedule information at the physical education building on the corner of University and 15th or at the U of O recreation desk (103 Gerlinger Hall; tel. 346-4113).

Headquarters for the **U of O Outdoor Program** (tel. 346-4365) is located in a southeast-corner basement room of the Erb Memorial Union (corner of 13th and University), festooned with maps, photos, and bulletins covering every sport from biking to bungee jumping. The program sponsors more whitewater activities than any other group in town, as well as backpacking trips outside the state to supplement area hikes. Outings are run on a cooperative shared-expense basis with the participants customizing the trip to their needs. In addition to these activities, you can also connect with people on your own through the office exchange bulletin board. The Outdoor Program also has camping equipment to loan for free. In addition, it's an excellent resource center for statewide travel information, with books, maps, pamphlets, and videos about Oregon wilderness locales and outdoor activities. You're privy to all this and more for a $5 membership fee.

Eugene Parks and Recreation (22 W. Seventh Ave.; tel. 687-5333) puts out free seasonal publications about their offerings, which include bus tours, hikes, arts and special-interest classes, as well as a heavy dose of fitness activities. These are largely coordinated through four community centers wherein staffed recreational facilities and bulletin boards offer programs for all ages. Sports equipment is rented inexpensively out of these offices. Especially popular are the pools and fitness centers at **Echo Hollow** (1560 Echo Hollow Rd.; tel. 687-5525) and **Sheldon** (2445 Willakenzie Rd.; tel. 687-5314). The drop-in user fee is $2, and a one-month pass is available for $25. These pools have fitness centers equipped with weights and exercise paraphernalia. Consult Parks and

Recreation literature or call for the schedule.

Lane County Ice (Lane County Fairgrounds, 13th and Monroe, Eugene; tel. 687-4ICE) offers ice-skating lessons and open public skating. Admission is $3 and adult skate rental is $3, $2 for students.

Bike rentals are available from a dozen different outlets. One store, **Collins Bike Shop** (60 E. 11th; tel. 342-4878), also has a TRIS display terminal (see the general Introduction) enabling bikers and hikers to gain access to info on trail conditions everywhere in the state at no cost.

Golf

Laurelwood Golf Course (2700 Columbia St., Eugene; tel. 687-5521 for info, or 484-4653 for tee times) is a city-owned regulation-length golf course. Greens fee (around $12) and rentals are reasonable, and there's a 250-yard driving range here.

Of the many courses in Lane County, **Tokatee** (54947 ORE 126, Blue River; tel. 822-3220 or 800-452-6376) is the best. In fact, *Golf Digest* once rated it among the top 25 courses in the nation, and *Back Nine* rated it the best public course in the Pacific Northwest. To get there, drive 47 miles east of Eugene on the McKenzie Highway (ORE 126). The 18 holes here are set in a mountainous landscape patrolled by elk and other forest creatures. It's always a good idea to call ahead for reservations.

Tennis, Jogging, And Horseback Riding

Of the many public tennis courts throughout Eugene, the best-lit facilities are at the U of O and at 24th and Amazon Parkway near Roosevelt Middle School.

Near the Amazon courts, runners will enjoy the bark-o-mulch trail that follows Amazon Creek in a one-mile loop. The best jogging of all, however, is found at the four-mile **Prefontaine Trail** along the Willamette River east of Alton Baker Park. Named after Steve Prefontaine, whose world-record times and finishing kicks used to rock the Hayward Field grandstands before his untimely death in 1975, this soft path meanders along the river not far from the university. To get there, follow the bikepath from Alton Baker Park east toward Springfield. Another route is the road behind Oregon West Fitness (1475

Franklin Blvd.) that's closed off to motorized traffic. This leads to the footbridge that takes bikers, hikers, and joggers to the Prefontaine Trail, Willamette bikepath, Autzen Stadium, and other facilities found along the Willamette River Greenway. Exercise equipment can break up your run on the "par course" section of the Prefontaine Trail.

If you're more interested in taking to the trails on your trusty steed, **Bow Wow Ranch** (33435 Van Duym Rd.; tel. 345-5643) is located off I-5 at exit 199, four miles north of Beltline Highway. Rentals and lessons are also available at **Pruitt's Equestrian Center** (83260 Rattlesnake Rd., Crow; tel. 726-1545) southwest of Eugene. Call ahead for schedule and reservations.

ENTERTAINMENT

Keeping up with Eugene's multifaceted entertainment offerings involves previewing the listings put out by two local newspapers, the weekly *What's Happening* and the daily *Eugene Register Guard*. Calling the U of O ticket office for athletic event information (tel. 346-4461) and reading the bulletin boards on the ground floor of the Fifth Street Public Market or at Sundance Natural Foods can supplement these sources.

Spectator Sports

Each spring, the U of O track team, a perennial contender for the best team in the nation, has meets at **Hayward Field** (Agate and 15th Avenue). This site has hosted world-class events like the NCAA Finals and the United States Olympic Trials in addition to the U of O schedule. Track fans come here each June to enjoy the **Twilight Meet,** in which the elite of the sport compete. Tickets to all U of O sporting events will usually cost you a little more than seeing a first-run movie, but at least the money goes toward a fine educational institution.

Fall means Duck football at **Autzen Stadium** (Centennial Blvd. on Day Island). To get there, head north on Ferry Street. Just after crossing the Willamette River, take a hard right on Centennial Boulevard. The U of O football team has produced several NFL players of note, including Dan Fouts, Chris Miller, and Ahmad Rashad. In winter, the townsfolk cram into

MacArthur Court, located just south of the physical education building on University St., which is a funky anachronism from 1939, the year the Ducks won the first NCAA basketball championship. Even if you're not a fan, you're bound to get caught up in the frenzied decibels of "quacker backers" who support a team known for its never-say-die attitude.

In summer, the **Eugene Emeralds** play ball at Civic Stadium (2077 Willamette St.; tel. 342-5367) for honor, glory, and a chance to break into the big leagues. This Class-A team is most famous for once having all-time great Mike Schmidt on its roster and for serving some of the best concession food you'll ever taste at a ballpark. Barbecued chicken along with hot dogs and burgers are grilled outside, and microbrews are on hand to help wash it all down. Tickets cost $3.50 for adults, $2 for kids. Come Fourth of July to see the best fireworks display in town (or watch it free from Amazon Park or College Hill).

Dancing And Music
If you tire of watching other folks in action, the best spot for frenetic dancing in town is the **W.O.W. Hall** (291 W. Eighth Ave.; tel. 687-2746). This old Wobblie (International Workers of the World) meeting hall has remained as a monument to Oregon's activist past in labor history. Despite having all the ambience of a junior-high-school gym, it hosts some surprisingly big names, including the likes of Queen Ida, Taj Mahal, and other venerated rock, roots, and blues performers. The W.O.W. bills itself as having the best hardwood dance floor in the Pacific Northwest. In any case, it's probably the most crowded and features an interesting cross section of Eugenians. Beer and wine are served downstairs.

Another major concert venue featuring dancing to live bands is the **Erb Memorial Union Ballroom** (13th and University; tel. 346-4000, tickets tel. 346-4362). Local-guy-who-made-good Robert Cray, Los Lobos, and other nationally known performers have played here. The dance floor is more spacious than the W.O.W. Hall's but can actually exceed its downtown counterpart in BTUs generated by the mass of writhing bodies.

The **Eugene Hilton Ballroom** (66 E. Sixth Ave.; tel. 342-2000) also hosts big names, including John Lee Hooker, Asleep at the Wheel, and other acts running the gamut of popular music. For more sedate listening, the **Hult Center** (see "Sights" above) is next door to the Hilton. The Eugene Symphony, under the dynamic direction of Marin Alsop, and other estimable local groups like the Chamber Singers perform here along with a wide-ranging array that has included the Neville Brothers, George Winston, Merle Haggard, Andre Watts, and George Carlin. The Hult Center's summer series, **Eugene Festival of Musical Theater** (834 Pearl, Suite 240; tel. 345-0028), puts on shows like *The King and I* and *Peter Pan* under the direction of Ed Ragazzino. At Christmastime, the *Nutcracker* is always a treat at the Hult.

Live jazz in the basement of **Jo Frederigo's** (295 E. Fifth Ave.; tel. 343-8488) is made more enjoyable by crayons, paper, and one of their famous Long Island iced teas. Decent Italian food is served upstairs.

Down the block, the **Oregon Electric Station Restaurant and Lounge** (Fifth and Willamette; tel. 485-4444) hosts live jazz and rhythm-and-blues acts. This historic landmark features excellent dinner (best prime rib in town) and lunch entrees, a full bar, as well as a back room with couches, wing chairs, and the ambience of an English club. Opposite the Electric Station and the downtown post office, **Delbert's Cafe** (525 Willamette; tel. 342-5234) serves up tasty soups, light entrees, baked items, and espresso. The adjoining branch of Smith Family Bookstore and live folk music in the evening are other attractions.

In the same neighborhood, **Allan Brothers Coffeehouse and Bakery** (152 W. Fifth Ave.; tel. 342-3378) has live folk and blues at night and the same excellent coffee as its Corvallis outlets. This spacious coffeehouse is in a charming old building across from the Lane County Jail and attracts everyone from off-duty cops to madmen playing speed chess. Home-baked goodies and breakfast, lunch, and dinner entrees can be ordered at the counter.

Another coffeehouse hangout is the **Coffee Corner** (28th and Oak; tel. 342-7238). The entertainment might be limited to an occasional magician or pianist, the coffee prices may be a tad higher than elsewhere, but there's a bright cheery ambience thanks to windows on all sides and a staff that dispenses good vibes along with cups of ambition. In addition to quality java, this place is quietly one of the better places to eat in town. The Mexican scramble for breakfast ($4.75) is filling, and the fresh fish, quiche, and homemade soup during the rest of the day are top-notch. Leave room for dessert.

Closer to campus is **Taylor's College Side Inn** (894 E. 13th Ave.), situated directly opposite the academic buildings and the university bookstore. Quality blues acts frequently take the stage here, but local bands of different genres also show up. A dance floor, a big-screen cable hookup, espresso drinks, and a selection of microbrews are other enticements. In addition, expensive but substantial burgers, sandwiches, soups, and breakfast fare will also help you bop till you drop. The $2 or $3 cover here is well worth it. Another campus hangout is **New Max's Tavern** (550 E. 13th Avenue). Reggae and new-wave acts often pop up here, with $2 or $3 asked at the door.

Two of the "in" places to be out are **Good Times Cafe and Bar** (375 E. Seventh Ave.) and **Harpo's** (211 Washington Street). Both are blues-oriented, though Harpo's leans more toward rock and heavy metal. An admission of $3 is commonly charged at both establishments.

Theaters

While there's no shortage of movie screens in this town, the real cinematic gems are usually found at the university (consult the *Oregon Daily Emerald,* the U of O student newspaper, which is distributed free at Fifth Street Market, the U of O Bookstore, and Sundance Natural Foods) and the **Bijou Theatre** (492 E. 13th Ave., Eugene; tel. 686-2458). The university series favors cult films and classics *(Yellow Submarine, The Last Wave, The Bicycle Thief, King of Hearts,* etc.) and the $1-2 admission helps you forget the oppressiveness of the lecture halls that serve as theaters. The Bijou is the place to see foreign films, art flicks, and less commercial mainstream movies. This old converted church is intimate, and has great munchies and late-night presentations.

If you want first-run motion pictures, chances are you can find whatever flick you're looking for at **Movies 12** (Gateway Mall, 2850 Gateway St., Springfield; tel. 741-1231). A dozen features, a $5 admission for adults, $3 for children, and discounted admissions before 6 p.m. make this Eugene's leading moviehouse.

ACCOMMODATIONS

A few bed and breakfasts and an AYH hostel provide the best values for the dollar in town. Seniors, however, can use various discount cards (AARP et al.) to offset the high prices of such upscale accommodations as the Valley River Inn and the Eugene Hilton. Otherwise, you just have a choice of cheap motels on E. Broadway, moderately priced ones on Franklin Blvd., as well as others detailed in the accomodations chart. The best bets for the budget traveler are the campsites and rustic digs east of town on the McKenzie River Highway (see "ORE 126—The McKenzie River Highway" in "The High Cascades" chapter, following).

The Eugene-area hostel is located at **Lost Valley Center** (81868 Lost Valley Ln., Dexter 97431; tel. 937-3351), a 25-minute drive on ORE 58. This four-bed facility is open 24 hours a day and features environmental programs. In downtown Eugene, more information on the hostel as well as other resources is available at the **Hostelling International Travel Center** (311 E. 11th St.; tel. 683-3685).

Visiting parents of U of O students, college lecturers, and folks willing to spend a little for quality head for the **Campus Cottage Bed and Breakfast** (1136 E. 19th Ave.; tel. 342-5346). Bedroom amenities like down comforters, antiques, and fresh flowers are in keeping with rates of around $75 a night. The three bedrooms have private baths, and guests can also enjoy a living room with a fireplace, an outside deck, two cats, and a dog. A full breakfast of special egg dishes, fresh fruits, and pastries is included. As its name implies, the Campus Cottage is located one block south of the U of O.

Twenty minutes south of Eugene, **Ivanoff's Inn** (3101 Bennett Creek Rd., Cottage Grove; tel. 942-3171) is a more moderately priced alternative for those seeking the best of the country near the city. To get to Bennett Creek Rd., take the Cottage Grove exit off I-5. This will run into ORE 99, which leads into River Rd. in a quarter mile. Bennett Creek is an eighth of a mile down on the right. Beautiful trees and lush greenery line Bennett Creek Rd., which is paralleled by the Hidden Valley Golf Course on one side and hills leading up to the Willamette National Forest on the other. Ivanoff's is set on five hilly acres with forested trails. These appealing surroundings are only five minutes (three miles) from Cottage Grove downtown shopping and close to covered bridges and the Bohemia

EUGENE ACCOMMODATIONS

Angus Inn Motel, 2121 Franklin Blvd., tel. 342-1243, $40-55, cable TV, wheelchair access, pool, restaurant/lounge, exercise room, nonsmoking rooms.

Barron's Motor Inn, 1859 Franklin Blvd., tel. 342-6383, $42-52, cable TV, wheelchair access, pets, restaurant/lounge.

Best Western Greentree Motel, 1759 Franklin Blvd., tel. 485-2727, $55-70, cable TV, wheelchair access, pets, restaurant/lounge, pool.

Best Western New Oregon Motel, 1655 Franklin Blvd., tel. 683-3669, $55-70, cable TV, wheelchair access, pets, restaurant/lounge, covered pool, laundry, nonsmoking rooms.

Budget Host Motor Inn, 1190 W. 6th Ave., tel. 342-7273, $25-30, cable TV, pets, nonsmoking rooms.

Campus Inn, 390 E. Broadway, tel. 343-3376, $40-50, cable TV, wheelchair access, pool, pets, nonsmoking rooms.

Downtown Motel, 361 W. 7th Ave., tel. 345-8739, $35-42, laundry, nonsmoking rooms, complimentary continental breakfast.

Eugene Motor Lodge, 476 E. Broadway, tel. 344-5233, $30-35, cable TV, pool, kitchenettes, nonsmoking rooms.

Eugene Travelers Inn, 540 E. Broadway, tel. 342-1109, $35-40, cable TV, pool, pets, nonsmoking rooms.

Executive House Motel, 1040 W. 6th Ave., tel. 683-4000, $30-50, cable TV, nonsmoking rooms.

Franklin Inn, 1857 Franklin Blvd., tel. 342-4804, $36-48, cable TV, restaurant, kitchenettes, pets, nonsmoking rooms, complimentary continental breakfast.

Motel Six, 3690 Glenwood Drive., tel. 687-2395, $25-35, cable TV.

Nendels Inn, 3540 Gateway St., tel. 726-1212, $55-100, wheelchair access, pets, restaurant/lounge, pool, laundry, live entertainment, nonsmoking rooms.

Pacific Nine Motor Inn, (Springfield), 3550 Gateway St., tel. 726-9266, $30-35, cable TV, wheelchair access, pool.

Red Carpet Motel, 1055 W. 6th Ave., tel. 345-0579, $25-30, cable TV.

Red Lion Inn Eugene, 205 Coburg Rd., tel. 342-5201, $78-86, cable TV, wheelchair access, pets, restaurant/lounge, pool, live entertainment, nonsmoking rooms.

Red Lion Inn, Eugene/Springfield, 3280 Gateway St., tel. 726-8181, $75-285, cable TV, pool, restaurant/lounge, tennis courts, nonsmoking rooms.

Shilo Inn, (Springfield), 3350 Gateway St., tel. 747-0332, $50-60, cable TV, wheelchair access, pets, restaurant/lounge, pool, laundry, nonsmoking rooms, complimentary continental breakfast.

Sixty Six Motel, 755 E. Broadway, tel. 342-5041, $28-35, cable TV, nonsmoking rooms.

Timbers Motel, 1015 Pearl St., tel. 343-3345, $30-35, cable TV, pets, nonsmoking rooms.

Valley River Inn, 1000 Valley River Way, tel. 687-0123, $98-140, wheelchair access, restaurant/lounge, pool, sauna, Jacuzzi, nonsmoking rooms, river view.

EUGENE BED AND BREAKFAST

B & G's Bed and Breakfast, 711 W. 11th Ave., tel. 343-5739, $39-59, cable TV, lunch/dinner available, laundry, nonsmoking rooms, breakfast included.

Campus Cottage Bed and Breakfast Inn, 1136 E. 19th Ave., tel. 342-5346, $78-93, meals available, fireplace, nonsmoking rooms.

Lorane Valley Bed and Breakfast, 86621 Lorane Hwy., tel. 686-0241, $69-79, wheelchair access, meals available, nonsmoking rooms.

Shelly's Guest House Bed and Breakfast, 1546 Charnelton St., tel. 683-2062, $55-65, meals available, fireplace, cable TV, laundry.

Wheeler's Bed and Breakfast (Coburg), 404 E. McKenzie, tel. 344-2276, $40-50, cable TV, lunch/dinner available, pets, laundry, nonsmoking rooms, breakfast included.

mining country (see "Dorena Reservoir"). Three rooms (one with private bath) range from $60 to $70 a night. This includes a full breakfast featuring Swedish specialties.

Eugene-area Camping

If you're looking for campsites in the covered-bridge country above Cottage Grove try **Baker Bay,** which has 54 sites at $7 per night. Located approximately 18 miles from Eugene; get there by I-5 south to Mosby Creek Rd. (take the Cottage Grove exit), turn left, then left again on Row River Rd., then take the right fork.

Near the quaint town of Coburg north of Eugene is a **KOA Kampground** (tel. 343-4832). Take the Coburg exit off I-5 and head west and you'll find the KOA a mile or so down the road. Twelve bucks a night buys a tent site for two people; $14.50 is charged for a vehicle hookup.

Between the coast and the Oregon Country Fair grounds, **Triangle Lake Park** (tel. 927-6189) has three sites for $5 a night. Proceed 25 miles west from the fairgrounds on ORE 126. Take a right onto Poodle Creek Rd., then a left on ORE 36 to Triangle Lake. You'll find the campsites just after the lake.

Whiteaker Creek near Kentucky Falls (see "Off The Beaten Track" above) has 30 sites at $4 per night. Take ORE 126 30 miles west of Eugene. Turn left one mile past Wildcat Creek Bridge six miles east of Mapleton.

Close to the Oregon Country Fair is **Fern Ridge Shores** (tel. 935-2335), located in a quiet family park 12 miles west of Eugene. Take Jeans Rd. off ORE 126 near Veneta. Unlike the other previously mentioned sites, reservations are not accepted. Campsites go for $12 per night; hookups are $14.

EUGENE CUISINE

While there are a number of good restaurants in Eugene, you'll probably be more impressed by the staggering array of locally made gourmet products and natural foods available at markets here. Whether it's Tsunami sushi, Toby's tofu pâté, or Euphoria chocolate truffles, it's not hard to find exotic munchies right on the grocer's shelves. Even less arcane local fare offers surprises as one taste of Nancy's honey yogurt, Humble bagels, Prince Puckler's ice cream, Genesis juice, or Metropol French bread will confirm. As you might have guessed, many of these delectables come free of chemicals and often with nutritional concerns foremost. Produce labels in many Eugene specialty food stores intone "fresh," "home-grown," and "organic" with the constancy of a mantra, and meat and poultry markets carry products that are rabinically pure. Not surprisingly, two of the nation's leading granola producers are headquartered here.

Two of the leading purveyors of Eugene cuisine began as hippie health-food stores around 20 years ago. Today, **Sundance Natural Foods** (748 E. 24th; tel. 345-6153) and the **Kiva** (125 W. 11th; tel. 342-8666) stock more than just grains, sprouts, and vitamins, and feature some of the best selections of wine and organic produce in the state. Such relatively recent arrivals upon the scene as **Friendly Foods** (2757 Friendly; tel. 688-3944) and **Oasis Fine Foods** (2489 Willamette; tel. 345-1014) have expanded the largely vegetarian inventory of their hippie forefathers with more meat and takeout items.

Campus Area
The eateries on the campus periphery are a cut above those found in most college towns. Start the day at **Campus Glenwood** (1340 Alder; tel. 687-0355) or at the southside **Glenwood** (2588 Willamette St.; tel. 687-8201). The menu is standard American breakfast fare, with a few entrees paying deference to eclectic college-town tastes. What they all have in common are large portions in the $5 range. Try the turkito, a turkey burrito with melted cheese that comes with hash browns, or various tofu dishes. Many folks will tell you that the huevos rancheros here are the best in town. You can also get good and reasonably priced lunches (like the veggie burger) and dinners (seasonal specials like fresh salmon) here.

If your tummy can only handle coffee and a croissant in the morning, head to **Espresso Roma** (825 E. 13th Ave.; tel. 484-4848) or **Fall Creek Bakery** (881 E. 13th Ave.; tel. 484-1662). Espresso Roma has a delightful outside courtyard which fills up when the rain stops. The Fall Creek Bakery is distinguished for award-winning cinnamon rolls and chocolate-chip cookies.

Oriental lunchtime favorites include combination lunch specials (dim sum on Sunday) at **China Blue** (879 E. 13th Ave., Eugene, tel. 343-2832; and 2307 N.W. 9th St., Corvallis, tel. 757-3088). The **Bamboo Pavilion** nearby could well be the best dollar value around thanks to huge portions for under $3. **Sy's New York Pizza** (1211 Alder; tel. 686-9598) would make his mentor, Original Ray's of New York, proud with a by-the-slice operation that lines 'em up at lunch and dinnertime.

Also in the shadow of the campus is one of the best restaurants in town, the **Excelsior Cafe** (754 E. 13th Ave.; tel. 485-1206). Set in a charming old colonial home, the menu changes monthly, highlighting what's in season. It can be spendy, but lighter "bistro dinners" and hors d'oeuvres let you appreciate the restaurant's innovative approaches to seafood, veal, game, and salads at cheaper prices. While lunch and dinner are served here every day, there's also a Sunday

brunch, and service till 2:30 a.m. on Saturday. Despite a reputation for fine food, it's their wonderful decadent assortment of desserts and cozy bar that pull in the lion's share of the clientele.

Up the street from the Excelsior, **Napoli** (686 E. 13th Ave.; tel. 485-4552) serves gourmet pizza, soups, pasta, and an array of baked goods and desserts (try the cannoli). Omelettes and frittatas give breakfast here an Italian flair.

Rennie's Landing (1214 Kincaid; tel. 687-0600) serves breakfast, gourmet burgers, homemade soups, beer, and wine. Late-night and predawn hours, a second-floor outside deck, and a location right across from the U of O campus make this a favorite with the campus crowd—particularly after Duck games.

Farther away from campus, the McMenamin brothers have two **brewpubs.** One is on the corner of Agate and 19th, the other at 1243 High St. (tel. 345-4905). Each repeats the successful formula of the establishments discussed in the Portland chapter. The High Street pub is ensconced in a comfy converted oak house, with a tree-shaded brickwork back patio that makes the perfect hangout on a hot afternoon.

Chez Ray's (1473 E. 19th Ave.; tel. 342-8596) is the brainchild of former Grateful Dead personal chef Ray Sewell. With dinners between $8 and $12 and such lunchtime entrees as salmon burgers and polenta lasagna, this little hole-in-the-wall behind the Hayward Field track is the perfect blend of sophisticated tastes, moderate prices, and friendly atmosphere. Close by, the **Gazebo Restaurant** (1646 E. 19th Ave.; tel 683-6661) has a bright, cheerful ambience and Middle Eastern specialties. While this is a great place for an intimate dinner, you can get the same dish for a slightly cheaper price at lunch.

Fifth Street Market Eateries
A local newspaper once gave the nod to **Terry's Diner** (Fifth Street Market; tel. 683-8190) for the best burgers and best omelettes (thanks to the lemon in the eggs, which makes them extra fluffy) in town. Old advertising billboards and jukebox tunes from the '50s, thick malteds that come in the metal mixing container, and laugh-a-minute waitresses stylishly reinvent the all-American diner for those born too late. Terry's is open for all meals till 10 p.m. except Sundays, when it closes at 6 p.m.

Upstairs in the market is **Mekala's** (tel. 342-4872). Despite elegant decor and exotic Thai dishes (try the duck, pad thai, any of the curries, and coconut ice cream for dessert), prices are reasonable. Because few people smoke in Eugene, request the smoking section for intimate dining and a window on Fifth Ave., a people-watching perch extraordinaire.

Downstairs in the market, **Casablanca** (tel. 342-3885) has Middle Eastern cuisine with pita sandwiches, babbaghanoush hummus, and other regional specialties. This restaurant was voted Eugene's favorite lunch spot in a local poll.

Downtown Dining

In the heart of downtown are two other popular restaurants. **Anatolia** (992 Willamette; tel. 343-9661) features Greek and Indian food par excellence. Spicy curries and vindaloo chicken are complemented by saganaki (fried cheese), spanakopita (spinach cheese pie), and gyro sandwiches here. The best baklava in town for dessert and a shot of ouzo or retsina can finish off a richly flavored and moderately priced repast. Folks who remember Poppi's, a fabled Greek taverna in the campus district that was forced to close when Sacred Heart hospital expanded, will especially relish Monday nights here when the menu of one of Eugene's all-time favorite restaurants is re-created. Anatolia's is quickly gaining the following of Poppi's, so get there early.

Dominating the first floor of the Atrium building, **De Frisco's** (99 W. 10th Ave.; tel. 494-2263) has built its reputation on the more than 20 microbrews, imports, and domestic beers it has on tap. A pool table and big-screen TV, a wall paneled with books, and live jazz on Wednesday nights also explain De Frisco's enthusiastic following. A variety of hearty soups and barbecued-chicken sandwiches are lunchtime mainstays here.

A few blocks east is downtown's gourmet gulch. Two places stand out from the pack. **Cafe Zenon** (898 Pearl St.; tel. 343-3005) has a multi-ethnic menu which is constantly changing. Despite this challenge, the Zenon manages to pull off dishes ranging from Italian to Thai in fine style. The only problems you'll run into here are getting in—reservations aren't taken and there's

often a wait—and getting out without stopping at the eye-popping dessert display.

Across the street is a spacious two-story Italian restaurant, **Ambrosia** (174 Broadway; tel. 342-4141). Antique furnishings and stained glass set the stage for Old World cuisine prepared to suit contemporary tastes. The individual-sized gourmet pizzas (cooked slowly in a wood-burning oven), a wonderful squid-in-batter appetizer, and northern Italian specialties will make spaghetti and meatballs seem like old hat here. Ambrosia restaurant was honored by *Wine Spectator* for having one of the most outstanding wine lists in the world.

Some of the best restaurant values are located on the fringes of downtown. On Fifth Ave., the **Keystone Cafe** (395 W. Fifth Ave., tel. 342-2075) is also known for huge portions, low prices, and its support of community activism. Home-style breakfast features eggs and potatoes and whole-grain pancakes. Highly recommended is the Mexican chorizo (a spicy sausage) made by a local butcher shop specializing in chemical-free meat. Mexican dinner specials on Friday and Saturday are particularly good. The chicken mole or chiles rellenos with black beans and rice are as tasty as you'll find in many area Mexican restaurants and only cost around $5.

Perhaps the busiest neighborhood during lunchtime is around Willamette and 16th. The biggest reason for this is the **French Horn** (1891 Willamette; tel. 343-7473). For $2.25, the restaurant's soup of the day with fresh French bread is the salvation of scores of people with little time and a taste for home cooking. Hot entrees and salads with homemade mayonnaise round out the menu. At breakfast, the $2 scrambled eggs come with your choice of additional ingredients (bacon, cheese, spinach, etc.), each 25 cents. The French Horn's baked goods are also scrumptious.

The large white colonial building down the street is the **Vets Club,** where you can sit in the same dimly lit vinyl booths where such visiting literati as William S. Burroughs, Gregory Corso, and Hunter S. Thompson have raised a glass with local writer/god Ken Kesey. Drinks here are inexpensive and quite strong.

A block south from the Vets Club on the corner of Willamette is **Euphoria Chocolate Co.** (6

W. 17th Ave.; tel. 343-9223), a chocolatier of national repute. Their Grand Marnier truffle and other confections are sold around town. Come here after holidays and buy the bite-size Santas, hearts, and bunnies at reduced price.

Though the corner of 15th and Willamette may not conjure up the "gunfight at the OK Corral," **Tino's** (tel. 342-8111) is fighting off a most unlikely challenger across the street. The **Pizza Stop** (1478 Willamette St.; tel. 345-4811), a small whole-grain bakery, has managed to commit the ultimate heresy and get away with it—a pizza with an organic whole-wheat crust that actually tastes good. Compounding the felony, condiments like artichoke hearts and chopped raw garlic grace these nontraditional pies. By contrast, Tino's straight-ahead approach emphasizing a crisp crust, copious amounts of cheese, and a low grease factor has made it a Eugene tradition for 40 years. If pizza isn't on your wish list, Tino's does a fine job on calzone and fresh pasta dishes. The Bread Stop is also known for sandwiches, microbrews, cookies, scones, and the ultimate survival food—hiker's bread. This yeast-free bread contains amaranth, which, when combined with other ingredients, provides a complete protein.

Beyond the downtown are three of Eugene's better restaurants. **Hilda's** (400 Blair Blvd.; tel. 343-4322) specializes in South American food. Brazilian marinated flank steak strips with black beans and rice typifies this hearty cuisine, reminiscent of Mexican cooking but not as hot or greasy. The restaurant is small enough to create long waits on weekends. **Tom's Tea House** (788 W. Seventh Ave.; tel. 343-7658) is *the* place for Szechuan and Hunan stir-fry. Kung pao chicken and mu shu pork are reliable choices here.

The **Valley River Inn's** (1000 Valley River Way, Valley River Center; tel. 687-0123) riverside outdoor deck might offer Eugene's most delightful dining experience on a warm summer night. The River Room's extensive menu draws largely on regional ingredients put together creatively to best bring out the flavors of mountain, valley, and coast. The lightly cooked vegetables, sautéed seafood, and other healthful fare seem to go with the Willamette River kayakers and shoreside joggers who whoosh by the dining patio. You can sip Oregon wines by

the glass or microbrews here if the moderate-to-upscale dinner prices are beyond your budget. Whatever you decide to do, take a sweater—it cools down fast here at night. Finally, leave room for the restaurant's marionberry cobbler.

Jazz Station (18th and Chambers; tel. 687-8157) sits on the edge of a shopping center parking lot remote from restaurant row on Willamette. Yet, the soups, salads, homemade bread, diverse dinner offers, gooey desserts, and great coffee of this informal bistro have more in common with its downtown counterparts than with the burger joints that surround it. And, as its name implies, the sound system provides a steady stream of tunes to enjoy it all by. Breakfasts and lunch also justify driving about a mile west of center city.

A few miles north of Jazz Station in an area some Eugeneans call Felony Flats is a local favorite. **New Day Bakery** (345 Van Buren; tel. 345-1695) serves filbert croissants, first-rate coffee, and the best turkey sandwiches in town.

EVENTS

There is a lot happening in this south Willamette Valley hub of culture and athletics. Several events, however, best impart the flavor of the area.

Oregon Bach Festival
Of these, only one enjoys international acclaim. The Oregon Bach Festival (write: U of O Music School, 18th Ave., Eugene 97403; tel 867-5000 for tickets, 346-5666 for business office) takes place over two weeks from late June into early July under the baton of famed Bach interpreter Helmut Rilling from Germany. *New York Times* critic Harold Schonberg once rated the festival the best of its kind in the country, and an influx of renowned visiting opera and symphonic virtuosi guarantees this will remain the case. Over two dozen separate concerts are featured, with musical styles ranging from the baroque era to the 20th century. Vocalist Bobby McFerrin, pianist Jeffrey Kahane and the Billy Taylor Jazz trio along with the Turtle Island String Quartet supplemented the festival's 1993 lineup of Bach instrumental virtuosi and opera singers. The centerpieces of the festival, however, are Bach

works like the *St. Matthew Passion,* numerous cantatas, and the Brandenburg Concertos.

Tickets range from $7 to $28, with performances taking place in the Hult Center and at the Beall Concert Hall at the U of O Music School. Free events, including "Let's talk with the conductor," mini-concerts, and children's activities take place at these venues during the festival. Particularly recommended is the festival's Discovery Series—eight concertos preceded by a short lecture-demo by Helmuth Rilling. Each 5 p.m. concert features a different Bach church cantata. Free noon concerts in the Hult lobby are also popular. The schedules are available at the U of O Music School and are also published in the *Eugene Register Guard* and *What's Happening.* A scheduled series of brunches, lunches, and dinners with the musicians also adds a special touch to the festival.

Appealing to lowbrow and highbrow alike is **Art in the Vineyard** (for info contact the Maude Kerns Art Gallery or the Eugene-Springfield Visitors and Convention Bureau, or call 223-8309), which generally takes place over the several days of the July 4 weekend in Alton Baker Park. This event brings together art, music, and wine in a tranquil park near the Willamette River. One hundred artists' booths and the offerings of a dozen vineyards frequently grace the affair, along with live music (jazz, country, blues, and folk) and food concessions. An admission of $2-5 is charged to yet another Eugene outdoor celebration of her cultural richness.

Oregon Country Fair

Just after the Bach Festival in late July, the Oregon Country Fair takes place (see callout) as the second major cultural event of the summer. There's no such thing as free love, but for $7-10 (kids 12 and under free, 55 and above are half price) you can buy a 1967 experience with a price to match. This annual fantasyland is staged among the trees west of Noti on ORE 126; for more information, contact the fair at Box 2972, Eugene 97402; tel 343-4298. Gates open at 11 a.m. and close at 7 p.m.

The best way to avoid traffic is to take the free shuttle from 13th and Monroe in Eugene, which goes directly to the wooded fair site near the Long Tom River. This shuttle emanates from the County Fairgrounds parking lot. Bus ser-

vice usually begins around 10:30 a.m., with the last departure from the fair site at 7 p.m. Car access to the fair is open 10 a.m.-6 p.m. Of special interest are the archaeology projects at the fair that detail the oldest known human presence documented in western Oregon, dating back 10,000 years.

Other Events

The fall is ushered in with the **Eugene Celebration.** This two-week fête in late September and early October includes such events as the mayor's Fine Art Show, readings by Oregon authors at the Hult Center, the Fifth Avenue Jazz Festival, and the coronation of the Slug Queen. Street performers all over town and food booths in the parking lot on Eighth Ave. and Willamette also help the community put its best foot forward. Contact the Eugene-Springfield Visitors and Convention Bureau for more details.

The university sponsors the **Eugene Folk Festival** (tel. 686-INFO) in the spring, which has attracted the likes of Tom Paxton and blues harpist James Cotton. Call for the schedule of the upcoming concerts. It generally takes place behind the student union on the second weekend of May.

On the second weekend in August, the **Junction City Scandinavian Festival** (Greenwood St., between Fifth and Seventh, Junction City) celebrates the town's Danish founders. Folk dancing, traditional crafts, and food make up the bulk of the activities. Skits of Hans Christian Andersen folk tales are enacted during the four-day event, along with guided bus tours into the city's Scandinavian past. The latter are hourlong tours and take you by Scandinavian pioneer farmsteads built in the 1800s. Tour tickets are available at the info windmill for $2.50. Swedish, Finnish, Norwegian, and Icelandic ethnicities also exert a presence in this festival. Junction City is 12 miles northwest of Eugene off ORE 99. Contact the local chamber of commerce (Box 3, Junction City 97484; tel. 998-6154) for more information on the festival. They can also tell you how to get to the mid-March **daffodil display** on Ferguson Road west of Junction City.

In the other direction from Eugene, **Bohemia Mining Days** (contact the Cottage Grove Chamber of Commerce, 710 Row River Rd., Box 587, Cottage Grove 97424; tel. 942-2411) convenes

OREGON COUNTRY FAIR

Time warp: 1969-1991

If you've been too busy to follow the growth of the '60s counterculture, put on your paisley and follow an eclectic caravan of handpainted schoolbuses, Volkswagen beetles, Volvos, and BMWs to the Oregon Country Fair.

After buying your ticket at the gatehouse, join the crowds of tie-dyed, fringed, and lovebeaded fairgoers. Entering, you wander through a kaleidoscope of natural fabrics, graceful ceramics, stained glass, rainbow candles, and thousands of other variously sculpted wares. Machine-manufactured items are simply unavailable. Every aspect of the fair, its booths, and participants is, in a sense, art.

What? Two hours gone by already? You need a cup of espresso and a piece of torte if you're going to make it through this day. Ah, the **Hilltop Bakery** is just around the corner with all the caffeine and sweet treats necessary. Or perhaps you want a **Rita's** burrito bulging with avocado, salsa, and sprouts. The choices are mouth-watering: get fried rice, Tsunami sushi, blazing salads, or even a tofuless tofu burger (100% ground beef), and more!

All fed and ready for a little entertainment? Overwhelmed by the constant parade of costumed stilt walkers, strolling musicians, winged "country fairies," children in face paint, bare-breasted women, and other ambient wonders? Not far from any burnout point is a stage.

Shady Grove is a quiet venue for acoustic folk, classical, new age, and other music.

The **Daredevil, W.C. Fields,** and **Energy Park** stages host contemporary New Vaudeville stars and other rollicking performances.

See the **Royale Famille du Carniveaux** debut a unique musical comedy.

Marvel as the **Reduced Shakespeare Company** performs *Romeo and Juliet* backwards in one minute flat.

Shake your head and mutter as **Up For Grabs** juggles circular sawblades and/or small children.

But wait, there's more. Try **The Circus** with its parade, orchestra, and veteran virtuosos. Ogle snake charmers and belly dancers at the **Gypsy Stage.** Or dance to the national and international stars of rock 'n' roll, reggae, and alternative music on the **Main Stage.**

Starting to sound less like a "hippie fair" and more like a well-catered and -established art convention? Don't worry; there's always a sojourn into geo-socio-political-eco-consciousness at **Community Village.** Several booths here and in **Energy Park** teach and demonstrate the latest in new and matured '60s activism and environmental awareness.

Tired already? So are we, but there's a whole year to rest up and reminisce before the next Oregon Country Fair.

To get there, head west from Eugene on ORE 126 and follow the signs. For additional information, contact the Oregon Country Fair, Box 2972, Eugene 97402; tel. 343-4298.

The Oregon Country Fair is where Renaissance-era arts and crafts meet Sixties activism and whimsy.

MARIA THOMAS

in mid-July. The five-day event is highlighted by the Prospector's Breakfast, gold-panning demonstrations, a half-marathon, a bake-off, a flower show, an ugly-dog contest, and other competitions. Many of the events take place at re-created **Bohemia City** near the chamber of commerce on Row River Road. Don't miss the Grand Miner's Parade, which happens on Saturday afternoon. Floats, horse teams, drill teams, and color guards make their way from Harrison Ave. to Row River Rd. with colorful costumes and the kind of enthusiasm last seen around here after turn-of-the-century lucky strikes.

PRACTICALITIES

Information And Services

The following list scratches the surface of Eugene's many service institutions and information outlets. A bevy of literature befitting Oregon's second-most-populated area can be obtained at the **Eugene-Springfield Visitors and Convention Bureau** (305 W. Seventh Ave.; tel. 484-5307 or 800-452-3670 in Oregon, 800-547-5445 outside Oregon).

Eugene Parks and Recreation has the following switchboard numbers: tel. 687-5333 for general information, 687-5360 for athletics, 431-5850 for arts, and 687-5311 for disabled recreation.

The **U of O Switchboard** (795 Willamette St.; tel. 346-3111) is a multipurpose referral line. Rides, housing, and emergencies can be taken care of Mon.-Fri. 8-5. The main **post office** is located at Fifth and Willamette (tel. 341-3611) and is open Mon.-Fri. 8-5, Sat. 9-noon.

Sacred Heart Hospital (1255 Hilyard; tel. 686-6962) is one of the leading institutions of its kind in the state. Emergency-room care is available 24 hours daily. A cheaper alternative is the **Whitebird Clinic** (341 12th Ave.; tel. 342-8255).

Across the street from Sacred Heart, the **Smith Family Bookstore** (768 E. 13th, tel. 345-1651; and 525 Willamette St., tel. 343-4717) is an excellent used-book store. The **U of O Bookstore** (13th and Kincaid) and the **Bookmart** (865 Olive; tel. 484-0512) have the best selection of new titles and periodicals. For travel books, you can't beat the **S.S. Adventure** (199 E. Fifth Ave.; tel. 485-7348). This store also carries U.S. Geological Survey maps and camping guides.

The **Eugene Public Library** (100 W. 13th; tel. 687-5450) has the most user-friendly periodicals section in the state.

Eugene's network of outdoor clubs and environmental organizations is extensive enough to preclude a thorough listing, but the vortex of the environmental community, the **U of O Survival Center** (Suite 1, Erb Memorial Union, U of O campus; tel. 346-4356), can steer you to the right adventure.

Club Wash, on the corner of 13th and Patterson, is a place to do laundry and cope with insomnia. Video games, munchies, espresso, a suntanning booth, and a big-screen TV offer ambience. Best of all, the machines, which do a load of wash for 50 cents (!), won't clean you out.

last-minute arrivals to the Oregon Bach Festival

JURETTA NIDEVER

Getting Around

Amtrak at Fourth and Willamette (tel. 485-1092), **Greyhound** at Ninth and Pearl (tel. 344-6265), and **Green Tortoise,** which picks up passengers in front of the U of O library at 15th and Kincaid (tel. 937-3603), are the major modes of long-distance public transport. Tortoise fares are the lowest to San Francisco ($49) and L.A. ($69). The northbound bus leaves at 1:15 p.m., the southern route departs at 3:45 p.m. Consult the general Introduction for info on days of service and other considerations.

Around town, **Lane Transit District** (tel. 687-5555) has canopied pavilions displaying the bus timetables downtown. Their business office on 10th and Willamette has pocket-sized schedules. Fares are 75 cents (children and seniors half price) and about a third less on weekends. The **ride board** on the bottom floor of the Erb Memorial Union at the U of O has a list of rides available for those willing to share gas and driving. **Emerald Taxi** (tel. 686-2010) is fast, reliable, and reasonably priced.

If you're in your own car, just remember that (1) the campus is in the southeastern part of town; (2) First Ave. parallels the Willamette River; and (3)Willamette St. divides the city east and west. The downtown mall, which encompasses the area between Sixth through 11th streets (north to south) and Pearl through Charnelton (east to west) allows through traffic north or south via Olive street. Navigation is complicated by many one-way roads and dead ends. Look for alleyways that allow through traffic, to avoid getting stuck.

The Eugene **airport** (tel. 687-5430) is a 20-minute drive northwest from downtown. Just get on the Delta Highway off Washington St. and follow the signs. It's served by Alaska (tel. 800-426-0333), American (tel. 800-547-7000), Northwest (tel. 800-692-7000), United and United Express (tel. 800-241-6552), and U.S. Air (tel. 800-428-

4322). Transfers to Portland are available through Horizon (1-800-547-9308). This new facility has food service on the second floor. The Sunday *Register Guard* lists the lowest fares to and from Eugene.

Media

Public radio stations are all clustered near the bottom of the FM dial, with the dominant presence being KLCC (89.7 FM). The station's programming ranges from new-wave jazz and "Blues Power" (Saturday afternoons) to a dynamic news department. On Saturday nights, 5-8 p.m., the campus and countercultural communities tune in to three hours of all-Grateful Dead programming. The University of Oregon station KWAX (90.1 FM) can be heard in eastern Oregon and on the coast and provides continuous classical music. Perhaps the most popular radio show in the area is KUGN (590 AM) morning show, which mixes news and local gossip with good music of different genres.

What's Happening (1251 Lincoln St.; tel. 484-0519) has the best entertainment listings in Eugene. This publication is available free at commercial establishments all over town.

A rundown of Eugene's ever-expanding list of live music venues, concert dates, reviews, etc. is available in a free monthly, *Music News,* available in commercial outlets around town.

The *Eugene Register Guard* (975 High St.; tel. 485-1234) was mentioned in the general Introduction. Travelers should especially look for *Guard* columnist Mike Thoele's coverage of offbeat Oregon locales, personalities, and local color. These in-depth profiles convey what is special about Oregon, contributing to the newcomer's sense of place as well as to Oregonians' understanding of their own state. While the column appears sporadically, you can catch up on Thoele's previous columns in an anthology, *Footprints Across Oregon* (Portland: Graphic Arts Center Publishing Co., 1988).

SOUTHERN OREGON

South of the Willamette Valley and west of the Cascades is a corridor of the state most residents call southern Oregon. To be more precise, this label refers to cities along Interstate 5 below Cottage Grove as well as towns in the shadow of the Siskiyou Mountains' eastern flank. What the Coast Range is to the Willamette Valley, the Siskiyou's rugged V-shaped canyons, wild rivers, and serpentine rock formations are to southern Oregon. The outstanding features of this region include world-class kulturfests, the biggest chunk of remaining wilderness on the Pacific coast, and California retirees who've come in search of cheap real estate and more sun than they'll see anywhere else west of the Cascades.

Initially it was gold finds on the Rogue River which drew prospectors into the territory in the 1850s. Settlers following the Applegate Trail, a southern alternative to the Oregon Trail, also migrated here around this time. A stagecoach line in the 1870s and a railroad a decade later established commerce with California markets. Forest products, orchard crops, and precious metals went south on these modes of transport until interstate trucking supplanted the iron horse in the 1930s.

Recently, attention has been focused on the northern part of the Siskiyou range and its 440,000 acres of old-growth Douglas fir. Many timber company contracts to clearcut these trees are being contested by environmental groups. The environmentalists claim that the forest represents one of the world's most botanically diverse regions—with eight different soil types and more living matter per hectare than any other forest on the planet. As always, timber companies see the trees as a renewable resource and suggest that logging would create minimal damage to the ecosystem.

The region is no stranger to activism and aberration in general. Back-to-the-land refugees came into the tiny hamlet of Takilma on the Smith River to pursue alternative life-styles decades ago and are still keeping the dream alive. So-called survivalists have chosen the Rogue Valley as the place to make their last stand in the Armageddon they say is inevitable. Several religious and new-age communities have also established themselves here.

SOUTHERN OREGON

TO EUGENE
OAKLAND
5
STEAMBOAT
BOULDER CREEK WILDERNESS
GLIDE
NORTH UMPQUA RIVER
LOOKINGGLASS
138
TO CRATER LAKE & DIAMOND LAKE
ROSEBURG
WILDLIFE SAFARI
99
ROGUE - UMPQUA DIVIDE WILDERNESS
42
TO COOS BAY
TO DIAMOND LAKE
230
SOUTH UMPQUA RIVER
UNION CREEK
62
CANYON CREEK PASS (ELEV. 2,020 ft.)
TO CRATER LAKE
STAGE ROAD PASS (ELEV. 1,830 ft.)
WOLF CREEK
WOLF CREEK
PROSPECT
LOST CREEK RESERVOIR
GRAVE CREEK
SHADY COVE
JOSEPH H. STEWART STATE PARK
GALICE
MERLIN
GALICE RD
RIVER
62
TO AGNESS
MERLIN
GRANTS PASS
ROGUE RIVER
ROGUE
RIVER
MT. McLOUGHLIN (ELEV. 9,495 ft.)
99
140
199
TO KLAMATH FALLS
FISH LAKE
APPLEGATE RIVER
SUMMIT (ELEV. 5,105 ft.)
JACKSONVILLE
MEDFORD
DEAD INDIAN CREEK
0   10mi
0   10km
238
238
HOWARD LAKE PRAIRIE COUNTY PARK
CAVE JUNCTION
99
HYATT RESERVOIR
ASHLAND
EMIGRANT RESERVOIR
OREGON CAVES NAT'L MONUMENT
SISKIYOU MOUNTAINS
MT. ASHLAND (ELEV. 7,523 ft.)
66
PARKER MTN. SUMMIT (ELEV. 4,362 ft.)
APPLEGATE LAKE
TO KLAMATH FALLS
OREGON
CALIFORNIA
SISKIYOU SUMMIT (ELEV. 4,310 ft.)
TO EUREKA
TO REDDING
5

© MOON PUBLICATIONS, INC.

Adding to this eclectic mix are whitewater rafters, fishermen, and culture vultures drawn to southern Oregon's Shakespeare Festival in Ashland and the Peter Britt Music Festival in Jacksonville. Travelers enjoy this dynamic region, where Oregon's past, present, and future come together.

ASHLAND AND VICINITY

With the possible exceptions of Stratford-upon-Avon and its Shakespeare presentations, and Oberammergau, Germany, and its passion play, there is no town so closely identified with a cultural event as Ashland and the Oregon Shakespeare Festival. You can immediately sense that this is not just another timber town from a Tudor-style McDonald's and some of the highest prices you'll encounter anywhere in the state (the average Ashland home price in 1991 was $132,000). The newcomer will also be struck by the dearth of neon and obtrusive signs in this population center of 18,000 people. Theater tickets are the coin of the realm here, with contemporary classics and off-off-Broadway joining presentations of the Old Bard.

Blessed with a bucolic setting between the Siskiyous and the Cascades, Ashland embodies the spirit of the Chautauqua movement of a century ago, which was dedicated to bringing culture to the rural hinterlands. Up until the 1930s, however, entertainment was mostly confined to the traveling vaudeville shows that came into the Ashland/Jacksonville area to entertain the residents of a gold-rush country in decline. Then Southern Oregon University started up the Shakespeare Festival under the direction of Professor Angus Bowmer. Such noted thespians as George Peppard, Stacey Keach, and William Hurt have graced Ashland's stages early in their careers, and the festival has garnered its share of Tonys and other awards.

Ashland's tourist economy is also sustained by an auspicious location roughly equidistant between Seattle and San Francisco. Closer to home, day-trips to Crater Lake, Rogue River country, and the southern Oregon coast have joined the tradition of "stay four days, see four plays" as a major part of Ashland's appeal.

SIGHTS AND DAY-TRIPS

Lithia Park

The centerpiece of Ashland is Lithia Park. Recognized as a National Historic Site, the park was designed by John McLaren, landscape architect of San Francisco's Golden Gate Park. A walk through 100-acre Lithia Park along Winburne Way's beautiful tree-shaded trail is a must on any itinerary here. This footpath and a scenic drive through the park start west of the Lithia Fountain. Redwoods, Port Orford cedar, and other species line the drive, which takes you along Ashland Creek to the base of the Siskiyous. The park owes its existence to Jesse Winburne, who made a fortune from advertising on the New York subways and tried to develop a spa around Ashland's Lithia Springs, which he said rivaled the venerated waters of Saratoga Springs, New York. Although the spa never caught on due to the Depression, Winburne was nevertheless instrumental in landscaping Lithia Park with one of the most varied collections of trees and shrubs of any park in the state. Winburne was also responsible for piping the famous Lithia water to the plaza fountains so all might enjoy its beneficial minerals. While many visitors find this slightly sulfurous, effervescent water a bit hard to swallow, many locals have acquired a taste for Ashland's acerbic answer to Perrier and happily chugalug it down.

The hub of the park in the summer months is the Bandshell, where concerts, ballets, and silent movies are shown. Children love to play at the playgrounds or feed the ducks in the ponds. Big kids enjoy tennis, volleyball, horseshoes, or traversing one of the many trails in the park. Every Tuesday on Water St. next to Lithia Creek the **Farmer's Market** is held. Rogue Valley farmers, craftspeople, and ranchers sell arts and crafts, fruit and produce, and dried flowers.

Another way to enjoy the park is by taking a nostalgic ride through it in a horse-drawn carriage. **Lithia Carriage Company** (tel. 482-5319) offers 25-minute excursions that begin at the information booth on the plaza near the park entrance.

Schneider Museum Of Art

The Schneider Museum of Art (Southern Oregon State College campus, Ashland; tel. 482-6245) features contemporary artforms from national and international artists. Hours are Tues.-Fri. 11 a.m.-5 p.m., Sat. 1-5 p.m.

Up, Up, And Away

Rogue Valley Balloon Flights (474 N. Main; tel. 855-1290) takes up to four passengers on an hour-long excursion high over the Rogue River Valley. Lift-off is shortly after dawn, but you'll be wide awake as you soar skyward with your FAA-approved pilots and aircraft. The valley wind blows gently one way, then gradually changes direction as the earth is warmed by the heat of the sun. A ground chase crew follows the balloon at all times, just in case the thermals are a little uncooperative that morning. Bring your Visa or MasterCard, because this is a spendy sort of attraction at well over $100 a person. Reservations required.

A slightly cheaper alternative to lighter-than-air-craft is a 30-minute flight over the valley in a vintage biplane with **Ashland Air** (403 Dead Indian Rd.; tel. 488-1626). The planes may be old-fashioned, but they are newly built and equipped with the latest in modern technology to ensure that your trip is both safe and enjoyable. Flightseeing includes downtown Ashland and Lithia Park, Emigrant Reservoir, and Pilot Rock.

To get to the airstrip, go a mile past the Ashland Hills Inn on ORE 66. Be sure to call ahead for reservations.

Day-trips

Jackson Hot Springs (ORE 99; tel. 482-3776) is two miles north of Ashland on the old highway and has a naturally heated public swimming pool as well as private mineral baths. Lighted tennis courts are found in Lithia Park, Hunter Park (on Summit St.), and on the Southern Oregon State College campus.

Meyer Memorial Pool (Hunter Park, Summit St., Ashland 97520; tel. 488-0313) includes a wading pool for infants and toddlers under age five, as well as a large swimming pool for grown-ups. The season kicks off with a splash Memorial Day weekend with lap and open swimming sessions Sat. and Sun. 1-6 p.m. Summer hours start mid-June with open swimming Mon.-Fri. 1:30-4:45 p.m., Mon. and Wed. 7:30-8:45 p.m., and the regular weekend hours of 1-6 p.m. Admission is 50 cents per session.

Six miles east of Ashland on ORE 66 is **Emigrant Reservoir.** In addition to water-skiing, sailing, fishing, and swimming, a 270-foot twin flume waterslide ($4 for 10 rides, plus $2.50 admission, open Mon.-Thurs 10-7 p.m., Fri.-Sun. 10-8 p.m.; tel. 776-7001), rental Hobie Cats, and sailboards add to the fun in the sun. Sailing lessons and boat rentals are available from the

the Oregon Shakespearean Festival's outdoor Elizabethan stage lake's **Hobie House Marina** (tel. 488-0595). Farther down ORE 66 on the summit of the Greensprings Highway, about a half hour outside of Ashland, is **Enchanted Rabbit Mountain** (tel. 488-1913). Here you can enjoy horse-drawn wagons (sleigh rides in winter) which wind leisurely through the mountaintop pine forests, taking in great views of the Rogue Valley and wildlife. Afternoon rides with an English picnic are $25; romantic moonlight rides are $15. Be sure to call ahead for reservations.

East of Ashland 20 miles on Dead Indian Rd. is **Howard Prairie Lake Resort** (tel. 482-1979). This 4,500-foot-high, six-mile-long lake has fa-

cilities for all water sports, horseback riding, and golf. A general store, restaurant, lodging, and 250-acre campground are also found at this retreat.

ASHLAND DRAMA

Shakespeare

While Lithia Park is the heart of Ashland, Shakespeare is the soul of this community. The festival began when Angus Bowmer, an English professor at Southern Oregon College, decided to celebrate Independence Day weekend in 1935 with a performance of *As You Like It*. He wasn't sure if the people *would* like it, so he scheduled cockfights and a boxing match during the show's intermission to ensure a large enough box-office draw. By the time he retired as artistic director of the festival in 1970, his Fourth of July dream had grown up into an internationally acclaimed drama company with three theaters, one named in his honor. Nowadays, the Shakespeare festival contributes $45 million annually to the area's economy, and four million people have purchased tickets over the last 55 years.

The three festival theaters are located at the southeast end of Lithia Park. Take the Shakespeare steps up the small hill by the Lithia water fountains to get to the complex known as the Shakespeare Plaza. The **Elizabethan Theater,** built on the site of Ashland's Chautauqua Dome, was modeled after the Fortune Theatre of London, circa 1600. This outdoor summer-only theater is the largest of the three and is primarily the domain of the Old Bard. While Shakespeare under the stars is incredibly romantic ("I knew she would be my wife after we saw the play together"—true story), it can also get very cold after sunset. Dress warmly, and consider investing a few bucks in the rental lap blankets and pillows for extra comfort.

The second-largest playhouse is the 600-seat **Angus Bowmer.** This indoor complex is a masterpiece theater, with excellent acoustics, computerized sound and lighting, and nary a bad seat in the house. The echoes of Shakespeare's immortal prose fill this hall during the wetter winter months when the outdoor stage is closed. Finally, the 150-seat **Black Swan** is the actors' and directors' theater, where modern works and experimental productions are the norm.

Tickets

Getting tickets to the **Oregon Shakespeare Festival** (15 South Pioneer St., Box 158, Ashland 97520; tel. 488-5406, for information tel. 482-2111) is as much a part of the show as the performance. Due to its tremendous popularity, seats will sell out months in advance, especially for the comedies. Your best strategy is to plan ahead and order well in advance. All seats are reserved, with the best seats up front (but not too close) commanding top dollar and prices de-

HANK KRANZLER

Sir John Falstaff is a basket case in
The Merry Wives of Windsor.

creasing for seats farther from the stage. Ticket prices are $18-24 for the Elizabethan Theater, and $24 for the Agnus Bowmer and Black Swan. If you are unable to get tickets ahead of time, your best bet is to get to the Shakespeare Plaza an hour or two before the show with a sign stating what show you want to see. If you are lucky, you will score tickets from someone with extras. Avoid bidding wars with other would-be theatergoers, as ticket scalping is frowned upon here. Otherwise, be at the ticket window at 6 p.m. for any available seats that will then be released. There are usually standing-room-only tickets ($10) if all else fails. And remember, there is no late seating at any of the theaters. As of the 1992 season, the rear third of the Elizabethan Theater's seats were roofed to improve acoustics and restrict street noise.

For a behind-the-scenes look at the action, backstage tours are given by the actors and actresses and lend an interesting inside perspective to the magic of the theater. Included in the tours are visits to the Exhibit Center (a museum with changing displays relating to current shows) and dressing rooms, and an opportunity to handle props from actual productions. The two-hour tours depart from the Black Swan Theatre during the festival season every performance day at 10 a.m. The charge is $8, half price for those under 11. Call 482-4331 for more info. Advance reservations are required.

That's Show Biz
Shakespeare isn't the only act in town. Some of the other local companies include the **Actors Workshop,** the **Lyric Theatre, Studio X, Children's Theatre,** the **Oregon Cabaret Theatre,** and **Southern Oregon State College** productions. Ashland is also home to the **State Ballet of Oregon,** which gives many summer performances. The **Ashland Visitor Information Center** (tel. 482-3486) has complete information on all the goings-on, as does the Southern Oregon Reservation Center (tel. 488-1011 or 800-547-8052).

A few miles north of Ashland is the town of Talent. The **Minshall Theatre** melodrama has been a popular favorite there for over 20 years, mainly because audience participation is openly encouraged. Here you get to cheer for the hero and boo and hiss the villain, and a splendid time is guaranteed for all.

SPORTS AND RECREATION

Skiing
Perched high atop the Siskiyou range and straddling the California-Oregon border is Oregon's highest point west of the Cascade mountains, 7,523-foot-high **Mt. Ashland** (tel. 482-2897 for info, 482-2754 for the snow report). To get there, take the Mt. Ashland exit off I-5 and follow the road for a few miles to the complex. Skiers of all levels enjoy the 22 different runs and breathtaking vistas. An average of 325 inches of snow falls on the mountain, making it possible to ski Thanksgiving through Easter. Night skiing Thursday through Saturday.

It is a good idea to check with the Southern Oregon Reservation Center (see "Information and Services" following) about any special ski packages available. Also, the spring and fall are good times to come to Ashland, as the rates are lower than during the peak summer tourist

7,525-foot-high Mt. Ashland is Oregon's southernmost ski area.

season. Many proprietors include free Mt. Ashland lift tickets with the price of the room. When the snow has melted off, the walk to the top of Mt. Ashland is an easy one, with good views of the Siskiyous and Mt. Shasta. It's prudent to bring along a sweater, as it gets fairly windy up there.

Adventure Center
The **Bicentennial Bikepath** crisscrosses through town before going down the valley to Medford along Bear Creek. If you like to ride a bike but are not big on pedaling, contact the **Adventure Center** (40 N. Main; tel. 488-2819 or 800-444-2819) for information about their Mt. Ashland downhill bike cruise. This half-day morning or picnic-lunch ride descends 4,000 feet on 16 miles of quiet paved roads through the countryside to Emigrant Reservoir. The three-hour morning cruise departs at 8 a.m., costs $34, and includes fruit, pastries, and drinks. The four-hour picnic cruise departs at 11 a.m., costs $40, and includes a great lunch in a beautiful mountain glade. Bicycles, safety equipment, roundtrip transfer from Ashland, and a friendly, experi-

enced guide are also provided. All you really have to do is steer! The Adventure Center also has mountain bikes for rent that include helmet, lock, and maps for $5 an hour, $15 for a half day, and $25 for a full day.

The Adventure Center also functions as a clearinghouse for other recreational activites. They will help you plan trips for any size party. There's never a charge for this service, and they also offer group discounts. Adventure Center rafting trips include all gear, guides, and transfer from Ashland. The four-hour half-day trip ($40, includes snack) runs 8 a.m.-noon or 1-5 p.m., and the five-hour picnic trip ($70, includes lunch) runs 10 a.m.-5 p.m. Rated one of the best floats in southern Oregon, the all-day ($85, all meals) upper Klamath River trip runs 7 a.m.-5:30 p.m.

Horseback Riding

To graduate from a two-wheeled coast to a four-legged gallop, **Mountain Gate Stables** (tel. 482-8873) has many horseback-riding packages to choose from. Short trail rides take in scenic views of the mountains and valleys, and longer rides deep into the woods of the Greentree Mountains include saddlebag lunches prepared by the Greentree Restaurant. Another option features an overnight stay in creekside cabins at Buckhorn Springs. And in the event of inclement weather, you can always practice your walk, trot, and canter in the arena. To get there, take Ashland St. (ORE 66) two miles east of the Ashland Hills Inn. Call ahead for additional information and reservations.

Equipment And Golf

You can rent outdoor-recreation equipment at reasonable rates from **Ashland Mountain Supply** (31 N. Main St.; tel 488-2749).

A few miles outside of Ashland on ORE 66 is **Oak Knoll Golf Course** (3070 ORE 66; tel. 482-4311). Get into the swing of things before the play; at $6 for nine holes and $10 for 18

ASHLAND ACCOMMODATIONS

Ashland Hostel, 150 N. Main, tel. 482-9217, members $10, nonmembers $13, reservations highly advised.

Ashland Motel, 1145 Siskiyou Blvd., tel. 482-2561, $30-50, pets, pool.

Ashland Super 8, 2350 Ashland St., tel. 482-8887, $55, wheelchair access, covered pool.

Best Western, 132 N. Main, tel. 482-0049, $60-85, heated pool.

Columbia Hotel, 262 E. Main, tel. 482-3726, $40-60, European-style inn.

Curl Up Motel, 50 Lowe Rd., tel. 482-4700, $44-56, pool.

Hillside Inn, 1520 Siskiyou Blvd., tel. 482-2626, $60-70, wheelchair access, pool.

Knight's Inn Motel, 2359 Ashland St. (I-5 exit 14), tel. 482-5111, $40-55, cable TV, pool.

Manor Motel, 476 N. Main, tel. 482-2246, $30-49, kitchenettes.

Mark Antony Hotel, 476 N. Main, tel. 482-2246, $60-105, National Historic Landmark.

Palm Motel, 1065 Siskiyou Blvd., tel. 482-2636, $40-120, wheelchair access, pool.

Stratford Inn, 555 Siskiyou Blvd., tel. 488-2151, $80-120, wheelchair access, covered pool.

Timbers Motel, 1450 Ashland St., tel. 482-4242, $45-50, kitchenettes, pool.

Valley Entrance Motel, 1193 Siskiyou Blvd., tel. 482-2641, $55-70, nonsmoking rooms, pool.

Vista 6 Motel, 535 Clover Lane (I-5 exit 14), tel. 482-4423, $35-45, pool.

Windmill's Ashland Hills Inn, 2525 Ashland St., tel. 482-8310, $80-225, free theater shuttle, many amenities.

holes, even if you triple bogey, you can't miss. For weekend rates, add a dollar or two onto the greens fee.

PRACTICALITIES

Bed And Breakfast

The warm traditions of England are represented in Ashland not only by Oregon's leading Shakespearean festival, but also by the town's numerous bed and breakfasts, the most of any locale in the state. Although they cost a bit more than plastic, carbon-copy motel units, you get so much more for your money. In addition to such extras as fresh flowers in your room, antique brass beds with down comforters, and complimentary evening aperitifs, hearty morning meals are also included. The romantic ambience of these homes away from home is ideal for a special occasion.

Another plus is that most of these establishments are within easy walking distance of the theaters. Chances are good you will be home from the show long before many other patrons of the arts are getting to their parked cars. The properties are small, with usually only a handful of rooms, but they are also quite popular, especially during the summer. Advance planning and reservations are crucial, for the odds of strolling in off the street and finding accommodations at an Ashland bed and breakfast are remote. One way to find a place to bunk is to call **Ashland B&B Reservation Network** (tel. 482-BEDS). This association of 22 inns assures you easy access to excellent-quality accommodations. As the network members are so fond of saying, "nobody does it bedder."

Ashland Main St. Inn (142 N. Main; tel. 488-0969; $50-85) is a Victorian-style home stocked with period furnishings. A continental breakfast is brought up to your room. **Chanticleer** (120 Gresham; tel. 482-1919; $90-155) rules the roost with six romantic rooms replete with fluffy comforters and private baths. Their gourmet breakfasts are the talk of Ashland. A full cookie jar on the kitchen counter and the green Adirondack chairs in the garden will also come to mind long after you leave.

The six rooms of the **Edinburgh Lodge** (586 E. Main; tel. 488-1050 or 800-643-4434; $65-95), four blocks from the theaters, have handmade quilts and private baths. **The Hersey House** (451 N. Main; tel. 482-4563; $120 a night, two-night minimum) is an elegantly restored Victorian with antique furniture and private baths. **The Iris Inn** (59 Manzanita; tel. 488-2286; $50-90) is a cheerful Victorian with a fitting decor. After a walk through the Iris's gardens, you'll probably agree with Shakespeare: "Of all the flowers, methinks a rose is the finest."

The McCall House (153 Oak St.; tel. 482-9296; $67-90) is a restored Victorian built in 1883 by Ashland pioneer John McCall. It's a block away from restaurants, shops, theaters, and Lithia Park. Iron beds and handmade quilts underscore **Adam's Cottages** (737 Siskiyou Blvd; tel. 482-0562; $59-105). Children are welcome here, and a baby-sitter is available. **The Morical House** (668 N. Main; tel. 482-2254; $50-70) is a restored 19th-century home tastefully decorated with antiques. Flower gardens surround a putting green.

Although **Romeo Inn** (295 Idaho St.; tel. 488-0884; $115-175) is eight blocks from the Shakespeare Plaza, the large bedrooms with private baths and the patio with a heated pool and Jacuzzi make it worth the walk. The **Royal Carter House** (514 Siskiyou Blvd.; tel. 482-5623; $60-85) has rooms with private baths, antiques, and a special breakfast fit for a king.

The Winchester Inn (35 S. Second St.; tel. 488-1113; $65-90) is a six-room Victorian with private baths and a gourmet restaurant. Breakfast is served out on the patio at the **Woods House** (333 N. Main; tel. 488-1598; $65-105). In addition to the six rooms with private baths in the main home, the adjacent carriage house has two-room suites that can comfortably sleep six.

A new guest house that specializes in suites is the superb **Waterside Inn** (70 Water St.; tel. 482-3315, $110-$200), with exquisitely decorated suites such as "Kafuzo" (Japanese decor, sleeps four) and "Taos" (sleeps five), whose spacious living rooms and kitchens make them ideal (and reasonably priced) for two couples who plan to stay more than a weekend. The entire complex overlooks Ashland Creek and includes a garden patio where continental buffet breakfast is served, as well as a formal restaurant.

If you're looking for a romantic hideaway for special events, **Duck Crossing** (750 Neil Creek

Rd.; tel. 488-4633; $110) offers a single cottage for a maximum of two guests. Airy and light with lots of windows, gorgeous views, and a private bath, it's only a 10-minute drive away from town.

Ashland AYH Hostel

Offering 35 beds and family rooms, the Ashland AYH Hostel (150 N. Main St.; tel. 482-9217) is a two-story 1902 house near the Pacific Crest Trail and only three blocks from the Elizabethan Theater and Lithia Park. The hostel also has a coin laundry.

Food

Ashand's creative talents are not just confined to theatrical pursuits. Some of Oregon's better restaurants are around Main St. here. Even the humbler fare served in Ashland's unpretentious cafes and burger joints can be memorable.

The **Greenleaf Restaurant**'s (49 N. Main; tel. 482-2808) patio on the second floor makes a wonderful spot to enjoy an evening snack. Healthful fare with Mediterranean flair, espresso, and a good selection of desserts pull in the evening crowds, just as the omelettes, frittatas, and fruit smoothies attract devotees of healthy breakfasts. The **Back Porch Barbecue** (88 N. Main; tel. 482-4131) lives up to its name. In addition to chicken, ribs, and the like, live music on summer weekends and extra tables outside the building along the creek round out the cookout motif. The **Ashland Bakery Cafe** (38 E. Main St.; tel. 482-2117) makes a mean breakfast, and the buckwheat pancakes come with real maple syrup. Later, try the chicken teriyaki sandwich. The only buffet champagne brunch in town is at the **Ashland Hills Inn** (2525 Ashland St.; tel. 482-8310). A seafood bar and an abundant array of salads, pastries, and entrees are featured here 11 a.m.-2 p.m. The brunch is held outside on the patio in warm weather.

Theresa's Cantina (76 N. Pioneer St.; tel. 482-1107) serves "heart smart" Mexican cuisine without all of the MSG, salt, and lard. **Omar's** (1380 Siskiyou Blvd.; tel. 482-1281), Ashland's oldest restaurant, is noted for its seafood. You'll also be impressed by the restaurant's chicken Dijon, steaks, and moderate prices. **Deli La France** (45 N. Main; tel. 482-6052) is open for breakfast, lunch, and dinner.

For $4, get two French Twists, a baked petite French bread stuffed with cheeses, tomatoes, sweet red peppers, and herb mayonnaise, all in your choice of three main varieties. For a fine picnic in nearby Lithia Park, order the Très Français Basket (for two or more).

If you're in the mood for some Mexican food, try **Munchies** (64 N. Main). The food here is made mostly from scratch and has no MSG or lard. They also make their own vegetarian refried beans and offer eight vegetarian specials, all for under $7. **Michael's Fine Hamburgers** (457 Siskiyou Blvd.; tel. 482-9205) not only has the best burgers in town, but Texas-style barbecue and chili as well. **Geppetto's** (345 E. Main; tel. 482-1138) is the place to go for Italian cuisine. Nothing fancy, just real food prepared and served by real people at real prices. **Brothers Restaurant and Deli** (95 N. Main; tel. 482-9671) specializes in gourmet soup and sandwiches. New York meets the Northwest here in a tasty marriage of deli delights and indigenous ingredients. **Rosie's Sweet Shop** (303 E. Main; tel. 488-0179) features hot dogs, burritos, and customized sandwiches, as well as gourmet ice cream. **Gen Kai Japanese Restaurant**'s (180 Lithia Way; tel. 482-9632) authentic Japanese home-style food is the Ishikawa family favorite. Tables surround a small indoor rock fountain, and Japanese-style seating is also available.

Chata (1212 S. Pacific Hwy., Talent; tel. 535-2575) is a few miles away from Ashland but worth the trip. Reflecting the warm traditions of Poland, *bigos* (hunter's stew), *golabki* (cabbage balls), and *mamaliga* (sautéed cornmeal with cheeses) are a few of the well-prepared dishes you'll find here. Also located in Talent is **New Sammy's Cowboy Bistro,** (2210 S. Pacific Highway; tel. 535-2779); bring cash (no credit cards) and plan ahead (way ahead). With only six tables, New Sammy's fills up fast. Don't be put off by the exterior (gas station upgrade) or the interior decor (it's been described as "looking like Pee Wee Herman's playhouse"); the restaurant uses only organically grown food, and everything is homemade. Open Tuesday-Sunday, $30-$40 per person including wine and dessert. No sign, but there's a neon star on the roof.

Off the main drag in beautiful Lithia Park, **Lithia Park Cafe** (85 Winburne Way; tel. 482-3559) serves up inexpensive international entrees along with good ol' American food. This is a great spot to grab a cappuccino and a light bite on the way to the show. Despite the fast-food facade, this place caters to sophisticated tastes.

The menu at **Crystal** (212 E. Main; tel. 482-1721) is as elaborate as the huge chandelier that looms over the dining room. A Paris-trained chef prepares sumptuous entrees, artful soups, and elegant desserts. Down the hill from the Elizabethan Theatre, **North Light** (120 E. Main; tel. 482-9463) serves low-priced, imaginative vegetarian food. **Chateaulin** (150 E. Main St.; tel. 482-2264) looks the most Shakespearean, with its dark wooden interior and lighted stained-glass behind the bar. Traditional French and nouvelle cuisines are offered in a menu that changes weekly. If you go there after the play for one of their 25 specialty coffee drinks, be careful what you say about the performance—Hamlet or Falstaff may show up wearing blue jeans.

Nightlife
Rogue Brewery and Publichouse (31 S. Water St., Bluebird Park; tel. 488-5061) is southern Oregon's only microbrewery and brewpub. A full selection of handcrafted ales is complemented by a unique menu designed to enhance the flavor of the beer. Another particularly pleasant feature is that this is a smokeless pub. Across the courtyard you'll find **Thai Pepper** (84 N. Main; tel. 482-8058), whose sauces go well with an after-dinner brew here. The only rock 'n' roll club in the valley is **Soc Hop** (1700 Ashland St.; tel. 488-1780). A live DJ plays your favorites of the '50s, '60s, and '70s. The standard soda fountain menu keeps you fortified and rockin' around the clock. What else can you say? Some of us never grow up!

Allann Brothers (1602 Ashland St.; tel. 488-0700) is a cozy coffeehouse with live music Friday and Saturday nights. Gourmet coffee drinks, soups and sandwiches, and fine desserts are available. **The Vintage Inn** (31 Water St.; tel. 482-1120) is right next door and features a potpourri of nightly entertainment. Jazz, classical, folk, and bluegrass are some of the musical strains you may hear here. Something always seems to be happening at the **Mark Anthony Hotel** (212 E. Main; tel. 482-1721), whether it be music in the lounge, piano bar in the lobby, or a play in the ballroom. Call ahead to find out what's scheduled. **Jazmin's** (180 C St.; tel. 488-0883) has a dance floor and live music Thurs.-Sat. evenings; cover $1 and up. The cheapest beer in town can be found at the **Log Cabin Tavern** (41 N. Main St.; tel. 482-9701).

Information And Services
Ashland Visitor Information Center (110 E. Main St., Ashland 97520; tel. 482-3486) offers brochures, play schedules, and other up-to-date information on what's happening. The chamber has two booklets in particular (available for a small fee) that will help you appreciate the unusual variety of trees and shrubs in Lithia Park: *Woodland Trails* and *Lithia Park—The History*. Another excellent source of information is the **Southern Oregon Reservation Center** (Box 477, Ashland 97520; tel. 488-1011 in Oregon, 800-547-8052 in U.S.A.). This agency specializes in arranging Shakespearean vacation packages with quality lodging, choice seats for performances in all three theaters, and other tour and entertainment extras.

Ashland is famous for having one of the more dynamic Elderhostel programs in the country. Seniors bed down at Southern Oregon State dorms and take Shakespeare classes at the university to enhance their appreciation of the plays. To find out about the offerings of this hostel as well as the programs of its counterparts in Corvallis and Lakeview, write **Elderhostel** (75 Federal St., Boston, MA 02110-1941; tel. 617-426-8056)

Regional books, out-of-town papers, and a delightful bakery-cafe upstairs make **Bloomsbury Books** (290 S. Main; tel. 488-0029) a place worth knowing about. The cafe's tables are topped off by a layer of glass showcasing excerpted pages from such immortal works as Hemingway short stories and *Oregon Handbook* to help make a cup of coffee here a literary interlude.

The **post office** (Lithia Way and First St.; tel. 482-3986) is open during regular business hours; for **police** call 482-5211 or 911. **Ashland Community Hospital** (280 Maple St.; tel. 482-2441) has 24-hour medical service.

Getting There And Getting Around
Greyhound (91 Oak St.; tel. 482-2516) serves Ashland with a handful of daily north and southbound departures. Local connections between Medford and Ashland are possible through **Rogue Valley Transportation** (tel. 799-BUSS). The #10 bus leaves every half hour from 5 a.m. to 8 p.m. The southbound **Green Tortoise** leaves from the Safeway (585 Siskiyou Blvd.) parking lot Mon., Fri. 11:45 p.m. (and Wed., Sat., June 1-Oct. 1). Northbound runs depart Tues., Sat. 5:15 p.m. (and Thurs., Sun., June 1-Oct. 1). Contact **Ski Ashland** (Box 220, Ashland 97520; tel. 482-2897) for information on the Mt. Ashland daily bus to and from Medford and Ashland. Twenty-four-hour **taxi** service is available from **Ashland Taxi** (tel. 482-3065). **Executive Rent-a-Car** (Butler Ford, 1977 U.S. 99; tel. 482-2521) picks up and delivers anywhere in the Bear Creek Valley. Used cars for $15 a day plus mileage are available through the **Ashland Hills Inn** (2525 Ashland St.; tel. 482-8310).

MEDFORD AND VICINITY

In the 1850s, gold discoveries drew people and commerce to the Rogue River Valley. The seat of the prosperity was Jacksonville, a major stagecoach stop whose boom went bust in the 1880s when the new railroad line bypassed the town for a train station known as Middle Ford. Middle Ford's name became shortened to Medford and the town was incorporated in 1885.

Today, along with a resource-based economy revolving around agriculture and timber products, Medford is becoming established as a retirement center. Proximity to Ashland's culture, Rogue Valley recreation, and Cascade getaways, as well as rainfall totals half those recorded in the Willamette Valley, are some of the enticements. Unfortunately, if the current population of 40,000 grows much larger, the already poor air quality here will become worse. Already smog alerts brought on by heat and inversions have some folks calling the city "Dreadford."

Call it what you will, but for cost of living, location, and employment opportunities, there is no better place to live in southern Oregon than Medford.

SIGHTS

Table Rocks
About 10 miles northeast of Medford are two eye-catching basaltic buttes, Upper and Lower Table Rock. They are composed of sandstone with erosion-resistant lava caps deposited during a massive Cascade eruption about four to five million years ago. Over the years, wind and water have undercut the sandstone. Stripped of their underpinnings, the heavy basalt on top of the eroded sandstone is pulled down by gravity, creating the nearly vertical slabs that we see today.

The Table Rocks were the site of a decisive battle in the first of a series of Rogue Indian wars in the 1850s. Major Philip Kearny, who later went on to distinguish himself as the great one-armed Civil War general, was successful in routing the Indians from this seemingly impervious stronghold. A peace treaty was signed here soon afterward by the Rogue (Takilma) Indians and the American government. For a time, this area was also part of the Table Rock Indian Reservation, but the reservation status was terminated shortly thereafter.

For nearly a century, the Table Rocks were the domain of vultures and rattlesnakes until the **Lower Table Rock Preserve** was established in 1979. This 1,890-acre preserve is near the westernmost butte, which towers 800 feet above the surrounding valley floor. Established by the Nature Conservancy and later turned over to the government, the preserve protects an area of special biologic, geologic, historic, and scenic value. Pacific madrone, white oak, manzanita, and ponderosa pine grow on the flank of the mountain, while the crown is covered with grasses and wildflowers. Newcomers to the region will be especially taken by the madrone trees. This glossy-leaved evergreen has a "skin" that peels in warm weather to reveal a smooth, coppery orange bark. It's found mostly in the Northwest and was noted by early explorers as fuel for long, slow, hot-burning fires.

MEDFORD

62

TO CRATER LAKE &
KLAMATH FALLS

JACKSON COUNTY
EXPO PARK

5

BEAR CREEK

TO GRANTS
PASS

99 TO ROGUE RIVER

ROGUE VALLEY BLVD

TABLE ROCK RD.

AIRPORT RD.

AIRPORT RD.

MEDFORD - JACKSON
COUNTY AIRPORT

CRATER LAKE AVE.

McANDREWS RD.

ROGUE VALLEY BLVD.

JACKSON ST.

HAWTHORNE
PARK

E. MAIN

OAKDALE

GRAPE ST.

ST.

COTTAGE ST.

238

238

W. MAIN

238

JACKSONVILLE HWY.
TO JACKSONVILLE

AVE.

8th ST.

10th ST.

ST.

RIVERSIDE

SISKIYOU BLVD.

MURPHY RD.

ROGUE VALLEY
MEDICAL CENTER

ROSS LN.

COLUMBUS

ST.

UNION PARK

MONROE

KENYON AVE.

ST.

DAKOTA AVE.

BEAR CREEK

BARNETT RD.

HAMILTON

STEWART AVE.

AVE.

FICHTER
MAIN WARING PARK

VETERANS
PARK

MILES
FIELD

TO ASHLAND

99

5

TO ASHLAND

0   0.75mi

0   0.75km

© MOON PUBLICATIONS, INC.

Park checklists show that over 140 different kinds of plants reside here, including dwarf meadow foam, which grows no place else on earth. One reason is because water doesn't readily percolate through the lava. Small vernal ponds collect on top of the butte, nurturing the wildflowers that flourish in early spring. The wildflower display reaches its zenith in April. A dozen different kinds of flowers cover the rock-strewn flats with bright yellows and vivid purples.

Hikers who take the two-mile trail to the top of horseshoe-shaped Lower Table Rock are in for a treat. Be on the lookout for batches of pale lavender fawn lilies peeking out from underneath the shelter of the scraggly scrub oaks on the way up the mountain. You'll want to walk over to the cliff's edge, which will take you past some of the "mima mounds" or "patterned ground" that distinguishes the surface of the butte. How the mounds were formed is a matter of scientific debate. Some scientists believe they represent centuries of work by rodents, others think they are accumulated silt deposits, while still others maintain that they have been created by the action of the wind. However they got there, the mounds are the only soil banks on the mountain that support grasses, which are unable to grow on the lava. Lichens and mosses manage to grow on the lava, however, painting the dull black basalt with luxuriant greens and fluorescent yellows during the wetter months.

The trail up Upper Table Rock is a little over a mile, but much steeper than the Lower Table Rock trail. Clay clings to the slopes of Upper Table Rock, making the going both sticky and slippery during the wet season. The trail affords wonderful vistas of the Rogue River and Sams Valley to the north. Two benches along the way are good places to stop and rest, savor the view, and scrape the heavy clay off of your shoes.

The trail reaches the top of the butte on the far eastern side. The ponds up here are smaller and fewer than on Lower Table Rock, but the mima mounds are more clearly defined. Upper Table Rock also shows less wear and tear from human activity, and the flower show is just as spectacular. Long black strips of hexagonal basalt look as though they were formed by tanks marching across the butte while the lava was cooling. You'll find that this irregular, knobby surface is difficult to walk on, but the colorful mosses and lichens love it. Also look for the tiny bouquets of grass widows, lovely purple flowers that dangle on long, graceful stalks. The odd-looking building off to the west is a navigation device maintained by the Federal Aviation Administration. It's easy to get disoriented out here, with hundreds of acres to explore. The point where the trail heads back down the mountain is marked by two large trees, a ponderosa pine and a Douglas fir, accompanied by a smaller cedar.

To get to the Table Rocks, take ORE 62 northeast out of Medford. Turn left on Table Rock Rd. and follow it until you reach Wheeler Road. Look for small directional signs pointing the way. The parking area and trailhead are located on the west side of Wheeler Road. Table Rock Rd. is also accessible from the north via ORE 234.

Harry And David's Country Store

About a mile south of Medford on U.S. 99 is the country store of famous fruit purveyors Harry and David Holmes (2836 S. Pacific Hwy., Medford 97501; tel. 776-2277). Harry and David took over their family's Bear Creek Orchards in 1914. Bear Creek Orchards was recognized for the size and quality of its pears, which were shipped to the grand hotels of Europe. But their lucrative export market collapsed during the Depression, so the brothers decided to sell their fruit by mail. To establish a new reputation domestically, they headed for both seaboards. Each carried sample gift boxes of fruit, which they personally delivered to high rollers like David Sarnoff, Walter Chrysler, Leland Stanford, and Alfred P. Sloan. Their first foray was an immediate success, and their mail-order business was born.

Today, Harry and David's is one of the world's leading shippers of food and fruit gifts. Here you'll find food, gifts, and fun in their old-fashioned store. Strolling through the aisles, you can enjoy many free samples of the merchandise. The fruit-stand section of the store offers farm-fresh fruit, vegetables, and produce. You can also find "rejects" from Harry and David's Fruit-of-the-Month Club that are nearly as good as the mail-order fruit but are too small or blemished to meet their high quality standards.

The gourmet-foods section features their complete line of freshly made baked goods, smoked meats and fish, and cheeses. Again, be on the lookout for products with slight imperfections that go for a fraction of the cost listed in the store catalog. The jams and fruit spreads in particular are less expensive here. Their deli stacks up a multitiered ice-cream cone, and the food in the restaurant includes tasty soups, salads, and sandwiches, as well as a delectable assortment of fresh-baked desserts.

For visitors unable to make it south from the Portland area, there is an outlet store east of the city. Take the Troutdale exit off I-84 into the Columbia Outlet Mall, and look for it on the west side of the complex.

To the north of Harry and David's is Jackson and Perkins Co., the world's largest private rose grower. The two merged together under the auspices of the Bear Creek Corporation.

Jackson And Perkins

The history of Jackson and Perkins began in 1872 in Newark, New York, where the company first began wholesaling nursery stock. Their mail-order business started at the 1939 World's Fair in New York. Many customers who had ordered roses appreciated having them shipped and requested the same service the following year. From this nucleus, their reputation quickly spread and orders for their roses came in from all over the country.

Jackson and Perkins moved to California's San Joaquin Valley in 1966 to take advantage of the 262-day growing season. The roses are raised in California, then harvested and sent to the Medford plant where they are prepared for nationwide shipment. The company's annual catalogs offer bulbs, seeds, and plants of all kinds, as well as their award-winning roses. Take a walk down the primrose path of their 43,000-square-foot Test and Display Garden (next to the warehouse) from May through October to enjoy the colorful sights and sweet smells of the floral displays.

Grist For The Mill

About 15 minutes away from Medford on ORE 62 is Oregon's last original water-powered gristmill that's still in operation, the **Butte Creek Mill** (Box 561, 402 Royal, Eagle Point, OR 97524; tel. 826-3531). To get there, take ORE 62 about 10 miles north to Eagle Point and follow the signs to the mill. Built in 1872, you can see that the foundation pillars were hand-hewn with an axe and that wooden pegs and square nails hold up the rest of the structure. The two 1,400-pound millstones were quarried in France and assembled in Illinois. From there, they were shipped around the Horn and then transported over the mountains by wagon. Genuine stoneground products are available in the mill shop, including 12 kinds of flours, four kinds of meal, four cracked grains, six cereals, four mixes (pancake, waffle, cornbread, and biscuit), and other

The Antelope Creek "Kissing Bridge" is located near Butte Creek Mill in Eagle Point.

STUART WARREN

grain products. A variety of health-food products rounds out the nutritious collection of edibles here. Open Mon.-Sat. 9-5 daily (except major holidays).

Adjacent to the mill is the **Oregon General Store Museum.** This museum is a re-creation of a typical late-1800s general store. Home remedies, giant coffee grinders, pickle barrels, and other common goods of the day are exhibited. A working music box, antiques and collectibles, and old advertising signs add to the decor. Open 11 a.m.-4 p.m. on Saturdays, donations eagerly accepted.

Ridin' The Rails

Just about anyone who likes trains will enjoy **Medford Railroad Park** (tel. 770-4586 or 779-7979) on Berrydale Ave. off Table Rock Rd., a few blocks away from the Rogue Valley Mall. The park features miniature steam trains that run the second and fourth Sundays of each month, April through October, 11 a.m.-3 p.m. Locomotives and other railway equipment are faithful reproductions of full-size trains, except that one inch here equals a foot out in the real world. Coal, wood, oil, and propane fire the steam boilers that propel the trains around a mile-long track. Passengers are carried in small cars across bridges, culverts, and over a small grade. Admission is free.

SPORTS AND RECREATION

Take Me Out To The Ball Game

Medford's **Miles Field** (tel. 770-5364), located about a mile south of town near the Armory on U.S. 99, is the home turf of the Medford Athletics baseball team, a farm club of the Oakland Athletics. Here you get the opportunity to watch budding hopefuls round the bases on their way up to the bigs, and might-have-beens shuffle back unnoticed to the dugout. Jose Canseco, home-run slugger and American League rookie-of-the-year in 1985, used to play here. While it's not exactly major-league action, you can sit closer to the field and the admission ($3-7) is definitely minor. The season runs from mid-June through Labor Day. Call ahead to see what team is in town.

Golf

Near Miles Field is **Bear Creek Golf Course** (2325 South Pacific Hwy.; tel. 773-1822). This is a compact little nine-hole course that's both a challenge and a bargain at $5 a round. If you would rather go for a regulation-sized course, **Cedar Links Golf Course** (3144 Cedar Links Dr.; tel. 773-4373) in northeastern Medford has 18 holes waiting for you. To get there, take ORE 62 north toward White City. Turn right on Delta Waters Rd., right again on Springbrook Rd., and then left on Cedar Links Drive. The greens fee is $10 for nine holes and $16 for 18 holes; add a dollar or two more on weekends.

Splish Splash

When the mercury heats up into the 90s and 100s during the summer, it's time to cool off in one of Medford's several public swimming pools. **Jackson Pool** (815 Summit; tel. 770-4586) is a popular family place to get wet. In addition to the 100-foot-long waterslide, a concession stand there sells ice cream, soft drinks, and other snacks. The swimming season starts June 11 and runs on into early September. An open recreational swim is held Mon.-Wed. 1-3 p.m. and also on Friday. Thursday evenings are reserved for family swims, 7:30-9:15 p.m. Admission is $2 for adults, $1 for ages 18 and under. **Hawthorne Pool** (505 E. Main St.; tel. 770-4586) features an open swim Sun.-Fri. 1-3 p.m. and 3:30-5:30 p.m.

The indoor **YMCA Pool** (1522 W. Sixth St.; tel. 772-6295) offers several open swim sessions year-round. Admission is $5 per session, $1.50 for ages 18 and under; be sure to call ahead to confirm scheduling.

PRACTICALITIES

Bed And Breakfast

A romantic bed and breakfast with a parklike ambience is the **Greenwood Tree** (3045 Bellinger Ln.; tel. 776-0000; $110-125). The rooms and suites here have private baths and are decorated with antiques, Persian rugs, and fabric art collections. A lavish breakfast and afternoon tea in the parlor, on the porch, or out in the garden, as well as chocolate truffles on your pillow at night, further enhance the atmosphere.

MEDFORD ACCOMMODATIONS

Cedar Lodge Motor Inn, 518 N. Riverside Ave., tel. 773-7361, $34-50, pool, nonsmoking rooms.

City Center Motel, 324 S. Central Ave., tel. 773-6248, $30-40, pool.

Harvey's Motel, 1510 S. Central Ave., tel. 779-6561, $25-30.

Horizon Motor Inn, 1154 E. Barnett Rd., tel. 779-5085, $60-120, wheelchair access, pool, lounge.

Millwood Inn Motel, 1034 N. Riverside Ave., tel. 773-1152, $35-50, pool, lounge.

Motel 6, 950 Alba Dr., tel. 773-4290, $25-35, pool.

Pine Tree Inn Motel, 525 S. Riverside Ave., tel. 772-6133, $35-50, pool, nonsmoking rooms.

Pony Soldier Motor Inn, 2340 Crater Lake Hwy. (ORE 62), tel. 779-2011, $60-70, wheelchair access, pets, pool.

Shilo Inn of Medford, 2111 Biddle Rd., tel. 770-5151, $55-60, wheelchair access, pets.

Sierra Inn Motel, 345 S. Central Ave., tel. 773-7727, $35-55, kitchenettes.

Red Lion Inn, 200 N. Riverside Ave., tel. 779-5811, $90-110, everything.

Valli Hai Hotel, 1034 Court St., tel. 772-6183, $25-30, cheap and funky.

Windmill Inn of Medford, 1950 Biddle Rd., tel. 779-0050, $56-80, wheelchair access, pool.

In addition to a hand-hewn and hand-pegged building dating back to the Civil War, a willow swing in a three-story barn, a hammock suspended between enormous 300-year-old oaks, and a gazebo beneath shady apple trees overlooking the rose garden also grace the grounds.

Another popular bed and breakfast is **Holly Street Suites** (304 North Holly St.; tel. 779-4716). Three historic structures here offer unique accommodations. The five-room Waverly Cottage was built around the turn of the century and is one of southern Oregon's most ornate Queen Anne-style homes. A magnificent red cedar archway with gold-leafed carvings and antique etched glass divides the dining room and parlor. The kitchen and pantry are tastefully painted to bring out the oak cabinets, counters, and plaster gingerbread. The bathroom is equipped with a clawfoot bathtub and a European temperature-controlled shower sprayer. The master bedroom has a canopied king-sized bed, the other bedroom has a double bed, and both rooms have antique dressers. All five of these rooms are yours to enjoy privately.

The Edwardian is a private three-room suite featuring a bedroom with a queen-sized brass bed, private bath, living room with cable TV, kitchen, and laundry room. Plants, flowers, a wraparound porch, and breakfast-in-a-basket delivered to your door add the finishing touches.

The Holly House holds two suites, the King and the Queen. The King Suite is a spacious three-room unit fit for royalty. The king-sized bed, private bath, and a kitchen/dining room featuring African mahogany and a rosewood wet bar will make you feel like the lord of the manor. The other half of the building houses the Queen Suite. The bedroom is large, with two queen-sized beds separated by an oak divider. The kitchen has an antique wood cook stove, and the solarium is bright and comfortable. Both suites have private entrances and breakfast is delivered between 7:30 and 9:30 a.m. at your convenience.

Rates range from $40 to $110; additional guests are $20 each. Reservations are advised, and the Waverly Cottage has a two-day minimum-stay requirement on weekends and holidays.

Food

The **Alpine Restaurant** (1011 Spring St.; tel. 772-2481) offers cuisine that reflects the traditions of old Germany. Open for breakfast, lunch, and dinner; the German apple pancake is a popular way to start the day. For dinner try some

LA BURRITA

If you are an aficionado of Mexican food, make sure that you plan for a lunch or dinner at La Burrita. The original La Burrita Restaurant is on ORE 238 between Jacksonville and Medford, and outlets of this popular establishment have recently opened up in Medford and Grants Pass. But as with many replicas, the copies never seem to be quite as good as the original, so visit the *genuine* La Burrita (2715 Jacksonville Hwy.—same as ORE 238—tel. 770-5770) if possible.

Half of this restaurant is a store that carries authentic Mexican foodstuffs and beverages, and this is where you order your meal also. The chiles rellenos here are the best in Oregon, and generous two-item combination plates with rice, beans, and chips go for under $5. The accompanying homemade salsa is hot enough for most people, but if you really want to do the Oregon version of the "Mexican Hat Dance," ask for the extra-hot salsa: this legendary green mixture is pure ground jalapeños. The dining room is also a throwback to old Mexico, with Day-Glo felt paintings on the walls that are so bad they're good. Enjoy your food along with the toe-tapping gay-sad strains of a distant accordion, *gracias* to the Norteño music that is always playing in the background. This is where the migrant workers come to fortify themselves and socialize in between gigs in the fields and orchards. The place may be funky, but it's got great food at a great price, as well as being a bite-sized slice of southern Oregon life.

sauerbraten served with red cabbage and spaetzle (homemade German noodles). Dinners are accompanied with soup, salad, and fresh-baked bread.

A family restaurant where you can find some elegance on a budget is **Apple Annie's** (1021 S. Riverside, tel. 776-0711; and 900 Alba Dr., tel. 779-4472). Many specialty items are featured on the menu here, as well as some of the more traditional favorites. Breakfast specials like the French-toast combo (two pieces of French toast, two breakfast meats, and one egg) and the deluxe pancake sandwich (two eggs, two meats, and two pancakes) go for $3.95. Dinner specials range from $5 to $12.

Deli Down (406 E. Main St. #6; tel. 772-4520) makes its own pasta every day. Specialties include pasta salads, meat pastries, overstuffed sandwiches, all-you-can-eat pasta bar, and homemade cheesecake. You'll find the restaurant in the Main St. Market.

If your taste buds are set for border food, **Mexicali Rose** (corner of Fourth and Fir, 17 W. Fourth St.; tel. 779-4289) can sate your cravings. Large dinners replete with rice and beans (be sure to ask for the special black beans) range from $6 to $10. The Super Nachos is a perfect complement to the list of Latin American import beers or giant margaritas on the menu here.

Stanley's (510 N. Riverside; tel. 772-5114) is open for breakfast, lunch, and dinner. Check the board for the daily specials; dinners range from $6 to $12. **The Sandpiper** (1841 Barnett Rd.; tel. 779-0100) is open weekdays for lunch and dinner and for dinner only on weekends. The Sunset suppers like teriyaki chicken, petite sirloin, prime rib, or the fresh catch of the day are served with soup, rice, and vegetables for $8.95. Full chicken, beef, and seafood dinners that run $12-20 come with choice of soup, salad or salad bar, potatoes or rice, vegetables, and bread. Turtle boats and mud pies are among the variety of sweet treats on the dessert tray.

The Wild Plum (1528 Biddle Rd.; tel. 772-5200) features fresh salads, soups, and sandwiches as well as light and full dinners. You may go "plum crazy" trying to decide which one of their 33 flavors of pie to enjoy. A favorite with loggers and truckers, **Withams** (2339 Biddle Rd.; tel. 772-9307) has inexpensive daily lunch and dinner specials that include soup or salad. The food's pretty good, and the price is right, even though you might think you're on the set for *Convoy*.

Events

The **Jackson County Fair** is held at the county fairgrounds just north of town the third weekend of July. Admission is $5 for adults, $2 for children, and parking is an additional $2. Frequent shuttle-bus departures provided by **Rogue Valley Transportation** (3200 Crater Lake Ave., Medford; tel. 799-2988) relieve you of fighting the crowds for limited parking spaces. The buses leave from downtown Medford, Poplar Square, Crater High School, and other points around town. The trip back from the fair is free, and the shuttles run approximately every 15 minutes.

Cowboys, ranchers, and farmers all come in with their families for fun and top-name entertainment. Country music seems to dominate the stage, with performers like Ricky Skaggs, Waylon Jennings, and Charley Pride drawling out their tunes. If the kids are going to spend the day at the midway, consider purchasing their ride tickets in advance and saving 50% off the regular $8.95 "one price for all rides" (except Saturday). Check with the Medford Chamber of Commerce (see "Information and Services" below) for presale ticket outlets.

Free rides on a 40-foot sternwheeler are offered on the south pond. Professional fishing guides will teach kids tricks of the trade at Huck Finn's Fishing Pier, which is also located on the pond. And in addition to the normal selection of jams, fruits, and vegetables, fly-tying and contemporary collections (like baseball cards) are other judged categories that are worth a closer look.

Information And Services

The **post office** (333 W. Eighth, Medford 97501; tel. 776-3604) is open Mon.-Fri. 8:30-5 and can help with passport information in addition to selling stamps and envelopes. **Providence Hospital** (1111 Crater Lake Ave.; tel. 773-6611) has 24-hour emergency care. This is where the flying angels of Air Medivac speedily bring in people from remote areas for immediate treatment. From basic home health services to intensive care, the staff of **Rogue Valley Medical Center** (2825 Barnett Rd.; tel. 773-6281) is ready around the clock to help you when you need help. **Medford Physicians and Surgeons Clinic** (1025 E. Main St.; tel. 773-6271) offers 24-hour pediatrics, surgery, and cardiology care as well as specialists for a host of other ailments.

The **police** (tel. 770-4783 or 911 for emergencies only) and state police (2700 N. Pacific Hwy.; tel. 776-6111, or 911 for emergencies only) can help out in case there's trouble. The **Medford Visitors and Convention Bureau** (304 S. Central Ave.; tel. 772-6293) and **Log Cabin Information Center** (88 Stewart Rd.; tel. 776-4021) have all kinds of useful maps, directories, and information for the asking. Both offices are open Mon.-Fri. 9-5. Additional information on recreational sites and parks in the Medford area can be acquired from the **Bureau of Land Management** office (3040 Biddle Rd.; tel. 770-2200). The **Medford Library** (413 W. Main; tel. 776-7287) has one of the best collections of books, magazines, and periodicals in southern Oregon.

Out of a half dozen coin-operated laundries in Medford, **B.J.'s Homestyle Laundromat** (1712 W. Main; tel. 773-4803) is the most pleasant establishment. With games, television, and a snack bar, it's almost like doing your laundry at home. Open seven days a week from 8 a.m. to 9 p.m., an attendant is always on duty, and dry-cleaning and drop-off washing services are available.

Getting There And Getting Around

The **Greyhound** (212 Barnett Rd.; tel. 779-2103) depot is open 6 a.m. to midnight daily. **Rogue Valley Transportation** (3200 Crater Lake Ave.; tel. 799-2988) provides connections to Jacksonville, Phoenix, White City, Talent, and Ashland. Most buses depart Medford at Sixth and Barnett, Mon.-Fri. 8-5, Sat. 9-5, no service Sundays. Linkages to Eagle Point and White City are courtesy of **Cascade Bus Lines,** but call 664-4801 for the schedule, as it fluctuates. **Courtesy Yellow Cab** (tel. 772-6288) has 24-hour service in the Medford area. A wheelchair van, senior-citizen discounts, and special rates on airport transfers are all available on request.

Medford/Jackson County Airport (administrative office tel. 776-7222) is the air hub for southern Oregon and is served by United, Horizon, and other carriers. Two rental-car agencies are at the airport, **Budget** (tel. 773-7023) and **National** (tel. 779-4863).

JACKSONVILLE

Oregon's pioneer past is tastefully preserved in Jacksonville. Located five miles west of Medford and cradled in the foothills of the Siskiyou Mountains, this small town of 2,100 residents retains an atmosphere of tranquil isolation. With about 90 original wooden and brick buildings dating back to the 1850s, it was the first designated national historic landmark district in Oregon and the third such site in the nation.

In early 1852, two itinerant prospectors, Cluggage and Poole, were returning to a northern California mining camp with supplies from the Willamette Valley. They camped by a creek in the area for a night's rest. The next morning, they found a good-sized gold nugget in a hoofprint made by one of their pack animals in what became known as Rich Gulch. They continued to California with their goods for the other miners, but in the excitement of their discovery, the secret slipped out. They hurriedly backtracked their way to southern Oregon and staked their claims along Rich Gulch and Daisy Creek. Within a matter of weeks, the mining camp population grew from two to 2,000. Tents, wooden shacks, and log cabins were hastily erected, and the town of Table Rock City was born. The name was changed to Jacksonville the following year, in honor of President Andrew Jackson and the town's namesake county.

The town grid was surveyed in September 1852 into 200-foot-square blocks. California and Oregon streets were then, as now, the hubs of business and social life in Jacksonville. But the city's tightly packed wooden structures proved to be especially prone to fire. Between 1873 and 1884, three major fires reduced most of the original buildings to ashes. These harsh experiences prompted merchants to use brick in the construction of a second generation of buildings, and the practice was furthered by an 1878 city ordinance requiring same. Most of the building blocks were made and fired locally. To prevent them from returning to the earth during the damp seasons, the porous bricks were painted to protect them from the elements; cast-iron window shutters and door frames further reinforced the structures.

Boomtown Jacksonville was the first and largest town in the region and was selected as the county seat. It was even nominated and briefly considered as the state capital. The prominence of Jacksonville was made manifest with the 1883 erection of a 60-foot-high courthouse with 14-inch-thick walls. But like the gold finds that quickly played out, Jacksonville's boisterous exuberance began to subside when the Oregon and California Railroad bypassed the town in the early 1880s in favor of the nearby hopeful hamlet of Medford. Businesses were quick to move east to greet the coming of the iron horse, and Jacksonville's stature as a trading center diminished. When the county seat was finally moved to Medford in 1927, Jacksonville's heady days had long since vanished.

During the Depression, families with low incomes took up residence in the town's unmaintained buildings, taking advantage of the cheap rents. Gold mining enjoyed a brief comeback, with residents digging shafts and tunnels in backyards, but it was not enough to revive the derailed economy. However, the following decades saw a gradual resurgence of interest in Jacksonville's gold-rush heritage. The Southern Oregon Historical Society was created after World War II, and individuals began to take interest in the many unaltered late-1880s buildings and restore them to their former glory. The **Beekman Bank** was one of the first structures to be spruced up, and the prominent **United States Hotel** was rehabilitated in 1964. The restoration movement was rewarded when the National Park Service designated Jacksonville as a National Historic Landmark in 1966.

Today, Jacksonville paints a memorable picture of a western town with its historic buildings, excellent museum, and a beautiful pioneer cemetery. In addition, a renowned music festival, colorful pageants, and a rich local folklore all pay tribute to Jacksonville's golden age.

Jackson County Museum
A good place to start your explorations is at the museum (206 N. Fifth St.; tel. 773-6536). This

imposing two-story brick-and-stone Italianate building was completed in 1883 and served as the county administration building until 1927, when the county seat was moved to Medford. For more than two decades, the structure didn't have any permanent tenants, but then became the Jackson County Museum and headquarters of the Southern Oregon Historical Society in 1950.

Nowadays, in addition to pioneer artifacts, a mock-up of Peter Britt's photo studio, and interesting old pictures, the museum also has a good walking-tour map of the other historical sites in the city. Another bonus is that admission is free, although donations are greatly appreciated. The stucco building next door to the courthouse used to be the county jail, but today it serves as the children's museum. Kids of all ages will enjoy the hands-on experience of seeing old-fashioned toys close up. A small bookstore is located here as well, specializing in local and regional historical publications.

Peter Britt Gardens
Peter Britt came to Jacksonville not long after gold was first discovered in Rich Gulch in 1851. After briefly trying his hand at prospecting, he redirected his efforts toward painting and photography. The latter turned out to be his specialty, and for nearly 50 years he photographed the places, people, and events of southern Oregon (Britt was the first person to photograph Crater Lake). He also incorporated new techniques and equipment in his studio as photographic advances were developed. You'll find his ambrotypes, daguerrotypes, stereographs, and tintypes on display at the Jackson County Museum.

The Swiss-born Peter Britt was also an accomplished horticulturalist and among the first vintners in southern Oregon. In addition to experimenting with several varieties of fruit and nut trees to see which grew best in the Rogue River Valley, he kept the first weather data records in the region. Another testimonial to his love of plants is the giant redwood tree you see on the western edge of the Britt Gardens (S. First and W. Pine streets), which he planted 130 years ago to commemorate the birth of his first child, Emil.

His house was a beautifully detailed Gothic revival home that was built in 1860 and then enlarged in the 1880s. Unfortunately, it was destroyed by fires in 1957 and 1960 and can now be remembered only through photographs. The stone-and-mortar wall visible today marks the site of the original foundation. Some of the remaining plantings are part of the original gardens and many others were lovingly put in place in 1976 by Robert Lovinger, a landscape architecture professor from the University of Oregon. The Peter Britt Music Festival was held on the grounds of the estate from 1962 until 1978, when the new Britt Pavilion was built just south.

A short half-mile hike begins 15 yards uphill from the Emil Britt redwood tree. A fairly level path follows the abandoned irrigation ditch that used to divert water from Jackson Creek to the Britt property. Soon you will notice Jackson Creek below the trail, as well as several overgrown sections of a nearly forgotten logging railroad bed. This is a particularly nice walk in the spring when the wildflowers are in bloom and the mosses and ferns are green.

Peter Britt Music Festival
On a hillside near the Britt homesite, a small classical music festival began in 1962. Over 30

BRITT FESTIVALS
Jacksonville, Oregon

years later, the scope of the **Britt Festival** (offices at 614 Medford Center, Medford 97504; tel. 773-6077 or 800-88-BRITT) has developed into a musical smorgasbord encompassing such diverse styles as jazz, folk/country/bluegrass, music theater, and dance, in addition to the original classical repertoire. Mel Tormé, B.B. King, Jean-Pierre Rampal, and the Nitty Gritty Dirt Band are just a few of the big-name artists who have performed here over the years.

The festival runs from the last week of June through the first week of September with a series of nearly 40 concerts. Tickets range from $10 to $20 for general admission. Seating is as much an integral part of the atmosphere of the Britt Festival as the music. Concert-goers often bring along blankets, small lawnchairs (allowed only in designated areas), wine, and a picnic supper to enjoy along with entertainment on balmy summer evenings.

Reserved seating was added in 1987, a move many thought would destroy the intimate ambience. However, these seats are built somewhat down into the ground, so the patrons on blankets and lawn chairs behind them are still able to see the action, while those with bad backs and tired bones are able to enjoy the show too. The reserved seats run $3-5 more than general admission. A large area in front of the seats is for those who like to sit on the grass or on blankets.

Wherever you decide you might like to sit, be sure to order your tickets well in advance to avoid having to stand outside. Like the Oregon Shakespeare Festival, the shows sell out months in advance, especially for the well-known performers.

Hello, Dolly

The comprehensive collection of dolls on display at the **Jacksonville Doll Museum** at the corner of Fifth and Jacksonville streets contains nearly every doll pictured in the *Blue Book of Dolls*. The oldest one on display here is a fragile 1640 Italian crèche doll with carved ivory head and hands. Carved wooden Queen Anne, Dutch or penny woodens, and papier-mâché types are representative of the styles from previous centuries. China heads, Parian, and stone bisques, which were popular from 1830 on, are also lined up for your inspection. But whatever your fancy—bisque, celluloid, cloth, composition, metal, plastic, or rubber—you'll find it here. Open daily 11 a.m.-3:30 p.m. May 30-Sept. 30, with admission $2 for adults, $1 for children under 12, and free for kids under six.

Tours And Tastings

During the summer, **Trolley Tours** (tel. 535-5617) offers 50-minute narrated tours every hour on the hour 10 a.m.-4 p.m. A motorized trolley car picks up passengers at the corner of Third and California streets for an informative and entertaining excursion into Jacksonville's pioneer past. Adult fares are $3.50, children under 12 are $1.50.

For a taste of some of the best of the Pacific Northwest, head for the **Tasting Room** (ORE 238, Jacksonville; tel. 899-1001). Here you can sample fine food and wine for free. After the tastings, you'll have a better idea of what to choose from in their store. Oregon wines, hickory-smoked meats and jerky, and cheeses are some of the goodies you'll want to take home with you. The Tasting Room packs special Britt Festival picnic baskets too.

Pioneer Days

The Wild West returns to life in mid-June in Jacksonville with the town's annual Pioneer Days. A parade in old-time regalia down the main streets of Jacksonville kicks off the party. Following the parade, a street fair featuring arts, crafts, and food booths is held along California St. for the rest of the day. A street dance follows in the afternoon with live music, as well as an old-time fiddlers' performance. Children's games and activities are also scheduled for the afternoon. One of the most popular is the haystack search, in which tots grub around in the straw for over $200 in hidden currency. At 2 p.m., another fun annual event called the Ugly Legs Contest takes place. Contestants wear paper sacks over their heads so they are judged solely on how bad their legs look. Mud, sandals, worn-out sneakers, and other cosmetic/artistic touches are allowed. Other special events are also planned for seniors, and bingo games are held all day long. Call the chamber of commerce (tel. 889-8118) for details.

PRACTICALITIES

Bed And Breakfast

The **Jacksonville Inn** (175 E. California St.; tel. 899-1900; $80-100) lies in the heart of the commercial historic district. In addition to eight air-conditioned rooms furnished with restored antiques and private baths, the inn has an excellent dining room with gourmet fare and an extensive wine list with well over 700 selections. Reservations are highly recommended, especially during the summer. A block down California St. is the **McCully House Inn** (240 E. California St.; tel 899-1942; $75-85). Built in 1861 in the classical revival style, this mansion has four beautifully decorated bedrooms with private baths. European and American antiques, Oriental rugs, delicate lace curtains, and a magnificent square grand piano (tuned a half step lower than today's A-440) add to the historical ambience. A full "country continental" breakfast is included with the price of your room.

Another historic alternative is the **Old Stage Inn** (883 Old Stage Rd., Box 579, Jacksonville 97530; tel. 899-1776 or 800-US-STAGE). Built in 1857 and lovingly restored, the inn provides the appeal of yesterday with the comforts of today. Farm-fresh local produce and home-baked goods are included in a full breakfast. Call ahead for reservations and information.

The Colonial House Bed and Breakfast (Box 1298, 1845 Old Stage Rd., Jacksonville 97530; tel. 770-2783) is a beautiful Georgian colonial revival home built in 1917. The five-acre grounds have graceful old oaks, well-maintained lawns, and a shady pond. Two suites are available, both tastefully decorated and with private baths. A full breakfast of gourmet omelettes, homemade muffins, and seasonal local fruits, or a traditional English breakfast, is also included. Afternoon tea is served at 4 p.m. Rates are $95 per night for one to two people; each additional person is $25. No smoking is allowed, and reservations are recommended.

The Reames House (Box 128, 540 E. California St.; tel. 899-1868) is a spacious Victorian built in 1868. Listed on the National Register of Historic Places, the house is furnished with antiques and is complemented by lovely flower gardens and a covered patio. The carved antique walnut double bed, lace curtains, and period lamps of the Victoria Room ($90) transport you back into the last century. The private bath features a pull-chain toilet and a claw-foot tub. The Peachtree Room ($90) also has a private bath, as well as twin mahogany sleigh beds, a dresser, and an armoire with stenciled walls and curtains. The Colonial Room ($80) shares a bath with the Gold Strike Room ($75). All guests receive a full breakfast of seasonal fruits, fresh-baked goods, gourmet egg dishes, and other breakfast entrees served with freshly ground coffee. The Reames House also offers the use of bicycles, Frisbees, tennis racquets, and even a gold pan if you care to try your luck at Rich Gulch.

A half mile out of old-town Jacksonville is the new **State Lodge** (830 N. Fifth St.; tel. 899-3953 or 800-253-8254; $50-70). The modern rooms here are large, clean, and comfortable, with a country feeling

Food

The **Jacksonville Inn** (175 E. California St.; tel. 899-1900) has consistently been rated one of the top restaurants in Oregon by *Oregon* magazine and *Pacific Northwest* magazine. Distinctive cuisine, served à la carte or table d' hôte, is prepared by master chefs for your enjoyment. While the gold-rich mortar sparkles in the walls of the dining room and lounge, the menu is what offers some real treasures. Steaks, seafood, and specialties of the inn like veal, duck, and prime rib are among the offerings. A selection of vegetarian dishes is also available. A connoisseur's wine cellar of over 700 vintages further enhances your gourmet meal. Open every day for lunch and dinner; reservations are suggested.

The **Bella Union Restaurant and Saloon** (170 W. California St.; tel. 899-1770) is another popular spot in town. Soups, salads, chicken, steaks, pasta, and pizza are some of the items you'll find on the menu here. Vegetarians can enjoy fare like steamed vegetables with cashews and three cheeses or spaghetti with a tangy marinara sauce, both of which include soup or salad and homemade bread for under $9. When the weather is right, the patio in back of the restaurant is a pleasant place to eat lunch or enjoy a beer.

If you're looking for dinner to take to the concert in the gardens or a place to catch a bite before the opening curtain, **Britt Landing** (150 S. Oregon St.; tel. 899-8248) can get you started out on the right note. The Britt Picnic Dinner features substantial sandwiches ($7-10) that are complemented by pasta salad, fresh fruit, and a triple-chocolate brownie. Early-bird dinners ($7-11) come with choice of soup or salad, herb rice, bread, and vegetable.

Calico Palace (605 N. Fifth; tel. 899-1866) serves up a tasty lunch and dinner. Dinners are served family style with plenty of salad, hot bread, potato, gravy, and vegetables for $8-15. Lunch features dozens of burger or hot dog combinations that come with garden veggies and soup, salad, or potato.

Lighter fare can be procured from the **Good Bean Company** (165 S. Oregon St.; tel. 899-9740). Snack items from the display case help enhance a cup of Jacksonville's best java.

Information And Services

The Jacksonville **library** (170 S. Oregon St.; tel. 899-1665) is open Mon.-Tues. noon-6 p.m., Wed.-Thurs. 11-5, Fri. 10-4. The **Jacksonville Chamber of Commerce** (Box 33, 185 N. Oregon St., Jacksonville 97530; tel. 899-8118) is open 10 a.m.-4 p.m. daily and has the scoop on events and activities. The Jacksonville **post office** (175 N. Oregon St., Jacksonville 97530; tel. 899-1563) is open 8:30 a.m.-5 p.m. weekdays. Public transportation connecting Jacksonville with Medford is available on the 30A and 30B buses. Call 799-BUSS for scheduling information.

GRANTS PASS AND VICINITY

The banner across the main thoroughfare in town proudly proclaims: It's the Climate. But while the 20-inches-a-year precipitation average and 52° yearly mean temperature might seem desirable, the true allure of Grants Pass is the mighty Rogue River, which flows through the heart of this community. More than 25 outfitters in Grants Pass and the surrounding villages of Rogue River and Merlin specialize in fishing, float, and jetboat trips. Numerous riverside lodges, accessible by car, river, or footpath, yield remote relaxation in the shadow of the nearby Klamath-Siskiyou Wilderness.

It was the climate that attracted back-to-the-land refugees of the '60s to nearby Takilma, a planned utopian community. More recently, survivalists, in expectation of nuclear Armageddon, have established a network of shelters in the area. They believe that forests filled with game and foraging opportunities coupled with prevailing winds that will keep radioactive fallout away improve their odds . . . good luck!

The climate is also responsible for the once-thick forests in the surrounding mountains, timber source for the numerous mills which in turn provided many jobs. However, decades of overcutting by the lumber companies has dramatically diminished the supply of saw timber, resulting in mill shutdowns and high unemployment rates. In response, the economic base has been gradually shifting away from wood products and now keys on the natural beauty of the area, the recreational opportunities, and of course, the benign weather.

SIGHTS

Palmerton Arboretum

Six miles down U.S. 99 in the town of Rogue River is the Palmerton Arboretum. Orginally a five-acre nursery, the park features plant representatives from around the globe, including Japanese pines and Mediterranean cedars in addition to redwoods and other trees native to the Northwest. A real treat in the spring, the ornamental arboretum offers over 40 species of mature trees complemented by several kinds

of azaleas and rhododendrons. Admission is free. While you're there, be sure to see **Skevington's Crossing,** a 200-foot-high swinging suspension bridge over Evans Creek that connects the arboretum to Anna Classick city park.

Oregon Vortex

About 10 miles south of Grants Pass on I-5 is the House of Mystery at the Oregon Vortex (4303 Sardine Creek Rd., Gold Hill 97525; tel. 855-1543). Called the "Forbidden Ground" by the Rogue Indians because the place spooked their horses, it is actually a repelling magnetic field where objects tend to move away from their center of alignment and lean in funny directions. For example, a ball at the end of a string would not hang straight up and down, and people would seem taller when viewed from one side of the field as opposed to the other. Visitors may bring balls, levels, cameras, or any other instrument they wish to test the vortex for themselves. Guided tours through the house built on this curious site are $4.50 adults, $3.50 children. Open March 1-Oct. 14, 9 a.m.-4:45 p.m., except on Sundays and sometimes Thursdays.

Gold Gulch

In the same area as the Oregon Vortex is Gold Gulch (contact address 8785 Blackwell Road, Central Point 97502; tel. 664-2847). To get there, take I-5, U.S. 99, or the Old Stage Rd. (ORE 228) north from Jacksonville and look for the brightly colored billboards around Gold Hill pointing the way.

Gold Gulch is a re-created early-day mining town that borders on being hokey but provides some worthwhile attractions. Mining and logging exhibits, antique mining equipment and tools, and an authentic arrastra gold mill offer insights into the rigors and dangers of the industries that first opened up the Oregon frontier. A gambling den, mining and assay office, blacksmith shop, Wells Fargo Express Depot, and, of course, the hangman's tree round out the picture of life in the gold country. One of the highlights of Gold Gulch is a walk down into the Millionaire Mine to see a true quartz gold vein and learn how gold is recovered from the depths of the earth. Open June 1 through Labor Day; the admission is $2 for adults and $1 for children.

Wolf Creek Tavern

Approximately 20 miles north of Grants Pass on I-5 in Wolf Creek is Oregon's oldest hostelry, the Wolf Creek Tavern (tel. 866-2474). Originally a hotel for the California and Oregon Stagecoach Line, this historic property is now owned by the state and operated as a restaurant and hotel. Legend has it that President Rutherford B. Hayes visited the tavern in the late 1880s and One Eyed Charlie used to chew the fat in the

dining room. You can also view the small room where author Jack London stayed and wrote part of his famous novel, *The End of the Story.* The staff wears early-19th-century clothing in keeping with the ambience of this famous roadhouse.

Some of the food in the restaurant is a little more modern, with such fare as hamburgers, hot dogs, and grilled-cheese sandwiches on the menu, mainly to keep the kids happy. However, other entrees are typical of those you might have found a hundred years ago when taking a road trip through southern Oregon, and they are quite good. And should the lure of tradition pall, fans of haute cuisine can enjoy such dishes as scampi and house-cut steaks here. Lunch, dinner, and Sunday brunch are served. Afterward, you might want to relax in the "ladies' parlour" or "gentlemen's tap room" or stroll amid the apple trees and roses on the lawn outside. Wolf Creek's boardinghouse had its heyday when it was a halfway house on the Portland-Sacramento stagecoach route, but it continues to serve road-weary travelers with rooms that range from $45 to $60. The period furniture imparts atmosphere, while the bed and baths here are modern enough to be comfortable.

Big Pine

About an hour outside of Grants Pass is the tallest ponderosa pine in the world. Standing a whopping 246 feet high and sporting a 57-inch diameter, Big Pine lives up to its name with an estimated volume of 12,500 board feet of wood. This 300-year-old giant lives in a grove of large pines, cedars, and Douglas firs at **Big Pine Campground.**

To get there, take the Merlin exit off I-5 just north of Grants Pass and proceed toward Galice. Just beyond Morrison's Lodge, a luxurious getaway on the Rogue River, turn left onto Taylor Creek Rd. 25. Big Pine Campground is about 10 miles farther. Another routing option is via U.S. 199. About 20 miles south of Grants Pass on U.S. 199, take Onion Creek Rd. on the north side of the highway and follow it 20 miles to Big Pine.

The campground features 12 picnic sites and 14 campsites. Picnic tables, fire rings, and vault toilets are provided. Water is available from a hand pump between campsites seven and nine. A small playground and primitive softball diamond are tastefully incorporated into the

THERE'S GOLD IN THEM THAR HILLS

Geologists estimate that the prospectors of the 1850s and commercial mining operations that followed found only 25% of Oregon's potential take. With the wild gyrations of the timber-dependent economy, and gold fetching several hundred dollars a troy ounce, it's no wonder that many out-of-work loggers and other people have taken to gold panning in the waterways of southern Oregon.

Almost all streams in Coos, Curry, Douglas, and Jackson counties are good sources of color. "Color" refers to the flecks and bright chips of metal sometimes called gold dust; larger odd-shaped lumps of gold are nuggets. The gold originally comes from veins in the mountains, where it is washed out by winter weather. Spring floods and heavy rains carry the gold downstream. The density of gold causes it to settle in obstructions (like moss), in quiet water behind boulders, or at the base of waterfalls. These deposits of gold can vary from fine gold flecks to a bonanza of nuggets.

But before you head for the hills, you will need some basic equipment. Specially designed gold pans with flaring sides three to four inches deep are available at many hardware stores. Widths range from six inches to two feet; pick one that is comfortable for you to handle. Keep in mind that a pan full of water and gravel can get pretty heavy! Your pan must also be "blued" before panning, otherwise the layer of oil on it will stick to the gold and cause the stuff to float out with the other lighter materials. Heat the pan on your stove until it is a deep blue color and the oils are burned off. Other useful tools include tweezers, a small vial or two, a trowel, and a small shovel or pick.

Panning takes finesse, but with practice it quickly becomes easier. Put some dirt from a likely location in your pan with some water. Pick out the larger pieces of rock and gravel or squeeze out the moss and discard. Swirl the pan gently around from side to side. This causes the gold to sink to the bottom, making it possible to scoop out more gravel from the top. Tilt the pan at a slight angle, and the gold will now fall to the bottom of the lower edge. Remember that gold is 19 times heavier than water and also heavier than most other minerals contained in the gravel of streams. Continue to dip, shake, and remove sand until you have only a small amount left. This is the stage where you have to be extra cautious not to wash away your gold. When you have taken out as much sand as possible, you will have (if you hit pay dirt) small strands of black sand and gold in your pan. Extract the color with tweezers, grab a beer, and start the process all over again. With some work and a little luck, you'll soon be singing the old refrain, "We're in the money!"

The marble halls of the Oregon Caves attract thousands of visitors.

grounds. Many trails take hikers to Big Pine and beyond for a short hike or an all-day adventure. A lazy creek meanders through the area, with alders, hazelnuts, and an array of colorful wildflowers growing along its banks. Deer and other wildlife are frequently spotted grazing in the fragrant meadows nearby. Foragers can pick their fill of blackberries in July and August. Cost is $7 a night.

The Oregon Caves

About 30 miles southwest of Grants Pass are the Oregon Caves. Take U.S. 199 to Cave Junction and then wind your way 20 miles up ORE 46 The last 13 miles of this trip are especially exciting. Just remember that there are few turnouts of sufficient size to enable a large vehicle to reverse direction. A beautiful old-growth Douglas fir forest lining the road might help divert the faint-of-heart from the nail-biting turns on ORE 46.

The cave itself—as there is really only one, which opens onto successive caverns—was formed over the eons by the action of water. As rain and snowmelt seeped through cracks and fissures in the rock above the cave and percolated down into the underlying limestone, huge sections of the limestone became saturated and collapsed—much as a sand castle too close to sea level always caves in. When the water table eventually lowered, these pockets were drained of water and the process of cave decoration began.

First, the limestone was dissolved by the water and carried in solution into the cave. When the water evaporated, it left behind a microscopic layer of calcite. This process was repeated countless times, gradually creating the beautiful formations visible today. When the minerals are deposited on the ceiling, a stalactite begins to form. Limestone-laden water that evaporates on the floor might leave behind a stalagmite. When a stalactite and a stalagmite meet, they become a column. Other cave sculptures you'll see include helicites, hell-bent formations that twist and turn in crazy directions; draperies, looking just like their household namesakes but cast in stone instead of cloth; and soda straws, stalactites that are hollow in the center like a straw, carrying mineral-rich drops of moisture to their tips.

Discovered in 1874, the Oregon Caves attract thousands of visitors annually. During the Depression, walkways and turnoffs were built to make the cave more accessible. Unfortunately, tons of waste rock and rubble were stashed into nooks and crannies in the cave, instead of being transported out. This had the ironic effect of obscuring the very formations intended for display. However, the National Park Service started to remove the artificial debris in 1985, exposing the natural formations once again. Little by little, the cave is returning to the way it looked before the manmade "improvements" were started.

The River Styx, another victim of Depression-era meddling, is enjoying a similar resurrection. This stream used to run through the cave but was diverted into pipes to aid trail and tunnel construction. The pipes ended up buried beneath tons of pulverized rock, and now the Park Service is hard at work undoing the hand of man to let the stream flow where God intended.

Tours of the cave are conducted year-round by National Park Service interpreters. Their presentations are both informative and entertaining, and you will leave the cave with a better understanding of its natural, geologic, and human history. Admission is $8 for adults and $4 for children ages 6-11. The tour takes a little under an hour and requires some uphill walking. Remember that during summer you can sometimes wait an hour in line to go on a tour. Also, from October through April, fewer tours are offered. Good walking shoes and warm clothing are recommended. It may be warm and toasty outside, but the cave maintains a fairly consistent year-round temperature of 41 degrees. Passageways can be narrow, ceilings low, and the footing slippery. Due to federal regulations, children under the age of six are not permitted inside the cave. However, a baby-sitting service is available. Tour times can be obtained by calling 592-3400.

Oregon Caves Chateau

From mid-June through early September, the six-story Oregon Caves Chateau (Box 128, Cave Junction 97523; tel. 592-3400) offers food and accommodations. Located about 50 miles west of Grants Pass on ORE 199, the six-story chateau stands at an elevation of 4,000 feet. Built in 1934, this rustic building blends in with the forest and moss-covered marble ledges. The rooms feature views of Cave Creek canyon, waterfalls, or the Oregon Caves entrance. Rates range from $55 to $75 per night for two to four people. Special "lovers' retreat" weekend packages including discount dinners and cave admissions are also available, but make reservations early, as the number of packages is limited.

The chateau has been nicknamed the "Marble Halls of Oregon," and you can see the huge marble fireplace in the lobby for yourself while you thaw out after your spelunking expedition. The food at the chateau is surprisingly good, and having Cave Creek running through the center of the dining room definitely adds to the unique atmosphere.

For a nice after-dinner hike, ask directions to the big Douglas fir tree, located a little over a mile from the Chateau. With a circumference of 38 feet, seven inches, it appears to be the largest standing tree in Oregon. The surrounding forests here are loaded with tan oak, canyon live oak, Pacific madrone, chinquapin, and manzanita.

Camping

Near the Oregon Caves, camping is available at **Grayback** (Illinois Valley Ranger District, Box 389, Cave Junction 97523), 12 miles from Cave Junction on ORE 46. There are 25 tent sites and 16 vehicular sites close to Sucker Creek. Electricity and piped water are provided, with a store, laundromat, and showers within a mile. Closer to the caves is **Cave Creek** (same address as above). Just take ORE 46 four miles south of the caves to Forest Service Rd. 4032. Piped water and pit toilets are provided, and showers are available five miles away. You'll also find a ranger station and informative campfire programs here on summer evenings. Both campgrounds charge $5.

ROGUE RIVER TRIPS

There are about as many ways to enjoy the Rogue as there are critters in and around it. Some people prefer the excitement and challenge of maneuvering their own craft down the treacherous rapids. Oar rafts (which a guide rows for you), paddle rafts (which you paddle yourself), and one-man inflatable kayaks are the most widely used boats for this sort of river exploration. The 40-mile section downstream from Graves Creek is open only to nonmotorized vessels, and river traffic is strictly regulated by the U.S. Forest Service. The limited float permits (25 a day) are prized by rafters around the world, as the Rogue not only has some of the best whitewater in America but also guarantees a first-rate wilderness adventure. And yet, it can be a civilized wilderness. Hot showers, comfortable beds, and sumptuous meals at several of the river lodges tucked away in remote quarters of this famous waterway welcome boaters after a day's voyage. Excellent camping facilities are available for those who want to experience nature directly.

But you don't have to risk life and limb in a fancy inner tube to see the Rogue, because several local companies offer jetboat tours. On a jetboat, powerful engines suck in hundreds of gallons of water a minute and shoot it out the back of the boat through a narrow nozzle, generating the necessary thrust for navigation. With no propeller to hit rocks and other obstacles,

One of the most popular ways to see the Rogue is by kayak.

these 20-ton machines can carry 40 or more passengers in water only six inches deep. This makes the jetboat an ideal way to enjoy the beauty of the Rogue and at the same time keep your feet dry. Finally, many outfitters charter drift boats to secret fishing holes for anglers to try their luck landing supper.

Fishing On The Rogue
The upper Rogue River is renowned for one of the world's best late-winter steelhead fisheries. Numerous highways and backroads offer easy access to 155 miles of well-ramped river between Lost Creek Reservoir east of Medford and Galice west of Grants Pass. With fall and spring chinook runs and other forms of river recreation, it's no accident that the Rogue Valley is home to the world's top three aluminum and fiberglass driftboat manufacturers. Add rafters, kayakers and plenty of bank anglers and you can understand why peak salmon or steelhead

season is sometimes described as "combat fishing." Contact southern Oregon visitor info outlets for rules, regulations, and leads on outfitters.

Float Trips
Paul Brooks Raft Trips (Box 638, Merlin 97532; tel. 476-8051) offers a one-day guided trip that gives you the choice of oar raft, paddle raft, or inflatable kayak. Enjoy an excellent lunch at one of the river lodges. **Eagle Sun Inc.** (Box 611, Ashland 97520; tel. 482-5139) has half-, full-, and multi-day trips on oar or paddle rafts. Their adventures range from the mild to the wild, and child care can be arranged through their office. **Galice Resort and Store Raft Trips** (11744 Galice Rd., Merlin 97532; tel. 476-3818) offers full-day raft or inflatable-kayak trips. All-day trips depart at 9 a.m., and half-day departures are at 9 a.m. and 1 p.m. **Noah's World of Water** (Box 11, Ashland 97520; tel. 488-2811) has been providing quality rafting and fishing trips since 1974. They have half-day and one- to four-day excursions that vary from exciting whitewater rafting highs to kinder, gentler floats. From late March to early October, they depart Ashland for the Rogue three times daily, and a roundtrip transfer from your lodging is included in the price.

Orange Torpedo Trips (Box 1111-S, Grants Pass 97526; tel. 479-5061 or 800-635-2925) has half-day and one- to three-day raft or inflatable-kayak (also affectionately known as orange torpedoes because of their color and shape) adventures. They also offer a unique VIP two-day package that combines the best on the river: jetboat tour, wagon ride, gourmet dining, lodging, wildlife park, and float trip all rolled into one.

Otter River Trips (12163 Galice Rd., Merlin 97532; tel. 476-8590) caters to families, offering one-day whitewater-rafting trips. They also operate fishing excursions year-round and special gold-panning trips. **River Adventure Float Trips** (Box 841, Grants Pass 97526; tel. 476-6493) has summer raft and fall fishing trips that vary from a half day to several days. **River Trips Unlimited, Inc.** (4140 Dry Creek Rd., Medford 97504; tel. 779-3798) has been guiding trips on the Rogue for over 30 years. They have one- to four-day raft, Tahiti, or summer-run steelhead fishing trips that include meals and overnight stays at some of the river lodges.

Rogue/Klamath River Adventures (Box 4295, Medford 97501; tel. 779-3708) has one- to three-day whitewater-rafting and inflatable-kayak trips that give you the option of camping out under the stars or roughing it in style at a river lodge. **Rogue/Klamath Whitewater Co.** (1202 E. Main St., Medford 97504; tel. 772-8467) has personalized high-quality trips for the lowest available rates. Exciting half-, full-, and two-day overnighter raft, inflatable kayak, and guided salmon-fishing trips are among the offerings. **Rogue Wilderness, Inc.** (Box 1647, Grants Pass 97526; tel. 336-1647) is here to tailor-make just about any length of trip you may care to take. Whitewater rafting, inflatable kayaking, and salmon and steelhead fishing are some of the available options.

For more information on scenic whitewater-rafting and fishing trips, contact the **Rogue River Guides Association** (Box 792, Medford 97501; tel. 772-5194).

Jetboat Trips

Hellgate Excursions (953 S.E. Seventh, Grants Pass 97526; tel. 479-7204) is the premier jetboat operator on this end of the river. Their trips begin at the dock of the Riverside Inn (971 S.E. Sixth St., Grants Pass) and proceed downriver through the forested Siskiyou foothills. En route, black-tailed deer, ospreys, and great blue herons are commonly seen. If you're lucky, a bald eagle or black bear might also be sighted. The scenic highlight is the deep-walled Hellgate Canyon, where you'll look upon what are believed to be the oldest rocks in the state. The rugged beauty here provided the backdrop for John Wayne and Katherine Hepburn in *Rooster Cogburn*. Trips including a champagne brunch ($28 for adults, kids 4-11 $16) and a weekday lunch of barbecued chicken and ribs ($34 for adults, kids $18) at a wilderness lodge are two popular additions to this itinerary. Another option is to tack on an extra foray into Grave Creek Whitewater beyond Hellgate at a price comparable to that of the regular luncheon cruise (lunch is available but not included). Finally, if you have limited time and/or a limited budget, you can just venture to Hellgate and turn around ($18 adults, $10 kids). These excursions run May 1 through Sept. 30 and feature commentary by your pilot, who knows every eddy in the river. Be sure to call ahead for reservations, as space on all of their runs books up fast.

THE CHRISTMAS FLOOD OF 1964: POSTSCRIPT TO DEVASTATION

Passing through the serene Rogue River Valley today, little indication can be seen of the ravages of the Christmas Flood of 1964. The autumn of that fateful year seemed to augur the coming of a peaceful winter in Rogue country. With the white snow on the mountains and a ring around the harvest moon, the only thing that seemed missing was ol' Saint Nick himself, riding through the night sky.

But then the rains came—slowly at first. Then little by little, almost imperceptibly, the downpour transformed into a deluge. The warm rains quickly melted the snowpack and the swollen streams spurred the foaming Rogue on its course to the sea. Logjams and abnormally high tides contributed to raising the water levels to record heights.

Whole towns had to be evacuated from the onslaught of water. Many families saw their hopes and dreams wash away, with their tears, in the rain—victims of the impartial hand of nature. The inundation was not confined to the Rogue, as the killer storm turned almost every western Oregon river into a frighteningly efficient generator of destruction. Governor Hatfield declared the region a disaster area. The damage statewide was in the millions of dollars, and many lives were lost by the time the muddy waters receded a week later. To avert a similiar castastrophe here in the future, the Army Corps of Engineers constructed Lost Creek Reservoir on the upper Rogue not long afterwards.

And while time has healed the effects of the Christmas Flood of 1964, you can still find high-water marks here and there in the valley. Tacked high up on trees and bridges, perched over 100 feet above the now placid waters of the Rogue, they serve as a silent reminder of the magnitude of this great disaster.

EVENTS

Boatnik Festival

The Boatnik Festival starts on Memorial Day weekend at Riverside Park in Grants Pass. A carnival, parade, and softball tournament are featured, but the top event is the whitewater boat races. Over two dozen modified speedboats and jetboats compete in a 46-mile course on the Rogue River. Warm-ups begin on Memorial Day morning, followed by the race at 1 p.m. The competition starts at the boat docks in Riverside Park.

Josephine County Fair

The Josephine County Fair normally takes place in mid-August at the fairgrounds in Grants Pass. In addition to the usual fair attractions such as the carnival, concessions, and 4-H livestock, entertainers like Johnny Cash and Three Dog Night perform for enthusiastic crowds. A popular annual competition held here is the four-wheel tractor pull, in which souped-up farm vehicles attempt to drag a bulldozer (with its blade down) 100 yards as fast as possible.

Rooster-crowing Contest

The nearby city of **Rogue River,** southeast of Grants Pass on I-5, has something to crow about. On the last day of June, the Rogue River Rooster Crow is held at the Rogue River Elementary School grounds, beginning with a parade and followed by live music and entertainment. A street fair featuring arts, crafts, and food is also set up on the premises. But the big event takes place early in the afternoon. Farmers from all over Oregon and northern California bring their roosters to strut their stuff and wing out songs to the enthusiastic crowds. A fowl tradition since 1953, the rooster to crow the most times in his allotted time period wins the prize for his proud owner.

Grants Pass Downs

Horse-racing aficionados will appreciate Grants Pass Downs. The season opens Memorial Day weekend with races on weekends through the Fourth of July. Place your bets on your favorite steeds to place, win, or show ($2 minimum). The cash-sell betting is all computerized, al-lowing for more exotic bets like the quiniela and the trifecta. The latter are "wheel" bets, in which you get to choose one of every possible combination of two or three horses ($1 minimum) to win. Even if you're not the betting sort, it's a kick watching the horses thunder around the bend and down the home stretch.

Growers Market

Farmers markets are an Oregon tradition, particularly in the southern part of the state. Grants Pass is said to have the largest one of all, boasting produce, crafts, prepared foods, and plants. As its location was in flux at the second edition's press time, call or write to determine where the market will be held (Growers Market, P.O. Box 576, Grants Pass 97526; tel. 476-5375). It's open Saturdays 9 a.m.-1 p.m., from mid-March till Thanksgiving, and also on Tuesdays at the same times, beginning in June.

PRACTICALITIES

Bed And Breakfast

The **Riverbanks Inn** (8401 Riverbanks Rd., Grants Pass; tel. 479-1118) is situated along a tranquil section of the Rogue. The Japanese gardens, hot tub, and Casablanca-meets-Caribbean decor complement this beautiful natural setting. Guests can choose among a log cabin, cottage, and three-bedroom riverside lodge that sleeps 10 ($250). Breakfast is included. The healthful gourmet meals and massage therapy available here are other enticements.

Campgrounds

Many fine campgrounds are found along the banks of the Rogue River near Grants Pass. The privately owned and operated RV parks in the KOA genre tend to be more expensive than their public counterparts but also offer more amenities like swimming pools, laundromats, and other conveniences. They range from about $10 to $15 a night and are found along U.S. 99 between Gold Hill and Grants Pass. The four county parks listed below cost $8 for hookup sites, $7 for tent sites. Contact the **Josephine County Parks Dept.** (Rogue River 97537; tel. 474-5285) for reservations and additional information.

GRANTS PASS ACCOMMODATIONS

IN TOWN

Best Western, Grants Pass, 111 Agness, tel. 476-1117, $55-90, many amenities.

City Center Motel, 741 N.E. 6th, tel. 476-6134, $30-40, kitchenettes.

Fireside Motel, 839 N.E. 6th St., tel. 474-5558, $35-50, pool.

Flamingo Inn, 728 N.W. 6th St., tel. 476-6601, $30-42, pool, pets, kitchenettes.

Golden Inn, 1950 N.W. Vine St., tel. 479-6611, $40-50, pool, food, pets.

Hawks Inn, 1464 N.W. 6th St., tel. 479-4057, $35-45, pool and air conditioning.

Knight's Inn Motel, 104 S.E. 7th, tel. 479-5595, $35-45, laundromat, pets.

Motel 6, 1800 7th St., tel. 474-1331, $25-35, pool and air conditioning.

Motel de Rogue, 2600 Rogue River Hwy., tel. 479-2111, $45-65, on the river.

Redwood Motel, 815 N.E. 6th St., tel. 476-0878, $35-45, playground, pool, pets.

Rogue River Inn, 6285 Rogue River Hwy. (old Hwy. 99), tel. 582-1120, $40-50.

Shilo Inn of Grants Pass, 1880 N.W. 6th, tel. 479-8391, $55-65, pool, pets.

Uptown Motel, 1253 N.E. 6th, tel. 479-2952, $35-45, pets.

ROGUE RIVER RETREATS

Morrison's Rogue River Lodge, 8500 Galice Rd., tel. 476-3825, $150-240, the super-deluxe treatment.

Paradise Ranch Inn, 700 W. Monument Dr., tel. 479-4333, $88-125, reservations recommended.

River Shore Resort, 2520 Rogue River Hwy., tel. 476-6203, $45-70, reservations required.

Riverside Inn Restaurant, 971 S.E. 6th St. tel. 476-6873, $70-90, home port of **Rogue Jetboat Excursions.**

Rogue Valley Resort, 7799 Rogue River Hwy., tel. 582-3762, $41-69, reservations required.

Indian Mary Park is the showcase of Josephine County parks. To get there, go about eight miles east of Merlin on the Merlin-Galice Road. Located on the banks of the Rogue River, this campground has 89 sites, several with sewer hookups and utilities, as well as showers, flush toilets, and piped water. A boat ramp, beautiful hiking trails, a playground, and one of the best beaches on the Rogue make this one of the most popular county campgrounds on the river.

Griffen Park is a smaller campground with 24 sites for tents and trailers. To get there, take the Redwood Highway (U.S. 199) to Riverbanks Rd., then turn onto Griffen Rd. and follow it about five miles to where it meets the Rogue. The park has a boat ramp, showers, flush toilets,

piped water, and RV dumping facilities. **Schroeder Park** is another complete campground near town. Located on Schroeder Lane off Redwood Ave., the park has 31 sites, some with hookups and utilities. Showers, flush toilets, and a boat ramp make this a favorite spot for fishing enthusiasts. In addition to a picnic area and an excellent swimming hole, a rope tied to a huge cottonwood on the opposite bank of the river near the park is waiting for any swingers who like to make a big splash.

Whitehorse Park is six miles west of Grants Pass on Upper River Road. Purchased by the county in 1958 from the Rogue Rovers Trail Club, this park has 44 campsites, many with hookups and utilities. Showers, piped water, lighting, and good hiking trails developed by the previous owners are found here. The river channel shifted away from the park in the wake of the Christmas flood of 1964, but it's only about a half-mile walk to a fine beach on the Rogue.

The only state park in the area is **The Valley of the Rogue**. Located about halfway between Medford and Grants Pass off of I-5, the park is set along the banks of its namesake river. The Rogue supports year-round salmon and spring steelhead runs. Although there are 97 sites for trailers and motor homes, and 77 tent sites, this place fills up fast, so reservations are recommended during the warmer months. Hookups, utilities, showers, laundromat, and some wheel-chair-accessible facilities make this campground worth the $10-a-night fee.

Food

Although it's not the gourmet capital of Oregon, Grants Pass is a town where many travelers pull in for a bite. Its proximity to Rogue River recreation and fishing, together with a wide range of dining alternatives, explain this popularity.

Granny's Kitchen (117 N.E. F St.; tel. 476-7185) has great breakfast omelettes, a full lunch menu that includes everything from pot pie to quiche, and all-American dinners. Their bakers are busy during the wee hours of the morning producing extraordinary pies that sell like hotcakes the rest of the day. The **Skinny Spot** (126 N.E. F St.; tel. 479-6234) is one of the few restaurants in Oregon that caters to those with special dietary needs. Restricted-calorie, low-cholesterol, and minimal-sodium-and-sugar items are emphasized on their menu. **Erik's** (1067 Redwood Spur, Grants Pass; tel. 479-4471) is for the serious eater. The 22-foot-long salad bar is a meal in itself, and there's a hot dinner buffet where you can fill any extra space left on your plate. A wide range of steak, seafood, chicken, and pasta dinners is also available.

R-Haus (2140 Rogue River Hwy.; tel. 476-4287), a local favorite dinner spot, is a formal dining room in a turn-of-the-century house. Check to see what the nightly early-bird specials are. The waitresses dress in Victorian style at **Yankee Pot Roast** (720 N.W. Sixth; tel. 476-0551), but the menu will bring you back to the future. Light dinners are only $7.95, and all other dinner se-

lections are $8.95 and $9.95 respectively.

The menu at **China Hut** (1434 N.W. Sixth; tel. 476-3441) features interesting entrees such as vegetarian chow yuk, Mandarin pineapple duck, and ma po tofu. Even if you don't always understand the lingo, don't worry; all you really need is a big appetite to finish their large portions. The **Hong Kong** (820 N.W. Sixth; tel. 476-4244) has a family-pack dinner to go that at $9.95 for two people is one of the best deals in town. **Pongsri's** (1571 N.E. Sixth, tel. 479-1345) is an Oriental restaurant with good vegetarian and seafood dinners. The price is right, and the helpings are generous.

Herb's La Casita (515 S.E. Rogue River Hwy.; tel. 476-1313) has a little bit of everything, featuring a full menu of Mexican and American dishes. **Maria's Mexican Kitchen** (105 N.E. Mill; tel. 474-2429) uses handmade tortillas and a special family recipe to make some of the best burritos around. **Little Italy** (201 S.W. Sixth; tel. 479-1066) was rated one of the top 200 restaurants in the state by *Oregon* magazine. In addition to downhome Italian dishes like saltimbocca, there's an ample selection of American food too.

Outside of Grants Pass proper are a few other restaurants of note. To satisfy your craving for nonmeat burgers and vegetarian fare, try the **Grayback Cafe** (120 Cedar Flat Rd., Williams; tel. 846-6900). Located in Williams, about 20 miles south of Grants Pass on the back road to the Oregon Caves, they also have ribs, chicken, and regular burgers. Northwest of Grants Pass, in Merlin, the **Blue Heron Dinner House** (330 Merlin Ave.; tel. 479-6604) serves everything from seafood fettuccine to chicken piccata, Wed.-Sun. 4-10 p.m. Dinner theater with the Col. Edwards Traveling Troupe, performing what can best be described as frontier vaudeville, is also featured in a separate dining room. And for home cooking and local color, **Buzz's Wheel-in Cafe** (450 Merlin Rd.; tel. 476-3912) is a safe bet. Breakfasts are the most popular, featuring a mean stack of pancakes that would satisfy even Paul Bunyan.

Information And Services

Josephine Memorial Hospital (715 Dimmick; tel. 476-6831) offers ambulance service around the clock. **Southern Oregon Medical Center** (1505 N.W. Washington; tel. 479-9717) is a participating member of Blue Cross health service and also features 24-hour emergency care. The **police** (tel. 474-6370) and state police (tel. 474-3175) are only a phone call away.

The **post office** (132 N.W. Sixth, Grants Pass 97526; tel. 479-7526) is open 8:30-5 weekdays. The **Grants Pass Chamber of Commerce** (1501 N.E. Sixth; tel. 476-7717) is open 9-5 daily.

Greyhound (460 N.E. Agness Ave.; tel. 476-4513) offers access to the I-5 corridor and the coast. The **Green Tortoise** picks up off I-5 at Denny's Restaurant (exit 58).

A pleasant air-conditioned and carpeted laundromat is **Maytag Laundry and Dry Cleaners** (1620 Williams Highway Plaza; tel. 479-1743). Located on the south side of Safeway in the Plaza, it's open seven days a week from 7:30 a.m. to 10 p.m. **Classic Auto** (414 N.E. F St.; tel. 476-8938) features new and used rental cars. Pick up and delivery is free anywhere within the city limits, nonsmoking cars are available, and all cars are air-conditioned.

Blind George's (G street between Fifth and Sixth) is a newsstand and smokeshop on the main drag. It's also a local institution. This is the place to come to get travel info, local gossip, and out-of-town newspapers. In addition to its array of printed media, its buttery, crunchy popcorn is justifiably famous.

ROSEBURG AND VICINITY

Many people just passing through the Roseburg area would probably quickly dismiss it as a hick town of lumberjacks and country bumpkins. A closer look, however, reveals many more interesting layers beneath the mill-town veneer. While about half of the folks here rely upon the woods as a workplace (and this fact is reflected in the no-nonsense cafes and businesses meeting their needs), growing pockets of refinement are found in between the pickup trucks and lumber mills. An award-winning museum, Oregon's only drive-through zoo, and some fine restaurants are a few examples of culture in the hinterland.

And yet, the true allure to Roseburg is not really in town, but in the surrounding countryside. The Mediterranean climate of the Umpqua Valley has proven ideal for producing world-class wines and contributes to wonderful winetasting tours. The beautiful North Umpqua River to the east offers rafting, camping, hiking, and fishing. In addition to catching trout, salmon, and bass, anglers come from all over to enjoy one of the world's last rivers with a native run of summer steelhead. Numerous waterfalls along the river and the frothy whitewater make the Indian word Umpqua ("Thunder Water") an appropriate name. And if you are really interested in a closer look at a lumber mill, you can visit the world's largest particleboard plant.

In short, there's more here than a hasty visual appraisal would suggest, and it's worth more time than it takes to top off a tank of gas and wolf down a hamburger. Check it out—you'll be glad you did.

SIGHTS

Art And Culture
The **Douglas County Museum of History and Natural History** (Box 1550, Roseburg 97470; tel. 440-4507 or 800-452-0991) is located at the Douglas County Fairgrounds (exit 123 off I-5). This nationally acclaimed museum has four wings of exhibits that range from a million-year-old saber-toothed tiger to 19th-century steam-logging equipment. Indian artifacts, a re-creation of the 1882 Dillard Oregon and California Railroad depot, an imaginative forest-industry exhibit, and an extensive collection of historical photos make your visit both entertaining and educational. Open Tues.-Sat. 10-4, Sun. 12-4.

The **Umpqua Valley Arts Center** (1124 W. Harvard; tel. 672-2532) has two galleries. The main gallery features monthly rotating shows of local, regional, and Northwest artists. The Gift Gallery offers one-of-a-kind gifts made by a wide variety of Oregon artists.

Flower Power
The **Lotus Knight Memorial Gardens** are in Riverside Park. Located between Oak and Washington streets on the banks of the South

Umpqua River, these gardens are a feast for the eyes with colorful azaleas and rhododendrons in the spring. Open daily 5 a.m.-10 p.m.

Something Fishy
The **Winchester Fish Ladder** is just off I-5 at exit 129 on the north bank of the North Umpqua River. Here visitors can watch salmon and steelhead in their native environment as they swim by the viewing window at Winchester Dam. The North Umpqua and the Columbia are the only rivers in Oregon that offer this attraction. Spring chinook and summer steelhead migrate upriver May through August, and coho, fall chinook, and more summer steelhead swim on by from September through November. From December through May, winter steelhead is the primary species seen going through the fish ladders and on past the window.

Mill Tours
The world's largest particleboard plant, **Rose-**

burg Forest Products (tel. 679-3311, ext. 392), south of Roseburg in nearby **Dillard,** offers tours by appointment only (with 24 hours' advance notice required) Wednesday and Friday at 1:30 p.m. This plant runs around the clock, seven days a week, producing this versatile building material. You'll see the entire process, from wood chip to finished product, accompanied by a cacophony of bells and whistles. The tour lasts approximately two hours, with some uphill walking and stair climbing. No open-toe shoes or high heels are allowed. Visitors must be 10 years of age or older. Contact the Roseburg Visitors and Convention Bureau for info on other local mill tours. As you drive down I-5 outside of town you'll be able to see piles of Roseburg Forest Products lumber on the east side of the highway. The enormity of these piles bespeaks this company's status as the largest privately held, for-profit company that is Oregon-owned and headquartered (1991 and 1992 figures).

Wildlife Safari

Tucked away in a 600-acre wooded valley is Wildlife Safari (Safari Rd., Winston 97496; tel. 679-6761), Oregon's drive-through zoo. To get there, take exit 119 off I-5 and follow ORE 42 for four miles. Turn right on Lookingglass Rd. and right again on Safari Road. Once inside the park gates, the brightly colored birds and semiexotic game animals transport you to other lands, with an oddly appropriate Oregon backdrop. Be that as it may, every possible step has been taken at Wildlife Safari to re-create African and North American animal life zones. Lest this conjure the image of lions, tigers, and bears eating Bambi and company for supper before your very eyes, rest assured that these critters are kept apart from their natural prey. Similar precautions are taken with humans. People must remain inside their vehicles except in designated areas, and windows and sunroofs must be kept closed in the big cats' and bears' areas.

The first loop takes you to see the tigers and cheetahs. These giant felines loll lazily about or catch catnaps in the tall grass. The next link takes you through the heart of "Africa," where the deer and the antelope play. Wildebeests, zebras, and other creatures scamper freely about, seemingly oblivious to the slow parade of cars and people watching them. Elephants, rhinoceroses, and other African big game are also represented here. Soon you are in "North America." Bears, bighorn sheep, pronghorns, moose, and buffalo are just a few of the animals that live down in the valley. Perhaps the most popular attraction is the petting zoo, where children get "hands-on" experience. When the weather is good, play sheik or sultan and take a memorable ride on the camel or the elephant. Open at 8:30 a.m. in the summer and 9 a.m. the rest of the year, the park closes at dusk regardless of the season.

WINERIES

Eight wineries in the Roseburg vicinity offer tastings and tours. The dry, Mediterranean climate

DOUGLAS COUNTY

A good look at just about any local mountainside tells the story of Douglas County. For years, the economy here has revolved around *Pseudotsuga menziessi* ("false hemlock"), the Douglas fir. Named after David Douglas of the English Botanical Society, who visited Oregon in the 1820s to research Northwest flora and fauna, the Douglas fir has enabled its namesake county to perpetually rank near the top of the state's timber-production levels. This distinction has given it the nickname of the "Lumberjack County."

After all of this fanfare, you probably think that Douglas County is named after David Douglas, right? Wrong! It's really named after Illinois Senator Steven A. Douglas, who gained fame for debating Abraham Lincoln in 1858 on the "peculiar institution" of slavery. Although Lincoln lost the senatorial election to Douglas, the debates helped Lincoln gain national prominence and polarized the issue, which James Madison called "a firestorm in the night." Douglas's notoriety out west, however, was due more to his ardent advocacy of Oregon statehood in Congress. It was no small honor to choose his name to grace this county where stagecoaches passed en route to Jacksonville gold country, where California-bound steamships plied the Umpqua, and where Oregon's most esteemed pioneer family, the Applegates, chose to settle.

OREGON STATE HIGHWAYS

Camels smile at passing motorists at Wildlife Safari.

and rich variety of soils in the area are ideal for chardonnay, Pinot Noir, gewürztraminer, riesling, zinfandel, and cabernet sauvignon varietals. A good wine-tour pamphlet with a fine map showing the location of the wineries is available from the Roseburg Visitors and Convention Bureau.

Hillcrest Vineyard, Callahan Ridge Winery

Hillcrest Vineyard (240 Vineyard Ln.; tel. 673-3709), in business since 1963, is one of the oldest vineyards in Oregon. Their first batch was a humble 240 gallons, but production has since grown to over 20,000 gallons annually. The winery is noted primarily for its rieslings but also produces cabernet sauvignon, Pinot Noir, and small quantities of other varieties. Callahan Ridge Winery (340 Busenbark Ln.; tel. 673-7901), open daily for tastings, tours, and sales, is the Umpqua Valley's newest vintner. They offer a very dry gewürztraminer, white zinfandel, and white riesling, as well as barrel-aged chardonnay and a late-harvest gewürztraminer. The tasting room hours are daily 11:30 a.m.-5 p.m., April-October.

Davidson Winery

Davidson Winery (2637 Reston Rd., Tenmile; tel. 679-6950) is located 22 miles southwest of Roseburg. The winery produces estate-bottled wines including Pinot Noir, chardonnay and riesling. Open Memorial Day through Labor Day, daily 10-5; rest of the year by appointment only.

Girardet Wine Cellars, Umpqua River Vineyards

Down the road from Davidson Winery is Girardet Wine Cellars (895 Reston Rd.; tel. 679-7252). Philippe Girardet, from a town at the headwaters of the Rhone River in Switzerland, brings European wine-blending techniques to Oregon. This process produces unique chardonnay, Pinot Noir, cabernet sauvignon, and riesling wines. Tastings, tours, and sales daily noon-5, May-Sept.; Sat. noon-5, Oct.-April. The winery is closed Dec. 20-Jan. 30. The Umpqua River Vineyards (451 Hess Lane; tel. 673-1975) offers tastings daily 11:30- 5:30.

Jonicole Vineyards (491 Vineyard Ln.; tel. 679-5771) offers cabernet sauvignon, chardonnay, Pinot Noir, and rosé. Open daily noon-5:30.

Lookingglass And Henry Wineries

The Lookingglass Winery (6561 Lookingglass Rd.; tel. 679-8198) endorses a philosophy of winemaking that includes quality fruit, strict temperature control, and the limited use of antioxidants like sulfites. Their first release in January 1990 was a rare Botrytised late-harvest white riesling. Open daily noon-5 p.m., April-December. The Henry Winery (Box 26, ORE 9, Umpqua 97486; tel. 459-5120 or 459-3614) has produced a string of award-winning varietals from chardonnay, gewürztraminer, and Pinot Noir grapes. Their 1984 Pinot Noir won the double gold award at the prestigious San Francisco Expo National Wine Competition, proving that Oregon wines can compete with California's best. Recent newcomers to their outstanding lineup include Pinot Noir blanc and Muller-Thurgau. In addition to tasting and tours daily from noon to 5 p.m., lunch at their shaded picnic tables near the vineyard and the Umpqua River can heighten your enjoyment of the fruit of the vine.

SPORTS AND RECREATION

Two area golf courses are open to the public. **Sutherlin Knolls** (tel. 459-4422) is 12 miles north of Roseburg to the west of Sutherlin on ORE 138. Golf nine holes for $7, 18 holes for $13. For a dollar or two more, you can use an electric golf cart to get you and your clubs over the hills and dales. A coffee shop and lounge provide sustenance and lubricants to keep you putting happily around. **Roseburg Municipal Golf Course** (1005 Stewart Park Dr., Roseburg 97470; tel. 672-4592) is closer to town. It costs $6 for nine holes, $10 for 18 holes; knock off a buck or two during winter. In addition to power carts, a lighted driving range, and rental golf clubs, a complete pro shop offers lessons and any peripherals you may need.

Tennis buffs will find free courts at the Douglas County Fairgrounds, Roseburg High School, and Umpqua Community College. Twelve lighted courts are located at Stewart Park off Stewart Parkway, but they require fees and reservations (tel. 673-8650). The YMCA (tel. 440-9622) is also located in Stewart Park and has racquetball and basketball courts as well as an indoor swimming pool. Umpqua Community College (tel. 440-4600, ext. 686) has a pool ($1.50) that's open to the public during the summer from 1 to 4 p.m. and 7 to 9 p.m. Roseburg also has two bowling alleys and two movie theater complexes.

DOUGLAS COUNTY FISHING

The Umpqua River system is home to a dozen species of popular eating fish that range from the big chinook salmon to the tiny silver smelt. The following overview will help you decide where and when to go and what to take to land some supper.

THE GOATS OF MOUNT EMIL

There's a saying that only a dude or a fool will predict the weather. But the folks here in Roseburg were once able to tell with 93% accuracy if it was going to rain. Their system was simple enough. A basalt mountain called Mt. Emil that rises up from the west bank of the South Umpqua River near downtown had been home to a herd of goats for as long as anyone could remember. When the goats came down from the top of Mt. Emil, that meant it was going to rain.

In the early 1960s, Mother Nature's barometer had to make way for the wheels of progress. Road-building crews blasted out huge chunks of Mt. Emil to make room for Interstate 5. The goats endured this incursion into their domain and still managed to faithfully make their pilgrimage down from the mountaintop when inclement weather was imminent. But 20 years later, the highway engineers decided that the freeway entrance at the base of Mt. Emil was too dangerous and needed more work. So in the early 1980s, the men and machines once again assaulted the goats' territory.

This time, the citizenry of Roseburg came together to protect their weather soothsayers. They circulated petitions to "save our goats" and sent them to Salem with an emotional plea to the governor to halt the construction, but to no avail. With their turf dynamited into oblivion and the gentle grassy glade turned into a steep cliff, the goats departed for points unknown. Today, Mt. Emil survives in the form of an ugly rock escarpment that echoes with the 24-hour roar of traffic, while the plaintive bleating of the goats of Mt. Emil is only a fading memory.

Chinook Salmon

Spring chinook enter the North Umpqua River from March to June, work their way upstream during July and August, and spawn from September to October. The average size is about 15 pounds, though occasionally people hook some big ones two to three times that weight. You'll need a stout rod, sturdy reel, drifting eggs or sand shrimp for bait, and some type of spinner. Fall chinook are mainly found in the warmer South Umpqua River. Their migration starts in midsummer and peaks in September when the rains increase water flow and lower the river's temperature. Bait and tackle for fall chinook fishing are pretty much the same as spring chinook gear.

Steelhead

The best fishing for summer steelhead on the North Umpqua is from June to October; the fish spawn from January to March. This fish averages only six to eight pounds, but it will make you think that you are trying to reel in a chinook by the way it struggles. Fly-fishing for summer steelhead is extremely popular—so much so that the 31-mile stretch from Rock Creek upriver to Soda Springs is for fly-angling only. Elsewhere on the North Umpqua, spin-casting with drift eggs, plugs, lures, or shrimp is allowed. There are no summer steelhead on the South Umpqua because there are no deep pools for them during the hot summer months.

Winter steelhead are found in both the North and South Umpqua rivers. They begin their migration upriver in November, so December and January are the best fishing months. The fish spawn from February to April. The success of the winter steelhead runs is in great part determined by the weather, which affects important variables like water temperature, level, and color. Generally speaking, if it's cold and wet (but not too wet), the fishing tends to be better. This makes it important to dress warmly in appropriate raingear so you don't turn as blue as the fish you're trying to catch.

Coho And Sockeye Salmon

Coho, alias "silvers," are found throughout the Umpqua River system. The coho life cycle lasts about three years. Each spends its first year in fresh water, heads for the ocean to spend one to

The South Umpqua River, an angler's mecca, winds through wooded southern Oregon hills.

two years, and then returns to fresh water to spawn. The adults weigh an average of 10 pounds each.

Far more rare in the Umpqua River system are crimson sockeye, affectionately nicknamed "reds" by local guides and everyone else. These river denizens usually weigh about five pounds; eggs are the preferred bait. Possessing more oil than the chinook, the sockeye is regarded as the number-one salmon for quality and flavor.

Rainbow Trout

You'll find this brightly speckled fish in nearly all rivers and streams of the Umpqua River system where the water is relatively cool and gravel bars clean. They don't like warm water and avoid the lower South Umpqua and Cow Creek for this reason. Rainbows do like the riffles at the entry or exit of pools. This is the most common game fish in the water, mainly because the rivers, lakes, and streams of the Umpqua are routinely seeded with over 100,000 legal-size (eight inches or longer) rainbows. The fishing season opens in April, with the best fishing in early summer when the fish are actively feeding. The best baits are salmon eggs, worms, or small flies; lures can also be used with success. The most popular tackle is spin-casting gear with a light leader.

Brown And Brook Trout
In the rapids of the upper North Umpqua you'll find browns, particularly around Soda Springs. Browns seem to like faster-moving water than rainbows. The average size is about a foot long, but sometimes 20-inchers are landed. Mid-summer is the best time to fish for browns. Worms and salmon eggs prove effective, but the best lure is one that resembles a small fish.

High in the icy blue upper reaches of the North Umpqua is a small population of brook trout. The adult brook averages about six inches, which is also the legal minimum size, so light tackle is best. Mid- to late summer is when the brook trout are biting, and they go for eggs and worms.

Smallmouth, Largemouth, And Striped Bass
The smallmouth is the most numerous of the three bass species commonly found in the Umpqua River system. The largest concentration of them is near Elkton, and they average between one and two pounds. The best time to fish for this species is when the water warms up to a high 50s-low 60s temperature range during spring and summer. Spinning gear with three-pound test line and a four-inch plastic worm are the most popular, with smaller deep-diving plugs right behind. So plentiful are smallmouth bass on the Umpqua that the river has its own set of guidelines that are more generous than the regulations governing other Oregon waterways. You are allowed 12 bass a day with no more than five over 17 inches.

Largemouth bass are found mainly in valley lakes and reservoirs. These fish average two pounds, with some big ones now and then tipping the scales at four pounds. The bait, tackle, and regulations are the same as for smallmouth. The key difference is that fishermen should have a boat to keep moving with the school.

Striped bass are found in the main Umpqua and seem to roam back and forth from brackish to sweet water continuously. The striped bass is the largest of the bass species found here, and the Umpqua has produced some world-record catches of the fish over the years. You'll need a boat to fish for "stripers" as the guides call them, as well as a stout rod, 20- to 30-pound test line, and a variety of bait. Minnow or eel imitations are good for trolling, herring or smelt work for bottom-fishing, and try hooks or plugs for surface casting.

Shad
Commerical fishing interests have been fishing for shad in the Umpqua River since the 1920s. Since 1964, about 60,000 shad a year are taken from the Umpqua. Shad eggs or roe are considered a delicacy, particularly on the East Coast.

Smelt
Smelt are found on the lower Umpqua near Reedsport around Dean Creek. They have no set timetable for their migrations, moving about the ocean and into the river whenever they deem it necessary. Smelt are usually caught with a small mesh net.

PRACTICALITIES

Bed And Breakfast
The Wood's Bed and Breakfast (428 Oakview Dr., Roseburg 97470; tel. 672-2927; $45-60) is located six miles northwest of town near scenic River Forks Park. Their guest suite overlooks a pond on their seven-acre wooded spread. Judy Wood, the hostess, has published her own cookbook, and gourmet meals are always featured.

The Gothic-revival-style **Hokanson's Guest House** (848 S.E. Jackson St.; tel. 672-2632; $55-75) was built in 1882 on land once owned by Aaron Rose, the founder of Roseburg. Listed in the National Register of Historic Places, each bedroom in the building has a private bath with a claw-foot tub and period furnishings. Hokanson's Hi-Ho Restaurant is five blocks away. Another classic home from the era when lumber was king is the **House of Hunter** (813 S.E. Kane St.; tel. 672-2335, $50-65). Two rooms

ROSEBURG ACCOMMODATIONS

Best Western Douglas Inn Motel, 511 S.E. Stephens St., tel. 673-6625, $52-62, restaurant.

Best Western, Garden Villa Motel, 760 N.W. Garden Valley Blvd., tel. 672-1601, (800) 547-3446, $50-75, pool, pets, nonsmoking rooms.

Budget 16 Motel, 1067 N.E. Stephens St., tel. 673-5556, $42-52, pool.

Casa Loma, 1107 N.E. Stephens St., tel. 673-5569, $25-50, cable, Jacuzzi.

City Center Motel, 1321 S.E. Stephens St., tel. 673-6134, $25-50, basic.

Dunes Motel, 610 W. Madrone, tel. 672-6684, $45-55, lounge, pets.

Hilltop Motel, 978 N.E. Stephens St., tel. 673-6223, $25-50, cable.

Holiday Motel, 444 S.E. Oak, tel. 672-4457, $30-50, pool, pets.

Motel Orleans, 427 N.W. Garden Valley Blvd., tel. 673-5561, $35-75, pool, restaurant, lounge.

Pine Motel, 2821 N.E. Stephens St., tel. 672-4063, $30-40, kitchenettes, pool.

Roseburg Travelodge, 315 W. Harvard, tel. 672-4836 or (800) 255-3050, $40-60, pool.

Rose City Motel, 1142 N.E. Stephens St., tel. 673-8209, $25-45, cable, pets.

Shady Oaks Motel, 2954 Old 99, tel. 672-2608, $30-40, air conditioning.

Sycamore Motel, 1627 S.E. Stephens St., tel. 672-3354, $30-40, restaurant.

Town House Motel, 525 N.E. Stephens St., tel. 672-4526, $25-40, cable, pets.

Vista Motel, 1183 N.E. Stephens St., tel. 673-2736, $30-50, showtime, HBO, pets.

Windmill Inn of Roseburg, 1450 N.W. Mulholland Dr., tel. 673-0901, (800) 452-5315 in Oregon, (800) 547-4747 in the U.S., $50-90, everything.

---

have private baths; two other rooms share a bath. Each room boasts an English wardrobe closet, a handmade quilt, and turn-of-the-century furnishings. Telephone and TV can be hooked up to your room upon request.

Campgrounds
Armacher County Park (tel. 672-4901; $5-10) is five miles north of town off I-5 on exit 129. The park is situated on the North Umpqua and has 10 tent sites and 20 RV/trailer sites with full hookups. A bathhouse and picnic area are also found here. **Twin Rivers Vacation Park** (433 Rivers Forks Rd.; tel. 673-3811; $6-15) is six miles out of town (via I-5, take exit 125) where the North and South forks of the Umpqua converge. Water, electricity, waste disposal, and a coin-op laundry are available at this 85-site park. **Fairgrounds RV Park** (210 Frear St.; tel. 440-4505; $10-12) has 50 hookups, water, and a drive-through dump station. **U-Haul RV Center** (1182 N.E. Stephens; tel. 672-6864) has a dumping station for self-contained vehicles.

Food
Roseburg is not exactly the fine-dining capital of Oregon. Most of the folks here are more interested in getting a big plate of food than titillating their palates. Since there is no shortage of fast-food joints, greasy spoons, and truck-driver restaurants, let's focus instead upon a few unique eateries in town.

A highly regarded Tex-Mex establishment is **La Hacienda** (940 N.W. Garden Valley Blvd.; tel. 672-5330). You'll know the place when you see it. In front of the cream-colored stucco building with green and orange stripes are tall arches of typical Spanish design. The food inside is equally inviting. In addition to the usual assortment of tacos, tostadas, and tamales, you'll find some dishes that break away from the Mexican-food norm. The shrimp and chicken fajitas are good, as are the combination dinners and seafood dishes. One of the latter you may care to try is langostinos Jalisco, prawns sautéed in butter, garlic, and white wine. A big basket of chips with green tomatillo salsa or the more traditional red salsa comes with your meal. La Hacienda also features a wide selection of Mexican beers to enhance your lunch or dinner.

If you're in the mood for some good, cheap, and plentiful Italian cuisine, head for **Momma's Home Cookin'** (834 N.W. Garden Valley Blvd.; tel. 672-4361). Spaghetti, linguine, fettuccine, canneloni, and manicotti are among the "pastabilities." Momma's also features calzone as well as a full line of pizzas. Open seven days a week for lunch and dinner. You'll find good deli sandwiches at **Between the Buns** (214 S.E. Jackson; tel. 672-8633). "Dagwood-style" sandwiches piled way too high with fillings come at a low price that makes them easy to swallow. Open Mon.-Fri. 11 a.m.-5 p.m.; call the night before to order a picnic lunch.

Brutke's Wagon Wheel (227 N.W. Garden Valley Blvd.; tel. 672-7555) is the place to go for prime rib. The chef's prime rib recipe dates back over 30 years and accounts for over a third of the food sales at the restaurant. But if you don't fit the beefeater's shoes, chicken and "heart smart" entrees are also featured on the menu. The restaurant has a colorful, homey atmosphere. You might see loggers wearing flannel shirts and denims while other folks sport formal wear and furs. It's not uncommon for couples to come by here for a special occasion and families to drop in for a good, wholesome meal. Open Mon.-Fri. for lunch and dinner, Sat.-Sun. for dinner only.

Those who enjoy the full fanfare of sumptuous soups and salads, flambé dinners, and sinfully rich chocolate desserts should consider a meal at **P.B. Clayton's Fine Food and Spirits** (968 N.E. Stephens; tel. 672-1142). This contemporary restaurant specializes in fresh seafood, chicken, and pastas. A dance floor and a live DJ in one section of the restaurant make P.B. Clayton's a popular nightspot. Open for lunch and dinner Mon.-Sat., with dinner only Sunday.

Chin's Cafe (1614 S.E. Stephens; tel. 673-3291) has Chinese food worth crossing the mountains for. Chin's makes a wide selection of beef, pork, chicken, and seafood specialties. Open for lunch and dinner Sun.-Fri., with dinner only Saturday. **Kuraya's** (5096 Old Hwy. 99 S; tel. 679-9701) features Thai food that is guaranteed to spice up your evening. A popular dish here is Pad Thai, which features noodles, sprouts, and scallions beneath a sauce blending hot, sweet, and peanut flavors. Their homemade coconut ice cream will soothe your stomach if you overdosed on the hot stuff. Open seven days a week for lunch and dinner.

For a lumberjack-sized breakfast, the **Timber Mill** (2455 Diamond Lake Blvd.; tel. 672-0705) will fill you up without breaking the bank. Open seven days a week from 4 a.m. to 9 p.m., early risers should be prepared to share the restaurant with mill workers fortifying themselves for the day's work. An old log-truck driver adage is "Never eat at a place called Mom's," but you can make an exception at **Mom's Place** (634 E. Cass; tel. 672-8459). Open seven days a week from 3 a.m. to 3 p.m., large platefuls and low prices make this place another workingman's friend.

Cafe Espresso (corner of Douglas and Jackson, 368 S.E. Jackson; tel. 672-1859) has a bright, many-checkered decor and a varied lunch menu. Daily specials on the order of quiche and lasagna washed down by caffeinated cups of premium brew are especially appreciated in a town low on good coffeehouses. Breakfast is also served here.

Events

Roseburg's big event is the **Douglas County Fair,** held annually at the fairgrounds the second week of August. Besides the usual assortment of 4-H prize bulls, mom's marmalade, and grandma's-secret-recipe apple pie, the bright lights of the midway rides, food booths, and horse and stock-car races add to the festive atmosphere. In the afternoon, big-name singers entertain the crowds with toe-tapping country music. While it's seven days of fun, and well worth seeing if you're in the neighborhood, high temperatures compel an early start.

Information And Services

The **Roseburg Visitors and Convention Bureau** (410 S.E. Spruce St.; tel. 672-9731) has all kinds of useful information free for the taking. One particularly useful pamphlet is a driver's guide to historic places. And while the staffmembers here are courteous and can offer decent travel-planning suggestions, they are tight-lipped when it comes to specific recommendations on food and lodging. Open Mon.-Fri. 8-5:30.

The **Douglas County Library** (1036 S.E. Douglas; tel. 440-4305 or 800-452-0992, ext. 311) is in the west wing of the Douglas County Courthouse. Hours are Mon. noon-9 p.m., Tues.-Wed. 10-9, and Thurs.-Sat. 10-6. From September through May, the library is also open Sun. 12-4. The **Douglas County Museum Lavola Bakken Research Library** (Douglas County Fairgrounds; tel. 440-4507) is a reference library on the first floor of the museum. It has a good collection on the historical and cultural development of Douglas County, as well as information on the county's botany, geology, and zoology.

Douglas Community Hospital (735 W. Harvard Blvd.; tel. 673-6641) offers a 24-hour physician-staffed emergency room treating everything from colds to major trauma. **Harvard Urgent Care Clinic** (1813 W. Harvard Blvd., Suite 110; tel. 673-1503) is the place to drop in for minor medical problems.

The Roseburg **police** (774 S.E. Rose; tel. 673-6633 or 911 for emergencies only) and the state police (tel. 440-3333) are always avail-able should any trouble occur. The **post office** (519 S.E. Kane, Roseburg 97470; tel. 673-5326) is open Mon.-Fri. 8:30-5 p.m. If you're recycling your dirty clothes, **Wash and Dry Laundry** (1820 N.E. Stephens; tel. 673-7701) and **Clothes Hamper Launderette** (2428 W. Harvard Blvd.; tel. 672-0240) both feature coin-operated machines.

Getting There And Getting Around

The **Greyhound/Trailways** bus depot (835 S.E. Stephens; tel. 673-5326) is open weekdays 7:30 a.m.-6:30 p.m., Sat. 8-5. Routes connect Roseburg with California, the Willamette Valley, and Washington, as well as the Oregon coast. **Pal Auto Rental** (1410 S.E. Stephens; tel. 673-5210) features new and late-model car rentals at reasonable rates. **The Mobile Tune** (1400 S.E. Stephens; tel. 673-5210) has vehicles ranging from compacts and economy cars to luxury sedans and pickup trucks in addition to trailers and RVs. **Roseburg Sunshine Taxi Express** (tel. 672-2888) can chauffeur you around the city.

OAKLAND

Many travelers drive by the exit marked Oakland on I-5 joking that maybe they made a wrong turn somewhere and ended up in California. But the curious who venture a few miles off the freeway to explore this National Historic Landmark discover that *this* Oakland is an interesting voyage into Oregon's past. Established in the 1850s, this hamlet today gives little indication of the caprices of fate and fortune it has experienced in its 140-year history.

Oakland was a stopover point for the main stagecoach line linking Portland and Sacramento until the Oregon and California Railroad came to town in 1872. With these two transportation linkages, Oakland thrived as a trading center for outlying hop fields and prune orchards. In the early 1900s, millions of pounds of dried prunes were shipped all over the world from Oakland. In the 1920s and '30s, raising turkeys became the prominent industry in the area, and Oakland became the leading turkey-shipping center in the western United States. During the '40s through the '60s, the lumber in-dustry dominated the local economy. Today, livestock ranching, farming, and tourism are the economic mainstays.

While not as built-up as its counterpart restoration farther south in Jacksonville, Oakland still provides a good place to pull off the interstate and reflect on the passing of time in a one-time boomtown turned rural hamlet.

SIGHTS

Old Town Oakland is a good place to start your tour, because this is where it all began. An excellent free history and walking-tour pamphlet is available at city hall (117 Third St.). The original wooden buildings were destroyed by fires in the 1890s, and most of the brick and stone structures in the historical district date back to this era of reconstruction. There are many antique stores, art galleries, and curio shops to browse through as well. The **Oakland Museum** (136 Locust) is worth visiting. The exhibit in the back

THE LEGENDS OF ONE-EYED CHARLIE AND BLACK BART

While it has been a century since southern Oregon has heard the pounding hoofbeats and grinding axles of an approaching Portland-to-Sacramento stagecoach, the West's first organized interstate transportation system hasn't been forgotten. Such stageline stopovers as Wolf Creek Tavern, north of Grants Pass, and Jacksonville, west of Medford, have been commemorated with National Historic Landmark and National Historic District status. In addition to these evocations of the era, the stories of two romantic figures, Black Bart and One-Eyed Charlie, help to bring back a time when the Wild West lived up to its name.

One-Eyed Charlie was a stagecoach driver, a job that commanded considerable respect back in 19th-century Oregon. A look at the roadbeds of such wagon-route remnants as I-5 between Grants Pass and Roseburg and ORE 238 north of Jacksonville might help you to understand why. Hostile Indians, ruthless highwaymen, and inclement weather plagued these frontier thoroughfares. Even without such hazards, bouncing along for days on end on a buckboard carriage, minus shock absorbers and air-conditioning, required considerable fortitude.

Of all the men on the Oregon-to-California line, One-Eyed Charlie was the driver of choice whenever Wells Fargo needed to send a valuable cargo. Despite a salty vocabulary, an opinionated demeanor, and a rough appearance, all of which might have rankled some passengers, no one was better at handling the horses or dealing with adversity.

When the stage would roll into Portland or Sacramento, One-Eyed Charlie would collect his paycheck and disappear for a few days. It was said he was a heavy drinker and gambler during his sojourns deep into the seamy frontier underworld. When it came time to make the next trip through, however, he'd be back at the helm, sober and cantankerous as ever.

One day, One-Eyed Charlie's hard-drivin' hard-drinkin' life caught up with him. When the coroner was preparing the body for burial, he made a surprising discovery. One-Eyed Charlie was really One-Eyed Charlene! Shock waves reverberated up and down the west coast at the realization that a woman had been best at what was considered exclusively a man's domain. But the real kicker was that she had voted in the 1860 and 1864 presidental elections for Abraham Lincoln, over half a century before a woman could legally vote! As the voting records have been lost, legal scholars have been unable to prove or debunk the persistent legend of One-Eyed Charlie.

Another personality from the stagecoach era, the outlaw Black Bart, has also become part of Western folklore. Between 1875 and his capture in 1883, he robbed 28 stagecoaches of their gold shipments. Known as the Gentleman Bandit due to his polite treatment of passengers, Black Bart had a penchant for verse. One of his finer efforts read:

"I've labored hard and long for bread, for honor and for riches.
But on my corns too long you've tread, you fine-haired sons of bitches.
Let come what will, I'll try it on, my condition can't be worse.
And if there's money in that box, tis munney in my purse."

But the Gentleman Bandit's chivalrous ways proved to be his undoing. A handkerchief much like one he offered to the ladies when he helped them off of the stage was found at the scene of a robbery. The initials "CB" were embroidered on the corner. Traced by its laundry mark to San Francisco, the owner was identified as Charles Bolton, an employee of Wells Fargo Bank. This explained why Black Bart was able to know the arrival time of gold shipments. After completing four years of a six-year sentence at San Quentin, Charles Bolton was let out for good behavior. He disappeared shortly thereafter, but will forever be remembered as the Gentleman Bandit for his refinement and the fact that he never shot anyone.

re-creates Oakland during its boom times. Open daily 1-4:30 p.m.; closed on holidays; admission is free.

PRACTICALITIES

Accommodations
Tolly's Beckley House (338 S.E. Second; tel. 459-9320) is a Queen Anne-style house dating back to 1890. Such touches as the antique-furnished suites and an included Tolly's Restaurant breakfast make the $60-70 rate well worth it.

Food
The **Lamplighter Inn** (126 Locust; tel. 459-4938) opens at 6 a.m. for breakfast and serves basic American food like omelettes, sandwiches, and burgers. The lounge in the back of the restaurant is the hot spot in town, where locals come to tilt glasses and play video poker. Even if you're not in the mood for a drink, go inside and check out their huge Maxfield Parrish-like painting of a naked lady petting a swan. It is based on William Butler Yeats's 1923 poem "Leda and the Swan." Leda was ravished by Zeus in the form of a swan, and subsequently gave birth to Helen of Troy. Oakland is noteworthy for these leftover touches of refinement from its golden age, which seem almost incongruous against its present-day small-town facade.

Fancier fare is found across the street at **Tolly's** (115 Locust; tel. 459-3796), "where sodas flow and friendships grow." Lunch is served 10 a.m.-6 p.m. and features deli, croissant, and Scandinavian sandwiches (like the Svensk Farsk Frukt, which is cream cheese, peanut butter, dried apricots, prunes, and bananas, guaranteed to give you that "get up and go" feeling), as well as creative entrees and salads. We recommend prawns Dijon. Elaborate gourmet dinners are served 5:30-10 p.m. (except Mondays) and are complemented by a fine wine list and mellow piano music. Whichever meal you are having, be sure to save some room for the homemade desserts proudly shown off in the lobby display case. The well-illuminated upstairs room is the nicest place to sit. Here, you can admire the sturdy 25-foot-long, 4-by 20-inch Douglas fir roof supports that tell of another era when lumber was king.

Information And Services
The small but quaint **Oakland Public Library** (100 N.E. Seventh) is in the historic Washington School Building (1910). Open Mon. 2-8, Tues. 10-2, Wed. 10-12 and 2-6, and Fri. 1-5. The **post office** (109 Locust St., Oakland 97462) is open Mon.-Fri. 8:30-5, closed one hour for lunch. The **chamber of commerce** is at city hall (117 Third St.). The **police** can be reached at 440-4471, and for **emergency medical care**, dial 911. For general visitor info on Oakland, call Cindy Whitaker of the **Oakland Business Association** (tel. 459-4688).

THE HIGH CASCADES
INTRODUCTION

The Cascades comprise one of the most magnificent natural playgrounds in the world. This collage of green forest and black basalt outcroppings is topped by extinct volcano cones covered with snow. Plenty of lakes, rivers, and waterfalls provide a pleasing contrast to the earth tones here. There are over 160 parks in the High Cascades, providing easy access to hiking, camping, climbing, and other recreational pursuits. Many of these parks are linked together by the Pacific Crest Trail, which traverses the entire range border to border. The famous thoroughfare is the backbone of an extensive network of footpaths that wind through this spectacular region. In addition, six national forests, six federal wilderness areas, and Oregon's only national park, Crater Lake, are also found in the Oregon Cascades. Add to this list the bevy of luxury resorts, nine developed ski areas, hundreds of miles of cross-country skiing and snowmobiling trails, as well as numerous waterways teeming with fish, and you have all the accoutrements for roughing it in style.

THE LAND

What fault scarps are to the California landscape, lava fields and snowcapped volcano cones are to Oregon. While remnants of the state's not-so-distant volcanic past abound, the most impressive and dramatic examples are found in the High Cascades, a chain of icy peaks stretching from northern California to British Columbia. The Oregon Cascades lie in the heart of this great range, and many have been named after former military commanders and heads of state. Given their stature and commanding presences, Mounts Hood, Jefferson, and Washington rate such distinction. Mount Hood (11,235 feet) is the tallest in the state, and many others top out at over 10,000 feet. Oregon's peaks are part of the great Ring of Fire which encircles the Pacific and includes Cotopaxi (Ecuador), Fuji (Japan), and Krakatoa (Indonesia), as well as the Cascades' notorious sister volcanoes, Lassen (California) and St. Helens (Washington).

SOUTH CASCADES REGION

They are linked together by the theory of continental drift and plate tectonics. According to the theory, the landmasses force the ocean floor to slip underneath the continental plate. This creates heat-generating friction, causing rocks to melt. The resulting hot, soupy subterranean mass feeds inland volcanoes with magma and molten rock, 20-plus miles beneath the earth's surface.

When water is added to this hellish brew, the melting point of the rocks is lowered by 1,000° F or more. Water also acts as the major explosive agent of volcanic eruptions, primarily due to the steam created in the reaction. Eventually, the vapors can no longer be confined, and the plugged vent is pierced by the tremendous pressures of the steam and other gases produced from the magma. The lighter materials are ejected first—ash, cinders, and pyroclastic debris, and oftentimes the earth spits up mouthfuls of its fiery interior as well. Once the water supply is spent, the lava usually becomes too viscous to flow, and the vent is once again sealed up by the cooling rock to start the process anew.

The Cascade Range is approximately 25 million years old, perhaps the youngest mountain range in the contiguous 48 states. However, geologists are uncertain when the Cascade volcanoes began to form. Guesstimates date their formation at several million years ago, during the Pleistocene epoch. And while the mountains appear to be dormant, keep in mind that nature's clock is unpredictable. Although the odds of Oregon becoming a Pompeii in our lifetime seem remote, the recent worldwide increase in earthquakes and volcanic eruptions suggests that the earth's internal burners are heating up again, and one of Oregon's slumbering giants may awaken soon.

There are four major types of volcanoes, and all of them are found in the Cascades. Cinder cones, like Lava Butte and Black Butte, are formed by the explosive ejection of ash and particles of lava and rarely exceed 1,200 feet in height. Shield volcanoes, like Mt. Washington and Three Fingered Jack, form gently sloping domes that tend to be wider than they are high. Erosion is responsible for their present ragged-edged appearance. Plug-dome volcanoes, like Beacon Rock in the Columbia River Gorge, are the result of lava cooling until it's too thick to flow beyond the vent, creating a massive dome. Finally, there are composite volcanoes, making up the bulk of the majestic Cascades, which are formed layer by layer from ash, cinders, and lava.

CLIMATE

The Cascades, never more than 100 to 150 miles from the Pacific, effectively divide the state into dramatically different biomes. The moisture-laden westerlies dump prodigious amounts of precipitation on western Cascade slopes, up to 150 inches a year in some locations. Having thus purged themselves, the clouds then pass over the east side of the range, retaining what little moisture they have left. While the wet-siders are busy picking the moss out from between their toes and enduring the seemingly endless succession of rainy days, the dry-siders enjoy an average of 200 days of sunshine and about 12 inches of precipitation a year.

When it's not raining in the Cascades, it's usually snowing. Willamette Pass, for example, gets an average of 300 inches of snow a year. Crater Lake, oftentimes the coldest place in the Cascades, has recorded a chilly -21° F. Mount Hood has experienced over 100 feet of snowfall in a year. The snow nourishes glaciers on the major peaks left over from the last ice age, 11,000 years ago, and feeds rivers, lakes, and streams with summer runoff as well. The snowpack also makes for some of the finest skiing in the Northwest.

Lest you think folks living on the western Cascades' flanks are confined to their log cabins all year by the lavish amounts of precipitation, the good news is that the weather is pleasant and dry most of the summer and into the early fall. Summer temperatures also usher in conditions favorable for a variety of outdoor pursuits. The flip side of the benign weather is that it brings higher numbers of visitors and dry, tinderbox conditions to the forest. The latter, along with frequent thunderstorms, makes forest fires a recurring seasonal menace.

FLORA AND FAUNA

Flora

The wet western slopes of the Cascades are dominated by the state tree, the Douglas fir. This towering evergreen requires abundant moisture and plenty of sunshine. The drier east side is comprised mostly of ponderosa and lodgepole pine forests. The trees often meet with almost no transition zone, because the changes in rainfall are so marked on Cascade summits. However, in southern Oregon, where precipitation levels are generally lower, pine trees have stolen over the crest into the Klamath, Rogue, and Umpqua river basins.

Fires and the hand of man can have more effect on the natural balance of a forest than fluctuations in weather. The changes in ground cover, shade, and soil make conditions more favorable for one species of tree over others. The aggressive Oregon oak is one such example, an easily established tree that can quickly challenge the kingdom of the Douglas fir. The oak's reign, however, is often cut short by the bitter cold, deep snow, and dry summers. Eventually, the Douglas fir is able to usurp the oak and regain its former rule over the forest.

The lodgepole pine is the primary benefactor in the southern Cascades, where frequent summer lightning storms take their annual toll of other species. The tough little cones of this tree endure fires and other adversities such as climatic extremes and barren soils, sprouting when favorable conditions return. The tree colonizes an area rapidly, growing up straight, true, and fine. As their name implies, these forthright trees were often used in the construction of lodges by the Indians and pioneers. But the lodgepole pine usually meets the same fate as the Oregon oak, sooner or later choked out by the larger and longer-lived climax species like Douglas fir, cedar, balsam fir, Engelmann spruce, white pine, and hemlock.

And the lodgepole pine is not entirely free of competition for turf in the wake of a fire. Oftentimes low brush quickly moves in, firmly establishing its territorial dominance over young pine seedlings. The tenacious manzanita, sticky laurel, and varieties of ceanothus, currants, and

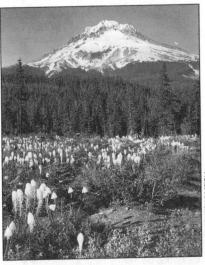

Bear grass, a common sight in the Cascades, blooms under Mt. Hood's shadow.

OREGON TOURISM DIVISION

other miscellaneous shrubs generically labeled as buckbrush or snowbrush are the predominant examples of this type of chaparral.

Wild rhododendrons, dogwoods, and myriad wildflowers are the smile of spring in the Cascades as Old Man Winter releases his frozen grip upon the land. Summer foragers can find blackberries, huckleberries, and salmonberries, as well as many exotic types of mushrooms, in the damp recesses of the forest. Fall color from hardwoods is limited on Cascade slopes. Bright splashes of gold are provided by ash, aspen, cottonwood, tamarack, and bigleaf maple, but the heavy hitters are the brilliantly colored Douglas and vine maples. The vine maples in particular can make the otherwise lackluster fall foliage of the Cascades come alive with vivid reds and yellows.

Fauna

The Cascades are Oregon's forest primeval. The black bear, wolf, mountain lion, lynx and bobcat compete with each other as well as man in the hunt for beavers, deer, elk (wapiti), and snowshoe hares. The smaller predators such as foxes, weasels, and martens prey upon chipmunks, squirrels, porcupines, and rats. Other commonly encountered forest creatures include the coyote, raccoon, and skunk. A half-dozen species of bats add to the diversity of mammals present in the Cascades. Indeed, this is where the wild things are.

The mountains are also home to a wide range of amphibians and reptiles. Generally speaking, most amphibians, such as frogs and salamanders, are found in cool and damp habitats west of the Cascades, whereas their cold-blooded reptilian fellow travelers (especially the lizard) prefer the warm and dry eastern flank. However, there always seem to be exceptions to every rule. Several of these critters are found on both sides of the Cascades, seemingly oblivious to the inherent climatic discrepancies.

The most widespread example of Cascade herpetofauna is the Pacific tree frog, *Hyla regilla*. It has been found on both sides of the range at elevations up to 7,000 feet. One secret to the frog's success is its versatility in using available breeding water for egg laying and larval development. While many mountain pools are strictly temporary or seasonal, they nonetheless allow enough time for the rapid growth and subsequent proliferation of the species. Also, the frogs are able to adapt to their terrestrial existence. During the dry summer months, tree frogs absorb moisture from the night air through their skin. The moisture is collected in their bladder and then excreted through the skin during the day to keep the frog cool. Furthermore, the frogs seem to have enough sense to take refuge during extreme weather conditions in abandoned rodent burrows or rock or log crevices and sit it out.

A handful of other species of frogs and toads also hop around the Cascades. If you are camping near a Cascade lake in the summer, you may be surprised at how loudly the frogs croak at night. While this deep-throated chorus may leave some campers tossing and turning on their air mattresses, others will undoubtedly rest assured that the frogs are also busy consuming an inordinate amount of insects, especially the pesky mosquito.

Visitors to the high country come upon many a giant Pacific salamander in mountain waterways. Common in high to low elevations, the timing of their metamorphosis into adults coincides with the seasonal fluctuations of their home stream. In addition to the Pacific giant, six other species of salamanders also call the Cascades home.

Reptiles prefer to slink around the warmer and drier east side. Over a dozen species of snakes and lizards are common to the Cascades. The most dangerous member of the family is *Crotalus viridis*, the western rattlesnake. Able to strike with blinding quickness and inject potentially lethal amounts of venom into its victim, this diamond-headed snake should be avoided at all costs. They like to sun themselves in warm open spots and can be difficult to spot until you step on them, as they tend to coil up. Listen for the telltale rattle of the snake's tail, and give them a wide berth. Baby rattlers, while smaller than the adults, are just as deadly, and more dangerous to wilderness adventurers because their rattles have not yet developed enough to make any noise. And while you may be tempted to smash a rattlesnake to smithereens with a handy rock or tree branch, keep in mind that these reptiles effectively police the exponential growth of rodent populations.

The Cascades have over 70 species of birds, ranging from the great horned owl to the pewee. The successional stages of forest management in the mountains play an important role in the habitat and territory of many species. When an area is first logged over, the grasses and small shrubs that grow soon afterward are favorite haunts of the state bird, the western meadowlark. The mountain quail prefers thicker brush and small trees, the second phase of forest regeneration. The mixed deciduous woods that comprise the next stage make the ideal habitat for warblers. Finally, when the conifers have once again become the climax species of the forest, sharp-shinned hawks will move in. Thus, changes in habitats often increase certain species of birds at the expense of others.

SKIING THE CASCADES

The Cascades are a haven for winter sports that range from Alpine and Nordic skiing to snowmobiling and snowshoeing. There are nine developed ski areas and hundreds of miles of backcountry trails for these wintertime recreational pursuits. And while other ski areas in Colorado, Idaho, and California have been hard-hit by drought, Oregon is still blessed with an abundant annual snowpack that makes for nearly year-round skiing. It is no wonder that ski pros like Billy Kidd and the famous Mahre brothers hold racing camps in Oregon, or that the Cascades are the official training ground for the U.S. Olympic Ski Team. While the Cascades don't have the mystique of the Rockies, the greater challenge here is due to the variability of conditions. People who ski in the Northwest can ski anywhere in the world.

Mount Hood

In addition to being the state's highest mountain, Mt. Hood also boasts the most ski areas, five in all. A popular destination for families and beginners is **Cooper Spur** (for info write; Box 977, Hood River 97032; tel. 352-7803). Located on the northeastern flank of the mountain, 24 miles south of Hood River on ORE 35, it usually offers protection from storms and prevailing westerlies, yet has more than enough snow for a good time. Operating hours are Wed.-Sat. 9 a.m.-10 p.m., Sun. 9-4. Call 386-5900 for holiday hours and the snow report. You can also find out about the Cloud Cap auto tour, an 11-mile scenic loop in the area. Also on the east side is **Mt. Hood Meadows** (Box 470, Mt. Hood 97028; tel. 337-2222), the peak's largest ski area. Ten miles from Government Camp on ORE 35, hundreds of acres of groomed slopes and seven double chair lifts plus one triple and one quad ensure plenty of room for all. Hours are Mon.-Tues. 9-4:30, Wed.-Sat. 9 a.m.-10 p.m., Sun. 9-7. Call 227-SNOW for the snow report. It's often sunny here on the east slope of the mountain when on the west side it's snowing and raining.

Ski Bowl

Ski Bowl (Box 280, Government Camp 97028; tel. 272-3206) is only 53 miles away from metropolitan Portland on ORE 26 and features the most extensive night skiing in the country. The upper bowl also has some of the most challenging skiing to be found on the mountain. Hours are Mon.-Thur. 9 a.m.-10 p.m., Fri. 9 a.m.-11 p.m., Sat. 8:30 a.m.-11 p.m., Sun. 8:30 a.m.-10 p.m. Call 222-BOWL for the snow re-

port. A mile further down ORE 26 is **Summit Ski Area** (Box 385, Government Camp 97028; tel. 272-3255), the place for families, beginners, and people who just like to play in the snow. Affectionately called "Snow Bunny" by many locals, this small 62-year-old ski area may have only one chair lift, one rope tow, and three half-mile trails, but it is always big on fun. Open only on weekends and holidays 8-4:30, call 272-3351 for the snow report. Rumors are circulating that Snow Bunny's facilities may close, so call ahead to check on public access.

Timberline

The undisputed king of the mountain is Timberline (Timberline Ski Area, Timberline Lodge 97028; tel. 272-3311). Located 60 miles east of Portland on ORE 26, the skiing starts where the trees end. With the highest vertical drop of any ski area in Oregon (3,600 feet) as well as the highest elevation accessible by chair lift (8,600 feet), 60% of Timberline's ski runs are in the intermediate-level category. Given this terrain, it should come as no surprise that the U.S. Olympic Ski Team trains here on Palmer Glacier during the summer months. Hours are Sun.-Tues. 9-4, Wed.-Sat. 9 a.m.-10 p.m. Call 222-2111 for the snow report. This is the mountain's only year-round ski area.

Attractive midweek ski packages are available that include lodging at the hall of the mountain king, **Timberline Lodge.** This National Historic Site was built in the 1930s as a Works Progress Administration project. Billed as the most magnificent wooden structure ever built, the lodge also features fine dining and a heated outdoor swimming pool. For lodging reservations and info on special packages, call 231-5400 from Portland, (800) 452-1335 from the rest of Oregon, and (800) 547-1406 from Nevada, northern California, Idaho, Utah, and Washington.

Here, at 6,000 feet, the frequently wet Cascade snow is less sloppy. While it's not as light as powder, the 31 runs are so well groomed that Timberline snow is easily navigable. The chair lifts (six in winter, two in summer) are mostly obscured by trees or topography, so you get a feeling of intimacy with the natural surroundings when you're schussing downhill. You can go up two lifts, enjoying a nearly two-mile-long run that drops 2,500 feet vertically. At the top of the Palmer chair lift is a sign that tells the scouting story of Joel Palmer, who climbed the mountain to this elevation to help pioneer the Barlow Road section of the Oregon Trail.

Though the first fresh snow usually comes in November or December, several years ago there were flurries on the Fourth of July, underscoring Timberline's claim of offering the only lift-serviced summer skiing in the U.S. Skiers can pay $22 for a one-day summer lift ticket at Timberline. The two summer chairs run daily through Labor Day 7 a.m.-1:30 p.m. The upper Palmer lift, highest on the mountain, is open only from late spring through fall, when conditions are safe for skiing on the Palmer glacier. The Magic Mile chair, directly below the Palmer, is open to the 7,000 foot level for sightseers as well as skiers. The price for non-skiing sightseers is $5 for adults, $3 for kids 12 and under, or $15 for a family of four. Remember that summer temperatures on Mt. Hood can vary from below freezing to 90° F. Along with sun cream, dark glasses, and other warm-weather gear, bring layered ski apparel to adapt to varied conditions.

Transportation direct from Portland airport to Timberline can be arranged through **Mt. Hood Express** (tel. 250-4379). This van service ranges from $15/person for six to as high as $60 for one person.

Hoodoo Ski Bowl

The state's oldest ski area, Hoodoo Ski Bowl (Box 20, ORE 20, Sisters 97759; tel. 342-5540), has the additional distinction of also being the least expensive. Located between Salem and Bend on ORE 20, this family-oriented resort is evenly divided into beginner, intermediate, and advanced terrain and also offers night skiing. Hours are Tues.-Sun. 9-4; night skiing Wed.-Sun. 4-10 p.m. For the snow report, call 345-7416 from Eugene, 585-8081 from Salem, or 752-8887 from Corvallis.

Willamette Pass

Willamette Pass, 69 miles southeast of Eugene on ORE 58 (write: 1899 Willamette St., Suite 1, Eugene 97401; tel. 484-5030), has some of the most challenging runs in the state as well as a multitude of beginner and intermediate trails. You'll find some of the steepest runs in the state here, as opposed to open chutes or powder bowls at other ski areas. Since Willamette Pass plows its own parking lot, you will not need a snow-park permit here. Hours before Jan. 1: Wed.-Sun. 9-4. After Jan. 1: Wed.-Sat. 9-9, Sun. 9-4. Call 345-SNOW for the ski report.

Mount Bachelor

The Northwest's largest and most complete ski area is Mt. Bachelor (Box 1031, Bend 97709; tel. 800-547-6858 outside Oregon, 382-8334 inside Oregon). Located 22 miles southwest of Bend on Century Dr., 10 ski lifts and trails that range from beginner to expert make for some of the most popular skiing in the state. This is the winter training grounds for the U.S. Olympic Ski Team. With a top elevation over 9,000 feet, skiing here can run well into the summer months. Hours are weekdays 9-4, weekends and holidays 8-4. Call 382-7888 for the snow report. *Ski* magazine ranks Mt. Bachelor among the top five ski resorts in North America.

Mount Bailey

Limited to only 12 skiers a day, Mt. Bailey Snowcat Skiing (Diamond Lake Resort, Diamond Lake 97731; tel. 793-3311) is a unique back-country adventure for the experienced skier. Located north of Crater Lake on ORE 138, Mt. Bailey does not have crowds and lines but does have virgin slopes of powder and dynamite scenery. Snowcat skiing tours begin at 7 a.m., by reservation only.

HEALTH

Tick Talk

While relevant Cascade health hazards have already been discussed in the general Introduction of this book (see "Health and Help"), a few words about ticks are also in order. The deer tick, found throughout the Cascades, has been fingered in the spread of Lyme disease. First discovered in Lyme, Connecticut, in 1975, this strain of disease is now extant in western Oregon. The first sign of an infected bite is a rash called erythema chronicum migrans. It starts at the site of the bite and gradually enlarges, clearing up at the center while staying red around the edges. The rash is accompanied by flulike symptoms, and it spreads all over the body in one out of two cases.

The second stage of the illness affects only about 15% of those infected, but the consequences are no less severe. Inflammation of the nerves and covering tissues of the spinal cord-brain can often result in headaches and memory and concentration problems. The heart can also be affected, resulting in decreased heart function and fainting spells.

The last stage occurs weeks to years after the bite. It is characterized by aching joints, and the knees appear to be particularly vulnerable. It is suspected that the illness also can contribute to arthritis in the victim's future.

The good news is that the disease can be cured with a 10-day dosage of tetracycline. If you see the telltale red rash days or weeks after your romp in the woods, see a doctor. A prescription for prevention would be to lay the insect repellant on real thick.

KLAMATH FALLS

"One person's conservation is another's unemployment." This bromide underscores life in Klamath County, which has one of the highest unemployment rates and lowest per-capita incomes in the state, largely due to recent cutbacks in logging.

Klamath Falls, or K Falls as locals call it, is the county's population hub, with 17,000 people. It's used to hard times after witnessing the decline of its previous economic base, the railroads. In an attempt to build a viable economic future, the Salt Caves Dam Project has been proposed on the Klamath River. In addition to producing enough megawatts in hydroelectric power to fuel a city the size of Medford (50,000 people), Klamath Falls stands to make tens of millions of dollars from paybacks on the sale of bonds.

But there is one snafu. The Bureau of Land Management's designation of the Klamath as a federal scenic river has given environmentalists, hikers, fishermen, and whitewater rafters a legal leg to stand on in a prolonged battle against the project. They allege that reduced fish runs and diminished scenic and recreational values along the Klamath will result from the coming of the dam. The orientation of the local populace is made evident by the fact that there isn't one whitewater rafting company listed in the Klamath Falls phone directory, despite the approximate half-million-dollar yearly take of commercial rafters on the Upper Klamath River.

Whatever happens with the project, everyone hopes that the locals can somehow improve their economic destiny without compromising the aesthetic and biological integrity of the Klamath River.

The town's economic doldrums could be relieved by recent interest in Klamath Falls as a retirement community and recreational center. A recent American Chamber of Commerce poll determined that its cost of living was the lowest among western cities surveyed. Other incentives for relocation include a dry climate with 280 days of sunshine, cold but not damp winters (but less cold and rainy than Bend), and the fact that it's a paradise for the outdoorsperson. Klamath River trout are legendary (average size 21 inches) and such draws as world-class whitewater rafting and the region's status as the preeminent North American winter roost of the bald eagle also could spur an influx of new population.

SIGHTS

Favell Museum
A fine collection of Indian artifacts and western art is found at the Favell Museum (125 W. Main St., Klamath Falls 97601; tel. 882-9996). Here you'll find beautiful displays of Indian stonework, bone and shellwork, beadwork, quilts, basketry, pottery, and Northwest coast carvings. A collection of over 60,000 mounted arrowheads, including an exquisite fire-opal arrowhead, also helps get the point across that this is no ordinary museum. Other exhibits of note include the Cougar Mountain Cave Collection, the Nicolarsen Cache Find, and Monte Sherman's silver treasure from an abandoned wagon train. Another attraction is the collection of miniature working firearms, ranging from Gatling guns to inch-long Colt .45s, displayed in the museum's walk-in vault.

KLAMATH FALLS

If artifacts aren't your bag, you're bound to appreciate one of the best collections of western art in the state. Oils, acrylics, and watercolors are featured here, as well as bronzes, dioramas, photography, taxidermy, and woodcarvings. Over 300 artists are represented, including eight from Oregon. Thirteen of the artists are members of the Cowboy Artists of America. The museum's gift shop and art gallery specializes in limited-edition prints and original western art. Open Mon.-Sat. 9:30 a.m.-5:30 p.m.; admission is $5 for adults, $4 for seniors, $2 for children 6-16, and kids under age six get in for free.

Klamath County Museum
A good background on the region can be gained from a visit to the free Klamath County Museum (1451 Main St.; tel. 883-4208). The natural-history section has exhibits on fossils, geology, minerals, and indigenous wildlife of the Klamath Basin. The exploration and settlement area depicts the hardships of pioneer life and the events leading to the Modoc Indian War. The general history section takes you through the world wars and on up memory lane to the present. Those who really want to revel in local history can make an appointment to pore through the mu-

seum's research library, which includes one of the largest regional collections of primary sources on Captain Jack and the Modoc Indian War. During the summer, a restored 1906 trolley will give you free transportation from the Klamath County Museum to the Favell Museum and the historic Baldwin Hotel. The Klamath County Museum is open daily 10-6, June through Labor Day.

Mares Eggs Springs

Not far west of Klamath Falls off of ORE 140 W. is Mares Eggs Springs. This shallow pond, about an acre in size, is one of the few places on earth where *Nostoc amlissimum gard,* also known as mares eggs, grow. This blue-green unicellular algae is actually groups of minute cells that are joined together in chains by a gelatinous substance, forming a spherical colony in a rusty green sac. When the colony, or mares egg, reaches maturity, it breaks up into small fragments which in turn form new colonies. The mares eggs found in this locale can range in size from a pinhead to an extra-large potato.

Nostoc thrive here in the cold, clear water. Snowmelt and icy springs feed this pond, and temperatures never exceed 40 degrees. Mares eggs have also been called witch's butter, star jelly, and spittle of the stars. They are considered a delicacy in China and Japan.

To get to Mares Eggs Springs, take ORE 140 W. to the first paved road past the Rocky Point turnoff, marked To Fort Klamath. Turn right and go past a marsh to a wooded area. The pond is on the right and marked by a sign, but look carefully because it can be easy to miss if you are not paying attention.

Collier Memorial State Park

About 30 miles north of Klamath Falls on U.S. 97 is Collier Memorial State Park. Donated to the state in 1945 by Alfred and Andrew Collier as a memorial to their parents, this 146-acre park documents the history of logging's technological improvements. The first building at the south end of the parking lot in the park's Pioneer Village is the logger's homestead cabin, stocked with a wide variety of tools and artifacts on display inside. Near the homestead cabin is the blacksmith shed, representative of the type of shop found in early logging camps. The next

building houses an assortment of logging machinery including log wagons with wheels made of cross-cut sections of logs bound in iron, and chain-drive trucks with hard rubber tires. Also on display are steam-propelled devices including tractors, a narrow-gauge locomotive, and a one-person handcart.

Thunderbeast Park

About 40 miles north of Klamath Falls on U.S. 97 is Thunderbeast Park. For the price of admission ($3 for adults, $2 for students, free for kids under age five), you can see life-sized replicas of the giant mammals that roamed western Oregon 50 million years ago. Two-horned rhinoceroses, zebralike horses, and large saber-toothed tigers are just a few of the critters that haunt this place. The size and shapes of these animals are based upon skeletons from the American Museum of Natural History in New York, and their outward appearances are based on paintings from nationally known paleontologists. Placards placed in front of each exhibit give the name and a concise history of the animal. While some are quick to scoff at the park as a hokey tourist trap, many people, especially youngsters, enjoy this well-presented glimpse into the past, when the land was semitropical.

KLAMATH BASIN WILDLIFE REFUGES

The Klamath Reclamation Project

One hundred years ago, about 185,000 acres of the Klamath Basin consisted of shallow lakes and marshes. These wetlands used to be a fall stopover for over six million waterfowl migrating south for the winter. In addition to the wide variety of birds winging their way through the territory, large concentrations of marsh birds like pelicans, cormorants, egrets, and herons resided here as well. The fertile web of life created by the wetlands further supported a host of other animals like mink, otter, beaver, deer, bear, and elk. Lunker trout and other fish grew fat in the nutrient-rich waters, providing an abundant food source for the largest concentration of osprey and bald eagles in the contiguous United States.

But our national bird didn't get to rule the roost for long. Many people believed that keeping the wetlands in their natural state was a waste of space. In 1905, the U.S. Bureau of Reclamation began to pull the plug on many of the lakes and marshes here with the initiation of the Klamath Reclamation Project. The drained land was converted to irrigated agricultural endeavors, which now support a major facet of the basin's economy. However, while this was good for ranchers and farmers, it was not so good for the birds. Faced with a habitat reduced over 75%, the peak fall concentrations of migratory Pacific Flyway waterfowl have dwindled over 80%.

Fortunately, some of the basin's original habitat has been protected as national wildlife refuges that are managed by the **U.S. Fish and Wildlife Service** (1400 Miller Island Rd. W, Klamath Falls 97603; tel. 883-5732). There are currently six such refuges, three in Oregon and three more just across the state line in California. Coniferous forests, grassy meadows, marshes, open water, sagebrush and juniper grasslands, and cliffs and rocky slopes are some of the habitats found in the parks. This variety of terrain and vegetation supports an abundant population of wildlife; park checklists show 411 different species present at the refuges.

Fall is the best time of year to observe waterfowl migrations. Starting in late August with

the arrival of pintails and white-fronted geese, the numbers of ducks and geese swell to nearly one million by early November. Canada, Ross's, and snow geese, mallards, green-winged teals, tundra swans, and pigeons are some of the other major migratory species represented. August and September are also good times to view marsh birds like cormorants, egrets, grebes, gulls, herons, pelicans, and terns. The latter group generally moves out of the basin by late October.

Eagles
From December through February, the Klamath Basin is home to the largest wintering concentration of bald eagles in the lower 48 states. The thousands of winter waterfowl that reside here provide a plentiful food source for these raptors. By January, 700-800 eagles coming from as far north as Saskatchewan and the Northwest Territories congregate here. While bald eagles can and do take live birds, they feed primarily on waterfowl that have died from hunting injuries, diseases like fowl cholera, or natural causes.

In addition to a readily available food supply, the eagles require night-roosting areas. The **Upper Klamath National Wildlife Refuge** (just south of Crater Lake) and the **Bear Valley Na-**

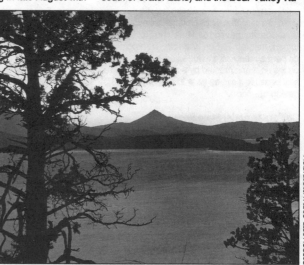

Oregon's largest lake, Upper Klamath, is also home to large bird populations.

tional Wildlife Refuge (between Keno and Worden) both have mature stands of timber that can support the weight of up to 300 eagles a night. The eagles prefer trees on northeastern-facing slopes that protect them from the cold southwest and westerly winds. They also like trees that have large open-pattern branches that give them easy landing and takeoff points. However, the eagles *don't* like it when people bother them. Hence, the roosting areas are closed from early Nov. through March 30.

The good news is that there are still ample viewing opportunities of our national bird, especially when it is very cold. When ice covers the shallow lakes and marshes, the waterfowl are forced to congregate in the few areas of remaining open water. With the food source concentrated like this, it doesn't take long for an eagle to swoop down out of the sky and grab some supper. Contact the Fish and Wildlife office for the latest information on the best eagle-watching locations. A good sighting can be had driving to Bear Valley at sunrise. To get there, drive one mile south of Worden on U.S. 97. Turn right on Keno Worden Rd., cross the railroad tracks, and take an immediate left on the gravel road. Travel for about a mile and pull off the road. From here you can sometimes see up to 100 bald eagles soar from their roosts at the top of the ridge to their daytime feeding area on the lake to the east.

A world-renowned eagle conference (for info write: Klamath Basin Eagle Conference, 4647 Miller Island Rd., Klamath Falls 97603; or Ralph and Charlotte Opp, 5803 Estate Dr., Klamath Falls 97603, tel. 882-8486) is held in February with lectures, a film festival, art and photography shows, road racing, field trips, and workshops. The highlight is a predawn field trip to the nearby Bear Valley roost. It's sponsored by the Audubon Society at Oregon Institute of Technology at Klamath Falls. The conference fee is $25.

Get a free map and bald-eagle brochure by sending a stamped, self-addressed envelope to: Klamath Basin National Wildlife Refuges, Route 1, Box 74, Tule Lake, CA 96134; tel. (916) 667-2231.

Water Birds

March through May is when waterfowl and shorebirds stop over in the basin on their way north to their breeding grounds in Alaska and Canada. They rest and fatten up during the spring to build up the necessary strength and body fat to carry them through their long migration. This time of year is also the nesting season for thousands of marsh birds and waterfowl. The **Klamath Forest National Wildlife Refuge** north of Klamath Falls on U.S. 97 is a good place during spring to observe sandhill cranes, shorebirds, waterfowl, and raptors.

The summer months are ideal for taking the self-guided auto tour routes and canoe trails. Descriptive leaflets are available for both attractions from the Oregon Fish and Wildlife office. Among the most prolific waterfowl and marsh bird areas in the Northwest, over 4,500 ducks, 2,600 Canada geese, and thousands of marsh and shorebirds are raised here each year. You may also see American white pelicans, *Pelecanus erythrorhynchos,* at the Upper Klamath National Wildlife Refuge during the summer. Unlike the brown pelican found on the Oregon coast, white pelicans prefer freshwater or estuarine areas. Another distinction that separates them from their seabound counterparts is that they paddle and dip their bills for food, whereas brown pelicans will dive into the water for fish.

The refuges are open during daylight hours, except when nesting and hunting seasons dictate schedule modifications. Overnight camping is not permitted at any of the refuges.

PRACTICALITIES

Bed And Breakfast

The **Klamath Manor** (219 Pine St., Klamath Falls 97601; tel. 883-5459) is a beautifully decorated turn-of-the-century home with French doors, period furnishings, four-poster beds, and oak floors. The master bedroom is the most luxurious bedroom available, with a fireplace and private bathroom. Further comfort is provided by a hot tub next to a flower-filled garden. Afternoon tea and a full English-American or vegetarian breakfast are included; rates are $45-65 per night double occupancy. No pets or small children are permitted.

Located on the southern shore of Klamath Lake is a rustic home called **The Stone House**

KLAMATH FALLS ACCOMMODATIONS

Best Western Klamath Inn, 4061 S. 6th St., tel. 882-1200, $54-75, covered pool, continental breakfast.

High Chaparral Motor Lodge, 5440 ORE 97, tel. 882-4675, $30, pool, pets.

Hill View Motel, 5543 S. 6th St., tel. 883-7771, $30-40, restaurant/lounge, pets.

Maverick Motel, 1220 Main St., tel. 882-6688, $35-45, pool.

La Vista Motor Lodge, ORE 97 or P.O. Box 761, Klamath Falls 97601, tel. 882-8844, $25-35, pool, laundry.

Molatore's Motel, 100 Main St., tel. 882-4666, $35-75, pool.

North Entrance Motel, 3844 ORE 97, tel. 884-8104, $25-35, covered pool, pets.

Oregon Motel 8, 5225 ORE 97, tel. 883-3431, $30-40, pool, kitchenettes, laundry.

Pony Pass Motel, 75 Main St., tel. 884-7735, $30-40, a/c.

Super 8 Motel, 3805 ORE 97, tel. 884-8880, $45-55, wheelchair access, restaurant, laundry.

Thunderbird Motel, 3612 S. 6th, tel. 882-8864, $60-75, pool, pets.

Value 20 Motel Klamath Falls, 124 N. 2nd St., tel. 882-7741, $30-40, wheelchair access, river views.

803 Front St., Klamath Falls 97601; tel. 883-8317). The bedrooms are modest yet cozy and stocked with antiques. A full country-style or continental breakfast is included, and the Stone House is happy to oblige special dietary considerations. The nicest thing about the property is its location on Oregon's largest lake, Upper Klamath Lake. From the front porch, several species of ducks, Canada geese, great blue herons, white pelicans, and bald eagles can be observed. The lucky visitor here in the spring can be treated to the spectacle of the courting dance of the western grebe. Rates are $45-60 per night double occupancy; reservations are recommended.

Locals are high on **Crystal Creek Lodge** (Box 489, Fort Klamath 97626; tel. 800-826-2968). Located close to the Upper Klamath Lake bald eagle nesting sites, this 19th-century homestead welcomes sportsmen, birdwatchers, and breakfast-lovers to its charming combination of guest rooms and restaurant. With room rates around $40, boat rentals and guided hunting and fishing trips available, you might want to reserve an extended stay. To get there, take ORE 62 to ORE 140. Then drive 45 miles east to the junction with Westside Road. Follow Westside en route to Fort Klamath and look for the sign on the right.

Campgrounds

Most of the campgrounds you'll find in the vicinity of Klamath Falls are privately owned operations. These facilities cater mostly to RVs with electric, water, and sewer hookups, as well as other creature comforts like swimming pools, laundromats, and recreational halls. These properties also tend to be in prime locations, which accounts for rates that are steeper than those of their public counterparts. Fortunately, there are several places to pitch a tent in both types of parks without having to deal with someone parked right next to your sleeping bag in a 40-foot-long mobile home watching "Wheel of Fortune" instead of the night sky.

On the north end of Upper Klamath Lake adjacent to the Upper Klamath National Wildlife Refuge lies **Harriman Springs Resort and Marina** (Harriman Route, Box 79, Klamath Falls 97601; tel. 356-2323). The campground features six tent and 17 RV sites with hookups. Flush toilets, showers, firewood, and a laundromat are also available. Open from April to late October, the fee is $7 per night. To get there, go 27 miles northwest of Klamath Falls on ORE 140 W and take a right onto Rocky Point Road. Proceed another two miles and you will see the resort on the right.

Another mile down Rocky Point Rd. is **Rocky Point Resort** (Harriman Route, Box 92, Klamath Falls 97601; tel. 356-2287), which also enjoys close proximity to the Upper Klamath National Wildlife Refuge. This resort has five tent and 28 RV sites with hookups. Flush toilets, showers, firewood, a laundromat, recreation hall, and other summer-camp trappings are available. Open April to mid-November, the camp charges $10 per night.

Several other campgrounds are also found on Upper Klamath Lake. The best deal around is **Hagelstein County Park** (County Parks Dept., Klamath Falls 97601; tel. 882-2501). The park can accommodate five tent campers and five RVs in sites that feature picnic tables and fire-grills, with flush toilets and water nearby. In addition to being the only campground on the east shore of the lake, it's the only free campground in the area. Open April to late November, reservations are advisable in this small park. To get there, head north of Klamath Falls for nine miles and look for the signs on the left side of the road.

About four miles north of Klamath Falls on U.S. 97 on the southeastern shore of Upper Klamath Lake is **Mallard Campground** (Route 5, Box 1348, Klamath Falls 97601; tel. 882-0482). Here you'll find 10 tent and 43 RV sites with hookups. Showers, flush toilets, laundromat, and pool are also on the premises. Open all year, $10 per night.

Approximately seven miles farther north of Mallard Campground on U.S. 97 is **KOA Klamath Falls** (3435 Shasta Way, Klamath Falls 97601; tel. 884-4644). Set along the shore of Upper Klamath Lake, the park features 18 tent and 73 RV sites with hookups. In true KOA style, flush toilets, showers, a pool, laundromat, recreation hall, and other amenities are available, Open all year, $10 per night.

Food
Klamath Falls is a small, unpretentious town that doesn't try to be anything more than what it is (which isn't much). As such, some locals suggest that visitors come here for the birds, not necessarily for the food. Fowl jokes aside, sandwiched in between the obligatory fast-food joints are a flock of eating establishments worthy of a brief mention.

You can get just about anything you want at **Alice's** (1012 Main St.; tel. 884-1444) restaurant. Open for breakfast, lunch, and dinner, Alice's recalls a San Francisco bill of fare. Fresh pasta, steaks, seafood, and fresh baked goods are complemented by good coffee, espresso, and imported beers and wines. Vegetarian meals are also available here.

For something Italian, try **Fiorella Italian Ristorante** (6139 Summers; tel. 882-1878). Open for dinner Tues.-Sat., the restaurant specializes in pasticcio (Venetian-style lasagna). Seafood and vegetarian meals are also found on the menu, as well as imported beers and wines. **Molatore's** (100 Main St.; tel. 884-6298) also features Italian cuisine, with moderately priced steak and seafood rounding out the offerings.

If you're in the mood for some Chinese food, head right for **Wong's** (421 Main St.; tel. 884-6578). In addition to an assortment of Chinese combination dinners and vegetarian dishes, you can also find American-style steak and seafood here. **King Wah** (2765 Pershing Way; tel. 882-0489), specializing in Cantonese cuisine and thick-cut steaks, is another option for Oriental fare.

The **Bagelry Company** (2542 Shasta Way; tel. 882-3419) produces fresh breads, bagels, and pastries. They make great sandwiches on bagels or deli breads stuffed with meats and cheese, ideal for birdwatching picnics. The veggie sandwich with avocado, cheese, sprouts, and tomato provides respite from meat between the buns. **Clasico Italian** (404 Main St.; tel. 883-6412) offers good food in an old brick hotel. Open Tues.-Sat., **Chez Nous** (3927 S. Sixth; tel. 883-8719), offers continental cuisine, moderately priced steak and seafood, and an extensive wine list. The best Mexican food in town can be found at **Los Dos Amigos** (4545 S. Sixth St.; tel. 883-3758). An excellent pizza is made at **Pizza by Campbell** (3020 Shasta Way; tel. 882-8500), located across from the Shasta Plaza.

Information And Services
The **post office** (317 S. Fourth; tel. 884-9226) is open 9 a.m.-5 p.m. weekdays. You can find additional information about the region by visiting the **Klamath County Library** (126 S. Third; tel. 882-8894). The **police** (Fifth and Walnut; tel.

883-5336 or 911 for emergencies only) and state police (2525 Biehn; tel. 883-5711) are always on call to assist. **Greyhound** (1200 Klamath Ave.; tel. 882-4616) can take you to California and the Willamette Valley. You can find the hard stuff at the **State Liquor Store** (4309 S. Sixth; tel. 884-3313). For health problems, the men and women of **Merle West Medical Center**

(2865 Dagget Ave., Klamath Falls 97601; tel. 882-6311, or 883-6176 for emergencies only) can help put all the pieces together again.

For more information on the area, the **Klamath County Tourism Department** (Box 1867, Klamath Falls 97601; tel. 884-0666) can help provide what you're looking for.

ORE 62: THE CRATER LAKE HIGHWAY

Many locals who live near the Crater Lake Highway sport bumper stickers on their vehicles that read, "I Survived Highway 62." The challenges of successfully navigating this challenging, precipitous, and circuitous thoroughfare, with its horrific winter weather and slow-moving summer crowds, help give it a killer reputation. Even so, there always seems to be traffic on this winding conduit between Crater Lake and southern Oregon. This isn't surprising when you consider the scenic appeals of the Rogue River and Cascade Mountains. Add excellent fishing on the Rogue below Oregon's largest fish hatchery, Eagle Creek, along with the swimming, boating, and rafting opportunities, and you too will be taking to the hills along Highway 62.

HIKES

Many choice hikes are found along the 50-mile stretch of the Rogue River Trail from Lost Creek Lake to the river's source at Boundary Springs just inside Crater Lake National Park. Tall waterfalls, deep gushing gorges, and a natural bridge are all easily accessible. Those interested in more than just a short walk from the parking lot to the viewpoint can design hikes of two to 18 miles with or without an overnight stay. Travelers with two cars can arrange shuttles to avoid having to double back.

Mill Creek Falls
One of the more scenic recreation spots is owned by Boise Cascade, a timber conglomerate. Boise Cascade has constructed paths through its land to a series of three waterfalls and an impressive, rock-choked section of the Rogue River called the Avenue of the Giant

Boulders. The largest of the three waterfalls is Mill Creek Falls, which plunges 173 feet down into the river. Signs along the highway and Mill Creek Drive (a scenic loop out of the community of **Prospect**) direct visitors to the trailhead. Boise Cascade has also posted a large map that further details the trail routes. The hike is short, but steep.

Takelma Gorge
A particularly wild section of the river is found at Takelma Gorge. Located one mile from River Bridge Campground on the upper Rogue River, the trail offers vistas of sharp, foaming bends in the river with logs jammed in at crazy angles on the rocks, and ferns growing in the mist of the waterfalls. Although the river's course is rugged, the grade on the trail is an easy one.

Natural Bridge
Even if you're in a hurry, you should take 15 minutes to get out of your car and stretch your legs at the Natural Bridge. Located a quarter mile from Natural Bridge Campground, a mile west of Union Creek on ORE 62, here the Rogue River drops into a lava tube and disappears from sight, only to emerge later a little way downstream. A short paved path takes you to a manmade bridge that fords this unique section of the river. Several placards along the way explain the formation of the Natural Bridge and other points of interest.

Rogue River Gorge
Just outside of **Union Creek** on ORE 62 is the spectacular Rogue River Gorge. The narrowest point on the river, the action of the water has carved out a deep chasm in the rock. A short trail with several well-placed overlooks follows

the narrow confines of the Rogue River Gorge

the rim of the gorge. Green mossed walls, log-jams, and a frothy torrent of water are all clearly visible from the trail. Informative placards discuss curiosities like the living stump and the pot-holes carved in the rock by pebbles and the action of the water.

National Creek Falls
Another short hike for hurried motorists is National Creek Falls. An easy half-mile walk down a trail bordered by magnificent Douglas firs leads to this tumultuous cascade. To get there, take ORE 230 to Forest Service Rd. 6530. Follow the road until you reach the trailhead marked by a sign.

Boundary Springs
A two-mile hike down a cool and shady trail takes you to the source of the mighty Rogue River, Boundary Springs. Situated just inside Crater Lake National Park, it's a great place for a picnic. About a mile down the path from the trailhead, hang a left at the fork to get to Boundary Springs.

Once at the springs, you'll discover small cataracts rising out of the jumbled volcanic rock that's densely covered with moss and other vegetation. While the temptation to get a closer look is great, the vegetation here is extremely fragile, so please refrain from walking on the moss. To get there, take ORE 230 north from ORE 62 to the crater rim viewpoint, where parking can be found on the left-hand side of the road.

PRACTICALITIES

Camping
For those who like roughing it in style with all of the amenities in their RVs, a couple of well-maintained trailer parks in the Rogue country can accommodate large vehicles. **Fly-Casters Campground and Trailer Park** (Box 1170, Shady Cove 97539; tel. 878-2749; $14-18 per night) and **Shady Trails RV Park and Campground** (Box 1299, Shady Cove 97539; tel. 878-2206, $14 per night) are both located about 23 miles north of Medford on ORE 62. Situated on the banks of the Rogue River, these parks feature hookups and picnic tables. Flush toilets, bottled gas, gray wastewater disposal, and showers are also available. A grocery store and restaurants are in the nearby town of **Shady Cove**. Both these parks are good home bases for RV owners who like to fish and hike.

Five miles below Lost Creek Lake on ORE 62 is **Rogue Elk County Park** (Jackson County Parks and Recreation, 10 South Oakdale, Medford 97501; tel. 465-2241). This campground features 20 sites for tents and RVs (15 feet maximum) with picnic tables and firegrills. Piped water and vault toilets are also on the premises. Open July to late October, the camp fee is $9 per night. The kids will enjoy swimming in Elk Creek, which, in addition to being adjacent to the campground, is warmer and safer than the Rogue. A rope swing tied to a tree adds to the fun at the swimming hole.

Along the shore of Lost Creek Lake is **Joseph Stewart State Park** (35251 ORE 62, Trail 97541; tel. 560-3334). Here you'll find 50 tent and 151 RV sites (40 feet maximum). Electricity, sewer hookups, firegrills, and picnic tables are provided. Flush toilets, water, gray wastewater disposal services, showers, and firewood are also available. Boat-launching facilities for Lost Creek Lake are located nearby. Open all year, the fee is $9 per night. Eight miles of hiking trails and bike paths crisscross the park. Lost Creek Lake also has a marina, beach, and boat rentals.

If you want to get away from the highway, head for **Abbott Creek** (Rogue National Forest, Prospect Ranger Station, Prospect 97536; tel. 560-3623). One of the few backwoods camps in the area that has potable water, it's seven miles northeast of the town of Prospect on ORE 62 and three miles down Forest Service Rd. 68. Situated at the confluence of Abbot and Woodruff creeks and not far from the upper Rogue River, this campground has nine tent and 12 RV sites (22 feet maximum) with picnic tables and firegrills. Hand-pumped water and vault toilets are also available. Open from late May to late October, the camp charges $6 per night.

Set along the bank of Union Creek where it merges with the upper Rogue River is **Union Creek** (Rogue National Forest, Prospect Ranger Station, Prospect 97536; tel. 560-3623). Located 11 miles northeast of Prospect, you'll find 72 tent and RV sites (16 feet maximum) with picnic tables, firegrills, piped water, and pit toilets. Open from late May to early September, the fee is $7 per night. Many fine hikes on the Rogue River Trail (see "Hikes" above) are within close proximity of the campground.

A half mile past Union Creek Campground on ORE 62 is **Farewell Bend** (Rogue National Forest, Prospect Ranger Station, Prospect 97536; tel. 560-3623). Located near the junction of ORE 62 and ORE 230, the camp has 61 tent and RV sites (22 feet maximum) with picnic tables and firegrills. Piped water and flush toilets are also within the campground boundaries. Open from late May to early September, the fee is $8 per night. This campground is situated along the banks of the upper Rogue near the Rogue River Gorge (see "Hikes" above).

A nice little campground tucked off the highway and yet fairly close to the Rogue River and Crater Lake National Park is **Huckleberry Mountain** (Rogue National Forest, Prospect Ranger Station, Prospect 97536; tel. 560-3623). To get there, go about 18 miles northeast of Prospect on ORE 62 and then four miles down Forest Service Rd. 60. There you'll find 15 tent and RV sites (21 feet maximum) with picnic tables and firegrills. Water and vault toilets are also available. Open July to late October, the campground is free of charge (14-day maximum stay). This campground is at an elevation of 5,400 feet, so be sure to have the proper gear to ensure a comfortable visit (see "Camping and Wilderness Travel" in the general Introduction).

Accommodations

The types of accommodations you'll find on ORE 62 are rustic and simple, catering mainly to fishermen and lovers of the great outdoors. The abundance of excellent campgrounds and RV parks also explains the dearth of lodgings.

The **Maple Leaf Motel** (20717 ORE 62, Shady Cove 97539; tel. 878-2169) has kitchenettes, cable TV, and a picnic and barbecue area to grill the day's catch or some burgers if the fish weren't biting. Rates range from $35-50. The **Two Pines Motel** (Box 182, 21331 ORE 62, Shady Cove 97539; tel. 878-2511) features kitchenettes with cable TV and runs $20-35 per night. The **Royal Coachman Motel** (Box 509, Shady Cove 97539; tel. 878-2481) has kitchenettes, cable TV, and HBO for $35-60 per night. Rooms with decks overlooking the river run $50-70.

The **Prospect Hotel and Motel** (391 Mill Creek Rd., Prospect 97536; tel. 560-3664) gives you a choice between something old and something new. The hotel, built in 1889 and listed on the National Register of Historic Places, has several small but comfortable rooms with bath. The rooms are named after local residents and famous people who have stayed at the hotel, including Zane Grey, Teddy Roosevelt, and Jack London. Because the hotel is small and old, no children, smoking, or pets are permitted. Rates are $55 a night per room. The adjacent motel features clean, spacious, and modern units that range from $40 to $60, with some kitchenettes available. You can smoke and bring the kids and family dog along, too.

Not far away from Prospect on the Crater Lake Highway is the **Union Creek Resort** (Prospect 97536; tel. 560-3339 or 560-3565). Built in the early 1900s, the Union Creek is listed on the National Register of Historic Places. Open year-round, it has rooms available in your choice of the original lodge, cabins, or housekeeping cabins. The lodge rooms, which range from $35 to $50, have washbasins in them and lodge guests share the bathrooms down the hall. The sleeping cabins with bath range from $40 to $60. The housekeeping cabins with bath and kitchen range from $50 to $75. The **Union Creek Country Store,** located at the resort, carries groceries and other essential items. Fishing licenses and snow-park permits can also be purchased here.

Food

ORE 62 parallels an old stagecoach road between Fort Klamath and the Rogue Valley. While the ruts in the road are gone, the tradition of frontier hospitality lives on in the establishments along this much-traveled mountain pass.

Loli's Hacienda (21666 ORE 62, Shady Cove; tel. 878-2144) is open for lunch and dinner. Though the Santa Fe pink-and-green interior and faux adobe may cause you to shake your head, the food gets a nod. Broasted chicken, pizza, and Mexican cuisine are some of the items you'll find on the menu here. Lunches range from $5 to $9, dinners range from $7 to $12. Perhaps part of Loli's charm is the old coin-operated puppet show machine located in the dining room. For two bits, brightly dressed señoritas dance about as the band plays on.

Down the road a little bit is the finest restaurant on this section of the Rogue River, **Beldi's.** From the cloth napkins to the crystal wine-glasses, you're assured a first-class dinner from start to finish. The dining room is perched on a bluff overlooking the river, further enhancing the visual appeal of the meal presentation. Chicken, veal, steak, and seafood dinners range from $10 to $20. Be sure to call ahead (tel. 878-2010) for reservations.

About halfway between Medford and Crater Lake in the vicinity of Prospect are a few eateries worth a mention. The **Prospect Cafe** (31 Mill Creek Rd., Prospect; tel. 560-3641) is open for breakfast, lunch, and dinner seven days a week. Breakfast with two eggs, hash browns, toast, and jam costs $3. Omelettes are cooked the way you like them with your choice of a dozen fillings. Best buys include the Mini Logger (one hotcake, one egg, two strips of bacon, and two links) and the Timber Feller (two hotcakes, two eggs, two strips of bacon, and two links).

While the names of the sandwiches on the menu (like Cougar Catch and Beefy Bobcat) match many of the stuffed critters adorning the walls, lunch is basic lumberjack fare, and lots of it. All sandwiches are accompanied with fries and choice of potato, coleslaw, or green salad.

Dinner entrees range from $7 to $14 and include soup and salad, vegetable, choice of potato, and fresh baked bread. Be sure to ask about the nightly special. Big wedges of home-baked pie are $2 a slice, or $2.50 with ice cream melting down the sides.

The dinner house at the **Prospect Hotel** (391 Mill Creek Rd., Prospect; tel. 560-3664) also comes recommended. Dinner is served family style with the works Tues.-Sat. 5-9 p.m. The menu offers a choice of two main courses that are different each night, and the menu changes monthly. One very special treat you can enjoy year-round here is huckleberry pie. A generous slice accompanied with a good strong cup of coffee costs under $3.

Beckie's (Union Creek Resort; tel. 560-3339) is an intimate place to stop for a bite to eat. One half of the building is an old log cabin; the other half is a modern design with plenty of windows. Breakfast runs $4-8 with all the trimmings. The lunch menu features sandwiches and burgers in the $3-6 bracket. Dinners that include chicken, pork, or steak entrees range $8-15. If you simply want to cool off on a hot day, the thick soda fountain-style shakes or malts at the ice-cream parlor next door to the restaurant will do the trick.

CRATER LAKE

INTRODUCTION

High in the Cascades lies the crown jewel of Oregon, Crater Lake. America's deepest lake (1,932 feet) glimmers like a polished sapphire in a setting created by a volcano blowing its top and collapsing thousands of years ago. Crater Lake's extraordinary hues are produced by the depth and clarity of the water and its ability to absorb all the colors of the spectrum except the shortest light waves, blue and violet, which are reflected and refracted skyward. Kodak used to send their apologies along with customers' photographs of Crater Lake, because they thought that they had goofed on the processing, so unbelievable are the colors of the water. In addition to a 33-mile rim drive around the main attraction, Oregon's only national park also features 210 campsites, dozens of hiking trails, and boat tours on the lake itself.

THE LAND

Geologically speaking, the name Crater Lake is a misnomer. A crater is an elliptical or circular depression in the surface of the earth that is surrounded by an inward-facing rim. Many craters are volcanic in origin, their walls formed by ash and lava fragments that were expelled explosively from the volcano's vent. Technically, however, Crater Lake lies in a caldera, which is produced when the center of a volcano caves in upon itself; in this case, the cataclysm occurred 6,600 years ago with the destruction of formerly 12,000-foot-high Mt. Mazama.

Klamath Indian legend has it that Mt. Mazama was the home of Llao, King of the Underworld. The chief of the world above was Skell, who sometimes would stand upon Mt. Shasta, 100 miles to the south. A fierce battle between these two gods took place, a time marked by great explosions, thunder, and lightning. Burning ash fell from the sky, igniting the forest, and molten rivers of lava gushed 35 miles down the mountainside, burying Indian villages. For a week the

night sky was lit by the flames of the great confrontation. The story climaxes with Skell's destruction of Llao's throne, as the mountain collapsed upon itself and sealed Llao beneath the surface, never again to frighten the Indians and destroy their homes. Although the lake became serene and beautiful as the caldera filled with water, the Indians believed that only punishment awaited those who foolishly gazed upon the sacred battleground of the gods.

The aftereffects of this great eruption can still be seen. Huge drifts of ash and pumice hundreds of feet deep were deposited over a wide area—up to 80 miles away. The pumice deserts to the north of the lake and the deep, ashen canyons to the south are the most dramatic examples. So thick and widespread is the pumice that water percolates through too rapidly for plants to survive, creating reddish pockets of bleakness in the otherwise green forest. The eerie gray hoodoos in the southern canyons were created by hot gases bubbling up through the ash, hardening it into rocklike towers. These formations have withstood centuries of erosion by water that has long since washed away the loosely packed ash, creating the steep canyons visible today. **Wizard Island,** a large cinder cone that rises 760 feet above the surface of the lake, and the **Phantom Ship,** located in the southeastern corner, offer evidence of volcanic activity since the caldera's formation.

The lake is confined by walls of multicolored lava that rise 500 to 2,000 feet above the water. Although it does not have a drainage outlet, Crater Lake is not saline because it is fed entirely by snow and rain, and the surrounding volcanic rocks are nearly salt-free. And yet, the level of the lake fluctuates only one to three feet a year, as evaporation and seepage keep it remarkably constant. Another surprise is that while Crater Lake often records the coldest temperatures in the Cascades, the lake itself has only frozen over once since records have been kept. The water stays around 38° F, although scientists have discovered hot spots 1,400 feet below the lake's surface that are 66°. Rainbow trout and kokanee (a landlocked salmon) were intro-

Oregon's crown jewel, Crater Lake

duced to the lake many years ago by man. Due to the lack of proper food, these fish are too small and scrawny to make good eating, but they nevertheless manage to eke out a meager existence in the frigid waters. Some types of mosses and green algae grow more than 400 feet below the lake's surface, a world record for these freshwater species.

HISTORY

Accounts differ on who "discovered" Crater Lake, but most sources agree that it was John Wesley Hillman, a prospector looking for the Lost Bucket Mine. He christened his find Deep Blue Lake. Successive discoverers named it Blue Lake, Lake Majesty, Great Sunken Lake, and finally, Crater Lake. Peter Britt first photographed it in the 1880s, bringing widespread attention to the lake. This, coupled with the tireless work of William Gladstone Steel, culminated in Crater Lake's establishment as a national park in 1902.

SIGHTS

Visitor Centers
The new visitor center is located below Rim Village near park headquarters and is a good place to start. Open daily from summer into fall (depending on snowfall), the center provides information, maps, and publications, as well as back-country permits and first aid. If the lake is socked in by lousy weather, you can still see it anyway: excellent films about Crater Lake are shown in the center's theater every half hour and by special arrangement. For additional information, contact the superintendent (Crater Lake National Park, Box 7, Crater Lake 97604; tel. 594-2211).

The original visitor center is on the rim. A rock stairway behind the small building leads to Sinnott Memorial and one of the best views of the lake. Perched on a rock outcropping, accompanying interpretive placards help you identify the surrounding formations and savor the vista.

Boat Tours
There are over 100 miles of hiking trails in the park, and yet only one leads down to the lake itself. This is because the 1.1-mile-long **Cleetwood Trail** is the only part of the caldera's steep, avalanche-prone slope safe enough for passage. The trail drops 700 feet in elevation and is recommended for those in good physical condition. There is no alternative transportation to Cleetwood Cove dock, located at the end of the trail, where the Crater Lake **boat tours** (tel. 594-2511) begin. These narrated excursions depart on the hour 10 a.m.-4 p.m. and cost $10 for adults, $5.50 for children under 12 (free for kids under 18 months).

In addition to cruising around the lake and giving you a close look at the Phantom Ship and other geologic oddities, the tour includes a

A WINTER'S TALE OF THE TAPE

Crater Lake is famed for massive snow accumulation. Roads are frequently closed due to drifts until the beginning of July, and 50-foot annual deposits are common. If this fails to impress, consider some of the following Crater Lake snow jobs: In the winter of 1932-33, the lake saw the most snow ever recorded in the state during a calendar year, 879 inches. The most snow to fall in 12 consecutive months fell here between April 1948 and March 1949, a grand total of 931 inches. The most snow that ever fell on an Oregon locale in one storm, 119 inches, occurred here March 16-25, 1975. Finally, the most snow ever recorded in Oregon in one month was at Crater Lake in 1933, 256 inches.

10-minute stop on Wizard Island. Passengers electing to hike the steep, one-mile spiral path to the top of the island volcano can catch a later boat back to the dock. However, keep in mind that boats have limited space, which means your return trip could be as late as 5 p.m., depending upon availability. And while it's a great place for a picnic, please be careful to leave this unique island in an unspoiled condition for future visitors.

Hikes
July and August are the most popular months. Colorful flowers and mild weather greet the summer throngs. One of the best places to view the mid-July flora is on the **Castle Crest Wildflower Trail.** The trailhead to this half-mile-long loop trail is a half mile from the park headquarters. Stop there for directions to the trailhead as well as a self-guiding trail booklet that will tell you what the flowers along the trail are called.

A suitable challenge of brawn and breath is the **Garfield Peak Trail.** The trailhead to this imposing ridge is just east of Crater Lake Lodge. It is a steep climb up the 1.7-mile-long trail, but the wildflower displays of phlox, Indian paintbrush, and lupine, as well as frequent sightings of eagles and hawks, give ample opportunity for you to stop and catch your breath. The highlight of the hike is atop Garfield Peak, which provides a spectacular view of Crater Lake 1,888 feet below.

When snow again buries the area in the wintertime, services and activities are cut to a minimum. However, many cross-country skiers, snowshoe enthusiasts, and winter campers enjoy this solitude. Park rangers lead snowshoe hikes (weather permitting) at 1 p.m. weekends, daily during Christmas week. Ski and snowshoe rentals are available at Rim Village.

Winter trekkers should be aware that there are no groomed cross-country trails. Thus, it's imperative to inquire about trail, avalanche, road, and weather conditions at the visitor center (open 8:30-4:30 p.m. daily). Circumnavigating the lake, which is visited by frequent snowstorms, takes two to three days, even in good weather. Only skilled winter hikers should attempt this 33-mile route that requires a compass and maps to traverse unmarked routes and avalanche paths. There are no overnight accommodations in the area mid-October through June (and you are not allowed to sleep in your vehicle), necessitating a long drive out of the park for any creature comforts. Prior to setting out on any extended journey, pick up a permit and some free advice at the visitor center.

PRACTICALITIES

Campgrounds
Mazama Campground, eight miles south of the rim, has 198 sites, restrooms, and a dump station. **Lost Creek Campground,** located on the eastern section of Rim Dr., has 12 sites, water, and pit toilets. Neither campground has showers or hookups. They are opened when the snow melts, and closed for the season when the snow returns. Contact the park superintendent (tel. 594-2211) for more information.

Accommodations And Food
One of the nicest things about 183,180-acre Crater Lake National Park is that it's not very developed. The services are concentrated on the southern edge of the lake at **Rim Village.** From May 19 to October 14, the only accommodations in the park, **Mazama Cabins** (tel. 954-2511), are found next to Mazama Campground. Each room features two queen beds and a bath, and two are designed for wheelchair access. Be sure to call ahead for reservations.

Although at press time there were no accommodations on the rim, you can at least still get a hot meal at the **Cafeteria** and the **Watchman Deli Lounge**. The Cafeteria is open all year, serving traditional breakfasts, with lunch and dinner offerings including a salad bar, cook-to-order entrees, and deli sandwiches. The Watchman Deli Lounge is located upstairs above the Cafeteria and is open from noon to 11 p.m., June 11 through Labor Day. The menu includes hamburgers, deli sandwiches, pizza, and snacks, as well as microbrews, espresso, wine, and spirits. Even though it's called a lounge, families are always welcome. The adjoining gift shop is stocked with postcards and knickknacks. A small grocery section there sells various foodstuffs and beverages in case you've run out of peanut butter and beer.

In 1994 or 1995, the Crater Lake Lodge will reopen to full capacity (71 rooms) after years of restoration. The lodge is situated on the rim south of the Sinnott Overlook and is hewn of indigenous wood and stone. The massive lobby boasts a picture window on the lake and will have decor echoing back to its 1915 origins. The stone fireplace is large enough to walk into and serves as a gathering spot on chilly evenings. Make reservations far in advance (Crater Lake Lodge Company, Box 97, Crater Lake 97604; tel. 594-2511) if you want to stay here.

Getting There And Getting Around
The only year-round access to Crater Lake is from the south via ORE 62. This highway makes a horseshoe bend through the Cascades, starting at Medford and ending 20 miles north of Klamath Falls. The northern route via ORE 138 (Roseburg to ORE 97, south of Beaver Marsh) is usually closed by snow mid-October through July. The tremendous snowfall also closes 33-mile-long Rim Drive, although portions are opened when conditions permit. Rim Drive is generally opened to motorists around the same time as the northern entrance to the park.

ORE 138: THE UMPQUA HIGHWAY

One of the great escapes into the Cascade Mountains is via the Umpqua Highway. This road runs along the part of the Umpqua River coveted by Zane Grey and Clark Gable as well as legions of less ballyhooed nimrods during steelhead season. The North Umpqua is a premier fishing river full of trout and salmon as well as a source of excitement for whitewater rafters who shoot the rapids. Numerous waterfalls, including the second highest in Oregon, Watson Falls, feed this great waterway and are found close to the road. Tall timbers line the road through the Umpqua National Forest, and many fine campgrounds are situated within its confines. Mountain lakes like Toketee Reservoir, Lemolo Lake, and Diamond Lake offer boating and other recreational opportunities. The Umpqua National Forest also boasts challenging and yet accessible mountain trails up the flanks of Mt. Bailey (8,603 feet) and Mt. Thielsen (9,182 feet). And when snow carpets the landscape in winter, you can go cross-country skiing, snowmobiling, and snowcat skiing on Mt. Bailey free from the crowds at other winter sports areas.

The main reason this place is still so wild is because of the ruggedness of the terrain. The first road was built in the 1920s, a crude dirt trail that ran from Roseburg to Steamboat. Travelers of the day who wanted to get to the Diamond Lake Lodge spent three days traversing this road by car, then had to journey another 20 miles on horseback to reach their final destination. The North Umpqua Road was expanded to Copeland Creek by the Civilian Conservation Corps during the Depression, but the trips to Diamond and Crater Lakes were still limited to a trailwise few.

It wasn't until the late 1950s, when President Dwight D. Eisenhower pushed for development of the nation's interstate freeways and state highways, that road improvement began in earnest. Douglas County responded to the president's call by allocating $2.76 million toward federal matching funds to construct the Umpqua Highway. The all-weather thoroughfare was completed in the summer of 1964, opening up the North Umpqua basin to timber interests, sportsmen, and tourists.

Numerous Indian rock paintings are found in the Umpqua region.

The economy of Douglas County feeds upon the timber of the Umpqua National Forest. Approximately three-fourths of all workers in the county are directly or indirectly dependent on the timber industry. Timber receipts from federal lands generate $60 million annually for county coffers, providing money for roads, schools, and other services. But with over a quarter-million truckloads of logs rolling out of the Umpqua National Forest each year, it's no wonder that the timber boom is going bust. The dwindling supply of trees after 25 years of unabated cutting, and huge cutbacks in the allowable harvest of old-growth timber due to endangered species like the spotted owl mean that the lumberjack county is in for a major transition in the near future.

The good news is that there are still many unspoiled areas that were spared the lumberman's axe and that are easily accessible to the traveler. Come and enjoy a beautiful green section of the Oregon Cascades on a road less traveled.

SIGHTS

Colliding Rivers
Just off of ORE 138 on the west side of the town of **Glide** is the site of the colliding rivers. The Wild and Umpqua rivers meet head-on in a bowl of green serpentine. The best time to view this spectacle is after winter storms and when spring runoff is high. If the water is low, check out the high-water mark sign from the Christmas Flood of 1964. Water levels from that great inundation were lapping at the parking lot.

Waterfalls
Visitors can get an unusual perspective of **Grotto Falls** because there's a trail in back of this 100-foot cascade. If you venture behind the shimmering water, watch your step because the moss-covered rocks are very slippery. To get there, take ORE 138 for 18 miles east of Roseburg to Glide. Follow Little River Rd. to the Coolwater Campground where you'll find the turnoff to Forest Service Rd. 2703 nearby. Take it for five miles until you reach the junction of Forest Service Rd. 2703-150. Proceed down Forest Service Rd. 2703-150 for another two miles until you reach the trailhead. It's only a short hike in to view Grotto Falls.

About 10 miles west of the town of **Steamboat** is 50-foot-high **Susan Creek Falls,** whose trailhead sits off ORE 138 near the Susan Creek picnic area. A one-mile trail winds through a rainforestlike setting to the falls. The cascade is bordered on three sides by green mossy rock walls that never see the light of the sun and stay wet 365 days a year. Another quarter mile up the trail are the **Indian Mounds.** One of the rites of manhood for Umpqua Indian boys was to fast and pile up stones in hopes of being granted a vision or spiritual powers. Also called the Vision Quest Site, you can see many different stacks of moss-covered stones in an area protected by a fence.

Four miles west of Susan Creek Falls is **Fall Creek Falls.** Look for the trailhead off of ORE 138 at Fall Creek. A good walk for families with young children and older people, the mild one-mile trail goes around and through slabs of bedrock. Halfway up the trail is a lush area called **Job's Garden.** Stay on the Fall Creek Trail and in another half mile you'll come to the falls. It's a double falls with each tier 35 to 50 feet in height. Back at Job's Garden, you may care to explore the Job's Garden Trail, which leads to the base of columnar basalt outcroppings.

During fish-migration season, it's fun to venture a little way off of ORE 138 at Steamboat and go up Steamboat Creek Rd. 38 to see the fish battle two small waterfalls. The first, **Little Falls,** is a mile up the road. It's always exciting to see the fish miraculously wriggle their way up this 10-foot cascade. Four miles farther down Steamboat Creek Rd. is **Steamboat Falls.** A viewpoint showcases this 30-foot falls, but not as many fish try to swim up this one because of the fish ladders nearby.

Back on ORE 138 about three miles east of Steamboat is **Jack Falls.** Look for the trailhead sign and follow the trail along the brushy bank of Jack Creek to a series of three closely grouped falls ranging from 20 to 70 feet in height.

Two big waterfalls are another 19 miles down ORE 138 near the Toketee Ranger Station. To get to **Toketee Falls,** follow Forest Service Rd. 34 at the west entrance of the ranger station, cross the first bridge, and turn left. There you'll find the trailhead and a parking area. The half-mile trail ends up at a double waterfall with a combined height of over 150 feet. The word *toketee* means "graceful" in the Indian dialect, and after viewing the water plunge over the sheer wall of basalt you'll probably agree it's aptly named.

Double back to ORE 138 and take Forest Service Rd. 37 near the east entrance of the Toketee Ranger Station. This road will take you to the trailhead of **Watson Falls,** a 272-foot-high flume of water. A moderate half-mile trail climbs through tall stands of Douglas fir and western hemlock and is complemented by an understory of green salal, Oregon grape, and

ferns. A bridge spans the canyon just below the falls, giving outstanding views of this towering cascade. The cool spray that billows up to the bridge always feels good on hot days after the hike uphill.

Another falls worth a visit is **Lemolo Falls.** *Lemolo* is an Indian word meaning "wild and untamed," and you'll see this is the case with this thunderous 100-foot waterfall. To get there, take Lemolo Lake Rd. off of ORE 138, then follow Forest Service Roads 2610 and 2610-600, and look for the trailhead sign. The trail is a gentle one-mile path that drops down into the North Umpqua Canyon and passes several small waterfalls on the way to Lemolo Falls.

Umpqua Hot Springs

The Umpqua Hot Springs is mostly unknown and far away enough from civilized haunts not to be overused, and yet it's accessible enough for those in the know to enjoy. The springs have been developed with wooden pools and a crude lean-to shelter. It's best to go during midweek, as weekends tend to have more visitors, forcing you to wait your turn for a soak. To get there, go north from the Toketee Ranger Station and turn right onto County Rd. 34, which is just past the Pacific Power and Light buildings. Proceed down 34 past Toketee Lake about six miles. When you cross the bridge over Deer Creek, which is clearly noted by a sign, you will be a little less than a half mile from the turnoff. The turnoff is a dirt road to the right that goes a mile and ends at a small parking area. Please note that in wet weather this road may be impassable, and it is not recommended for low-slung cars at any season. From the parking area, it's a half mile down the blocked road to the hot springs trailhead and another half mile to the pool.

SPORTS AND RECREATION

The North Umpqua has several distinctions. First, it is known as one of the most difficult North American rivers to fish. No boats are permitted from 15 miles in either direction of Steamboat, and no bait or spinners are allowed either. This puts a premium on skillful fly-fishing. You can wade on in and poke around for the best fishing holes on the North Umpqua, one of the few rivers with a native summer run of steelhead—or better yet, hire a guide.

Fishing Outfitters

"Fishing is our only business," proclaims the sign at **Umpqua Angler** (420 S.E. Main, Roseburg 97470; tel. 673-9809), and their staff is always eager to help you sink your hooks into some supper. This full-service shop features licensed and insured guides for spring and fall salmon as well as summer and winter steelhead. They have all kinds of fishing equipment, bait and tackle, and boats and boat supplies. If you have trouble with your rod and reel, this is the place to bring it in for repairs. Open at 7 a.m. seven days a week.

One of the decisions fishing-guide shoppers have to make is to choose from Gary, Larry, or Jerry. **Gary's Guide Service** (607 Fawn Dr., Roseburg 97470; tel. 672-2460) has been in the fishing business for over 20 years and can teach you tried-and-true secrets of the trade. Licensed, bonded, and insured, all equipment is provided for fly- or drift-fishing for salmon and steelhead on the North Umpqua. Rates are $150 for a one- to two-person full-day trip.

Larry's Guide Service (12736 N. Umpqua Hwy., Roseburg 97470; tel. 673-3099) can help you get out on the river year-round to fish for salmon, steelhead, and striped bass. The driftboats are large and heated; bait, tackle, and safety equipment are all provided. Rates are $150 for full-day trips; call ahead for reservations and additional information. **Jerry's Guide Service** (tel. 672-8324) mimics Gary's and Larry's offerings. Jerry Phelps, a teacher, naturalist, and guide with a master of science degree, offers an educational and entertaining fishing experience. Jerry's rates are also $150 for the full-day trip.

Bill Conners Guide Service (Box 575, Glide 97443; tel. 496-0309) offers trips on the North Umpqua River for winter steelhead Jan.-April, for chinook salmon May-June and Sept.-Oct., and for summer steelhead June-October. He uses drift boats and gives you a choice of fly-, bait, or lure fishing. Rates are $150 for a daytrip with one to two people and include bait, tackle, and a snack. Call ahead for reservations.

Rafting

It's no secret that the fishing is excellent on the North Umpqua River. And yet, the river has only recently been "discovered" and gained popularity with whitewater rafters and kayakers. But fishing and floating are not always compatible, so guidelines for boaters and rafters have been established by the Bureau of Land Management and the Umpqua National Forest. The area around Steamboat has the most restrictions, mainly because of the heavy fishing in the area that boaters would disturb. Be sure to check with the Forest Service (tel. 498-2531) prior to setting out to make sure that you are making a legal trip. A good way to get started rafting and avoid the hassle of rules, regulations, and gear is to go along with an experienced whitewater guide. They provide the safety equipment, the boats, and the expertise; all you have to do is paddle. There are, however, a few things to know before you go.

Don't bother to bring a camera; your hands will be too busy paddling to have time to take pictures. Besides, keeping a camera dry in a raft is not an easy task and often requires special protective equipment. Short pants are preferable, because a little water that splashes up on your leg can be brushed off easily, whereas soaked jeans will remain wet and continue to draw out heat from your body for the duration of your voyage. Ponchos can be effective at keeping the water off your upper body, but they breathe poorly. This means that your perspiration from the exertion will get you nearly as soaked as any souse hole. Another thing to remember is to wear a pair of worn-out sneakers that you don't really care about and leave the Gucci sandals at home. There always seems to be a little bit of water in the bottom of the boat, and shoes are always required for safety reasons. Finally, a hat and liberal layers of sunscreen are recommended to protect your skin from the ravages of the mountain sun.

Rafting Outfitters

North Umpqua Outfitters (Box 1574, 368 N.E. Garden Valley Blvd., Roseburg 97470; tel. 673-4599) offers raft, kayak, and drift-boat trips. Half-day raft trips are $30 per person; full-day raft trips with lunch are $45 per person. This company operates the North Umpqua Kayak School, which gives classes on how to paddle safely, to roll and handle surfing waves, and survive souse holes (exhilarating pools of foaming water that can be equally dangerous because of their strong eddies). Half- and full-day kayak lessons include all necessary equipment. Half- and full-day drift-boat trips are available for those who like to troll their fishing line in the water on their way downstream. They also rent boats, rafts, kayaks, and the appropriate accoutrements. If you make your reservation in advance, you are given a discount, and you can also knock off 10% on certain packages if you bring in their brochure, available at the Roseburg Visitors and Convention Bureau (see Roseburg "Information and Services").

If you want to rent your equipment, a good place to check out is **North Umpqua Equipment Rental Sales and Service** (14168 ORE 138, Roseburg 97470; tel. 673-5391). You'll find it 12 miles east of Roseburg on ORE 138 next to the Whistlers Park Mercantile Store. They feature one- and two-person inflatable kayaks (also called "orange torpedoes") and whitewater rafts for two to six people.

Hikes

Over 570 miles of trails crisscross the one-million-acre **Umpqua National Forest**. With elevations that range from 1,000 to over 9,000 feet, there are hikes to please families and mountain climbers alike. Wildlife and wildflowers, mountain lakes and mountain peaks, old-growth forest and alpine meadows are some of the attractions visitors see along the way.

If you're camping along the North Umpqua River, many pleasant day-hikes are possible on the **North Umpqua Trail**. Slated to be completed by the mid-1990s, this projected 76-mile thoroughfare will stretch from Rock Creek just east of Idleyld Park all the way up to the Pacific Crest Trail at Windigo Pass. The trail connects many of the campgrounds and has many access points from ORE 138. Check with the Umpqua National Forest Ranger Station (Diamond Lake Ranger District, HC 60, Box 101, Idleyld Park 97447; tel. 498-2531) for a map and brochure to plan your expedition along this beautiful walkway.

One completed segment of the North Umpqua Trail is the **Panther Trail**. This gentle one-mile hike begins near Steamboat at the parking lot of the former ranger station. Many wildflowers are seen late April through early June on the way up to the old fish hatchery. One flower to look for is the bright red snow plant, *Sarcodes sanguinea,* which grows beneath Douglas firs and sugar pine trees. Also called the carmine snowflower or snow lily, the snow plant is classified as a saprophyte, a plant that contains no chlorophyll and derives nourishment from decayed materials. Growing 8-24 inches in height, the red flowers are crowded at the crown of the stem.

A **five-mile hike** that ranges from easy to moderate is found on the south slope of 8,363-foot-high Mt. Bailey. Bring plenty of water and good sturdy hiking shoes because the last half mile of the ascent is steep, with many sharp rocks. To get to the trailhead, take ORE 138 to the north entrance of Diamond Lake. Turn off onto Forest Service Rd. 4795 and follow it five miles to the junction of Forest Service Rd. 4795-300. Proceed down 4795-300 another mile until you see the trail marker.

The easy two-mile **Diamond Lake Loop** takes hikers through a mix of lodgepole pine and true fir to Lake Creek, Diamond Lake's only outlet. There are many views of Mt. Bailey along the way, as well as some private coves ideal for a swim on hot days. But while the grade is easy, keep in mind that the elevation is nearly a mile high and pace yourself accordingly. To get to the loop, take Forest Service Rd. 4795 off of ORE 138 on the north entrance to Diamond Lake and look for the trailhead sign on the west side of the road.

For those who like to climb mountains for reasons other than just because they are there, the **Mt. Thielsen Trail** offers a million-dollar view from the top of the mountain. This four-mile moderate-to-difficult trail winds to the top of Mt. Thielsen's spire-pointed 9,182-foot-high volcanic peak. Bring along water and quick-energy snacks; hiking boots are also recommended due to the sharp volcanic rocks that could easily damage ordinary shoes. Extra care should be taken getting up and down the last 200 feet since the rocks weaken from ice and erosion during the winter and are prone to crumbling underfoot. If you make it to the top, be sure to enter your name in the climbing register found there. Then take a look at the view, which stretches from Mt. Shasta to Mt. Hood, and forget all the silly preoccupations that plague us mortals. You'll find the trailhead on the east side of ORE 138 one mile north of the junction of ORE 230.

Mount Bailey Snowcat Skiing

Located 80 miles east of Roseburg off of ORE 138 in the central Cascades is Mt. Bailey (tel. 793-3333). Snowcats transport no more than 20 skiers up the mountain from Diamond Lake Resort to the summit of this 8,363-foot-high peak. Experienced guides then lead small groups down routes that best suit the abilities of each group. The skiing is challenging and should only be attempted by those who can ski advanced runs at major ski areas in various snow conditions. Open bowls, steep chutes, and tree-lined glaciers are some of the types of terrain encountered during the 3,000-foot drop in elevation back to the resort.

The prices may also seem steep at $90 a day, but it's worth it given the pristine beauty of the area, dearth of crowds, and superlative skiing. You can save some money with the Powder Pass—six days of skiing for the price of five. Other attractive packages include overnight lodging in fireside cabins at Diamond Lake Resort as well as an "alpine lunch" of breads, meats, cheeses, vegetables, homemade pie, and coffee served up on the mountain. Rates are $240 for the two-day package, $345 for the three-day, and $550 for the five-day. Only a limited number of skiers can be booked, so be sure to call ahead for reservations.

Slip Slidin' Away

If you fit the bunny hill category, you might enjoy inner-tubing at Sliding Hill (tel. 793-333) near Diamond Lake Resort. A rope tow takes "tubers" to the top of the hill seven days a week, 9-5, for nonstop thrills and spills on the way back down. The hill has a ticket system similar to other ski lifts, with full-day, half-day, and two-hour passes available. Passes including an inner tube cost $10 for the full day, $8 for the half day, and $6 for two hours. A $5 refundable deposit is required for the equipment, and many sizes of inner tubes are available. If you bring your own inner tube, you can save a dollar or two.

Cross-country Skiing

Over 56 miles of designated Nordic trails are found in the Diamond and Lemolo lakes area along the upper reaches of ORE 138. The trails range in elevation from 4,200 feet to over 8,000 feet at the top of Mt. Bailey. Some of the trails are groomed, and all of them are clearly marked by blue trail signs. Contact the Umpqua National Forest (Diamond Lake Ranger District, HC 60, Box 101, Idleyld Park 97447; tel. 498-2531) and request maps and information on these trails.

The Nordic Center (tel. 793-3333) at Diamond Lake Resort has equipment, waxes, and rentals, and is open 8-5 daily. It costs $12 per day for a rental package including skis, boots, and poles. Lessons are also available. A great option to cross-country buffs is to take a snowcat from Diamond Lake to the north rim of Crater Lake for $50 per person. You have the option to ski the 10 miles back to Diamond Lake (which is mostly downhill) with a guide, or ride back on the snowcat for an additional $40. A hearty lunch is included in the package.

Motorized Snow Trails

Approximately 133 miles of designated motorized snow trails are concentrated around the Lemolo and Diamond lakes area. The trails are usually open in late November, when snow accumulations permit, and range from 4,000 to over 8,000 feet in elevation. Many of these trails are groomed on a regular basis, and all are clearly marked by orange trail signs and diamond-shaped trail blazes pegged up on trees above the snowline. Contact Umpqua National Forest (see "Cross-country Skiing" above) for maps and additional information.

One of the more exotic runs is into Crater Lake National Park. Snowmobiles and ATVs (all-terrain vehicles) must register at the north entrance of the park and stay on the road. The trail climbs up about 10 miles from the park gates to the north rim of the lake. Be aware that the mountain weather here can change suddenly, creating dangerous subzero temperatures and whiteout conditions. Also, watch for Nordic skiers and other people sometimes found on motorized-vehicle trails.

Snowmobile Tours

If you've ever wanted to ride on one of these motorized snow broncs, then this is the way to go. Each person is furnished with his or her own snowmobile and fuel. A half-dozen tours are available ranging from $30 for the one-hour, 17-mile ride around Diamond Lake to $125 for the eight-hour, 100-mile trip to Crescent Lake. The most popular trip is the Crater Lake rim tour. It costs $60 and takes four hours to cover the 50 miles of snowbound terrain. A hearty lunch is included. Make your reservations at the **Diamond Lake Resort Hilltop Shop** (tel. 793-3333). The only catch to the offer is that you must be a guest of the resort, due to the clauses in the liability insurance policy carried by the concessionaire.

PRACTICALITIES

Camping On The Little River

If the thought of a campground with good shade trees and a waterfall with a swimming hole sounds idyllic, head for **Cavitt Creek Falls** (Bureau of Land Management, 777 N.W. Garden Valley Blvd., Roseburg 97470; tel. 672-4491). To get there, head east of Roseburg on ORE 138 to Glide, take Little Creek Rd. (County Rd. 17) for seven miles, then continue three miles down Cavitt Creek Road. Eight sites for RVs (20 feet maximum) with picnic tables and firegrills are provided, with piped water, pit toilets, and firewood available on the premises. Open May to late Oct., Cavitt Creek runs $6 per night.

Another campsite five miles up Little River Rd. is **Wolf Creek** (North Umpqua Ranger District, 18782 ORE 138, Glide 97443; tel. 496-3532), which features five sites for tents and RVs (16 feet maximum) and three tent-only sites. Picnic tables, firegrills, vault toilets, and piped water are provided. Open mid-May to late Oct., the fee is $4 per night. The grounds also have a group-picnic site with a pavilion sheltering 14 picnic tables, plus barbecue grills, flush toilets, and chlorinated water. This facility is booked on a reservation-only basis for $35 per day. A softball field, horseshoe pits, and swimming in the Little River make this a fine place for family get-togethers.

An easy way to keep your cool is at **Coolwater** (North Umpqua Ranger District, 18782 ORE 138, Glide 97443; tel. 496-3532). Seven tent and RV sites (16 feet maximum) with picnic

tables and firegrills are available; vault toilets and well water from a hand pump are also on the grounds. Open mid-May to late Oct., the campground charges $4 a night. To get there, follow Little River Rd. 15 miles out of Glide. There are many good hiking trails nearby, including **Grotto Falls, Wolf Creek Nature Trail,** and **Wolf Creek Falls Trail.**

One of the best deals on the Little River is at **White Creek** (North Umpqua Ranger District, 18782 ORE 138, Glide 97443; tel. 496-3532). Open from mid-May to late Sept., this small five-site campground accommodates tents and RVs (31 feet maximum) free of charge. Picnic tables and firegrills are provided, and piped water and vault toilets are available. Situated on the confluence of White Creek and Little River, there is a good beach and shallow water that provide excellent swimming for children. The only catch to this oasis of tranquility is that your stay is limited to two weeks at a time. To get there, take Little Creek Rd. 17 miles to Red Butte Rd. and proceed a mile down Red Butte Rd. to the campground.

Tucked away at an elevation of 3,200 feet on the upper reaches of the Little River is **Lake in the Woods** (North Umpqua Ranger District, 18782 ORE 138, Glide 97443; tel. 496-3532). Here you'll find nine sites for tents and RVs (16 feet maximum), with picnic tables, firegrills, vault toilets, and hand-pumped water. Open from June to late Oct., the camp charges $4 per night. Set along the shore of four-acre, manmade Little Lake in the Woods, motorized craft are not permitted in this eight-foot-deep pond. Two good hikes nearby go to either **Hemlock Falls** or **Yakso Falls.** To get there, head 20 miles up Little River Rd. to where the pavement ends; proceed another seven miles until you reach the campground.

North Umpqua River Camping

Set along the bank of the North Umpqua River 15 miles east of Roseburg on ORE 138 is **Whistler's Bend** (Box 800, Winchester 97495; tel. 673-4863). Picnic tables and firegrills are provided at this county park, as are piped water, flush toilets, and showers. No reservations are necessary, and the fee is $8 per night. The fishing is good here, and even though it's fairly close to town, it doesn't usually get too crowded.

About 30 miles east of ORE 138 is **Susan Creek** (Bureau of Land Management, 777 N.W. Garden Valley Blvd., Roseburg 97470; tel. 672-4491). This campground has 33 tent and RV sites (20 feet maximum) with picnic tables and firegrills. Flush toilets, piped water, and firewood are also available. Open May to late Oct., the fee is $7 per night. Situated in a grove of old-growth Douglas fir and sugar pine next to the North Umpqua River, a fine beach and swimming hole complement the setting.

Within easy access to great fishing (fly-angling only), rafting, and hiking, **Bogus Creek** (Diamond Lake Ranger District, HC 60, Box 101, Idleyld Park 97447; tel. 498-2531) offers you the real thing. Here you'll find five tent sites and 10 tent and RV (20 feet maximum) sites with picnic tables and firegrills. Flush toilets, iodinated water, and gray wastewater sumps are available. Open May 1-Oct. 31, the fee is $5 per night. As the campground is a major launching point for whitewater expeditions and within a few miles of Fall Creek Falls and Job's Garden Geological Area (see "Waterfalls" under "Sights" above), it's hard to beat the feeling here.

About 38 miles east of Roseburg on ORE 138 near Steamboat is **Canton Creek** (Diamond Lake Ranger District, HC 60, Box 101, Idleyld Park 97447; tel. 498-2531). Take Steamboat Creek Rd. off ORE 138 and proceed 400 yards to the campground. This campground features 12 sites for tents and RVs (16 feet maximum) with the standard picnic tables and firegrills, plus piped water, flush toilets, and gray wastewater sumps. Open from mid-May to late Oct., Canton Creek costs $5 per night. Close to good fly-fishing on the North Umpqua, this site gets surprisingly little use.

Horseshoe Bend (Diamond Lake Ranger District, HC 60, Box 101, Idleyld Park 97447; tel. 498-2531) is 10 miles east of Steamboat. There are 34 sites for tents and RVs (22 feet maximum) with picnic tables and firegrills. Flush toilets, piped water, gray wastewater sumps, laundromat, and general store are also available. Open mid-May to late Sept., the fee is $8 per night. Located in the middle of a big bend of the North Umpqua covered with old-growth Douglas firs and sugar pines, this is a popular base camp for rafting and fishing enthusiasts.

Campsites At Diamond Lake

Several campgrounds are in the vicinity of beautiful 5,200-foot-high Diamond Lake; boating, fishing, swimming, bicycling, and hiking are among the popular recreational options here. The trout fishing is particularly good in the early summer, and there are also excellent hikes into the Mt. Thielsen Wilderness, Crater Lake National Park, and Mt. Bailey areas. While technically no reservations are necessary, the campgrounds here can fill up fast, so it's always a good idea to book a space ahead of time. For the campgrounds listed below, contact Diamond Lake Ranger District, HC 60, Box 101, Idleyld Park 97447; tel. 498-2531.

Though ORE 138 twists and turns most of the 80 miles from Roseburg to Diamond Lake, many people head straight for **Broken Arrow.** This 142-site campground with standard picnic tables and firegrills has plenty of room for tents

Many Umpqua River campgrounds are close to Eagle Rock.

and RVs (30 feet maximum); flush toilets, piped water, and gray wastewater sumps are available. Open from early May to late Sept., the fee is $5-12 per night, depending upon the site. Premium lakeshore sites command top dollar.

The next campground bears the name of its raison d'être, **Diamond Lake.** Here you'll find 160 campsites for tents and RVs (22 feet maximum) with picnic tables and firegrills. Piped water, flush toilets, and firewood are also available. Open from May 15 to Oct. 31, the fee is $7 per night. Numerous hiking trails lead from the campground, including the Pacific Crest National Scenic Trail. Boat docks, launching facilities, and rentals are nearby at Diamond Lake Lodge.

On the east shore of Diamond Lake is **Thielsen View.** It features 60 tent and RV sites (30 feet maximum) with picnic tables and firegrills. Piped water, vault toilets, gray wastewater sumps, and a boat ramp are also available. It's open late May to late Sept., and the fee ranges from $6 to $10 per night depending upon the site. As the name implies, this campground has picturesque views of Mt. Thielsen.

Accommodations

The number of lodgings on the North Umpqua is limited to a few properties that range from rustic lodging to full-service resorts. The abundance of campgrounds and wilderness getaways accessible via the Umpqua Highway partially explains the dearth of motel units. In short, most people come here to get close to nature's teachings and leave the trappings of civilization behind. However, if the weather takes a turn for the worse or you'd rather rough it in style, you have several options that will give you shelter from the storm.

Near Idleyld Park is the **North Umpqua Resort** (Box 177, Idleyld Park 97447; tel. 496-0149). Situated on ORE 138 along the north

---

STEAMBOAT INN

In the late 1800s, a steamboat chugged up the Umpqua River from Reedsport to Roseburg. Based upon this sole voyage, the Umpqua is still listed as a navigable river by the U.S. Coast Guard and all river traffic is regulated. While no vessels made it to the area 38 miles upriver from Roseburg that's called Steamboat today, the name comes from the common practice of unscrupulous gold speculators who would overestimate the value of holdings to buyers and after the sale would catch the first available steamboat out of the region.

The gold mines are worked out now, but the real treasure of the North Umpqua can still be found at the **Steamboat Inn** (Steamboat 97447; tel. 496-3495 or 498-2411). This is the premier dining and accommodations property on the river. The Inn is extremely popular and there are only 15 units, so reservations are a must. The grounds are beautifully maintained and blend in with the natural surroundings. It's an ideal getaway from civilization, near the hiking trails, waterfalls, and fishing holes for which the Umpqua is famous.

The food here is also top-notch. The sweet and cold water served here is devoid of chemicals and comes right out of the ground just the way God put it in. The breakfast specialty is the sour cream roll-up. This delectable concoction is a big pancake stuffed with homemade jam and sour cream. Omelettes, French toast, hotcakes, and eggs are other featured eye openers, and homemade cinnamon rolls and bran muffins round out the offerings. The health conscious will enjoy the homemade granola with yogurt and fresh fruit.

Lunch features burgers, sandwiches, soups, and salads. The veggie burger made with beans and lentils and topped with lettuce, tomatoes, onions and a thick slice of cream cheese is delicious. It also comes with the homemade soup of the day. The selection of fresh-baked pies ($2.25 a slice) makes for a perfect dessert.

In addition to a regular dinner menu, the special Fisherman's Dinner ($30) is served nightly during the summer and on weekends the rest of the year. The elaborate presentation begins about a half-hour after dusk with champagne and hors d'oeuvres. The entree of the day (vegetarian entrees are available upon advance request), freshly baked bread, vegetables, and other dishes are served up family style on the Inn's big wood-slab tables. An elegant dessert and hot beverage conclude the meal. Reservations are required for the Fisherman's Dinner.

bank of the Umpqua, the place is not fancy but it is at least clean. The rooms range from $27 to $50, and good fishing can be had from the private bank of the property on the river. About four miles east of Idleyld Park is the **Dogwood Motel** (HC 60, Box 19, Idleyld Park 97447; tel. 496-3403). Here you'll find clean modern units with or without kitchenettes located on tidy, well-kept grounds. Room rates range from $45 to $60.

Near the summit of the Cascade Mountains about 75 miles east of Roseburg is **Lemolo Lake Resort** (write HC 60, Box 79 B, Idleyld Park 97447; tel. 496-0900). Formed by a Pacific Power and Light dam, Lemolo Lake has German brown trout, as well as kokanee salmon, eastern brook trout, and rainbow trout. The lake is sheltered from wind by gently sloping ridges, and there are many coves and sandy beaches found along the 8.3 miles of shoreline. Water-skiing is permitted on the lake. Boats and canoes can be rented, and many miles of snowmobiling and cross-country skiing trails are nearby.

The resort itself has cabins, both housekeeping and standard, and rooms available. Each Swiss-chalet housekeeping cabin is equipped with a furnished kitchen, bathroom with shower, and wood-burning stove. They can sleep up to five and they cost $65 per night. The Swiss-chalet standard cabins (with bathroom but no kitchen) sleep six in two double and two single beds for $60. Rooms with two double beds go for $55 and rooms with one double bed cost $45.

Food

If you've got a craving for some junk food, the **Colliding Rivers Drive-In** (19162 ORE 138, Glide; tel. 496-3205) can satisfy you. Nothing fancy: burgers, chicken, and spuds. For the ultimate gut bomb, try the Overload, a three-quarter-pound hamburger with bacon, cheese, and ham for $6.99. Chicken dinners with spuds and dinner rolls are $14 for 15 pieces and $20 for two dozen pieces. Sixteen flavors of ice cream offer a sweet alternative to fried food.

Munchies (20142 ORE 138, Glide; tel. 496-3112) features Mexican food made mostly from scratch with no lard or MSG. They make their own vegetarian refried beans and offer eight vegetarian specials on the menu. Omnivores will enjoy the Munchie burrito, a large tortilla stuffed with beef or chicken and beans and topped with melted cheeses, lettuce, onions, olives, tomatoes, salsa, sour cream, and guacamole. The large burrito will fill you up in a hurry. Burgers, sandwiches, and all-day breakfasts can be found here, as well as homemade pie. Open seven days a week from 9 to 9.

Another option in Glide is **The Red Barn** (20641 ORE 138, Glide; tel. 496-0246). Breakfast here ranges from $2 to $6, and lunches featuring burgers or sandwiches come with fries or chips and potato or green salad. Vegetarians will enjoy the garden veggie sandwich with Swiss cheese, lettuce, tomato, cucumber, alfalfa sprouts, and cream cheese that comes garnished with cottage cheese or potato salad. Moderately priced steaks, poultry, and seafood are the primary dinners featured, which include salad, fries, rice or baked potato, and a light dessert ranging from $7 to $14. Lighter fare is available as well, and the best seats in the house are in the back room overlooking the Umpqua River. Open Mon.-Thurs. 7:30 a.m.-8:30 p.m., Fri.-Sat. 7:30 a.m.-4 p.m., and Sun. 7:30 a.m.-8:30 p.m.

In nearby Idleyld Park is **Dave and Ellen's** (Box 177, Idleyld Park; tel. 496-0855). This full-service restaurant makes its food from scratch and piles your plate high with lots of it. Breakfast ranges from $3 to $7, lunches from $3 to $8, and dinners $7 to $15. Homemade rolls and stir-fried vegetables accompany all dinners.

Information And Services

The **post office** (18404 ORE 138, Idleyld Park 97447; tel. 496-3412) is open Mon.-Fri. 8 a.m.-1 p.m. and 2-5 p.m. Get additional information on hikes, campgrounds, and fishing from the **Forest Service** (North Umpqua District Ranger Station, 18782 ORE 138, Glide 97443; tel. 496-3532).

ORE 58: OAKRIDGE AND VICINITY

Halfway between Eugene and the Cascades' summit on ORE 58 lies the town of Oakridge. Originally a Southern Pacific railway stop called Hazeldel, the name was changed in 1912 to fit the topography. Known also as the "Gateway City to the national forest," lumber, recreation, and tourism support this small community (pop. 4,000) tucked away in a foothill valley of the Cascades. The surrounding Willamette National Forest turns out billions of board feet of lumber each year, while it still retains some of the finest wilderness areas in Oregon.

There are over 100 lakes and streams near here, waiting for just about any nimrod to pull out his or her quota of rainbow, German brown, cutthroat, and Dolly Varden trout from the cool waters. A short drive from town are Waldo Lake and Diamond Peak Wilderness Area, as well as summer sailing and water-skiing at Odell Lake. Winter sport enthusiasts can find excellent downhill skiing at Willamette Pass, and there are plenty of beautiful trails available for Nordic skiers too. If you like to fish, hike, camp, sail, ski, or just hang out in the woods, it's all only minutes away from Oakridge.

SIGHTS

The **Oakridge Pioneer Museum** (76433 Pine St.; tel. 782-2666 or 782-2703) is open Saturdays 1-4 p.m., or by special request. Pioneer artifacts that range from tools to toys are on display here. Two colorful exhibits in particular recreate the 1880s—a grocery and a typical kitchen of the early Oregon settlers. A large collection of old dolls and children's toys fills up a showcase that today's kids still find fascinating. The Chain Saw Tree, an interesting presentation on the evolution of the saws that conquered the forest, is worth taking a look at too.

McCredie Hot Springs is found 10 miles southeast of Oakridge on ORE 58 near mile marker 45. A short walk down to Salt Creek brings you to a small hot spring that is adjacent to the river. This location allows the visitor to enjoy the rush of simultaneously hot and cold water. Depending on how you position yourself, you can take a bath at any temperature you choose. There are plans to develop McCredie Hot Springs into a resort, so it is recommended

OREGON TOURISM DIVISION

Clear Creek in winter finery

WILLAMETTE NATIONAL FOREST

In the middle of Oregon's Cascade Range is the Willamette National Forest (Supervisor's Office, 211 E. 17th, Eugene 97440; tel. 687-6521). Encompassing over 1.6 million acres of land stretching from the Mt. Jefferson area east of Salem to the Calapooya Mountains northeast of Roseburg, this enormous forest is about the size of New Jersey.

Eight wilderness areas take up one-quarter of its land, and seven major Cascade peaks lie within its boundaries. In addition to three national recreation trails (Fall Creek, McKenzie River, and South Breitenbush Gorge) and the famed Pacific Crest Trail, over 1,300 miles of developed trails weave throughout Willamette National Forest.

Recreational opportunities abound. Two developed ski areas, Willamette Pass and Hoodoo Ski Bowl, serve schussers. Near each ski park are snowmobile areas, at Waldo Lake and Big Lake respectively. Cross-country skiing is also available on many of the National Forest Service roads and trails. Precipitation in the Willamette National Forest ranges 40-150 inches a year, providing the Willamette and McKenzie rivers with excellent conditions for whitewater rafting, drift-boat fishing, canoeing, and kayaking. Dozens of lakes and reservoirs round out the boating picture with sailing, rowing, and water-skiing. Big-game hunters can stalk black bear, Roosevelt elk, and deer (blacktailed deer west of the Cascades, mule deer east). Anglers can try their luck catching dinner in one of the forest's many lakes, rivers, and streams.

And yet, this playground in the woods is also the workplace for a significant percentage of the population in the six counties that occupy the Willamette National Forest. The area is usually the top timber producer of all 159 national forests in the United States. Supplying approximately eight percent of the total cut on National Forest Service lands in the country, the Willamette National Forest generates over $130 million annually in timber receipts. In addition to providing a steady source of employment for thousands of people, 25% of the forest's timber revenues go to local coffers to help fund public schools and roads.

Besides the Douglas fir, another Willamette Forest tree has become a source of revenue. The discovery that the Pacific yew

tree yields taxol, effective against some kinds of cancer, has focused the eyes of the country here. Just look for a small twisted tree with sparse dark needles, moss-laden branches, peeling reddish bark, and sprouting burls in damp, shady areas. From April to the fall, a small red berrylike growth decorates yew branches. Birds and deer love them but they're poisonous to humans. The fact that the yew thrives in the shade of an old-growth forest has thrust this species into the middle of debates over the importance of preserving the biodiversity of this ecosystem.

Four major highways lead to the Willamette National Forest: ORE 58 (the Willamette Highway), ORE 126 (the McKenzie Highway), U.S. 20 (the Cascadia Highway), and ORE 22 (the Santiam Highway). Whichever route you choose to follow, William Cullen Bryant's words should apply: ". . . Go forth, under the open sky, and list to Nature's teachings . . . the hills rock-ribbed and ancient as the sun—the vales stretching in pensive quietness between; the venerable woods—rivers that move in majesty, and the contiguous woods where rolls the Oregon . . ."

that you partake of this experience while it's still in its raw, natural state. Another hot springs in the area is **Meditation Pool** (Wall Creek). Directions are best obtained at the Oakridge Ranger Station, as the routing is a little complicated.

HIKES

Fall Creek National Recreation Trail

The Fall Creek National Recreation Trail is about 30 miles southeast of Eugene. To get there, take ORE 58 about 15 miles to Lowell, then go north for two miles to the covered bridge at Unity Junction. Take a right onto Forest Service Rd. 18 (Fall Creek Rd.), and stay to the left of the reservoir. Follow the road for 11 miles to Dolly Varden Campground, where the trail starts.

The 14-mile-long Fall Creek Trail is ideal for short day-hikes or longer expeditions; several national forest entry/exit points crop up along the way. Another plus is the low elevation of the trail, which makes it accessible year-round. Strolling through the wilderness, you will pass many deep pools, whitewater rapids, and over a dozen small streams. Giant Douglas firs, bigleaf maples, vine maples, dogwoods, and red alders are some of the predominant vegetation you'll see along the way. In the spring, visitors are treated to shooting stars, trillium, bleeding heart, and other vibrant wildflowers.

There are five campgrounds en route and three other spur trails that merge into the Fall Creek Trail. **Bedrock Campground** is a particularly popular spot for swimming. Those without a fear of heights can jump off the bridge into the deep waters of the creek 40 feet below, or perhaps attempt a dive off of the adjacent rock escarpment.

Larison Creek Trail

The Larison Creek Trail (Trail 3646) is less than 10 minutes away from Oakridge. To get there, take ORE 58 to Oakridge. Turn onto Kitson Springs County Rd. and proceed for a half mile. Turn right on Forest Service Rd. 21 and follow it three miles to the trailhead, which you'll find on the right side of the road.

Multicolored mosses cover the valley floor and its walls simulate a brush-stroked backdrop to stands of old-growth fir. Further contrast is supplied by waterfalls and swimming holes. The mild grade and low elevation of this trail make it accessible year-round.

Tufti Creek Trail

Another good hike close to Oakridge is the Tufti Creek Trail (Trail 3624). To get there, take ORE 58 to Oakridge. Turn onto Kitson Springs County Rd. and proceed for about a mile. Turn left onto Forest Service Rd. 23 and follow it for six miles. This will take you along the northeast bank of Hills Creek Lake and on past Kitson Hot Springs (which is also worthy of investigation). Look for the trailhead sign on the right, about a mile past the hot springs.

This short and friendly half-mile trail winds through large Douglas firs and cedars and overlooks Hills Creek Gorge. There are many small waterfalls and deep swimming holes along the way. This trail is also accessible year-round.

Rigdon Lakes

A more ambitious hike is up to Rigdon Lakes (Trails 3590 and 3583). To get there, follow ORE 58 for 24 miles southeast of Oakridge. Take a left on Forest Service Rd. 5897. Follow it 10 miles to North Waldo Campground; the trailhead is to the right of the restrooms. This three-mile walk starts at North Waldo Lake Campground on Trail 3590. The trail is mild and scenic, paralleling the north shore of Waldo Lake for about two miles until the Rigdon Trail junction (Trail 3583). Head north (turn right) at the trail intersection for another mile to get to the first of the three Rigdon lakes, which has several peninsulas that are ideal for a picnic, and several small islands that might tempt swimmers who don't mind cold water. A hike afterward up to the top of Rigdon Butte is highly recommended. You will have to bushwack, as there is no clear trail, but it is not a difficult climb if you follow the saddle of the ridge. From this vantage point, you can see all three Rigdon lakes as well as many other nearby Cascade landmarks. If you want to take a closer look at the two other Rigdon Lakes, they're only another mile or so down Trail 3583 from the first lake.

PRACTICALITIES

Accommodations

Three reasonable options in the area are **Hall's Motel and Mobile Home Park** (48229 ORE 58; tel. 782-2611); **Silver Star Motel** (47487 ORE 58; tel. 782-2602); and the **Best Western Oakridge Inn** (47433 ORE 58; tel. 782-2212), which has 30 nice units that during the June 1-Oct. 30 summer season range from $45 to $60. Winter rates are about $5 less.

Odell Lake, 30 miles southeast of Oakridge on ORE 58, deserves a special mention. There are two resorts, several summer homes, and five campgrounds around this 3,582-acre lake. Located in a deep glacial trough, the lake probably filled with water about 11,000 years ago when a terminal moraine blocked the drainage of Odell Creek. Due to the depth of the lake and the nearly perpetual west-to-east winds that blow through Willamette Pass, the water averages a cold 39° F. Those breezes, however, help to keep the pesky mosquitoes and other obnoxious insects away and make for some of the best sailing in the Cascades. The premier property on Odell Lake is the **Odell Lake Lodge** (P.O. Box 72, Crescent Lake 97425; tel. 433-2540). To get there, take the East Odell exit off of ORE 58 and follow the road a couple of miles. The hotel rooms range from $40 to $50 a night, with the cabins going for $50-110. Skiers may want to take advantage of large cabin 12, which

comfortably houses as many as 16 people for $185 a night. As the lodge is extremely popular, reservations are strongly recommended, as much as a year in advance for weekends.

Moorages are available for rent, as are canoes, powerboats, and sailboats. The lodge has a complete tackle shop to help outfit you to catch the kokanee and mackinaw that inhabit the icy waters, and rental equipment is also available if you don't bring your own. The restaurant at the lodge will cook your bounty for you and serve it along with soup or salad, potatoes, vegetables, and bread for $8 per person. The lodge also maintains its own system of trails, which provide good biking in the summer and cross-country skiing in the winter. Bikes and ski equipment can be rented from the lodge. In addition to these outdoor pursuits, basketball, volleyball, badminton, and horseshoes round out the fun. Tots and toddlers will enjoy the sandbox, the toy library, and the swings. Every Sunday afternoon, the lodge restaurant features Cajun food, which is accompanied biweekly throughout the summer by hot licks from the Étouffee Cajun Band.

Across the lake from the lodge is **Shelter Cove Resort** (West Odell Lake Rd., Cascade Summit; tel. 433-2548), which features eight cabins complete with kitchens ($50-115), 69 campsites with picnic tables and electricity ($7-10), and 65 moorages ($3-7) in the marina. The General Store store handles everything from groceries, tackle, and boat rentals to snow-park

mile-high Waldo Lake

TED LONG ISHIKAWA

permits and fishing/hunting licenses. The September to October displays of Odell Lake's landlocked salmon spawning are unforgettable.

Campgrounds

Blue Pool Campground, on the banks of Salt Creek, is 10 miles from Oakridge on ORE 58. During the summer, water is available for flush toilets and general use. Each of the 18 sites features a picnic table and a fireplace grill. It costs $6 for a family per site, or $12 for two families on one site. A Golden Age passport grants the holder a 50% discount. Contact the Oakridge Ranger Station (46375 ORE 58, Westfir 97492; tel. 728-2291) for information.

Six miles west of Oakridge on the banks of the Willamette River and not too far from Lookout Point Lake is **Black Canyon Campground.** Open May through late October, there are 72 sites for tents, trailers, or motor homes up to 22 feet long for $6 a night. Picnic tables and fireplace grills are standard; piped water, firewood, and vault toilets are also available. Boat docks and launching facilities are nearby on the south end of Lookout Point Lake. For additional information, write to Willamette National Forest (46375 ORE 58, Westfir 97492; tel. 782-2291).

There are two very nice campgrounds up at Waldo Lake called **Shadow Bay** and **North Waldo.** To get there, take ORE 58 for 24 miles southeast of Oakridge. Take a left on Forest Service Rd. 5897. It is five miles to Forest Service Road 5896, which takes you to Shadow Bay, and 10 miles down Forest Service Rd. 5897 to North Waldo. Both campgrounds charge $7.

Since there are 150 campsites between the two campgrounds, this usually ensures enough views of this mile-high lake for everyone to enjoy. Open June to late September, the fee is $8 a night. Boat docks and launching facilities are available, plus good sailing and fishing at Waldo. Many trails lead to small backcountry lakes from here; this is a good place to establish a base camp. Contact the Oakridge Ranger District for additional information.

If you want to get away from the traffic of ORE 58 and don't mind bouncing down Forest Service roads for over half an hour, you might consider **Blair Lake Campground.** To get to Blair Lake, head east out of Oakridge on County Route 149 for one mile. Turn left onto For-

est Service Rd. 24 and go eight miles until you hit Forest Service Rd. 1934. It's another seven miles down Forest Service Rd. 1934 to Blair Lake. For further information, contact Willamette National Forest (46375 ORE 58, Westfir 97492; tel. 782-2291).

On the shore of little Blair Lake, a picturesque setting at 4,800 feet with nine tent sites awaits the determined explorer. Open June through mid-October, the fee is $5 per night, no reservations necessary. Picnic tables and fireplace grills are provided, with piped water, firewood, and pit toilets available. Boat docks are nearby, but no motorized craft are permitted on the lake.

Food

Sandwiched in between the roller rink (where the tri-state competition is annually held) and the bowling alley is **Taco Villa** (47961 ORE 58; tel. 782-2935). You might think the artwork and decor are funky, but one look at the menu and you'll see that the price is right. The fajita dinner (chicken or beef, grilled onions/bell peppers on a tortilla spread with guacamole, cheddar cheese, lettuce, and tomato) comes complete with potatoes, beans, salsa, and sour cream. You can complement your meal with a fresh old-fashioned milkshake from the soda fountain or top it off with one of 16 different ice creams for dessert.

After a hard day skiing, head on down the hill to **Timber Jim's** (45727 ORE 58; tel. 782-4310). This restaurant can best be described as the house that Jack built—lumberjack, that is. Huge rough-hewn wooden beams provide the roof support, the walls are paneled with latticework, and thick slabs of wood provide tables and benches for eating. "Misery whips" (two-man crosscut saws), pictures of logging crews from over 50 years ago, and other lumber paraphernalia round out the decor. A barroom piano sits proudly in the middle of the room, and sing-alongs after ski parties are not uncommon. Big Jim serves beer and wine, and the salad bar is decent. Try the Logger's Favorite pizza with the works. Dinners range from $4 for spaghetti to $9 for steak and prawns.

Latecomers or early risers should remember that the **Sportsman Cafe** (48127 ORE 58; tel. 782-2051) is open 24 hours a day (except Christmas Eve and Day). This is where you can hear many a fish story about the day's catch or the big one that got away. If the fish weren't biting, you can still find something good on the menu to get your hooks into here. Dinners that come with salad, fries, and toast range from $3.50 for veal cutlets to $5.25 for grilled halibut or batter-dipped jumbo prawns.

Information And Services
The **chamber of commerce** (47811 ORE 58, Oakridge 97463; tel. 782-4146) offers a wide assortment of info on the area.

The **post office** (48264 E. First, Oakridge 97463; tel. 782-2730) is open during business hours. To get there, turn at the town's only traffic light, cross over the bridge, and go right.

The post office is about a half mile down. The **Oakridge Medical Clinic** (47815 ORE 58; tel. 782-2221) offers family and emergency medicine. Hours are Mon.-Fri. 9-5, Sat. 9-noon. For after-hours emergencies, call 911. The **Liquor Store** (48019 Hwy. 58; tel. 782-3405) is open Mon.-Sat. 11 a.m.-7 p.m., closed on holidays.

Getting There
Greyhound serves ORE 58 to Klamath Falls and points beyond and stops at the Taco Villa restaurant (47961 ORE 58; tel. 782-2935). **Amtrak**'s Starlight Express serves Oakridge. The southbound train arrives/departs at 6 p.m., the northbound at 10:45 a.m. Be sure to call ahead (800-USA-RAIL) for reservations.

ORE 126: THE MCKENZIE RIVER HIGHWAY

The best way to get to this scenic road from the Willamette Valley is to take I-105 east from I-5 near Eugene. Take a left at the end of the interstate near the outskirts of Springfield and you will be on the McKenzie River Highway. There are four lanes for a couple of miles, and this is one of your best chances to ease by any slow-moving vehicles. However, beware of The Man, who often patrols the road here—he loves to write those tickets!

In any case, just past where the four lanes merge into two, the McKenzie River Recreation Area begins. For the next 60 miles, you will not see any major population centers, as most of the towns out here consist of little more than a post office. However, you will see beautiful views of the blue-green McKenzie River with heavily forested mountains, frothy waterfalls, jet-black lava beds, and snowcapped peaks as a backdrop.

The first 15 miles of the McKenzie River Highway pass through many fruit and nut orchards (primarily apples, cherries, and filberts), Christmas-tree farms, and berry patches (blueberry, raspberry, and marionberry). McKenzie River farmers enjoy plentiful water supplies from the McKenzie diversion canal, as well as fertile soils

and a mild climate. Walterville is located in the middle of this agricultural section of the McKenzie Recreation Area.

The Leaburg Dam on the right signals your entry into the middle section of the McKenzie, where there are many vacation homes. A total of six dams on the McKenzie provide power, irrigation, and what the Army Corps of Engineers calls "fish enhancement." A favorite haunt of fishing enthusiasts, the mellow waters of the middle McKenzie teem with trout, steelhead, and salmon. You'll notice many driftboats parked in driveways. These boats have bows at both ends to prevent water inundation from either front or back. Mild whitewater rafting and driftboat fishing are popular here, and there are many local guides and outfitters ready to help you float your expeditions (see "Guides and Outfitters" following).

The Willamette National Forest boundary is near Blue River. Huge, old-growth Douglas firs usher the clear blue waters of the McKenzie through the mountains. In addition to the McKenzie River National Recreation Trail, waterfalls, mountain lakes, and lava formations are all a short trek from the road.

TED LONG ISHIKAWA

Oregon produces most of the world's supply of filberts.

NORTH CASCADES REGION

TO SEATTLE

COLUMBIA RIVER

WASHINGTON

OREGON

PORTLAND

WILLAMETTE RIVER

TO PENDLETON

LOST LAKE

MT. HOOD
(ELEV. 11,239 ft.)

GOVERNMENT CAMP

TIMBERLINE LODGE

BARLOW PASS
(ELEV. 4,155 ft.)

BLUE BOX PASS
(ELEV. 4,024 ft.)

TO BIGGS

PINHEAD BUTTES
(ELEV. 5,585 ft.)

SILVER FALLS S.P.

TO SALEM

WARM SPRINGS
INDIAN RESERVATION

KAH - NEE - TA

BREITENBUSH SPRINGS

NORTH SANTIAM RIVER

DETROIT LAKE S.P.

DETROIT

DETROIT L.

PACIFIC CREST TRAIL

DESCHUTES RIVER

MT. JEFFERSON
(ELEV. 10,495 ft.)

METOLIUS RIVER

MADRAS

SOUTH SANTIAM RIVER

GREEN PETER RES.

MARION L.

PALISADES S.P.

FOSTER RES.

TOMBSTONE SUMMIT
(ELEV. 4,236 ft.)

THREE FINGERED JACK
(ELEV. 7,841 ft.)

BLACK BUTTE
(ELEV. 6,415 ft.)

HAYSTACK RES.

SWEET HOME

HOODOO BUTTE
(ELEV. 5,721 ft.)

BLUE L.

CLEAR L.

SUTTLE L.

SMITH ROCK S.P.

TO ALBANY

MT. WASHINGTON
(ELEV. 7,800 ft.)

SISTERS

TO JOHN DAY

PRINEVILLE

BELKNAP CRATER
(ELEV. 6,877 ft.)

SISTERS S.P.

CLINE FALLS S.P.

REDMOND

TO EUGENE

McKENZIE BRIDGE

McKENZIE RIVER

NORTH SISTER
(ELEV. 10,085 ft.)

THE HUSBAND
(ELEV. 7,520 ft.)

MIDDLE SISTER
(ELEV. 10,047 ft.)

TUMALO S.P.

SAWYER S.P.

PILOT BUTTE S.P.

COUGAR RES.

SOUTH SISTER
(ELEV. 10,358 ft.)

BROKEN TOP
(ELEV. 9,152 ft.)

BEND

SPARKS L.

FALL CREEK RES.

LOWELL

ELK L.

MT. BACHELOR
(ELEV. 9,060 ft.)

LAVA BUTTE
(ELEV. 5,016 ft.)

TO BURNS

OREGON HIGH
DESERT MUS.

LAVA L.

LAVA RIVER CAVE

TO LA PINE

LITTLE LAVA L.

OAKRIDGE

CULTUS L.

0   10mi

0   10km

© MOON PUBLICATIONS, INC.

BRUCE BUSH

*Koosah Falls thunder
on the McKenzie.*

SIGHTS

Proxy Falls

To get to Proxy Falls, follow the old McKenzie Pass (ORE 242) from the new McKenzie Pass (ORE 126) for 10 miles. Look for a small hiker-symbol sign on the right-hand side of the road. This is the only marker for the trail to a spectacular pair of waterfalls, Upper and Lower Proxy Falls.

An A+ trail, it's an easy half-mile walk to Upper Proxy. The trail goes through a lush forest that changes with the season. There are giant rhododendrons that bloom in late spring, tart huckleberries in summer, and brilliant red foliage from the vine maples in the fall. Take a left at the first fork in the trail. This will take you to Upper Proxy Falls. A particularly good view of the falls can be obtained near the giant Douglas fir at the base of the pool.

Now that you've seen Upper Proxy Falls from the bottom up, check out Lower Proxy Falls from the top down. Go back to the fork in the trail and take a left. In less than a half mile, you will suddenly be on a ridge looking across a valley at Lower Proxy falls. A good time to photograph both of these falls is around midday, when the sun's angle best illuminates the water.

Dee Wright Observatory

The Dee Wright Observatory on ORE 242 (which is closed in winter) is about halfway between ORE 126 and Sisters. Built in the early '30s as a Civilian Conservation Corps project, it was christened after the building's supervisor, who died prior to its completion. The tower windows line up with views of Mt. Jefferson, Mt. Washington, and the Three Sisters, as well as the eight-mile-long, half-mile-wide lava flow that bubbled out of nearby Yapoah a little less than 3,000 years ago.

Unfortunately, the Dee Wright Observatory was struck by lightning in September of 1989, and the building suffered heavy structural damage from the ensuing fire. Built mostly out of lava rock, the supporting timbers sustained the bulk of the damage. With tight state and federal budgets and the estimated high price tag for repairs, the fate of this historic landmark remains unclear. However, all was not lost: the half-mile-long **Lava River Trail** next to the observatory offers a fine foray into the surrounding hills of rolling black rock. In addition to helpfully placed and concise interpretive placards explaining the lava formations, the trail is wheelchair-accessible. But while the walk is easy enough, the 5,300-foot elevation can sometimes make it seem a little more difficult.

Koosah Falls

This cascade is about 20 miles from McKenzie Bridge on ORE 126. The visitor facilities here have recently been improved and now provide wheelchair access and excellent views of this impressive 70-foot-high falls on the McKenzie. The blue water bounces and bubbles over and through a basalt formation that flowed into the McKenzie thousands of years ago. If you look carefully, you can see many small springs flowing from crevices at the base of the falls. The blue water may have inspired the name Koosah, which comes from the Chinook Indian word for sky.

Sahalie Falls

Another beautiful waterfall is only a half mile farther east on ORE 126 from Koosah Falls. It is only a few yards from the parking lot to the viewpoints of the falls. Also the result of a lava dam from the Cascade Range's not-so-distant volcanic past, here the river tumbles 100 feet into a green canyon. The highest falls on the McKenzie river, Sahalie means "high" in the Chinook Indian dialect. It's said that this waterfall churns out the highest volume of water of any falls in the state. Anyone who might want to take a shower is welcome to hike the slippery, unimproved trail to the base of the roaring cascade. Most people, however, are content to enjoy the view from benches and observation posts along the paved path.

Sawyer's Cave

This ice cave is on the right just past the junction of ORE 126 and U.S. 20, near mile marker 72. You'll need a flashlight and a sweater to explore Sawyer's Cave; watch your head and watch your step. Classified as a lava tube, it's the result of a lava flow that cooled faster on the top and sides, forming a crust. Underneath, the hotter lava continued to drain downhill, leaving the lava tube behind. There are also small stalactites hanging down from the ceilings, formed from lava drippings. The basalt rock is a poor heat conductor, and like a natural refrigerator it keeps the coolness of winter and night inside the cave. Ice can be found on the floor of the cave during the hottest summer months.

HIKES

McKenzie River National Recreation Trail

The McKenzie River National Recreation Trail runs for 26 miles. It starts just outside the small town of **McKenzie Bridge** and goes to the Old Santiam Wagon Road, about three miles from the junction of ORE 126 and U.S. 20. But don't let that scare you. There are enough access points to let you design treks of three, five, eight, or more miles along this beautiful trail. It is hard to say which section of the footpath is the best, as each portion has its own peculiar charms; the following highlights give you a sample of what to expect.

Start up at the top of the McKenzie River Trail at the **Old Santiam Wagon Road.** Completed in the early 1860s, this was the first link of the route from the mid-Willamette Valley to central and eastern Oregon. Way stations were established a day's journey apart to assist the pioneers along their weary way. While most of these primitive establishments are no more, some of these historic buildings have survived and are still used today by packers. There isn't much left of the Old Santiam Wagon Rd. either, as much of it was destroyed with the construction of ORE 126. However, a seven-mile stretch remains from ORE 126 through the rugged lava country to the Pacific Crest Trail. A short walk on this former road to the promised land helps you to appreciate both the hardiness of the pioneers and the comforts of modern travel.

From the Old Santiam Wagon Rd., the McKenzie River Trail surveys many remarkable volcanic formations. Lava flows over the last few thousand years have built dams, created waterfalls, and even buried the river altogether. At the northern end of **Clear Lake,** you can see the remains of an ancient forest preserved for nearly 3,000 years in the lake's cool waters. When nearby Sand Mountain erupted, the lava dammed up the McKenzie River and created Clear Lake. Koosah and Sahalie falls were also created by lava dams, and the view of these whitewater cascades from the McKenzie River Trail is much different than the accessible version from the highway. Another interesting sight is the **Tamolitch Valley,** where the McKenzie gradually sinks beneath the porous lava, disappearing altogether until it reemerges three miles later at Tamolitch Pool. This area is accessible only on the National Recreation Trail.

If at all possible, arrange your McKenzie outing with friends and take two cars. This way you can have a car stationed at the beginning and ending segments of your hike, and thus avoid doubling back. Also keep in mind that hikes starting at the upper end of the trail take advantage of the descending elevation.

Robinson Lake Trail

The quarter-mile-long Robinson Lake Trail takes you to a heart-shaped lake with some fishing and swimming. To get there, turn off of ORE 126 onto Robinson Lake Road. Be on the lookout for logging trucks and rocks on the gravel road. Follow the signs marked Forest Service Rd. 2664. At the unmarked junction, go straight onto the red pumice road (Forest Service Rd. 2664) and continue until you reach the parking lot. It takes about 10 minutes to drive the four miles in. The trail is in good condition; the left fork takes you to the center shore of Robinson Lake. The shallow lake warms up considerably during the summer, making a swim all the more inviting.

GUIDES AND OUTFITTERS

McKenzie River Adventures (Box 567, Sisters 97759; tel. 549-1325 or 822-3806 evenings) has half-day, full-day, and two-day whitewater rafting trips May-September. The half-day (four-hour) trip (lunch included) is $40 per person, $25 per child; the full-day (six-hour) trip (lunch included) is $50 per person, $30 per child; and the two-day overnighter (meals included) is $150 per person, $100 per child. The cruises range from seven to 18 miles and take in some Class-II and -III rapids. Reservations are recommended.

Jim's Oregon Whitewater (56324 ORE 126, McKenzie Bridge 97413; tel. 822-6003) charters whitewater rafts April-September and fly-fishing driftboats April-October. The half-day whitewater-rafting trip (lunch included) costs $40 per person; the full-day (lunch included) is $50 per person; and the two-day overnighter (meals included) is $120 per person. For those interested in

some serious fly-fishing, it's $150 per boat (one to two people) per day. A more mellow fishing trip is the scenic drift boat package for $100 per boat (one to two people) per day. Reservations are recommended.

Spencer Outfitters and Guide Service (656 N. 71st St., Springfield 97478; tel. 747-8153) charters whitewater-rafting, fishing, and hunting trips. The half-day raft trips (lunch included) are $25; full-day trips (lunch included) are $35; and the one- to three-day overnighters (meals included) are $50 per day. Fishing and hunting trips (one to two persons) are $150 a day. Fly-fishing is Bob Spencer's specialty, and all fishing equipment is provided.

Prince River Outfitters (Box 116, Vida 97488; tel. 896-3941) charters whitewater rafting trips May-September. The half-day trips (no lunch) cost $25, the full-day (lunch included) is $40, and the two-day overnighter (all meals) is $129. Fishing for spring chinook or summer steelhead (April 15-Oct. 31) costs $90 per person; fly-fishing for rainbow trout (May 1-Oct. 31) is $50 half-day, $75 all day. Food, tackle, and rain gear are provided on all fishing charters.

PRACTICALITIES

Accommodations

Fry's Double JJ Motel (Ore 126, Vida 97488; tel. 822-5304) is a small family operation that rents out two housekeeping cabins. Depending upon the time of year and the number of people, the units range between $30 and $55. Ask the innkeeper for directions to the Goodpasture covered bridge (22 miles east of Eugene, one mile west of Vida) outside of town. Its 165-foot length and classic gothic windows make it the most photographed bridge in Oregon.

Sleepy Hollow Motel (54791 ORE 126, Blue River 97413; tel. 822-3805) is located within walking distance of one of the finest public golf courses in the country, Tokatee. This property is open from April 1 to Nov. 1. The motel has 14 air-conditioned units that range from $45 to $85, $5 each additional person. Reservations are recommended.

The Cedarwood Lodge (Ore 126, McKenzie Bridge 97413; tel. 822-3351) is tucked away in a grove of old cedars just outside of the town of McKenzie Bridge. The lodge has nine vacation housekeeping cottages that feature fully equipped kitchens, bathrooms (with showers), fireplaces (wood provided), and portable barbecues. Rates vary from $50 to $85 for two people, depending on the cabin and the season, $10 each additional person. Pets are allowed, but only by advance arrangement. Minimum three-day advance reservations are required July-Sept. and holidays.

The **Sportsman's Lodge Resort** (56228 Delta Dr., McKenzie Bridge 97413; tel. 822-3243) is a popular retreat for golfers who come here to enjoy the award-winning Tokatee Golf Course. The lodge has two small cabins that cost $70 and $90 each, plus the huge Delta House, which can comfortably take in up to eight people with its four bedrooms, four bathrooms, kitchen, dining room, living room, and fireplace. Delta House rates (per night) decrease with the length of the stay.

The historic **Log Cabin Inn** (ORE 126, McKenzie Bridge 97413; tel. 822-3432) is an excellent bed and breakfast. The inn was built in 1906, and President Hoover, Clark Gable, and the Duke of Windsor are among the many notables who have stayed here over the years. With its homey decor, wraparound porch, and cedar-paneled dining hall, the Log Cabin Inn would make a wonderful label on a bottle of maple syrup. There are also nine guest cottages, each one of them boasting a fireplace, a porch, and a view of the McKenzie River. For $4 per person, the inn will bring a continental breakfast to your cabin in the morning for you to enjoy along with the scenery. The Log Cabin's restaurant features game dishes and salmon. Room rates range from $50 to $60 double occupancy, each additional person $5. Reservations required.

Belknap Springs Lodge (Box 1, McKenzie Bridge, 97413; tel. 822-3512) offers rooms, cabins, and camping. The rooms range from $40 to $85 per couple, $10 each additional person. The five cabins range from $25 to $45, $5 each additional person. Camping sites are $5 per person per day, or $25 per person per week. The main attraction on the property is **Belknap Springs.** The water (which contains 26 different minerals) is gently filtered piping hot into a swimming pool on the south bank of the McKenzie.

The property is clean, the scenery is beautiful, and the price is right. For $3, you can use the mineral pool facilities, just what the doctor ordered to ease the aching muscles from that killer hike or the ski marathon. But don't wait too long to fill this prescription—the pool closes at 9 p.m. If you forget your towel, you can rent one.

Campgrounds
The following campgrounds are under the jurisdiction of the Willamette National Forest (McKenzie Ranger District, McKenzie Bridge 97413; tel. 822-3381). Contact the office for reservations and additional information. All are open late May to early September. Many of these campsites connect with the beautiful McKenzie River National Recreation Trail. The fishing is also quite good on the McKenzie and the many lakes and reservoirs within this bailiwick. Its prime location halfway between Eugene and Bend also helps make the area a popular vacation spot during the summer, so advance reservations are recommended.

A mile west of McKenzie Bridge on ORE 126 is **McKenzie Bridge Campground.** As the name implies, this 20-site multi-use park is along the banks of its namesake river. The fee is $5 a night. Piped well water, vault toilets, and a boat launch are provided. East of McKenzie Bridge about three miles on ORE 126 is **Paradise Creek Campground.** Although there are 54 tent/RV (up to 22 feet) campsites, flush toilets, and piped water, only 20 of the sites are in premium riverside locations. The summer trout fishing here can be very good, and the fireplace grills and wooden tables make it easy to cook and eat a fresh-caught meal. Welcome to paradise! The fee is $10 a night and reservations are recommended.

Olallie Campground is 11 miles outside of McKenzie Bridge on ORE 126 and has 17 multi-use sites. Olallie is situated on the banks of the McKenzie River; boating, fishing, and hiking are some of the nearby attractions. Piped water, vault toilets, and picnic tables are provided. The fee is $4 a night. A couple more miles past Olallie on ORE 126 is **Trailbridge Campground.** Located on the north shore of Trailbridge Reservoir, piped water, vault toilets, and picnic tables are provided at this 24-site multi-use campground. Boat docks are close by, and the reservoir is noted for its good trout fishing.

Another ideal campground for boating enthusiasts is **Lake's End** on nearby Smith Reservoir. One of the few boat-in campgrounds in Oregon, the only way to reach this park is via a two-mile sail across the lake. To get there, take ORE 126 for 13 miles northeast of McKenzie Bridge and turn right on Forest Service Rd. 1477. Follow the road for three miles to the boat ramp, and bon voyage! Be sure to take along plenty of water, because the campground does not provide any. You will, however, find picnic tables, vault toilets, and plenty of peace and quiet away from the cars and traffic of the other mainstream parks. There is no fee for this escape from the ordinary.

On the south shore of Clear Lake, 14 miles northeast of McKenzie Bridge on ORE 126, is **Coldwater Cove Campground.** Piped water, vault toilets, and picnic tables are provided at this 34-site multi-use park. The fee is $5 a night. **Crocket Lodge** (no phone) is adjacent to the campground and has a store, cafe (serving breakfast 6:30-10 a.m. and lunch 11-2), and cabins, as well as boat docks, launches, and rentals. But before you haul your 426-horsepower Glastron jetboat up McKenzie Pass to cut some mean 20-foot-high rooster tails with your CX-202 competition waterskis, keep in mind that small electric fishing-boat motors are the only mechanical means of propulsion allowed here by the Forest Service.

A handful of campgrounds dot ORE 242, the old McKenzie Pass, but only **Alder Springs** has piped water. This remote campground with seven tent sites charges $3 a night.

Food

It's easy to zip by the tiny restaurant near Vida called the **Village Cafe** (tel. 822-3891). But if you have a sweet tooth, be on the lookout for milepost 35 and a small red building nearby with a sign on top that reads Mom's Homemade Pies. This place has established quite a reputation, as the hundreds of business cards pinned to the ceiling will attest. The food is simple and straightforward: hamburgers, hot dogs, grilled-cheese sandwiches, and the like. However, Mom's pies are the main attraction that keep the parking lot full and the customers coming back for more.

Fifteen minutes up the road is the **Forest Glen Restaurant** (51774 Cascade St., Blue River; tel. 822-3714). This is the place to go if you want a fine-dining experience in the wilderness. Chicken, steak, seafood, and pasta are among the elegant offerings here. Ranging from $10 to $25, dinners come with a shrimp appetizer, bread, soup and salad bar, and your choice of brown rice with vegetables, baked potato, or French fries. There are also reasonably priced burgers and fries for the kids to keep your budget balanced.

If you've been camping out in the woods for a few days and you're getting tired of freeze-dried food, you might want to time your return to civilization with the Forest Glen's Sunday brunch buffet. This all-you-can-eat extravaganza includes such delectables as custom-made omelettes, crab and shrimp crepes, French toast with fresh strawberries and whipped cream, eggs Benedict, and roast top sirloin. Add this to a smorgasbord of homemade pastries, bagels, and croissants, a soup and salad bar, and the chef's choice entrees, and you'll understand why reservations are recommended. It's a good place to bring a hungry brood, because it costs only 50 cents per year through age 11; adults are charged $9.95.

If you're in the mood for a good lunch or dinner served with a generous helping of historical ambience, head for the **Log Cabin** (see "Accommodations" above). Built in 1906, the inn's cedar-paneled dining room reflects the soft hues of a different era. Their sandwiches cost between $3 and $7 and are served with potato salad. For a couple of bucks extra, you can wash lunch down with a glass of smooth port. Dinners range from $7 to $20 and feature salmon and game dishes with all the trimmings. Whatever meal you choose to take in, try the beer-cheese soup, and save some room for one of their homemade cobblers or pies (especially the marionberry).

Getting There

The best way for carless travelers to get to the McKenzie National Recreation Trail from Eugene is via Lane Transit District (tel. 687-5555). Their bus starts at downtown Eugene and goes up the McKenzie River Highway, stopping at many small communities along the way. The terminus point is the McKenzie River Ranger Station at McKenzie Bridge, and the fare is $4. The schedule changes with the season and weather conditions, so be sure to call ahead to plan your trip and return.

SISTERS AND VICINITY

Sisters, established in 1888 when nearby Camp Polk was deactivated, is named after its backdrop to the south, the Three Sisters. These over-10,000-foot-high peaks were the last major obstacle for the pioneers to circumnavigate on their journey to the fertile Willamette Valley. The emigrants named the mountains after some of the virtues that helped propel them through the hardships of the frontier: faith, hope, and charity. Over the years, no one could agree upon exactly which mountain was named what, so the Oregon Legislature settled the dispute by labeling the mountains as the North, Middle, and South Sisters respectively.

In any case, while most of the Old Santiam Wagon Rd. has long since been replaced by asphalt and forest overgrowth, the 19th-century flavor has been preserved in the town of Sisters. Wooden boardwalks, 1880s-style storefronts, and plenty of good ol'-fashioned western hospitality grace this small town of about 1,000. Some people are quick to lambast the thematic zoning ordinances of Sisters as cheap gimmicks to lure tourists, while others seem to enjoy the lovingly re-created ambience. As well

as being a food, fuel, and lodging stop, Sisters is also a jumping-off point for a wealth of outdoor activities. Skiing at Hoodoo Ski Bowl, fly-fishing and rafting on the Metolius River, and backpacking into the great Three Sisters Wilderness are just a few of the popular local pursuits. Nearby luxury resorts such as Black Butte Ranch, an annual rodeo, and North America's largest llama ranch add to the appeal of this vintage-1888 village.

SIGHTS

Dick Patterson's Arabian Ranch

Dick Patterson's Arabian Ranch (15425 U.S. 20, Sisters 97759; tel. 549-3391) is located just outside the city limits. In addition to a large herd of these fine-looking horses, the ranch is also home for over 500 llamas. These critters are used as pack animals on expeditions into the mountains, as well as for pets and wool production. Sheep ranchers in particular like to have a llama or two around their livestock because predators such as wolves and coyotes abhor their scent. The Pattersons do not give

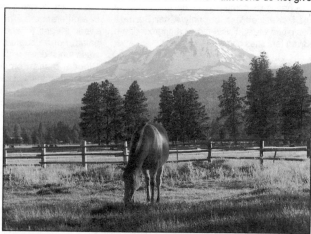

the Three Sisters Wilderness, backyard to the vintage town of Sisters

BRUCE BUSH

guided tours of the ranch. However, they will try to accommodate people who would like to visit and see the animals, provided they call ahead and make an appointment.

Llama Treks

It's easy to fall in love with llamas. Their regal manner, soft dark eyes, and gentleness engender an immediate connection. In addition, outfitters who rent them out for guided trips (or solos) point out that their padded feet hardly leave a trace on the trail. Two area outfitters, **Last Camp Llamas** (4555 N.W. Pershall Way, Redmond 97756; tel. 546-6828) and **Oregon Llamas** (Box 6, Camp Sherman; tel. 595-2088), make their animals available for \$25-30 a day with a minimum of two llamas. Remember to procure a Forest Service permit for overnights in the Three Sisters, Mt. Washington, and Mt. Jefferson wildernesses if you elect to go by yourself. These permits (obtainable from ranger stations) specify grazing etiquette for your animals. An orientation class offered by the outfitter for those traveling independently will review such procedures before you hit the trail.

Metolius River

About 10 miles from Sisters is the second-largest tributary of the Deschutes River, the Metolius. To get there, take the Camp Sherman Hwy. off of ORE 20 five miles west of Sisters. This road will take you around Black Butte. On the north face of this steep, evergreen-covered cinder cone lies the source of the Metolius. Known simply as "the Spring," the water wells up out of the earth at a constant 48° F. The warm, spring-fed waters of the upper Metolius are ideal for insect egg and larval development, which in turn provides an abundant food source for rainbow, brown, brook, and bull trout, kokanee salmon, and whitefish. Consequently, some of the best fly-fishing in the state is found on the upper Metolius. This was no secret to the Indians. The name Metolius derives from the Indian word for "white fish," after the lightly colored salmon found in the river. A beautiful riverside trail follows the Metolius as it meanders through the ponderosas past many excellent fishing holes. Driftboats are used to tackle the harder-to-reach places along this 25-mile-long river.

Other streams merge with the Metolius, lowering the water temperature to an average of 35° F. While the fishing isn't as good as in the warmer upper reaches, the whitewater rafting is actually better downstream. The increased water volume coupled with steeper flow gradients provide plenty of exciting rapids for river-runners to splash around in.

Hoodoo Ski Bowl

A little over a half hour west of Sisters on ORE 126 is one of Oregon's most family-oriented skiing areas, Hoodoo Ski Bowl (tel. 342-5540). Generally operating from Thanksgiving to Easter (snow conditions permitting), it's open Tues.-Sun. 9 a.m.-4 p.m. Hoodoo features 17 ski runs serviced by three chair lifts and a rope tow. The maximum vertical drop is 1,035 feet, and the runs are fairly evenly divided between advanced, intermediate, and beginner levels of difficulty. The rates at this 55-year-old ski bowl are equally attractive. Adult all-day passes are \$17, and seniors (65 and over) and children under six accompained by a paying adult ski free. The rates on the rope tow are \$8 per day. The "sno-fone" (tel. 354-7416 from Eugene, 585-8081 from Salem, 753-8887 from Corvallis) has the latest information on weather and snow conditions.

Inexpensive lodging is found across the highway from the ski area at **Santiam Lodge** (tel. 342-5540). Built by the Civilian Conservation Corps during the Depression, this facility offers dormitory-style accommodations for groups of 15-75. A fully equipped kitchen, dining room, and large lounge with a fireplace are upstairs; the rooms and bathrooms are downstairs. The rates are quite reasonable—as little as \$15 per night per person. "Lodging and three meals" packages start at \$35, and reduced rates on lift tickets and rental equipment are also available to groups making advance reservations. After a weekend at Santiam Pass, there will be no doubt "Hoodoo" you love.

PRACTICALITIES

Accommodations

Sisters Motor Lodge (600 W. Cascade, Sisters 97759; tel. 549-2551) is within easy walking distance of the shops and boutiques of Sisters.

Bedrooms and kitchenettes go for $45-70 a night, and you can bring the dog along too. The **Best Western Ponderosa Lodge** (505 ORE 20, Box 218, Sisters 97759; tel. 549-1234 or 800-528-1234) is a new, ranch-style resort motel. Rooms ($65-80) feature private balconies with views of the mountains and the adjacent Deschutes National Forest, as well as dial-direct phones and cable TV. Other amenities include a spa, heated pool, and free continental breakfast.

The **Fourth Sister Lodge** (Box 591, Sisters 97559; tel. 549-6441) offers bedrooms and bedroom suites ($50-125). Each of the bedroom suites has a fully equipped kitchen, a dining room, and a large living room with a fireplace, as well as one or two bedrooms. The recreation room in the center of the lodge complex has a sauna, spa, and swimming pool. Reservations are requested two weeks in advance, but since this popular property fills up fast, extra lead time is advised.

The **Metolius River Lodge** (P.O. Box 110, Camp Sherman 97730; tel. 595-6290) is a 12-unit complex featuring six pine-paneled cabins. The latter vary in price ($60-100) depending on room configuration and accoutrements. The most coveted pair have decks extending over the river, and the majority have fireplaces. The price includes continental breakfast brought to your door and all the firewood you need.

Lake Creek Lodge (Sisters 97759; tel. 595-6331) is located in the nearby Metolius Recreation Area. This full-service resort has individual houses and cottages that range from $60 to $250 depending upon the unit and number of people. Tennis, swimming, and fishing are some of the many activities available here. Dinner is in the pine-paneled main lodge and features a different entree each day, complemented by homemade breads, salads, and desserts. The establishment caters especially well to families.

Another Metolius retreat can be found at **Cold Springs Resort** (Cold Springs Resort Ln., HCR 1270, Camp Sherman 97730; tel. 595-6271). Open from mid-April to mid-October, the cabins here ($75-95) feature naturally pure artesian well water. A footbridge across the Metolius connects the resort to Camp Sherman, where groceries, a church, and a cafe are within easy walking distance. Pets are allowed here for $5

per night, but must be kept on a leash at all times and never left unattended.

Northwest of Sisters about 18 miles is the **Blue Lake Resort** (13900 Blue Lake Dr., Sisters 97759; tel. 595-6671; $50-100). Situated in the Deschutes National Forest at 3,500 feet, the resort offers accommodations that range from cabins and A-frames to townhouses and condos. All units have kitchens with utensils, dishes, and appliances. Their marina has boats, canoes, kayaks, and paddleboats for rent. It's a beautiful spot to relax and enjoy a lake that rivals Crater Lake in color.

Food

The **Ranch House** (310 S.E. Hood St., Sisters; tel. 549-8911) specializes in sandwiches and take 'n' bake pizza and also has a good selection of domestic and imported beers and wines. The **Lonetree Restaurant** (160 E. Cascade, Sisters; tel. 549-8940) features good old American food. Check the board for the daily specials.

The **Gallery Restaurant** (230 W. Cascade, Sisters; tel. 549-2631) offers chuckwagon dinners that range from $6.50 to $9. Surprisingly tasteful paintings on Old West themes as well as flintlocks and other ancient armaments pay homage to the area's pioneer past. Many eastern Oregonians will tell you that **Papandrea's** (325 S.W. Hood, Sisters; tel. 549-6081) makes the best pizza in the state. While such claims are highly subjective, outlets in Bend and Oregon City attest to this small chain's dedicated following.

The hot spot in town is undoubtedly the **Hotel Sisters and Bronco Billy Saloon.** Built in 1912, the upstairs rooms of this historic structure have been refurbished into intimate mini-dining rooms. Barbecued ribs are the specialty of the house, but you can also find fresh seafood, steaks, chicken dishes, and Mexican fare here. In one corner of the building, on the other side of the western-style saloon doors, is Bronco Billy's. This funky watering hole must look much the same as it did 80 years ago. A racy painting that used to grace the local brothel is proudly displayed behind the bar, and cowboy hats on most heads complete the picture of a town whose Old West ambience gets better with age. For the price of a beer, you can get one of the local Stetson-hatted good ol' boys to tell you the inside scoop on where to go and what to do in this neck of the woods.

Campgrounds

A handful of campgrounds open only in summer are near Sisters on the old McKenzie Highway, ORE 242. **Cold Springs** (Contact Sisters Ranger Station; tel. 549-2111; $6) is five miles west of town on ORE 242. This campground, 3,400 feet in elevation, has 23 sites for tents and small trailers (22 feet maximum). Picnic tables, firegrills, pits toilets, and water are provided. It's a pretty spot, near the source of Trout Creek.

Six miles farther down the road is **Whispering Pine** (same contact). No fees are charged at this primitive campground with six tent sites, mainly because there is no water available. Another six miles up the pass at 5,200 feet is **Lava Camp Lake** (same contact). Two tent sites and 10 RV sites (22 feet maximum) are available at this rustic campground. There is no fee, but there's also no water. The main allure is its close proximity to the Pacific Crest Trail and the Three Sisters Wilderness.

Events

The annual **Sisters Rodeo** opens the second weekend of June. In addition to the normal assortment of calf-roping and bronco-bucking, country dances, a "buckaroo breakfast," and a 10-km Stampede Run round out the fun. Contact the **Sisters Chamber of Commerce** (Box 476, Sisters 97759; tel. 549-0251) for the schedule of events.

Services

The Sisters **post office** (160 First St., Sisters 97759; tel. 549-3561) is open for service Mon.-Fri. 9-5. The office is also open Sat., but without window service. The **liquor store** (216 Cascade; tel. 549-9841) is open Mon.-Sat. 10-6, Oct. 1-May 31; Mon.-Sat. 10-7, June 1-Sept. 30. Three miles outside of Sisters, a **laundromat** is found at the KOA campground (67667 U.S. 20, Bend 97701; tel. 549-3021), which is open 9 a.m.-10 p.m. all week long.

BEND AND VICINITY

Since 1980, Deschutes County has been the state's fastest-growing population center, largely due to its hiking trails, fishing streams, golf courses, whitewater runs, and ski slopes. Proximity to all this recreation has made the city of Bend Oregon's number-one destination for the active traveler. While the resulting increase in traffic and prices can sometimes make you forget that you're in Oregon, Bend's location between the eastern flank of the Cascades and the desert provides respite from what the locals call "Californication." The boom in real estate can be appreciated by the fact that the average price for a three-bedroom, two-bath house here was $60,000 in 1987. By 1991, the price had jumped 50%.

The seeds of growth were planted several decades ago when a onetime military encampment a dozen miles south of town was transformed into the Sunriver Resort community. Black Butte Ranch, the Inn of the Seventh Mountain, and other destination resorts soon

the Deschutes River

national parks, preserves, monuments, BLM wilderness, and the country inside the proposed Oregon High Desert Protection Act.

Info on native American history, wildlife, and plant communities, as well as descriptions of such areas as the Abert Rim, Hart Mountain Wildlife Refuge, and Owyhee Canyonlands, can be found on the reverse side of the map.

Drake Park

The Deschutes River has a dam and diversion channel just above downtown Bend. It provides valuable irrigation water for the farmers and ranchers of the dry but fertile plateau to the north, and creates a placid stretch of water called Mirror Pond that is home to Canada geese, ducks, and other wildlife. Drake Park is on the east bank of this greenbelt and is a nice place to relax, have a quiet lunch, or maybe toss a Frisbee around.

However, you had better be careful where you step, as the birds leave behind numerous land mines. The folks living in those nice houses on the west bank of Mirror Pond got tired of scraping the guano off of their shoes, but unfortunately for them, they were legally unable to do anything against their fowl neighbors due to their protected status. They came up with a rather ingenious solution to the geese and their offensive droppings. The residents chipped in $1500 to buy a pair of swans from Queen Elizabeth's Royal Swannery in England. Since geese and swans do not get along, the citizens reasoned that the blue-blooded swans would chase away the common Canada geese. While the geese are still here, you will notice that they tend to congregate in Drake Park, while the swans have a decided preference for the private estates.

Pilot Butte

On the east side of town is Pilot Butte. A road barber-poles its way up to the top of this 511-foot-high volcanic remnant. Here, you can enjoy a sweeping view of nine snowcapped Cascade peaks and their green forests. It is also pretty at night, with the twinkling lights of the city below and the stars above. Full moons are especially awesome, illuminating the ghostly forms of the mountains in icy, light-blue silhouettes.

followed. South of the city is some of the best skiing in the state on Mt. Bachelor; to the north, world-class rock-climbing routes at Smith Rock State Park and famed fishing holes on the Metolius River await. Add Cascade hiking, Deschutes River rafting and fishing, and other nearby locales for rockhounding, golf, horseback riding, and water sports, and you'll understand why it's often hard to find a place to bed down for the night here on weekends.

SIGHTS

Getting The Big Picture

A 28- by 38-inch relief map and brochure produced by **Emerald Imagery** (Send $5.50 to Box 3429, Eugene, OR 97403) is perhaps the best linear intro to the area. Entitled *Visitors Guide to Oregon High Desert Wilderness*, it demarcates the region's mountains, deserts, and grasslands, as well as boundaries of wildlife refuges,

Pine Mountain Observatory

Another peak experience worth investigating is the Pine Mountain Observatory (tel. 382-8331), located about 40 miles east of Bend on U.S. 20. Take the road out of Millican to the top of 6,395-foot-high Pine Mountain to reach the installation. Three Cassegrain telescopes with 15-, 24-, and 32-inch mirrors are used by University of Oregon teachers and students to unlock the secrets of the universe. The friendly astronomers here will often allow visitors an intriguing peek at the neighboring stars and planets. Call ahead for information and weather conditions before making the trip. A donation of $2 per person is suggested.

Newberry Volcano National Monument

The West's newest national monument enshrines the obsidian fields, deep mountain lakes, and lava formations left in the wake of a massive series of eruptions. While lacking the visual impact of Crater Lake, this preserve is more accessible and less crowded than her southern Cascade counterpart. Beyond Newberry Crater itself, the monument extends north 25 miles along a volcanic fracture zone to Lava Butte. A 1981 U.S. Geological Survey probe drilled into the caldera floor found temperatures of 510°F, the highest recorded in an inactive Cascade volcano.

Lava Lands Visitor Center, Lava Butte

About 11 miles south of Bend on U.S. 97 are the Lava Lands Visitor Center (tel. 593-1221) and Lava Butte. The center has some interpretive exhibits that explain the region's volcanic history, as well as a small but good selection of local geology books and an assortment of free pamphlets on local attractions; their bulletin board has the latest activities and goings-on posted. Open 9-4 daily.

After your orientation, cruise on up to the top of 500-foot-high Lava Butte, located just behind the visitor center. During the summer, to get to the top you must take the shuttle, which leaves the parking lot every half hour; adults $1, children 50 cents. The rest of the year you can take your own vehicle up, although the road is not recommended for trailers and RVs. The observation platform on top of the fire lookout established here in 1928 offers the best viewpoint.

Be sure to talk to Joe, the fire lookout, who has spotted more forest fires in Oregon than anyone else. Nearly a mile above sea level, the butte affords a commanding panorama of the Cascade Range. On a clear day you can see most of the major peaks, with Mounts Jefferson and Hood looming prominently on the northern horizon. These snowcapped turrets backdrop a 10-square-mile lava field. You can venture out into this eerie landscape by taking the trail that starts from the visitor center and makes its way to the Phil Brogan lookout.

A short trail circumnavigates the 150-foot-deep crater on Lava Butte and is complemented by informative placards that help you interpret this otherworldly environment. From the trail you can see how the lava flow from the butte changed the course of the Deschutes River. You can also see the "kipukas," small islands of green trees surrounded by a sea of black lava. Along the trail, look for some of what geologists call splatter. You'll know it when you see it, because it looks exactly like what it sounds like. Pick up a couple of red pumice rocks for the children, who will be fascinated by the way the stones float in the bathtub.

Lava River Cave

About 12 miles south of Bend on U.S. 97 is Oregon's longest known lava tube, the Lava River Cave (tel. 593-2421). Open from mid-May to mid-Sept., the admission is $1.50, and lantern rentals (available at the Lava Lands Visitor Center) are also $1.50. The cave is a cool 40° F year-round, so dress warmly. Since the walking surface is uneven, flat-heeled shoes are recommended. Bring a flashlight to guide you through this lava tube, or rent one at the entrance for 50 cents. The trail is an easy 2.4-mile roundtrip from the parking lot.

The first chamber you enter is called the Collapsed Corridor. Volcanic rocks that fell from the roof and walls lie in jumbled piles. Freezing water in cracks pries a few rocks loose each winter, which is why the cave is usually closed during the cold months. Stairs take you out of the Collapsed Corridor into a large void called Echo Hall. Here the ceiling reaches 58 feet high and the cave is 50 feet wide. Conversations return from the opposite side of the hall as eerie noises in the dark. The lateral markings you see

CENTRAL OREGON ~ WHERE EAST MEETS WEST

It's a paradox in Oregon that one goes east to reach what feels like the West. Driving from lush wet western Oregon to the sage-covered cowboy country east of the Cascades changes your perspective like a fun-house mirror. In a transformation so abrupt it can be blinding, the muted light and thick forest canopy part to reveal chaparral, buff-colored desert flora or green lollipop-shaped junipers. This growth is lower to the ground and more spread out than the fir and hemlock of western Oregon, enlarging your field of vision. The low humidity here gives a clarity to starry night skies and so sharpens the outlines of distant objects that mountains fifty miles away seem within easy walking distance. The marked contrasts between conditions on each side of the Cascades are best appreciated when there's an opportunity to observe a stormfront approaching from the west. Darkened cloud masses on the crest of the Cascades can often be seen from a central Oregon vantage point bathed in sunlight.

etched on the walls here show the various levels of past volcanic flows.

At Low Bridge Lane, watch your head because the ceiling dips down to five feet. Look for the "lavacicles" in this and other areas of the cave. (This term comes from a geologist's 1923 publication on the cave called *The Lava River Tunnel.*) Two kinds of them are found here: the hollow cylindrical "soda straws" were formed by escaping gases, and the other cone-shaped formations were created by remelted lava dripping down from the ceiling.

The next curiosity you'll come across is a cave inside the cave, the Two Tube Tunnel. Here two tubes are found running for 95 feet with intermittent connections between them. The smaller tube was formed when the level of the lava flow dropped, and the cooling lava created a second roof and tube inside the existing cave.

The terrain changes again in the Sand Gardens. Rain and snowmelt carry volcanic ash down through cracks and openings in the cave and deposit them here. The process continues today with the nearly constant dripping water carving out spires and pinnacles in the sand. These formations take hundreds of years to grow, so please stay behind the fenced-off area. The sand gets thicker and thicker until it completely blocks off the lava tube, forcing an abrupt about-face. The walk back to the light of the sun affords a different perspective on this remarkable natural attraction.

It is important to avoid littering the cave, collecting samples, or doing anything else to mar this national treasure. Don't light flares, paper, or cigarettes, because the fumes kill off insects, the food source of the cave's bat population. Roosting bats should not be disturbed, because waking them from hibernation results in certain death for these winged mammals. In short, "Leave nothing but footprints, take nothing but pictures, and kill nothing but time."

Benham Falls

Four miles down Forest Service Rd. 9702 from the Lava Lands Visitor Center is Benham Falls. Give other cars a wide berth and plenty of following distance, as the road's pumice and fine dust are hard on paint jobs and engines. The road leads to a small picnic area in a grove of giant ponderosa pines on the bank of the Deschutes River. With tables, pit toilets, firegrills, and plenty of shade, this is a nice place for a picnic. Be sure to tote your own fluids though, because there is no water. Day use only, no fees and no camping.

The hike to the falls is an easy one-mile jaunt downstream. Take the footbridge across the river, and enjoy your stroll past a spectacular section of untamed whitewater. While the water here in the Deschutes is much too cold and dangerous for a swim (except perhaps on very hot days), it's always ideal for soaking your feet a little after you've completed your hike. Benham Falls was created when magma from Lava Butte splashed over the side, flowing five miles to the Deschutes. When the molten rock collided with the icy water, the churning rapids and crashing waterfall were created here.

High Desert Museum

Six miles south of Bend on U.S. 97 is the High Desert Museum (59800 South U.S. 97, Bend

97702; tel. 382-4754). This five-million-dollar center for natural resources, native animals, and cultural history of the intermountain, western high desert is well worth the price of admission (adults $5, seniors $4.50, children ages 6-12 $2.50, and kids under five free). Along the many trails that wind through the 150-acre facility, visitors can observe river otters at play, porcupines sticking it to each other, and birds of prey dispassionately watching over the whole scene. Replicas of a sheepherder's cabin, a settler's cabin, forestry displays, and other historical interpretations are also along the museum walkways.

Inside the museum's main building, unique exhibits, slide and movie shows, galleries, and pioneer history demonstrations are presented. The Orientation Center has lizards, snakes, and toads on display, and other animals can be seen at the Wildlife Observation Pavilion. The **Earle A. Chiles Center** exhibit on the Spirit of the West features eight "you are there" life-sized dioramas. This walk through time begins 8,000 years ago beside a still marsh and takes you to a fur brigade camp, into the depths of a gold mine, and down Main Street of a boisterous frontier town. The **Spirit of the West Gallery** has representative arts and artifacts of the early American West, as well as tools, clothing, and other personal belongings from the 19th century.

Newberry Volcano

Lava Butte is one of over 400 cinder cones in a family of over 1,000 other smaller volcanoes that together comprise Newberry Volcano. This vast shield volcano covers 500 square miles. In the caldera of this immense million-year-old mountain lie two alpine lakes called Paulina and East lakes.

Composed of rocks ranging from basalt to rhyolite, the black obsidian flow that's found at Newberry Volcano has been the source of raw material for Indian spearpoints, arrowheads, and hide scrapers for thousands of years. Prized by the original inhabitants of the area, the obsidian tools were also highly valued by other Indian nations and were a medium of exchange for blankets, firearms, and other possessions at the Taos Fair in New Mexico. These tools and other barterings helped to spread Newberry Volcano obsidian all across the West and into Canada and Mexico. Centuries later, NASA sent astronauts to walk on the volcano's pumice-dusted surface in preparation for landing on the moon.

Paulina And East Lakes

South from Bend 27 miles on U.S. 97 is the turnoff to Paulina and East lakes. The 16-mile paved but ragged County Rd. 21 twists and turns its way up to the lakes in the caldera of Newberry Crater. Several campgrounds and two resorts are located along the shores of these lakes, which are noted for their excellent trout fishing. Be sure to take the four-mile drive (summer only) to the top of 7,985-foot-high Paulina

The Paulina Peak drive is one of the highest in the state.

TED LONG ISHIKAWA

Peak on Forest Service Rd. 500. Towering 1,500 feet over the lakes in Newberry Crater, the peak also allows a perspective on the forest, obsidian fields, and basalt flows in the surrounding area.

Fishing in the area is said to be best in the fall. In Lake Paulina, fisherman can troll for kokanee as well as brown and rainbow trout. Paulina's twin, East Lake, features a fall run of German brown trout which move out of the depths to spawn in shoreline shallows. **Paulina Lake Resort** (tel. 536-2240) books up early with a dozen three-bedroom log cabins going for $50-115 a night. Hearty lunches and dinners ($3-15) can be had in the resort's log-paneled dining room. Boat rentals and a general store are also on-site. **East Lake Resort** (tel. 536-2230) offers 11 cabins with housekeeping facilities for $55-85 per night. A snack bar, general store, and boat rentals are on-site, and the nearby RV park has a laundry, public showers, and pay phones. Each year, 225,000 trout are planted in East Lake, and in 1990, Atlantic salmon were introduced here. The cold water and abundant fresh water shrimp make for excellent-tasting fish. Camping is also available; contact the Bend Ranger Station for details. Paulina Resort is open in the summer for fishing and Dec.-March for cross-country skiing. East Lake Resort is open mid-May through mid-October.

SPORTS AND RECREATION

Horsing Around
Several public stables in the vicinity of Bend offer horseback rides that satisfy everyone from the dude to the experienced equestrian. Whether it be a mild-mannered pony for young children or a lively steed for the wannabe buckaroos, you'll find appropriate mounts and trail rides for all ages and skill levels.

Black Butte Stables (Box 402, Sisters 97759; tel. 595-2061 or 595-1297) at Black Butte Ranch has several packages that take you down trails in the shadow of the Three Sisters. The Big Meadow pony ride for children is $5 for 15 minutes and $10 for a half hour. The one-hour Big Loop ride costs $18, the one-hour Gobblers Knob ride costs $22, the two-hour Glaze Meadow ride costs $25, and the Hole-in-the-Wall Gang ride (for experienced riders only) costs

Rock-climbers will enjoy the diverse terrain of Smith Rock.

$30. The half-day Reata Trail ride costs $45, and the full-day Oregon Trail ride costs $65.

If you want a box lunch on the Oregon Trail ride, it's an additional $5. Evening meal rides include the Buckaroo Barbecue for $30 and the Steak ride for $35. If you want to start your day in the saddle, consider the Buckaroo Breakfast ride for $30. Reservations are suggested for the short rides and are required for the half-day, full-day, and meal rides. Riding lessons are also available.

Located 15 minutes west of Sisters on ORE 126 is **Blue Lake Corrals** (tel. 595-6681). The half-hour pony ride for children on Jeepers costs $5. The one-hour Crater Rim ride ($20) takes you through alpine meadows to the top of the crater that holds 314-foot-deep Blue Lake. The two-hour Waterfalls ride ($25) incorporates views of several waterfalls as well as Three Fingered Jack. The two-hour Lakes Loop trip ($25) meanders through the forest past three crystal-clear mountain lakes. The two-hour Twilight ride ($26) offers cooler temperatures, lovely sunsets and skyscapes, and views of wildlife coming out of the woods to feed.

Blue Lake Corrals' three half-day rides, the Discovery Trail, Meadow Lake Trail, and Cache Mountain Trail, all cost $45. The all-day Alpine trip ($60) goes into the Mt. Jefferson Wilderness. Summer is the best time to go on this trip due to the abundance of wildflowers, and lunch is also included. Meal rides, like the Cowboy Breakfast and the Chuck Wagon Supper, are also available and run from $28 to $38. Two-day wilderness pack trips are featured too. Reservations are requested at least one hour before the trail rides, and the meal rides need 24 hours' advance notification.

Five miles west of Redmond at the Eagle Crest Resort is **Eagle Crest Equestrian Center** (Box 1194, Redmond 97756; tel. 923-2072. The half-hour kids' pony ride on Geronimo costs $6. The one-hour Juniper Trail ride takes you through the junipers and sagebrush of the high desert and costs $17. The two-hour Cline Butte ride ($30) goes to the top of Cline Butte, where you get a good view of the interface between Cascade and desert life zones. The half-day Skyline Trail ride takes you out into the wilds of the desert, where you and your guide blaze your own trails (reservations required). Wagon rides, cookout rides, and riding lessons are also available.

About 15 miles south of Bend on U.S. 97 at Sunriver Resort is **Sunriver Stables** (Box 3254, Sunriver 97709; tel. 593-2538). The 15-minute Smallest Buckaroo pony ride costs $7. A good ride for beginners is the half-hour Bald Eagle Loop ($14), which goes along the Deschutes River. The one-hour Nature's Cove ride ($20) takes in views of the Deschutes River, wildlife, and wildflowers. The two-hour Ramsey Ridge ride climbs to a panoramic viewpoint overlooking the resort. For those who want to do some serious riding, you can create your own ride (three hours minimum) into the Deschutes National Forest for $36 for the first two hours, then $14 per additional hour. Private lessons, surrey, covered wagon, and sleigh (winter only) rides are also available.

Fishing

With over 100 mountain lakes and the Deschutes River within an hour's drive of Bend, your piscatorial pleasures will be satisfied in central Oregon. The high lakes offer rainbow, brown, and brook trout as well as landlocked Atlantic and coho salmon. The Deschutes River is famed for its red-sided rainbow trout and summer steelhead. You will need appropriate fishing gear like chest waders, rod 'n' reel, and fishing license/steelhead tags. All gear and permits are available locally.

A full-service pro shop with everything for the fly fisher is **The Fly Box** (923 S.E. Third St., Bend 97701; tel. 388-3330). Custom-tied flies and a full selection of fly-tying tools and materials provide you with the goodies to keep the fish biting. Fly-fishing classes, fishing guide services, and equipment sales, rentals, and repairs can also be found here.

Lacy's Whitewater and Wild Fish (57 Pinecrest Court, Bend 97701; tel. 389-2434) offers guided float trips on the Deschutes and John Day rivers, fly-fishing on the high Cascade lakes, and walk-in river treks on Fall River, Crooked River, and the upper Deschutes River. Lacy's floats nearly 100 miles of the Deschutes River on a year-round basis. Stable water temperatures from the spring-fed river and abundant water hatches of baetis, midges, stoneflies, salmonflies, goldenstones, mayflies and caddisflies keep the fish here in top condition. The wild red-sided trout of the Deschutes River are there all year, and the summer steelhead are found in the river from July through December. The John Day River is noted for being the only river in the state that hosts an all-wild run of summer steelhead. All-day float trips on either river cost $225 for one person, $300 for two, and $350 for three people. A deli-style lunch is also included. Rates for multiday trips (minimum two people, three days) run $160 per person per day and include all meals.

Guided trips to High Cascades lakes are $160 for one person and $205 for two. Walk-in river treks reach the good fishing holes not accessible by boat and are good for beginners. Half-day treks cost $80 for one person and $110 for two, and the full-day treks with deli-style lunches cost $110 for one person and $150 for two.

High Desert Drifter (721 N.W. Ogden, Bend 97701; tel. 389-0607) also offers guided fly-fishing float trips on the Deschutes River. The full-day trip that includes lunch, the necessary riverboater pass, and Warm Springs Indian Reservation fishing permit costs $225 for one person, $300 for two, and $375 for three. Multiday trips including all meals run $375 for two days, $550 for three days, $725 for four days, and $875 for five days.

Both outfitters require completion of a trip application form and a deposit.

Whitewater Rafting

The Deschutes River offers some of the finest whitewater in central Oregon. The numerous lava flows have diverted the river to create tumultuous rapids that attract raft, kayak, and canoe enthusiasts. From short rafting trips to multiday adventures, you'll find many options available to enjoy the exciting Deschutes River.

Hunter Expeditions (Box 346, Bend 97709; tel. 389-8370) features several rafting packages. The two-hour Mini Expedition ($27) takes you down a three-mile section of the Deschutes River that has Class I-IV rapids. Six daily departures from Bend include transfer to and from the river. The all-day trip ($65) takes in 12 action-packed miles of whitewater, including some exciting Class IV rapids like Box Car, Oak Springs, and Elevator. A deli-style lunch and plenty of drinks are included. The transfer pick-up point for the day-trips is in the town of Maupin (80 miles north of Bend via U.S 97 and U.S. 197) in front of the Oasis Cafe, and leaves promptly at 11 a.m.

The Inn of the Seventh Mountain (18575 Century Dr., Bend 97701; tel. 389-2722) offers a short two-hour raft trip ($28) down a three-mile section of the Deschutes that takes in some Class I-IV rapids. With names like Pinball Alley and the Souse Hole, you can be assured of a good ride! Transfer between the Inn and the river is included.

Rapid River Rafters (60107 Cinder Butte Rd., Bend 97702; tel. 382-1514 or 800-962-3327) offers a series of full- and multi-day packages on the Deschutes River. The one-day trip ($65) takes in 13 miles of the river between Wapinitia Rapids and Sherar's Falls. Toward the end of the run, you can sometimes see natives dip-net fishing off of rocks and wooden platforms in the river. A deli-style lunch with fresh fruit and beverages is provided. The two-day trip ($170) floats 29 miles of exciting whitewater. The three-day trip ($250) runs 44 miles between Trout Creek rapids and Sherar's Falls. The four-day trip ($330) takes in 55 miles of the Deschutes and is designed to allow you free time

for additional options like hiking, sunbathing, swimming, and fishing. On all of the multiday trips, the camping and meal preparations at pleasant riverside locations are taken care of by your guides.

Sun Country Tours (Box 771, Bend 97709; tel. 382-6277) is based at the Sunriver Resort. Their three-hour, three-mile whitewater adventure takes in Class I-IV rapids on the Deschutes River. It costs $25 for children 8-12 and $27 for adults. The full-day trip ($65) runs 13 miles through a dozen minor rapids and seven major ones including Wapinitia, Train Hole, and Oak Springs. A deli-style lunch is included. Multiday packages from 29-55 miles in length are also available. The two-day trip costs $170, the three-day costs $250, and the four-day costs $330. All meals on multiday trips are included, and the transfer from Sunriver to Maupin is also part of the day-trip packages.

If you would rather shoot the rapids on your own, you can rent canoes, kayaks, and rafts from **Bend Whitewater Supply** (Box 461, 2245 N.E. Division, Bend 97709; tel. 389-7191). This locally owned and operated full-service whitewater store can provide you with everything necessary for a safe and enjoyable whitewater experience. Bend Whitewater Supply also offers canoe and kayak lessons.

Juniper Aquatic And Fitness Center

One of the finest aquatic and fitness centers east of the Cascades is found at Juniper Aquatic and Fitness Center (800 N.E. Sixth St., Bend 97701; tel. 389-7665). Part of the Bend Metro Park and Recreation District, the center is located in 20-acre Juniper Park and features two indoor pools and a large 40-yard outdoor pool providing plenty of space for splashing around. Serious swimmers can enjoy frequent lap swims and adults-only swim times daily. An aerobics room, weight room, jogging trail, and tennis court offer other exercise options. A sauna and Jacuzzi provide you with yet another way to sweat it out. Call ahead to see what's on the schedule for the day's activities.

Cycle Coasting

If you like to bike but would rather have gravity do all of the work, consider the Paulina Plunge with **High Cascade Descent** (333 Riverfront, Bend 97702; tel. 389-0562). They provide qual-

Mt. Bachelor as seen from Sunriver

ity 15- and 18-speed mountain bikes, helmets, experienced guides, and the shuttle transfer from Bend and back. The action starts at Paulina Lake, where you begin your coast down forested trails alongside Paulina Creek. You'll pass by 50 waterfalls on your 3,000-foot descent, as well as abundant wildlife and varied vegetation. A deli-style lunch (vegetarian meals available upon request) and numerous opportunities for photography and fishing round out the fun. The tour costs $35 per person, $30 for children under 12. Large groups of over 10 people can receive discounts if they book trips in advance. If you have your own bicycle, you can deduct $5 from the tour price.

S.P.L.A.T.

One new sport that has gained over a million fans in the U.S. is paintball. A rugged 10-acre paintball playing-field 14 miles east of Bend on ORE 20 is operated by S.P.L.A.T. (Special Purpose Live Action Targets) (tel. 385-5721). Most paintball games are basically like steal the flag, except that team players fire balls of paint from CO_2-powered guns at each other. First developed by the U.S. Forest Service to mark trees and cattle, paintball has grown in sophistication to be an internationally recognized sport. All guns are set to fire the paintballs at less than 300 feet per second, and approved eye, face, and ear protection are mandatory. The paintballs themselves are made of nontoxic biodegrad-able vegetable matter that rinses clean in water. For $25 here, you can rent a gun, ammo, and safety equipment. Anyone over 10 years of age may play, although minors must have a waiver signed by a parent or guardian.

Golf

Central Oregon has recently gained recognition for world-class golfing. And no wonder. With a dozen courses and six more slated for construction, you can find just about every kind of golf challenge here. The warm sunny days, cool evenings, and spectacular mountain scenery make every shot a memorable one.

Two well-groomed courses, Big Meadow and Glaze Meadow, are found at **Black Butte Ranch** (tel. 595-6689). Big Meadow is more open and forgiving, while Glaze Meadow demands precise shots. Both have tall trees and lush fairways from tee to green. Greens fees are $24 for nine holes and $40 for 18 holes. Reservations for weekdays must be made at least one day in advance, while weekend bookings must be made no later than the Monday before.

Crooked River Ranch (tel. 923-6343), a nine-hole par-32 course, is wide open with few trees, but that doesn't detract from the challenge or the scenic vistas. Rates are $10-12 for nine holes and $18 for 18 holes. Weekend reservations must be made by Thursday.

A blend of open and tight holes can be found on the popular course at **Eagle Crest Resort** (tel. 923-4653). The two nine-hole segments of this par-72 course differ in character. The first set allows you to swing away, while the second places a premium on club and shot selection. The stand of 1,000-year-old junipers in mid-fairway and excellent greens add to the challenge and enjoyment. The greens fees are $17 for nine holes and $28 for 18 holes for registered guests; $20 and $34 for visitors. Weekend reservations must be made by Thursday.

Eighteen new holes opened up recently at the **Inn of the Seventh Mountain** (tel. 382-8711). Designed by Robert Muir Graves, the course's strategically placed trees, lakes, and sand traps have already given this place the reputation as the "mean green" golf course of central Oregon. The 18 holes here are spoken in the same breath as Sunriver's North Course and Black Butte's Glaze Meadows—fast company indeed. The greens fees are $25 for nine holes, $40 for 18 holes.

A true desert course found in Redmond that requires shot accuracy is the **Juniper Golf Club** (tel. 548-3121). This is an 18-hole par-72 course that snakes through the juniper and lava of the high desert. The prevailing winds and abundance of rocks off of the fairway challenge the golfer's shot-making abilities. Rates are $11-13 for nine holes and $20-25 for 18 holes. Reservations are required at least one day in advance.

Sixty miles north of Bend is the well-maintained 18-hole par-72 course at **Kah-Nee-Ta Resort** (tel. 553-1112, ext. 371). While shorter than many other resort courses in the area, it's nonetheless both a challenge and a delight to play. In addition to water to contend with from the Warm Springs River that meanders through the course, several holes have elevated greens that require blind shots to reach. The greens fees are $15 for nine holes and $25 for 18. Reservations can be made at any time.

A beautiful course in Bend with tight fairways, large greens, sand, and "water, water everywhere" is **Mountain High Golf Club** (tel. 382-1111). Two tricky par-four dogleg holes, three par-fives, and the necessity of placing shots over and around the junipers add to the test.

Rates are $20 for nine holes and $30 for 18. Reservations can be made anytime for weekdays, but must be made at least four days in advance for weekends.

About 45 miles north of Bend on U.S. 97 at the Madras Golf and Country Club is **Nine Peaks** (tel. 475-3511). This short par-36 nine-hole course is flat and more forgiving than most courses in the area. The name comes from the nine Cascade peaks that provide a stunning visual backdrop. Rates are $7-9 for nine holes and $12-16 for 18. Reservations are required at least one day in advance.

A course popular with seniors, ladies, and beginners is found at **Orion Greens** (tel. 388-3999) in Bend. This short executive course with no homesites lining the fairways can be deceptively tough. Water comes into play on four holes and shot accuracy is a must. Rates are $10 for nine holes and $17 for 18. Reservations are required at least one day in advance.

The hilly, rocky terrain of **River's Edge** (tel. 389-2828) in Bend makes it both beautiful and an extreme challenge. This testy nine-hole par-36 course has tiered greens and one of the region's most demanding water holes. Shot accuracy is more important here than at any other course in the vicinity. Rates are $14 for nine holes and $22 for 18 on weekdays; $15 for nine holes and $25 for 18 on weekends. Reservations are required one week in advance.

Two distinct 18-hole courses are found at **Sunriver Resort** (tel. 593-1221), 15 miles south of Bend on U.S. 97. The South Course is long, with fast greens that require a soft touch. The North Course, the premier course in the area, has been rated among the top 25 in the country, and is the site of the annual Oregon Open. Water, abundant bunkers, and constricted approaches to the greens make club selection and shot accuracy very important. The rates for either course are $24 for nine holes and $40 for 18 for registered guests; $30 for nine holes and $50 for 18 for visitors.

Prineville Meadows Course, west of the city on U.S. 26, adds another public course to the region's already formidable array of places to putter around.

PRACTICALITIES

Accommodations

Bend has exploded into the largest full-fledged resort town in the state. On holidays or ski weekends, it's hard now to find a decent room here if you don't have reservations, and it's bound to get worse. As such, expect many room rates to be significantly higher than what was listed in the accompanying chart at press time. One place where price won't ever be an inhibiting factor ($12-17) is Bend's **Alpine Hostel** (19 S.W. Century Drive, Bend 97702; tel. 389-3813), located on the road to Mt. Bachelor ski slopes. Added inducements to stay here include a free ski shuttle and 10% discounts on both Powder House ski rentals and hot tubbing at Soaks Unlimited.

Central Oregon Resorts

There are five premier resorts in Deschutes County that have helped transform it from a primarily agricultural area to the Aspen of the Northwest. Golf, horseback riding, tennis, swimming, biking/jogging/hiking trails, saunas, and hot tubs grace these all-year playgrounds, along with first-rate lodgings and restaurants. Ski packages and other special offers are also available at each establishment. While all of them feature recreation amid pleasant surroundings, subtle distinctions among them bear mention.

Located 31 miles west of Bend on ORE 20, **Black Butte Ranch** (Box 8000, Black Butte Ranch 97759; tel. 595-6211 or 800-452-7455) sits on the plain of the seven peaks. Ponderosa pines, lush meadows, and aspen-lined streams round out the metaphor of mountains' majesty. Over 16 miles of trails thread through the 1,800 acres of forested grounds. Accommodations range from deluxe hotel-type bedrooms to one-to three-bedroom condominium suites and resort homes. Rates for these digs range from $70 to $300.

Eagle Crest Resort (Box 1215, Redmond 97756; tel. 923-2453 or 800-682-4786) is five miles west of Redmond. This recent newcomer to the central Oregon resort scene offers hotel rooms, two-bedroom suites, and condos in the $70-250 range. The terrain and vegetation are representative of the high desert, and backdropped by views of eight Cascade peaks.

A great place for families is **The Inn of the Seventh Mountain** (Box 1207, Bend 97709; tel. 382-8711 or 800-452-6810). Located five miles outside of Bend on Century Drive in the Deschutes National Forest, bedroom units, fireside studios, and condos are available here in the $60-275 range. Their outstanding recreation department plugs the kids into nonstop fun, leaving the parents free to enjoy grown-up pursuits. Ice skating, cross-country skiing, and snowmobile trips are available during the winter months here.

Another place to bring the tribe is **Kah-Nee-Ta Resort** (Box K, Warm Springs 97761; tel. 553-1112 or 800-831-0100). Located at the bottom of a canyon about a dozen miles off U.S. 26 from the town of Warm Springs, Kah-Nee-Ta basks in 300 days of sunshine a year. Owned by the Confederated Tribes of Warm Springs, this arrow-shaped hotel is the centerpiece of the 600,000-acre reservation, which includes a working ranch and wild horses. Lodging possibilities include authentic Indian tepees (from $20), hotel rooms, and condo cottages that range from $50 to $250. The hot mineral baths and spring-fed swimming pool are among the highlights here. Such native-inspired dishes as salmon cooked outside in the traditional way (with roots and wild herbs) and bird-in-clay (a game hen stewing in its own juices inside a clay mold) also impart a unique flavor to a vacation here.

The Northwest's most complete resort **Sunriver Lodge** (Box 3609, Sunriver 97707; tel. 800-547-3922) not only has proximity to Mt. Bachelor skiing, Deschutes river canoeing/whitewater rafting, and hiking/horse trails in the Deschutes National Forest but also boasts golf courses, pools, tennis courts, and biking routes. An on-site astronomical observatory and nature center together with Sunriver's shopping mall compound the impression of a recreation mecca with something for everybody. Larger parties will find the spacious lodge suites (limit four persons to a suite) to be well worth the $165-180 asking price. Each of these units features a floor-to-ceiling fireplace, a fully equipped kitchen, a sleeping loft, and tall picture windows which open up to a patio. During the summer, complimentary bicycles and a two-hour float

BEND ACCOMMODATIONS

Bend Super 8 Motel, 1275 ORE 97, tel. 388-6888, $50-70, wheelchair access, covered pool, laundry.

Best Western Entrada Lodge, 19221 Century Dr., tel. 382-4080, $55-79, pool, Jacuzzi, pets, restaurant.

Best Western Woodstone Inn, 721 N.E. 3rd St., tel. 382-1515, $55-79, pool, Jacuzzi, pets.

Cascade Lodge Motel, 420 S.E. 3rd St., tel. 382-2612, $35-55, pool, pets, restaurant.

Cimarron Motel, 201 N.E. 3rd St., tel. 382-8282, $35-45, pool, pets.

Chalet Motel, 510 S.E. 3rd St., tel. 382-6124, $30-40, TV, a/c, small rooms.

Dunes Motel, 1515 N.E. 3rd St., tel. 382-6811, $40-50, pool, pets.

Edelweiss Motel, 2346 N.E. Division, tel. 382-6222, $30-40, clean.

Hill Crest Motel, 61405 ORE 97, tel. 389-5910, $30-50, kitchenettes, pets.

Maverick Motel, 437 N.E. 3rd St., tel. 382-7711, $38-50, pool, pets, restaurant/lounge.

Motel West, 228 N.E. Irving, tel. 389-5577, $30-40, kitchenettes, pets.

Palmer's Motel, 645 N.E. Greenwood Ave., tel. 382-1197, $30-40, covered pool.

Rainbow Motel, 154 N.E. Franklin Ave., tel. 382-1821, $30-40, kitchenettes, nonsmoking rooms.

Royal Gateway Motel, 475 S.E. 3rd St., tel. 382-5631, $30-50, HBO.

Sonoma Lodge, 450 S.E. 3rd St., tel. 382-4891, $30-45, pets.

Sportsman's Motel, 3705 ORE 97, tel. 382-2211, $35-55, kitchenettes, pets.

Tom Tom Motel, 3600 ORE 97, tel. 382-4734, $30-50, pets, laundry.

Westward Ho Motel, 904 S.E. 3rd St., tel. 382-2111, $31-35, covered pool, fireplaces, pets.

down the Deschutes in a canoe are included with room rental.

Campgrounds

With the Three Sisters Wilderness and the Deschutes National Forest flanking the western edges of Bend, there are many wonderful spots to enjoy a night camping out under the stars. But for those who want to stay within a two-mile radius of civilization, four decent RV parks can be found near Bend. **Bend Keystone** (305 N.E. Burnside, Bend 97701; tel. 382-2335; $14), **Crown Villa** (60801 Brosterhous, Bend 97701; tel. 388-1131; $16-24), **John's Trailer Park** (61415 U.S. 97 S., Bend 97701; tel. 382-6206; $15), and **KOA Bend** (63615 U.S. 97 N., Bend 97701; tel. 382-7728; $14-20) offer all of the major amenities. However, while a swimming pool, recreation room, and cable TV hookups are pleasant enough, they can ultimately take the spotlight away from the main attraction: around Bend, nature is the star.

Tumalo State Park (tel. 382-2601; $11 tents, $13 hookups) provides a middle ground between the rugged wilderness and tamed RV parks. Located five miles northwest of Bend off of U.S. 20 along the banks of the Deschutes River, 68 tent sites and 20 sites for RVs up to 35 feet long are available here. Showers, flush toilets, hookups, utilities, and a laundromat are also accessible. Open mid-April to late October.

A more secluded setting is **Tumalo Falls** (contact Deschutes National Forest, 1230 N.E. Third St., Bend 97701; tel. 388-5664; no fee). Located 16 miles west of town down Forest Service Roads 4601 and 4603, this small campground is situated along Tumalo Creek. Many fine hiking trails are in the area, including a short one to 97-foot-high Tumalo Falls. However, the facilities are primitive—pit toilets and no water.

Another exceptionally beautiful but equally rustic National Forest Service campground is **Todd Lake** (also contact the Forest Service for more info). To get there, take Century Dr. toward Mt. Bachelor. About a mile or two past the ski area, take the first Forest Service Rd. on the right. While this road eventually arrives at Sisters, it is not recommended for passenger cars. However, you will have to venture less than a mile on a well-maintained section to reach the parking area for Todd Lake. It's a short walk up the trail to the campsites at this 6,200-foot-high alpine lake. While tables, firegrills, and pit toilets are provided, you will need to pack in your own water and supplies, as no vehicles are allowed. It's a good thing, because the drone of a Winnebago generator into the wee hours of the night would definitely detract from the grandeur of this pristine spot. You'll find good swimming and wading on the sandy shoal on the south end of the lake, and you can't miss the captivating views of Broken Top to the north.

Farther away from the city is **Lapine State Park** (Box 5309, Bend 97708; tel. 536-2428 after Labor Day; before Labor Day tel. 800-452-5687 in Oregon, tel. 284-7388 outside of Oregon). Located eight miles north of Lapine off U.S. 97, look for a sign on the west side of the highway marking the three-mile-long entrance road. With 14 campsites, swimming, canoeing, and trout fishing, this place fills early on a first-come, first-served basis. This area also has one of the taller ponderosa pines in Oregon (191 feet) and close proximity to the Cascade Lakes Drive, the High Desert Museum, and an array of volcanic phenomena. Open from mid-April to late October depending upon snowfall, such amenities as flush toilets, firewood, showers, and a laundromat are available. Fees run $12 for a full hookup site, $11 for an electricity-only hookup.

Food

The scenery around Bend feeds the soul, and restaurants here do the rest. While area restaurants run the gamut from fast-food franchises to elegant dinner houses, many travelers also want something in between those extremes. Some alternatives for every budget are listed below.

Beef and Brew (Bend River Mall; tel. 388-4646) is a good dinner house for choice beef, seafood, and a tall cool one. Reservations are recommended. Many locals concur that **Cyrano's** (119 N.W. Minnesota Ave.; tel. 389-6276)

is one of central Oregon's premier dining experiences. With a reputation built around thick-cut steaks that are grilled to perfection over red oak, the menu also features fresh seafood and other gourmet specialties. If the weather is pleasant, enjoy lunch outside at their sidewalk cafe. Wholesome home-cooked food is available at **D & D Bar and Grill** (927 N.W. Bond St.; tel. 382-4592). Open every day (except Christmas) for breakfast, lunch, and dinner, the Grill has reasonably priced breakfasts and a good selection of hamburgers.

A popular Portland chain has opened up an outlet in Bend. **De Nicola's** (811 N.W. Wall St.; tel. 389-7364) offers a fine selection of Italian dishes, pizza, soups, and salads. If you love Italian food but are trying not to add more notches to your belt, ask for their special low-fat menu. Bend also boasts central Oregon's first brewery and brewpub, **Deschutes Brewery and Public House** (1044 N.W. Bond St.; tel. 382-9242). This is the place to come and relax with fresh, handcrafted ales and good homemade food. Large viewing windows in the pub enable you to watch next month's batch being concocted in the brewery.

For a healthy, low-fat, low-cholesterol vegetarian breakfast or lunch with many organic items available, **Cafe Santé** (718 N.W. Franklin; tel. 383-3530) is the place to go. **Great Harvest Bread Co.** (835 N.W. Bond) is a bakery chain with outlets in Eugene and Portland, and will be a hit with those who like hearty whole-wheat breads from stone-ground flour, or such intriguing muffin combinations as oat bran/raspberry/applesauce. Cinnamon rolls, cookies, and other Great Harvest confections are made without eggs, dairy products, or oils. You'll also appreciate the chance to sample these products prior to making a purchase.

Rated as "one of the ski country's great restaurants" by *Ski* magazine, **Players Grille** (61 N.W. Brooks St.; tel. 382-5859) offers lunch, dinner, and cocktails. Try the Northwest blueberry chicken—boneless breast sautéed with shallots, blueberry vinegar, and cream accented with fresh blueberries. Decent Chinese cuisine is found at the **Hong Kong Restaurant and Lounge** (580 S.E. Third; tel. 389-8880). A wide selection of Cantonese, Szechuan, and American food, as well as many vegetarian and "health food" dishes are prepared here.

Giuseppe's Ristorante (932 N.W. Bond St.; tel. 389-8899) brings the taste of northern Italy to Bend. Dinner specialties include chicken, veal, and 17 pasta dishes. Another Italian fine-dining experience is available at the **Italian Cottage** (1564 N.E. Division St.; tel. 382-5062). You can choose from over 30 entrees here, and their pastas and breads are made fresh daily. For some of the largest portions in central Oregon, head down to **Jake's Diner** (61260 U.S. 97 South; tel. 382-0118). Hearty breakfasts are served here 24 hours a day, and the tasty giant cinnamon rolls are a treat. Truckers everywhere in the West sing the praises of this place. Nonetheless, lunch and dinner might disappoint you if you're looking for "cuisine" instead of basic food.

Le Bistro (1203 N.E. Third St.; tel. 389-7274) is consistently rated the region's best French restaurant by the American Automobile Association and the Mobil Guide. Situated in an old church and designed with an open kitchen, the European chef/owner treats you to fresh seafood, chicken, lamb, veal, and steak dinners. Complement your fare with a bottle from the impressive wine list. **Mexicali Rose** (301 N.E. Franklin; tel. 389-0149) has the best Mexican food around Bend. Open every evening for dinner; be sure to ask for their special black beans with your entree. Call ahead for reservations, because the restaurant is very popular with locals.

The **Pine Tavern Restaurant** (967 N.W. Brooks St.; tel. 382-5581) has been in business since 1919, so they must be doing something right. The restaurant is located in a garden setting overlooking Mirror Pond, and ponderosa pines coming up through the floor enhance the interior ambience. Fresh mountain trout, prime rib, lamb, and hot sourdough scones with honey butter are among the many specialties here. Reservations are recommended. **Yoko's Japanese Restaurant** (1028 N.W. Bond St.; tel. 382-2999) is Bend's preeminent Japanese restaurant and sushi bar. While the teriyaki, tempura, and sukiyaki dinners are prepared to suit American tastes, it's not uncommon to see Japanese visitors here enjoying their native cuisine.

What the Salishan Dining Room is to the western part of the state, Sunriver's **Meadows Restaurant** (Sunriver Resort, tel. 800-547-

3922) is for gourmets east of the Cascades. When you enter the high-ceilinged confines of the Meadows, your eyes will be immediately drawn to the massive stone fireplace on the left. You'll also notice lead crystal, bronze, and wood sculptures adorning the restaurant's interior. The picture window view of Mt. Bachelor across the Sunriver Meadow at sunset, however, overshadows everything here—everything that is except for the lamb, duck, sturgeon, and wild game specialties for which the restaurant is famous. A more casual dining experience is also available at Sunriver Resort's **Provision Company.** This full service (breakfast, lunch, and dinner) restaurant also has a window on the mountain as well as an excellent array of creatively prepared salads, seafood, and pasta dishes. The only downside to dining here is the long line of people waiting for tables during peak seasons (ski weekends and late July through Labor Day). Because this is a first-come, first-served restaurant, you might want to come here very early or very late to avoid the wait list.

Finally, located at the Inn of the Seventh Mountain, **El Crab Catcher** (18575 Century Dr.; tel. 389-2722) also rates an ardent recommendation. This restaurant chain got its start on Maui, and now has come to Bend to share regional delights with a Polynesian flair. Try the flash-frozen-and-flown-in-fresh king crab legs with lemon butter, salad (go for the house dressing topped with crumbled blue cheese), vegetables, and hot sourdough rolls. Fresh seafood, steaks, poultry, and a variety of light suppers are also featured here. The staff is extremely friendly and goes out of its way to ensure you a prompt and delicious repast. Be sure to call in your reservations early, as this restaurant is as popular with the après-ski crowd as it is with the locals.

Information And Services

The **police** (720 N.W. Wall St.; tel. 388-5530 or 911) and the state police (63319 U.S. 20 W.; tel. 388-6300 or 911) are at your beck and call. The **post office** (2300 N.E. Fourth, Bend 97701; tel. 388-1971) is open Mon.-Fri. 8:30-5:30. If you like to make your own cocktails, the **liquor store** (939 N.W. Bond; tel. 382-6450) is open noon-8 p.m. Warm Springs Indian Reservation's

KWSO (91.9 FM) features an intriguing blend of progressive country music, morning chants by tribal elders, and discussions of issues concerning native Americans.

For additional information on the Bend area, the **chamber of commerce** (63085 U.S. 97 N., tel. 382-3221) is open Mon.-Thurs. 9-5, Fri. 8-6, Sat. 8-5, and Sun. 11-4. The **Deschutes County Library** (507 N.W. Wall St.; tel. 388-6677) is open Mon.-Sat. 9-6. The Bend and Fort Rock **Ranger Station** (1230 N.E. Third St.; tel. 388-5664) is the place to go for permits and information on the vast array of lands in central Oregon managed by the Forest Service.

St. Charles Immediate Care Center (1302 U.S. 97; tel. 388-7799) can be of assistance for minor medical problems and emergencies. The parent hospital, **St. Charles Medical Center** (2500 N.E. Nelf; tel. 382-4321, or 382-4321 ext. 7100 for emergencies only) treats major trauma and other health-care problems. If you're out in the boondocks and time is of the essence, **Air Life of Oregon** (tel. 800-621-5433 or 911) can get you to the medical center in a hurry. The **Bend Memorial Clinic** (1501 N.E. Medical Center Dr.; tel. 382-2811) is another option to remedy minor aches, pains, and ailments.

Events

The **Cascade Festival of Music** is held the third week of June on the banks of the Deschutes River. In addition to world-class performances of classical, pop, and jazz in the pavilion tent, children's concerts, music workshops, and strolling minstrels round out the pageant. Tickets and information are available through the Cascade Festival of Music office (tel. 382-8381).

The **Sunriver Music Festival,** held in the magnificent log-and-stone structure called the Great Hall at Sunriver Resort, has been pleasing capacity crowds since the festival's inception in 1977. The five-concert series features top performers from around the world. Highlights include the gala pops concert and the gourmet dinner as well as four traditional classical concerts and two children's concerts. Tickets and information are available through the Sunriver Music Festival office (tel. 593-1084).

GETTING THERE AND GETTING AROUND

By Air

The air hub of this section of the state is in Redmond (Redmond Air Center, Redmond 97756; tel. 548-5071), located 16 miles north of Bend on U.S. 97. **Alaska Air** (tel. 800-426-0333) has nonstop jet flights out of L.A. and Seattle; **Horizon Air** (tel. 800-547-9308) services the region from Portland and Seattle; and **United Express** (tel. 800-241-6522) provides flights to and from Portland and San Francisco. Taxi, limo, and bus transfers connect the traveler to Bend at nominal costs.

By Bus

Greyhound (1068 N.W. Bond St.; tel. 382-2151) is open Mon.-Fri. 7:30 a.m.-5:30 p.m., Sat. 7:30 a.m.-noon, Sun. 8-noon, and every evening 8:30-9:45 p.m. Bus service connects Bend with Klamath Falls to the south and Biggs, Maupin, and The Dalles to the north. **Resort Bus Lines** (767 S.E. Glenwood Dr.; tel. 389-7755) handles service to most outlying areas not serviced by Greyhound. **Central Oregon Shuttle Service** (tel. 382-0800) serves Bend to and from Portland International Airport. It's reasonably priced (around $20) and offers pick-ups and drop-offs at downtown hotels. **Redmond Airport Shuttle** (tel. 382-1687 or 800-955-8267) offers door-to-door service to and from the Redmond airport. A free **ski shuttle** run by Mt. Bachelor (tel. 382-2442) links downtown Bend to West Village on the mountain. **Yellow Cab** (tel. 382-3311) can always haul you around if you need a ride.

By Train

The closest you can get to Bend via Amtrak (tel. 800-872-7245) is Chemult, 60 miles to the south on U.S. 97. Amtrak will assist you in scheduling your transfer to Bend.

By Car

The automobile is still the vehicle of choice for exploring this quadrant of the state. Highways 97 and 20 converge on Bend, much as the Indian trails and pioneer wagon roads did 150 years ago when this outpost on the Deschutes was called Farewell Bend. Portland is three hours away via U.S. 97 and ORE 26, Salem is two hours away via ORE 20 and ORE 22, and Eugene is two hours away via ORE 20 and ORE 126. Crater Lake National Park is about two hours south down U.S. 97. There are also many loops worth investigating, like the Cascade Lakes Highway, Newberry Crater, and the Lava Lands, as well as other touring corridors.

You can rent a car for around $20 per day with 50 free miles daily from **Dorn Bothers Rentals** (148 N. Sixth, Redmond 97756; tel. 923-2027 in Redmond, tel. 382-2783 in Bend). They offer compact and midsize cars, passenger vans, four-by-fours, and pickups. Ski racks are also available. **Hertz** (1057 S.E. Third St., Bend; tel. 382-1711) and **Budget** (2060 U.S. 20 East, Bend; tel. 389-3031) are two national rental outfits also represented here.

NORTH OF BEND

North of the Bend-Redmond area, the roadsides lined with juniper and sage, and the fields of mint and wheat stand in welcome contrast to the malled-over main drags of central Oregon's biggest urban complex. The 500-foot-deep Crooked River Gorge (15 miles south of Madras off U.S. 97 at Ogden Scenic Wayside) and snow-capped vistas of Oregon's two highest mountains to the northeast (Mt. Hood and Mt. Jefferson) add further variety to the topography.

Rajneeshpuram
Throughout its history, north-central Oregon's topographic variety has been paralleled by the diversity of the human landscape here. Let's look at some of the more interesting fellow travelers:

The name Madras evokes the mystic East. While this central Oregon town has no such ties, it would have been hard to tell anyone that 10 years ago. Between 1981 and 1984 the population base of ranchers and farmers was augmented by thousands of red-clad disciples of Indian guru Bhagwan Shree Rajneesh. A 175,000-acre ranch was bought for the faithful near Antelope, a tiny community 30 miles northeast of Madras.

Although the commune demonstrated agricultural and architectural ingenuity, it was the Bhagwan's fleet of 96 Rolls Royces that got the headlines. When the Rajneeshees recruited homeless people to stuff the ballot box in local elections and then sent them away shortly thereafter, they compounded the bad first impression Oregonians had of their new neighbors. Before long, adverse publicity over the community's arsenal of combat weapons and their stated intent to use them alerted authorities to a potential threat. Fortunately, the Rajneeshees turned out to be more of a threat to themselves, with the Bhagwan's second-in-command implicated in everything from plots to murder the guru to the embezzlement of millions. Shortly before the dissolution of Rancho Rajneesh, the guru himself was deported because his vow of silence was inconsistent with a teaching visa. Today, the ranch is being converted into an environmental education campus.

Warm Springs Indian Reservation
In contrast to the here-today, gone-tomorrow legacy of Rajneeshpuram, the past lives on as more than a memory at the Warm Springs Indian Reservation, which straddles U.S. 26. Within this 600,000 acre bailiwick, you can see the age-old practice of dip-net fishing on the Deschutes, as well as the richest collection of tribal artifacts in the country at a 27,000-square-foot museum. Along with these touches of tradition, the reservation is the embodiment of the modern-day American dream, operating a dam, a resort hotel, and a lumber mill successfully. It's interesting to note that the employees of these enterprises are the descendants of the same Indians who greeted Lewis and Clark on the Columbia in 1805, as well as such Deschutes explorers as Peter Skene Ogden (in 1826), John Frémont, and Kit Carson (both in 1843).

Warm Springs Museum
Many travelers are eagerly awaiting the grand opening of the Warm Springs Museum. In addition to the rich cultural heritage of the Confederated Tribes of the Warm Springs, art and artifacts (over 20,000 pieces) from other regional native peoples will be displayed in this definitive interpretive center. If you're looking

ON THE TRAIL OF THE FIRST OREGONIANS

About five miles south of Warm Springs on U.S. 26, there's an eye-popping view of Mt. Jefferson's snow-capped volcano cone looming across 50 miles of sagebrush. The base of the mountain marks the western extent of the Warm Springs tribe's 1,000-square-mile reservation. You'll find a smaller but equally impressive display of the tribe's wealth at the **Museum at Warm Springs** (P.O. Box C, Warm Springs 97761; tel. 553-3331) located below the viewpoint at the bottom of the Deschutes River Canyon. Audiovisual displays, old photos, and tapes of traditional chants of the Paiute, Warm Springs, and Wasco peoples are aesthetically arrayed here. Each tribe's distinct culture and their coming together to form a thriving social and economic community define the major themes in the Northwest's only tribal museum. Replicas of a Paiute mat lodge, a Warm Springs tepee, and a Wasco plank house, along with recordings of each tribe's language, underscore this cultural richness and diversity. The exhibits, including items culled from a collection of more than 20,000 artifacts, range from a display of primitive prehistoric hand tools to a high-tech, push-button activated Wasco wedding scene. The museum is open daily 10-5 except Thanksgiving, New Years and Christmas Day; $5 admission, discounts for seniors and children.

Aficionados of Northwest native lore might want to take in the foregoing museum as part of a circuit including two other world-class exhibit halls: The High Desert Museum and The Maryhill Museum. Begin at the **High Desert Museum** (see "Bend and Vicinity" in the "High Cascades" chapter), a 90-minute drive south of Warm Springs on U.S. 97, 10 miles south of Bend. Exhibits here will give you an overview of the native peoples of the intermountain West and their land. Start with the "big picture" here, followed by the tribal exhibits at Warm Springs, then continue north on ORE 26 to ORE 35. Follow ORE 35 to I-84 in Hood River, head east on I-84 to The Dalles, and cross over the Columbia past The Dalles Dam via ORE 197. Once in Washington, take a right (north) on Highway 14. Keep an eye out for the Horsethief Lake State Park sign shortly and the petroglyphs on the rocks after you arrive on the Columbia's north shore. A little more than 20 miles up the road, near Goldendale, is the **Maryhill Museum** (Maryhill Museum Drive; tel. 509-773-3733). It's pretty hard to miss this large French chateau-style building surrealistically planted on the sparsely vegetated bluff above the Columbia. The museum is open daily 9-5, March 15-Nov. 15; adults pay $4 admission, seniors $3.50 and children 6-16 $1.50. Built by Sam Hill of Columbia Gorge Scenic Highway fame, the museum includes impressive Rodin plasters and chess sets spanning time and the globe, but the native baskets and clothing steal the show. The ground floor collection of native artifacts pays particular attention to the tribes along the Columbia, completing your perspective on the first residents of the Northwest.

It's best to take two or three days to complete this 170-mile museum circuit to do justice to the tribal legacy on display at all three museums.

---

for some fortification to help get you through the museum's extensive collections, get some wild huckleberry pie and a cup of coffee at the nearby **Deschutes River Crossing Restaurant.** A good place to pick up Indian crafts and souvenirs is the **Warm Springs Trading Post,** just across the parking lot from the Deschutes Crossing Restaurant on U.S. 26. Both are a quarter-mile south of the museum on the west side of the highway.

Petersen's Rock Garden

What began as one man's flight of fancy over the years has metamorphosed into a full-fledged rock fantasy. Petersen, a Danish immigrant farmer, created four acres of intricately detailed miniature castles, towers, and bridges made of agate, jasper, obsidian, malachite, petrified wood, and thunder eggs. The rock garden (7930 S.W. 77th St., Redmond 97756; tel. 382-5574) is free of charge and open 365 days a year 7 a.m.-9 p.m. (or till dusk in winter). To get there, take Gift Rd. off of U.S. 97 seven miles south of Redmond and 10 miles north of Bend. Follow the signs; it's only three miles off the highway. There is a very nice museum and gift shop in the rear of the complex that features many types of rocks, crystals, and semiprecious gemstones. In the back of the museum is the Fluorescent Room, in which little castles made of zinc, tungsten, uranium, and manganese glow in the dark. The staff will help direct rockhounds to promising sites in the vicinity to further their own collections. Admission is $2 for adults, $1 for children 6-16.

Richardson's Recreational Ranch

If you're a rockhound, you'll want to visit Richardson's Recreational Ranch (Gateway Route Box 440, Madras 97741; tel. 475-2680). This family-owned and -operated enterprise has extensive rock beds loaded with thunder eggs, moss agates, jaspers, jasper-agate, Oregon sunset, and rainbow agates. If you want to chip agates out of one of the many exposed ledges on the ranch, you will need to brings chisels, wedges, and other necessary hard-rock mining tools. Once you've completed your dig, you drop your rocks off at the office and pay for them by the pound. And if you don't care for dirt under your fingernails, you can always find rocks for sale from all over the world in the ranch's rock shop.

The motto here is "fun for everyone," and you're sure to meet many interesting "rocky fellers" back at the ranch. To get there, take U.S. 97 north of Madras for 11 miles and turn right at the sign near milepost 81. Follow the road for three miles to the ranch office.

Smith Rock State Park

The majestic spires towering above the Crooked River north of Redmond on U.S. 97 are part of this 623-acre state park. Named after a soldier who fell to his death off of the highest promontory (3,230 feet) in the configuration, the park is a popular retreat for hikers, rockclimbers, and casual visitors. Seven miles of well-marked trails follow the Crooked River and wend up the canyon walls to emerge on the ridgetops. Because the area is delicate and extremely sensitive to erosion, it's important not to blaze any trails because they may leave visible scars for years. Picnic tables, drinking water, and restrooms can be found near the parking area. The more adventurous can camp out in the park's primitive walk-in camping area.

While it's not exactly Yosemite, some of the climbing routes at Smith Rock are as difficult and challenging as any you'll find in the United States. Chocks, nuts, friends, and other clean-climbing equipment and techniques are encouraged here to reduce damage to the rock. On certain routes where these methods would prove impractical, permanent anchors have been placed. Climbers should use these fixed bolts (after testing them first for safety, of course) to minimize impact on the rock face. *Oregon Rock: A Climber's Guide* by Jeff Thomas has listings of all the routes at Smith Rock that do not require mounting of additional fixed protection. Climbers should never disturb birds of prey and their young in the lofty aeries.

As for more down-to-earth concerns, we recommend **La Siesta Mexican Restaurant** (8320 U.S. 97, Terrebonne; tel. 548-4898). Located on the south side of town in a nondescript crackerbox of a structure, this climber's favorite features such hard-to-find south-of-the-border specialties as nopal cactus, chorizo, and mole sauce. Moderate prices and dishes made from scratch make this an oasis in the culinary wastes of the high desert.

Shaniko

A half hour northeast of Madras is the ghost town of Shaniko. In its day, Shaniko was the largest wool-shipping center in the United States. The Columbia Southern railroad transported wool, sheep, cattle, gold, and people deep into the remote Oregon outback, and the city at the terminus prospered. Boomtown Shaniko had 13 saloons, stores, hotels, a schoolhouse, and a city hall. But when the railroad's mainline was diverted to the Deschutes River, Shaniko's prominence quickly faded.

Today you can still see many old buildings in Shaniko. The water tower provides a remarkable display of the jerry-rigged but nonetheless efficient water-distribution system. The three-room Shaniko schoolhouse (built in 1901) and City Hall, featuring the Constable's office and the jail, are also still standing. If you'd like to overnight here, the moderately priced **Shaniko Historic Hotel** (Shaniko 97057; tel. 489-3441) has been restored and combines the ambience of the past with modern comforts.

MOUNT HOOD

HIKING AND CAMPING

Mount Hood Climbs

Mt. Hood, at 11,235 feet the highest mountain in Oregon, has the additional distinction of being the second-most-climbed glacier-covered peak in the world. Nicknamed the "Fujiyama of America," there are hikes up Mt. Hood that cater to everyone, from beginners to advanced climbers. Another similarity to its Japanese counterpart is that there are only about two months out of the year that are safe for climbing, from May to mid-July. (Many mountaineers feel that the safe climbing season terminates at the end of July.)

Since the summer heat brings on the threat of avalanche danger and rockfall hazards, the time of day of your departure is just as important as the time of year. Most expeditions depart in the wee hours of the morning when the snow is firm and rockfall danger is lessened. Though you won't get as much sleep, you will be able to enjoy beautiful sunrise scenery as you venture to the top of the world—in Oregon, that is.

There are a few short and easy hikes from Timberline Lodge that require basic day-hiking equipment—hiking boots, water, snacks, sunglasses, sunscreen, and warm, waterproof clothing (since the weather can change rapidly, even in midsummer). Those intent upon reaching the top of the mountain, however, had best go prepared. In addition to the previously mentioned supplies, an ice axe, crampons and extra straps, extra clothing and food, first-aid kit, at least a quart of water, CB radio, topographic map and compass, and a 120-foot rope are necessary. Your boots should be waterproof and well insulated, because the final 3,000 feet in elevation is over glaciers and snowfields. Wool is the best material for keeping warm; wool socks (take an extra pair for emergency mittens), mittens, hat, sweater, and pants will keep you warm even when wet. A warm, water-resistant jacket is also a good idea.

While the climb looks like only a few miles on the map, it takes 10-15 hours to make the trip from Timberline Lodge to the top and back. The four primary routes up Mt. Hood—Hogsback, Mazama, Wyeast, and Castle Crags—are all *technical* climbs; there is no hiking trail to the summit. Having the right equipment means little if you don't know how to use it. It takes a minimum of three people to compose a safe party (many solo adventurers here have ended up decomposing), and you should have a competent and experienced leader in command. Always register at the lodge before climbing and check out when you return.

Most climbing deaths and injuries are avoidable. Dangers like falling ice, rock, and snow, gaping crevasses, and the temperamental mountain weather can all be surmounted with planning, preparedness, and common sense. The ultimate safety device became available several years ago. For $5 (for three days), climbers can rent a one- by two-inch transmitter at several Portland-area mountain shops. It gives off a signal which will enable search and rescue teams to find you. Be one of the hundreds of thousands of happy hikers who have successfully reached the summit and back, not another unfortunate statistic claimed by Old Man Mountain. For info on climbing guides (as well as Alpine and Nordic ski instructors), contact the **Mt. Hood Recreation Association** (68260 E. Welches Rd., Welches 97067; tel. 622-3017).

Hogsback

Of the four routes to the summit departing from Timberline Lodge, Hogsback is the most climbed. A good trip for beginners, the climb takes an average 10-12 hours roundtrip. The first mile ascends 1,000 feet and ends at the Silcox Warming Hut. Built in 1939, this rustic stone-and-timber shelter used to house the upper terminal of the original Magic Mile chair lift. This was the second chair lift built in the country, the first to use steel towers, and the nation's oldest operating chair lift until it was discontinued in 1962. This first leg of the climb is a good short hike for those who want to stay in the mellow zone. Now undergoing restoration, Silcox will soon be a dorm-style lodging unit with all of the amenities. Call the main desk at Timberline Lodge (tel. 231-7929) for details.

The trail continues up Palmer Glacier and onto White River Glacier. You climb up the glacier between Crater Rock and the Steel Cliffs and soon reach the saddle above Crater Rock. From here you stay on the saddle and head for the chute that leads to the summit. **Mazama** is a variation on Hogsback, and is a good route for your second climb. You would cross the saddle above Crater Rock and reach the summit going up the chute on the far left of the rock outcroppings.

Wyeast
An intermediate route for experienced climbers is Wyeast, which averages 12-14 hours roundtrip. About a half mile above Silcox Warming Hut, you would cross over White River Glacier and reach the saddle of the Steel Cliffs. From there you follow the saddle on up to the top. It doesn't go over as much snow, but the rocks on the ridge of the Steel Cliffs are dangerous and require expertise.

Castle Crags
Castle Crags offers an advanced route for experienced climbers. Because this trail goes over Illumination Rock and the Hot Rocks, climbers must go when the ice and rock are solid during January through April. Adding to the dangers of bona fide rock-climbing is the everpresent threat of winter weather. Disorienting whiteout conditions, frigid cold, and wicked gale-force winds compound the hardships already imposed by the grueling trail. This 12- to 14-hour roundtrip should only be attempted by serious climbers when the weather conditions are right.

Buried Forest Overlook
If the snowbound summit is not for you, an easier one-mile roundtrip hike is the Buried Forest Overlook. This overlook provides a dramatic view of the White River Canyon, where a thick forest was buried during one of the mountain's major eruptive periods about 200-250 years ago. Superheated gases blew down giant trees like matchsticks, and in the next instant, all was buried underneath a mixture of water, ash, and mud. The erosional forces of wind and water have since exposed the remains of the Buried Forest. To get there, follow one of the trails behind Timberline Lodge up the mountain about a quarter mile until you reach the Pacific Crest National Scenic Trail. Turn east (right) onto the Pacific Crest Trail and follow it another quarter mile or so to the overlook.

Mt. Hood Hiking
Hikes in the **Zigzag Ranger District** (70220 E. U.S. 26, Zigzag 97049; tel. 666-0704, or tel. 622-3191 from Portland) are an excellent introduction to the wealth of recreation options in the

glacier-covered Mt. Hood, above Trillium Lake

OREGON STATE HIGHWAYS

THAR SHE BLOWS!

In the past, Mt. Hood and Mt. St. Helens in Washington have shared many periods of volcanic activity. Although the 1980 eruption of Mt. St. Helens has given her more name recognition and public awareness than her Oregon counterpart, Mt. Hood is nonetheless a slumbering giant that occasionally snores loudly. Consider that six eruptions were recorded on Mt. Hood in the mid-1800s, with the last one in 1907. According to a carbon-dated four- to six-inch layer of ash found on the northeast and southeast flanks of the mountain, Lewis and Clark just missed the 1804 eruption. And with smoky emissions coming out of Mt. Hood fumaroles in the 1980s, scientists have placed sensitive seismic monitoring equipment to keep tabs on the volcano.

While Old Man Mountain still appears to be sleeping, the Portland Office of Emergency Management has drafted contingency plans for worst-case scenarios. Portland is located far enough away to be out of range of most volcanic debris, but its water source would be cut off. Portland relies upon the bountiful Bull Run watershed located on Mt. Hood, and ash and mudflows from a major eruption would have devastating effects upon the city's water supply. Giant mudflows into the Columbia River present another threat, which could precipitate downstream flooding.

The federal government has also gotten involved by developing complex evacuation plans for the foothill communities of Sandy and Hood River. The residents may be lucky enough to escape with their hides intact, but the lush fields and well-groomed orchards on the northeastern side of the mountain would very likely be blanketed with ash and debris and sound the death knell to the local way of life. The loss of this major agricultural resource would have statewide repercussions. The timber industry would also be hard hit by a major eruption. In addition to thousands of square miles of stumpage destroyed by mud, ash, and lava flows, scientists suggest that there would be a high probability of forest fires as well. Like the fruit growers of the Hood River Valley, the region's loggers would be hard-pressed to eke out a living from the charred ground should the mountain ever blow.

The good news is that the aftereffects of a volcanic eruption are eventually softened with time. In the wake of the Mt. St. Helens blast, insects, vegetation, and wildlife returned to the area within a year or two. Farmers in eastern Washington who saw their crops destroyed in 1980 are now enjoying bumper yields due to the soil's increased fertility. Nonetheless, in an era of worldwide earthquakes and volcanic eruptions, many locals look to the mountain and wonder if it will soon be Mt. Hood's turn to roar.

Mt. Hood National Forest off U.S. 26. Whether you're driving the whole Mt. Hood Loop (U.S. 26 to ORE 35 to I-84) or just looking for a nice day-trip from the Portland area, the Zigzag District's relatively low elevation and spectacular views of the state's highest mountain can be enjoyed by neophyte hikers or trailwise veterans.

Coming from Portland, take I-84 to the Wood Village exit and follow the Mt. Hood Loop signs to U.S. 26. After leaving Sandy, you'll notice fruit stands and the Wasson Brothers Winery tasting room (41901 U.S. 26, Sandy; tel. 668-3124) which can help provision a picnic on the slopes. En route to the trailheads, U.S. 26 is often lined with vehicles during winter ski weekends and summer vacation, with less traffic during the best hiking seasons, spring and fall.

The first stop you'll want to make is at the **Mt. Hood Visitor Center** (65000 E. U.S. 26, Welches 97028), located in Mt. Hood RV park

on the south side of the highway. This facility will help you get your bearings, with a wealth of pamphlets and an information desk. Pick up the free Forest Service flier "Mt Hood Hikes" here or a few miles up the road at the Zigzag Ranger Station. Of the 15 trails outlined in the Zigzag District, we've chosen one hike as a maiden voyage into this magical realm. Our criteria include ease of hiking, proximity to Portland, and aesthetic appeal. Unfortunately, the latter qualities have also made the **Ramona Falls Trail** perhaps the most traveled wilderness byway on the mountain. With judicious planning, however, you can avoid peak-use times. To reach Ramona Falls drive 18 miles east of Sandy on U.S. 26 to Lolo Pass Rd., close by the ranger station. This route (Route 18) heads north from the Zigzag store, eventually leading up to Lost Lake, whose views of Mt. Hood have graced many a postcard.

But instead of going all the way to the lake, you will want to go five miles up Lolo Pass Rd. to Forest Service Rd. 1825. From here, you'll take the road about four miles to its end. Just prior to reaching the main parking area, ignore the spur to the upper lot unless you have an especially roadworthy vehicle. The trip on this back road can create misgivings, as there are a dearth of signs indicating Ramona Falls. Once you've parked, however, all you need to do is follow the trail paralleling the Sandy River. In a little more than a mile you'll come to a bridge over the river with a pretty view of Mt. Hood. On the other side of the river, Trail 797 will get you to Ramona Falls in about two miles. The grade of the slope is gentle throughout, and while much of the trail isn't especially scenic (except for a bridge over the Sandy River, June rhododendrons, and views of Mt. Hood), Ramona Falls itself makes it all worthwhile. Imagine a multitude of cascades coursing over a 100-foot-high, 50-foot-wide series of basalt outcroppings. This weeping wall is set in a grove of gargantuan Douglas firs. The spray beneath this canopy of trees can drop the temperature 20° F, making the place a popular retreat on hot summer days. In the winter the trail makes a great cross-country ski run. In warmer times of the year, Ramona Falls is a popular equestrian trail.

After you've tackled Ramona Falls, other daytrips include the **Old Salmon River Trail** through lush old growth and the **Flag Mountain Trail** for extraordinary views of Mt. Hood. Supplement your hiking information with the TRIS screen at the ranger station. In addition to Zigzag-area jaunts, you could spend a year hiking all the trails described by the pamphlet in the several other ranger districts around the mountain.

More ambitious trekkers will take on the 36-mile Timberline Trail, a three- to five-day backpack usually begun at Timberline Lodge. If you undertake this loop, you'll finish up back at the lodge to cool off in the showers or swimming pool. While the alpine meadows on the Timberline Trail are beautiful, consult the rangers to see if water in the half-dozen creeks passed en route is too high during the June and July snowmelt seasons.

With almost two dozen trails branching off the Timberline, opportunities for shorter daytrip loop hikes abound. Most of the main trail follows the base of the mountain near timberline at elevations of 5,000 to 7,000 feet. On the northwest side, however, it drops to 3,000 feet and merges with the Pacific Crest Trail.

Camping
Set along the banks of the Salmon River is **Green Canyon** (Zigzag Ranger District, 70220 E. U.S. 26, Zigzag 97049; tel. 622-3191 or 666-0704 from Portland). This is the same contact for the next six campgrounds. Here you'll find 15 campsites for tents and RVs (31 feet maximum), with picnic tables and firegrills, piped water, pit toilets, and firewood available. Green Canyon is open from May to late Sept., and the fee is $5-7 per night, depending upon the site. Nearby is a trail that goes through the old-growth forests lining the Salmon River and past several waterfalls. A store and a cafe are about five miles away. To get there, go to Zigzag on U.S. 26 and take Salmon River Rd. (2618) four miles to the campground. Superlative hiking is close by. The Salmon River Gorge, with many waterfalls, volcanic plugs, and forested cliffs, is accessed by a trail several hundred feet above the river.

Near the replica of the Barlow Road Tollgate is **Tollgate.** Set along the banks of the Zigzag River, this campground has 23 tent sites and nine RV sites (22 feet maximum) with picnic tables and firegrills. Water, pit toilets, and firewood are also available. Open from late May to late Sept., the campground costs $5-7 per night. While it's one of the more primitive campgrounds in the area, it's close to the Mt. Hood Wilderness and many hiking trails. Take U.S. 26 one mile past Rhododendron to get there.

Situated on the Clear Fork of the Sandy River, **McNeil** has a good view of Mt. Hood. The campground has 34 sites for tents and RVs (22 feet maximum) with picnic tables and firegrills. Piped water, vault toilets, and firewood are also available. Open May to late Sept., McNeil charges $3-7 per night. To get there, turn onto Lolo Pass Rd. (County Route 18) at Zigzag and follow it for four miles. Turn right onto Forest Service Rd. 1825 and follow signs to the campground, about a mile farther. For a beautiful drive, go back to Lolo Pass Rd. and make a right, heading over the pass 25 miles to Dee. It takes about an hour if you drive straight there, but allow another 15 minutes for photo stops from Lost Lake, located on a spur road. Lolo Pass Road's gravel surface sees a fair amount of log trucks during the week so be careful. From Dee it takes 25 minutes to reach I-84 to loop back to Portland.

A popular place for a night out in the woods is **Camp Creek.** This campground has 30 sites for tents and RVs (22 feet maximum), with piped water, picnic tables, and firegrills. Flush toilets and firewood are also available. Open from late May to late Sept., Camp Creek charges $5 per night. Situated along Camp Creek not far from the Zigzag River, the campground has double campsites that two parties can share. To get there, go three miles east of Rhododendron on U.S. 26 and turn south to the campground.

About a mile down the road from Timberline Lodge is **Alpine.** The high-elevation setting here lives up to its name, with snow remaining on the ground until late in the summer during heavy snow years. There are 16 campsites for tents and trailers (22 feet maximum), plus piped water, picnic tables, and firegrills. Alpine is open July to late Sept., and the fee is $6 per night. In addition to summer skiing up at Mt. Hood, the Pacific Crest Trail passes by very close to the camp.

Near the junction of U.S. 26 and ORE 35 is **Still Creek.** Here you'll find 27 sites for tents and RVs (30 feet maximum), with picnic tables and firegrills. Piped water, pit toilets, and firewood are also available. Open from mid-June to late Sept., Still Creek costs $7 per night. The campground has many large trees and is close to the Old Swim Hot Springs Resort, a pioneer cemetery, and Trillium Lake.

A good place for a base camp for those who like to canoe is at **Trillium Lake.** There are 30 sites for tents and RVs (30 feet maximum), with picnic tables and firegrills. Piped water and vault toilets are also available; boat docking and launching facilities are nearby, but no motorized craft are permitted on the lake. The campground is open from late May to late Sept., and costs $6-8 per night, depending upon the site. To get there, take U.S. 26 two miles southeast of Government Camp, then turn right onto Forest Service Rd. 2656. Proceed for one mile to the campground.

The area also holds landmarks for the history buff. Near the lake is Summit Meadow, where Barlow Trail emigrants camped. The Barlow

Road completed the Oregon Trail as a land route from Independence, Missouri, to the Willamette Valley. The route spared the emigrants hazardous passage on the Columbia from The Dalles to Ft. Vancouver. The Barlow Road parallels U.S. 26 for much of the way here. Near Summit is a pioneer cemetery with names scratched into the surfaces of boulders. The Zigzag Ranger Station can supply good maps and describe other historic sites on the old Barlow Trail.

On ORE 35, signs a few miles north of its junction with U.S. 26 indicate Barlow Road in the Barlow Pass area. The Barlow Road opened in the fall of 1845, when an estimated 145 wagons and 1,000 emigrants attempted the crossing. They brought with them 1,600 horses, mules, and cattle, plus 13 sheep. The toll was $5 per wagon and 10 cents a head for the livestock. The road continued to serve as an east-west conduit over the Cascades long after it gained its status as the last leg of the Oregon Trail, seeing significant traffic until 1919.

As you climb up Barlow Pass on ORE 35, look for the sign on the right-hand side of the highway. By following the access road in, you can veer left (on foot) to the Barlow Road or continue by car to the end of the lot, where a foot trail to a pioneer woman's grave is indicated by a sign on the west side of the parking area. Less intrepid hikers can avoid the steep walk down to the grave and still get a "you-are-there" feeling by going 70 yards to the trail's junction with the original wagon road. Here on these steep slopes, it's easy to imagine the wagons being hitched to trees along the slope to prevent runaways. In an area called Laurel Hill farther down the trail, rope marks from this effort still remain as testimonials to pioneer travails.

A spot that offers good fishing, swimming, and sailboarding is **Clear Lake** (Bear Springs Ranger District, Route 1, Box 222, Maupin 97037; tel. 328-6211). Here you'll find 28 tent and RV sites (22 feet maximum) with picnic tables and firegrills. Piped water, vault toilets, and firewood are also available. Clear Lake is open late May to early Sept., and the fee is $6-8 per night. Boat docking and launching facilities are nearby, and motorized craft are allowed on the lake. To get there, go nine miles southwest of Government Camp on U.S. 26, then one mile south on Forest Service Rd. 449 to the campground.

A midsized county park called **Toll Bridge** (7360 Toll Bridge, Parkdale 97041; tel. 352-6300) is located 18 miles south of Hood River on ORE 35. This campground has 18 tent and 20 RV (20 feet maximum) sites with electricity, piped water, sewer hookups, and picnic tables. Flush toilets, showers, firewood, a recreation hall, and a playground are also featured. Open April-Nov. (and weekends during the off-season, weather permitting), $13-20 per night. Set along the banks of the Hood River, this campground includes bike trails, hiking trails, and tennis courts.

PRACTICALITIES

Accommodations

Since Mt. Hood is only an hour away from Portland, most people return to the city instead of staying at one of the commercial properties on the loop. But if you do want to make a night of it on Mt. Hood, forgo the ersatz Swiss ski chalets, follow the signs from ORE 26, and step into history at **Timberline Lodge** (Timberline 97208; tel. 800-452-1335 from outside Oregon, 231-7979 in-state). This is Oregon's Hall of the Mountain King, whose alpine setting and WPA-commissioned interior decor make it a cherished landmark of the Northwest. Room rates ranging between $50 and $150 make it as affordable as a garden-variety ski condo, and numerous bargain ski packages also help lay out the welcome mat.

The Lodge's "chalet rooms" with bunk beds are $50 a night, with $8 charged for each additional guest. Minutes away from Timberline's 1,100-pound door is a ski lift, your magic carpet to the slopes and, during the summer, to an array of wildflowers and superlative views. Other Timberline claims to fame are pioneer and Indian motifs to match the mountain. Hand-forged wrought-iron light fixtures and handwoven draperies and upholstery complement the 92-foot-high fireplace and floor-to-ceiling windows in the lobby. Finally, listen to FDR's dedication speech in the Exhibition Center on the main entry level and take in the scale model of Mt. Hood in the day lodge (push buttons to call up information).

The food in the award-winning Cascade Dining Room is outstanding, particularly the vine-maple-cured salmon. Spirits can be purchased there, and in the Ram's Head bar, and the Blue Ox bar. After a long day skiing the challenging slopes here, you'll relish a soak in the outdoor heated pool, especially enjoyable in the middle of a snowstorm or on cold, clear nights under a full moon.

There are plenty of cabin rentals available to those looking for après-ski ambience in an intimate setting. One that has enjoyed particularly good word of mouth is **Cedar Grove Cottage** (23782 E. Sampson Ave., Welches 97067; tel. 622-3952). Reservations are a must on this secluded forested acre a quarter mile away from the Sandy River. En route to the banks of the Sandy, you'll enjoy birdwatching and huckleberries during summer. Back inside the cottage, there's one bedroom with a queen-sized bed and a loft with a double futon (sleeps four). Added amenities include a well-appointed kitchen, a redwood shower, a fireplace, a stocked bookshelf, prints by Northwest artists adorning the walls, and a five-person outdoor spa on the connecting deck. Cedar Grove Cottage sits 30 minutes away from Timberline's ski slopes, about an hour from Portland, and within walking distance to shops and restaurants in nearby Welches. With rates of $100 per night for two or more nights (Mon.-Thurs. get three nights for the price of two), this hideaway is perfect for a special romantic retreat or a get-away-from-it-all family vacation.

Food

It doesn't really matter what you've been up to on the mountain. Whether you've been skiing, hiking, climbing, or biking, the end result is usually the same by the time you get down the hill. You're hungry. The Mt. Hood corridor is blessed with several eateries that fit most any mood and pocketbook. From fast food on the fly to leisurely gourmet dining, it's all here on the loop.

Twenty years ago, chef Kurt Mezger got tired of cooking for the Benson Hotel in Portland, so he bought the **Chalet Swiss** (U.S. 26 at Welches Rd., Welches; tel. 622-3600). The formality and high prices of his alma mater are left far behind, but the quality of the cuisine remains outstanding. Ten Swiss and other continental entrees are backed up with Northwest seafood specialties and premium cuts of beef. The Chalet also boasts one of the best wine lists on the mountain. Full-course meals range from $10 to $25 and can take an hour or two from appetizer to aperitif. À la carte selections ranging from $5 to $15 and wine by the glass provide quicker and lighter alternatives. Open for dinner only Wed.-Sat. 5-10 p.m., 5-9 on Sunday.

One mile west of Zigzag on U.S. 26 in Wemme is **The Inn Between** (tel. 622-5400). Open for lunch and dinner, here you can tour the taps (a dozen draft beers are available) and enjoy a steak cooked just the way you like it (because you can supervise how it's cooked yourself). Tuesday night is when steak prices drop to $7.95 for the 12-ouncer and $6.95 for the smaller version. If you've got a beef against red meat, the Inn can prepare a feast to suit even the most discriminating of vegetarian palates. Seafood specialties, teriyaki chicken, and gourmet sandwiches are also among the many offerings. For lighter appetites, a variety of salads and delicious homemade soups are also available. On Monday nights, in addition to the football game on the big-screen TV, the Inn features 75-cent tacos that will fill you up in a hurry. If you're only here for the large selection of microbrews, try some barbecued ribs in the Inn's secret zesty sauce, or perhaps the "Macho Nachos" to keep your blood-alcohol level reasonable.

European specialties on the order of goulash and pasta typify the hearty dishes on the menu of the **Ivy Bear** (U.S. 26, eight miles east of Sandy; tel. 622-3476). It's open for dinner Tues.-Sun., 4-10 p.m.

Follow U.S 26 to the west end of Government Camp and you'll find the **Mt. Hood Brewing Company** (tel. 272-3724). Fresh, casual foods can be washed down by microbrews, espresso drinks, and local wines here. Also in town is the **Huckleberry Inn,** which deserves mention if only for its 24-hour, seven-days-a-week restaurant and, you guessed it, wild huckleberry pie. The Inn's $15 pp dormitory rooms also provide welcome respite for rained-out campers on a budget.

Another popular eatery in the shadow of Mt. Hood is the **Barlow Trail Inn** (9580 East U.S. 26, Zigzag; tel. 622-3877). Open from 6 a.m. to 2 a.m., the Inn features excellent three-egg omelettes that will keep you energized all day long. Vegetarians are sure to enjoy the marinara spaghetti ($5.25) or the veggie garden burger made with mushrooms, nuts, oats, and low-fat mozzarella. Homemade chili, chicken dinners, and moderately priced steak and seafood round out the menu.

If you want to spice up your evening, consider **Los Amigos Spanish Restaurant** (46881 S.E. U.S. 26, Sandy; tel. 668-5444). You won't need a cast-iron stomach to eat here, because the food is cooked Spanish style, not jalapeños-by-the-truckload Tex-Mex style. The sauces, tamales, and chorizo are all prepared on the premises, delicately seasoned with chili powder, Mexican oregano, cumin, garlic, and onions. Try the enchilada grande, a flavorful blend of ground beef and chorizo rolled in a corn tortilla and topped with a delectable sauce. The Los Amigos sopaipilla also differs from what other south-of-the-border greasy spoons provide. Instead of a flat, oily, and overly sugared concoction, the sopaipilla here is a yeast-risen bread that's grilled up fresh for you. Prepare to feast in a pleasant, smoke-free environment without having to mortgage the homestead to pay for it.

SOUTHEASTERN OREGON
LAKE COUNTY

One of Oregon's three largest counties, Lake County covers 8,359 square miles and yet has only a smidgen over 8,000 inhabitants. In other words, there's lots of elbow room, with the population density working out to about one person per square mile. This land of open spaces and geologic marvels is home to a hardy breed that clings to the traditions of the Old West. Cowboys herd cattle on horseback, itinerant prospectors dig for color in the Quartz Mountains, and homesteaders tend to their farms in the remote outback. The county is called the Gem of Oregon because of the stark beauty of wide-ranging vistas beneath skies of pastel blue, and because the region is the best place to find Oregon's official gemstone, the Plush diamond, a type of spangled glass also called aventurine.

Visitors can climb the ancient citadel of Fort Rock, camp along a high mountain stream in Fremont National Forest, soak their bones in the soothing mineral waters of Hunter Hot Springs, or watch the graceful strides of antelope as they cross the uplands of Hart Mountain National Antelope Refuge. In addition to enjoying outdoor activities year-round, the people of Lake County are an active bunch with a busy calendar of rodeos, fairs, and celebrations.

The climate here is generally cool and semiarid with 250 days of sunshine a year. Summer temperatures stay in the mid-80s, while winter temperatures drop to the low 30s with precipitation averaging about 16 inches a year. This area can be a harsh land with little tolerance for the foolish, so take sensible precautions like toting extra water and gas. Despite a low density of creature comforts, you'll enjoy exploring this high desert country loaded to its sandy brim with wonders found nowhere else.

HISTORY

The history of human occupation here has been dated back 13,200 years through Dr. Luther Cressman's exploratory work at Fort Rock Cave. Early desert dwellers who roamed the Great

SOUTHEAST OREGON

© MOON PUBLICATIONS, INC.

Basin in search of game and food witnessed the eruption of Mt. Mazama 6,000 years ago. Their descendants, the Northern Paiutes, were also hunter-gatherers. This Lake County tribe was known as the "Groundhog Eaters."

The first Europeans to venture into the area were French Canadian trappers working for the Hudson's Bay Company in the early 1800s. Seeking out beaver pelts for the fashion trade back east and in Europe—the guard hairs of North America's largest rodent were used in the manufacture of felt hats, much coveted by the aristocracy of the time—these trappers were eventually joined by American mountain men. It wasn't until 1825 that Peter Skene Ogden, chief trader for the HBC, made an "official" tour of the area when he sensed the threat of an American incursion. John Frémont and a party guided by Kit Carson marched through here in 1843, naming Summer and Abert lakes.

The journals kept during these expeditions noted broad valleys with grasses "belly-high to a horse." This information attracted a new cast of players to the Great Basin, the cattle and sheep barons. With the passage of the Homestead Act in 1862, homesteaders moved in and started up more modest spreads. The white influx resulted in frequent tensions with the original occupants, which often culminated in bloodletting on both sides. But after the Bannock-Paiute uprising in 1878, the local natives were herded up and banished to a reservation.

This predictable quick fix eased the trouble on the frontier and led to a growth spurt. The town of Lakeview was chartered in 1889; it burned to the ground the following year and was rebuilt with brick and corrugated-iron roofs. Other hopeful hamlets with names like Arrow, Buffalo, and Loma Vista sprang up around the county. Many of these tiny burgs dried up and blew away after the two-year drought of 1918-20. However, the larger communities like Lakeview, Paisley, and Summer Lake held on. With the advent of refrigerated railroad cars, big ranchers prospered, selling beef to our "hamburger nation." Local farmers figured out how to irrigate and cultivate this ornery land, and those tough enough to survive eventually came to terms with life on the dry side. Nonetheless, because riparian rights are still being clarified, many underground water tables are being drained, raising the specter of another prolonged dry spell here.

SIGHTS: LA PINE TO LAKEVIEW

Lake County has some of the most intriguing geological formations in the Northwest. The following is a tour of a few of these marvels, starting at the junction of U.S. 97 and ORE 31 at La Pine. Evidence of the cataclysmic forces that shaped the Columbia plateau and the Great Basin are on display in this starkly beautiful part of the state. Ruptures in the ground and wave patterns left by ancient lakes on the flanks of mountains are some of these fingerprints left here by the hand of nature. Many sites described in the itinerary are annotated in the BLM's "Christmas Valley" brochure (BLM Lakeview office, 1000 E. Ninth St., Lakeview 97630) and a Forest Service brochure (Fort Rock Ranger District, 1230 N.E. Third, Bend 97701). Better yet, refer

OREGON DEPT. OF TRANSPORTATION

The 325-foot-high Fort Rock is visible from miles away.

to pages 101-105 of *Back Country Byways* by Stewart Green (Falcon Press, 1991) for a complete description of the remote routes to these phenomena. A four-wheel-drive vehicle is indispensable in this region if you value your oil pan.

Cracks And Caves

Twenty-six miles down ORE 31 is **Hole-in-the-Ground,** a curiosity located a mile off the highway. Although this 500-foot-deep indentation looks like a meteor crater, scientists believe that molten lava came into contact with water here, causing a massive explosion that quarried out the quarter-acre pit. Astronauts came here in 1966 to experience its lunarlike terrain. About five miles farther down the road is **Fort Rock Cave.** Sandals woven from sagebrush and dated at over 9,000 years old were found here in 1938 by anthropologist Luther Cressman.

Not far from the cave is **Fort Rock,** which towers 325 feet above the sagebrush plains. At the base of this tuff ring is an area of wave erosion cut by a long-disappeared lake. Fall and winter here offer wildlife viewing par excellence, particularly large herds of mule deer, mid-November to mid-April. Pronghorn can be seen year-round in the alfalfa fields. **Fort Rock State Park** offers trails and amenities for climbers and sightseers. The nearby town of Fort Rock has an old-time flavor that has been accentuated by the recent restoration of homestead cabins in a pioneer village managed by the **Fort Rock Valley Historical Society** (tel. 576-2327).

An interesting journey down into the bowels of the earth is offered at **Derrick Cave,** located 22 miles north of Fort Rock. This large lava tube is a half-mile long, with rooms up to 40 feet wide and 60 feet high. During the Cuban missile crisis of the early 1960s, the cave was turned into a fallout shelter. Metal doors were installed and provisions for 1,000 people were stockpiled. Fortunately, cooler heads prevailed and a nuclear confrontation was avoided. The supplies were plundered by vandals and the cave's civil-defense status was eventually dropped.

If you drive six miles north of Christmas Valley on a rough BLM road, you'll come to another break in terra firma that'll keep your imagination working overtime. **Crack-in-the-Ground** is about two miles long, 10-15 feet wide, and

up to 70 feet deep. According to geologists, this dramatic fissure has been open for at least 1,000 years. A BLM picnic area is at one end of this curious landmark.

Five miles northwest of Crack-in-the-Ground (on rough BLM Road 6109C) is Green Mountain Campround and fire lookout, which sits high above the previously mentioned Derrick Cave site. This primitive campground (large enough for three cars but without water or toilets) atop a small cinder cone overlooks hundreds of square miles of high desert, lava beds, and forest from 5,190 feet above sea level. In addition to Christmas Valley and Fort Rock Valley, snowcapped Diamond Peak lies 70 miles to the west, and Wagontire Mountain is 50 miles east.

Fossil Lake

Fossil Lake is two miles east of Christmas Valley. This was once a watering hole for camels, mammoths, and miniature horses during wetter times thousands of years ago. It was once part of a much larger body of water in the Fort Rock basin that was perhaps 40 miles wide and 200 feet deep. The water and animals disappeared when the climate changed, but their fossilized remains are still unearthed by paleontologists on sanctioned digs. Be aware that it is illegal to remove *any* fossils from the beds without proper authorization. Unfortunately, unscrupulous profiteers have been looting these timeless treasures from the lake and other fossil-rich sites in eastern Oregon. Be sure to notify the authorities immediately if you see any suspicious characters pilfering these valuable relics.

Lost Forest

An unusual sight in this area is located 10 miles northeast of Christmas Valley on a rough but passable BLM road. A 9,000-acre stand of ponderosa pines intermixed with the largest juniper trees in Oregon is all that is left of an ancient grove that dates back thousands of years. Surprisingly, studies of tree rings show that this area has received only nine inches of rain a year for the last 600 years, half the amount normally needed to sustain growth of ponderosa pines. But here, a layer of sand beneath the surface traps and retains enough moisture to allow the trees to survive. This island of green is 40 miles away from the nearest forest, accentuating the isolation and solitude of these stately sentinels. Many of the junipers here are over a thousand years old. On hot summer days, this place is a welcome source of shade. Any time of year, the sound of the desert wind through the trees can stir contemplation. The final three miles of the approach to Lost Forest require high vehicle clearance. To reach the area, drive eight miles east of the Christmas Valley post office, go eight miles north, and then eight miles east. The forest borders the largest inland sand dunes in the state.

Summer Lake

Summer Lake lies 15 miles beyond Silver Lake. The old Harris school on ORE 31 in the town of Summer Lake is worth a picture. This classic one-room schoolhouse, complete with bell tower, is straight out of *Little House on the Prairie*. The highway also passes through the **Summer Lake Wildlife Area**, home to 170 species of migratory birds. Spring is the best time to see snow geese, avocets, black-necked stilts, and snowy plovers. Summer Lake Hot Springs, on the southern tip of Summer Lake, is a private operation open seven days a week 9 a.m.-9 p.m. during summer, and Sat.-Thurs. 9-6 during winter. A dip in the concrete pool costs $2 for people six and over, free to children under six.

The region surrounding Summer Lake sits at the interface of desert and mixed conifer forest. Abundant wildlife, geological wonders, Indian sites, and historic structures here beckon further investigation. A good base for such explorations is **Summer Lake B&B Ranch** (Summer Lake 97640; tel. 943-3983). Situated along the shore of the lake, this reconstructed pioneer homestead is paneled with a variety of wood including redwood, cedar, oak, pine, fir, and myrtlewood. The feeling of warmth is enhanced by Darrell Seven, the innkeeper, whose flair for interior decorating, gourmet cooking, and sharing of local anecdotes compels a stay here as much as the beautiful outdoor environment does. Rates are $50 to $60 a night.

Paisley

A few miles south of the lake is the cowtown of Paisley. At the **Paisley Ranger Compound** there are several structures built by the Civil-ian Conservation Corps during the Depression. Check out the pine dugout canoe carved by CCC workers for Forest Service personnel.

If you're getting a little hungry, there are a couple of eateries in Paisley that will satisfy your cravings. The **Homestead Restaurant** (tel. 943-3187) is the full-service establishment in the locale, serving breakfast, lunch, and dinner. The soup du jour complemented with a sandwich makes a good lunch, and be sure to save room for the homemade cobbler. The local watering hole, **Pioneer Saloon** (tel. 943-3289), doubles as a family eating place. Pizza, steaks, and Mexican food are among the offerings on the menu here.

Lakeview

The "big city" of the county (population 1,800, elevation 1,800) is Lakeview, where some interesting repositories of history can be found. The **Schminck Memorial Museum** (128 S.E. Lakeview; tel. 947-3134) has over 5,000 antiques assembled by the Oregon chapter of the Daughters of the American Revolution, and is open Tues.-Sat. 1-5 p.m. or by appointment. **Indian Village** (508 N. First; tel. 947-2833) boasts one of the west's largest arrowhead collections. The complex also has a restaurant and lounge that features eye-opening specials like scrambled eggs with diced mushrooms, toast, and coffee for $2. The gift shop offers turquoise and silver jewelry and, oddly enough, is where many working people buy their flannel shirts and cowboy hats. If you're in the mood for something different, cruise 15 miles south of Lakeview on U.S. 395 to **Stringer's**. In addition to fine gifts, they claim to produce the world's only wild-plum wine and wild-plum jam.

Abert Rim

Fifteen miles north of Lakeview on U.S. 395 is the Abert Rim, the highest fault escarpment in the United States. The rim rises 2,000 feet above Lake Abert. This unusual body of water has no outlet and is rich in brine shrimp, which attract countless waterfowl and shorebirds. Due to its high alkalinity, it is hazardous to swim in the lake. Forest Service roads (see "Lakeview Ranger Station" under "Information and Services," following, for routing on obscure byways) lead through the North Warner Mountains to

BLM trails up the back side of Abert Rim. While it is an arduous journey down bumpy back roads and a steep hike up the mountain, the view from the rim is spectacular.

Gearhart Mountain Wilderness Area

About 40 miles west of Lakeview off of ORE 140 is the 22,000-acre roadless Gearhart Mountain Wilderness Area. Accessible only on foot or horseback, two major trails take adventurers into a challenging outdoor environment. **Gearhart Trail** (#100) incorporates 12 of the area's 16 miles of improved trails. This trail runs from **Lookout Rock** in the southeast corner of the wilderness, up over the mountain, down to **Blue Lake,** and to a trailhead on North Creek. The **Boulder Springs Trail** (#100A) runs from the west side of the wilderness to a junction with the other trail a half mile from the mountain summit. For maps and more information, contact the U.S. Forest Service ranger stations in Lakeview, Paisley, or Silver Lake (see "Services and Information" following).

While you're in the neighborhood, you might want to visit the **Mitchell Monument,** on ORE 140 between the wilderness area and Bly, which commemorates a tragedy that occurred on May 5, 1945. Reverend Archie Mitchell and his wife were escorting five children on a picnic near Corral Creek when one of the kids discovered a bomb dropped by a balloon from a Japanese plane. Unfortunately, the child triggered the bomb, and all but the good reverend were killed. This is the only recorded incident of World War II fatalities in the 48 contiguous states. Balloon bombs came down all over the western states, but only Oregon recorded civilian deaths due to their detonation.

Hart Mountain National Antelope Refuge

At the far eastern end of the county is a wildlife refuge that stretches across a high plateau rising above Warner Lakes. To get there from Adel, the first town east of Lakeview on ORE 140, go northeast 29 miles to Plush and take the road to the refuge headquarters. The station has information and a display describing this 275,000-acre sanctuary for pronghorns. The refuge is also home to bighorn sheep, mule deer, 213 species of birds, and many small mammals. A dunk in the hot springs a short distance from the station is highly recommended to take out the stiffness from bouncing down the dirt roads to get there. A campground is near the hot springs.

Despite the name of the preserve, you won't find any antelope here. In fact, there are no antelope living in North America—only pronghorns. Because these animals shed the outer sheaths of their horns each year, they differ from their Asian and African counterparts, which have permanent horns. Male pronghorns have prongs, protrusions extending from their sheaths, to further distinguish them from antelopes. The lingering misnomer was bestowed on these Oregon animals by Lewis and Clark. At any rate, many scientists believe that pronghorns could be the world's fastest land mammals over a long distance, barely edging out the cheetah on distances exceeding 1,000 yards. It's said they can cruise at more than 35 miles an hour, maintain 60 mph for half a mile, and reach 70 mph in short bursts.

Lake County is where the deer and the antelope—that is, pronghorn—play.

SPORTS AND RECREATION

In Town
The **Lakeridge Country Club** (ORE 140; tel. 947-3855) has a nine-hole golf course with a pro shop, a putting green, lessons, and cart rentals. **Christmas Valley Golf Course** (Christmas Valley; tel. 576-2333) is another nine-holer next to a 130-acre man-made lake that's served by a pro shop in the nearby Christmas Valley Lodge. The restaurant here is the only full-service dining room in these parts.

On Friday, Saturday, and Sunday, the **Alger Theatre** (22 F St., Lakeview; tel. 947-2023) shows top-name films for $3.75 adults, $2 children ages 2-11.

Fishing
With a name like Lake County, you'd be right in thinking that fishing holes are plentiful here. Known for excellent trout fishing in the mountainous areas, the region is also gaining a reputation for bass, crappie, catfish, and other warm-water fishing. **Crump, Flagstaff, Anderson,** and **Campbell** lakes in eastern Lake County provide the hottest action for crappie.

Friday Reservoir, located between Adel and Plush, is stocked with Lahontan cutthroat trout, and **Rock Creek,** which flows out of the Hart Mountain National Antelope Refuge, has redbanded trout. In western Lake County, **Goose Lake,** half in California, half in Oregon off U.S. 395, is also home to the native red-banded trout, but it's hard to fish for this unique subspecies in the shallow water. **Drews Reservoir,** 25 miles west of Lakeview on ORE 140, offers excellent fishing for channel catfish—some as large as 10 pounds. In the northern section of the county, **Thompson Valley Reservoir,** reached by driving south from Silver Lake on County Road 4-12, has yielded large rainbows. The **Chewaucan River,** which flows into Abert Lake, is heavily stocked with trout.

Skiing
Winter sports play a major role in Lake County's recreational schedule. **Warner Canyon Ski Area,** seven miles east of Lakeview on ORE 140, can accommodate almost any level of Alpine and Nordic skier, with 14 runs and three miles of cross-country trails. Thanks to a mile-high base elevation and the dry southeastern Oregon climate, excellent dry powder conditions are common. The area has a day lodge near the base of the hill with a snack bar that serves breakfast and lunch. The season may start as early as mid-December and run through the end of March. During this time the hill is open Thurs.-Fri. 1-4 p.m., Sat.-Sun. 10-4.

Rockhounding
Rockhounding is a popular hobby in Lake County. Best known for its abundance of sunstones (also known as aventurine or Plush diamonds), the area also has jasper, agates, petrified wood, fire opal, wonder stones, thunder eggs, and obsidian. To get to the sunstone-hunting grounds, go east on ORE 140 to the Plush junction and turn north. At the first junction take Valley Falls Rd. and follow the signs. Another spot for rockhounding can be reached by taking Hogback Rd. just north of the upper section of the Abert Rim; the Hogback junction is about 50 miles north of Lakeview on U.S. 395. For more info visit the **High Desert Rock Shop** (244 N. M St., Lakeview).

PRACTICALITIES

Campgrounds
Junipers Reservoir RV Resort (tel. 947-2050) is 10 miles west of Lakeview on ORE 140. This private reservoir with campgrounds is situated on a working cattle ranch that's open April 15-Oct. 31, depending on the weather. Designated as one of six private wildlife-viewing areas in the state, a visit to this spread offers an excellent chance to view longhorn cattle, deer, eagles, ospreys, and coyotes.

Goose Lake Campground is a large facility 15 miles south of Lakeview on U.S. 395. The campground has tent sites, RV hookups, and a boat launch on the shore of this huge lake that dips down into California. **Corral Creek Campground** is a good headquarters for an exploration of the Gearhart Mountain Wilderness, an area of high meadows, cliffs, and worn-down volcanoes. To get to the campsite turn off ORE 140 at Quartz Mountain, 24 miles west of Lakeview, and drive north on Forest Service Rd.

LAKE COUNTY ACCOMMODATIONS

AA Motel, 411 N. F St., Lakeview, tel. 947-2201, $30-35, modern, air-conditioned units.

Best Western Skyline Motor Lodge, Skyline 414 N. G St., Lakeview, tel. 947-2194, $45-60, covered pool, air-conditioning, laundry, nonsmoking rooms, complimentary continental breakfast.

Desert Inn, Christmas Valley, tel. 576-2262, $25-35, kitchenettes with refrigerators.

Hart Mountain Store & Bed & Breakfast, Plush, tel. 947-2491, $35-50.

Hunter's Hot Spring Resort, U.S. 395, Lakeview, tel. 947-2125, $30-40, pool, kitchenettes, restaurant/lounge, live entertainment.

Interstate 8 Motel, 354 N. K St., Lakeview, tel. 947-3341, $30-40, pets, kitchenettes, restaurant, laundry, complimentary continental breakfast.

Lakeside Terrace Motel and Restaurant, Christmas Valley, tel. 576-2309, $25.

Lakeview Lodge Motel, 301 N. G St., Lakeview, tel. 947-2181, $45-60, pets, kitchenettes, air-conditioning, nonsmoking rooms.

Rim Rock Motel, U.S. 395, Lakeview, tel. 947-2185, $25-35, cable TV, air-conditioning, complimentary continental breakfast.

3600. **Wildlife Refuge Campground** is on the Ana River just north of Summer Lake on ORE 31. Birdwatchers like to camp here and walk the dikes of Summer Lake looking for waterfowl and swamp mammals.

Food
Like most parts of the sagebrush side of Oregon, Lake County isn't known for its nouvelle cuisine. Be prepared for basic American food with an emphasis on hearty, home-cooked meals. Here's a list of eateries that won't enchant your palate, but will refuel your tank.

The **AA Restaurant** (Lakeview; tel. 947-2563) has dinners that range from $4.25 for liver and onions to $9.95 for a steak and shrimp combo. **Papa Dan's** (1217 N. Fourth, Lakeview; tel. 947-2248) serves Mexican food, pizza, and sandwiches. Complete dinners $4-5 with à la carte available, including chiles rellenos for $2 and tostada supreme for $4. They also deliver.

For authentic Chinese cuisine, try **King's Cafe** (27 N. F St., Lakeview; tel. 947-2217). For homemade grub like chicken baskets, pizza, burgers, and Mexican food, **Dan's Chuckwagon** (N. P St. and ORE 140, Lakeview; tel. 947-3436) is the place to go. Whenever you're hungry, **Jerry's** (508 N. Second, Lakeview; tel. 947-2600) is always open. The **Safeway** in Lake-

view is also open 24 hours and is a good place to stock up on groceries prior to heading out into the boondocks. The **Duck Inn Restaurant** at Hunter's Hot Springs Resort offers steaks, seafood, and Chinese food. Many locals consider the best place in the county to be **Plush West** (9 N. F St., Lakeview; tel. 947-2353). They are open for dinner only from 5:30 p.m.

Entertainment And Events
The **Christmas Valley Rodeo** runs the last weekend in May. Local cowboys and cowgirls compete in bareback riding, roping, and races. The following weekend is the **Silver Lake Rodeo** with more of the same. During the last weekend in June, the **Lake County Junior Rodeo** is held at the Lake County Fairgrounds in Lakeview. Finally, the fall **Lake County Round-Up** and fair held Labor Day weekend at the county fairgrounds includes a carnival, several parades, a barbecue, a buckaroo breakfast, and the annual rodeo.

Many of the earliest pioneers in Lake County were Irish immigrants who worked as sheepherders, some of whom turned to cattle ranching. To celebrate St. Patrick's Day, Lakeview merchants hold **Irish Days**, with a parade led by the Grand Leprechaun, usually the town's oldest Irishman. Other popular events are the potato stick races and the cow-chip fling. The community of Paisley prides itself on having some the largest mosquitoes in the state. To raise funds for controlling these pests, the town stages the **Mosquito Festival** in late July. The action includes a parade, a raft race, a turkey shoot, spitting, lying, cussing, and hollering contests, and the crowning of Ms. Quito. You'll also enjoy the relief provided by Paisley's oasis of greenery in the midst of the surrounding sagebrush desert.

Around Christmastime people flock to Christmas Valley's little blue post office to request a timely postal cancellation (done by hand and larger than machine-franking symbols). Collectors send a letter addressed to themselves with a request for a Dec. 24 or 25 cancellation. Such noel niceties can be obtained by addressing an envelope to Christmas Valley 97641, and enclosing instructions.

In case you're interested, this nondescript alfalfa-farming town got its romantic name by accident. Southeast of here, John C. Frémont spent Christmas at a lake during one of his mid-19th-century treks and called it Christmas Lake. A turn-of-the-century mapmaker mistakenly affixed this name to a lake adjacent to the present-day town site, which also took on the merry moniker.

Information And Services
The **Lake District Hospital and Nursing Facility** (700 S. J St., Lakeview; tel. 947-2114) has 24-hour emergency services. The **Lake County Chamber of Commerce** (tel. 947-2249) is located at the Lake County Courthouse. The **Lakeview Ranger Station** (U.S. 395 N., Lakeview 97630; tel. 947-3334) has info on the nearby wildernesses. The **post office** (18 S. G St., Lakeview 97630; tel. 947-2280) is open 9-5. The Lakeview **police** (525 N. First St.; tel. 947-2029) are here if you have any trouble. **Fire and ambulance** service is available by calling 947-2345.

Finally, should you ever need to call on someone here, be aware that the code of the frontier is fully operative. People gladly help each other out and expect nothing in return. Although the small population in a harsh land is extremely close-knit, people passing through need not ever fear being shunned as outsiders.

Getting There And Around
Buses depart twice a day from the **Red Ball Stage Lines Depot** (619 Center St., Lakeview; tel. 947-2255) for Klamath Falls and other connecting points. The depot is open 9-11 a.m. for the 9:15 departure (10 a.m. on Saturday), and 4:15-5:15 p.m. for 5:05 departure. Public **airports** are located in Lakeview, Paisley, Christmas Valley, and Alkali Lake, with private and government strips at Silver Lake, Fort Rock, Adel, and Wagontire. There are no regular commercial flights, but **Goose Lake Aviation** (tel. 947-4222) provides air-taxi service and an air ambulance at the Lakeview field.

BURNS AND VICINITY

Harney County occupies 10,185 square miles of sagebrush, rimrock, and grassy plains that are shared by only 7,100 inhabitants. With an average elevation of 4,000 feet above sea level, this northern edge of the Great Basin has a short growing season, a yearly snowfall of 36 inches, and clear skies at least 250 days per year. The main industries are logging, milling, and cattle ranching, with farming limited to hardy grains and hay. An index of the sparse population density here is the fact that the Burns area has one of the few public boarding schools in the United States. Students reside in dorms on campus because most come from ranches located many miles from town.

For travelers, the towns of Burns, Hines, and a few wide spots along U.S. 20 hold few points of interest—just places to refuel your rig and yourself. But off the main thoroughfares traversing the southeastern portion of the state are recreational retreats worthy of closer investigation. The Malheur Wildlife Refuge is nationally recognized as one of the best birdwatching sites in the country; the Steens Mountain Recreation Area is also famous for its stunning scenery; and the Ochoco and Malheur national forests are renowned for their fishing, boating, camping, backpacking, and hiking opportunities.

HISTORY

Oregon's high desert county was first inhabited by Bannocks, Northern Paiutes, and Shoshone Indians. When French-Canadian trappers arrived in the area, they were promptly ripped off by the natives. After losing horses and supplies, the trappers named the nearby river "Malheur" ("Unhappiness," or "Misfortune"). The surrounding region's alkali flats and parched hills also suggest this moniker.

Explorer Peter Skene Ogden scouted the area in 1826 while leading a fur brigade for the Hudson's Bay Company. He wasn't impressed with the region as a place for settlers, but the Idaho gold rush of 1860 brought prospectors through the area on their way to the gold fields, and they told stories of rich grasslands, plentiful water, and broad forests.

Pony soldiers under the command of General William Harney explored the region in 1848 and again in 1858, opening up southeastern Oregon to settlement. The most noted military adventure was the construction of a wagon road built between Harney County and Eugene. The leader of this work party, Enoch Steen, gave his name to Steens Mountain.

In 1878, 2,000 Bannocks, fed up with their loss of territory and poor treatment, took to the warpath. Troops from forts all over the west were sent to fight the natives in a war that dragged on until 1880.

The town of **Burns,** named after the Scottish poet Robert Burns, was founded on January 22, 1884. By 1889 it had a population of 250, which has since grown to over 3,000. A significant boost to the town's economy came in

Steens Mountain, rising abruptly above Mann Lake

THE CATTLE KINGS OF EASTERN OREGON

Cattle barons, those early-day entrepreneurs who ran the huge livestock operations of the 19th century, have typically been portrayed as imperious characters in old Western movies. More recently, the "crusty but benign" Ben Cartwright of television's "Bonanza," has added to our image of these men as two-fisted hardheads who brooked little interference in their affairs. Indians, sheepherders, and homesteaders beware! A quick look at the lives of three eastern Oregon cattle kings confirms some of this stereotype, yet John Devine, Pete French, and Bill Brown were unique individuals with personalities that are still talked about today.

John Devine came to Oregon in 1868 and started snapping up land by the simple method of squatting on it. He grabbed U.S. government land, Indian territory, and acreage ostensibly owned by road companies, which he quickly covered with vast herds of cattle. Part of his holding included the Alvord and the Whitehorse ranches on the east side of the Steens. After the devastating winter of 1889-90, during which he lost 75% of his stock, Devine's fortunes plummeted. He was bought out by another cattle baron, Henry Miller, and held on to only the Whitehorse Ranch until his death in 1901 at the age of 62.

Another rancher whose fate is still debated in this arid country is Pete French, an arrogant, forceful man with a bushy mustache that gave him the appearance of Wyatt Earp. Born in Red Bluff, California in 1849, French moved to Oregon in 1873 to manage the stock ranch of Dr. Hugh Glenn in the Donner and Blitzen Valley. French married the boss's daughter, and after Glenn was murdered by his bookkeeper, French built the French-Glenn Livestock Company into one of the largest spreads in the West. At its peak, the ranch had 100,000 acres on which roamed 30,000 head of cattle and 3,000 horses. Five hundred miles of barbed wire defined this empire stretching from the Donner and Blitzen River to Harney Lake.

While he was developing the P Ranch, French earned the enmity of hundreds of local homesteaders, many of whom were evicted from their squatter's shacks. One of his enemies, homesteader Ed Oliver, rode up to French one day and shot him dead. Oliver was arrested but later acquitted by a jury of settlers.

Bill Brown was a more popular and certainly more eccentric rancher than Pete French. His Gap Ranch, headquartered a few miles east of Hampton, halfway between Brothers and Riley, was at its largest 38,000 acres spread throughout four counties. Bill Brown didn't start out rich and he died penniless. In between he earned and lost a number of fortunes. His first enterprise was running a flock of 400 sheep. During that era he was so hard up he only owned one sock, which he switched from one foot to the other every day. Brown added horses to his holdings with such zeal that by the advent of WW I he owned 25,000 head, many of which he sold to the U.S. Cavalry. After the war, and with the advent of mass production of automobiles, Brown lost his shirt and his land. Many stories have been told about this balding six-footer with a square jaw and a mild manner. He never cussed, drank, or gambled, unless his faith in his store customers could be considered gambling. The operator of a mercantile, Brown was seldom behind the counter, relying instead on the honesty of his customers, who were asked to toss their cash in a cigar box. Another quirk was Brown's legendary habit of writing checks on anything available, from tomato-can labels to wooden slats. Local bankers had no problem cashing the "checks" for Brown's hired help or suppliers.

1924 when a rail line reached Burns. Its sister city, **Hines,** was incorporated in 1930. Named after Chicago lumberman Edward Hines, this town of 1,400 residents is primarily a bedroom community for Burns.

SIGHTS

Sagehen Hill Nature Trail

The Sagehen Hill Nature Trail is 16 miles west of Burns at the Sagehen Rest Stop on U.S. 20. This half-mile nature trail has 11 stations on a route that takes you around Sagehen Hill through sagebrush, bitterbrush, and western juniper. Other plants found along the way include lupine, larkspur, owl clover, and yellowbell. The lucky visitor in early May might also catch the sage grouse courtship ritual. The male will display his plumage and make clucking noises to attract the attention of the ladies. If these feathered friends are not visible, the views of Steens Mountain (elevation 9,733 feet) to the southeast can make the hike worthwhile.

Harney County Museum

The Harney County Museum (18 W. D St., Burns 97720; tel. 573-2636) started its career as a brewery and then became a laundry and a wrecking yard. Local pioneer families have donated its displays of quilts, furniture, a complete kitchen, a wagon shed, and machinery. Of special interest are artifacts from Pete French's ranch. The museum is open June-Sept., Tues.-Fri. 9-5, Sat. 9-noon. Admission is $1.50 adults, $2 for a family, and 50 cents for children.

Diamond Craters

Diamond Craters have been described by scientists as the most diverse basaltic volcanic features in the United States. To tour these unique formations, drive 55 miles south of Burns on ORE 205 until you reach the Diamond junction. Turn left and begin a 40-mile route ending at New Princeton on ORE 78. On the way you'll see why this area is called "Oregon's Geologic Gem." There are craters, domes, lava flows, and pits that give an outstanding visual lesson on volcanism. To aid your self-guided tour, pick up the *Diamond Craters* brochure at the BLM office in Hines.

Round Barn

While on the road to New Princeton, stop at the Round Barn, a historic structure built by rancher Pete French to break his saddle horses. Located 20 miles northeast of Diamond, the barn is 100 feet in diameter with a 60-foot circular lava-rock corral inside. Twelve tall juniper poles support a roof covered with 50,000 shingles. Hundreds of cowpokes have carved their initials in the posts of this famous corral.

Malheur National Wildlife Refuge

Malheur and Harney lakes, fed by the mountain snow runoff from the Blitzen and Silvies rivers, have been major nesting and migration stopovers since prehistoric times. The contrast between the stark, dry basin land, with its red sandstone monoliths and mesas, and the lush green marshes is startling. These vast marshes, meadows, and riparian areas surrounded by the eastern Oregon desert attract thousands of birds and hundreds of birdwatchers. The refuge is dominated by three fluctuating lakes—Malheur, Mud, and Harney. These are nourished by a scant eight inches of rain a year.

Refuge officials say that 250 species have been counted within its boundaries. Prime bird-watching times are spring and fall. In the spring, the flocks come from the Great Basin south of the refuge. They generally nest for several months here and then head north to Canada. In March, the first Malheur arrivals include Canada and snow geese, and in the vast Malheur Marsh, swans, mallards, and other ducks. Also look for sandhill cranes in the wet meadows. Shorebirds are followed by warblers, sparrows, and other songbirds in spring. Birds of prey such as golden eagles and red-tailed hawks can be seen swooping over the sage-covered prairies throughout spring, summer, and fall. Ponds and canals at Malheur occasionally host the trumpeter swan in the late spring. This is one of the few places where you can observe this endangered species, with its seven-foot wingspan, nesting. Flocks of pelicans are a summertime spectacle worth catching. See them before they head south to Mexico in the fall.

Late spring is a good time to visit before summer's scorching heat and mosquitoes. Beyond the barrackslike Malheur Field Station, where students study desert ecology and wildlife, is a gravel road. If you follow the signs you'll come to the refuge headquarters in a grove of cottonwoods looking out over the huge expanse of Malheur Lake. Here you can pick up maps for the self-guided auto tour of the refuge. A short distance downhill is a small museum where more than 250 bird specimens are beautifully arrayed. Also of interest is the charming park on the edge of the lake.

While the groupings of birds at Malheur are not so numerous as they are in such birder haunts as the Klamath Lakes and the Oregon coast, the variety here is unsurpassed. Among birders, however, it is the "accidental list" of 55 infrequently sighted species that makes the preserve special. Many of these "exotics" are sighted nowhere else in the region.

In the late 1800s, settlers enjoyed unrestricted hunting here, and at the turn of the century hunters killed thousands of swans, egrets, herons, and grebes for feathers for the millinery trade. In 1908, President Theodore Roosevelt put a stop to the slaughter by protecting the area as a bird sanctuary. The Blitzen Valley and P Ranch were added to the refuge in 1935. Today, 185,000 acres are protected.

To get to the refuge drive 25 miles south from Burns on ORE 205 and then nine miles east on the county road to Princeton.·The last six miles to the refuge headquarters are gravel surfaced. For general info on Malheur, call 493-2612. For details and reservations in dorm rooms or trailers within the refuge, write Malheur Field Station, HC 72, Box 260, Princeton 97721. These spartan accommodations range between $11 and $20. Most of the time you'll be sharing a bath, and it's necessary to bring your own bedding and a towel. Cafeteria-style meals are available here (reservations required). Call 493-2629 to put dibs on these creature comforts; otherwise you might have to drive 35 miles to Burns for bed and board.

Frenchglen

Named for famous rancher Pete French and his wealthy father-in-law, Dr. Hugh Glenn, the town of Frenchglen was originally known as P Station and was part of the nearby P Ranch. Today, this historic community with its hotel, store, corral, and post office remains essentially the same as it was 50 years ago. To get there, drive about 60 miles south on ORE 205 from Burns.

Steens Mountain

Steens Mountain, named after Major Enoch Steen, an Army officer assigned the task of building a military road through Harney County, is one of the great scenic wonders of Oregon. A 30-mile fault block, the mountain rises straight up from the Alvord Desert to a row of glacial peaks. On the western side, huge gorges carved out by glaciers a million years ago descend to a gentle slope drained by the Donner and Blitzen River, which flows into Malheur Lake. Steens Mountain has five vegetation zones ranging from tall sage to alpine tundra. The best way to see the transition is to drive the **Steens Mountain Road** out of Frenchglen to the top of Steens Mountain. This is the highest road in Oregon, rising 9,720 feet in elevation. The first 15 miles of the road are gravel and the last nine miles are dirt. The latter portion is not recommended for low-slung passenger cars.

Steens Mountain Loop

A good way to see the Steens area is via the Steens Mountain Byway, a 52-mile adventure starting and ending at Frenchglen. The route up the highest mountain in the state without conifers or significant tree cover of any kind (save for some beautiful aspens) can be compared to a visit to Alaska's alpine tundra. Multicolored low-to-the-ground wildflowers and a sense of vastness give the feeling of being on top of the world. This impression is accentuated by standing in snow while you look 5,000 feet straight down into the sun-scorched Alvord Desert, which records seven inches of rain annually.

The first four miles of the trek lead across the Malheur Wildlife Refuge and up to the foothills of Steens Mountain. **Page Springs,** the first campground on the route, is a popular spot offering campsites along the bank of the Donner and Blitzen River. Approximately 13 miles beyond Page Springs is **Lily Lake,** a good place for a picnic. This shallow lake has an abundance of water lilies, frogs, songbirds, and waterfowl. After Lily Lake, you really start to climb up the mountain to **Fish Lake, Jackman Park** (both with campsites), and viewpoints of Kiger Gorge and the East Rim. **Kiger Gorge** is a spectacular example of a wide, U-shaped path left by a glacier.

The **East Rim** is a dramatic example of earth-shifting in prehistoric epochs. The lava layers that cap the mountain are thousands of feet thick, formed 15 million years ago when lava erupted from cracks in the ground. Several million years later, the Steens Mountain fault block began to lift along a fault below the east rim. The fault block tilted to the west, forming the gentler slope that stretches to the Malheur Lake Basin. At the summit (9,670 feet) you can see the corners of four states on a clear day—California, Nevada, Oregon, and Idaho. A good time to visit is August to mid-September—Indian summer. Nights are cold but daytime temperatures are more pleasant than summertime scorchers. Later in the fall, red bushes and yellow aspens attract photographers. Some of the aspens are located at Whorehouse Meadow and are indirectly responsible for its name. Lonely shepherds would scratch love notes and erotica in the tree bark, pining away for a visit from the horse-drawn bordellos that serviced these parts.

The area has off-highway vehicle restrictions to protect the environment. Five gates controlling access to the Steens are located at various elevations and are opened as road and weather conditions permit. Normally, the Steens Byway is not open until mid- to late July and is closed by snow in October or November. Gas is available only in Burns, Frenchglen, and Fields. Take reasonable precautions when driving the loop: sudden storms, lightning, flash floods, and extreme road conditions can be hazardous to travelers. The loop returns to ORE 205 about 10 miles south of Frenchglen.

Catlow Valley/Alvord Desert Loop

Another equally ambitious loop is the drive around Steens Mountain along the Catlow Rim and Alvord Desert and back to Burns. Starting at Burns, head south on ORE 205 through the Malheur Wildlife Refuge, past Frenchglen, and up over the divide into the Catlow Valley, which was once a massive inland lake. A side trip to the ghost town of **Blitzen** starts at a right turn (to the west) four miles south of the Steens Loop Road. This eight-mile jaunt will take you to the ruins (a half-dozen dilapidated buildings) of a little town founded in the late 1800s. Blitzen was named after the Donner and Blitzen River, which

flows nearby. *Donner und blitzen* is German for thunder and lightning, the label given this stream by Captain George Curry, who tried to cross it during a fierce thunderstorm.

The next point of interest on the loop is **Roaring Springs Ranch,** tucked under the west rim of Steens Mountain. Originally homesteaded by Tom Wall, the ranch was sold to Pete French and in later years developed into the largest cattle operation in the county. The dramatic backdrop, well-kept classic ranch building, and the surrounding meadows make Roaring Springs Ranch an ideal Western movie set.

After driving 33 miles through the Catlow Valley you'll come to **Fields,** the largest community on the east side of Steens. Homesteaded by Charles Field, the town was established as a supply station in 1881. Fields now has a gas station, store, cafe, and motel. The cafe next to the tiny motel and store here serves great milkshakes. A root beer shake made with hard ice cream flavored with bananas or oreos tastes great on a hot summer day. Field's original stone cabin is across the road.

From Fields head north into the Alvord Desert, site of the dry Alvord Lake and the Alvord Ranch. Along the way you'll pass through **Andrews,** a small community at the edge of the alkali flats. Another stop worthy of attention, particularly if you're in need of revitalization after your travels, is **Alvord Hot Springs,** a few miles north of Andrews. This rustic spa is recognizable by its corrugated-steel shack on the east side of the road. Two pools of hot mineral water piped in from spring runoff will cook your bones and soak away your aches and pains at no charge. The road continues until it connects with ORE 78, which leads back to Burns or south to Burns Junction. The panorama of the east side of Steens Mountain alone is worthy of a trip, but views of the **Pueblo Mountains** to the south and the Great Basin country to the east are also impressive.

Oard's Free Museum

Oard's Free Museum (tel. 493-2535) is located 23 miles east of Burns on U.S. 20. The museum has antique guns, clocks, barbed wire, spinning wheels, and dolls as well as native artifacts, including a Yakima chief's costume. Hours are 7 a.m.-8 p.m. every day.

Paiute Reservation
If you want a livelier encounter with native American culture, visit the Burns Paiute Reservation. Contact the tribal headquarters first for information; either call them at 573-2088 or write to HC-71, 100 Pa' Si' Go Street, Burns 97720.

SPORTS AND RECREATION

Golf
Harney County's "Oasis in the Desert" is the nine-hole **Valley Golf Club** (345 Burns-Hines Hwy., Burns 97720; tel. 573-6251). This challenging course is open to the public, but clubhouse facilities are reserved for members and guests.

Rockhounding
Harney County is rockhound country. Each year, thousands of these enthusiasts flock to this far-flung corner of the state to collect fossils, agates, jasper, obsidian, and thunder eggs. The **Stinking Water Mountains,** 30 miles east of Burns, are a good source of gemstones and petrified wood. Thunder eggs can be dug up four miles south of Oard's Museum on U.S. 20 after getting permission from the Don Robbins family. Contact them through the museum. **Warm Springs Reservoir,** just east of the Stinking Water Mountains, is popular with agate hunters. **Charlie Creek** and **Radar,** west and north of Burns respectively, produce black, banded, and brown

obsidians. Be sure to collect only your limit—be a rockhound, not a rockhog. Also keep in mind that it is illegal to take arrowheads and other artifacts from public lands.

Fishing
Rainbow and red-banded trout occur naturally in most streams in this area and many lakes and rivers are also stocked. Good fishing is available on the Donner and Blitzen and Malheur rivers, Emigrant Creek, Chickahominy Reservoir, Delintment Lake, and Yellowjacket Lake. Krumbo Reservoir on the Malheur Wildlife Refuge is a good bet for trout or largemouth bass.

PRACTICALITIES

Accommodations
If you're seeking shelter in Burns, you'll find that the properties here are generally inexpensive, have air-conditioning to help you beat the heat, and allow you to bring the family dog along, too. The **Orbit Motel** (Hwys. 20/395, Burns 97720; tel. 573-2034) features a pool, nonsmoking rooms, cable TV, and wheelchair access; their rates range from $24-40. Another bargain is the **Silver Spur Motel** (789 N. Broadway, Burns 97720; tel. 573-2077), which offers nonsmoking rooms, a weight workout room, and a complimentary continental breakfast for $32. You get treated like a king at the **Royal Inn** (999 Oregon Ave., Burns 97720; tel. 573-5295). Enjoy the

OREGON DEPT. OF TRANSPORTATION

The Frenchglen Hotel is a restored turn-of-the-century hotel.

tennis courts, two swimming pools, and a decent restaurant without paying a king's ransom. Rates range $36-40. The **Best Western Ponderosa Motel** (577 W. Monroe, Burns 97720; tel. 573-2047) features a swimming pool, nonsmoking rooms, and large spacious rooms for $36-40.

The **Frenchglen Hotel** (Frenchglen; tel. 493-2825) is 60 miles south of Burns on ORE 205 and is an excellent place to stay while visiting Steens Mountain or Malheur Wildlife Refuge. Built in 1914 as a stage stopover in historic Frenchglen, the hotel has eight smallish rooms (with shared bath down the hall) for $40-48 and ranch cooks ready to fix you a family-style breakfast, lunch, or dinner. The family-style evening repast here costs $12 and you must be there at 6:30 p.m. Watching thunderstorms sweep across Steens Mountain from the hotel's screened-in porch can provide after-dinner entertainment. The hotel's season runs March to November.

Campgrounds

There are three high-elevation campgrounds along the Steens Mountain Loop Road. **Page Springs,** four miles southeast of Frenchglen, is open all year. Close to the Malheur Wildlife Refuge, the campground is a good headquarters for birdwatching, fishing, hiking, and sightseeing. **Fish Lake** is the next campground, located 17 miles east of Frenchglen. Open July 1-Nov. 15, the lake is stocked with eastern brook, cutthroat, and rainbow trout. Aspens surround the campsites, which have toilets, well water, and firepits with wood included with campsite fee. **Jackman Park** is three miles east of Fish Lake and is particularly popular with backpackers who use it as a takeoff point. There are six sites with toilets and potable water. All of these campgrounds cost $4 per night for each vehicle. Write the BLM, Burns District HC-74, P.O. Box 12533, Hwy. 20 West, Hines 97336; tel. 573-5241. As for summertime Steens weather, the 100° F temperatures in the high desert give way to 50-80° daytime temperatures atop the mountain. Nonetheless, be aware that the summit can have severe thunderstorms and lightning. At night, the mercury will often drop below freezing, even on days with high noontime temperatures.

A couple of campgrounds to the north of Burns up in the Malheur National Forest are **Yellowjacket** and **Idlewild.** Yellowjacket is on the shore of Yellowjacket Lake, 30 miles northwest of Burns on Forest Service Rd. 2170. As the name implies, be sure to keep your food under wraps, especially meats, if you want to avoid being visited by the namesake hosts of the lake. Idlewild is 17 miles north of Burns on U.S. 395. There is no charge for overnighting in either spot, but don't expect amenities either.

Food

The culinary highlight of Burns is coffee in the **Safeway** deli (Monroe St.). In other words, B.Y.O. food here. A little west of Burns, a sign in Hines proclaims "Worst Foods of The World—70's prices."

Steens Mountain Cafe (195 Alder, Burns; tel. 573-7226) is an anomaly—a first-rate restaurant in a town known for its lousy chow. Chef Tony is proud of his sourdough breads, pancakes, waffles, and pizza crust. He also has a big selection of deli sandwiches for $2.95-$4.95, and chicken parmesan or spaghetti dinner for $4.95. His deep-dish and regular pizzas run $8.95-11.95.

Silver Sage (239 N. Broadway, Burns; tel. 573-7878) has both American and Mexican meals, a salad bar, and beer, wine, and cocktails. Their buckaroo burger with ham, cheese, fries, and salad is $4.30. Dinner entrees include fajitas for $7 and rib steaks with salad bar and homemade bread for $10.75.

Entertainment And Events

In mid-April, the **John Scharff Migratory Waterfowl Festival** held in Burns celebrates the spring return of waterbirds to the region with lectures, movies, slides, and guided birdwatching tours. For information on the festival call 493-2612. Harney County, once the trapping territory of mountain men like Peter Skene Ogden and Joe Meek, has two blackpowder clubs that relive those days with a yearly **Blackpowder Shoot and Rendezvous.** The **Steens Mountain Men** hold their shoot in September and the **Harney Free Trappers** hold theirs in June. These rendezvous attract colorful gatherings of folks in buckskin, talkin', shootin', lyin', and renewing friendships from "afore last winter." For information on dates and locations call Bigfoot at 573-7814 or Silver Fox at 573-7554.

Steens Mountain Days is held in early August. Centered in Frenchglen, the fun includes a 10-km run along the Steens rim, a sagebrush roping contest, a barbecue, a street dance, and a beer garden. During the last weekend in June, the sky is filled with lighter-than-air ships for the **High Desert Hot Air Balloon Rally** at the Burns Union High School. Burns is also the site of **Obsidian Days** in mid-June, as well as the **Harney County Fair** and the Rodeo and Race Meet held in early September. First-run flicks can be enjoyed at **Desert Community Theatre** (68 Broadway, Burns; tel. 573-4220).

Information And Services
For general information on the region, contact the **Harney County Chamber of Commerce** (18 W. D St., Burns 97720; tel. 573-2636). For information on recreation, stop by the **Bureau of Land Management** office (12533 W. U.S. 20, Hines 97738; tel. 573-5241). The **Burns and Snow Mountain Ranger District** is also near-

by (Box 12870, U.S. 20, Hines 97738; tel. 573-7292).

If you need the law, the Burns and Hines City **police** (tel. 573-6028) and the Harney County **sheriff** (tel. 573-7281, or after 5 p.m. and weekends, 573-6028) are there to help. The **post office** (222 N. Broadway, Burns 97720, tel. 573-2931) is open 9-5 weekdays.

Burns is serviced by **Trailways Bus Lines** (682 N. Broadway; tel. 573-2736). The Burns Airport (87A, Rural Route HC 71; tel. 573-6139) is five miles from town.

Lindberg's Highland Rock Shop (1316 Hines Blvd., Burns; tel. 573-5118) might be the best rock shop for certain kinds of specimens in the Northwest. Even if you're not buying, check out the thunder eggs and petrified wood. Also ask to see the glow-in-the-dark rocks and the fireplace hacked out of local treasures in the back of the store. Info on where to look yourself is also available for rockhounds (pamphlets for sale).

U.S. 26: PRINEVILLE TO SUMPTER

Prineville, the geographic center of Oregon, is a fitting starting point for this route across the northcentral section of the state (see map p. 426). Coming from the west, you drop down from tall bluffs into the Crooked River Valley and, nearing the city, cruise through hills dotted with juniper. White-and-black magpies dart in front of your car and red-winged blackbirds observe your passing from their fenceposts. A thriving community and the seat of Crook County, Prineville has a population of 5,000, gets a meager 10 inches of rain a year, and relies on agriculture, wood products, and tourism for its economy. The town is also known as the Gateway to the Ochocos, a heavily wooded mountain range that runs east-west for 50 miles. One of Oregon's least-known recreational areas, the Ochocos are still ruggedly pristine. Beyond these mountains stretches the long valley of the John Day River. In the vicinity are also the famous John Day Fossil Beds, the historic gold-mining camps of Canyon City and Sumpter, and another wild area called the Strawberry Mountain Wilderness.

Just as the fossil beds provide a cross section of the earth's history, a trip down U.S. 26 will give you a feel for the leather-tough countryside of central eastern Oregon and the people who settled here: the second-generation pioneers from the Willamette Valley, the Basques, Scots, and Irishmen from the old countries, and the Chinese who came to pick over the tailings left by gold miners in a hurry. Their combined heritage is here for the finding, along with night skies unobscured by city lights and diverse wildlife roaming the surrounding plains and forests.

HISTORY

The Ochocos
The Ochoco country, named after a Paiute Indian word for willows, was heavily populated by natives who lived off a bounty of deer, elk, fish, and camas roots. The first significant passage of Europeans other than trappers through the area was the Lost Wagon Train of 1845.

Led by Stephen Meek, brother of the Oregon Territory spokesman Joe Meek, the pioneers were seeking a route to the Willamette Valley easier than the arduous trek over the Blue Mountains. Instead, they found hardship, starvation, thirst, and death on a tortuous journey through the deserts of Malheur and Harney counties and along the rugged ridges of the Ochoco Mountains. Their hardships finally ended when they found the Crooked River and followed it north to The Dalles. Somewhere during the trek, members of the party scooped up gold nuggets and kept them in a blue bucket. Though the legend of the Blue Bucket Mine has since captivated fans of Oregon history, its actual site has never been found.

In 1860, Major Enoch Steen led an expedition through the region, which resulted in a number of geographic areas being named after him, including Steens Mountain and Stein's Pillar. Eight years later, Barney Prine built a blacksmith shop, a store, and a saloon near the bank of Ochoco Creek, which grew into the city of Prineville, the only town in 10,000 square miles. It was settled by the sons of the pioneers who came west in the wagon trains. It was their turn to carve out a life from the wilds.

At the turn of the century, cinnabar, the raw ore in which mercury is found, was discovered in the Ochocos, which brought an influx of miners. About the same time, a range war broke out between the cattlemen and sheepherders. Groups like the Ezee Sheep Shooters and the Crook County Sheep Shooters Association bragged that they had slaughtered 8,000-10,000 sheep in 1905 alone. Incensed by this lawlessness, the citizens of Oregon moved to stop the killing, but troubles continued for cattle and sheep ranchers and farmers. Harsh winters took their toll on livestock, and the hope that the plains would be receptive to wheat farming didn't work out.

During WW I, many homesteaders gave up and moved to the cities to work for the war effort. In 1917, Prineville made a decision that wound up boosting the local economy. They built a railroad to Redmond, linking their line with the Union Pacific. Used primarily to haul ponderosa pine logs, the railroad remains the only city-owned railroad still in operation in the United States. In the 1950s a new industry was added to the mainstays of logging, ranching, and farm-

ing. Gemstones of high quality were discovered in the Ochocos, prompting a rockhound/tourism boom that continues to this day.

One peculiar historical note of interest: for most of its 11-decade existence, Crook County was a bellwether county, giving the majority of its vote to the winner of every presidential race. However, the county lost its distinction as the nation's last election-eve litmus test as a result of its choice of George Bush over Bill Clinton.

John Day Region

A string of communities runs east from Prineville and includes Mitchell, Dayville, Mt. Vernon, John Day, Canyon City, and Prairie City. The early history of this stretch of the John Day Valley centers around the discovery of gold in 1862. According to most estimates, 26 million dollars

---

ADOPT-A-WILDERNESS PROGRAM

Most of eastern Oregon is public land under the jurisdiction of the Bureau of Land Management. One of the laws that governs the BLM's management of these millions of acres of semiarid steppes is the Federal Land Policy and Management Act (FLPMA) of 1976, which mandates a review of all BLM roadless areas for possible inclusion in the Wilderness Preservation System. Of the five million acres inventoried, the BLM is recommending protection of 1.1 million acres. Conservationists are calling for twice that amount. To convince Congress to meet the conservationists' acreage requests, an Adopt-A-Wilderness Program has been initiated with the goal of preparing a collection of on-site reports called the Sage Alternative.

Sponsored by the Oregon Natural Desert Association, the program invites desert-lovers to pick an area to adopt as their own. The "parents" go on field trips, gather information, take photographs, prepare slide shows, brochures, portfolios, and other profiles as evidence that their small portion of the desert needs to be preserved in its natural state.

To get involved, contact ONDA (Box 1005, Bend 97709; tel. 385-6908), the central clearinghouse for the program. Then lace up your boots, grab your hat, and get out there!

in gold was taken out of the Strawberry Mountain Wilderness. At the peak of the gold rush, Whiskey Flat, later called Canyon City, was populated by 5,000 miners, which made it larger than Portland at the time. Thousands of Chinese immigrated to the area to work the tailings, or leftovers, from the mines. The impact of the Chinese miners is celebrated every year during Kam Wah Chung Days (see "Entertainment and Events" following) in John Day.

One of the more colorful denizens of Canyon City was the celebrated poet Joaquin Miller, who served as the first elected judge in Grant County. Known as the "Byron of Oregon," this dashing figure dressed like Buffalo Bill and orated his florid sonnets to a baffled audience of miners.

Lastly, the area generated an irony common in history: John Day, the man whose name was attached to a river, a valley, and a town, never saw any of them. A hunter from Virginia, Day was hired to provide meat for the Pacific Fur Company Expedition led by Wilson Price Hunt. Thirty miles east of The Dalles, near what was then known as the Mau Hau River, Day and another mountain man were attacked by Indians and left naked and injured. The river soon became known as Day's River; mapmakers later changed it to the John Day River.

SIGHTS

Prineville

A good place to begin your travels in Ochoco country is at the **A.R. Bowman Museum** (246 N. Main St., Prineville 97754; tel. 447-3715), open Mon.-Fri. 10-5, Sat. noon-5. This museum's two floors of exhibits and displays are a notch above most small-town historical museums. Fans of the Old West will enjoy the tack room with saddles, halters, and woolly chaps. Rockhounds will be delighted with the displays of Blue Mountain picture jasper, thunder eggs, and fossils. Other classic displays are a campfire setup with a graniteware coffee pot and a pound of Bull Durham tobacco, a moonshine still, a country store, and an upstairs parlor of the early 1900s.

Stein's Pillar

Once out of town, the country east of Prineville starts to shift from juniper flats to pine ridges. One landmark that stands out is Stein's Pillar, a 300-foot monolith that rises like a rocky forefinger out of the pines. To get to this impressive column of stone, take the Mill Creek Rd. at Ochoco Lake, six miles east of Prineville. Stein's Pillar will be on your right. The scenic route back to Prineville from the Mill Creek Wilderness on McKay Road takes you by some exquisite meadows and clear mountain streams.

Lookout Mountain

Another side trip of note is a visit to the Lookout Mountain Special Management Area. Located in the Ochocos, it's a unique biosphere with 28 plant communities, one of the finest stands of ponderosa pines in the state, lots of elk and deer, and creeks full of rainbow and brook trout. A seven-mile trail starts at the Ochoco Ranger Station 22 miles east of Prineville on County Rd. 22 and ends at the summit of Lookout Mountain, from which 11 major peaks are visible. Friends of Lookout, a coalition of environmental and recreational groups, invites you to visit the area and lend your support to efforts to secure legislation protecting this unique habitat.

John Day Fossil Beds

The next sights as you travel east are among the most prominent tourist stops in eastern Oregon. In the 1860s, self-taught geologist Thomas Condon discovered what is now known as the John Day Fossil Beds. These archives of stone provide a paleontological record of the 70 million years and five geologic epochs of life on this planet. The days of 50-ton brontosaurs and 50-foot crocodiles, as well as delicate ferns and flowers, are captured in the rock formations of the three beds, easily visited in a day's excursion. This is the richest concentration of prehistoric mammalian fossils in the United States. More than 120 species have been identified here.

The first stop, the **Painted Hills**, is 50 miles east of Prineville on a spur road off U.S. 26. Turn left at the sign outside Mitchell and go six miles along Bridge Creek to the site. Stop first at the visitor center to get oriented and fill your canteen. Continuing on, you'll soon notice the startling, deep red colors of the hills. Although the view from the road is impressive, you really have to get out and hike the trails to literally get the picture. The **Fossil Leaf Trail** will lead you to remnants of a 30-million-year-old hardwood forest. The **Carroll Rim Trail** takes you to the top of Carroll Rim for a spectacular view of the Painted Hills. The **High Desert Trail** is a three-mile loop out into the desert for those seeking the quiet and solitude of the big empty. Enjoy deep yellows, browns, and reds thanks to the multihued volcanic debris that piled up centuries ago.

The next bed, the **Clarno Formations,** can be reached by taking ORE 207 north of Mitchell to Service Creek, then ORE 19 to Fossil and ORE 218 to Clarno. These beds are the oldest (40-60 million years) and northernmost of the three units comprising the national monument. After passing through Fossil, the Clarno Formations are 18 miles west. The **Clarno Arch Trail** will get you up into the formations to the base of the Eroded Palisades, the Petrified Logs, and the Clarno Arch. The Clarno Unit is one of the few places in the world where stems of plants, seeds, leaves, and nuts are all preserved in the same location. These species point to a different climate here millions of years ago—warm enough to support subtropical forest with flowering trees. Palm ginkgo and magnolia leaf imprints lend credence to this assertion. A scenic little side loop through the ghost town of Twickenham will take you down through a canyon with sandstone pillars looming like gargoyles, huge juniper trees, and green creek-bottom meadows—just follow the signs through this little wayside. The banded cliffs are so close you can almost reach out and touch them! The road connects with ORE 19 at Butte Creek Pass.

The third area of the John Day Beds, the **Sheep Rock Unit,** can be reached by driving back down ORE 19 to Service Creek, where you turn east and follow the John Day River to **Spray** and **Kimberly** and then south for 20 miles. The trails here include the **Sheep Rock Overlook Trail, Island in Time Trail,** and the **Blue Basin Trail.** These last two are just north of Sheep Rock. The ground at Blue Basin is cobalt blue and the creek water is green. The

Sheep Rock Unit is also home to the **Cant Ranch Visitor Center,** headquarters for the National Park Service, which maintains the John Day Fossil Beds National Monument. The center has an excellent interpretive exhibit, books and informational pamphlets, and a knowledgeable staff who will answer your questions.

The address is John Day Fossil Beds National Monument, 420 W. Main, John Day 97845; tel. 575-0721. There's not much camping here but *Selected Local Campgrounds of Grant County,* put out by the Grant County Chamber of Commerce (281 W. Main, John Day 97845; tel. 575-0547), lists what's available.

Where East Meets West

After visiting the John Day Fossil Beds, head east to the town of John Day. A must stop while in town is the **Kam Wah Chung and Company Museum** (250 N.W. Canton; tel. 575-0028). It's open May-Oct., Mon.-Thurs. 9 a.m.-noon, Sat.-Sun. 1-5 p.m. No admission is charged to this collection of numerous artifacts; also featured are replicas of a general store, a pharmacy with over 500 herbs, a doctor's office, Chinese temple, and home. The building was constructed as a trading post on the Dalles Military Road in 1866-67. It soon became the center of Chinese life in the John Day area, serving as a general store, herbal pharmacy, hotel, fortune-teller's studio, casino, assay office, and Taoist shrine. When you consider that John Day had twice as many Chinese residents as Caucasian in the 1880s, it's clear that this museum is not some arcane exhibit but rather an important window to the past.

It's the little touches in the faithfully restored building that stay with you. First your eye will be drawn to the metal shutters and outside wooden staircase on this rough stone edifice. Inside, there's a locked and barred herb cage where Ing Hay prepared medicine and where gold dust was weighed. A Taoist shrine graces the room where groceries and opium were dispensed. Finally, the meat cleaver by Doc Hay's bed bespeaks the fear and despair of Chinese life here near the turn of the century. For more information, the reader is referred to *The Chinese Doctor of John Day* by Jerry Barlow and Christine Richardson (Binford and Mort, 1979).

Museums

Another repository of local history is the **Grant County Historical Museum** in Canyon City, a couple of miles south of John Day on U.S. 395. The museum is open June 1-Sept. 30, Mon.-Sat. 9:30-4:30, Sun. 1-5. Centered in the heart of Oregon's mining and ranching country, the facility's wealth of memorabilia depicts the early days of Grant County and includes an extensive rock collection plus Chinese and native American items.

The **Dewitt Museum** (South Main, Prairie City) is housed in the old western terminus of the Sumpter Valley Railroad, which operated between Baker and Prairie City from 1909 until 1947. The depot was restored in 1979 and today has 10 rooms full of artifacts from Grant County's early days. Open May 15-Oct. 15, Thurs.-Sat. 10-3.

While not an official museum, the ghost town of **Whitney,** located 12 miles up ORE 7 from its junction with U.S. 26 (about 15 miles east of Prairie City), has a story to tell to those who visit its ruins. Whitney was the terminus for stage lines to the mining and cattle towns of Unity, Bridgeport, and Malheur City. Now abandoned buildings are all that remain of this bustling community of the early 1900s. An interpretive sign just off ORE 7 explains the local history.

Sumpter

Traveling north of Whitney, you come to the **Sumpter Valley Wildlife Area,** a 158-acre site located between Phillips Reservoir and Sumpter on ORE 7. Canada geese, ring-necked ducks, bitterns, and Virginia rails can be seen in the wetlands and gravel dredge remains along the Powder River.

A few miles north of the refuge is Sumpter, a gold-mining town in the Elkhorn Mountains. To get there, turn off U.S. 26 at Austin and drive 22 miles on ORE 7 through the Sumpter Valley to this historic little town. The first settlers here were five Southerners who built a stone cabin and christened it Fort Sumter after the South Carolina garrison that was shelled in April of 1861, signaling the start of the Civil War. In 1883, the U.S. Post Office rejected the name, so locals changed it by dropping the "Fort" and adding a *p*. The heyday of gold mining in the area was 1900-05, when over 3,000 miners worked the hard-rock mines and dredged the Powder River. By 1905, most of the gold was gone, but dredging continued until 1954.

One of the attractions of the Sumpter area is the **Sumpter Valley Railroad Excursion** (Box 389, Baker City 97814; tel. 894-2268). Passengers ride in two observation cars pulled by a wood-burning, narrow-gauge steam en-

Sheep Rock looms over the John Day Fossil Beds.

gine originally used to haul logs and ore in addition to people. There is also a restored 1920 car and an 1890 caboose. The seven-mile run from Phillips Lake to Sumpter costs $8 for adults, $6 for children under 16. The railroad is open from Memorial Day weekend through the last weekend in September with four runs daily at 10 a.m., noon, 2 p.m., and 4 p.m. Call or write the railroad to find out about special moonlight rides featuring live entertainment and hobo stew.

When you're ready to leave Sumpter, you have three travel options. You can retrace your route back to U.S. 26 and continue east to Vale and Ontario or head west toward U.S. 97 and Bend. Another possibility is to drive 19 miles east on ORE 7 to ORE 245, and then north nine miles to Baker. The third choice, the **Elkhorn Drive National Scenic Byway,** takes you northwest from Sumpter through the gold-mining territory to Granite, across the north fork of the John Day, past Anthony Lake, and on to Baker.

SPORTS AND RECREATION

Lakes
Prineville Reservoir, 17 miles south of Prineville on ORE 27, was built for irrigation and flood control and covers 310 acres. A popular year-round boating and fishing lake, it is famous for its huge bass. **Ochoco Lake,** six miles east of Prineville on U.S. 26, is a favorite recreational spot for locals, with year-round fishing, boating, and camping (see "Camping" following).

Rockhounding
The Ochocos are prime rockhound territory, with free public collecting areas operated by the Rockhound Pow-Wow Association. Two good sites are off of U.S. 26. **Whistler Springs** is between mileposts 49 and 50. Turn left on Forest Service Rd. 27 for about six miles, then turn right onto Forest Service Rd. 500 and follow it to the springs. The collection area is near the campground. **White Fir Springs** is a good spot for jasper-filled thunder eggs. To get there, drive to milepost 41, turn left on Forest Service Rd. 3350, and follow it five miles to the diggings. For more info on rockhounding and where to dig, **Elkins Gem Stones** (833 S. Main St., Prineville; tel. 447-5547) can help.

Riding The Ranges
Ever dreamed of going on a cattle drive? You can do it for real in the John Day River Valley with the cowboys of the **Cottonwood Ranch** (Box 334, Dayville 97825; tel 987-2134). The two-day trip includes chuckwagon dinners and breakfast, a barbecue, a hayride, and camping in tepees. The cost is $250 per person.

A more civilized way to spend the day might include a round of golf at the **Mountain View Country Club** (tel. 575-0179). Located just west of John Day on U.S. 26, this nine-hole golf course accepts greens fees from nonmembers.

PRACTICALITIES

Accommodations
The **Rustlers Roost Motel** (960 W. Third, Prineville 97754; tel. 447-4185) was designed in the Old West style. Art by local artists and antique furniture grace the rooms. Rates start at $29.95 for a single and $34.25 for a double. The **Prineville Reservoir Resort** (HC 78, Box 1300, Prineville 97754; tel. 447-7468) is on the shoreline of Prineville Reservoir, 17 miles southeast of Prineville on the Paulina Highway (ORE 27). This resort offers motel accommodations with kitchenettes starting at $48 for a double. Camping units go for $12. The resort also rents fishing boats, paddleboats, and motors. Those driving U.S. 26 to the Painted Hills, Prineville to Mitchell, will enjoy comfort and moderate prices at the **Carolina Motel** (1050 E. Third, Prineville; tel. 447-4132) east of downtown. Housekeeping units, air-conditioning, and a large multiroom family unit are just some of the amenities here.

The **Elliot House Bed and Breakfast** (305 W. First, Prineville 97754; tel. 447-7442) is a classic Queen Anne-style home that was entered on the National Register of Historic Places in 1989. In keeping with the 19th-century flavor of the house, the hosts serve a sumptuous breakfast in the morning and a formal tea at 3 p.m. Not as fancy, but handy if you find yourself in Fossil for the evening, is the **Fossil Motel and Trailer Park** (Box 282, Fossil 97830; tel. 763-4075). Owner Nancy Grimm invites you to "sleep in a fossil bed." Rates are $25-45.

If you find yourself in a similar situation in John Day, try the **Dreamer's Lodge** (144 Canyon Blvd., John Day 97845). There's air-conditioning and a fridge in every room. Rates are $36-45. **Bed and Breakfast by the River** (Route 2, Box 790, Prairie City 97869; tel. 820-4470), located on a working ranch by the John Day River, is a good takeoff spot for hiking in the nearby Strawberry Mountain Wilderness, fishing or rafting on the river, or just basking in country hospitality. Rates are $30 and $60 per day for double occupancy.

Camping

For good campsites in the Ochocos, take Ochoco Creek Rd. approximately 10 miles east of Ochoco Lake. Choices include **Ochoco Camp, Walton Lake** (where you can fish, boat, or hike the trail to Round Mountain), **Wildwood,** and **Ochoco Divide.** Open from mid-April to late October, these campsites cost $8 per night. While on this loop, stop at the mining ghost town of **Mayflower.** Founded in 1873, the community was active until 1925. A stamp mill is still visible.

Strawberry Fields Forever

The **Strawberry Mountain Wilderness,** a pocket mountain range southeast of John Day, offers a good system of trails, seven lakes, volcanic rock formations, and if you're lucky, glimpses of bighorn sheep. Set up your base camp at **Strawberry Campground,** eight miles south of Prairie City on County Route 60, then two miles on Forest Service Rd. 6001. Open from June to mid-October, Strawberry's fees are $5 per night. The campground is next to Strawberry Creek and is the trailhead for jaunts to Strawberry Lake, Strawberry Falls, and Strawberry Mountain. As you might guess, chances are good you'll find some of these wild berries along the way!

If your travels find you in this neighborhood in winter, try the groomed snowmobile and cross-country ski trails, which run from the Austin House in Bates (at the junction of U.S. 26 and ORE 7) to Sumpter, a distance of 23 miles. For more information on the trails, contact this roadhouse (Box 8, U.S. 26, Bates 97817; tel. 488-2387).

Food

If you get hungry while in Prineville you can try a folksy little spot called **Barr's Cafe** (887 N. Main,

Prineville; tel. 447-5897). It's open 24 hours, with breakfast served around the clock. The top-of-the-line restaurant in town is the **Ochoco Inn and Cinnabar Restaurant** (123 E. Third, Prineville; tel. 447-3888). You'll find the ubiquitous Western motif in a building built on the site of the Jackson Hotel, which burned in 1922, and the Prineville Hotel, which went up in flames in 1966. The restaurant makes generous bunkhouse deli sandwiches and also features a hazelnut pesto fettuccine dish. The eclectic menu is highlighted by a seven-ounce steak marinated in whiskey, Worcestershire sauce, red wine, and herbs for $9.95. Cheers!

Those heading to the Painted Hills via ORE 26 are encouraged to stop off at the **Blueberry Muffin Restaurant** (tel. 462-3434), located on the west side of Mitchell just past the turnoff to the John Day Fossil Beds. This is likely to be the only restaurant worthy of the name encountered after leaving Prineville. Expect decent American food, with homemade pies a highlight.

A more traditional approach to beefsteak is favored by the **Grubsteak Mining Company** (149 E. Main St., John Day; tel. 575-1970). Their best deal is an eight-ounce rib-eye steak for $13. Thirteen miles east of John Day you come to **Prairie City,** currently going through a transition into a tourist town similar to Sisters in central Oregon. One of the prime examples of this renovation is **Ferdinand's** (128 Front St., Prairie City; tel. 820-9359). This colorful watering hole in a refurbished butcher shop built in 1902 has a carving of a bull over the front door, and inside sports a collection of antiques, cougar hides, and old photos on the walls. Be sure to check out the two carved maidens, called the Twin Virgins, over the classic long bar. The figures were sculpted in Milan, Italy, in 1879, and they and the bar furniture made the trip around the Horn, up the Columbia River on a sternwheeler, and then to Prairie City by wagon. Ferdinand's has a full menu of surprisingly urbane fare that can be washed down with microbrewery beer and ale from Portland.

Finally, if you have a car full of hungry children, you might want to fill them up in the **Elkhorn Saloon and Family Restaurant** (tel. 894-2244) in Sumpter. The claim to fame here is a homemade combo pizza, weighing in at five pounds, for $18.95.

Entertainment And Events

The **Central Oregon Timber Carnival** is held in Prineville during the second week in May with a parade, equipment display, logging show, men's and women's logrolling, and a tug-of-war between loggers and Forest Service workers. For more information call 447-5031. Another popular Prineville get-together is the **Annual Prineville Rockhound Show and Powwow** (Box 671, Prineville 97754; tel. 447-6760), held in mid-June. The powwow attracts prospectors and rockhounds from all over the country.

The first week in July is the time and Prineville is the site for the **Crooked River Roundup,** with pari-mutuel horse racing. The restored cars of the Prineville Railroad make special trips during the summer, including a **Fourth of July barbecue run.** Check with the Prineville Chamber of Commerce for details.

Down the road a ways, Mt. Vernon holds its **Cinnabar Mountain Rendezvous** May 26-28. The rendezvous includes a parade, dance, community potluck, and lumberjack contest. **Kam Wah Chung Days** in John Day are held in late April to celebrate the Chinese heritage of the area. A full schedule of events includes rickshaw races, a Chinese checkers tourney, flower-arranging demos, a puppet theater, and a Chinese parade. Another midsummer festival is **'62 Days** in Canyon City, just south of John Day on U.S. 395, which celebrates the local discovery of gold in 1862 with a medicine-wagon show, can-can girls, and a reenactment of the opening of historic Sel's Brewery. The **Elkhorn Crest Sled Dog Races** in January and the **Rooster Crowing Contest** in July are two popular Sumpter events. On the first weekend of August the town sponsors the **Old Time Fiddler's Contest** and the **Sumpter Valley County Fair and Flea Market,** one of the largest crafts shows and flea markets in the Northwest.

Information And Services

For general information, the **Prineville-Crook County Chamber of Commerce** (390 N. Fairview St., Box 546, Prineville 97754; tel. 447-6304) is a valuable resource. If you need the law, the **Prineville City Police** (400 E. Third St.; tel. 447-4168), the **Crook County Sheriff's Office** (308 E. Second St., Prineville; tel. 447-6398), and the **state police** (400 E. Third St., Prineville; tel. 447-4168) are always ready to serve you. In the next county over, the **John Day Police** (240 S. Canyon Blvd., John Day 97845; tel. 575-0030) and the **Grant County Sheriff's Office** (200 S. Canyon City Blvd., Canyon City 97820; tel. 575-1131) are also at your beck and call. Out here in the wide-open spaces, these numbers can sometimes prove useful.

The two newspapers in the area are the *Central Oregonian* (558 N. Main, Prineville 97754; tel. 447-6205), which publishes twice a week, and the *Blue Mountain Eagle* (714 E. Main, John Day 97845; tel. 575-0710), circulated weekly on Thursdays.

The Prineville **post office** (155 Court, Prineville 97754; tel. 447-5652) is open Mon.-Fri. 6:30 a.m.-5:15 p.m., Sat. 6:30 a.m.-4:30 p.m. The John Day post office (151 Canyon Blvd., John Day 97845; tel. 575-1306) keeps similar hours.

The Ochoco National Forest is administered from the following offices: **Prineville Ranger District** (2321 E. Third., Prineville 97754; tel. 447-3825), **Paulina Ranger District** (6015 Paulina Star Route, Paulina 97751; tel. 447-3713), **Big Summit Ranger District** (Box 225K, Mitchell Star Route, Prineville 97754; tel. 447-3845), **Snow Mountain Ranger District** (Star Route 4, Box 12870, ORE 20, Hines 97738; tel. 573-7292), and the **Malheur National Forest Office** (139 N.E. Dayton St., John Day 97845; tel. 575-1731).

Pioneer Memorial Hospital (1201 N. Elm, Prineville 97754; tel. 447-6254) has 24-hour emergency services. In John Day, medical help is available at the **Blue Mountain Hospital** (170 Ford Rd., John Day 97845; tel. 575-1311). The **Third St. Shell and Food Mart** (550 W. Third, Prineville 97754; tel. 447-4476) is open 24 hours. The **Laundry and Dry Cleaners** (250 E. Fourth St., Prineville; tel. 447-3126) is also open 24 hours, with dry cleaning available Mon.-Fri. 9-5. In John Day, you can get your clothes clean at the aptly named **Weary Traveler Laundromat** (755 S. Canyon Blvd., John Day; tel. 575-2076).

Getting Around
Prineville Airport (tel. 447-2833), two miles west of Prineville, is a fixed-base operator facility serviced by Rimrock Aviation. The **John Day Airport** (Airport Rd., John Day 97845; tel. 575-1151) has no commercial flights but does have a charter service. Prineville is served by **Greyhound** (1825 E. Third., Prineville 97754; tel. 447-5516), but no buses serve John Day and vicinity.

ANNE LONG

NORTHEASTERN OREGON
ALONG THE OLD OREGON TRAIL

The pioneer trek along the Oregon Trail, a tide of migration starting in 1841 and lasting over 20 years, is one of this country's great epochs, celebrated in novels, films, books, and songs. It's almost the largest voluntary human migration ever recorded. The wagon trains started in Independence, Missouri, as soon as the spring grass was green. Then the race was on to get across the far mountains before the winter snows. Although the first few hundred miles were easy traveling across the plains, the hardships were not long in coming. Indian attacks, cholera, exhaustion, drownings, and in some cases, bad directions gave this 2,000-mile journey the nickname "The Longest Graveyard." Some historians believe that by 1859, at least 30,000 immigrants had died on the Oregon Trail. This would amount to an average of one unmarked grave for every 100 yards between Independence and Oregon City. By some estimates, over 300,000 people made the trek from the midwest to Oregon between 1841 and the turn of the century.

At Fort Hall in eastern Idaho, there was a fork in the trail and a sign, which read To Oregon. It was here that the pioneers had to make a key decision. They could head south to California and the gold fields shining with the promise of instant wealth, or they could continue west to Oregon, where the fertile valley of the Willamette offered its own allure as a New Jerusalem for serious farmers and homesteaders. Those who chose Oregon crossed the Snake River near Ontario, the Malheur River at Vale, and followed the wagon ruts north to lose sight of the Snake at Farewell Bend. The route is now paralleled by I-84 through Baker, La Grande, Pendleton, and on down the Columbia River Gorge to Portland. The towns along this modern Oregon Trail reflect the heritage of the pioneer era. The character and tenacity of those who chose Oregon over California can be seen in the sunburned, windcreased faces of these sagebrush citizens. The following section offers a tour of this region, starting with Ontario and traveling northwest.

Located midway between Portland and Salt Lake City in Oregon's far east, Ontario is where "Oregon's day begins." It's the biggest city in Malheur County, with a population of 9,750. Ontario ships over five percent of the nation's onions and provides a good portion of the sweet russet potatoes used for French fries. Other local crops include sugar beets, peppermint, grains, and ornamental flowers. This abundance derives from a location on the fertile plain at the junction of the Snake and Malheur rivers.

Baker, set in a valley between the Wallowas and the Blue Mountains, is the jumping-off spot for Hells Canyon, the deepest gorge in the world. Ranchers still drive their herds down the highways here, and folks wave howdy to passersby. It's a friendly place that has held on to its pioneer spirit.

La Grande, located in what the indigenous peoples called Copi Copi (the surrounding "Valley of Peace"), is now known as the Grande Ronde Valley. Home of Eastern Oregon State College, La Grande enjoys a brisk economy based on beef ranching, wheat farming, and timber. Tourism is on the rise as well. In addition to being the gateway to Wallowa Lake and the northern flank of the Wallowa Range, the region has a rich history, which is detailed at a new Forest Service visitor area along a section of trail in the Blue Mountains between Pendleton and La Grande.

HISTORY

Ontario, the town at the beginning of the Oregon section of the Oregon Trail, began as a cattle-shipping depot. The 1883 completion of the Oregon Short Line Railroad connected it to the Union Pacific and markets in the east. In 1939, manmade reservoirs began irrigating the Snake River Valley, turning it into a rich agricultural region. During WW II, relocation centers for Japanese-Americans were built here. The only crime these citizens had committed was having the wrong ancestry. Stripped of their rights by a single executive order signed by President Roosevelt, about 5,000 Americans of Japanese ancestry were forced to liquidate their property and move into prisonlike barracks in remote sections of the west. This serious breach of constitutional freedoms remains one of the saddest chapters in American history. It's also worth noting that many of these unjustly incarcerated pariahs fought in the European theater of war in some of the most decorated units in the American Armed Forces.

In any case, a good percentage of the internees stayed in the area and now are well represented in the local business and agricultural communities. As in the Columbia Gorge, Japanese surnames grace many a ranch or farmstead in eastern Oregon. The U.S. Senate has appro-

Leslie Gulch in Malheur County

OREGON TOURISM DIVISION

NORTHEAST OREGON

TO BOISE

IDAHO

HELLS CANYON NATL. REC. AREA

SNAKE RIVER

IDAHO
OREGON

FAREWELL BEND STATE PARK

ONTARIO

VALE

ENTERPRISE
JOSEPH

MT. HOWARD
(ELEV. 8,200 ft.)

CHIEF JOSEPH MT.
(ELEV. 9,617 ft.)

EAGLE CAP
(ELEV. 9,685 ft.)

HALFWAY

WALLOWA LAKE

MATTERHORN
(ELEV. 10,004 ft.)

WALLOWA Mountains

TO WALLA WALLA TO LEWISTON

GRANDE RONDE RIVER

WALLOWA RIVER
WALLOWA

ELGIN

THIEF VALLEY RESERVOIR

NORTH POWDER

HAINES

BAKER

PHILLIPS RESERVOIR

MILTON-FREEWATER

LA GRANDE

EMIGRANT SPRINGS STATE PARK

McKAY CREEK RESERVOIR

LEHMAN HOT SPRINGS

GRANITE

SUMPTER

BLUE MTN. HOT SPRINGS

20mi

20km

WASHINGTON
OREGON

COLD SPRINGS NATL. WILDLIFE REFUGE

PENDLETON

PRAIRIE CITY

STRAWBERRY MTN.
(ELEV. 9,038 ft.)

TO SPOKANE

HERMISTON

UMATILLA

DIXIE PASS
(ELEV. 5,260 ft.)

JOHN DAY

CANYON CITY

STRAWBERRY MTN. WILDERNESS

TO BURNS

COLUMBIA RIVER

JOHN DAY FOSSIL BEDS NATL. MONUMENT SHEEP ROCK UNIT

WASHINGTON
OREGON

CONDON

PAULINA

CROOKED RIVER

TO PORTLAND

FOSSIL

JOHN DAY RIVER

JOHN DAY FOSSIL BEDS NATL. MONUMENT PAINTED HILLS UNIT

OCHOCO SUMMIT
(ELEV. 4,720 ft.)

OCHOCO LAKE STATE PARK

PRINEVILLE RESERVOIR STATE PARK

PRINEVILLE

TO PORTLAND

TO BEND

JOHN DAY FOSSIL BEDS NATL. MONUMENT CLARNO UNIT

© MOON PUBLICATIONS, INC.

OREGON'S NEW GOLD RUSH

California's "Days of '49" and other historic gold rushes in Alaska, Colorado, and Oregon have given us a colorful image of gold mining, with bushy-bearded miners in plaid shirts and red long johns panning for the glitter in sparkling mountain streams. But a new gold rush in Oregon has a less romantic edge to it—the use of cyanide to leach gold dust from pulverized earth.

At Grassy Mountain near Vale in Malheur County, Quartz Mountain in southern Lake County, Farewell Bend north of Ontario, and the Bohemia Mountains near Cottage Grove in the Willamette Valley, mining corporations are investing millions in a new process that promises to extract the last flakes of the yellow stuff, which is now worth between $300-400 an ounce. The process is called heap leach-mining and it's a lot cheaper than underground mining. A grid-work of ammonia nitrate and diesel fuel is detonated, and the tons of earth loosened by the explosion are ground up and spread out in huge plastic-lined ponds. Then a solution of cyanide and water is sprayed over the ore. The solution leaches out the gold and other metals. The mining corporations expect to get $370 million from the Grassy Mountain project and up to $1.5 billion from the Quartz Mountain mine. The jobs that these operations bring to local areas will be welcomed in a time of uncertain employment in rural Oregon. But there is a definite down side.

Gary Brown of Ontario is a member of Concerned Citizens for Responsible Mining. He states that the cyanide leaching is dangerous and destructive. It contaminates the water table, attracts and poisons birds and animals, and uses up 50 times more earth than underground mining.

Like offshore oil exploration, the harvesting of ancient forests, and the damming of scenic rivers, this new gold rush will be another battleground for the ongoing conflict between environmentalists and natural resource-dependent industries.

---

priated money for a museum here documenting the internment. It's expected to be built at Treasure Valley Community College and should be open by the time you read this book. An influx of Hispanic migrant workers who came to work the crops in the '50s and '60s also stayed to start new lives, adding yet another ethnic flavor to the cultural stew in Ontario.

Baker, the next major town up the line, was named after Col. Edward Baker, Oregon's first senator and a one-time law partner of Abraham Lincoln. Baker City got its charter in 1874 and soon became known as the "Queen City," for all roads led to this commercial center. In 1861, it became the hub of the eastern Oregon gold rush and its population swelled to 6,600, making it bigger than Boise. Stop by the U.S. National Bank there and check out the 80.4-ounce Armstrong gold nugget, found in 1913.

Pioneer cattleman Herman Oliver recalls his visits to Baker as a young boy. He remembers the trolley car that ran the length of Main Street for a nickel. When the conductor reached the end of the line, he pulled a pin holding the horse and led the animal to the other end of the trolley and hooked it up for the return trip. Today, this frontier-era cattle, lumber, and gold-mining crossroads recaptures its 120 years of history with stone and brick buildings, many of which date from 1880-1915. Local historians say the town's architectural styles include Italianate, classic revival, Victorian, and Carpenter Gothic. East of town, along Route 7 and its offshoots, ghost towns like Granite and Cornucopia give new meaning to Gertrude Stein's description of another place: "There's no there there."

La Grande, the third city on the Oregon Trail, is in a valley where the Nez Percé once gathered for their summer encampments until the Oregon Trail cut through their territory. More than a few of the pioneers were impressed with the possibilities of the Grande Ronde country. They stayed to build a town that became the market center for a broad stretch of wheat and grass-seed farms. Lumber from the Blue Mountains and livestock that fattened easily on lush fields of tall grass also helped the Oregon Trail pioneers' dreams come true.

SIGHTS

Vale And Oregon Trail Sites

Vale, the seat of Malheur County, is located on the Malheur River at the spot where the wagons crossed the river, 28 miles west of Ontario on

U.S. 20/26. If you're intrigued by the drama of the pioneers, this little town offers an abundance of historic insight. On your visit to Vale, look north to **Malheur Butte** at mile marker 254. This long-extinct volcano was used as a lookout point by Indians watching for the wagon trains. The next historical site is **Malheur Crossing** on the east edge of Vale. The pioneers stopped here to take advantage of natural hot water from underground thermal springs to bathe and do their laundry.

The **Keeney Pass Oregon Trail Historic Site,** on the southern outskirts of Vale, has a display of the deep ruts cut into the earth by ironclad wagon wheels. This exhibit marks the most-used route of the wagon trains as they passed through the Snake River Valley on their way to Baker Valley to the north. From the top of this pass you can see the route of a whole day's journey on the trail to Oregon, 150 years ago. Ponder the fact that one pioneer in 10 died on this arduous transcontinental trek as you gaze out at the Snake River crossing near Old Fort Boise to the southeast. In June and July, Indian paintbrush and penstemon add a dash of color to the sagebrush and rabbitbrush that surround the ruts in the trail. Another site of interest is the **Stone House,** one block east of the Courthouse on Main Street. Built in 1872, it replaced a mud hut way station on the trail.

National Historic Oregon Trail Interpretive Center

Six miles east of Baker is the 23,000-square-foot Oregon Trail Interpretive Center (Box 854, Baker 97814; tel. 523-6391), which houses a theater, artifacts, photographs, and diaries of Oregon Trail pioneers. To get there, take exit 302 off I-84 and ORE 86. Exhibits on native Americans, fur traders, and soul seekers round out the historical perspective. Outside the building you see the panorama of the Blue Mountains, the Lone Pine Valley, and the Oregon Trail itself. A recreation of living history is featured at the **Pioneer Encampment,** where interpretive demonstrations give you an up-close view of what life was like on the trail.

Your next stop is an authentic **mining camp,** site of one of the earliest gold strikes along the trail. Get a taste of gold fever through the exhibited remnants and depictions here. There are five miles of nature walks and trails that have much the same flora and fauna that the pioneers saw, compounding the impression that the sky and the land were the only signposts along the 2,000-mile-long Oregon Trail. At last, you come to the famous thoroughfare itself and you can follow the footsteps of the several hundred thousand people who made the epic transcontinental trek. When you consider that 90% of the original 2,170-mile wagon route was destroyed by human activity, the eight miles of 150-year-old wagon ruts spread over Virtue Flat below the visitor center take on a deeper meaning. Natural grandeur is added to the scene by the breathtaking 10,000-foot Elkhorn Mountains to the west, the Blues to the south, and the craggy Eagle Cap Wilderness to the northeast. Some say that if you are out here alone, and you close your eyes and tilt your head to one side, you can still hear the grunts and groans of man and beast as they wearily slog along on their way to the promised land.

Oregon Trail Regional Museum

The Oregon Trail Regional Museum (Campbell and Grove streets, Baker 97814; tel. 523-9308) is open daily 10-4 from the second weekend in May through the third weekend in September. As well as exhibits depicting the great migration, the museum houses an extensive collection of seashells and corals and one of the most comprehensive exhibits of rocks, minerals, and semiprecious stones in the west.

Crossroads Center

Crossroads Creative and Performing Arts Center (2020 Auburn Ave., Baker 97814; tel. 523-3704) is in the old Carnegie Library. It has monthly exhibits, a gift shop, and an Arts and Crafts Fair held July 17-19. While you're at the Crossroads Center, ask for a pamphlet describing the **Baker's Dozen,** a tour of the town's historic homes.

Eastern Oregon Museum

The Eastern Oregon Museum (Third and School, Haines 97833; tel. 856-3568) is open every day 9-5 April 15-Oct. 15 and has an outstanding collection of farming, mining, and pioneer artifacts.

Geographical Center Of The United States

According to local wags, the geographical center of the United States shifted dramatically with the addition of Hawaii and Alaska, to a spot 12 miles north of Medical Springs, where ORE 203 meets Catherine Creek.

Hot Lake

Hot Lake Mineral Hot Springs was considered "Big Medicine" by the western tribes that camped near its healing waters. In 1810, Astor Pacific Fur Company trappers described elk crowding around this spring. Thereafter, the lake, located five miles east of La Grande on ORE 203, became a popular spot for explorers and emigrants. In 1864, Samuel Newhart built a hotel and bathhouse here. A hospital was added at the turn of the century and it soon became known as the Mayo Clinic of the West, a polite euphemism for one of the Northwest's first "fat farms." During that era, the healing waters here were also thought to give relief from arthritis and rheumatism. The resort is not currently in operation.

North Powder Elk Views

North Powder Elkhorn Wildlife Management Area is a winter elk feeding station open for visits (by permit) Dec. 1-April 15, but viewing is possible from nearby county roads in late afternoon and evening. To get there, go west 10 miles from exit 285 off I-84. Viewpoints are one mile south of the headquarters on River Rd. and two miles north of headquarters on Tucker Flat Road. These Rocky Mountain elk are somewhat smaller than the Roosevelt elk commonly seen on the west side of the Cascades.

Deadman's Pass

Deadman's Pass, at exit 228 on I-84, led emigrants out of the Blue Mountains into the Umatilla Valley. This was the last big hump they had to cross before the raft trip down the Columbia. The name comes from three incidents during the Bannock Indian War of 1878 in which seven men were killed. Look for a sign directing you up a trail to a sampling of still-visible wagon ruts.

SPORTS AND RECREATION

The country through which the Oregon Trail passes is filled with recreational choices. **Ontario-Shadow Butte Golf Course** (tel. 889-9022) is an 18-hole municipal course with pro shop and lounge, two miles west of Ontario. **Bully Creek Reservoir,** 30 minutes' drive west of Ontario near the small town of Vale, has boat-launch facilities, picnic and camping areas, swimming, and water-skiing. The fishing includes crappie, bass, trout, and perch. **Anthony Lakes Ski Area** (tel. 800-762-7941) is between Baker and La Grande, 18 miles west of North Powder and Haines on I-84. Open Nov.-April, daily 9-4, this ski resort offers a chair lift, Nordic trail system, day lodge, ski shop, and ski lessons. All-day tickets are $16.50; children under 10 pay $11.

Camping

Of the many campsites in the Wallowa-Whitman National Forest, here are four of the best. **Grande Ronde Lake Campground** along the shore of the lake has all the amenities and good trout fishing as a bonus. The fee is $5 per night. To get there drive 17 miles northwest of Haines on ORE 411, then eight miles west on Forest Service Rd. 73. The camp is one-half mile northwest on Forest Service Rd. 43. **Sherwood Forest Campground** is a small site on the banks of the Grande Ronde River. There is no fee for this campground, which is open late May-late November. Go nine miles northwest of La Grande on I-84, then 13 miles southwest on ORE 244. From there, drive six miles south on Forest Service Rd. 51.

A third site, **Hilgard Junction State Park,** is also on the Grande Ronde River, at the foot of the Blue Mountains. Fees for this 18-site (no hookups) campground are $7 per night. To get there drive eight miles west of La Grande on I-84 to Starkey Road. This campground is very popular during deer- and elk-hunting seasons and is expected to also be very busy during the 1993 Oregon Trail celebration as its location is on the original route of this pioneer pathway. The fourth site is **Emigrant Springs State Park,** a large facility with flush toilets, a laundromat, and a playground, right off I-84. The fee is $10 per night. This park has a display on the Oregon Trail and is a good spot to stop while traveling on the interstate.

PRACTICALITIES

Accommodations

These lodgings, ranging from affordable to fancy, should make your own trek along the Oregon Trail far more comfortable than it would have been 150 years ago. Baker City is the hub, with 11 motels (455 motel rooms) plus two bed and breakfasts and three RV parks. During Oregon Trail Festivities, the Baker City Visitor and Convention Bureau also has motel listings for La Grande, 45 miles north on I-84, should local rooms be filled up. The **Fireside Motel** (1737 N. Oregon, Ontario 97914; tel. 889-3101) will run you $18-28. The **Tapadera Motor Inn** (1249 Tapadera Ave., Ontario; tel. 889-8621) ranges $34-40 per night.

Closer to the other end of the scale, the **Grant House Bed and Breakfast** (2525 Third St., Baker 97814; tel. 523-4364) charges $50. This large, four-story inn boasts an outdoor hot tub and five sleeping chambers, including the Gore Vidal and Cybill Shepherd rooms. The **Sunridge Inn** (1 Sunridge Lane, Baker 97814; tel. 523-6444) has a heated pool and private patios and is this town's high-priced spread with rates of $52-62. The **Western Motel** (3055 10th St., Baker 97814; tel. 523-4646) is a more economical choice, with rates of $26-33. If you don't feel like dining in their restaurant, you can whip up something in your own kitchen. **Stange Manor** (1612 Walnut, La Grande 97850; tel. 963-2400) is a Georgian colonial mansion built by a timber baron. Period furniture and views of the mountain make this a steal at $45-65 for two. All rooms except two have baths.

The **Union Hotel** (326 N. Main, Union 97883; tel. 562-5417) will take you back to another era, with a room and bath for around $20. The town of Union is 11 miles southeast of La Grande on ORE 203, and shows off lots of great old brick buildings and old-time atmosphere. The **Moon Motel** (2116 Adams Ave., La Grande 97850; tel. 963-2724) is the most affordable lodging in town, with rates of $23-30. Lastly, the **Pitcher**

Inn Bed and Breakfast (608 N. Street, La Grande 97850; tel. 963-9152) is a 1925 Georgian home with a honeymoon suite with private bath and three more rooms sharing two baths. It's open all year except Jan. 2-15. Rates are $55-75.

Food

Not too many recommendations on this route, but here are a few worth tucking in your napkin for. The **Cheyenne Social Club and Lounge** (11 S.W. First, Ontario; tel. 889-3777) was named after a bawdyhouse run by Jimmy Stewart in a 1970 Western. Lunches run $4.25-9 and dinners $9-25, primarily steak and seafood entrees, all in a late-19th-century setting.

Blue and White Cafe (1825 Main, Baker; tel. 523-6792) is an institution. For nearly 40 years this cafe has been selling coffee for a dime and cinnamon rolls for 25 cents. You'll have to vie for counter space here with a bunch that calls itself the Main Street Nearly Honest Senile Businessmen. For a more hearty breakfast try the biscuits and gravy!

The Front St. Cafe (1840 Main St., Baker City; tel. 523-7526) is a good bet for lunch. Burgers and 14 varieties of salad can fortify your wanderings along the Oregon Trail. A sure bet for a good all-American meal is the **Farm House Restaurant** (401 Adams, La Grande; tel. 963-9318). Sandwiches cost $3 and dinners $6. If you appreciate "gourmet" (by La Grande standards) Mexican food try **Mamacita's** (110 Depot, La Grande; tel. 963-6223). Entrees run $4.25-$6.25, including a Guadalajara tostada for $5.25, flautas for $4.50, and arroz con pollo for $6.25. Save room for dessert if only for Mamacita's flan or, if you're really hungry, Kahlua pie. **Ten Depot Street** (10 Depot St., La Grande; tel. 963-8766) might be a harbinger of things to come. Such interesting plates as teriyaki tofu for $7.95, Oregon-raised lamb chops for $12.95, and a delicious salmon pâté for $3.95 will evoke bistros west of the Cascades. To complete the effect they also serve Portland microbrewery beer and ale.

Ten miles north of Baker City is the well-regarded **Haines Steakhouse** (ORE 30; tel. 856-8639). Open Wed.-Mon. for dinner, you can sup on charcoal-grilled steak (there's also fish, chicken, and barbecued steak), garlicky potato salad, and smoky baked beans, if you're still hungry after a trip to the well-stocked salad bar. Antiques and cowboy Americana decorate the restaurant, enhancing what may be described as first-rate chuckwagon fare. Stetson-hatted diners and log-cabin style booths will get you in the mood for all this frontier hospitality. The restaurant's blond-wood false front stands out in this town of stone and brick structures like a Conestoga wagon on an open prairie.

Entertainment And Events
Like every town in America, each town on our route has a special festivity in which the locals whoop it up in their own way. The **Obon Odori Festival** celebrating Ontario's Japanese heritage is held the third week in July at the Buddhist temple. On the schedule are tours of the temple, a dinner featuring Asian cuisine, arts-and-crafts displays, and an evening of dancing with audience participation.

The **Vale Rodeo** is a four-day fête that takes place July 1-4. It's highlighted by the Suicide Race, an event held at nearby Vale Butte in which cowboys race their horses off a steep slope into the arena. The **Miner's Jubilee**, the big shivaree in Baker, is traditionally celebrated during the third week in July. On the bill are a fiddle festival, an arts and crafts fair, bed and raft races, a cowbelles' breakfast, and the World Championship Porcupine Sprint Race. On the Fourth of July in Haines, a wide spot on ORE 30 between Baker and North Powder, they have a competition to name the oldest working cowhand in the Northwest. If you think you qualify call 856-3211. La Grande's major celebrations of the year are the **Oregon Trail Days and Rendezvous** in mid-August and **Blue Mountain Days** in late June, which features a parade, rodeo, and motorcycle rally.

Health
Ontario's hospital is **Holy Rosary Medical Center** (381 S.W. Ninth; tel. 889-5331). It has 24-hour emergency service. **St. Elizabeth Hospi-**

tal (3325 Pocahontas Rd., Baker) also has a 24-hour emergency room. **Grande Ronde Hospital** (900 Sunset Dr., La Grande; tel. 963-8421) has an air ambulance service called Blue Mountain Aeromedical (tel. 800-426-5554).

Information And Services
The Malheur County **Chamber of Commerce** office (173 S.W. First Street, Ontario 97914; tel. 889-8012), the Vale County Chamber of Commerce (272 N. Main, Vale 97918; tel. 473-3800), the Baker County Chamber of Commerce (490 Campbell St., Baker 97814; tel. 523-5855) and the La Grande-Union County Chamber of Commerce (1502 N. Pine, La Grande 97850; tel. 963-8588) all have useful information to aid your explorations along the Old Oregon Trail. Better yet, contact the **Baker City Visitor and Convention Bureau** (490 Campbell St., Baker City 97814; tel. 800-523-1235) for updates on all sesquicentennial events.

You can find a **post office** in Baker (1550 Dewey Ave., Baker 97814; tel. 523-4237) and in La Grande (1202 Washington, La Grande 97850; tel. 963-2041). The **state police** have offices in Baker (1050 S. Bridge; tel. 523-5866) and La Grande (3014 Island Avenue; tel. 963-7174). The **local police** also have offices in Baker (tel. 523-3644) and La Grande (tel. 962-1017).

Getting Around
There is very little public transit in this land of large distances and small population. Here's what is available: **Greyhound** has terminals in Baker (515 Campbell; tel. 523-5011) and in La Grande (2108 Cove Ave.; tel. 963-5156). **Grande Ronde Transportation Company** (1901 Jefferson, La Grande 97850; tel. 963-6119) has a bus charter service. **La Grande Aviation** (Route 2, Box 2546, La Grande 97850; tel. 963-6572) will fly you where you want to go. **Amtrak** (tel. 800-872-7275) has two unmanned stations, in Baker (2803 Broadway) and La Grande (Depot and Jefferson).

THE WALLOWAS

Acclaimed as the "Switzerland of America," the Wallowa Mountains and the broad valley to the north are not just another spectacular alpine region. Thanks to the outdoor-recreation boom and a publicity mill fueled by magazines like *Outside* and *Backpacker,* these mountains have become the new hot mecca for lovers of life on the wild side. Come now, before the word gets out about this backpackers' paradise where snowcapped Teton-like spires and blue-green glacial lakes are still relatively unvisited.

Ask most any Oregonian who has been there and they will tell you that the Wallowa range is one place in Oregon "you gotta see—you just gotta." With 17 of the state's 29 mountains over 9,000 feet and 50 glacial lakes sprinkled throughout 300,000 acres, the Eagle Cap Wilderness is a recreational area that should figure prominently in your travel plans. Here, campers and cross-country skiers are regularly treated to glimpses of bighorn sheep, mountain goats, elk, and mule deer, as well as snow-streaked granite peaks rising above meadows dotted with an artist's palette of wildflowers.

The Wallowa Valley, formed by the drainages of the Wallowa, Minam, and Grande Ronde rivers, has lots of open space. The area's economy is fueled by the traditional eastern Oregon triad of timber, farming, and cattle ranching. Enterprise is the commercial center of it all, while Joseph is the hub of a growing arts community and the gateway to Wallowa Lake, a recreational haven at the end of the road. After a visit to this "larger-than-life" countryside, it is easy to see how it sustained the proud and indomitable Nez Percé, the native people who once roamed its river canyons, glacial basins, and grassy hills.

HISTORY

The Wallowa Valley, set apart by deep river canyons and mountain ranges, is the ancestral home of the Nez Percé, a tribe known for its horse-raising skills and fierce independence. These regal people, astride their spotted Appaloosas, first encountered Europeans when mountain men wandered onto their land. At first they were friendly, feeding and caring for the Bonneville Party, which had struggled up out of the Snake River Canyon in 1834. Later, when a dry spell in the Grande Ronde Valley to the south prompted homesteaders to give the Wallowas a try, the two cultures clashed.

A tense era followed, in which various drafts of different treaties added to the confusion. The settlers later successfully lobbied the United States government to evict the natives, which led to the Nez Percé War of 1877. Chief Joseph and his people fought a running battle that covered 1,700 miles and ended with his surrender in the Bear Paw Mountains, 50 miles from the Montana-Canada border. Meanwhile, back at the ranch in the Wallowa Valley, the toughest of the settlers endured the winters, droughts, and other hardships of life on the frontier. One bachelor, in an attempt to ease his loneliness, sent the following note to a friend in Missouri: "Send at once C.O.D. a good-looking maid or widow, 30 years or under. Widow with a few children preferred."

In 1908, a passenger train steamed into Wallowa on a newly laid track from Elgin, thus expanding a route that had previously seen only horsemen and wagons. Not much has changed since those early days. The people of the Wallowa Valley believe that they inhabit paradise, and they seem to enjoy sharing it with visitors drawn by its natural beauty and vivid history.

SIGHTS

Wildlife

Two wildlife-viewing areas await you as you sweep down into the Wallowa Valley. The **Spring Branch Wildlife Area,** a woodland marsh, is two miles east of Wallowa on ORE 82, on the north side where the road leaves the Wallowa River. The eight-acre viewing area, managed by the Oregon Department of Fish and Wildlife, has beaver dams and lots of waterfowl, including the black tern, an insect-eating bird found in eastern Oregon marshes. The **Enterprise Wildlife Area** is two miles west of Enterprise off ORE 82. To get there, turn south on

CHIEF JOSEPH

The Nez Percé Indians had lived in peace with white explorers and neighboring tribes of the Northwest for generations. They gave the Lewis and Clark Expedition much needed horses and promised that they'd never make war on the white man. But with the incursion of miners and settlers, and because of misunderstandings surrounding the annexation of Indian land through a series of treaties never signed by Chief Joseph, tension increased to the breaking point. White disregard of native property spurred on some rash young Nez Percé to retaliate. The ensuing 11-week conflict, during which the Nez Percé engaged 10 separate United States military commands in 13 battles (the majority of which the Nez Percé won), guaranteed Chief Joseph's fame as a brilliant military tactician. However, after many hardships, Chief Joseph surrendered with the following words to Generals Miles and Howard on October 5, 1877, only 50 miles from the sanctuary of the Canadian border.

Tell General Howard I know his heart. What he told me before, I have in my heart. I am tired of fighting. Our chiefs are killed. Looking Glass is dead. Too-hool-hool-suit is dead. The old men are dead. It is the young men who say yes and no. He who led on the young men is dead. It is cold and we have no blankets. The little children are freezing to death. My people, some of them, have run away to the hills and have no blankets, no food; no one knows where they are, perhaps freezing to death. I want to have time to look for my children and see how many I can find. Maybe I shall find them among the dead. Hear me, my chiefs. I am tired; my heart is sick and sad. From where the sun now stands, I will fight no more forever.

In 1879, Chief Joseph spoke to the Department of Indian Affairs in Washington D.C., detailing the broken promises of the government, the suffering of his people, and the unjust treatment of the Indians by white society.

I have heard talk and talk, but nothing is done. Good words do not last long unless they amount to something. Words do not pay for my dead people. They do not pay for my country, now overrun by white men. They do not protect my father's grave. They do not pay for all my horses and cattle. Good words will not give me back my children. Good words will not make good the promise of your War Chief General Miles. Good words will not give my people good health and stop them from dying. Good words will not get my people a home where they can live in peace and take care of themselves. I am tired of talk that comes to nothing. It makes my heart sick when I remember all the good words and all the broken promises. There has been too much talking by men who had no right to talk. Too many misrepresentations have been made, too many misunderstandings have come up between the white men about the Indians. If the white man wants to live in peace with the Indian

continues

ANNE LONG

he can live in peace. There need be no trouble. Treat all men alike. Give them the same law. Give them all an even chance to live and grow. All men were made by the same Great Spirit Chief. They are all brothers. The earth is the mother of all people, and all people should have equal rights upon it. You might as well expect the rivers to run backward as that any man who was a free man should be contented when penned up and denied liberty to go where he pleases. If you tie a horse to a stake, do you expect he will grow fat? If you pen an Indian up on a small spot of earth, and compel him to stay there, he will not be contented, nor will he grow and prosper. I have asked some of the great white chiefs where they get their authority to say to the Indian that he shall stay in one place, while he sees white men going where they please. They cannot tell me.

I only ask of the government to be treated as all other men are treated. If I cannot go to my own home, let me have a home in some country where my people will not die so fast. I would like to go to Bitter Root Valley. There my people would be healthy; where they are now they are dying. Three have died since I left my camp to come to Washington.

When I think of our condition my heart is heavy. I see men of my race treated as outlaws and driven from country to country, or shot down like animals.

I know that my race must change. We cannot hold our own with the white men as we are. We only ask an even chance to live as other men live. We ask to be recognized as men. We ask that the same law shall work alike on all men. If the Indian breaks the law, punish him by the law. If the white man breaks the law, punish him also.

Let me be a free man—free to travel, free to stop, free to work, free to trade where I choose, free to choose my own teachers, free to follow the religion of my fathers, free to think and talk and act for myself—and I will obey every law, or submit to the penalty.

Whenever the white man treats an Indian as they treat each other, then we will have no more wars. We shall all be alike—brothers of one father and one mother, with one sky above us and one country around us, and one government for all. Then the Great Spirit Chief who rules above will smile upon this land, and send rain to wash out the bloody spots made by brothers' hands from the face of the earth. For this time the Indian race are waiting and praying. I hope that no more groans of wounded men and women will ever go to the ear of the Great Spirit Chief above, and that all people may be one people.

Fish Hatchery Rd. to this 32-acre site located just before the fish hatchery. Walk down the dike that goes through a grove of trees to view marsh wrens, snipe, mink, beavers, and muskrats.

Culture In The Hinterland

If you have an afternoon to spare in **Enterprise,** the Wallowa County Centennial Committee has organized a **walking tour** for you. Stop by the chamber of commerce booth in the Enterprise Mall and pick up their brochure. It has descriptions and locations of many of the historic buildings in the area, like the Wallowa County Courthouse, the Enterprise Hotel, the Oddfellows Hall, and a number of private homes. After an hour of edification and exercise, take a break at the **Bookloft-Skylight Gallery** (107 E. Main, Enterprise; tel. 426-3351), just across the street from the county courthouse. This gathering spot for artists and community activists sells bestsellers and local-history books and offers monthly shows of guest artists, as well as freshly brewed coffee and home-baked cookies.

Joseph

Cruising farther into the valley, you reach the lively community of Joseph, named after the famous Nez Percé chief. A must-stop for history buffs is the **Wallowa County Museum** on Main St. (tel. 432-6095). Open from the last weekend in May to the third weekend in Sept., hours are daily 10-5. Built in 1888, the museum building has served as a bank, a newspaper office, a private hospital, and a meeting hall. Its current incarnation as a museum started in 1960. The theme of the museum is Wallowa history, including displays of pioneer life and the Nez Percé tribe, the valley's original inhabitants. Near the museum during summer, a reenactment of the Great Joseph Bank Robbery takes place every Wed. and Sat. at 1 p.m.

Joseph is also the center of a blossoming art community in the Wallowas. Take a walk down Main St. and you'll find a number of art galleries and antique stores, among them the Wallowa Lake Gallery, Wild Goose Antiques, and the Edge of the Wilderness Gallery. The Gene Hayes Gallery specializes in the outdoors and the Old West, and Eagle Mountain Gallery and Valley Bronze is a casting foundry that uses the lost-wax casting process to create monumental sculptures.

Wallowa Lake

The brightest gem in the Wallowas setting is Wallowa Lake, which at 5,000 feet in elevation is the highest body of water in eastern Oregon. This classic moraine-held glacial lake is a few miles south of Joseph on ORE 62. The lake is ringed with lodges, amusement rides, a large state park with an overnight campground, packhorse corrals, boat launches, and marinas. It is also home to the Wallowa Lake Monster, a creature with a gentle disposition and a length varying from 30 to 100 feet, depending on the sighting. Reports of the critter go back several centuries to native American tales and are also the current focus of the Monster Observation and Preservation Society (MOPS).

A real treat for visitors is a ride in the Mt. Howard Gondola. Open during the summer 10-4, the gondola route is the steepest and longest in North America, lifting passengers from the edge of Wallowa Lake up 3,200 feet to the 8,200-foot summit of Mt. Howard. As the lift floats upward, the pastureland and wheatfield views near Wallowa Lake give way to forests of lodgepole pine, tamarack, and quaking aspen. The 15-minute trip in the closed gondola car costs $9 for adults, $8 for seniors, and $5 for children 10 and under. It operates mid-May-June on weekends only; thereafter it's open daily through September. The ride ends at a snack

bar and gift shop on top of the peak. But forget about the snacks, knickknacks, and trinkets; the best reason for taking the trip is the view of 26 mountain peaks, including the Wallowa Range, Snake River country, and Idaho's Seven Devils area. As you see the eight peaks of Eagle Cap Wilderness mirrored into the lake below and the gorges of the Snake and Imnaha rivers to the east, you'll understand the tenacity of Chief Joseph to remain in the area.

SPORTS AND RECREATION

Camping

Camping out in the Wallowa Valley and the Eagle Cap Wilderness can be as easy as pulling off ORE 82 just 15 miles east of Elgin and pitching your tent at Minam State Recreation Area ($6), or as rigorous as using one of the following three campsites as a jumping-off point for backpacking into the high country.

Boundary Campsite is five miles south of Wallowa on County Route 515, then two miles south on Forest Service Rd. 163. There's no

Wallowa Lake is the largest lake in northeastern Oregon.

OREGON DEPT. OF TRANSPORTATION

At Eagle Cap you can hike where eagles soar.

fee for this site set along the banks of Bear Creek, but there's also no water. A trailhead provides access to the dazzling grandeur of the Eagle Cap basin.

The next campsite/trailhead is **Two Pan,** one of the most popular gateways into the Wallowas. To get there, head south from Lostine on County Route 551 for seven miles and down Forest Service Rd. 5202 for 11 miles. This is a rough and rocky washboard grade, so take your time. Firewood and vault toilets are available; there are no fees or water. Trails leave Two Pan for the Lostine River Valley and the glacial lakes at the base of Eagle Cap.

The third campsite is **Hurricane Creek,** three miles southwest of Joseph. There's no charge for overnight camping, and piped water and firewood are available. The Hurricane Creek trailhead leads to a hike along the east slope of the Hurricane Divide past Sacajawea Peak and the Matterhorn to the glacial lakes basin. An ambitious trek would start at Two Pan and end at Hurricane Creek.

Then there's always **Wallowa State Park** campground (Wallowa Lake, Rt. 1, Box 323, Joseph 97846). This is one of 13 Oregon campgrounds that operate on a reservation system (see the general Introduction); reserve by mid-

spring or you're outta luck. Lake views, large campsites (89 tent and 121 RV sites), clean bathhouses, and covered kitchen shelters make it worth the $15-17 nightly fee. A marina, a sports field, and the cultural diversions of nearby Joseph (home to the Jazz at the Lake Festival in July) also recommend an early reservation.

Skiing

The recreational delights of the Wallowas are not reserved for summer only. The skiing in this alpine wonderland is excellent. **Ferguson Ridge Ski Area** (tel. 426-3493) is a good example. To get there, drive east from Joseph about five miles on the Wallowa Loop Hwy., then follow signs south on Tucker Down Road. This small facility has a rope tow and T-bar that climb from a 5,100-foot base to 5,800-foot-high Ferguson Ridge. Lift tickets are $7 a day. Nordic skiers can try a mile loop trail or take an eight-mile marked and packed route to Salt Creek Summit.

Another popular spot is **Salt Creek Summit,** about 20 miles southeast of Joseph on Wallowa Loop Highway. The facility has five miles of marked but ungroomed ski trails and a plowed snow park. A European approach to a skiing adventure is a tour of **Wallowa Alpine Huts.** Three- to five-day hut-to-hut tours of the Eagle

Cap Wilderness cost $185-465. Also available are lessons, helicopter skiing, and telemark camps. For information write to Alpine Huts (Box 9252, Moscow, ID 83843; tel. 208-882-1955).

For cross-country skiers, the **Wallowa Lake Nordic Center** (Wallowa Lake State Park; tel. 426-4611) maintains 13 miles of Nordic ski trails around Wallowa Lake. Finally, **Sacajawea Park Cross-Country Ski Trail** challenges the ambitious. Take Hurricane Creek Rd. west from Joseph to the Hurricane Creek trailhead. This cross-country ski route will take you up into a basin on the northeast side of Sacajawea Peak. After two steep miles through the forest, the trail opens up into a clear area with a view of the surrounding glacial peaks. For more information on this trek call the Eagle Cap Ranger District office at 426-3104.

Outfitters

If your budget allows for a guided adventure into the Wallowa wilds, here are two excellent services. The **Eagle Cap Wilderness Pack Station** (Route 1, Box 416, Joseph; tel. 432-4145) charges fees starting at $7 an hour per person for short trips to lakes and streams in the Eagle Cap high country, and going up to $750 for deluxe excursions to Hells Canyon or along the Imnaha River. **Wallowa Llamas** (Route 1, Box 84, Halfway 97834; tel. 742-2961) will show you a unique way to venture into the wilderness. One surefooted, even-tempered llama will carry 20 pounds of your gear; you carry the rest. The outfit offers trips to Hells Canyon, Imnaha Falls, Eagle Meadows, and across the rugged Wallowas. The expeditions are designed for those with some backpacking experience or anyone in reasonably good shape. Costs range from a three-day jaunt for $225 to a seven-day journey for $595.

Fishing

Fishing in this high country is a matter of choosing your favorite game fish. You can catch kokanee (landlocked salmon) and mackinaws in **Wallowa Lake,** trout and steelhead in the streams that flow out of the ice-capped mountains, or bass, crappie, and sturgeon in the **Snake River.** According to experts, the **Imnaha River** is one of the best late-season fishing streams in the Pacific Northwest.

PRACTICALITIES

Accommodations

Rather than list the usual motel information, here are lodgings in the Wallowas that reflect the special flavor of this unique outback:

On the Imnaha River 14 miles south of Imnaha is **Diamond W Ranch** (Route 1, Box 466, Imnaha 97842; tel. 577-3157). Rates start at $60 for adults and $30 for children and include meals and horses. The **Flying Arrow Resort** (Route 1, Box 370, Power House Rd., Joseph 97846; tel. 432-2951) not only has a great name but also a chocolate shop, bookstore, and village market. Rates start at $51 for one- and two-bedroom cottages.

Red's Wallowa Horse Ranch (Box 26, Joseph 97846; tel. 432-9171) is one of Oregon's best-known retreats. The lodge is tucked away in a high mountain valley with no phones or electricity and is famous for its home cooking and hospitality. You either fly in or arrive by an eight-mile pack trip. Guests stay in the lodge or in log cabins equipped with hot water, kerosene lamps, and fireplaces. Horseback rides, hiking, fishing, snowshoeing, and cross-country skiing trips can be arranged. Package rates are $75-100 a day for the whole shootin' match.

Other accommodations near Joseph are **Eagle Cap Chalets** (Route 1, Box 419, Wallowa Lake Hwy., Joseph 97846; tel. 432-4704). Tucked into the pines, this cluster of cabins and condos has all you need to visit Wallowa Lake in comfort and style. Rates run $49-75. The folks at the **Wallowa Valley Guest House** (Box 843, Joseph 97846; tel. 432-9765) have rooms for $35 and up for two. Close to Nordic and downhill ski areas, this B&B can also arrange pack trips and llama treks.

A couple of hostelries on the shore of Wallowa Lake are good bets for those who want comfort rather than campouts. The **Wallowa Lake Lodge** (Box 1, Joseph 97846; tel. 432-4082, or 426-4336, Jan. 1-April 15) is a renovated 1923 hotel with room for two starting at $40 in winter and $55 in summer. Cabins with fireplaces and kitchens start at $55 in winter and $75 in summer. The Nordic center is a five-minute walk away and there are a store and gas station on the grounds. **Matterhorn Swiss Village** (Route 1,

Box 350, Joseph 97846; tel. 432-4071) has rates from $41 to $48. In keeping with the notion that the Wallowas are the Switzerland of America, this facility has six cottages with names like the Alpenhof and Berghof, a gift and sports shop, and water-ski, bike, and sailboard gear rentals.

Food

Like most frontier outposts in the American West, the Wallowa Valley has lots of standard takeout joints and few eateries worth a special stop. However, the following restaurants will not only keep you going during your visit but give you a few tasty surprises as well.

The **T'N'T Kitchen** in Wallowa (tel. 886-7705) grills a tasty buffalo burger with soup, salad, and fries for under $5. They also sell stuffed buffalo toys in case the kids would rather play with their food than eat it. **Cloud Nine** (105 S.E. First, Enterprise; tel. 426-3790) serves up deli sandwiches, good coffee, and homemade soups in an old firehouse. Sandwiches run $3-5. **A Country Place on Pete's Pond** (Box 459, Montclair St., Enterprise; tel. 426-3642) is a charming lunch spot on the edge of a five-acre lake. Pete invites you to feed the fish, enjoy the swans, and eat indoors or out on the lawn. A floating bandstand has musical entertainment on some occasions. Their sandwiches run $4-5, are made with homemade bread, and come with fries, salad, or soup.

Another spot in Enterprise with good food is **Sonita's Cafe Olé** (107 S.W. First St.; tel. 426-4888). Located in the Enterprise Mall, the cafe has both Mexican and American dishes with combination dinners running $6-15. Specialties include the Burrito Del Mar with shrimp and Monterey jack for $10.95 and chimichangas for $6.95.

Your best bet in Joseph is **Pam's Country Inn Restaurant** (500 N. Main; tel. 432-1195). Pam's has an ambience reminiscent of a French country inn. Their "country cooking" menu features dinners starting at $6 and house specialties like beef Wellington and chicken teriyaki from $10. Their eight-ounce filet mignon runs $14.95. Close to Wallowa Lake, **Vali's Alpine Delicatessen** features great cinnamon rolls at breakfast (9-11 a.m.) and a different dinner menu each day (seatings at 6 and 8 p.m.). Dinner runs $6 to $8.50. Open Tues.-Sun. in summer, weekends only in winter.

Entertainment And Events

Most of the local celebrations here revolve around cowboys and Indians and the arts community. The **Wallowa Valley Festival of the Arts** held at the Joseph Civic Center happens in the third week of April. Along with awards for Northwest artists, there are winetasting parties, a silent auction, and a quick-draw competition. A recent addition to the festivities is a reading by cowboy poets. For information on the festival call the Wallowa Valley Arts Council at (800) 635-2000. The **Bookloft-Skylight Gallery** (107 E. Main, Enterprise 97828; tel. 426-3351) is a gathering spot across from the courthouse where books and monthly shows by guest artists keep alive the Spirit of the Arts Festival. The flame of knowledge is also kept burning by **Sunflower Books** (1114 Washington St., La Grande; tel. 963-5242). The **Wallowa County Fiddlers' Contest** brings fiddlers from throughout the Northwest to mix it up with music, good grub, and the spirit of the pioneer days. Held in Enterprise on the third weekend in July, the contest is a treat for both the performers and their appreciative audiences.

The tiny town of **Lostine** celebrates the **Fourth of July** with artists, craftspeople, and collectors plying their wares in the Lostine Sidewalk Flea Market.

Chief Joseph Days is a week-long cowboy-and-Indian festival hosted by Joseph, the little town near Wallowa Lake. Held in late July, the list of events includes dances, a carnival, a Grand Parade, a ranch-style breakfast, and a three-day rodeo, which has grown to be one of the largest in the Northwest. For tickets and information call 432-1015. Another echo of the Wild West can be witnessed at 1 p.m. every Wednesday, Friday, and Saturday during the summer as four outlaws ride into town and rob the First Bank of Joseph. This dramatic re-creation of a historic robbery is played out on the spot of the original heist. The bank building now houses the Wallowa County Museum.

Alpenfest is a three-day festival held the third weekend after Labor Day in Edelweiss Hall next to the tramway at Wallowa Lake. This gala is a return to the old country and all that's Bavarian, sending echoes into the mountains with music, alpenhorn blowing, and yodeling competitions. Dancing, sailboat racing, and a bounty of Northern European cuisine are also featured. For reservations and information call the Wallowa Lake Tourist Committee at 432-6325.

Hells Canyon Mule Days, held the second weekend after Labor Day at the Enterprise Fairgrounds, is where pack-animal fanciers can get their kicks. The action includes mule races, a parade, a speed mule-shoeing contest, and endurance races.

Information And Services
The Wallowa **post office** is at 104 N. Stories (tel. 886-3422), while the one in Enterprise is at 201 W. North (tel. 426-3555). The local office of the **Oregon State Police** is at 522 River, Enterprise (tel. 426-3036). Contact the Wallowa sheriff's office at 426-3131, Wallowa police at 886-2422, Enterprise police at 426-3755, and Joseph police at 432-3832. The only hospital in Wallowa County is the **Wallowa Memorial Hospital** (410 E. First, Enterprise; tel. 426-3111).

The **Wallowa County Chamber of Commerce** (Box 427A, 107 S.W. First St., Enterprise; 97828; tel. 426-4622) has a booth in the Enterprise Mall with a full complement of brochures, maps, and other information on the area. The county has two newspapers, the *Wallowa County Chieftain* (106 N.W. First, Enterprise; tel. 426-4567) and the *Joseph Eagle* (Box 549, Joseph; tel. 432-5585). If you need to get in touch with the **Forest Service,** the Eagle Cap Ranger District office is at 612 S.W. Second, Enterprise (tel. 426-3104); the Wallowa Valley Ranger District is one mile north of Joseph on ORE 82 (tel. 432-2171).

Getting There And Getting Around
Moffit Brothers Transportation (Lostine; tel. 569-2284) makes a daily roundtrip between La Grande and Wallowa Lake. **Wallowa Valley Stage** (tel. 432-3531) leaves from Paul's Chevron in Joseph. Don't worry about finding this gas station; it's the only one in town.

Two air services operate in Wallowa County. **Joseph Air Service** (Airport Rd., Joseph; tel. 432-6305) and **Spence Air Service** (Box 217, Enterprise; tel. 426-3288) are both listed in the *Oregon Pilot's Guide* and are available for charter flights.

HELLS CANYON

Hells Canyon, carved out by the Snake River, is the deepest gorge in the world, averaging 6,600 feet in depth. A 67-mile stretch of the Snake at the bottom of this canyon is one of the nation's protected Wild and Scenic Rivers. In 1975, Congress established the **Hells Canyon National Recreation Area,** comprised of 650,000 acres of stunning vistas, archaeological sites with petroglyphs and native ruins, as well as a mighty river thundering through rugged canyon lands. It's a hard place to get to, so be sure you check the local weather and road conditions before visiting the area. Also, it's a good idea to pack a snakebite kit. There are rattlesnakes in this country!

There are several ways to get to Hells Canyon from the Oregon side. The first route is easiest and on paved roads. From Baker take ORE 86 for 50 miles east to **Halfway.** Stop here to stock up on groceries and gas and then continue on ORE 86 another 16 miles to Oxbow Dam and then another 20 miles to Hells Canyon Dam.

This site affords a spectacular view of the canyon. Another paved approach is via ORE 82 through the Wallowa Valley to Enterprise, Joseph, and Imnaha. From Imnaha, one of the most isolated towns in America, take a rough road for 24 miles to Hat Point Lookout. Once you get there you'll be convinced that the all-encompassing view was worth the hassle.

Sights
The interior of Hells Canyon is a rugged wilderness framed by basalt cliffs. Cheatgrass, primroses, sunflowers, and prickly pear cactus are included in the canyon's varied botany. Bear, elk, mule deer, bighorn sheep, eagles, otters, and chukhar partridges are frequently seen here. Many outfitters can steer you to the canyon's pictographs, which some sources place at 10,000 years of age. In addition to Chief Joseph and his Nez Percé tribe, the area was also occupied by miners and pioneers, as turn-of-the-century log cabins and shacks attest.

SPORTS AND RECREATION

Backpacking
Before your trip into Hells Canyon, consider what the authors of *Hiking Guide to the Great Northwest* (Spring and Manning; Seattle: The Mountaineers, 1991) have to say about hiking here: "Hells Canyon is definitely not paradise. Summer temperatures soar above 100 degrees, rattlesnakes abound, and . . . despite the river, drinkable water can be hard to find." Nonetheless, over 900 miles of trails provide hikers with a wide variety of recreational choices in the Hells Canyon Recreation Area. Major trails are maintained but others are difficult to follow. Ticks and poison oak can be problems here too. Black widow and brown recluse spiders constitute the biggest danger, however. There are 12 campgrounds on the Oregon side of Hells Canyon. Here are a few of the better ones.

Lake Fork Campground is 18 miles northeast of Halfway on Forest Service Rd. 39. There are 10 sites with drinking water, and the fishing is good at nearby Fish Lake. Indian Crossing is located 45 miles southeast of Joseph on Forest Service Rd. 3960 and has drinking water as well as a trailhead for backpacking into the Eagle Cap Wilderness. On the northern end of the recreational area, Buckhorn Springs is 43 miles northeast of Enterprise and features a great view, spring water, and berry-picking in season.

River Outfitters
Hells Canyon Challenge (Star Route, Box 25, Lostine 97857; tel. 569-2445) offers an excursion full of excitement and gorgeous views. You start out at the mouth of the Grande Ronde River and then power up the Snake River in a jetboat. The rates start at $45 per person for a one-day trip and go up to $150 for a two-day trip for four persons. Other river guides offering trips up and down the Snake are Hells Canyon Adventures (Box 159, Oxbow 97840; tel. 785-3352) and Anderson River Adventures (Route 2, Box 192-H, Milton-Freewater 97862; tel. 558-3629). They both have one-day trips for

under $100. The *Oregon Guides and Packers* publication is a good resource in which to locate other outfitters (see the general Introduction).

Fishing for trout, catfish, smallmouth bass, and, if you're lucky, 100-year-old sturgeon can add to the pleasure of a raft trip.

PRACTICALITIES

Accommodations
Clear Creek Farm Bed and Breakfast (Route 1, Box 138, Halfway 97834; tel. 742-2233) is in a comfy old farmhouse on 160 secluded acres with a creek and pond for swimming and a great view of the upper Hells Canyon and Eagle Cap Wilderness. Best of all, it's all yours for $45. Birch Leaf Lodge (Route 1, Box 91, Halfway 97834; tel. 742-2990) is in a turn-of-the-century farmhouse on 42 acres at the foot of the Wallowa Mountains. A special feature of this B&B is a resident excursion planner who will help you schedule your recreational activities. Particularly recommended is a loop taking in the Oregon Trail Visitor Center at Baker City, and McGraw Point, the most accessible Hells Canyon overlook from Halfway, en route north to Joseph. Rates at this B&B (including a full country breakfast) run $50-65.

Food
If you're on your own, it would be prudent to pack a few picnic items. Restaurants are few and far between in this country. But there is a good restaurant in Halfway called Wild Bill's, named after the owner. Their dinners run $4.95 -$12.95 with two specials of the house—chicken teriyaki for $7 and chicken-fried steak made with their homemade gravy for $6.50. Also worth a stop here is the Old Church Restaurant (Main St., Halfway), which serves surprisingly urbane fare with homemade flair. Pasta dishes are highly recommended.

Information
Hells Canyon National Recreation Area Headquarters (Box 490, Enterprise 97828; tel. 426-3151) has additional information on Hells Canyon.

PENDLETON

The title of Sam Shepard's play *True West* is an appropriate moniker for this outpost on the prairie. People are really at home on the range here, leaving the city streets pretty quiet until a mid-September rodeo draws cowboys, cowgirls, and wannabes from all over the West. The transformation of Pendleton from a refueling and supply stop for surrounding ranchers to "party central" takes place in September during the Round-Up, with brewtaps going full tilt and streets filled with tourists in straw cowboy hats and bright new bandanas. When you're done whooping it up with the local good ol' boys, a town rich in history and memory awaits.

With a population of 15,000, Pendleton is one of the largest towns in eastern Oregon. It's an economic force thanks to vast wheat fields (Umatilla County ranks fifth in the U.S. in wheat production), rows of green peas, famous woolen mills, and tourism from the Pendleton Round-Up. The

climate is mild and dry, with an average temperature of 51 degrees and annual rainfall of 13 inches. Locals joke that this is where summer spends the winter. Located on I-84 equidistant from Portland, Seattle, Spokane, and Boise, Pendleton sits pretty much by itself in the midst of wide-open spaces. Residents like it that way.

HISTORY

Pendleton, originally called Goodwin's Station, is situated two miles downriver from the Oregon Trail's crossing at Emigrant Springs State Park. For millennia the ancient homeland of the Umatilla Indians, the area was visited by Lewis and Clark in 1805 and John Jacob Astor's American Fur Company in 1812. No Europeans put down roots until 1843, when Methodist missionaries led by Dr. Marcus Whitman brought a

Pendleton Round-Up brings back the glory of the Old West.

thousand settlers and 1,300 cattle to the region. The town itself, named after Senator George Hunt Pendleton, was founded in 1868 and incorporated in 1880. At that time, Pendleton consisted of a hotel and five houses. But it grew through the late 1880s to a ripsnorting cattle and farming center with 18 bawdyhouses and 32 saloons. It quickly gained the reputation of being the town that couldn't be tamed. The feistiness of the citizens here was demonstrated by the theft of the county seal and records from Umatilla Landing, thus making Pendleton the county seat.

Many of Pendleton's streets are named after Confederate generals—a legacy of hundreds of Southern emigrants who drifted west after the Civil War. Still other streets are numbered chronologically, but with confusing directional considerations. This has resulted in two First Streets (one southeast, one southwest.), two Second Streets, and so on—good luck.

SIGHTS

Round-Up Hall Of Fame

The Round-Up Hall of Fame (13th and S.W. Court Ave.) exhibit can be found under the south grandstand area at the Round-Up Stadium. The history of America's biggest rodeo is depicted in photos of past champions and famous bucking broncos along with displays of artifacts. The star of the show is a stuffed horse named War Paint. Admission is free and guided tours are available. The Pendleton Round-Up itself costs $5-10 and takes place over four days in September (see "Entertainment and Events" following).

Pendleton Woolen Mills

Next to the Pendleton Round-Up, the town is best known for the Pendleton Woolen Mills (1307 S.E. Court Place; tel. 276-6911), where they make those immortal plaid shirts. After shearing, the wool goes to a scouring mill in Portland where it's graded, sorted, and washed. Then the dried wool returns to the Pendleton mill for dyeing, carding, spinning, rewinding, and weaving.

The business began over in the Willamette Valley in Brownsville when Thomas Kay, a Yorkshireman whose family was in the woolen business in England, started a weaving mill. His descendant, Clarence Bishop, founded the Pendleton facility. Production began in 1909 with Indian-style blankets, which are still going strong, along with men's and women's sportswear.

Tours run Mon.-Fri. at 9 a.m., 11 a.m., 1:30 p.m., and 3 p.m. Large groups are asked to make an appointment. To get to the mills on I-84 going east, take exit 207 through Pendleton on Dorion. Do not cross the viaduct but turn left and proceed four blocks. For additional information, write Box 969, Pendleton 97801.

Umatilla County
Historical Society Museum

In 1881 the Oregon-Washington Railway and Navigation Company, a subsidiary of the Union Pacific Railroad, constructed the northern branch of its transcontinental railroad through northeast Oregon, and Pendleton served as an important stop on the route. By 1910, Pendleton had become the second-largest city in eastern Oregon and merited a new railroad depot. The building (Box 253, 108 S.W. Frazer, Pendleton 97801; tel. 276-0012), an adaptation of the California mission style, boasted multipaneled windows, decorative brickwork, and wide, flaring eaves. The depot no longer serves railroad passengers but instead houses the museum's collection of Oregon Trail pioneer and Indian artifacts.

Native Peoples Museum
In 1995, a unique exhibit will provide much needed balance to the saga of Oregon pioneer migration. The Confederated Tribes of the Umatilla Reservation just outside town are putting together a 43,000-square-foot museum dedicated to describing the effects of the white man's arrival here. The beginning of the end of their way of life will be well documented with exhibits on what Indian life was like prior to the pioneers arrival, an examination of the impact of the horse (brought to North America by Europeans) on Indian people, and an Oregon Trail retrospective from the point of view of the Cayuse, Umatilla, and Walla Walla tribes. The trail passed right through the current reservation site and meant long-term environmental problems for the native people, including diminished salmon runs and the dying forest of the Blue Mountains. The trail also brought chicken pox and measles, and the railroad that paralleled the trail brought tobacco, syphilis, and tuberculosis. Today, nuclear wastes are transported along I-84, also paralleling the ruts where prairie schooners once traveled. In addition to human historical perspectives, an inquiry into the future of the land will look at once-flourishing animal and plant populations that are now extinct, as well as the deleterious effects of newly introduced "exotics" from Europe and Asia. Call the Pendleton Chamber of Commerce Visitors and Convention Bureau for further details.

Tours
One of the area's liveliest attractions is **Pendleton Underground Tours** (Box 1072, 37 S.W. Emigrant Ave., Pendleton 97801; tel. 276-0730). This visit to the wild and woolly days of the Old West takes you through the tunnels underneath Pendleton's historic district. The tour starts at S.W. First and Emigrant and continues on to the old Shamrock Cardroom, filled with the boun-

cy sounds of honkytonk music. From there, it's on to the Cozy Rooms Bordello and other secrets of the town's past, ending with the inevitable gift shop.

At one time a series of 90 passageways, originally built as freight tunnels, crisscrossed beneath the downtown area. During the Prohibition era, bootleggers, gamblers, opium dealers, and Chinese railroad laborers frequented the businesses that grew up here. Three tours are available; the Underground tour, the Cozy Rooms Bordello tour, or a combination of both excursions. Open Mon.-Sat. 9-5. For each tour, admission is $5 for adults, $3 for kids under 12. The combination tour charge is $9 for adults, $5 for kids. Tours are 45 minutes each and reservations are recommended. To get there from I-84, take exit 209 and turn north into Pendleton. Continue up Emigrant Ave. to S.W. First Street. The tour begins on the northeast corner of S.W. First St. and Emigrant Avenue.

Hamley's Western Store (30 S.E. Court Ave.; tel. 276-2321) is internationally known for its western saddles and custom leathercraft. The second floor is a gallery of native American artists. Stop by and join one of the tours of saddle-making in progress, held Mon.-Sat. 9-5:30.

A good place to learn more about the local scene is **Armchair Books** (39 S.W. Dorion; tel. 276-7323), a store that specializes in regional titles and authors.

Those interested in local native (Umatilla and Cayuse) art should visit the **Collectors Gallery** (223 S.E. Court; tel. 276-6697) across from the post office. Armchair books supply background info on local Indian lore, with an excellent selection of regional titles.

SPORTS AND RECREATION

Lots of sun is conducive to such outdoor activities as golf at **Pendleton Country Club,** seven miles south of town on U.S. 395, and boating and water-skiing on **McKay Reservoir** near the country club. In a little over an hour, fishing enthusiasts can head north and arrive at the Columbia River for salmon, steelhead, and bass, or try the area's man-made lakes for bluegills, bass, and catfish. During the winter months, skiing is on tap up at

Spout Springs, one of the oldest ski resorts in the Northwest. To get there, drive north on ORE 11 to Weston, turn east on Ore 204, and travel a few miles past Tollgate to the ski area.

PRACTICALITIES

Accommodations

The cost for lodging in this town is reasonable. But if you show up at rodeo time without a reservation or unprepared to pay double the room rate, you might be out of luck. The Chamber of Commerce has a list of private homes that rent for a little less than a motel room, but they are normally booked well in advance. If you bring a tent, camping is usually available in schoolyards and other special sites set up for the several days of the Round-Up.

A tonic to modern life is a stay at the **Bar M Ranch**, 31 miles northeast of Pendleton on ORE 11. Built on the site of the historic Bingham Springs Resort, the ranch lies at the base of the Blue Mountains in the Umatilla National Forest. A stable of 50 horses, a natural warm springs, a recreation barn, and eight rooms in a hand-hewn log house let you rough it in style. Rates are $545 per week for a single and $505 each for double occupancy, which includes horse rides, meals, and all amenities.

Food

The Rainbow Bar and Grill (209 S. Main; tel. 276-4120) is a famous saloon/restaurant for rodeo fans and local buckaroos. The walls are covered with photos of Round-Up champions and Indian princesses, and the place was recently mentioned in Craig Lesley's novel *Winterkill,* the tale of a modern-day Indian bronc rider trying to scrape by. The Rainbow serves passable American diner food, which you shouldn't pass up, if only for local color.

The **Harvester Restaurant and Lounge** (2220 S.E. Court Ave.; tel. 276-9046) is home of the giant chicken-fried steak. **Cimmiyotti's** (137 Main St.; tel. 276-4314) is a dark cozy spot evoking an Old West bordello that has both American and Italian cuisine. The **Great Pacific Wine and Coffee Co.** (403 S. Main; tel. 276-1350) offers evidence that "hip" has come to Pendleton. They feature imported cheeses, desserts, croissant sandwiches, an espresso bar, and gourmet products.

The **Circle S** (210 S.E. Fifth; tel. 276-9637) is a Western-style restaurant that serves up a

PENDLETON ACCOMMODATIONS

Chaparral Motel, 620 S.W. Tutuilla, tel. 276-8654, $40-50, cable, wheelchair access, pets, kitchenettes, restaurant, nonsmoking rooms.

Econo Lodge, 201 S.W. Court Ave., tel. 276-5252, $35-50, cable, pets, pool.

Longhorn Motel, 411 S.W. Dorion, tel. 276-7531, $35, cable, pets, restaurant, nonsmoking rooms.

Motel 6, 325 Nye Ave., tel. 276-3160, $25-35, clean and basic.

Pillars Motel, 1816 S.E. Court Ave., 276-6241, $21 per person.

Pioneer Motel, 1807 S.E. Court Ave., tel. 276-4521, $25-35.

Ranch Motel, 7 I-84, Barnhart Exit, tel. 276-4711, $35-75, cable, wheelchair access, pets, pool, restaurant.

Red Lion Motor Inn, 304 S.E. Nye, tel. 276-6111, $79-89, cable, wheelchair access, restaurant/lounge, pool, live entertainment, nonsmoking rooms.

Tapadera Motor Inn, 105 S.E. Court Ave., tel. 276-3731, $50-85, cable, pets, restaurant/lounge, non-smoking rooms.

Thrifty Motel, 102 S.W. 18th St, tel. 276-1920, $25-35.

Travelers Inn, 310 S.E. Dorion Ave., tel. 276-6231, $40-60, cable, pets, pool, restaurant, laundry.

great barbecue sandwich for $3.50. Billed as Pendleton's oldest restaurant, **A&R Burger Island** (912 E. Emigrant; tel. 276-3352) has carhop service after 11 a.m. Its facade of palm trees taking root on painted burgers is reason enough for a visit. **The Health Nuts** (1700 S.W. Court Place; tel. 276-2251) is an oasis of natural foods in Pendleton, with a complete selection of whole grains, nuts, yogurt, and organic vegetables in season.

The **Bread Board and Catering Service** (141 S. Main St.; tel. 276-4520) has scrumptious homemade soups and sandwiches—a great place to provision a picnic. **Rachel's** (233 S.E. Fourth; tel. 276-8500) serves up steak and seafood at moderate prices. The native American art here adds a nice touch.

Entertainment And Events

In 1910, Pendleton farmers and ranchers got together to celebrate the end of the wheat harvest. This was the first year of the **Pendleton Round-Up,** which now draws 45,000 rodeo fans in the grand tradition started by legendary rodeo stars like Jackson Sundown and Yakima Canutt. Usually held in mid-September at Raley Park, the fun begins with the **Westward Ho Historical Parade,** including covered wagons, mule teams, buggies, and hundreds of Indians in full regalia. There's also a **Happy Canyon Pageant,** which portrays the native American culture, the coming of the emigrants, clashes between the two, and the birth of a frontier town. The Round-Up features such classic competitions as bulldogging, calf-roping, and wild-horse races Wed.-Saturday.

A **tepee encampment** of hundreds of Indians (Umatilla, Cayuse, Warm Springs, Blackfoot, and Nez Percé) on the Round-Up grounds and the **cowboy breakfast** of ham, eggs, flapjacks, and coffee served every morning at 6:30 a.m. in Stillman Park exemplify the traditions here, which take the Old West beyond the rodeo ring.

Tickets for each day run $5-10 depending on location. Phone orders will be accepted for Visa or MasterCard by dialing (800) 524-2984, or you can write for an order form to Pendleton Round-Up (Box 609, Pendleton 97801; tel. 276-2553). The **Northwest Cowboy Poetry Round-up** (tel. 276-2321) takes place the end of June at the Convention Center.

Information And Services

St. Anthony's Hospital (1601 S.E. Court Ave.; tel. 278-3214) has 24-hour emergency service. The **Pendleton Chamber of Commerce Visitor and Convention Bureau** (25 S.E. Dorion, Pendleton 97801; 276-7411 or 800-452-9403 in Oregon, 800-547-8911 outside Oregon) can steer you to local sights and special events. If you run into trouble during the Round-Up, the **police** can be reached at 276-4411. The **post office** (104 Dorion Ave., Pendleton 97801; tel. 278-0203) is down the street and open 8:30-5.

Pendleton Airport (2016 Airport Rd.; tel. 278-0947) is located 3 1/2 miles west of town center and is served by Horizon Air (tel. 800-547-9308). Aerowest Aviation (tel. 276-3835) provides charter rentals. At the airport, Hertz Rent-a-Car (tel. 276-3183) is the only such outfit in these parts. **Greyhound** (320 Court Ave.; tel. 276-1551) and **Pendleton Bus Co.** (tel. 276-5621) offer charters and transportation. The main line of the Union Pacific Railroad passes through Pendleton, with **Amtrak** passenger service available. However, the shelter station at S. Main and Frazer St. is unstaffed, and anyone planning to catch a train here should call (800) 872-7245 in advance.

BOOKLIST

In addition to the titles cited in the text, Oregon-bound travelers would do well to acquaint themselves with these books.

Atlases

Two publications authored by Samuel Dickman make Oregon's cultural and geological landscapes come alive. *Oregon Divided* (Portland: Oregon Historical Society, 1982) and *The Making of Oregon* (Portland: Oregon Historical Society, 1979) address the human history, economics, and topography of each part of the state.

Oregon Geographic Names by Lewis MacArthur (Portland: Oregon Historical Society, 1982) might physically be a weighty tome, but its alphabetical rundown of the history of the place-names here makes for light and informative reading.

The Coast

There are many good books on the coast, but the only one we've found that'll give something beyond what you'll find in conventional guidebooks was written by out-of-staters. East Coast residents and former *Rolling Stone* writers Parke Puterbaugh and Alan Bisbort's *Life is a Beach* (New York: McGraw-Hill Book Company, 1988) portrays Oregon's western edge with humor, insight, and graceful prose.

Oregon Coast Hikes by Paul Williams (Seattle: Mountaineers Books, 1983) is the best regional hiking guide.

Eastern Oregon

The classics for this area are *The Oregon Desert* by E. R. Jackson and R. A. Long (Caldwell, Idaho: Caxton Ltd.,1964) and *Steens Mountain in Oregon's High Desert Country* (Caldwell, Idaho: Caxton, Ltd., 1967). Within the volumes, history and local color fill in the east side's wide-open spaces.

Fiction

The book to read before coming here is *Sometimes a Great Notion* by Ken Kesey (New York:

Viking, 1964). This book is a fictional portrayal of what Mark Twain called the "westering spirit."

General Interest

The hottest new "reads" on the region are *The Good Rain* by Timothy Egan (New York: Alfred A. Knopf, 1990) and *Stepping Westward* by Sallie Tisdale (New York: Holt and Co., 1991). While both books depict the past, present, and future of the Northwest, each work stakes out different bailiwicks in the psychic landscape here. Egan brings the practiced eye of a *New York Times* correspondent to towns along the Columbia and other parts of Oregon and Washington caught in the transition from a resource based economy. The historical perspectives of a 19th-century diarist's entries underscore his descriptions of local color and contemporary issues throughout this book. Tisdale's treatment of similar terrain and themes emphasize a native world view and myths. Fact and fancy are deftly interwoven by this author who is also an award-winning essayist.

Other Northwest vignettes worth perusing are found in the final chapters of the late Supreme Court Justice William O. Douglas's autobiography, *Of Men and Mountains* (San Francisco: Chronicle Books, 1985). Particularly evocative are his descriptions of the Wallowas.

The Best of Oregon by Ken Metzler (Portland: Timber Press, 1986) is a loving look at the state by a longtime Oregon journalist and University of Oregon professor.

Guidebooks

Ralph Friedman is Oregon's King of the Road. Of his half-dozen books, *Oregon for the Curious* (Caldwell, Idaho: Caxton Ltd., 1972) is most recommended. It still is the best mile-by-mile description of the state ever done.

Another writer who can stake a claim as the Dean of Oregon Travel Writers is Mimi Bell, simply on the strength of *Off Beat Oregon* (San Francisco: Chronicle Books, 1983). Charming essays about travel in all four corners of the state will get you out of the armchair and onto the road.

Other excellent supplements to *Oregon Handbook* are penned by William L. Mainwaring for West Ridge Press in Salem, Oregon. His *Exploring Oregon's Central and Southern Cascades* (1979) and *Exploring the Oregon Coast* (1985) outline activities, hikes, camping, history, and local color.

History

The best concise history of Oregon can be found in the back of **Oregon Blue Book** (published biannually by the state of Oregon in Salem). This section of Oregon's political "Who's Who" is written by noted historian Terrence O'Donnell. His work in that book as well as in *Portland: An Informal History and Guide* (Portland: Oregon Historical Society, 1964) should disabuse any notions you might have that history is boring.

The grandaddy of them all, the *WPA Guide to Oregon* (Federal Writers' Project, 1941) was reissued a decade ago as *Oregon, the End of the Trail* (editor, Carol Stream: Somerset Press, 1982) and is the primary inspiration for *Oregon Handbook*. The product of dozens of authors working in the Federal Writers' Project, this post-Depression guidebook still sets the standard for completeness and vividness of description. Although much of the info is dated, its rundown of pioneer history and glimpses of early 20th-century Oregon make it a valuable tool for any modern traveler interested in understanding the Beaver State.

Photo Essays

The western part of the state is effectively profiled by Marnie McPhee in *Western Oregon: A Portrait of the Land and Its People* (Helena: American Geographic Publishing, 1987). Excellent color photos make the wetside's landscape and cultural geography come alive. In the same series, Mark Hoy's *Backroads of Oregon* (Helena: American Geographic Publishing, 1987) is also a winner.

Insight Guides: Pacific Northwest, edited by Hans Hoefer (Portland: Graphic Arts Center Publishing Co., 1986) and featuring Oregon chapters by state residents (including the *Oregon Handbook* writers), is a cross between a coffee-table book and a guidebook. Despite the relative lack of hard information, lavish illustrations covering the whole state paint an evocative portrait in broad strokes.

The preeminent coffee-table books of Oregon photos were done by Ray Atkeson (Portland: Graphic Arts Center Publishing, 1968-1987). The once-costly hard-covered editions of his *Oregon I, Oregon II,* and *Oregon III* are now available in paperback.

Statewide Hiking Guides

The best of this genre is undoubtedly *Exploring Oregon's Wild Areas* by William L. Sullivan (Seattle: Mountaineers Books, 1988). Activities for hikers, backpackers, climbers, cross-country skiers, and saddlers are outlined in this well-organized book. Geology and botany are also addressed.

INDEX

Page numbers in **boldface** indicate the primary reference to a given topic. *Italicized* page
numbers indicate information in captions, callouts, charts, illustrations, or maps.

Stuart Warren

Stuart Warren

Stuart Warren refers to himself and the coauthor of *Oregon Handbook* as "roads scholars." Together they've worked over two decades as motorcoach tour directors and Stuart himself has penned several guidebooks, taught and translated technical English for the Colombian national oil concession, and imported Guatemalan textiles. When not indulging lifelong passions for chess and hiking, he can usually be found prowling the stacks of Powell's Bookstore with his family (Rebecca, Liam, and Phineas) near their home in Portland, Oregon.

Ted Long Ishikawa

Ted Long Ishikawa

I'm more of a pianist than writer. Performing for the Queen of England in Yosemite National Park and recording my album, *Heart of Yosemite,* seemed much more glamorous than writing a book. But I've kept on typing and in the process learned about the many special things my home state has to offer. It is my wish that more people will enjoy Oregon and that *Oregon Handbook* will enhance their visits.

Ted lives in Eugene, Oregon with his wife Sawako.

MOON HANDBOOKS—THE IDEAL TRAVELING COMPANIONS

Open a Moon Handbook and you're opening your eyes and heart to the world.
Thoughtful, sensitive, and provocative, Moon Handbooks encourage an intimate
understanding of a region, from its culture and history to essential practicalities. Fun to
read and packed with valuable information on accommodations, dining, recreation, plus
indispensable travel tips, detailed maps, charts, illustrations, photos, glossaries, and
indexes, Moon Handbooks are ideal traveling companions: informative, entertaining,
and highly practical.

To locate the bookstore nearest you that carries Moon Travel Handbooks or to order
directly from Moon Publications, call: (800) 345-5473, Monday-Friday, 9 a.m.-5 p.m. PST.

THE PACIFIC/ASIA SERIES

BALI HANDBOOK   by Bill Dalton
Detailed travel information on the most famous island in the world. 428 pages.   **$12.95**

BANGKOK HANDBOOK   by Michael Buckley
Your tour guide through this exotic and dynamic city reveals the affordable and accessible
possibilities. Thai phrasebook. 214 pages.   **$10.95**

BLUEPRINT FOR PARADISE: How to Live on a Tropic Island   by Ross Norgrove
This one-of-a-kind guide has everything you need to know about moving to and living
comfortably on a tropical island. 212 pages.   **$14.95**

FIJI ISLANDS HANDBOOK   by David Stanley
The first and still the best source of information on travel around this 322-island archipelago.
Fijian glossary. 198 pages.   **$11.95**

INDONESIA HANDBOOK   by Bill Dalton
This one-volume encyclopedia explores island by island the many facets of this sprawling,
kaleidoscopic island nation. Extensive Indonesian vocabulary. 1,000 pages.   **$19.95**

JAPAN HANDBOOK   by J.D. Bisignani
In this comprehensive new edition, award-winning travel writer J.D. Bisignani offers to
inveterate travelers, newcomers, and businesspeople alike a thoroughgoing presentation of
Japan's many facets. 800 pages.   **$22.50**

MICRONESIA HANDBOOK: Guide to the Caroline, Gilbert, Mariana, and Marshall Islands
by David Stanley
Micronesia Handbook guides you on a real Pacific adventure all your own. 345 pages.   **$11.95**

NEW ZEALAND HANDBOOK   by Jane King
Introduces you to the people, places, history, and culture of this extraordinary land. 571 pages.
$18.95

OUTBACK AUSTRALIA HANDBOOK   by Marael Johnson
Australia is an endlessly fascinating, vast land, and *Outback Australia Handbook* explores the
cities and towns, sheep stations, and wilderness areas of the Northern Territory, Western
Australia, and South Australia. Full of travel tips and cultural information for adventuring,
relaxing, or just getting away from it all. 355 pages.   **$15.95**

PHILIPPINES HANDBOOK   by Peter Harper and Evelyn Peplow
Crammed with detailed information, *Philippines Handbook* equips the escapist, hedonist, or
business traveler with thorough coverage of the Philippines's colorful history, landscapes, and
culture. 587 pages.   **$12.95**

SOUTHEAST ASIA HANDBOOK   by Carl Parkes
Helps the enlightened traveler discover the real Southeast Asia. 873 pages.   **$16.95**

SOUTH KOREA HANDBOOK   by Robert Nilsen
Whether you're visiting on business or searching for adventure, *South Korea Handbook* is an
invaluable companion. Korean glossary with useful notes on speaking and reading the
language. 548 pages.   **$14.95**

SOUTH PACIFIC HANDBOOK   by David Stanley
The original comprehensive guide to the 16 territories in the South Pacific. 740 pages.   **$19.95**

TAHITI-POLYNESIA HANDBOOK   by David Stanley
All five French-Polynesian archipelagoes are covered in this comprehensive guide by
Oceania's best-known travel writer. 235 pages.   **$11.95**

THAILAND HANDBOOK   by Carl Parkes
Presents the richest source of information on travel in Thailand. 568 pages.   **$16.95**

THE HAWAIIAN SERIES

BIG ISLAND OF HAWAII HANDBOOK   by J.D. Bisignani
An entertaining yet informative text packed with insider tips on accommodations, dining, sports
and outdoor activities, natural attractions, and must-see sights. 347 pages.   **$11.95**

HAWAII HANDBOOK   by J.D. Bisignani
Winner of the 1989 Hawaii Visitors Bureau's Best Guide Award and the Grand Award for
Excellence in Travel Journalism, this guide takes you beyond the glitz and high-priced hype and
leads you to a genuine Hawaiian experience. Covers all 8 Hawaiian Islands. 879 pages.   **$15.95**

KAUAI HANDBOOK   by J.D. Bisignani
Kauai Handbook is the perfect antidote to the workaday world. Hawaiian and pidgin glossaries.
236 pages.   **$9.95**

MAUI HANDBOOK   by J.D. Bisignani
"No fool-'round" advice on accommodations, eateries, and recreation, plus a comprehensive
introduction to island ways, geography, and history. Hawaiian and pidgin glossaries. 350 pages.
$11.95

OAHU HANDBOOK   by J.D. Bisignani
A handy guide to Honolulu, renowned surfing beaches, and Oahu's countless other diversions. Hawaiian and pidgin glossaries. 354 pages.   **$11.95**

THE AMERICAS SERIES

ALASKA-YUKON HANDBOOK   by Deke Castleman and Don Pitcher
Get the inside story, with plenty of well-seasoned advice to help you cover more miles on less money. 384 pages.   **$13.95**

ARIZONA TRAVELER'S HANDBOOK   by Bill Weir
This meticulously researched guide contains everything necessary to make Arizona accessible and enjoyable. 505 pages.   **$14.95**

BAJA HANDBOOK   by Joe Cummings
A comprehensive guide with all the travel information and background on the land, history, and culture of this untamed thousand-mile-long peninsula. 356 pages.   **$13.95**

BELIZE HANDBOOK   by Chicki Mallan
Complete with detailed maps, practical information, and an overview of the area's flamboyant history, culture, and geographical features, *Belize Handbook* is the only comprehensive guide of its kind to this spectacular region. 263 pages.   **$14.95**

BRITISH COLUMBIA HANDBOOK   by Jane King
With an emphasis on outdoor adventures, this guide covers mainland British Columbia, Vancouver Island, the Queen Charlotte Islands, and the Canadian Rockies. 381 pages. **$13.95**

CANCUN HANDBOOK   by Chicki Mallan
Covers the city's luxury scene as well as more modest attractions, plus many side trips to unspoiled beaches and Mayan ruins. Spanish glossary. 257 pages.   **$12.95**

CATALINA ISLAND HANDBOOK: A Guide to California's Channel Islands
by Chicki Mallan
A complete guide to these remarkable islands, from the windy solitude of the Channel Islands National Marine Sanctuary to bustling Avalon. 245 pages.   **$10.95**

COLORADO HANDBOOK   by Stephen Metzger
Essential details to the all-season possibilities in Colorado fill this guide. Practical travel tips combine with recreation—skiing, nightlife, and wilderness exploration—plus entertaining essays. 422 pages.   **$15.95**

IDAHO HANDBOOK   by Bill Loftus
A year-round guide to everything in this outdoor wonderland, from whitewater adventures to rural hideaways. 275 pages.   **$12.95**

JAMAICA HANDBOOK   by Karl Luntta
From the sun and surf of Montego Bay and Ocho Rios to the cool slopes of the Blue Mountains, author Karl Luntta offers island-seekers a perceptive, personal view of Jamaica. 213 pages. **$12.95**

MONTANA HANDBOOK by W.C. McRae and Judy Jewell
The wild West is yours with this extensive guide to the Treasure State, complete with travel practicalities, history, and lively essays on Montana life. 393 pages. **$13.95**

NEVADA HANDBOOK by Deke Castleman
Nevada Handbook puts the Silver State into perspective and makes it manageable and affordable. 400 pages. **$14.95**

NEW MEXICO HANDBOOK by Stephen Metzger
A close-up and complete look at every aspect of this wondrous state. 375 pages. **$13.95**

NORTHERN CALIFORNIA HANDBOOK by Kim Weir
An outstanding companion for imaginative travel in the territory north of the Tehachapis. 800 pages. **$19.95**

OREGON HANDBOOK by Stuart Warren and Ted Long Ishikawa
Brimming with travel practicalities and insiders' views on Oregon's history, culture, arts, and activities. 461 pages. **$15.95**

PACIFIC MEXICO HANDBOOK by Bruce Whipperman
Explore 2,000 miles of gorgeous beaches, quiet resort towns, and famous archaeological sites along Mexico's Pacific coast. Spanish-English glossary. 450 pages. **$15.95**

TEXAS HANDBOOK by Joe Cummings
Seasoned travel writer Joe Cummings brings an insider's perspective to his home state. 483 pages. **$13.95**

UTAH HANDBOOK by Bill Weir
Weir gives you all the carefully researched facts and background to make your visit a success. 445 pages. **$14.95**

WASHINGTON HANDBOOK by Dianne J. Boulerice Lyons and Archie Satterfield
Covers sights, shopping, services, transportation, and outdoor recreation, with complete listings for restaurants and accommodations. 433 pages. **$13.95**

WYOMING HANDBOOK by Don Pitcher
All you need to know to open the doors to this wide and wild state. 495 pages. **$14.95**

YUCATAN HANDBOOK by Chicki Mallan
All the information you'll need to guide you into every corner of this exotic land. Mayan and Spanish glossaries. 391 pages. **$14.95**

THE INTERNATIONAL SERIES

EGYPT HANDBOOK   by Kathy Hansen
An invaluable resource for intelligent travel in Egypt. Arabic glossary. 522 pages.   **$18.95**

MOSCOW-ST. PETERSBURG HANDBOOK   by Masha Nordbye
Provides the visitor with an extensive introduction to the history, culture, and people of these
two great cities, as well as practical information on where to stay, eat, and shop. 260 pages.
$13.95

NEPAL HANDBOOK   by Kerry Moran
Whether you're planning a week in Kathmandu or months out on the trail, *Nepal Handbook* will
take you into the heart of this Himalayan jewel. 378 pages.   **$12.95**

NEPALI AAMA   by Broughton Coburn
A delightful photo-journey into the life of a Gurung tribeswoman of Central Nepal. Having lived
with Aama (translated, "mother") for two years, first as an outsider and later as an adopted
member of the family, Coburn presents an intimate glimpse into a culture alive with humor,
folklore, religion, and ancient rituals. 165 pages.   **$13.95**

PAKISTAN HANDBOOK   by Isobel Shaw
For armchair travelers and trekkers alike, the most detailed and authoritative guide to Pakistan
ever published. Urdu glossary. 478 pages.   **$15.95**

STAYING HEALTHY IN ASIA, AFRICA, AND LATIN AMERICA
by Dirk G. Schroeder, Sc D, MPH
Don't leave home without it! Besides providing a complete overview of the health problems that
exist in these areas, this book will help you determine which immunizations you'll need
beforehand, what medications to take with you, and how to recognize and treat infections and
diseases. Includes extensively illustrated first-aid information and precautions for heat, cold,
and high altitude. 200 pages.   **$10.95**

MOONBELTS

Made of heavy-duty Cordura nylon, the Moonbelt offers maximum protection for your money
and important papers. This all-weather pouch slips under your shirt or waistband, rendering it
virtually undetectable and inaccessible to pickpockets. One-inch-wide nylon webbing, heavy-
duty zipper, one-inch quick-release buckle. Accommodates traveler's checks, passport, cash,
photos. Size 5 x 9 inches. Black.   **$8.95**

New travel handbooks may be available that are not on this list.
To find out more about current or upcoming titles,
call us toll-free at (800) 345-5473.

IMPORTANT ORDERING INFORMATION

FOR FASTER SERVICE: Call to locate the bookstore nearest you that carries Moon Travel Handbooks or order directly from Moon Publications:

(800) 345-5473 • **Monday-Friday** • **9 a.m.-5 p.m. PST** • **fax (916) 345-6751**

PRICES: All prices are subject to change. We always ship the most current edition. We will let you know if there is a price increase on the book you ordered.

SHIPPING & HANDLING OPTIONS: 1) Domestic UPS or USPS first class (allow 10 working days for delivery): $3.50 for the first item, 50 cents for each additional item.

Exceptions:
  • **Moonbelt** shipping is $1.50 for one, 50 cents for each additional belt:
  • Add $2.00 for same-day handling.
  • UPS 2nd Day Air or Printed Airmail requires a special quote.
  • International Surface Bookrate (8-12 weeks delivery):
    $3.00 for the first item, $1.00 for each additional item. Note: Moon Publications cannot guarantee international surface bookrate shipping.

FOREIGN ORDERS: All orders that originate outside the U.S.A. must be paid for with either an International Money Order or a check in U.S. currency drawn on a major U.S. bank based in the U.S.A.

TELEPHONE ORDERS: We accept Visa or MasterCard payments. Minimum order is US$15.00. Call in your order: (800) 345-5473, 9 a.m.-5 p.m. Pacific Standard Time.